ENTER A SAMURAI

ENTER A SAMURAI

*Kawakami Otojirō
and Japanese Theatre
in the West*

VOLUME TWO
Endnotes, Bibliography, and Index

Joseph L. Anderson

Enter a Samurai: Kawakami Otojirō and Japanese Theatre in the West, Volume 2

Cover design by Hayley Love
Interior design by Susan Wenger

Published by Wheatmark®
610 East Delano Street, Suite 104
Tucson, Arizona 85705 U.S.A.
www.wheatmark.com

International Standard Book Number: 978-1-60494-368-9
Library of Congress Control Number: 2011922206

Contact the author: jlanderson29@aol.com
Visit the author's website: www.kawakamiotojiro.com

Contents

ENTER A SAMURAI

Endnotes

Introduction

1 Takahashi, "Zadankai," 92–93. Citations are abbreviated in Endnotes. Full identification of these citations appear in the Bibliography section of this Volume Two.

2 Ibid., also 74–97; Kurata, *Kindaigeki*, 260.

3 Fischer-Lichte, *Show*, 136–37, 130. She studied developments that took place primarily in Europe after Kawakami's tours.

4 Pavis, *Intercultural*, 8.

5 Marleigh Ryan, "Modern Japanese Fiction: 'Accommodated Truth,'" *Journal of Japanese Studies* (Summer 1976), 257–58.

6 *Microcosmische Vorspiele Des neuen Himmels und der Neuen Erde; Von einem Liebhaber göttlicher und natürlicher Geheimnisse* (Frankfurt and Leipzig, 1744, n.p.), quoted by Helmar Schramm, "The Open Book of Alchemy in/on the Mute Language of Theatre: 'Theatricality' as a Key for Current Theatre/Research," *Theatre Research International* 20:2 (Summer 1995), 159.

7 Computer-based digitization can significantly improve preservation of both print and image. Unfortunately, many originals are now flakes of paper or inexplicably lost in archival preservation.

8 Matsumoto, *Meiji engekiron*, 203. *Gendaigeki* has been the dominant form and milieu for shimpa, shingeki, motion pictures, and television drama.

9 Tsubouchi Hakubutsukan, *Kokugeki*, 339.

10 Puccini, *Butterfly*, 15.

Prologue

1 Gluck, *Japan's*, 73–74.

2 Stephen Vlastos, "Opposition Movements in Early Meiji, 1868–1885," in Jansen, *Cambridge*, 402.

3 Gluck, *Japan's*, 60–62.

4   The basic issue: "freedom for Japanese people" or "freedom for the Japanese people as a nation"?

5   Gluck, *Japan's,* 17–35.

6   Ichioka, *Issei,* 10.

Chapter 1

1   Inoue, *Kawakami,* 8, 10.

2   Matsunaga, *Kawakami,* 5, 17–18. The Hakata area developed a distinctively regional *niwaka* (Inoue Seizō, *Hakata niwaka tokuhon* [The Hakata *niwaka* reader] [Hakata: Yoshi Shobō, 1987], 5–45).

3   Inoue, *Kawakami,* 10–11; Matsunaga, *Kawakami,* 18, 23.

4   Yanagi Keitarō, *Kawakami,* part 1.

5   Matsunaga, *Kawakami,* 24–26.

6   Katō, *History,* 79.

7   "Nihon engekikai no fūunji Kawakami Otojirō" [Kawakami Otojirō: soldier of perilous fortune in the Japanese theatrical world], in *Nihon no sōzōryoku* [Japanese creative power], ed. Makino Noboru (Nihon Hōsō Shuppan Kyōkai, 1992), 8:114–16; also Inoue, *Kawakami,* 146.

8   Matsunaga, *Kawakami,* 34–40; Scalapino, *Democracy,* 105–7; Bowen, *Rebellion,* 287–88.

9   Jason G. Karlin, "The Gender of Nationalism: Competing Masculinities in Meiji Japan," *Journal of Japanese Studies* 28:1 (Winter 2002): 58–60; Bowen, *Rebellion,* 287–88.

10   "Soshi-ism in Japan," *Nation* (U.S.) (April 25, 1895): 321.

11   Kurata, *Kindaigeki,* 10–16, 28–33, 262; Matsunaga, *Kawakami,* 41–46; "Shimpageki to Kawakami" [Shimpa and Kawakami], *Miyako shimbun,* November 12, 1911, in Shirakawa, 504–5.

12   Komota, *Nihon.* 24–26; G. T. Shea, *Leftwing Literature in Japan: A Brief History of the Proletarian Literary Movement* (Tokyo: Hosei University Press, 1964), 5–7; 60; Mita, *Social,* 14–19, 28–29, 144–47.

13   Kurata, *Kindaigeki,* 26–33, 262–67; "Meika shinsoroku," 21–22; Matsunaga, *Kawakami,* 40.

14   Faith Bach, "Breaking the *Kabuki* Actors' Barriers: 1868–1900," *Asian Theater Journal* 12:2 (Fall 1995): 267–71.

15   Ihara, *Kabuki,* 8:320–22. This was on a bill with the famous featured play, *Satomi Hakkenden* (The story of the eight dogs [warriors]). Kawakami apparently had a bit part in *Satomi.*

16   Mita, *Harukanari,* 60–61; Kurata, *Kindaigeki,* 34; Yanagi, *Shimpa no rokujūnen,* 65–67, 79; Matsunaga, *Kawakami,* 51–53.

17   Faith Bach, "Breaking the *Kabuki* Actors' Barriers," 268, 271.

18   Kawatake Shigetoshi, *Gaisetsu,* 373.

19   Miyake Shūtarō, *Engeki,* 81; Kurata, *Kindaigeki,* 37; Matsunaga, *Kawakami,* 46–47; Kawakami Otojirō Kenshōkai, *Otojirō shimpageki,* part 2.

20   The principal oral storyteller forms were *rakugo, jōruri, kōdan,* and *naniwabushi.*

21   Muramatsu Shunkichi, *Tabishibai,* 90–91.

22   Kyôgen is the classic comic form related to nô.

23   Dōmoto, *Kamigata,* 263; Ihara, *Kabuki,* 7:344–47. Faith Bach; "Breaking the *Kabuki* Actors' Barriers," 268–70. Kurata, *Meiji,* 4:71, listed thirty-five to forty-five different kinds of *misemono* shows.

24   Gerald Groemer, "Nō at the Crossroads: Commoner Performance During the Edo Period," *Asian Theater Journal* 15 (Spring 1998): 131–33.

25   Raz, *Audience,* 218; also 186–89.

26   In the late nineteenth century, the medley program was more popular in Osaka than in Tokyo.

27   Kawatake Shigetoshi, *Nihon engeki zenshi,* 801–9, 815–24.

28   Ihara, *Meiji,* 387; also Hagii, *Shimpa,* 14–15; Kawatake Shigetoshi, *Gaisetsu,* 344–47.

29   Japanese officials who saw theatre abroad apparently did not attend or report on foreign popular theatres so there was little awareness of raucous behavior in the lesser theatres of the West.

30   Kawatake Shigetoshi, *Nihon engeki zenshi*, 801–8.

31   Ibid., 793–97; Ihara, *Meiji*, 387–88, 391–93, 455; Sekine, *Meiji*, 114–24; Toita, "Kabuki, *Shimpa*," 194–201; Toita Yasuji, *Kabuki kono hyakunen* [Kabuki: the past one hundred years] (Mainichi Shimbunsha, 1978), 9.

32   Toita, "Kabuki, *Shimpa*," 204–6; Brandon, *Kabuki*, 4; Okazaki, *Japanese Literature*, 460–65; Hagi, *Shimpa*, 16–19.

33   *Zangirimono* may be considered an updating of kabuki *sewamono* as well as a predecessor of the contemporary drama of shimpa (Kawatake Shigetoshi, *Nihon engeki zenshi*, 783–89).

34   Ibid., 798–800; Ihara, *Meiji*, 389, 393; James R. Brandon, "Kabuki and Shakespeare: Balancing Yin and Yang," *Drama Review* (TDR 162) 43:2 (Summer 1999): 22–23; Toita, "Kabuki, *Shimpa*," 217–19.

35   Kawatake Shigetoshi, *Gaisetsu*, 346–47; Raz, *Audience*, 220; Toita, "Kabuki, *Shimpa*," 225.

36   Okamoto, *Meiji*, 266; Ogasawara, *Kabuki*. 71.

37   The great unresolved diplomatic problem Japan faced during the mid-Meiji period was how to terminate the unequal treaties with Western countries (Donald H. Shively, "The Japanization of the Middle Meiji," in Shively, *Tradition*, 89).

38   Graham Squires, "Yamaji Aizan's Traces of the Development of Human Rights in Japanese History," *Monumenta Nipponica* 56:2 (Summer 2001): 139; Gluck, *Japan's*, 60–64.

39   Mita, *Harukanari*, 63; Raz, *Audience*. 213–14.

40   Leonard Pronko, "From Insularity to Internationalism," in *Rethinking Japan, Volume 1: Literature, Visual Arts, and Linguistics*, eds. Adriana Boscaro et al. (New York: St. Martin's, 1991), 167–68.

41   Soeda, *Hayari*, 37–54; Komota, *Nihon*, 24–27; Ozaki, *Taishū*, 193–94; Hagii, *Shimpa*, 23; Mita, *Social*, 14–19, 28–29, 64.

42   Ozaki, *Taishū*. 194; also Yamaguchi, *Joyū*, 43; Kawatake Shigetoshi, *Gaisetsu*, 374.

43   Kawatake Shigetoshi, *Nihon engeki zenshi*, 990–91.

44   Matsunaga, *Kawakami*, 48–49; Kawakami Otojirō Kenshōkai, *Otojirō shimp-geki*, part 2.

45   Kurata, *Kindaigeki*, 68–72; Kurata, *Meiji*, 5:61, 65; Sansom, *Western*, 372, 378.

46   A 1900 recording of "Oppekepē bushi" sung by a Kawakami substitute is on the CD, Miller, *Yomigaeru*, cut 1. Additional information appeared in both the booklet that accompanied this record and in J. Scott Miller, "Dispossessed Melodies: Recordings of the Kawakami Theatre Troupe," *Monumenta Nipponica* 53:2 (Summer 1998): 225–35.

47   Soeda, *Hayari*, 67–70. "Oppekepē" lyrics appeared in print many times with many variations. Among the first was the illustrated booklet *Shinsaku: Oppekepē bushi* [New work: the Oppekepē song] (n.p., 1891). There is no definitive version.

48   In some renderings that are probably more original and less censored this line is "Expanding liberty and the right to be free."

49   My translation here attempted to duplicate original cadences. Alternative translations appeared in William P. Malm, "The Modern Music of Meiji Japan," in Shively, *Tradition*, 282–84, and in Miller, "Dispossessed Melodies," cited above. Other Japanese verses were in Akiba, *Tōto*, 247–48 and seven full stanzas in "Kawakami Otojirō no 'Oppekepē,'" *Kabuki* (December 1911): 107–9.

50   Komota, *Nihon*, 210; Toita Yasuji, *Kabuki*, 79.

51   *Kairyō* was often a code word for Europeanization.

52   Kurata, *Kindaigeki*, 36–37; Kurata, *Meiji*, 5:153; Shirakawa, *shimbun*, 15.

53   Inoue, *Hakata*, 17–20, 45.

54   Kurata, *Kindaigeki*, 38–39, 263. Kawatake Shigetoshi, *Gaisetsu*, 375; Kurata. *Meiji*, 5:71–72; Shirakawa, *shimbun*, 16.

55   Kurata, *Kindaigeki*, 48–52, 57–58; Yanagi, *Shimpa no rokujūnen*, 31, 40; Kawatake Shigetoshi, *Nihon engeki zenshi*, 991; Mita, *Harukanari*, 74–76; Shirakawa, *shimbun*, 16.

56   Yanagi, *Shimpa no rokujūnen*, 33.

57   Ibid., 60–61; Ogasawara, *Kabuki*, 161–65; Akiba, *Tōto*, 235.

58   Okamoto, *Meiji*, 33, 62; Kurata, *Kindaigeki*, 149; untitled death notice, *Engei gahō* (February 1907): 104.

59   Kawatake Shigetoshi, *Gaisetsu*, 374.

60   Matsunaga, *Kawakami*, 4–5.

61   Miyake Shūtarō, *Engeki*, 82–84; "Meika shinsoroku," 22; Raz, *Audience*, 139.

62   "Kairyō engeki," advertisement, *Ōsaka asahi shimbun*, February 5, 1891, in Shirakawa, 53, also 16.

63   Kawatake Shigetoshi, *Gaisetsu*, 372–73; "Meika shinsoroku," 22.

64   Kurata, *Kindaigeki*, 263; Sansom, *Western*, 400; Ogasawara, *Kabuki*, 175–78.

65   "Meika shinsoroku," 22–23; Shirakawa, *shimbun*, 17.

66   Kurata, *Kindaigeki*, 263. There were earlier kabuki plays about Itagaki but, following long established custom as well as avoiding police suppression, they obscured the actual historical circumstances, period, and personages (Kurata, *Kindaigeki*, 18–25; Kawatake Shigetoshi, *Nihon no engeki*, 166).

67   Hagii, *Shimpa*, 24; "Shimpa hanseiki o kataru 7" [Discussing a half century of shimpa], *Miyako shimbun*, n.d. January 1937, n.p.; "Shimpa gojūnen kaiko kiji" [Articles recalling fifty years of shimpa], in file *ro* 2/74, Waseda.

68   Yanagi, *Shimpa no rokujūnen*, 136–38; Akiba, *Nihon*, 1:303.

69   "Keikoku bidan de fushō" [Wounded in *Keikoku bidan*], *Yomiuri shimbun*, August 7, 1891, in Shirakawa, 68; "Kawakami ichiza ishi o heisu" [Doctor summoned to Kawakami troupe], *Yomiuri shimbun*, September 24, 1892, in Shirakawa, 74.

70   Hagii, *Shimpa*, 24.

71   "Meika shinsoroku," 23–24.

72   When preceded by a proper name, *za* means either a troupe or a theatre. In this study, when a hyphen precedes *za* it indicates the name of a theatre.

73   Ihara, *Meiji*, 656–57. The Nakamura-za, established in 1624, was one of the original *Edo sanza* (three [major] theatres of Edo). Throughout the subsequent two and half centuries, it was frequently rebuilt after many fires and its location changed. There were at least nineteen active drama theatres in Tokyo when Kawakami first arrived in the capital city (Ihara, *Kabuki*, 7:368–69.)

74   Akiba, *Nihon*, 1:279; Matsumoto, *Meiji*, 146–47; Akiba, *Tōto*, 237–38; Ihara Seiseien, "Kaneizumi Ushitarō nikki" [The diary of Kaneizumi Ushitarō], *Kabuki* (October 1911): 69 and 138 (December 1911): 110–12.

75   "Kawakami ichiza ni hikimaku o okuru" [Horizontal draw curtain given to the Kawakami troupe], *Yomiuri shimbun*, August 4, 1891, Shirakwa, 67. Yoshiwara, the largest brothel district of Japan, was adjacent to Asakusa where Kawakami was playing.

76   Shirakawa, *shimbun*, 17.

77   Ibid., 18–19, 47, 50–52, 58.

78   The unresolved irony was that Japanese officialdom was calling for theatre (by which they meant kabuki) to become less frivolous and more "educative," while the early plays of Kawakami (and Sudō) that police attempted to suppress were primarily vehicles for teaching. The motives of the officials and the sōshi/shosei were similar but their ideologies were radically different.

79   Akiba, *Nihon*, 1:279–81; Kurata, *Kindaigeki*, 263; "Torigoe-za," *Chūō shimbun*, January 1, 1892, in Shirakawa, 79; Hagii, *Shimpa*, 23; Shirakawa, *shimbun*, 17–22.

80   Shirakawa, *shimbun*, 2.

81   Ibid., 17–18. 8; Hagi, *Shimpa*, 24.

82 Bertolt Brecht, *Stücke* (Berlin: Suhrkamp, 1966), 3:276, trans. in Ronald Gray, *Bertolt Brecht* (New York: Grove, 1961), 70.

83 Shirakawa, *shimbun*, 19, 66–67; Akiba, *Nihon*, 1:52–57; Matsumoto, *Meiji*, 144–45; Yanagi, *Shimpa no rokujūnen*, 148–49, 155; Ihara, *Kabuki*, 7:381, 391.

84 David R. Ambaras, "Social Knowledge, Cultural Capital, and the New Middle Class in Japan, 1895–1912," *Journal of Japanese Studies* 24 (Winter 1998): 1–33.

85 Shirakawa, *shimbun*, 2; Yanagi, *Shimpa no rokujūnen*, 141; Hagii, *Shimpa*, 26.

86 Fukuchi Ōchi, *Hirano Jirō* (Hakubunkan, 1893); Akiba, *Nihon*, 1:182–83.

87 "Meika shinsoroku," 27; Meiji Nyūsu Jiten Hensan Iinkai, comp., *Meiji nyūsu jiten* [Dictionary of Meiji news articles] (Mainichi Komyunikēshonzu, 1985), 4:126; Kurata, *Kindaigeki*, 264; Hagii, *Shimpa*, 26; Matsunaga, *Kawakami*, 92; Yamaguchi, *Joyū*, 51–52.

88 Theatrical nagauta is a vocal form that in kabuki is primarily recitative for narration passages but includes lyrical interludes (Akiba, *Tōto*, 240–44).

89 Akiba, *Tōto*, 170–81; Kawatake Shigetoshi, *Nihon engeki zenshi*, 827–28, 834–35; Toita, "Kabuki, Shimpa," 213–14; Yanagi, *Shimpa no rokujūnen*, 64–67, 78–79; Hagii, *Shimpa*, 13, 47–48; Leiter, *Kabuki Encyclopedia*, 261.

90 Kawatake Shigetoshi, *Nihon engeki zenshi*, 83; Hagii, *Shimpa*, 11.

91 Hagii, *Shimpa*, 104–7.

92 James R. Brandon, "Kabuki and Shakespeare: Balancing Yin and Yang," *Drama Review* (TDR 162) 43:2 (Summer 1999): 21.

93 Yanagi, *Shimpa no rokujūnen*, 64.

94 Hagii, *Shimpa*, 25–26.

95 Yanagi, *Shimpa no rokujūnen*, 324; Miyake, *Engeki*, 83.

96 Akiba, *Nihon*, 1:287–89.

97 Takahashi, "Zadankai," 76; Kurata, *Kindaigeki*, 264; Yanagi, *Shimpa no rokujūnen*, 134; Yanagi, *Ebanzuke*, 252.

98 Kawashima, *Nihon*, 91–92; Kurata, *Kindaigeki*, 263; Kawatake Shigetoshi, *Sōgō*, 337; Matsumoto, *Meiji*, 153–54, 167–70; Akiba, *Tōto*, 182–85.

99 Ogawa, *Nihon*, 96; Ōzasa, *Nihon*, 1:61.

100 Kawatake Shigetoshi, *Gaisetsu*, 374–76; Ihara, *Meiji*, 233–35; Hagii, *Shimpa*, 182–82. Chitose disappeared from the theatre world after the Seibikan broke up although the males of the troupe continued on to successful shimpa careers.

101 Akiba, *Nihon*. 1:283–897; Cody Poulton, "Drama and Fiction in the Meiji Era: The Case of Izumi Kyōka," *Asian Theater Journal* 12:2 (Fall 1995): 288; Marui, *Shimpa*, 15; Kawatake Shigetoshi. *Gaisetsu*, 374–76; Ihara, *Meiji*, 233–35; Hagii, *Shimpa*, 182–83.

102 Yamaguchi, *Joyū*, 17–19, 25–34, 37–40; "Meika shinsoroku: Kawakami Sadayakko" [Celebrity facts: Kawakami Sadayakko], *Engei gahō* (October 1908): 80; Downer, *Madame*, 48.

103 "Yakko no Kawakami netsu" [Yakko's passion for Kawakami], *Chūō shimbun*, November 18, 1892, in Shirakawa, 115; also Yamaguchi, *Jōyū*, 261.

104 Yamaguchi, *Jōyū*, 59, 261; Dōmon, *Kawakami*, 191; "Yakko, Kawakami to fūfu ni naru" [Yakko and Kawakami become husband and wife], *Yorozu chōbō*, October 13, 1893, Shirakawa, 136–37; Kano, *Acting,* 46–49.

105 "Meika shinsoroku 23: Kawakami Sadayakko," *Engei gahō* (October 1908): 80.

106 Her roles included the short-tempered younger brother Gorō and the villain Kudō in familiar kabuki plays about the Soga brothers.

107 Yamaguchi, *Joyū*, 34–36, 261; Dōmon, *Kawakami*, 74; "Joyū rekishō roku" [Report on visits with actresses],

Engei gahō (February 1911), 43; "Yūrakkan no geisha shibai" [Geisha play at the Yūrakkan], *Chūō shimbun*, December 6, 1891, in Shirakawa, 77.

108 Yamaguchi, *Jōyū*, 261.

109 Kano, *Acting*, 39–119.

110 Kathryn Ragsdale, "Marriage, the Newspaper Business, and the Nation-State: Ideology in the Late Meiji Serialized Katsei Shōsetsu," *Journal of Japanese Studies* 24:2 (Summer 1998): 244; Kurata, *Kindaigeki*, 142–43.

111 Ellen P. Conant, "The French Connection: Emile Guimet's Mission to Japan, a Cultural Context for *Japonisme*," in Conroy, *Japan*, 113–146.

112 Meiji Nyūsu Jiten Hensan Iinkai, comp., *Meiji nyūsu jiten*, 3:90.

113 Otojirō no yorokobi" [Otojirō's delight], *Chūō shimbun*, January 1, 1892, in Shirakawa, 81; "Kawakami ichiza futatabi Kyōto ni en su" [Kawakami troupe again performs in Kyoto], *Ōsaka mainichi*, September 11, 1892, in Shirakawa, 113.

114 "Meika shinsoroku," 24; also Kurata, *Kindaigeki*, 143; Matsunaga, *Kawakami*, 84.

115 Kawashima, *Nihon*, 90; Yanagi Keitarō, *Kawakami Otojirō*, part 5. Sadayakko and Kawakami were not yet married.

116 Advertisements in *Yorozu chōbō*, January 5, 1893, in Shirakawa, 123.

117 Matsunaga, *Kawakami*, 95; Shirakawa, *shimbun*, 22; Kurata, *Kindaigeki*, 143;

118 Shirakawa, *shimbun*, 22, Kurata, *Kindaigeki*, 143, 164.

119 "Meika shinsoroku," 27–28.

120 Noël, *Annales 1893*, 53–494.

121 Matsumoto, *Meiji*, 182; Noël, *Annales 1893*, 297; Marvin A. Carlson, *The French Stage in the Nineteenth Century* (Metuchen, New Jersey, 1972), 200. *Prise de Pékin* was first staged in 1861.

122 "Kawakami-jō no Furansu miyage" [Mr. Kawakami's present from France], *Chūō shimbun*, May 24, 1893, in Matsumoto, *Meiji*, 182.

123 Noël, *Annales 1893*, 299–301, 469–73; Matsumoto, *Meiji*, 182–84.

124 Kurata, *Kindaigeki*, 143–46; Shirakawa, *shimbun*, 22.

125 "Hamada Yakko no Shikago yuki," [Yakko of the Hamada to go to Chicago], *Yorozu chōbō*, June 8, 1893, in Shirakawa, 130; also 124. Dozens of Japanese went to Chicago to work in the Japanese exhibits at the Exposition.

126 "Meika shinsoroku," 28; Kurata, *Kindaigeki*, 144–46; Toita, "Kabuki, *Shimpa*," 222; Kikou Yamata "Saddo Yakko et la Théâtre Japonais," *Revue de France* 19:1 (January 1939): 85–109.

127 Kawatake Shigetoshi, *Sōgō*, 248, 337; Shiragawa, *shimbun*, 22–23, 140.

128 Shirakawa, *shimbun*, 15–23, 53–131. I found it impossible to make a precise record of Kawakami's productions because of insufficient documentation and because the same play or story sometimes appeared under a different title. Identification was further complicated by the Japanese practice of referring to plays by the names of their principal characters rather than by play titles. That same character might appear in several different plays.

129 Kawatake Shigetoshi, *Sōgō*, 248, 337.

130 Kurata, *Kindaigeki*, 264. Like most Japanese theatrical performances, there was more than one play on the program.

131 Kawatake Shigetoshi, *Sōgō*, 523–34; Kurata, *Kindaigeki*, 145–47; Matsunaga, *Kawakami*, 102; Akiba, *Nihon*, 1:403.

132 Kawatake Shigetoshi, *Gaisetsu*, 377. Mokuami wrote only for kabuki while Iwasaki later became a pioneer playwright in the new theatre.

133 Ihara, *Meiji*, 668; Yanagi, *Ebanzuke*, 82–85.

134   Kurata, *Kindaigeki*, 147; Matsunaga, *Kawakami*, 103; Akiba, *Nihon*, 1:403; "Meika shinsoroku," 28; Matsumoto, *Meiji*, 405.

135   Some sources have suggested that for *Mata igai* Kawakami borrowed parts from *Oedipus Rex*, a play that he was alleged to have seen in Paris. This connection was denied in Takahashi, "Zadankai," 75. I found no record of an *Oedipus* production while Kawakami was in Paris.

136   "Kawakami, dentō no kōka o tsukau" [Kawakami uses electric lighting effects], *Yorozu chōbō*, January 24, 1894, in Shirakawa, 145; Kurata, *Kindaigeki*, 264.

137   Ihara, *Meiji*, 666–69; Kawatake Shigetoshi, *Sōgō*, 523–24. This French play by Émile Erckmann and Alexandre Chatrian was the basis for Henry Irving's 1871 success, *The Bells*, that was remade in English by Leopold Lewis and was possibly seen in 1899 by Kawakami in Boston.

138   Ihara, *Meiji*, 667–68; Okamoto, *Meiji*, 207, 275–77.

139   "Kabuki-za no bawari" [Description of scenes at the Kabuki-za], *Chūō shimbun*, August 7, 1898, in Shirakawa, 270.

140   Kawatake Shigetoshi, *Sōgō*, 524. In *Nihon engeki zenshi*, 1006, Kawatake claimed this play with its "natural dialog" was a landmark in the development of a distinctive shimpa style.

141   Matsumoto, *Meiji*, 405; Shirakawa, *shimbun*, 23–24.

142   Kurata, *Kindaigeki*, 264; "Meika shinsoroku." 27–28; Matsumoto, *Meiji*, 405.

143   Shirakawa, *shimbun*, 23–24; Kawatake Shigetoshi, *Gaisetsu*, 377.

Chapter 2

1   Keene, "Sino-Japanese," 127–28.

2   Matsunaga, *Kawakami*, 105.

3   Matsumoto, *Meiji*, 55, 184–86; Shirakawa, *shimbun*, 5.

4   Kawatake Shigetoshi, *Sōgō*, 446; Jean-Jacques Tschudin, "Le théâtre en territoire interdit ou la mise en scène de la guerre sino-japonaise," in *Le nation en marche: Etudes sur le Japon impérial de Meiji*, ed. Jean-Jacques Tschudin and Claude Hamon (Arles: Picquier, 1999), 197; Yanagi Keitarō, *Kawakami*, part 7; Matsunaga, *Kawakami*, 111.

5   Kurata, *Kindaigeki*, 151–53; Kano, *Acting*, 63.

6   Toita, "Kabuki, *Shimpa*," 269.

7   Inoue, *Kawakami*, 40; Miyake Shūtarō, *Engeki*, 13–14; Kawatake Shigetoshi, *Gaisetsu*, 377–78; Keene, "Sino-Japanese War," 135–38, 143–44.

8   Matsunaga, *Kawakami*, 109; Keene, "Sino-Japanese," 157; Yanagi Keitarō, *Kawakami*, part 7.

9   Ibid., 771–72; Ogawa, *Nihon*, 80; Waseda, *Nihon*, 213; Ihara, *Kabuki*, 7:379; Okamoto, *Meiji*, 260. Danjūrō was in Mokuami's *Okige no kumo harau asagochi* [The morning east wind clears the southeast clouds].

10   Kurata, *Kindaigeki*, 152; Ogasawara, *Kabuki*, 235.

11   Keene, "Sino-Japanese," 173.

12   Booth, *Hiss*, 23, 33.

13   "Shibai tayori" [Theatre news], *Miyako shimbun*, November 22, 1894, in Shirakawa, 173–74. While actors' doubling and tripling lowered labor costs, this kind of casting was also a strong additional attraction because they displayed a wider range of their talents.

14   Kurata, *Kindaigeki*, 154; Sekine, *Meiji*, 213–14; Matsumoto, *Meiji*, 54; "Meika shinsoroku, 29."

15   Kawatake Shigetoshi, *Gaisetsu*, 377. The documentary aspect was accented by the increased conversational—but still heroic—tone of dialogue in the play (Miller, *Yomigaeru*, cut 22 *Sōzetsu kaizetsu Nisshin sensō*).

16 Donald Keene, "Realism and Unreality in Japanese Drama," *Drama Survey* 3 (February 1964): 336.

17 Kurata, *Kindaigeki*, 153; Kawatake Shigetoshi, *Sōgō*, 446; Ihara, *Kabuki*, 8:422–23; Keene, "Sino-Japanese," 128–40.

18 Gluck, *Japan's*, 135–37.

19 Kawatake Shigetoshi, *Nihon engeki zenshi*, 855–57.

20 Ogasawara, *Kabuki*, 229–31; Matsunaga, *Kawakami*, 113; Kawatake Shigetoshi, *Nihon no engeki*, 356–59; Keene, "Sino-Japanese," 143–44; Kurata, *Kindaigeki*, 153.

21 Akiba, *Nihon*, 1:282.

22 Kurata, *Kindaigeki*, 154; "Kōtaishi denka Kawakami engeki goran" [His Highness the Crown Prince sees Kawakami play], in Shirakawa, 176–77.

23 Kawatake Shigetoshi, *Nihon engeki zenshi*, 856–57.

24 Ibid., 1008. This uncertain tale is part of cherished Japanese theatrical lore.

25 Kurata, *Kindaigeki*, 155; Sekine, *Meiji*, 213–14; Matsumoto, *Meiji*, 54.

26 Kawatake Shigetoshi, *Sōgō*, 446.

27 Kurata, *Kindaigeki*, 154.

28 Matsumoto, *Meiji*, 185; Kawatake Shigetoshi, *Sōgō*, 446.

29 Matsunaga, *Kawakami*, 115–20; Dōmon, *Kawakami*, 97.

30 Ibid., 124; Yanagi, *Shimpa no rokujūnen*, 170.

31 Yanagi, *Shimpa no rokujūnen*, 170–71; Yanagi Keitarō, *Kawakami*, part 7. This was accurate for New Actors but not always for kabuki.

32 Ubukata, "Kawakami," 169; Matsunaga, *Kawakami*, 124–27.

33 Kawakami Otojirō Kenshōkai, *Otojirō Sadayakko-jo*, 4, 22.

34 Kurata, *Kindaigeki*, 156–58.

35 Enjōji, *Tōkyō*, 26–27; Dōmon, *Kawakami*, 99.

36 Ogawa, *Nihon*, 112; also Kawatake Shigetoshi, *Gaisetsu*, 378.

37 Ubukata, "Kawakami," 170; Kurata, *Kindaigeki*, 158–59; Ihara, *Kabuki*, 7:555, 565, 570, 573–75, 8:15.

38 Ihara, *Kabuki*, 7:420, 8:422–23.

39 Kawatake Shigetoshi, *Nihon engeki zenshi*, 832–33.

40 Ihara, *Kabuki*, 7:297–335; Seidensticker, *Low*, 160–63; Donald H. Shively, "The Japanization of the Middle Meiji," in Shively, *Tradition*, 112–14.

41 "Shimpa gojūnen seisuiki, 7" [Record of the trials and tribulations of fifty years of shimpa, part 7], *Tōkyō nichinichi shimbun*, n.d., October 1937, n.p.; Ogasawara, *Kabuki*, 188–91, 193–94; Ihara, *Kabuki*, 7:540–57; Yanagi, *Ebanzuke*, 254.

42 Kawatake Shigetoshi, *Nihon engeki zenshi*, 856; Marui, *Shimpa*, 17–24.

43 Kurata, *Kindaigeki*, 155; Yanagi, *Shimpa no rokujūnen*, 11–19.

44 Ibid., 158.

45 Yanagi Eijirō and Endō Shingo, "Taidan: shimpa to 'Taki no Shiraito,'" [Conversation: shimpa and *Taki no Shiraito*]; Kokuritsu Gekijō, *Taki no Shiraito*, program, June 1972, 44–48; Kawatake Shigetoshi, *Sōgō*, 371; Cody Poulton, "Drama and Fiction in the Meiji Era: The Case of Izumi Kyōka," *Asian Theater Journal* 12:2 (Fall 1995): 285–89, 295. *Taki no Shiraito* was adapted from Izumi Kyōka's 1894 newspaper serialized novel, *Giketsu kyōketsu* (Loyal Blood, Valiant Blood). Kawakami's house playwright, Hanabusa Ryūgai, first dramatized this shimpa classic. Novels and plays by Kyōka have been a major source for shimpa drama and film. Between 1990 and 2000, there were at least seven different productions of *Taki no Shiraito* in Tokyo, although not all were performed by shimpa actors (Poulton, "Drama," 321–23). As there has been no definitive dramatic version of *Taki no Shiraito*, it continues to be performed with different scripts by different playwrights.

46 Matsumoto, *Meiji*, 55; Ochi Haruo, *Kyōka to gikyoku* [(Izumi) Kyōka and drama] (Sunoko shobō, 1987), 13.

47 Okazaki Yoshie, *Japanese Literature in the Meiji Era*, trans. V. H. Viglielmo (Tokyo: Ōbunsha, 1955), 66, 126; Samson, *Western*, 410–11.

48 Shirakawa, *shimbun*, 3, 21–31; Matsumoto, *Meiji*, 412–13.

49 Shirakawa Nobuo, annotator, "Honkoku: Kawakami Otojirō ichiza shiyō jōen daihon: *Mekura shisha*" [Reprint of *The Blind Messenger* script used by the Kawakami Otojirō troupe], *Engeki kenkyū* 10 (1983): 79–212. Many historians have claimed that Kawakami's earlier war plays borrowed extensively from a revival of Verne's *Michel Strogoff* that he saw while in France (Shirakawa, *shimbun*, 6; Takahashi, "Zadankai," 92). That production opened on April 2, 1893, when Kawakami was en route back to Kobe (Noël, *Annales 1893*, 297; Yamaguchi, *Joyū*, 7).

50 Ihara, *Kabuki*, 7:531; "Kawakami-za kyōgen to yakuwari" [The play and cast at the Kawakami Theatre], *Kabuki shimpō* No. 1666 (1897), in Shirakawa, 225–26; Ransome, *Japan*, 90–96; Kano, *Actress*, 99–102.

51 "Kawakami-za gogatsu kyōgen" [Plays at the Kawakami Theatre in May], *Miyako shimbun*, May 18, 1897, in Shirakawa, 228; Osman Edwards, *Japanese Plays and Playfellows*, (New York: Lane, 1901), 65–72, 83–85; Shirakawa Nobuo, comp., "Meijiki seiyōshu gikyoku jōen nempyō, 1, Meiji gonen–Meiji yonjūnen" [Chronology of performances during the Meiji era of plays based on Western works, part 1: 1872–1907)], *Engeki kenkyū* No. 17 (1993): 49–86.

52 Typical of Japanese theatre, each long performance, whether kabuki or shimpa, consisted of two or more plays. This was similar to the earlier Anglo-American practice of several plays (the featured play with one or more lesser works) on one bill.

53 Marui, *Shimpa*, 16–22.

54 Ōzasa, *Nihon*, 68.

55 Yanagi, *Shimpa no rokujūnen*, 167.

56 Donald H. Shively, "The Japanization of the Middle Meiji," in Shively, *Tradition*, 78, 103–10; Gluck, *Japan's*, 135.

57 Gunji, *Kabuki*, 18; Mori Mitsuya, "Thinking and Feeling: Characteristics of Intercultural Theatre," in Scholz-Cionca, *Japanese*, 362–64.

58 Kabuki acting in the Kansai area has historically been less dependent on rigid kata.

59 James R. Brandon, "Kabuki and Shakespeare: Balancing Yin and Yang," *Drama Review* (TDR 162) 43:2 (Summer 1999): 15.

60 Natsume, *And Then*, 143.

61 Knepler, *Gilded*, 33.

62 Sauter, *Theatrical*, 149, 184–86. Italics *sic*.

63 Ihara, *Meiji*, 492–93; Keene, "Sino-Japanese," 158–61; Kawatake Shigetoshi, *Gaisetsu*, 343–44.

64 For one discussion of postmodern achievement, see Yukihiro Goto, "The Theatrical Fusion of Suzuki Tadashi, *Asian Theater Journal* VI 6 (Fall 1989): 103–23.

65 Donald Keene, "Realism and Unreality in Japanese Drama," *Drama Survey* 3:3 (February 1964): 332. A page later, Keene did consider what he called the "varieties of realism" in kabuki.

66 Eustace B. Rogers, "The Japanese Theatre," *Outing* 25 (December 1894): 195.

67 F. C. Walter Parr, "The Japanese Theatre," *Theater* (London) (October 1, 1884): 187; also Morse, *Japan*, 404. In his *Japan*, 214, Kawatake Toshio condemned the excess of realistic blood in nineteenth-century kabuki.

68 "Japanese Theatre I," *Appleton's Journal* 2 (November 27, 1869): 450.

69 Kawatake Shigetoshi, *Nihon engeki zenshi*, 1008, 1014; Kurata, *Kindaigeki*, 159–60.

70 Matsunaga, *Kawakami*, 132–33.

71   Kurata, *Kindaigeki*, 155. Shirakawa, *shimbun*, 125–354, included numerous newspaper articles that used *shinhaiyū*, *shin'engeki*, and *sōshi haiyū* for New Actor/Theatre plays. The word *shin'engeki* (new drama or new theatre) had been used in the 1880s to designate kabuki reform efforts.

72   "Shimpa gojūnen seisuiki, 7" [A record of the trials and tribulations of fifty years of shimpa, part 7], *Tōkyō nichinichi shimbun*, n.d. October 1937, n.p.

73   Yanagi, *Shimpa no rokujūnen*, 30; Kawatake Shigetoshi, *Nihon engeki zenshi*, 874–77.

74   Kawatake Shigetoshi, *Gaisetsu*, 378; Akiba, *Nihon*, 1: 240, 263, 324, 673. In an authoritative 1910 theatrical directory, actors were classified as either *kyūha* or shimpa (Kawajiri, *Engei*). The suffixes *-ha* and *-pa* are phonetic variations meaning "school," "clique," or "faction."

75   "Shimpa gojūnen seisuiki 7," *Tōkyō nichinichi shimbun*, October 1937, n.p.

76   Kawatake Shigetoshi, *Gaisetsu*, 378.

77   Yanagi, *Shimpa no rokujūnen*, 2–5; "Shimpa gojūnen kaiko kiji" [Articles recalling fifty years of shimpa], in file *ro* 2/74, Waseda; "Kawakami Otojirō ōmote" [Big welcome for Kawakami Otojirō], *Niroku shimpō*, March 17, 1900, in Shirakawa, 312.

78   Ortolani, *Japanese*, 155–56; Natsuko Inoue, "New (Neo) [*sic*] *Kabuki* and the Work of Hanagumi Shibai," in Leiter, *Kabuki Reader*, 193.

79   Toita, "The Kabuki, the *Shimpa*," 233–34; Minami, *Kabuku*, 31.

80   Okamoto, *Meiji*, 93–94.

81   "Eikoku kabuki no hanashi" [Speaking of British kabuki], *Kabuki* (April 1901): 1–5.

82   "Kaintsu" [Obituary] for Josef Kainz, *Kabuki* (January 1911): 43–47.

83   "Meika shinsoroku," 29–30; Kurata, *Kindaigeki*, 161.

84   Kurata, *Kindaigeki*, 159–60. 83 Matsunaga, *Kawakami*, 132–33.

85   Yanagi Keitarō, *Kawakami*, part 8; Kurata, *Kindaigeki*, 159.

86   Matsunaga, *Kawakami*, 132–33.

87   His candidacy has been called the "tarento giin no tanjō" (the birth of the show-business Diet representative).

88   Kurata, *Kindaigeki*, 159, 161.

89   Robert Scalapino, *Democracy and the Party Movement in Prewar Japan* (Berkeley: University of California Press, 1953), 112–13.

90   "Tōkyō-fu dainijū-ku" [Tokyo 12th district]," in Shirakawa, 253; Kurata, *Kindaigeki*, 159–61; "Meika shinsoroku," 29–30; Marui, *Shimpa*, 21.

91   Robert Scalapino, *Democracy and the Party Movement*, 173. Upper House members were all appointed.

92   Matsunaga, *Kawakami*, 85, 136–38; Kurata, *Kindaigeki*, 162.

93   Kurata, *Kindaigeki*, 162–64; multiple articles in Shirakawa, 265–68.

94   "Daijūni-ku" [Twelfth district], *Jiji shimpō*, 13 August 1898, in Shirakawa, 272; Matsunaga, *Kawakami*, 136–38; Kurata, *Kindaigeki*, 162.

95   "Fish and Ricksha Man," *New York Sun*, March 25, 1900, 2:8.

96   Yanagi, *Shimpa no rokujūnen*, 173.

97   Matsumoto, *Meiji*, 421–22; Édouard Pailleron, *Le monde où l'on s'ennuie* (Boston: Heath, 1894).

98   Yanagi, *Ebanzuke*, 89–93.

99   Akiba, *Nihon*, 1:307–8; Yanagi, *Shimpa no rokujūnen*, 174; multiple adverse reviews in Shirakawa, 274–82.

100 Yanagi, *Ebanzuke*, 256–57; Akiba, *Nihon*, 1:273; "Kawakami no rakujō" [The fall of Kawakami], *Tōkyō asahi shimbun*, August 6, 1898, in Shirakawa, 269.

101 Toita, "Kabuki, Shimpa," 273; Yanagi, *Shimpa no rokujūnen*, 174.

102 Kaneo, *Ōbei*, 2. "*Nippon* is an alternative pronunciation of *Nihon*. The written characters (kanji) for both pronunciations are the same. *Maru* denotes a Japanese boat or ship.

103   Matsunaga, *Kawakami*, 141–42.

104   Shirakawa, *shimbun*, 281–83.

105   Kaneo, *Ōbei*, 3.

106   Yanagi Keitarō, *Kawakami*, part 8; Matsunaga, *Kawakami*, 143; Kaneo, *Ōbei*, 3.

107   Yamaguchi, *Jōyū*, 76.

108   Jason G. Karlin, "The Gender of Nationalism: Competing Masculinities in Meiji Japan," *Journal of Japanese Studies* 28:1 (Winter 2002): 70–72.

109   "Kawakami no yake tokai" [Kawakami's desperate sea voyage], *Yorozu chōbō*, September 16, 1896, in Shirakawa, 285–86; Yanagi Keitarō, *Kawakami*, part 8.

110   "Kawakami Otojirō umi ni tadayou" [Kawakami Otojirō adrift at sea], *Jiji shimpō*, September 15, 1898; "Kawakami Otojirō to saishi no hyōryū" [Kawakami Otojirō and family drifting], *Tōkyō asahi shimbun*, September 16, 1898, in Shirakawa, 282–83; Kurata, *Kindaigeki*, 166; Matsunaga, *Kawakami*, 142.

111   Kaneo, *Ōbei*, 3; Kaneo, *Sadayakko*, 3.

112   Matsunaga, *Kawakami*, 144.

113   Kaneo, *Sadayakko*, 3; Okamoto, *Meiji*, 277.

114   Matsunaga, *Kawakami*, 144–45; Fujisawa Asajirō, "Kawakami fūfu o kataru" [Speaking of Mr. and Mrs. Kawakami)], in Fujii, *Jiden*, 261–63; miscellaneous articles on the progress of the boat, Shirakawa, *shimbun*, 290–95.

115   Kaneo, *Ōbei*, 5.

116   Kaneo, *Sadayakko*, 3.

117   Kaneo, *Ōbei*, 5–6. I based my calculation of the distance traveled on various accounts of their irregular route.

118   Ibid., Kawakami Sadayakko, "Kawakami Sadayakko," in Kawajiri, *Engei*, 53.

119   Kipling, *From*, 1:307.

120   Yokohama, *Meiji*, 146–50; Ochiai Yoshinobu, *Kōbe no rekishi: kodai kara kindai made* [History of Kobe: from the ancient past to modern times] (Kōbe: Gotō Shoten, 1989), 196–205; La Farge, *Artist's*, 4, 8.

121   Harold S. Williams, *Tales of the Foreign Settlements in Japan* (Rutland, Vermont: Tuttle, 1958), 130–31.

122   Kaneo, *Ōbei*, 6; "Kawakami fūfu Kōbe ni chakasu" [Mr. and Mrs. Kawakami arrive in Kobe], *Tōkyō shimbun*, January 10, 1899, in Shirakawa, 298. Fukui was a Kawakami protégé who had become a star.

123   "Kawakami Otojirō Kōbe ni mukō" [Kawakami Otojirō heads towards Kobe], *Tōkyō asahi shimbun*, January 7, 1899, in Shirakawa, 296.

124   "Fukui Mohei, Kawakami o sukuu" [Fukui Mohei saves Kawakami], *Yorozu chōbō*, January 17, 1899, in Shirakawa, 298.

125   Fujii, *Jiden*, 193.

126   Yamaguchi, *Joyū*, 76.

127   Ezaki, *Jitsuroku*, 97; "Kawakami zenshin ni suishu okosu" [Kawakami's entire body afflicted with dropsy], *Miyako shimbun*, February 10, 1899, in Shirakawa, 299; Matsunaga, *Kawakami*, 139.

128   Kawakami Sadayakko, "Kawakami Sadayakko," in Kawajiri *Engei*, 53; Kaneo, *Sadayakko*, 4.

129   Kawakami mentioned this to a newspaper reporter a year earlier ("Pari no Nihon engeki" [Japanese drama to Paris], *Jiji shimpō*, June 4, 1898, in Shirakawa, 264). He also mentioned taking a Japanese drama troupe to the forthcoming Paris Exposition.

130   Kurata, *Kindaigeki*, 157.

131   "Parii e norikomi" [Embarking for Paris], *Chūō shimbun*, December 28, 1898, in Shirakawa, 295–96.

132   The more familiar version was made into a novel in French, *Tcho-chin-goura: ou vengeance japonaise; roman japonaise*, traduit en englais avec notes et appendice par Frederick V. Dickins, traduction française de Albert Dousdebès (Paris: Ollendorff, 1886). The original English-language book by Dickins was first published

in Yokohama in 1875. Although Dickins claimed he translated the standard version of the play, his work was actually a loose adaptation in the form of a typical mid-nineteenth-century short novel (Frederick V. Dickins, *Chiushingura; or, The Loyal League: A Japanese Romance*, first edition 1875, reprinted Yokohama: Maruya and Kelley and Walsh, 1879). Another English-language version of *Chūshingura*, translated by Edward Greey and Shiuichiro Saito, was *The Loyal Ronins: An Historical Romance* (New York: Putnam, 1880). The "translators" acknowledged that they worked from an illustrated story that appeared in the *Iro ha bunko* of Tamenaga Shunsui (Edo: Nakamuraya, 1,836–48). Greey's introduction claimed that B. H. Gausseron translated a full version of the book into French in 1882 and that condensations appeared in German, Italian, Spanish, and Swedish. An abbreviated version of the basic story, "The Forty-Seven Rōnins," appeared in Mitford (1871), *Tales*, 15–41, and this may also have been translated into other European languages.

133 Miyaoka, *Ikoku*, 44–45; Akiba, *Tōto*, 105–6.

134 Ōzaki first adapted the Molière play into a *hon'an* novel in 1892. He then did the same with *A Doctor in Spite of Himself*. In the late 1890s, young kabuki playwright Matsui Shōō wrote *hon'an* versions of *The Bourgeois Gentleman* and *The Misanthrope*, but I found no record that these were produced prior to 1900. An earlier Japanese introduction to Molière was *The School for Wives* that appeared as a serialized *hon'an* novel in an 1879 newspaper (Shirakawa, *shimbun*, 3–4; Matsumoto, *Meiji engekiron*, 378).

135 Yanagi, *Ebanzuke*, 255; Kawatake Shigetoshi, *Sōgō*, 432. Ii Yōhō and Yamaguchi Sadao produced a less successful *Koi no byō* (Love sick) that was a *hon'an* of *A Physician in Spite of Himself* (Matsumoto, *Meiji engekiron*, 413–14).

136 "Pari e norikomi," *Chūō shimbun*, December 28, 1898, and "Pari ni okeru Nihon kabuki oyobi engeki hyōban" [Report on Japanese kabuki and drama in Paris], *Yomiuri shimbun*, April 8, 1900, in Shirakawa, 295–96, 313–14.

137 Fujii, *Jiden*, 263; Matsunaga, *Kawakami*, 149–50.

138 Miyaoka, *Ikoku*, 53, 57.

139 Charles E. Funnell, *By the Beautiful Sea: The Rise and High Times of That Great American Resort, Atlantic City* (New York: Knopf, 1975), 24, 155; "Atlantic City Society by the Sea," *Philadelphia Inquirer*, July 12, 1896, 18; "Atlantic City," *Philadelphia Inquirer*, July 24, 1898, 22.

140 "Kissa'en to shinhaiyū Kawakami" [A tea garden and New Actor Kawakami], *Miyako shimbun*, March 1, 1899, in Shirakawa, 299.

141 *Beikoku*, 1333. Several years later, Kushibiki produced *Japan at Night*, a vaudeville spectacular at the roof garden of Madison Square Garden ("Plays and Players," *Theatre* [New York] 3:30 [August 1903]: 184; Mantle, *Best Plays*, 413).

142 Ishimaki Yoshio, *Katsudō shashin keizai ron* [On the economics of moving pictures], (Bungadō, 1923), 162; Yoshida Chieo, "Katsuben no rekishi: 1" [History of the *katsuben* (narrators of silent motion pictures)]: 1; *Eiga shi kenkyū* 1 (1973): 19–20; Yamaguchi, *Joyū*, 77.

143 "Kissa'en to shinhaiyū Kawakami," *Miyako shimbun*.

144 Kaneo, *Sadayakko*, 4.

145 Kaneo, *Ōbei*, 2.

146 Fujii, *Jiden*, 29; Kaneo, *Sadayakko*, 4.

147 Quoted in Keene, *Dawn: Fiction*, 102.

148 Kaneo, *Sadayakko*, 4; Kaneo, *Ōbei*, 2.

149 Kentarō Kaneko "Views Concerning the World's Great Exhibition at Paris," *Far East* 2:5 (May 1897): 189, 194–95. He was writing about government oversight to assure full realization of the commercial potential of Japanese industrial manufactures.

150 Hosley, *Japan*, 31–42; Finn Dallas, "Japan at the Centennial," *Nineteenth Century* (Autumn 1976): 33–40.

151 William Walton, *World's Columbian Exposition: Art and Architecture* (Philadelphia: George Barrie, 1893), 1:87.

152 Ibid.

153 Also transliterated as Liao-Tung.

154 "Kawakami Otojirō yotto o uru [Kawakami Otojirō sells yacht], *Yorozu chōhō*, January 31, 1899, in Shirakawa, 298–99; Kaneo, *Ōbei*, 4; "Kawakami ketsubetsu no kōgyō" [Kawakami's farewell performance], *Miyako shimbun*, January 18, 1899, in Shirakawa, 298. The cities were Osaka, Kyoto, and Kobe.

155 Ezaki, *Jitsuroku*, 97–98; Yanagi, *Ebanzuke*, 257.

156 The Aioi-za was adjacent to the main brothel district of Kobe in an area that was once the site of a twelfth-century imperial palace (Ochiai Yoshinobu, *Kōbe no rekishi*, 205–06; Harold S. Williams, *Tales of the Foreign Settlements in Japan* [Rutland, Vermont: Tuttle, 1958], 187; Yokohama, *Meiji*, 151).

157 Yanagi, *Shimpa no rokujūnen*, 175–76.

158 Matsunaga, *Kawakami*, 151; Yanagi, *Shimpa no rokujūnen*, 242.

159 Marui, *Shimpa*, 23. The show opened March 31, 1899, at the Osaka Naka-za.

160 Ogawa, *Nihon*, 106; "Kawakami ichiza" [The Kawakami troupe], *Yomiuri shimbun*, December 9, 1893, in Shirakawa, 141; Hagii, *Shimpa*, 25; Okamoto, *Engeki*, 170.

161 Inoue, *Kawakami*, 62. Evidence about when and where Sadayakko received her stage name and where and when she first appeared professionally onstage has been highly contradictory. She later claimed that her name was created for her at the Palace Hotel in San Francisco later in 1899 (Fujii, *Jiden*, 194–96).

162 Ibid., 62–63.

163 Matsunaga, *Kawakami*, 151.

164 "Meika shinsoroku 23: Kawakami Sadayakko" [Celebrity facts 23: Kawakami Sadayakko], *Engei gahō* (October 1908): 88.

165 Yanagi Keitarō, *Kawakami*, part 9; "Meika shinsoroku 23: Kawakami Sadayakko," 88. Sadayakko claimed her first professional performance was at Himeji on this bill.

166 Sugimoto, *Madamu*, 124–25.

167 Ihara, *Kabuki*, 7:15; Marui, *Shimpa*, 23.

168 Yanagi, *Kido*, 161.

169 Fujii, *Jiden*, 264; "Kawakami Otojirō," *Miyako shimbun*, March 28, 1899, in Shirakawa, 300; "Kawakami Otojirōra kaigai ni tobu ka" [Kawakami group to fly abroad?], *Yomiuri shimbun*, March 18, 1899, Shirakawa, 300; Matsunaga, *Kawakami*, 152–53.

170 "Kissaẹn to shinhaiyū Kawakami," *Miyako shimbun*.

171 Discussed in Gluck, *Japan's*, 94.

172 Iwai, *Shimpa*, 113, 121–22, 136, 151, 162, 164, 186, 192; Kaneo, *Ōbei*, 6–7.

173 The numbers that follow descriptions were the ages at the time of departure and were calculated according to the European method of counting years. There may be discrepancies.

174 Kaneo, *Sadayakko*, 4.

175 Kaneo, *Ōbei*, 14.

176 Ibid, 33.

177 Toita, *Monogatari*, 26.

178 Inoue, *Kawakami*, 63. It was a centuries-old practice for traveling troupes to include a child actor or two. This Tsuru was the younger sister of Shige from the *Nippon Maru*.

179 Kineya is name of the principal "family" (school) of shamisen players. Most theatres hired from this specialist pool. Kimisaburō's own family name was Sugibashi (Kaneo, *Ōbei*, frontispiece 2).

180 Koyama was eager for the foreign trip because he had was deeply depressed for several years after his wife's death (Dōmon, *Kawakami*, 107).

181 "Kushibiki Yumito," advertisement, *Yomiuri shimbun*, March 19, 1899, in Shirakawa, 301; "Kawakami Bei e shuppatsu" [Kawakami departs for America], *Miyako shimbun*, April 21, 1899, in Shirakawa, 301.

182 "Ocean and Waterfront," *San Francisco Chronicle*, May 21, 1899, 9.

183 Kaneo, *Ōbei*, 6–7.

184 "Ocean and Water Front," *San Francisco Chronicle*; also Sawada, *Tokyo*, 47. The *Chronicle* did not explain how these Chinese got into the United States when the Chinese Exclusion Act was supposedly in force.

185 Yamaguchi, *Joyū*, 78.

186 "Ocean and Waterfront," *San Francisco Chronicle*.

187 Edward D. Beechert, *Honolulu: Crossroads of the Pacific* (Columbia: University of South Carolina Press), 55; William R. Castle, Jr., *Hawaii: Past and Present* (New York: Dodd, Mead, 1916), 85, 87–88; Jack Rankin and Ray Jerome Baker, *Panorama Hawaii* (Honolulu: Mutual Publishing, 1984), n.p.

188 Eleanor Robson Belmont, *The Fabric of Memory* (New York: Farrar, Straus, 1957), 9; A. S. Twombly, *Hawaii and Its People* (New York: Silver, Burdett, 1899), 23.

189 Julius W. Pratt, *Expansionists of 1898: The Acquisition of Hawaii and the Spanish Islands* (Gloucester, Massachusetts: Peter Smith, 1959), 216–26, 260–78, 319–20.

190 A touring kabuki troupe from the Kansai area played Hawaii as early as 1893. The Asahi-za was an active theatre by 1897 (James R. Brandon, "Kabuki: Changes and Prospects: An International Symposium," *Asia Theater Journal* 15:2 [Fall 1998]: 255).

191 Kaneo, *Ōbei*, 8.

192 Hazama, *Okage*, 28–29; Yukiko Kimura, *Issei: Japanese Immigrants in Hawaii* (Honolulu: University of Hawaii Press, 1988), 146; Takie Okumura, "Drive against the Gangsters," in *Kodomo no tame ni, For the Sake of the Children*, ed. Dennis M. Ogawa (Honolulu: University Press of Hawaii, 1978), 61–65.

193 Lawrence H. Fuchs, *Hawaii Ponoi: A Social History* (New York: Harcourt, Brace, 1961), 35–36; Hazama, *Okage*, 28–29; Research Committee on the Study of Japanese Americans in Honolulu, *Honolulu's Japanese Americans in Comparative Perspective* (Tokyo: Institute of Statistical Mathematics, 1984), 6; Alan Takeo Moriyama, *Imingaisha: Japanese Emigration Companies and Hawaii, 1894–1904* (Honolulu: University of Hawaii Press, 1985), 1–17, 78–85, 202–3.

194 Hazama, *Okage*, 26–29.

195 This replaced the earlier Royal Hawaiian Theatre which was built and monopolized by the Yankees who controlled the kingdom (Samuel Smiles, Jr., *Boy's Voyage round the World*, 235–36).

196 Eleanor Robson Belmont, *The Fabric of Memory*, 9; "Hawaii. Bubonic Plague Closes the Theatres," *NYDM*, April 7, 1900, 8; Hawaiian Opera House, Honolulu, program, November 1898; A. S. Twombly, *Hawaii and Its People*, 19. The Opera House was also known as the Orpheum.

197 Kaneo, *Ōbei*, 8. The Asahi-za burned down in January 1900 in a fire that destroyed fourteen blocks of Chinatown and left thousands homeless (Hazama, *Okage*, 27–28).

198 Kaneo, *Ōbei*, 9. Harris had been affiliated with the Sapporo Agriculture College in Hokkaidō and later returned to Japan as a bishop. As one of the foremost foreign apologists for Japanese imperialist policies, he received more high honors and decorations from the Japanese government than any foreigner had up to the time of his death in 1921 (*Kodansha Encyclopedia of Japan*, s.v. "Harris, Merriman Colbert;" Yoshio Markino, *When I Was a Child* [Boston: Houghton Mifflin, 1912], 212, 214).

199 Kaneo, *Ōbei*, 8–9.

200 Ibid; Malm, *Japanese*, 191.

201 Kaneo, *Ōbei*, 9.

202 In kabuki performance, the usual nagauta ensemble has Japanese drums (both shoulder-hand drum and side-hand drum) and flute, although a singer and player duo is also common.

203 William P. Malm, *Nagauta: The Heart of Kabuki Music* (Tokyo: Tuttle, 1963), 49.

204   Kaneo, *Ōbei*, 9; Gilbert, *American*, 41. Kineya's brilliant playing can be heard on record cuts 2, 5, 10, 15, 17, 28, and particularly on cut 12 in Miller, *Yomigaeru*, recorded in 1900 in Paris. His performance (although he was unidentified) of an *ōzatsuma* is on a 1901 recording made in Berlin (Hornbostel Collection, Berlin Phonogramm-Archiv, Federal Cylinder Project, Archive of Folk Culture (Washington: Library of Congress, AFS No. 10,054: B10, Cylinder No. 4,076; Original No. 24).

205   Malm, *Japanese*, 185–87.

206   Kaneo, *Ōbei*, 9.

207   Chamberlain, *Japanese*, 342–43.

208   Clara Whitney, *Clara's Diary: An American Girl in Meiji Japan* (Tokyo: Kodansha International, 1979), 93. Whitney was fifteen when she wrote her diary in 1876.

Chapter 3

1   "Personal Notes," *San Francisco Chronicle*, May 21, 1899, 18.

2   Siefkin, *City*, 14.

3   DeWitt, *Illustrated*, 79–80; Kennedy, *Great*, 55.

4   Siefkin, *City*, 14.

5   Ibid., 15.

6   Kipling, *American*, 18; Kipling, *From*, 1:439.

7   Jun'ichirō Tanizaki, *In Praise of Shadows (In'ei raisan)*, trans. Thomas J. Harper and Edward G. Seidensticker (New Haven: Lette's Island Books, 1977), 4–5.

8   *Crocker-Langley 1899*, 170. In 1899, Grant Avenue after it crossed Bush Street was called Dupont Street.

9   See also Noguchi, *American*, 33.

10   Kaneo, *Ōbei*, 12; Kaneo, *Sadayakko*, 4; Matsunaga, *Kawakami*, 154.

11   *Crocker-Langley 1899*, 1233. There was no Mitsuse in the comprehensive listings of attorneys in this directory. Background from: *Beikoku*, 411; Tsurutani, *America*, 68–72, 90–92; Niiya, *Japanese*, 31; Ezaki, *Jitsuroku*, 100.

12   Muramatsu Shōfu, *Kawakami*, 1:244.

13   "California Theatre," advertisement, *NYDM*, September 2, 1899, 6.

14   Fujii, *Jiden*, 195; Makimura, *Kawakami*. 127–28. Also Ezaki, *Jitsuroku*, 99; Yamaguchi, *Joyū*, 79; "Meika shinsōroku, 28–29.

15   "Sadayakko," *Niroku shimpō*, April 11, 1900, in Shirakawa, 314–15; Fujii, *Jiden*, 194; Yamaguchi, *Joyū*, 36; Kawakami Sadayakko, "Kawakami Sadayakko," in Kawajiri, *Engei*, 53, 56–57.

16   Dōmon, *Kawakami*, 108, 110.

17   Ezaki, *Jitsuroku*, 99.

18   Natsume, *And Then*, 139.

19   Dickson, *Streets*; "Kawakami Sadayakko," Kawajiri, *Engei*, 55–56; Ogi Shinzō and Maeda Chikashi, eds, *Meiji Taishō zushi, Tōkyō* [Pictures from the Meiji and Taishō Eras, Tokyo] (Chikuma Shobō, 1978), 158; K[iyoshi] K. Kawakami, "The Japanese in New England," *New England* 35 (December 1906): 440–44; Kipling, *American*, 19.

20   Novelist Nagai Kafū found smelly Americans had the "the stink of meat-eating people" ("Nezame" [Waking up], in Nagai's *Amerika*, 47).

21   Noguchi, *American*, 29, 104.

22   Baedeker, *United*, xxxi; Nagai, "Akuyū" [Bad Companions], in his *Amerika*, 37.

23   Yamaguchi, *Joyū*, 194.

24   Ezaki, *Jitsuroku*, 99.

25 DeWitt, *Illustrated*, 42; Bronson, *Earth*, 50, 53, 55.

26 Beikoku, 411.

27 Dickson, *Streets*, 107–8; Levy, *920 O'Farrell*, 4, 259.

28 Kiyoshi Kawakami, *Asia*, 122; U.S. Congress, Senate, 59th Congress, 2d session, Document No. 147, December 18, 1906, "Japanese in the City of San Francisco, California," 9–10. Very few Japanese names appeared in San Francisco city directories: Crocker-Langley 1899, 1900, and 1901.

29 Ichioka, *Issei*, 14–16. Students supported by the Japanese government usually went to the East Coast.

30 Herman, *Japanese*, 133.

31 Smith, *Americans*, 231; Kiyoshi Kawakami, *Asia*, 122; Tsurutani, *America*, 51; Wilson, *East*, 48. After 1900 many socialists returned to Japan to organize labor unions (Ichioka, "Early Issei Socialists," 2–3).

32 "Japanese Day at the Art Exhibition," *San Francisco Examiner*, May 25, 1899, 2; Smith, *Americans*, 231.

33 Daniels, *Politics*, 6.

34 Ichioka, *Issei*, 14–16; Wilson, *East*, 48–50.

35 Kiyoshi Kawakami, *Asia*, 122.

36 Walter G. Beach, *Oriental Crime in California* (Stanford: Stanford University Press, 1932), 14, 75; DeWitt, *Illustrated*, 82.

37 Daniels, *Politics*, 8, 19; Tsurutani, *America*, 68.

38 Noguchi, *American*, 139; Smith, *Americans*, 206–9.

39 Ichioka, *Issei*, 185; Frederick Palmer, "The Japanese School Question," *Collier's Weekly* (January 19, 1907): 24.

40 Tsurutani, *America*, 163.

41 Kiyoshi Kawakami, *Asia*, 121–22.

42 Tsurutani, *America*, 37. An alternative estimate was twenty Japanese males to one female (Masako Herman, *The Japanese in America, 1843–1973* [Dobbs Ferry, New York: Oceana, 1974], 133).

43 "A Japanese Tragedian," *NYDM*, June 3, 1899, 2; Kaneo, *Ōbei*, 9–10.

44 Kaneo, *Ōbei*, 9–10. *Kusunoki Masahige* was one of the first kabuki *katsurekigeki* ("living history [historically correct] plays") (Kawatake Shigetoshi, *Nihon engeki zenshi*, 797).

45 Okamoto, *Meiji*, 131–32; Yanagi Keitarō, *Kawakami*, part 9.

46 T.V.V. clubs were organized in independent chapters across the United States.

47 Ben Graf Hennecke, *Laura Keene: Actress, Innovator, and Impresario; a Biography* (Tulsa: Council Oak Books, 1990), 237.

48 Miyaoka, *Ikoku*, 44–45, 54–55; *Beikoku*, 133–34.

49 Estavan, *San*, 5:1:96, 255.

50 "Beikoku naru Kawakami Otojirō-ra no hyōban" [Popularity of the Kawakami Otojirō troupe in America], *Yomiuri shimbun*, July 5, 1899, in Shirakawa, 303–4; "The Japanese Historical Company Enacting Japanese Drama at the California Theatre," *Wave* (San Francisco) (June 24, 1899): 6. Although not documented, it was likely that nagauta singer Fujita Sennosuke and shamisen player Kineya Kimisaburo also performed solo or together as they had on ship.

51 There was no definitive version. English language approximations are in *Introduction to Classic Japanese Literature* (Tōkyō: Kokusai Bunka Shinkokai, 1939), 212; George Sansom, *A History of Japan: 1334–1615*, (Stanford: Stanford University Press, 1969), 126; Varley, *Warriors*, 196. A fuller account of the Kusunoki parting scene appeared in Y. Tan, "Sakurai no eki," *Far East* (Tokyo) 1 (1896): 2:23–25, 3:28–30.

52 Komota, *Nihon*, 219. My rendering here was a variation of a more complete translation in Morris, *Nobility*, 132.

53 In Morris, *Nobility*, 133, Kusunoki's brother, not Kusunoki, is said to have delivered this quintessential

speech as "I should like to be reborn seven times into this world of men ... so that I might [each time] destroy the enemies of the Court." See also Varley, *Warriors,* 196.

54   Helen Craig McCullough's translation of parts of this epic appeared in her *The Taiheiki: A Chronicle of Medieval Japan* (1959, reprint; Rutland, Vermont: Tuttle, 1979). McCullough discussed Kusunoki's early life but omitted the Sakurai and Minatogawa episodes.

55   Matsumoto, *Meiji engekiron,* 501, 903; Toyotaka, *Japanese,* 199; Kawatake Shigetoshi, *Sōgō,* 181–82, Hagii, Shimpa, 73.

56   Matsumoto, *Meiji engekiron,* 137, 144–45; Okamoto, *Meiji,* 131–32, 134; Kawakami Otojirō Kenshōkai, *Otojirō,* shimpageki, 14.

57   Akiba, *Nihon,* 1:307–8; Yanagi, *Ebanzuke,* 59; Yanagi, *Shimpa no rokujūnen,* 148–49; "Kawakami katsubetsu no kōgyō" [Kawakami's farewell performance], *Miyako shimbun,* January 18, 1899, in Shirakawa, 298.

58   In *The Nobility of Failure,* Ivan Morris investigated the Japanese celebration of these doomed heroes.

59   For late twentieth-century evaluations of Kusunoki, see Kon Tōkō, "Kusunoki Masashige: Chiryaku jūō no meishō" [Kusunoki Masashige: the thoroughly resourceful famous commander], and Nagai Michiko, "Nazo no jimbutsu: Kusunoki Masashige" [Enigmatic personality: Kusunoki Masashige], in Tsubota, *Nihon,* 4:54–59, 60–61; also Morris, *Nobility,* 106–42. For a contrasting nineteenth-century account, see Griffis, *Mikado's,* 152, 182, 190–91, 220, 406.

60   The patriotic emotional effects of *Kusunoki* on an early 1900 Japanese audience were described by Mrs. Hugh [Mary C.] Frazer in "The Japanese Stage," *Living Age* 248 (March 17, 1906): 681–86. Until the end of the Second World War, school textbooks had extraordinary coverage of Kusunoki as the ideal imperial subject (Mita, *Social,* 259–60 fn. 12).

61   Morris, *Nobility,* 137–38, 386 fn. 6.89.

62   Ortolani, *Japanese,* 93.

63   Kaneo, *Ōbei,* 10; Kellermann, *Sassa,* 55–56.

64   "Theatrical Managers Arrested for Permitting These Children on the Stage," *San Francisco Examiner,* May 27, 1899, 12; "Children Allowed to Sing in Public," *San Francisco Call,* May 30, 1899, 6. Police were acting on complaints from the raging Society for the Prevention of Cruelty to Children.

65   Marui, *Shimpa,* 17.

66   "Beikoku no Kawakami" [Kawakami in America], *Miyako shimbun,* July 4, 1899, in Shirakawa, 302–3.

67   Matsumoto, *Meiji engekiron,* 415, 417–19; Ihara, *Kabuki,* 7:568. An English language adaptation, *The Two Orphans,* was a major 1874 success in New York. Subsequent productions toured the United States for thirty years while the original was popular on French stages for over half a century (Hughes, *History,* 233–34; Strang, Players, 207–8; Marvin Carlson, *The French Stage in the Nineteenth Century* [Metuchen, New Jersey: Scarecrow, 1972], 170).

68   "Japanese Play Ends Abruptly," *San Francisco Chronicle,* June 23, 1899, 10.

69   "Beikoku naru Kawakami Otojirō-ra no hyōban" [Popularity of the Kawakami Otojirō troupe in America], *Miyako shimbun,* July 4, 1899, in Shirakawa, 303–4. This report, probably written by Kawakami, could not be confirmed because apparently nothing of the local vernacular press survived in archives. The National Japanese American Historical Society of San Francisco informed me that they knew of no surviving copies of San Francisco newspapers of this period.

70   Smith, *Americans,* 231; *Zaibei,* 12.

71   Kaneo, *Ōbei,* 11; *Beikoku,* 302.

72   Wilson, *East,* 31–32. The massive importation of "picture brides" began several years later and brought a domestic normalcy to the previously rough Japanese community.

73   Kaneo, *Ōbei,* 10–11.

74   Estavan, *San*, 15:1:68; Aya Mihara, "Professor Risley and Japanese Acrobats: Selections from the Diary of Hirohachi Takano, a Manager for the Risley Troupe, during the World Tour 1866–1869," *Nineteenth Century Theater* 18:1–2 (1990): 62. "Professor Risley" managed the first Japanese troupe to arrive in the United States. His name lives on as the American progenitor, or at least the introducer, of the "Risley act" in which one or more performers lie on their back and use their feet to juggle people or objects over their prone bodies. Risley himself had previously been a people juggler but found Japanese acrobats so much more skillful that he spent the rest of his life managing Risley acts from Japan.

75   Nishiyama Matsunosuke, *Edo Culture: Daily Life and Diversions in Urban Japan, 1600–1868*, trans. and ed., Gerald Groemer (Honolulu: University of Hawaii Press, 1997), 244–4; Miyaoka, *Ikoku*. 13–62.

76   Miyaoka, *Ikoku*, 14, 49–62.

77   "Glen Park Great Circus," *Wave* (May 20, 1899): 14.

78   Based on contemporary articles in the *San Francisco Bulletin, Call, Chronicle*, and *Examiner*.

79   *San Francisco Chronicle*, June 10, 1899, 1.

80   *San Francisco Chronicle* and *Examiner*, and to a lesser extent, the *Bulletin* and *Call*, June 10–12, 1899.

81   "Interstate Panorama Company; Battle of Manila Bay**!**" advertisement, *Wave* (May 6, 1899): 14; "You stand near Dewey on the Bridge," advertisement, *San Francisco Chronicle*, August 27, 1899, 3. Seven Japanese serving in the U.S. Navy went down with the *Maine*, and other sailors who were native Japanese participated in the Battle of Manila Bay (Herman, *Japanese*, 5). During the war, plays about the heroism of the American military were popular in the United States but were overshadowed by competitive flag-waving acts of vaudeville (Strang, Players, 1:14).

82   Peter Robertson, "Foyer and Footlights," *San Francisco Chronicle*, June 5, 1899, 5; "Why This City Will Soon Be without Good Drama," *San Francisco Bulletin*, June 15, 1899, 6.

83   Old opinion but now even more prevalent in "The Cursed Chinamen," *Figaro*, July 22, 1870, 2.

84   Gagey, *San*, 167, 172–177, 206; "Things and People," *Wave* (May 27, 1899): 6; Hornblow, *History*, 2:317; Muscatine, *Old*, map.

85   Advertisements in *San Francisco Chronicle*, May 7 and August 27, 1899; Joseph L. Backus, "Commentaries," in *Behind the Scenes*, by Gelett Burgess (San Francisco: Book Club of California, 1968), 33, 121.

86   Estavan, *San*, 17:3:171.

87   For discussions of American theatre patronage see Krows, *Play*, 253, 263, 271; "The Local Theatres," *San Francisco Chronicle*, June 4, 1899, 5.

88   "'The Turtle' an Offense," *San Francisco Examiner*, June 12, 1899, 10.

89   "Filthy 'Turtle,'" *San Francisco Call*, June 12, 1899, 8.

90   "'The Turtle,' a Big Crowd and a 'Sell,'" *San Francisco Examiner*, June 13, 1899, 12. Joseph W. Herbert adapted *The Turtle* from a French play that ran two years in Paris (Manhattan Theatre, New York, program, week of September 19, 1899, in program file: The Turtle, BRTC).

91   Fred S. Myrtle, "In Other Cities. San Francisco," *NYDM*, June 17, 1899, 2.

92   "Henry Miller Season," *San Francisco Chronicle*, June 11, 1899, 5; L. Du Pont Syle, "Two Very Interesting Plays," *San Francisco Examiner*, June 18, 1899, 12.

93   "'Chimes of Normandy' Well Acted and Sung," *San Francisco Examiner*, June 20, 1899, 6.

94   "The Local Theatres," *San Francisco Chronicle*, May 14, 1899, 5. Inspired by its orientalist success, the Tivoli's next attraction was the recent New York hit, *The Mandarin*, in which the principal characters were an overbearing Emperor of China and a young mandarin disguised as a wandering musician ("A New Opera Is a Good Deal," *San Francisco Chronicle*, May 23, 1899, 7).

95   *The Geisha* was more popular in Europe than *The Mikado*. Its initial London production ran 760 performances. The score was by Sidney Jones who made a career writing operettas about maidens in distress in such strange places as Japan, China, Greece, Persia, and Utah (Kurt Gänzl, *The Encyclopedia of the Musical*

Theater [New York: Schirmer, 1994], 920; J. Walker McSpadden, *Operas and Musical Comedies* [New York: Crowell, 1954], 506–7).

96   Tivioli Opera House, San Francisco, program, week of May 1, 1899, in theatre program file: SFPLSC; "At the Play," *Theater* (London) 27 (June 1, 1896): 351; Greenbank, *The Geisha*. The original title of the show was *Happy Japan*.

97   Noguchi, *Story*, 16. He most likely saw this Tivoli production.

98   Greenbank, *Geisha*, 77–84. "Chonkina" was suggestive of the sound made by a *shamisen* and was adapted from a Japanese song that Pierre Loti mentioned in his popular novel *Madame Chrysanthemum*. Male foreigners were most likely to hear "Chonkina" sung in a brothel for foreigners, where it accompanied a game of strip tease and musical chairs (without chairs). In the game, someone sang "Chonkina" and when it unexpectedly stopped the last person still moving had to remove an article of clothing.

99   *Madame Butterfly* had yet to appear as play or opera.

100   "Dramatic and Musical," *San Francisco Chronicle*, May 7, 1899, 5; Fred S. Myrtle, "In Other Cities. San Francisco," *NYDM*, May 27, 1899, June 3, 1899, 3; Alcazar Theatre, San Francisco, program, week of September 24, 1900, in program file: His Japanese Wife, BRTC.

101   "'The Little Tycoon' and Other Show Bills," *San Francisco Examiner*, May 9, 1899, 6.

102   Fred S. Myrtle, "In Other Cities. San Francisco," *NYDM*, May 27, 1899, 3; "Willard Spencer's Celebrated American-Japanese Comic Opera. Grand Opera House," advertisement, *San Francisco Examiner*, May 7, 1899, 5; McSpadden, Light Opera and Musical Comedy, 261–63.

103   The word "tycoon" and its Japanese origins were widely known.

104   "At the Theatre," *San Francisco Bulletin*, May 7, 1899, 19; Bordman, *American Musical*, 85–86.

105   Orpheum Theatre, advertisement, *San Francisco Chronicle*, May 2, 1899, 10; "The Willow Pattern Plate," clipping, in RLS NAFR+ Ser. 2 Vol. 97, p.119, BRTC.

106   Lafcadio Hearn, *Japan: An Attempt at Interpretation* (reprint, Rutland, Vermont: Tuttle, 1960), 391.

107   Kipling, *American*, 23. "O-Toyo, ebon-haired, rosy cheeked, and made throughout of delicate porcelain;" Kipling, *From*, 1:302.

108   Lehmann, *Image*, 91–90.

109   Said, *Orientalism*, 207.

110   Lehmann, *Image*, 87; Edwin Arnold, *Japonica* (London: Osgood, McIlvaine, 1891) and *Seas and Lands* (London: Longmans, Green, 1891).

111   The word disappeared from English usage while the icon lingered (J. L. Anderson, "Representing the Musmé: Before and After Belasco's *Madame Butterfly*," in ms).

112   See later references.

113   Masao Miyoshi, *As We Saw Them: The First Japanese Embassy to the United States* (Berkeley: University of California Press, 1979); Chitoshi Yanaga, "The First Japanese Embassy to the United States," *Pacific Historical Review*, 9:2 (June 1940): 113–38.

114   "Things Theatrical," *Spirit of the Times*, May 26–July 28, 1860, 192–304; Odell, *Annals*, 7:223. Both were short pieces on bills with other plays. I found no evidence that the Japanese visitors attended *Our Japanese Embassy*, and they were gone from New York before Jefferson's second show opened.

115   Odell, *Annals*, 7:273; 7:283, 350.

116   Masao Miyoshi, *As We Saw Them*, 43, 45, 160; "The Welcome to the Japanese," *Spirit of the Times*, June 30, 1860, 241; "Tommy," *Spirit of the Times*, June 23, 1860, 229; "Tommy," *Harper's Weekly* 4 (June 23, 1860): 389.

117   "Tommy Polka" (Philadelphia: Lee and Walker, 1860). Tommy's portrait on the cover of this sheet music included the requisite two swords of the samurai. Also Lester S. Levy, *Give Me Yesterday: American History in Song, 1890–1920* (Norman: University of Oklahoma Press, 1975), 382.

118   Odell, *Annals*, 7:350, 431, 534. The performer called Japanese Tommy was still active in 1882 (Odell, *Annals*, 11:624).

119   Aya Mihara, "Professor Risley and Japanese Acrobats: Selections from the Diary of Hirohachi Takano, a Manager for the Risley Troupe, during the World Tour 1866–1869," *Nineteenth Century Theater* 18:1–2 (1990): 62–74; Odell, *Annals*, 8:218. In this decade, there were so many comic Japanese, particularly in minstrel shows, that chronicler George C. D. Odell, looking at contemporary records, called them "the raging Japanese epidemic" (Odell, *Annals*, 8:249).

120   Mihara Aya, "Beikoku kōgyō ni kaketa geinō rokuza no dōkō: 1687nen o chūshin ni" [What happened to the six troupes of entertainers who took their chances in American show business: focusing on the year 1867], *Geinō shi kenkyū* No. 127 (1994): 1–24; Odell, *Annals*, 8:218–19, 249, 461, 485.

121   Odell, *Annals*, 8:220; also 8:219, 249.

122   New York Theatre, New York, program, week of January 8, 1906, and "The Mayor of Tokio," unidentified New York newspaper, January 9, 1906, in Erlanger Collection, microfilm *ZAN-*T33 reel 12, BRTC. The evolution of the "Jolly Jap" stereotype was more complex than what I have outlined here.

123   Miner, *Japanese*, 53–55; Gänzl, *British*, 273, 284, 656–57, 1068.

124   Edwin Arnold, "The Musmee," *Argonaut* (San Francisco) June 26, 1899, 10. The poem first appeared several years earlier in Arnold's *Japonica*.

Chapter 4

1   Kaneo, *Ōbei*, 11; "Beikoku no Kawakami Otojirō" [Kawakami in America], *Miyako shimbun*, July 4, 1899, in Shirakawa, 302–3.

2   "Japanese Play Ends Abruptly," *San Francisco Chronicle*, June 23, 1899, 10.

3   Greenbank, *Geisha*, 28–29

4   "Japanese Henry Irving—Ellen Terry," *San Francisco Examiner Magazine*, 27. Bernhardt played *Camille* (*La dame aux Camélias*) in December 1893 (Noël, *annales 1893*, 358). Kawakami was in Paris in February and March 1893.

5   Ibid.

6   "A Japanese Tragedian," *NYDM*, June 3, 1899, 2; also "Japanese Stars to Shine on the American Stage," *San Francisco Call*, May 20, 1899, 9; Peter Robertson, "Dramatic and Musical," *San Francisco Chronicle*, June 25, 1899, 5. Japanese summary of this coverage was in "Kawakami Otojirō to Beikoku shimbun" [Kawakami Otojirō and American newspapers], *Miyako shimbun*, June 22, 1899, in Shirakawa, 301–2.

7   Sada Yacco was the spelling of her name used in America and Europe. I have spelled it Sadayakko in accordance with the transliteration scheme used in this study.

8   Miln, *When*, 232.

9   Fujii, *Jiden*, 196–97.

10   "Japanese Play Ends Abruptly," *San Francisco Chronicle*.

11   Levi Damon Phillips, "Arthur McKee Rankin's *The Dainties* 1877–1881: Prime Example of the American Touring Process," *Theatre Survey* 25 (November 1984): 240. "Gross" or "net" receipts" were and are dicey show business conceptions.

12   Franklin Fyles, "The Theatre and Its People," *Ladies' Home Journal* 16 (October 1899): 4; Krows, *Play*, 266; Poggi, *Theatre*, 9–10.

13   Hughes, *History*, 325.

14   "First Performances of Japanese Dramas," *San Francisco Chronicle*, June 19, 1899, 5; also "California Theatre," advertisement, *NYDM*, May 13, 1899, 9; "California Theatre—Special!" advertisement, *San Francisco Examiner*, June 15, 1899, 5.

15 "California Theatre," advertisement, *Wave* (San Francisco) (June 17, 1899): 30. The latter piece was called *Miho no Matsubara* in Japanese.

16 "Professional Pickings," *Figaro* (June 13, 1899): 2.

17 "Thespians From Mikado's Land," *San Francisco Examiner*, June 20, 1899, 6.

18 DeWitt, *Illustrated*, 23–24.

19 Japanese backstage areas usually had a mezzanine (*chūnikai*) even when the auditorium (audience section) was confined by law to two floors.

20 "The California. Sketch of the Elegant Theatre," unidentified San Francisco newspaper, c. 1890, in Scrapbook MWEZ+ n.c. 4287, BRTC; Estavan, *San*, 16:158.

21 Cahn, *Theatrical 1899–1900*, 193; *San Francisco Theatrical Guide*, 6:21 (September 26, 1903): 39; "California Theatre," advertisement, *NYDM*, December 30, 1899, 87.

22 Gagey, *San*, 166–67, 206.

23 Quoted in Estavan, *San*, 16:157.

24 Jackson, *Victorian*, 89 fn. 1. These entrances were also confusingly called "stage doors."

25 "The California. Sketch of the Elegant Theatre;" Estavan, *San*, 16:158.

26 Gagey, *San*, 166. Local lore maintained that during the first shock of the 1906 earthquake, the high tower of the California building fell on the public safety headquarters next door and immediately cut off the communication system needed to coordinate fighting the fires that destroyed the city.

27 "First Japanese Actress to Appear in America," *San Francisco Bulletin*, June 18, 1899, 12. The original play was set prior to the Meiji Restoration when Tokyo was called Edo.

28 "Novelty in the Drama Troupe of Japanese," *San Francisco Examiner*, June 18, 1899, 29; Ashton Stevens, "Jap Players Present Their Native Drama," *San Francisco Call*, June 19, 1899, 3; "Thespians from Mikado's Land," *San Francisco Examiner*.

29 "Japanese Are Good Actors," *San Francisco Bulletin*, June 19, 1899, 6.

30 "About Drama and Opera," *San Francisco Chronicle*, June 19, 1899, 5.

31 The characters Nagoya Sanzaburō and Fuwa Banzaemon turn up in other plays in the ever intertextural world of kabuki.

32 The narrow right-hand hanamichi was disappearing as a permanent feature of Japanese theatres before 1899. When it was required in a kabuki theatre for a scene such as *Sayaate*, it was temporarily erected and called the *kari* (temporary) *hanamichi* or the *higashi no ayumi* (eastern walkway).

33 Seigle, *Yoshiwara*, 222–24. The geisha population rapidly increased from 1870. Sadayakko's early career as a geisha was part of this boom.

34 "Geisha" meant entertainer or performer and initially referred to male entertainers in brothels.

35 During a kabuki troupe tour of the United States in 1960, the Japanese Foreign Ministry was still concerned about the possibility of unfavorable opinions about Japan caused by the *seppuku* (harikiri) scenes of *Chūshingura* (Toshio Kawatake, *Japan*, 6–7).

36 Ashton Stevens, "Jap Players Present Their Native Drama;" "The Japanese Historical Company Enacting Japanese Drama at the California Theatre," *Wave* (June 24, 1899): 6; Takahashi, "Zadankai," 83.

37 I found no pictures of the San Francisco *Sayaate* production. Kawakami later had scenery made for this play with a representation of the Yoshiwara Nakanochō main street ("Plays to June 1905," seen in scrapbook MWEZ+ n.c. 297, pp. 99, 101, BRTC; photographs in Holmes, *Travelogues* 2:243).

38 Miller, *Yomigaeru*, p. 26 and record cut 6; *Shibai meiserifu shū*, 41–42.

39 Extensively explored in Gunji Masakatsu, *Kabuki to Yoshiwara* [Kabuki and Yoshiwara] (Asaji Shobō, 1956). The subsequent association of shimpa with the world of geisha parallels that of kabuki with its many brothel settings.

40 A random sampling: Chikamatsu Monzaemon's 1711 *Meido no Hikyaku* (*The Messenger from Hell*);

Tsuuchi Jihei's 1713 *Sukeroku yukari Edo zakura* (*Sukeroku*); Chikamatsu's 1720 *Shinjū ten no Amijima* (*The Love Suicides at Amijima*); Takeda Izumo, Namiki Senryū, Miyoshi Shōraku's 1748 *Kanadehon Chūshingura* (*The Treasury of the Forty-Seven Loyal Retainers* [*rōnin*]); Fukumori Kyusuke's 1816 *Sono kouta yume no Yoshiwara* (*Dream Song in the Yoshiwara*); Kawatake Mokuami's 1864 *Soga moyō tateshi no Gosho zome* (a.k.a. *Otokodake Gosho no Gorōzō*); and Kawatake Shinshichi III's 1888 *Kago tsurube sato no eizame* (a.k.a. *Sanno Jirōzaemon* or *Sobering up in the Yoshiwara*).

41   Donald H. Shively, "The Social Environment of Tokugawa Kabuki," Brandon, *Studies*, 32.

42   Seigle, *Yoshiwara*, 170–75, 217–19, 223–24.

43   Yone[jirō] Noguchi, "The Geisha Girl of Japan," *Theatre* (New York) No. 47 (January 1905): 22.

44   For high-class courtesans in earlier times, acts of sex and acts of art were more or less equal responsibilities of the job.

45   "About Drama and Opera," *San Francisco Chronicle*, June 19, 1899, 5; Porter Garnett, "The Theatres," *Wave* (June 24, 1899): 14.

46   Okamoto, *Meiji*, 130–31l; Yanagi Keitarō, *Kawakami*, part 3.

47   Nagata, *Tate*, 11–15.

48   Ibid.; Fujiwara, *Tachimawari*; James R. Brandon, "Form in Kabuki Acting," Brandon, *Studies*, 91–93.

49   In standard kabuki, but not in Kawakami's plays, important characters who are killed often move quickly off stage hidden behind a small black (sometimes red) cloth held by two stage assistants dressed in black.

50   Fujinami, *Shibai*, 92–93.

51   Nagata, *Tate*, 12–19; Mukai, *Nippon*, 237.

52   "Those Japanese Actors," *New York Times*, March 18, 1900, 18.

53   Josefita, "Drama," *Argonaut* (June 26, 1899): 10; also Porter Garnett, "The Theatres," *Wave* (June 24, 1899): 14; Ashton Stevens, "Jap Players Present Their Native Drama."

54   "Japanese Are Good Actors," *San Francisco Bulletin*, June 19, 1899, 6.

55   "About Drama and Opera," *San Francisco Chronicle*.

56   Fred S. Myrtle, "In Other Cities. San Francisco," *NYDM*, July 8, 1899, 3.

57   Peter Robertson, "Dramatic and Musical," *San Francisco Chronicle*, June 25, 1899, 5.

58   Described in Josefita, "Drama," *Argonaut* (San Francisco) (June 26, 1899): 10; "Those Japanese Actors," *New York Times*, March 18, 1900, 18; "The Japs at the Coronet," *Era* (London) (May 26, 1900): 11; "The Japanese at the Criterion," *Pall Mall Gazette* (London) June 20, 1901, 9.

59   Hopkins, *Magic*, 342–43.

60   Ashton Stevens, "Jap Players Present Their Native Drama." The word "Jap" appears in this book when it occurs in original quotations. I fully acknowledge that it is a racist term even though one hundred years ago, while degrading, it was sometimes less pejorative.

61   Josefita, "Drama," *Argonaut*.

62   Fred S. Myrtle, "In Other Cities. San Francisco," *NYDM*, July 8, 1899, 3.

63   "Japanese Are Good Actors," *San Francisco Bulletin*.

64   Peter Robertson, "Dramatic and Musical," *San Francisco Chronicle*.

65   Josefita, "Drama," *Argonaut*. In nineteenth-century American theatre, it was not uncommon for young women, not necessarily as young as Tsuru, to play boys (J. S. Bratton, "Irrational Dress," in Gardner, *New*, 83–84).

66   Ibid. In agreement: Ashton Stevens, "Jap Players Present Their Native Drama," *San Francisco Call*.

67   "Thespians From Mikado's Land," *San Francisco Examiner*, June 20, 1899, 6; "First Japanese Actress to Appear in America," *San Francisco Bulletin*, June 18, 1899, 12; "Japanese Play Ends Abruptly," *San Francisco Chronicle*, June 23, 1899, 10.

68   "First Japanese Actress to Appear in America," *San Francisco Bulletin*.

69   Ibid.; also "Behind the Flaring Footlights," *San Francisco Chronicle,* June 18, 1899, 5; "Thespians From Mikado's Land," *San Francisco Examiner*; Porter Garnett, "The Theatres," *Wave* (June 24, 1899): 14; "First Japanese Actress to Appear in America," *San Francisco Bulletin*; Ashton Stevens, "Jap Players Present Their Native Drama."

70   "Japanese Are Good Actors," *San Francisco Bulletin.*

71   A fuller synopsis of a later Kawakami performance of *Dōjōji* that mentioned the temple bell was in "Drama of Japan," *Seattle Daily Times,* September 16, 1899, 18. "Geisha and the Knight," *Portland Morning Oregonian,* September 30, 1899, 3, also reported a large bell on stage.

72   "Thespians from Mikado's Land," *San Francisco Examiner.*

73   Peter Robertson, "Dramatic and Musical," *San Francisco Chronicle,* June 25, 1899, 5.

74   In the kabuki canon version the dancer was a *shirabyōshi,* an itinerant female entertainer active during the twelfth and thirteenth centuries.

75   Performances of the full dance section of *Dōjōji* take thirty to forty-five minutes.

76   At this point the play usually ends. In an alternative kabuki version, the action continues with the arrival of a super-samurai subduer of serpents who overpowers the demon dancer. A fuller description of *Dōjōji* as danced by Sadayakko appeared in Lady Colin Campbell, "A Woman Walks," *World* (June 13, 1900): 13. As this was an impression of a performance in London a year later, it may not accurately reflect the staging in San Francisco.

77   The complete title is *Kyōganoko musume Dōjōji* (The gorgeously dressed maiden at Dōjōji).

78   Watanabe, *Musume,* 18–34; Toshio Kawatake, *Japan,* 34–35; Kawatake, *Engeki hyakka,* s.v. "Dōjōji mono;" Kabuki-za, Tōkyō, program, November 1983, 14. As a nō play, *Dōjōji* belongs to one of the principal genres of nō dramatic forms, *shūnenmono* (revenge plays), in which an avenging ghost returns. In San Francisco, Kawakami added comic bits that suggested the parodic *kyōgen* play also called *Dōjōji. Kyōgen* is a comic dramatic form allied with nō although its actors belong to a separate acting tradition.

79   Kawatake Shigetoshi, *Engeki hyakka,* s.v. "Dōjōji mono;" Watanabe, *Musume,* 451–55. For English language summaries of the basic play, see Halford, *Kabuki,* 229–30; Leiter, *Kabuki Encyclopedia,* 57, 250.

80   Brazell, *Traditional,* 507. For a translation of the play and a description of its dance components, see Mark Oshima in Brazell, 508–24.

81   Fujita, *Nihon,* 23. Ten to sixteen different dances may be incorporated into a "full" *Dōjōji* (Watanabe, *Musume,* 449–76; Fujita, *Nihon,* 294).

82   Sadayakko shed her costumes without an on-stage assistant.

83   Hanayagi Chiyo, *Nihon,* 189–90, 244; Watanabe, *Musume,* 455–71, 475; Japanese, *Theatre,* 67–68.

84   Gunji, *Buyō,* 123–24; Kawatake Shigetoshi, *Gaisetsu,* 314–15; James R. Brandon, "Form in Kabuki Acting," in Brandon, *Studies,* 81.

85   Watanabe, *Musume,* 449–85.

86   Toshio Kawatake, *Japan on Stage,* 11.

87   Geinō Shi, *Nihon,* 139–40, 283–84. There are at least two dozen kabuki versions of *Dōjōji* and even more stand-alone dance compositions (Kawatake Shigetoshi, *Engeki hyakka,* s.v. "Dōjōji mono;" Watanabe, *Musume,* 450; Kabuki-za, Tōkyō, program, November 1988, 53–55; Fujita, *Nihon,* 29, 76, 293, 296–97).

88   Fred S. Myrtle, "In Other Cities. San Francisco," *NYDM,* July 1, 3, and 8, 1899, 3.

89   Miho was the site of the legend recounted in Zeami's nō play, *Hagoromo (The Feather Robe),* which was subsequently adapted into a kabuki play.

90   This Kawakami miscellany resembled the earliest days of kabuki when minimal plots linked disparate short dances in a kind of variety show.

91   "First Japanese Actress to Appear in America," *San Francisco Bulletin,* June 18, 1899, 12.

92   Ibid.

93   Kellermann, *Sassa*, 55–59; Ubukata, "Kawakami," 172.

94   Fuller, in her revolt against body-centered ballet, was a pioneer of modern dance working in France. She was apparently unaware of "Sarashi" and similar Asian dances with waving fabric (Fuller, *Fifteen*, 59; Margaret Haile Harris, *Loïe Fuller: Magician of Light* [Richmond: Virginia Museum, 1979], 16–19, 36; also "Amusements. Madame Yacco," *Seattle Daily Times*, September 19, 1899, 12).

95   "Thespians From Mikado's Land," *San Francisco Examiner*, June 20, 1899, 6. An 1879 performance in Japan for U.S. ex-president General Ulysses Grant had geisha performing in especially made kimono with stars-and-stripes patterns (Takahashi Yuichiro, "Kabuki Goes Official: The 1878 Opening of the Shintomi-za," *TDR* No. T147 [Fall 1995]: 143–44).

96   "About Drama and Opera," *San Francisco Chronicle*, June 19, 1899, 5.

97   "Japanese Are Good Actors," *San Francisco Bulletin*, June 19, 1899, 6.

98   Richard D. Altick, *The Shows of London* (Cambridge: Harvard University Press, 1978), 97, 126, 176. A *naumachia* is a miniature representation of a sea battle in a theatrical venue.

99   Its most familiar appearance in Japan was in Chikamatsu Monzaemon's *Heike nyōgo no shima* (The Heike Clan and the island of women a.k.a. *Shunkan*) first produced in 1719.

Chapter 5

1   Josefita, "Drama," *Argonaut* (June 26, 1899): 10; Porter Garnett, "The Theatres," *Wave* (San Francisco) (June 24, 1899): 14.

2   "Thespians from Mikado's Land," *San Francisco Examiner*, June 20, 1899, 6.

3   Examples: "Japanese Are Good Actors," *San Francisco Bulletin*, June 19, 1899, 6; "Jap Players Present Their Native Drama," *San Francisco Call*, June 19, 1899, 3; "Japanese Play Ends Abruptly," *San Francisco Chronicle*, June 23, 1899, 10.

4   Fred S. Myrtle, "In Other Cities. San Francisco," *NYDM*, June 8, 1899, 3.

5   Josefita, "Drama," *Argonaut*.

6   "About Drama and Opera," *San Francisco Chronicle*, June 19, 1899, 5.

7   Josefita, "Drama," *Argonaut*; Ashton Stevens, "Jap Players Present Their Native Drama," *San Francisco Call*, June 19, 1899, 3; "Thespians from Mikado's Land," *San Francisco Examiner*, June 20, 1899, 6; "Japanese Play Ends Abruptly," *San Francisco Chronicle*, June 23, 1899, 10.

8   "The Japanese Historical Company Enacting Japanese Drama at the California Theatre," *Wave* (June 24, 1899): 6; Josefita, "Drama," *Argonaut*; Porter Garnett, "The Theatres."

9   Josefita, "Drama," *Argonaut*. Also Fred S. Myrtle, "In Other Cities. San Francisco," *NYDM*, July 8, 1899, 3.

10   "The Japanese Historical Company Enacting Japanese Drama," *Wave*.

11   "Thespians from Mikado's Land," *San Francisco Examiner*.

12   "Japanese Are Good Actors," *San Francisco Bulletin*.

13   Josefita, "Drama," *Argonaut*.

14   Peter Robertson, "Dramatic and Musical," *San Francisco Chronicle*, June 25, 1899, 5.

15   Noguchi, *Collected*, 36–38; Noguchi, *Japan*, ii–iii. He was referring to their background as sōshi.

16   Noguchi, *American*, 210.

17   Kaneo, *Ōbei*, 11

18   Ashton Stevens, "Jap Players Present Their Native Drama."

19   "About Drama and Opera," *San Francisco Chronicle*, June 19, 1899, 5.

20   Kaneo, *Ōbei*, 11. In his other record of the trip (Kaneo, *Kawakami Otojirō Sadayakko man'yūki*) neither *Sayaate* nor "Nunozarashi" were recorded on the bill for the California. Instead, this source listed *Kojima Takanori*. American documentation of the California Theatre performances made no mention of this play.

21 In Japan this is known as *arau* (washing).

22 Kaneo, *Ōbei*, 33, 34.

23 "Japanese Are Good Actors," *San Francisco Bulletin*; "Geisha and the Knight," *Tacoma Daily Ledger*, September 22, 1899, 3; "Amusements," *Seattle Daily Times*, September 14, 1899, 3; "There is a vast difference," *Seattle Post-Intelligencer*, September 17, 1899, 18.

24 "'Chimes of Normandy' Well Acted and Sung," *San Francisco Examiner*, June 20, 1899; 6.

25 "Tacianu, World's Greatest Female Impersonator," advertisement, *Figaro*, June 27, 1899: 2; also "Sex-Shifting and Gag-Stealing," *San Francisco Call*, June 16, 1899, 6.

26 "Japanese Are Good Actors," *San Francisco Bulletin*.

27 Kaneo, *Ōbei*, 10. See also Ezaki, *Jitsuroku*, cover; Dōmon, *Kawakami*, 93.

28 Josefita, "Drama," *Argonaut*.

29 After painting over their eyebrows with *oshiroi* (white makeup), Japanese actors drew black eyebrows about a half inch above the natural ones.

30 Kaneo, *Ōbei*, 10, 34. I found no San Francisco reviews other than the one in the *Argonaut* that commented on makeup. Neither that critic nor Kawakami seemed aware that French classical actors used off-white facial makeup to heighten the artificiality of their performances (Sauter, *Theatrical*, 129).

31 "There is a vast difference," *Seattle Post-Intelligencer*.

32 Nakamura, *Kabuki*, 144; Muramatsu Shunkichi, *Tabishibai*, 78; Yamaguchi, *Joyū*, 90; Tsubouchi, *History*, 190; "Kabuki nikki" [Theatre diary], *Kabuki* (March 1901): 67–70. As late as 1908, lead was still an ingredient in some *oshiroi* ("Oshiroi no yōsō" [Makeup components], *Engei gahō* [September 1908]: 132; "Haiyū to oshiroi" [Actors and white makeup], *Engei gahō* [April 1907]: 109).

33 The troupe did not perform any plays that called for *kumadori*.

34 Kaneo, *Ōbei*, 34.

35 "There is a vast difference," *Seattle Post-Intelligencer*. The troupe used the four Japanese makeup powders: off-white, pink, red, and yellow. Lines were drawn using *sumi* (Japanese black ink) and a writing brush.

36 "Kawakami no yōkō miyage" [Kawakami's souvenirs from abroad], *Kabuki* 34 (March 1903): 32. Kawakami observed that a major difference was the way foreign actors made up their eyes.

37 Wilton Lackaye, "The Actor and His Makeup," in Young, *Making*, 136, 138; J. E. Dodson, "Look the Part—Then Play It," in Young, *Making*, 167–68; Edward Fales Coward, "Masters of Makeup," in Young, *Making*, 178–79.

38 C. Leslie Allen, "Makeup of the Olden Time," in Young, *Making*, 17–71; Hammerton, *The Actor's Art*, 56–57; James O'Neill, "Grease Paint," in Young, *Making*, 164–66. Before factory-made commercial makeup, black was obtained from burnt cork or India ink, white from chalk or oxide of zinc, red from crushed cochineal insects, and yellow from ochre.

39 Young, *Making*, 2, 6; W. H. Crane, "Some Developments of the American Stage during the Past Fifty Years," *University of California Chronicle* 15 (April 1913): 211; Edward Fales Coward, "Masters of Makeup," in Young, *Making*, 178–79; Edith Davids, "The Art of Makeup," 355.

40 P. C., "The Theatre," *Speaker* 4 New Series (July 28, 1900): 462.

41 Hammerton, *Actor's*, 54–57; also Young, *Making*, 2, 10; Edith Davids, "The Art of Makeup," in Young, *Making*, 3–5; C. Leslie Allen, "Makeup of the Olden Time."

42 Fitzgerald, *Art*, 33–34, 36.

43 Label on a makeup exhibit in Theatre Museum, London, November 1994.

44 Booth, *Theatre*, 116.

45 Franklin Fyles, "The Theatre and Its People," *Ladies' Home Journal* (March 1900): 10; Edith Davids, "The Art of Makeup," 350; Young, *Making*, 12, 25; Sarah Bernhardt, "The Art of Making Up," *Cosmopolitan* (March 1896): 532.

46   Edith Davids, "The Art of Makeup," 352.

47   Bernard Shaw, "Sardoodledom," in his *Our*, 1:146–47.

48   Kaneo, *Ōbei*, 34–35; "Kawakami no yōkō miyage" [Kawakami's souvenirs from abroad], *Kabuki* (March 1903): 32; Sōya, *Honoo*, 73–74.

49   The #16 Chinese makeup was more yellow and not nearly as dark as the #19 Japanese which was a dark chocolate brown. The #20 Negro was off-black, not the charcoal black of minstrel shows (Young, *Making*, 12).

50   "The Japanese Ambassadors in Their State Costume" and "The Africans of the Slave Bark 'Wildfire,'" *Harper's Weekly* 4 (June 2, 1860): 337 and 344–45.

51   "Scene from 'The Darling of the Gods,' at the Belasco Theatre" and "The War Minister at Prince Saigon's Festival," photographs in unidentified periodicals, c. Dec. 1903, in RLS NAFR+ v. 44, pp. 20, 94, 95, BRTC; photograph files A and B: *The Mikado* in Wm. A Brady Scrapbook MWEZ+ n.c. 6615, BRTC.

52   Young, *Making*, 116. There was no evidence that the Kawakami troupe used the #19 Japanese or other dark skin grease paint of American makeup kits.

53   "The California," *San Francisco Bulletin*, June 20, 1899, 5.

54   Kaneo, *Ōbei*, 12; Kaneo, *Sadayakko*, 4; "Kawakami ichiza Sōkō ni shippai su" [Kawakami troupe fails in San Francisco], *Tōkyō asahi shimbun*, July 28, 1900 [sic], in Shirakawa, 320 (although the reprint was marked June 1900, the article appeared in June 1899); "Japanese Play Ends Abruptly," *San Francisco Chronicle*, June 23, 1899, 10; Fred S. Myrtle, "In Other Cities. San Francisco," *NYDM*, July 8, 1899, 3.

55   Fujii, *Jiden*, 197.

56   Hungerford, *Personality*, 294; Baedeker, *United*, xxxi.

57   Cahn, *Theatrical 1899–1900*, 183.

58   Fred S. Myrtle, "In Other Cities. San Francisco," *NYDM*, July 8, 1899, 3. Also "Japanese Play Ends Abruptly," *San Francisco Chronicle*, June 23, 1899, 10.

59   Kaneo, *Sadayakko*, 4.

60   Jerry Stagg, *The Brothers Shubert* (New York: Random House, 1968), 15–16.

61   Fred S. Myrtle, "In Other Cities. San Francisco," *NYDM*, July 8, 1899, 3.

62   "California Theatre," advertisement, *NYDM*, December 30, 1899, 87. New management took over in August ("Latest by Telegraph. San Francisco," *NYC*, August 19, 1899, 486). The American press earlier noted that Mitsuse had a Japanese partner "Oaano" [sic] or "Oano" [sic] ("Professional Pickings," *Figaro*, June 13, 1899, 2; Fred S. Myrtle, "In Other Cities. San Francisco," *NYDM*, July 8, 1899, 3).

63   *Crocker-Langley 1900* plus earlier and subsequent editions. Mitsuse spoke to a reporter after the Kawakami troupe was evicted and claimed Kawakami had simply run out of money ("Japanese Play Ends Abruptly," *San Francisco Chronicle*, June 23, 1899, 10).

64   Ibid.

65   "Kawakami ichiza Sōkō ni shippai su" [Kawakami troupe fails in San Francisco], *Tōkyō asahi shimbun*, July 28, 1899, in Shirakawa, 320.

66   "Japanese Play Ends Abruptly," *San Francisco Chronicle*.

67   Kaneo, *Sadayakko*, 5; Kawakami Sadayakko, "Sadayakko," 198.

68   "Kawakami ichiza Sōkō ni shippai su," *Tōkyō asahi shimbun*; Kaneo, *Ōbei*, 12; Kaneo, *Sadayakko*, 5; *Crocker-Langley 1899*, 170.

69   Kaneo, *Sadayakko*, 5–6; Kawakami Sadayakko, "Sadayakko," 198. Also Bronson, *Earth*, 57, 84.

70   Kaneo, *Sadayakko*, 4–5; Kaneo, *Ōbei*, 12.

71   Kawakami Sadayakko, "Sadayakko," 198; Kaneo, *Sadayakko*, 5.

72   Kaneo, *Sadayakko*, 5.

73 Kennedy, *Great*, 80, 86–87; Levy, *920 O'Farrell*, 259–61. Morton Street is now called Maiden Lane after its former occupants.

74 Kaneo, *Ōbei*,12; Kaneo, *Sadayakko*, 5; "Kawakami ichiza Sōkō ni shippai su," *Tōkyō asahi shimbun*. Also *Crocker-Langley 1899*, n.p.

75 "Meika shinsoroku 23: Kawakami," 31.

76 Kaneo, *Sadayakko*, 5; "Kawakami ichiza Sōkō ni shippai su," *Tōkyō asahi shimbun*.

77 *Beikoku*, 65; Kaneo, *Ōbei*, 12, 15; "Players of Mikado-Land," *Seattle Post-Intelligencer*, September 7, 1899, 6. Arai continued his financial and managerial interest in the troupe while they were on the West Coast.

78 Kaneo, *Ōbei*, 12.

79 Mihara, "Professor," 62–74; Aya Mihara, "Little 'All Right' Took the Stage: A Tour of the Japanese Acrobats in Western Europe," *Ōtani Joshi Daigaku eigo eibungaku kenkyū* (March 1996): 99–114.

80 "Mikado to His People," *San Francisco Chronicle*, June 20, 1899, 2.

81 "Zaibei Nichijin jōyaku shukugaikai" [Japanese residents in America at treaty celebration party], *Mainichi shimbun*, August 11, 1899, in Shirakawa, 305–6.

82 Ichioka, *Issei*, 17; Herman, *Japanese*, 133.

83 Smith, *Americans*, 231.

84 Herman, *Japanese*, 133; Wilson, *East*, 31–32.

85 Noguchi, *Story*, 29.

86 Apparently an adaptation of the earlier *Kawakami Otojirō senchi kembun nikki* [Diary of Kawakami Otojirō's observations at the front].

87 Kaneo, *Ōbei*, 13; Wilson, *East*, 48–50.

88 Shirakawa, *shimbun*, 23, 181–83. First produced by Kawakami in 1895.

89 Kaneo, *Ōbei*, 13. Elsewhere his play was variously titled *Hidari Jingorō* (Left-handed Jingorō), *The Ernest Statue Maker*, or *The Statue Maker*. In the 1880s and 1890s, various *Hidari Jingorō* plays were popular in kabuki (Ihara, *Kabuki*, 7:336, 398, 511). A short account of the historical Jingorō appears in English in Chamberlain, *Japanese*, 84–85.

90 Kawakami originally produced this at his Kawakami-za in January 1897 with great success (Ihara, *Kabuki*, 7:531).

91 Kaneo, *Ōbei*, 13.

92 Kisen was a *warumi* role, a kabuki character type equivalent to what was then called a "swish role" in American theatre. *Kisen* was a *hengemono* with several quick costume changes. It was part of the longer kabuki dance play, *Rokkasen sugata no irodori* (Variations on six great poets) written in 1831. This was very popular in the 1890s when Ichikawa Danjūrō IX and Onoe Kikugorō V, performed it (Misumi, *Nihon*, 132–34). The famous central story relates how several famous ninth-century poets unsuccessfully pursued the beautiful courtesan and female poet Ono no Komachi.

93 Kaneo, *Ōbei*, 13.

94 A Kikusui-za did not appear in any San Francisco city directories. It may have been a temporary conversion of one of the halls that Caucasian fraternal organizations had available for rent near the downtown Japanese area (*Crocker-Langley 1900*, 59–60).

95 Kaneo, *Ōbei*, 13.

96 Daniels, *Asian*, 112.

97 "S'kebei" is a rough Japanese word meaning "sex fiend" in this context.

98 Noguchi, *Story*, 215; Markino, *Japanese*. 5–6. Kawakami described West Coast hostility in "Kawakami no tegami" [A letter from Kawakami], *Miyako shimbun*, October 28, 1899, in Shirakawa, 307–8.

99 Kaneo, *Ōbei*, 14–15; Kaneo, *Sadayakko*, 6.

100 Daniels, *Politics*, 11; "The Lounger," *Critic* 37 (October 1900): 296. For autobiographical descriptions of schoolboy jobs, see Yoshio Markino, *When I Was a Child* (Boston: Houghton Mifflin, 1912), 213, 215–17 and Noguchi, *Story*, 35. Despite employers' promises to allow time for studies many required their servants to work sixteen hours a day, seven days a week.

101 "To Exclude Japanese from Public Schools," *San Francisco Call*, May 16, 1899, 12.

102 Ichioka, *Issei*, 24. Isajirō eventually returned to Japan to become a shimpa actor. In the interim it was likely that he attended the American Academy of Dramatic Arts in New York (Fujii, *Jiden*, 33; Iwai, *Shimpa*, 79).

103 "Kawakami ichiza no shōseki" [News of the Kawakami troupe], *Jiji shimpō*, September 6, 1899, in Shirakawa, 306; Kaneo, *Ōbei*, 14.

104 First produced by Kawakami in November 1892 (Marui, *Shimpa*, 15).

105 First produced by Kawakami in September 1896.

106 First produced by Kawakami in June 1898 (Marui, *Shimpa*, 21).

107 Kaneo, *Ōbei*, 14.

108 Louise Scher "A Flower of Japan," *Photoplay* (June 1916): 110–11. Aoki advertised his services as "Japanese artist" in *Crocker-Langley 1899*, 195.

109 Ki no Tsurayuki, *Log of a Japanese Journey from the Province of Tosa to the Capital (Tosa nikki)*, trans. Flora Best Harris (Meadville, Pennsylvania: Flood and Vincent, 1891).

110 Kakii, *Hariuddo*, 64–65; C. K. Field, "A Japanese Idol on the American Screen," *Sunset* 37 (July 1916): 25.

111 *Beikoku*, 153; Kevin Brownlow, *Behind the Mask of Innocence* (New York: Knopf, 1990), 344.

112 "Ince to Make Japanese Picture," *Moving Picture World* (January 31, 1914): 554; "Miss Tsura [*sic*] Aoki," *Moving Picture Herald* (May 16, 1914): 982; Kakii, *Hariuddo*, 65–66.

113 Based on perusal of "Studio Directory, Actresses—Leads," *Motion Picture News* (April 12, 1917): 91; "Mrs. Sessue Hayakawa Is Newest of Universal Stars," *Moving Picture World* (August 2, 1919): 687. In Japan Tsuru was later called the "The First [Japanese] International Actress" (Kakii, *Hariuddo*, 63).

114 *Beikoku*, 153; Kakii, *Hariuddo*, 65–66.

115 Kevin Brownlow, *Behind the Mask of Innocence*, 35.

116 Conversation with Hollywood veteran Frank Tokunaga, Nara, summer 1956; Anderson, *Japanese*, 40–43.

117 "Obituaries. Tsuru Aoki," *Variety* (November 8, 1961), n.p.

118 Yanagi, *Shimpa no rokujūnen*, 155.

119 Kita Jun'ichirō, "Usui Rokurō," in Tsuboda, *Nihon*, 8:118–19; *Fukuoka hyakunen, jōkan* [A hundred years of Fukuoka, vol. 1] (Ōsaka: Naniwasha, 1967), 140–44.

120 Kaneo, *Ōbei*, 14.

121 This was my estimate of the gross but it was impossible to verify paid expenses, cash donations, gifts in kind, and admission scales. One source indicated the T.V.V. hall held 450 and was filled for many of the Kawakami performances ("Beikoku nara Kawakami Otojirō-ra no hyōban" [Popularity of Kawakami Otojirō in America], *Yomiuri*, July 5, 1899, in Shirakawa, 303–4). Using newspaper reports cited previously, I estimated that 150–230 Japanese attended each of the three performances at the California Theatre.

122 Keene, *Pleasures*, 118.

123 Ichikawa Ennosuke III, lecture, New York Japan Society, September 13, 1989.

124 Leonard C. Pronko, "Creating Kabuki for the West," *Contemporary Theatre Revew* 1:2 (1995): 120.

125 Objections to female actors onstage were not only their actual presence as females but also doubts about their ability to project the classic androgyny of onnagata (Tamura Toshio, "Ne hanashi" [Talking about "Ne" (root)], *Engei gahō* (Jan. 1913): 144–46).

126 Androgynous attraction by both genders was pervasive. According to "The Period," *Far East* (Yokohama)

3:10 (October 16, 1872): 120, geisha paraded at festivals in full male attire and manner to advertise their female geisha services.

127 Noguchi Yonejirō, "Onnagata," in Hasegawa, *Onnagata*, 1–2. My translation.

128 "The Theatres Last Night," *San Francisco Chronicle*, August 1, 1899, 5; Fred S. Myrtle, "In Other Cities. San Francisco," *NYDM*, August 12, 1899, 4.

129 Ibid., 14–15. The Alcazar was at 116 O'Farrell between Stockton and Powell; the Morosco south of Market Street on Mission between Third and Fourth Streets, and the Columbia at 11 Powell Street.

130 Gagey, *San*, 167, 172–176, 206; Muscatine, *Old*, 370; "Dramatic Notes," *Wave* (San Francisco) (June 24, 1899): 14.

131 Franz von Suppé, *Gems from Clover*, libretto by Zell, Genée and Zappert (Boston: Ditson, 1889), n.p.

132 Cahn, *Theatrical 1899–1900*, 195. The 1906 earthquake and fire destroyed the Columbia (Hornblow, *History*, 2:317).

133 "The Theatres Last Night," *San Francisco Chronicle*, August 22, 1899, 8; "Clay Clement," *Louisville Courier*, November 23, 1897, n.p.; Clement, Clay, miscellaneous unidentified clippings in RLS NAFR+ Ser. 2 vol. 72, BRTC.

134 "Records of the Theatrical Circle," *Seattle Daily Times*, September 2, 1899, 18. There was no evidence that this troupe went to Japan.

135 Gagey, *San*, 174–76. The Alcazar was destroyed in the 1906 earthquake and fire.

136 Ibid., 176; Weldon B. Durham, "The Revival and Decline of the Stock Company Mode of Organization 1886–1930," *Theatre History Studies* 6 (1986): 165, 182.

137 L. Du Pont Syle, "Two Very Interesting Plays," *San Francisco Examiner*, June 18, 1899, 12.

138 Adolph Lehman, "Mr. Lewis Morrison," *Dramatic Magazine* (Chicago) 8 (September 1899): 101–2.

139 "Florence Roberts—An Actress from the West," *Theatre* (New York), June 1906, n.p.; Peter Robertson, "Foyer and Footlights," *San Francisco Chronicle*, June 4, 1899, 5.

140 Fred S. Myrtle, "In Other Cities. San Francisco," *NYDM*, August 12, 1899, 4.

141 "The Theatres Last Night," *San Francisco Chronicle*, August 22, 1899, 8; Parker Anderson, "The Rose of San Francisco," *Days Past* (January 8, 2006) Prescott, Arizona: Sharlot Hall Museum.

142 Kaneo, *Sadayakko*, 6; Kaneo, *Ōbei*, 15.

143 Dickson, *Streets*, 141; *Souvenir and Guide to San Francisco* (San Francisco: n.p., c. 1900), 45.

144 Kaneo, *Sadayakko*, 5.

145 "Kawakami Otojirō Beikoku nagare no uta" [Kawakami Otojirō's song about wandering about America], *Yomiuri shimbun*, November 4, 1899, in Shirakawa, 308.

Chapter 6

1 Kaneo, *Ōbei*, 15.

2 "Seattle, the Queen City of the Northwest," *Wave* (May 27, 1899): 8; *Polk's Seattle*, 71, 89–90; Writers', *Washington*, 219; Gerald B. Nelson, *Seattle: The Life and Times of an American City* (New York: Knopf, 1977), 27; Sale, *Seattle*, 50, 57.

3 Kaneo, *Ōbei*, 15.

4 Smith, *Americans*, 224–25; Nagai Kafū, "Akuyū" in his *Amerika monogatari*, 37, 39; *Beikoku*, 1006–7; Edward and Elizabeth Burke, *Seattle's Other History* (Seattle: Profanity Hill, 1979), n.p.; Charles D. Raymer, *Raymer's Dictionary of Seattle* (Seattle: Raymer, 1908), 65; "Miscellaneous," *Orient* (March 1899): 36; Niiya, *Japanese*, 308. In these sources estimates of the Seattle Japanese population at this time ranged from 1,000 to 5,600.

5 Morgan, *Skid*, 96–102; Sale, *Seattle*, 56–58.

6   Ōta, "Amerika," 5; Wilson, *East*, 33.

7   Former Jiyūtō leader Itagaki Taisuke (Kawakami's idol) was an active promoter of immigration to America (Tsurutani, *America Bound*, 51).

8   Ichioka, "*Ameyuki-san*," 10, 18 fn. 15. Ichioka claimed there were 600 Japanese prostitutes in Seattle around 1899. Flesh traders sometimes smuggled young Japanese women into Seattle hidden in barrels or crates (Mikiso Hane, *Peasants, Rebels, and Outcastes: The Underside of Modern Japan* [New York: Pantheon, 1982], 220).

9   Nagai Kafū, "Akuyū," 38, also 36, 38–39.

10   Yamazaki, *Story*, 72; Ōta, "Amerika," 4–5; Ichioka, "*Ameyuki-san*," 10; Morgan, *Skid*, 113.

11   Ōta, "Amerika," 4–5.

12   Most Japanese actors were bachelors. (Muramatsu Shunkichi, *Tabishibai*, 198–200).

13   My lengthy conversations with a former shimpa actor (name lost) who was a waiter at the Lenge Restaurant, New York, autumn 1981.

14   The boxes in Seattle were similar to the *baignoire* of French theatres where occupants could be hidden from view.

15   Hughes, *History*, 309; Morgan, *Skid*, 116, 123–31; Writers', *Washington*, 268.

16   Kaneo, *Ōbei*, 15; "Players of Mikado-Land," *Seattle Post-Intelligencer*, September 7, 1899, 6.

17   Kaneo, *Ōbei*, 15–16. The Jefferson Street Theatre, at the corner of Fourth and Jefferson, had an uneven history. At first cheaply constructed of wood for a few thousand dollars by the Seattle Turn Verein and called Turners Hall, it was later transformed into the fancier Seattle Opera House. Finally, with further renovations, it became the Jefferson Street Theatre. It held six hundred on two floors (Eugene Clinton Elliott, *A History of Variety-Vaudeville in Seattle: From the Beginning to 1914* [Seattle: University of Washington Press, 1944], 36; Howard Grant, *Story*, 31, 35, 44; Ladd, "Survey," 38–39).

18   Alice Ernst, *Trouping*, 119; Mary Katherine Rohrer, *The History of Seattle Stock Companies from their Beginnings to 1934* (Seattle: University of Washington Press, 1945), 12–13; "Washington," *NYC*, September 2, 1899, 537.

19   "Washington. Seattle," *NYC*, September 23, 1899, 605; "Records of the Theatrical Circle," *Seattle Daily Times*, September 2, 1899, 18.

20   "The Stage," *Seattle Daily Times*, September 9, 1899, 11; "Amusements," *Seattle Daily Times*, September 13, 1899, 8.

21   "Players of Mikado-Land," *Seattle Post-Intelligencer*.

22   "Mme. Yacco," *Seattle Post-Intelligencer*, September 10, 1899, 15. This newspaper carried not more than four or five small photographs throughout a typical week.

23   "There is a vast difference," *Seattle Post-Intelligencer*, September 17, 1899, 18.

24   "Why We Do Not Advertise in the P.-I. [*Post-Intelligencer*], May 15, 1899," *Stage* (Seattle: Seattle Theatre) No. 14 (October 22–24, 1900): 8.

25   Based on my examination of 1898–1900 American newspapers and from my own direct experience in theatre management in the 1950–60s.

26   "Mme. Yacco," *Seattle Post-Intelligencer*.

27   Howard Grant, *Story*, 35, 40; Ethel Grant, "Old Buildings," 38, 40–42; Ladd, "Survey," 38–39; Sale, *Seattle*, 50; *Polk's Seattle*, 872. The Seattle was the first theatre in the region to abandon overhead grooves and wing scenery and substitute a large grid-house. Located at Third Avenue and Cherry Street, it was across from the Occidental Hotel where Kawakami and Sadayakko were staying. The Seattle Theatre building was torn down in 1915 for construction of a much larger office structure.

28   Ladd, "Survey," 39; Ethel Grant, "Old Buildings," 42; O. M. Moore, compiler, *Washington Illustrated Including Views of the Puget Sound Country* (Seattle: Puget Sound Bureau of Information, c. 1901), n.p.

29   Howard Grant, *Story*, 41.

30   Nathan, *Another*, 307.

31   "Japanese Henry Irving," *Portland Morning Oregonian*, September 26, 1899, 8.

32   "Players of Mikado-Land," *Seattle Post-Intelligencer*.

33   "The Stage," *Seattle Daily Times*, September 9, 1899, 11; "The Fortson Relief Corps Benefit," *Seattle Daily Times*, September 13, 1899, 8. Shaw's third-class traveling repertoire company drew so well during its first week that it was held over for a second week opposite Kawakami ("Rounds of the Theatrical Circle," *Seattle Daily Times*, September 2, 1899, 18; "Third Avenue Theatre," advertisement, *Seattle Post-Intelligencer*, September 15, 1899, 5).

34   "Kawakami ichiza Sōkō ni shippai su" [The Kawakami troupe fails in San Francisco], *Tōkyō asahi shimbun*, July 28, [1899], in Shirakawa, 320; "Japanese Play Ends Abruptly," *San Francisco Chronicle*, June 23, 1899, 10

35   Multiple-item bills of shorter pieces continue to be the format in Japan, although from the 1960s when it first opened, the Kokuritsu Gekijō (National Theatre) countered this modern practice by playing complete or nearly complete kabuki plays. Earlier in the nineteenth century, American and British theatres balanced their major plays with shorter but complete pieces (often a farce) on a night's bill.

36   Kaneo, *Ōbei*, 16.

37   Nakamura, *Kabuki*, 38.

38   Kawakami played Kojima as *Bingō no Saburō* at the Asakusa Nakamura-za in March 1892 and as *Kojima Takanori* in 1893 (Inoue, *Kawakami*, 145–54; Kurata, *Kindaigeki*, 262–67; Shirakawa, *shimbun*, 22, 69; Akiba, *Nihon*, 1:307–8; Ihara, *Kabuki*, 7:389, 394; Akiba, *Nihon*, 1:307–8). As reports of play titles were often vague and contradictory, Kawakami may have produced two different Kojima plays.

39   Because this title came so late, it did not appear in most Seattle publicity. There were later variations in English and other European languages. In Japanese, Kawakami preferred to call his assemblage *Geisha to bushi* (Kaneo, *Ōbei*, 16). Equivalent to samurai, *bushi* was a close enough synonym for knight. The play also appeared abroad as *The Geisha and the Samurai* and *Geisha to somary. Somary* was a crude transliteration of samurai (the "*to*" was "and"). Kawakami himself often identified *The Geisha and the Knight* by the familiar titles of its three individual play components.

40   "There is a vast difference," *Seattle Post-Intelligencer*.

41   "Drama of Japan," *Seattle Daily Times*, September 16, 1899, 8. Although Kawakami apparently used some familiar kabuki dialog for a part of his *Sayaate*, the language in the *Kojima* segment was more like ordinary Japanese but still spoken in a highly heroic tone (Miller, *Yomigaeru*, cuts 3, 6, and 25).

42   Morris, *Nobility*, 117.

43   Griffis, *Mikado's*, 153.

44   Toda Ichigai, "Shōmura Sakura Jinja to Kawakami fūfu; Sadayakko to Fudōson [The Shōmura Sakura Shrine and Mr. and Mrs. Kawakami; Sadayakko and the deity Fudō], *Engei gahō* (January 1908): 79–81; "Shōsoku" [Correspondence], *Engei gahō* (February 1907): 99.

45   *The Taiheiki: A Chronicle of Medieval Japan*, trans. Helen Craig McCullough (1959, reprint; Rutland, Vermont: Tuttle, 1979), 108–25.

46   Henri L. Joly, *Legend in Japanese Art* (London: Bodley Head, 1908), 290; also Griffis, *Mikado's*, 153; Morris, *Nobility*, 116.

47   The bark-of-the-tree story likely originated in China.

48   For consistency in this work, the component plays of *The Geisha and the Knight* will be identified as *Kojima, Sayaate*, and *Dōjōji*.

49   In the familiar (i. e., more kabuki-authentic) *Sayaate* performed in San Francisco, Banza had no connection with a Kojima story.

50   "Amusements. The Japanese Company," *Seattle Daily Times*, September 14, 1899, 3.

51   "Drama of Japan," *Seattle Daily Times*.

52   Ibid.

53   Edward and Elizabeth Burke, *Seattle's Other History*, n.p.

54   "Drama of Japan," *Seattle Daily Times*.

55   "There is a vast difference," *Seattle Post-Intelligencer*, September 17, 1899, 18.

56   "Drama of Japan," *Seattle Daily Times*.

57   Ibid.

58   "There is a vast difference," *Seattle Post-Intelligencer*.

59   Ibid.

60   The nagauta performer, backed by shamisen, shifts between a chanting, declamatory mode and a singing style.

61   Scott, *Kabuki*, 70–74.

62   "Drama of Japan," *Seattle Daily Times*.

63   J. Thomas Rimer, *Modern Japanese Fiction and Its Traditions* (Princeton: Princeton University Press, 1987), 70–80.

64   Earl Miner, "The Collective and the Individual: Literary Practice and Its Social Implications" in *Principles of Classical Japanese Literature*, ed. Earl Miner (Princeton: Princeton University Press, 1985), 55.

65   Gunji, *Kabuki*, 18.

66   Nishiyama, *Daily*, 219. In both Nishiyama's comments and mine, neither of us was describing all kabuki plays.

67   Leiter, *Kabuki Encyclopedia*, 395.

68   "Amusements. The Japanese Company," *Seattle Daily Times*, September 14, 1899, 3.

69   In the canon *Sayaate*, courtesan Katsuragi was married to protagonist Nagoya.

70   The best-known *tereko* formation is the popular kabuki play *Sukeroku* in which the central character reveals that he is really one of the Soga brothers who were the protagonists of the famous revenge that took place five hundred years before events in *Sukeroku*. Once disclosed, this identity for the *Sukeroku* play evoked the many stories connected with the Soga brothers. Recycling is further evident in *Sukeroku* as parts of it also suggest events in the original kabuki *Sayaate*. Both *Sayaate* and *Sukeroku* have a Yoshiwara Nakanochō setting, comic country bumpkins in the brothel area, complications arising over a stolen object, and two male adversaries fighting over a courtesan (Thornbury, *Sukeroku's*, 7–28; Brandon, *Kabuki*, 5).

71   Mickel, *Footlights*, 67; Schaffner, *Fabulous*, 14, 52, 57; informal conversations with old time prairie actors at the Theatre Museum of Repertoire Americana, Mt. Pleasant, Iowa, summers 1980s.

72   Mori Mitsuya, "Intercultural Problems and the Modernization of Theatre in Japan," *Theatre Research International* 20:2 (Summer 1995): 149–55.

73   Gunji, *Kabuki*, 41–42; Tamiya Shirogoro, "Sequel to 'Dust in the Ears,'" in Dunn, *Actors*,' 20.

74   Hagii, *Shimpa*, 63–64.

75   Kaneo, *Ōbei*, 16.

76   Fujita Hiroshi, *Nihon*, 76, 295; Watanabe, *Musume*, 51–58; Kawatake Shigetoshi, *Engeki hyakka*, s.v. "Dōjōji mono."

77   Geinō Shi, *Nihon*, 117–46; Kawatake Shigetoshi, *Engeki hyakka*, s.v. "Dōjōji mono."

78   Kabuki-za, Tōkyō, program, April 1975, 24–26. This exotic music had precedents. In 1896, the innovating Ichikawa Danjūrō IX substituted violin and piano for the traditional accompaniment of *Musume Dōjōji* (Gunji, *Buyō*, 197).

79   Quoted in Rimer, *Toward*, 9. The spectator's pleasure, Kinoshita maintained, was experiencing actors' skills in bridging the gaps, particularly the emotional gaps.

80   Fergusson, *Idea*, 159.

81   Keene, *Pleasures*, 119–20; James R. Brandon, "Performance and Text in *Kabuki*," in Scholz-Cionca, *Japanese*, 177–78, 185–86; Gunji, *Kabuki*, 41–42; "Tabi shibai" [Touring companies], *Engei gahō* (April 1907): 65–68. In scripts, places designated for ad libbing were indicated with the term *sutezerifu* ("throw away dialog"). Despite the prevalence of such extemporaneous performance, many kabuki plays had dialog strictly set to be precisely delivered.

82   James R. Brandon, "Performance and Text in *Kabuki*," in Scholz-Cionca, *Japanese*, 177–78, 185–86; Gunji, *Kabuki*, 41–42.

83   James Thomas, *The Art of the Actor-Manager: Wilson Barrett and the Victorian Theatre* (Ann Arbor: UMI Research, 1984), 5.

84   Kendal, *Dramatic*, 100–1, 108.

85   Michael Booth in his *Theatre*, 10–11, discussed improvisation in the context of British troupes that played in booths and fit-ups.

86   Leiter, *Kabuki Encyclopedia*, 208; Makino Masahiro, *Katsudōya ichidai* [The life of a movie man] (Eikō Shuppansha, 1968), 17.

87   In the twenty-first century, *kuchidate* is the principal performing technique of small traveling troupes usually identified as *taishū engeki*.

88   Katherine Goodale, *Behind the Scenes with Edwin Booth* (Boston: Houghton Mifflin, 1931), 116. Booth performed in polyglot performances of Shakespeare at different times with foreign actors Ristori, Salvini, and Janauscheck who spoke in their own native languages opposite his English. Audiences already knew the story.

89   Artaud, *Theatre*, 71. Artaud did not seek to eliminate all coherent speech but to reduce its dominance and substitute more abstract but expressive sounds (Artaud, *Theatre*, 72, 107, 118).

90   Sauter, *Theatrical*, 64.

91   Ibid., 47. Italics in original.

92   Dunn, *Actors*, 80. General aspects of this proposition discussed in Terence Hawkes, *Structuralism and Semiotics* (Berkeley: University of California Press, 1977), 85–87.

93   Brooks, *Melodramatic*, 67.

94   Mitsuya Mori, "Thinking and Feeling: Characteristics of Intercultural Theatre," in Scholz-Cionca, *Japanese*, 360.

95   The obvious difference is that Kawakami adapted foreign "realism" to Japanese materials while today's transcultural theatre tends to seek foreign nonrepresentational means to enrich the staging of Euro-American dramas.

96   New York: Scribner's, 1893. Kawakami later produced *Kesa* based on the same story.

97   New York: Macmillan, 1915. Discussed in Miner, *Japanese*, 57–78, 216–18.

98   Neither of these English language plays was commercially successful.

99   "There is a vast difference," *Seattle Post-Intelligencer*, September 17, 1899, 18.

100   Ibid.

101   Ibid.

102   The props were for the *Kojima* segment.

103   "There is a vast difference," *Seattle Post-Intelligencer*.

104   Ibid. The troupe had not yet acquired replacements for male costumes seized in San Francisco.

105   Ibid.

106   Rimer, *Toward*, 35.

107   Kawatake Shigetoshi, *Engeki hyakka*, s.v. "katsura" (wigs).

108   "The Japanese Historical Company Enacting Japanese Drama at the California Theatre," *Wave* (June 24, 1899): 6; Scott, *Kabuki*, 132.

109   The *tokoyama* with his wigs remains a ubiquitous support person in kabuki and in Japanese period films.

110   Booth, *Theatre*, 116.

111   "There is a vast difference," *Seattle Post-Intelligencer*

112   "Drama of Japan," *Seattle Daily Times*, September 16, 1899, 8.

113   "There is a vast difference," *Seattle Post-Intelligencer*; Kaneo, *Ōbei*, 16.

114   "Wigs," *Stage* (London) (October 19, 1883), reprinted in Booth, *Victorian*, 5.

115   Ibid.; Hammerton, *Actor's*, 53, 58.

116   Lifson, *Yiddish*, 49.

117   Hammerton, *Actor's*, 53, 58.

118   Young, *Making*, 49–50.

119   Family crest = *mon*. Kusunoki's *kikusui* (chrysanthemum and flowing water) design is visible in the San Francisco photograph in Chapter 3.

120   "There is a vast difference," *Seattle Post-Intelligencer*.

121   Ethel Grant, "Old Buildings," 42.

122   It was possible that a new *kido* was made in Seattle.

123   The *kido* scenic element used on stage should not be confused with the identically named *kido* that was the audience entrance of a Japanese theatre (Itō, *Butai*, 32–33).

124   "Amusements. A Season of Opera," *Seattle Daily Times*, September 9, 1899, 12; "At the Marquam Grand" and "Old Friends Will Dine Him," *Portland Sunday Oregonian*, October 1, 1899, 3.

125   "Washington. Seattle," *NYC*, September 30, 1899, 628.

126   Alice Ernst, *Trouping*, 130–31. Manager Howe was subsequently an important figure in the rebellion against shoddy road companies sent out by the Theatrical Syndicate to the West Coast. See also Grant, *Story*, 33–36.

127   Kaneo, *Ōbei*, 17. The Seattle branch of the Turn Verein owned Germania Hall at the corner of Second Avenue and Seneca Street (*Polk's Seattle*, 71). Thirteen years earlier this Turn Verein club had been a leading hostile force in the anti-Asian confederation that ran Chinese out of Seattle (Morgan, *Skid*, 88).

128   *Beikoku*, 167.

Chapter 7

1   Kaneo, *Ōbei*, 17. The distance was forty miles.

2   "Hotel Arrivals," *Tacoma Daily Ledger*, September 21, 1899, 7; Kaneo, *Ōbei*, 17.

3   Martin, *Tacoma*, 61, 149; Writers' Program, *Washington*, 268, 272. Fire destroyed this hotel in 1935.

4   Nagai Kafū, "Saiyū nisshishō" [Diary of a journey to the West], in Nagai, *Amerika*, 393; *The New Northwest and Tacoma, Its Metropolis* (Tacoma: Chamber of Commerce, 1890), 6. In Seattle they called that same mountain Mount Ranier.

5   Kaneo, *Ōbei*, 17; Martin, *Tacoma*, 149.

6   Sale, *Seattle*, 51; *Polk's Tacoma City Directory, 1899* (Tacoma: Polk, 1899), 60, 75; Wilson, *East*, 33.

7   Nagai Kafū, "Amerika no omoide" [Memories of America] in *Kafū zenshū dainijūroku-kan* [The complete works of Kafū vol. 26] (Iwanami Shoten, 1985), 365–68. Kafū, like other Japanese, thought that a proper autumn had to have three distinct periods: *hatsuaki* or *shoshū* (the beginning of autumn), *chūshū* (middle autumn), and *banshū* (late autumn).

8   Murray Morgan, *Puget's Sound* (Seattle: University of Washington Press, 1979), 275–80.

9   Cahn, *Theatrical 1899–1900*, 681; *Polk's Tacoma City Directory, 1899*, 61; "Washington. Tacoma," *NYC*, September 23, 1899, 605.

10 "Tacoma Theatre," advertisement, *Tacoma Daily Ledger*, September 22 and 25, 1899, 5; "Washington. Tacoma," *NYC*, September 23 and October 7, 1899.

11 Ethel Grant, "Old Buildings," 63–64, 66, 70; Alice Ernst, *Trouping*, 109, 148–49, Martin, *Tacoma*, 61; Murray Morgan, *Puget's Sound*, 269. Fire destroyed the Tacoma Theatre in 1963.

12 Cahn, *Theatrical 1899–1900*, 681; "Tacoma Theatre," advertisement, *Tacoma Daily Ledger*, 25 September 1899, 5.

13 "Kawakami no yōkō miyage" [Kawakami's souvenirs from abroad], *Kabuki* (March 1903): 32.

14 *Tacoma New Herald Annual* (Tacoma: Bell, 1907), 63.

15 "Was an Artistic Success," *Tacoma Daily Ledger*, September 28, 1899, 3. Also "'Geisha and the Knight,'" *Portland Morning Oregonian*, September 30, 1899, 3.

16 "Was an Artistic Success," *Tacoma Daily Ledger*. This was apparently the "Sarashi" danced in San Francisco.

17 Kaneo, *Sadayakko*, 6.

18 Kaneo, *Ōbei*, 17; *Portland Guide Book, 1902* (Portland: Chamber of Commerce, 1902), 6; *Views of Portland and Glimpses of Oregon Scenery* (Portland: Averill, 1904), n.p.

19 Kaneo, *Ōbei*, 17; O'Donnell, *Portland*, 30; *Portland City Directory 1900–1901* (Portland: Polk, 1901), 376, 775

20 Sale, *Seattle*, 51; Hungerford, *Personality*, 281; O'Donnell, *Portland*, 18, 24, 37.

21 O'Donnell, *Portland*, 24.

22 Ibid., 140.

23 "Japanese Henry Irving," *Portland Morning Oregonian*, September 26, 1899, 8. The same connection to Irving was made in "Wants to Reform the Mimic Stage," *Portland Evening Telegram*, September 26, 1899, 3.

24 "Japanese Henry Irving," *Portland Morning Oregonian*.

25 "Wants to Reform the Mimic Stage," *Portland Evening Telegram*.

26 Schilling, "History," 214; "Kawakami no yōkō miyage," *Kabuki*; Alice Ernst, *Trouping*, 147; Matson, *Seven*, 58, 79; Percy Maddux, *City on the Willamette* (Portland: Binfords and Mort, 1952), 121, 131. The Marquam Building was at the northeast corner of S. W. Madison and S. W. 6th Avenue.

27 Alice Ernst, *Trouping*, 147; Matson, *Seven*, 59.

28 Schilling, "History," 239.

29 Alice Ernst, *Trouping*, 109; *The Hotel Portland* (Portland: Crocker, 1897), 23; Henry Irving, "The American Audience," *Fortnightly Review* 37 (February 1, 1885): 198; *Encyclopedia Britannica*, 1959, s.v. "Theatre;" McLean, *American*, 201.

30 Cahn, *Theatrical 1900–1900*, 588; Fuji Maro, "Tabiyakusha no nikki" [Diary of a traveling actor], *Kabuki* (September 1908): 119; 101 (December 1908): 101–3; 102 (January 1909): 123–24, 101–3.

31 According to Noguchi Yonejirō, American audiences in first class theatres were much less noisy than those in Japan (Noguchi; *American*, 122).

32 Yone[jirō] Noguchi, "Sada Yacco," *NYDM*, February 17, 1906, 11.

33 Mortimer Menpes, *Japan: A Record in Colour* (London: Adam and Black, 1901), 8.

34 Hamamura, *Kabuki*, 81.

35 Raz, *Audience*, 183–87.

36 Muramatsu Shunkichi, *Tabishibai*, 77–78. Actors with the itinerant booth theatres of Britain also beat large drums to attract audiences (Ann Featherstone, "Shopping and Looking: Trade Advertisements in the *Era* and Performance History Research," *Nineteenth Century Theatre*, 28 [Summer 2000]: 28–61).

37 *Portland Evening Telegram*, September 10–October 11, 1899; *Portland Morning Oregonian*, September 14–October 8, 1899; "Oregon. Portland," *NYC*, September 23, 1899, 598.

38   "Music and Drama," *Portland Evening Telegram*, September 23, 1899, 3; "Oregon. Portland," *NYC*, September 23, 1899, 598.

39   "Amusements," *Portland Evening Telegram*, October 3, 1899, 4; "Attendance Is Still Growing," *Portland Evening Telegram*, October 7, 1899, 6.

40   Kaneo, *Ōbei*, 17; "Geisha and the Knight," *Portland Morning Oregonian*, September 30, 1899, 3; "The Geisha and Knight," *Portland Evening Telegram*, September 30, 1899, 8.

41   "Geisha and the Knight," *Portland Morning Oregonian*; Schilling, "History," 346.

42   "Geisha and the Knight,'" *Portland Morning Oregonian*. It was identified as a "three-act play" ("Japanese Drama, *Portland Morning Oregonian*, September 28, 1899, 5).

43   "Amusements. Japanese Drama Tonight," *Portland Evening Telegram*, September 29, 1899, 4.

44   See images 4.6, 27.7, 27.8.

45   "Geisha and the Knight," *Portland Morning Oregonian*.

46   Kawakami identified *Miho no Matsubara* as *Nunozarashi*.

47   "Geisha and the Knight," *Portland Morning Oregonian*.

48   "Drama of Japan," *Seattle Daily Times*, September 16, 1899, 8.

49   Julian Mates, "American Musical Theatre: Beginnings to 1900," in Williams, *American*, 224–45.

50   Anecdotal references to specialties appear in Bernheim, *Business*, 99; Marian McKennon, *Tent Show* (New York: Exposition, 1964), 42, 45, 76, 100; Mickel, *Footlights*, 180, 186–88; Schaffner, *Fabulous*, 35; Slout, *Theatre*, 50; "Amusements. Change of Bill," *Seattle Daily Times*, September 8, 1899, 6.

51   Slout, *Theatre*, 13, 14, 26. Despite discussion and statistics about the shrinking road after 1910 in most histories of the American theatre, hundreds of these provincial rep companies were touring small-town America. Throughout the 1920s, there were at least three hundred of them. They frequently played in tents (Bernheim, *Business*, 98–99; Slout, *Theatre*, ix; Museum of Repertoire Americana, Mt. Pleasant, Iowa, exhibits).

52   I was there in the audience.

53   "Drama of Japan," *Seattle Daily Times*.

54   Geinō Shi, *Nihon*, 117–46; Ted Shawn, *Gods Who Dance* (New York: Dutton, 1929), 20.

55   Suzuki, *Way*, 8.

56   Barba, *Dictionary*, 83.

57   This is yet another manifestation of the essential *jo, ha, kyū* (prelude, development, crest) structure of Japanese art.

58   Gunji, *Buyō*, 73; Minami Hiroshi, ed., *Ma no kenkyū: Nihonjin no biteki hyōgen* [Studies of *ma*: an aesthetic expression of the Japanese] (Kōdansha, 1983). *Ma*, in this context, was "empty" space or time—the interval between elements).

59   Marcelle Azra Hincks, "The Art of Dancing in Japan," *Fortnightly Review* (London) 80 (July 2, 1906): 98.

60   Fujita Hiroshi, *Nihon*, 92, 102–18; Sakakibara, *Nihon*, 21–25, 59–62, 162–67.

61   These descriptions covered only what was relevant to Kawakami's repertoire.

62   "Amusements," *Portland Evening Telegram*, September 29, 1899, 4; also "Oregon. Portland," *NYC*, September 23, 1899, 598; Matson, *Seven*, 30, 100. Portland also had two vaudeville/variety venues in rundown buildings, the Metropolitan Opera House and the Fredricksburg Musical Hall ("Oregon. Portland," *NYC*, September 16, 1899, 579).

63   "Music and Drama," *Portland Evening Telegram*, September 23, 1899, 3; "Six More Performances," *Portland Morning Oregonian*, October 1, 1899, 17. O'Neil's *Oliver Twist* centered on her as Nancy Sykes.

64   *Magda* (Suderman's *Heimat*, 1893) and *Camille* (Dumas fils, 1852) were frequent vehicles for female stars of all nations. Both were among the first foreign plays to be staged in Japan. O'Neil's repertoire in Portland also included *Peg Woffington*, *The Jewess*, and *Elizabeth Queen of England* ("Oregon. Portland,"

NYC, September 23, 1899, 598). There was no certain evidence that Kawakamai or Sadayako saw O'Neil perform.

65   "'Elizabeth' Tonight," *Portland Morning Oregonian*, September 27, 1899, 5.

66   Kaneo, *Sadayakko*, 7; Kaneo, *Ōbei*, 18. Touring American actors had large steamer trunks. Japanese traveled with small luggage made of wicker (*kōri* and *tsuzura*) ("Tabi shibai" [Touring companies], *Engei gahō* [April 1907]: 65–68).

67   William Young, *Famous*, 1:889; also "Rounds of the Theatrical Circle," *Seattle Daily Times*, September 2, 1899, 18.

68   Maureen A. Shea, "Nance O'Neil: Power and Passion on the 'Modern' American Stage," *Theatre Studies* 21 (1974–75): 61, 66; William Young, *Famous*, 1:889; unidentified clipping, in scrapbook MWEX+ n.c. 16, BRTC; S. L. Watson, "Miss Nance O'Neil," *Metropolitan* (December 1897): 417–19. After a debut in singing parts, O'Neil's career extended over six decades and included performances in silent and talking films. She played Hamlet in 1924 and last appeared on Broadway in 1948 (*Who Was Who*, s.v. "O'Neil, Nance").

69   Horton, *Driftwood*, 204. This practice, of course, was not confined to Portland.

70   Kaneo, *Ōbei*, 17–18.

71   O'Donnell, *Portland*, 30, 104; *Portland City Directory 1899–1900*, 93, 810; Wilson, *East*, 34; Alice Ernst, *Trouping*, 98–100; *Souvenir of Portland and Oregon* (Portland: Oregon Editorial Association, 1899), n.p.

72   Kaneo, *Sadayakko*, 7. Dragging their luggage through the streets may have occurred only once when they moved to the UOAW Hall.

73   Kaneo, *Ōbei*, 18; *Portland Oregon in 1900*, (Portland: Thomson, 1900), 40–41; "O. R. & N.," advertisement, *Portland Morning Oregonian*, October 7, 1899, 11; "Are You Going East?" *Seattle Post-Intelligencer*, September 10, 1899, 18.

74   Emory R. Johnson, *American Railway Transportation* (New York: Appleton, 1903), 148; Chamberlain, *Japanese*, 407, 444; Ransome, *Japan*, 24; Wm. Bradley Parsons, "Railway Opportunities in the Orient," *Engineering* (New York) 19 (May 1900): 181.

75   "Shin'engeki no sossensha toshite Ōbei man'yū" [Going to Europe and America as a pioneer of the New Theatre], *Miyako shimbun*, July 25, 1900, in Shirakawa, 317.

76   Baedeker, *United States*, xxxi.

77   "Hunt for Bandits," *Chicago Daily Inter Ocean*, October 15, 1899, 1.

Chapter 8

1   Kaneo, *Ōbei*, 18.

2   "Weather," *Chicago Tribune*, October 12, 1899, 1; Kipling, *From*, 2:185.

3   Kaneo, *Ōbei*, 18; "Keller House," advertisement, *NYC*, June 10, 1898, 299; DiMeglio, *Vaudeville*, 92, 148; McArthur, *Actors*, 73.

4   DiMeglio, *Vaudeville*, 92.

5   "McVicker's 4th immense week," advertisement, *Chicago Tribune*, October 29, 1899, 40; "Amusements. McVicker's," *Chicago Daily Inter Ocean*, October 16, 1899, 5.

6   "Amusements. Grand Opera House," *Chicago Daily Inter Ocean*, October 29, 1899, 34; "Money in Cyrano," unidentified newspaper, January 8, 1899, clipping in RLS NAFR+ v. 321, p. 45, BRTC.

7   "At the Play," *Chicago Tribune*, October 22, 1899, 45; "Columbia," advertisement, *Chicago Tribune*, October 22, 1899, 44.

8   "From Other Points. Chicago," *NYC*, October 28, 1899, 718.

9   Kaneo, *Ōbei*, 18. The Kabuki-za held over 1,800 (Enjōji, *Tōkyō*, 26–27). Kawakami was mistaken about the number of large Chicago theatres.

10   Information about all of the theatres in Chicago was difficult to determine because those at the lowest end of the economic scale did not advertise in newspapers, were not listed in directories, and were located away from places where travel writers and city boosters ventured. Available statistics on seating capacities varied widely because of numerous renovations, misinformation, and hype. In addition to contemporary newspapers and the nearly definitive Cahn, *Theatrical 1899–1900*, 143–55, other sources were Flinn, *Chicago*, 121–28; Hill, *Souvenir*, 162–63, 206; G. W. Orear, *Commercial and Architectural Chicago* (Chicago: Orear, 1887), 53–60; Joseph N. Parker, *Columbian Exposition and Chicago's Wonders* (Chicago: Parker, 1893), 25–26; Vynne, *Chicago*, 34–52, 68. Published capacities of theatres in the United States were based on the finite number of fixed seats, although theatres had additional standing room and could add folding chairs. The typical Tokyo theatre could readily expand capacity an additional fourth by squeezing in more people to sit on the floor.

11   In Tokyo, the official count at this time was ten major and twelve minor theatres. These two classifications were determined by tradition and regulation rather than by physical measurement, audience capacity, admission charges, or potential gross (Miyake Saburō, *Koshibai*, 4–5; Ogawa, *Nihon*, 112).

12   Cahn, *Theatrical 1899–1900*, 145; William H. Birkmire, *The Planning and Construction of American Theatres* (New York: Wiley, 1896), n.p.

13   Daniel H. Perlman, *The Auditorium Building: Its History and Architectural Significance* (Chicago: Roosevelt University, 1976), 7–12, 17. The Auditorium Building was an early landmark in the Chicago school of skyscraper architecture that by 1899 was making a transition from massive masonry to steel frame construction. Louis Sullivan and Dankmar Adler were the architects of the Auditorium. Frank Lloyd Wright was a junior draftsman on the project.

14   "Auditorium. Chicago Orchestra," advertisement, *Chicago Tribune*, October 22, 1899, 44; "The Auditorium Opera Season," advertisement, *Chicago Daily Inter Ocean*, October 29, 1899, 25; Richardson, *Chicago*, 25.

15   Hill, *Souvenir*, 162.

16   Kaneo, *Sadayakko*, 9.

17   Matsunaga, *Kawakami*, 156; Yamaguchi, *Joyū*, 82.

18   "*Burōken ingurisshu*" in the original (Kaneo, *Sadayakko*, 11).

19   Ibid., 9; Kawakami Sadayakko, "Sadayakko," 200.

20   Kawakami Sadayakko, "Sadayakko," 200.

21   Kaneo, *Ōbei*, 18; Kaneo, *Sadayakko*, 7–8.

22   Kaneo, *Sadayakko*, 8. The *takuan* image was Kawakami's playful humor. *Takuan* was pickled *daikon* (radish) and "*daikon*" was theatrical slang for inept actor.

23   Kaneo, *Ōbei*, 18; Kawakami Sadayakko, "Sadayakko," 200; Reuben H. Donnelley, compiler, *The Lakeside Annual Directory of the City of Chicago, 1899* (Chicago: Chicago Directory, 1900), 2,183.

24   Kawakami Sadayakko, "Sadayakko," 201. Accounts of the troupe's Chicago hotel and rooming house experiences varied in different sources (Dōmon, *Kawakami*, 116; Kaneo, *Sadayakko*, 7–8).

25   In Seattle, the local press had identified Mikami incorrectly as Kawakami's "page" ("There is a vast difference," *Seattle Post-Intelligencer*, September 17, 1899, 18).

26   Muramatsu Shunkichi, *Tabishibai*, 28–31, 65; Sugimoto, *Madamu*, 162; Yanagi, *Shimpa no rokujūnen*, 155–56. A troupe sleeping and eating inside the theatre was called "*toya ni tsuku*" (going to roost).

27   "Joys and Comforts, Trials and Tribulations of the Actress 'On the Road,'" *New York World*, March 25, 1900, 2E.

28   Kaneo, *Sadayakko*, 8–9.

29   Hill, *Souvenir*, 52.

30   Julian Street, "Chicago's Individuality," in Pierce, *As Others*, 453; Kipling, *From*, 2:31; Michael and Ariane Batterberry, *On the Town in New York* (New York: Scribner's, 1973), 146; Schlereth, *Victorian*, 228. Free lunches were usually available from eleven in the morning to three in the afternoon.

31 Quoted in Lester S. Levy, *Give Me Yesterday: American History in Song 1890–1920* (Norman: University of Oklahoma Press, 1975), 111.

32 Stephen Crane, "Maggie: A Girl of the Streets," in *Stephen Crane: Prose and Poetry* (New York: Library of America, 1984), 46; also Kipling, *American*, 19.

33 DiMeglio, *Vaudeville*, 92; Stead, *If Christ*, 142–43.

34 Marilyn Thornton Williams, *Washing "The Great Unwashed"* (Columbus: Ohio State University Press, 1991), 29; also Schlereth, *Victorian*, 127.

35 Lillie Hamilton French, "The Development of the Modern Bath," *Harper's Bazar* 33 (March 31, 1900): 292.

36 Edward S. Morse, *Japanese Homes and Their Surroundings* (c. 1888; reprint, Rutland, Vermont: Tuttle, 1972), 202–3.

37 La Farge, *Artist's*, 35.

38 Lawrence Wright, *Clean and Decent* (Toronto University of Toronto Press, 1967), 2, 24, 165.

39 Caro Lloyd, "Municipal Public Baths in England and the United States," *Independent* 53 (January 3, 1901): 31; Robert Hunter, *Tenement Conditions in Chicago* (Chicago: City Homes Association, 1901), 108–9.

40 Kaneo, *Sadayakko*, 10.

41 Information about the overall theatre situation was principally derived from *Chicago Daily Inter Ocean*; *Chicago Daily News*; *Chicago Evening Post*; *Chicago Journal*; and *Chicago Tribune* for the period October 8–22, 1899. Other material was in *Map of the Business Center of Chicago* (Chicago: Blanchard, 190?) and Glover, *Story*, 106–11. Although Kawakami in Kaneo, *Sadayakko*, 10, recalled visiting managers of "first, second, and third class" theatres, he did not name any. I classified theatres based on information in the Chicago sources cited here.

42 Kaneo, *Sadayakko*, 10; Kaneo, *Ōbei*, 18.

43 Sturgis, *Influence*, 31; "Theatrical Season of 1893," unidentified newspaper c. 1894, in Alfred Edgar Mullet Scrapbook **T.11.9, RBC BPL.

44 Muramatsu Shunkichi, *Tabishibai*, 28–31.

45 "Mansfield Company Arrives," *Chicago Daily Inter Ocean*, October 16, 1899, 5.

46 "Studebaker," advertisement, *Chicago Tribune*, October 22, 1899, 44; "Amusement Notes," *Chicago Weekly Amusement Guide*, July 30, 1899, 9; "Where to Go," *Chicago Weekly Amusement Guide*, January 7, 1900, 1.

47 An extravaganza was a theatrical production constructed with a vague dramatic situation that linked numerous specialty acts amid spectacular scenic effects. Gerald Bordman in his *American Musical Theatre*, v, called extravaganzas "prototypical musical comedies." Extravaganzas in Chicago at this time were *Superba* and *A Trip to Chinatown* ("Bills of the Week," *Chicago Times-Herald*, October 15, 1899, 2:6; "Great Northern," advertisement, *Chicago Daily Inter Ocean*, October 29, 1899, 25; "Notes on Amusements," *Chicago Daily News*, November 1, 1899).

48 Amy Leslie, "Dearborn Has Good Attraction," *Chicago Daily News*, November 6, 1899, 3; "Notes on Amusements," *Chicago Daily News*, November 6, 1899, 3; "The Year's Review of the Local Stage," *Chicago Weekly Amusement Guide*, January 7, 1900, 24; "Amusements. Hopkins," *Chicago Daily Inter Ocean*, October 19, 1899, 5.

49 "Bills of the Week," *Chicago Times-Herald*, October 15, 1899, 2:6; "Amusements. Theatrical Notes, *Chicago Daily Inter Ocean*, October 29, 1899, 24. "Alahambra" and "Howard's," *Chicago Journal*, October 21, 1899, 4.

50 "Music and the Drama," *Chicago Journal*, October 9, 1899, 7.

51 Vynne, *Chicago*, 50–67. This source mentioned a theatre where it was rumored female dancers appeared totally nude (Stead, *If Christ*, 258).

52 Odell, *Annals*, vols. 7–15 (1857–1894); Jack Rennert, *100 Years of Circus Posters* (New York: Avon, 1974),

7, 26, 42. These accounts were fragmentary and suggested even greater unrecorded activity by Japanese performers. For instance, "Elks Street Fair," advertisement, *NYDM*, March 4, 1899, 20.

53   Kaneo, *Sadayakko*, 10.

54   "Amusements. Academy," *Chicago Daily Inter Ocean*, October 29, 1899, 34.

55   "Music and the Drama," *Chicago Journal*, November 1, 1899, 4.

56   Kaneo, *Ōbei*, 19.

57   Kaneo, *Sadayakko*, 10.

58   "Amusements," *Chicago Daily Inter Ocean*, October 22, 1899, 34; et sub.

59   Edwin Milton Royle, "The Vaudeville Theatre," *Scribner's* 26 (September 1899): 485–95. First-class vaudeville houses often sold out two regular daily performances and four on holidays. Only a few top legitimate attractions sold out all of their eight performances a week.

60   McLean, *American*, 7, 13.

61   "Plays and Players," *Chicago Daily Inter Ocean*, October 15, 1899, 34.

62   Edwin Milton Royle, "The Vaudeville Theatre," *Scribner's* 26 (September 1899): 485–95.

63   Noguchi, *Story*, 89, 91–93, 97–99.

64   Ibid., 85; also William Archer, "Chicago—Its Splendor and Squalor," in Pierce, *As Others*, 410–11.

65   Henry Justin Smith and Lloyd Lewis, *Chicago: The History of Its Reputation* (New York: Blue Ribbon, c. 1929), 191; also Schick, *Chicago*, 101; "Four Injured in a Collision," *Chicago Daily News*, October 9, 1899, 3; "Cable Car Runs Away," *Chicago Daily Inter Ocean*, October 11, 1899, 5; "Cable Car in a Wreck," *Chicago Daily Inter Ocean*, October 14, 1899, 3; "Three Slain by Street Cars," *Chicago Daily News*, November 14, 1899, 3.

66   Kaneo, *Sadayakko*, 7.

67   R. J. Murphy, *Chicago at a Glance* (Chicago: Walsh, 1909), 51.

68   Kaneo, *Sadayakko*, 9, 11.

69   Ibid.

70   Sawada, *Tokyo*, 47.

71   Those three men were Hattori Kintarō, the clock magnate and founder of the Seiko company, who was looking for precision machinery; a Mr. Yoshii who was the new American representative of the major Japanese steamship company NYK; and Dr. Katayama Otokura [*sic*], the imperial household architect who was investigating structural steel for construction of a new earthquake-proof royal residence ("Prominent Japanese Here," *Chicago Daily Inter Ocean*, October 23, 1899, 7; "Chicago to Build an Earthquake Palace in Japan," *Boston Evening Record*, November 20, 1899, 20).

72   Kawakami Sadayakko, "Sadayakko," 200.

73   Miyaoka, *Ikoku*, 68.

74   Quoted in Tsurutani, *America*, 50.

75   Matsunaga, *Kawakami*, 157.

76   Other contemporary examples of the hard-up actor song genre: William Jerome, lyricist; Frank David, composer, "I Took the Heavy Part" (New York: Shapiro, Bernstein, and Von Tilzer, 1900) and Augusta Howe Chambers, lyricist; Charles Coleman, composer, "The Night That She Played Her Last Part" (New York: Charles Coleman, 1899).

77   "Bills of the Week," *Chicago Times-Herald*, October 15, 1899, 2:6; "Haymarket," advertisement, *Chicago Tribune*, October 22, 1899, 44; "Chicago Opera House Continuous Vaudeville," advertisement, *Chicago Journal*, November 2, 1899, 4; John McCabe, *George M. Cohan* (Garden City, New York: Doubleday, 1973), 52, 55–56.

78   "Walking (or counting) the ties" was an expression for penurious actors who had to follow railroad tracks to a town where they could wire for money.

79 "Supe" = supernumerary.

80 "Ministrel troupe" referred to any cheap touring troupe and not necessarily to the blackface genre at the low end of show business.

81 George M. Cohan, lyricist and composer, "I Won't Be an Actor No More" (New York: Shapiro, Bernstein, and Von Tilzer, 1900).

82 Kaneo, *Sadayakko*, 11–12; "At the Play," *Chicago Tribune*, October 22, 1899, 45.

83 Kaneo, *Ōbei*, 18; Kaneo, *Sadayakko*, 12; Kawakami Sadayakko, "Sadayakko," 202. Although there were all kinds of exceptions, the standard box office split (after deduction of certain house and advertising expenses) was 60 percent for the company and 40 percent to the theatre (W. J. Henderson, "The Business of a Theatre," *Scribner's* 25 (March 1899): 308.

84 A show business expression for a show that opened with little advance publicity or reputation (Howells, *Story*, 287).

85 George C. Jenks, "Turning Theatrical Failures into Semi-Successes," *Theatre* (New York) No. 110 (April 1910): 120.

86 "Amusements. A Japanese Matinee," *Chicago Daily Inter Ocean*, October 23, 1899, 5; "Burton," *Chicago Times-Herald*, October 22, 1899, 2:6; "Central Music Hall. Burton Holmes Lectures," *Chicago Tribune*, October 22, 1899, 44).

87 Kaneo, *Sadayakko*, 12.

88 "Where to Go," September 17, 1899, 5; "Music and Drama," *Chicago Journal*, October 21, 1899, 5.

89 Leavitt, *Fifty*, 276, 579; Lincoln Theatre, Chicago, programs, March 31 and July 18, 1895, in Lincoln Theatre programs box Misc. 2 (LIN), CTPC CPL; "The New Lyric," *Chicago Weekly Amusement Guide*, September 10, 1899, 9; Glover, *Story*, 108.

90 Leavitt, *Fifty*, 579.

91 "The Year's Review of the Local Stage," *Chicago Weekly Amusement Guide*, January 7, 1900, 23; also "Where to Go," *Chicago Weekly Amusement Guide*, January 2, 1898, 1, and January 1, 1899, 7; Biff Hall, "Telegraphic News. Chicago," *NYDM*, October 28, 1899, 13; "The New Lyric," *Chicago Weekly Amusement Guide*, September 10, 1899, 9.

92 "Where to Go," *Chicago Weekly Amusement Guide*, September 3, 1899, 5. Also "The Year's Review of the Local Stage," *Chicago Weekly Amusement Guide*, 23; "From Other Points. Chicago," *NYC*, September 16, 1899, 578; Lyric Theatre, Chicago, program, September 24, 1899, item 9F 38RN PG L985, CHS; "The New Lyric," *Chicago Weekly Amusement Guide*, September 10, 1899, 9.

93 "The Year's Review of the Local Stage," *Chicago Weekly Amusement Guide*, 23; "Where to Go," *Chicago Weekly Amusement Guide*, 5.

94 Cahn, *Theatrical 1899–1900*, 151; Lyric Theatre, Chicago, program, September 24, 1899.

95 "Plays and Players," *Chicago Daily Inter Ocean*, October 15, 1899, 34; Flinn, *Chicago*, 121; Richardson, *Chicago*, 26.

96 G. W. Orear, *Commercial and Architectural Chicago* (Chicago: Orear, 1887), 20. Built only seventeen years earlier, this imposing municipal structure was already falling apart as if it were a monument to or metaphor for the city's notorious political corruption (Flinn, *Chicago*, 563; Schick, *Chicago*, 112). According to one source, the doors of City Hall were left open at night to allow for up to two thousand well-behaved homeless to sleep in the hallways (Stead, *If Christ*, 35–36).

97 Kaneo, *Sadayakko*, 12–13.

98 Noguchi, *American*, 224; Noguchi, *Story*, 85.

99 Kaneo, *Sadayakko*, 13.

100 Ibid., 8, 13.

101 Kawakami Sadayakko, "Sadayakko," 201.

102 Matsunaga, *Kawakami*, 155.

103 "Shin'engeki no sossensha" [New Theatre pioneer], *Miyako shimbun*, May 17, 1900, in Shirakawa, 317.

104 Jefferson, *Autobiography*, 333.

105 Muramatsu Shunkichi, *Tabishibai*, 60–62; "Yakusha no machimawari ni tsuite" [About actors' parades through town], *Kabuki* (July 1906): 98; Daigudō Seitan, "Tabiyakusha" [Traveling players], *Engei gahō* (February 1907): 58–59.

106 Kaneo, *Sadayakko*, 13–14. This account confused aspects of the first *machimawari* on October 21 with subsequent ones on November 2 and 3.

107 Kaneo, *Sadayakko*, 14; "Weather Indicators," *Chicago Daily Inter Ocean*, October 22, 1899, 5.

108 Sante, *Low*. 59. For anecdotes about show business street parades in the United States: Philip C. Lewis, *Trouping*, 70–71; Schaffner, *Fabulous*, 101, 105–6, 204–5; Jerry L. Martin, *Henry L. Brunk and Brunk's Comedians: Tent Repertoire Empire of the Southwest* (New York: Harper and Row, 1973), 47–48, 52; Will H. Locke, "Memories of Rep Trouping," *Winging It* (Mt. Pleasant, Iowa) 2:2 (Fall 1995): 2, 5; Marian Spitzer, "Ten-20–30; the Passing of the Popular-Priced Circuit," *Saturday Evening Post* (August 22, 1925): 42.

109 Kawakami Sadayakko, "Sadayakko," 200, 202–3. Lakefront Park was later renamed Grant Park.

110 "At the Play," *Chicago Tribune*, October 22, 1899, 45; also "Amusements," *Chicago Daily Inter Ocean*, October 22, 1899, 34; "The Current Bills," *Chicago Times-Herald*, October 22, 1899, 2:6.

111 "Where to Go. Lyric," *Chicago Weekly Amusement Guide*, October 22, 1899, 11.

112 Nicoll, *History*, 5:59–60.

113 Some props and scenery may have been lost in transit from Portland to Chicago (Kawakami Sadayakko, "Sadayakko" 200–1).

114 "Amusements. A Japanese Matinee," *Chicago Daily Inter Ocean*, October 23, 1899, 5; "The Stage," *Toledo Bee*, November 22, 1899, 4. *Catalog [of] Sosman and Landis Scene Painting Studio* and Poggi, *Theatre*, 252, listed the minimum number of stock sets for the smallest American theatres as parlor, kitchen, street, and wood[s]. These four scenes were familiarly known as front room, back room, town, and timber. The Theatre Museum of Repertoire America, Mt. Pleasant, Iowa, exhibits many surviving stock scenics (primarily backdrops) from this era. When small touring companies did not carry their own scenery, they had to rely on the limited range of sets found in a theatre. Regardless of whether a stock set was appropriate, the stock sets of a theatre tended—month after month, year after year—to become too familiar to a theatre's regular audience.

115 This connection was explicit in "Music and the Drama," *Chicago Times-Herald*, October 23, 1899, 6.

116 William Walton, *World's Columbian Exposition: Art and Architecture* (Philadelphia: Barrie, 1893), 1, 87, quoted in Hosley, *Japan Idea*, 14. The exhibits at the Chicago Exposition rekindled the Japan craze throughout the United States which began with the 1876 Philadelphia exposition ("The Sino-Japanese War," 172–73).

117 Lloyd Lewis, *Chicago*, 213; Richardson, *Chicago*, 28. Another measure of Chicagoan fascination was the creation of a Japanese garden in 1899 as an attraction at the San Souci Park, an amusement park and open-air summer vaudeville venue ("Where to Go," *Chicago Weekly Amusement Guide*, August 6, 1899, 1; "Amusement Notes," *Chicago Weekly Amusement Guide*, January 7, 1900, 27).

118 Impressions of traditional Japanese architecture were already appearing in designs of "Chicago School" architects Louis H. Sullivan, Frank Lloyd Wright, and others (Lancaster, *Japanese*, 83).

119 Herman and Rick Kogan, *Yesterday's Chicago* (Miami: Seemann, c. 1975), 98–100.

120 Amy Leslie, "Lazy Week for Theatres. Japanese Actors at Lyric," *Chicago Daily News*, October 23, 1899, 9.

121 It was not clear whether the *Dōjōji* bell seen onstage in Portland was three-dimensional or a painted cutout ("'Geisha and the Knight," *Portland Morning Oregonian*, September 30, 1899, 3). The bell was not mentioned in any Chicago or subsequent review.

122 Kaneo, *Sadayakko*, 14.

123 Lyric Theatre, Chicago, program, September 24, 1899, item 9F 38RN PG L985, CHS. This ticket scale differed from the regular Lyric Wednesday and Saturday afternoons that were billed as "bargain matinees" with all seats at 25¢. Established evening prices at the Lyric ran from 75¢ for orchestra seats to 15¢ in the gallery.

124 In Japan, deadheads were called *aburamushi* (cockroaches) and a papered house was an *aoda* (unripe green field) (Gunji, *Kabuki*, 63; Leiter, *Kabuki Encyclopedia*, 14).

125 "Plays and Players," *Chicago Daily Inter Ocean*, October 15, 1899, 34.

126 James Lear Allen, *The Choir Invisible*, pamphlet, Boston: Park Theatre, October 1900, 4–5, in program file: *The Choir Invisible*, BRTC.

127 Ibid.

128 "At the Play," *Chicago Tribune*, October 22, 1899, 45; "Amusements," *Chicago Daily Inter Ocean*, October 22, 1899, 34; D. M. H[albert], "Music and the Drama," *Chicago Evening Post*, October 18, 1899, 5.

129 "Drama of Today," *Chicago Times-Herald*, October 22, 1899, 2:6.

130 Amy Leslie, "Offered at the Theatres," *Chicago Daily News*, October 17, 1899, 3.

131 "The Stage," *Toledo Bee*, November 26, 1899, 10; "Theatrical Matters," *Boston Post*, December 8, 1899, 5.

132 "Henry Jewett," chapter in unidentified book, c. 1901, 212–15 and "An article dealing very briefly …," unidentified newspaper c. 1919, clippings, in Locke Collection Envelope 840, BRTC; "Henry Jewett, Actor, 68, Dead," *New York World*, June 25, 1930, n.p.; "Henry Jewett," *Boston Herald*, June 24, 1930, 10; "Henry Jewett, Veteran Actor Is Dead at 68," *New York Tribune*, June 24, 1930, n.p.; "About the Huntington Theatre Company," Huntington Theatre Company, Boston, program, March 1995, 5; Grandgent, "Stage," 398–99.

133 Exhibits at the Theatre Museum of Repertoire America.

134 Harlowe R. Hoyt, *Town Hall Tonight* (Englewood Cliffs, New Jersey: Prentice-Hall, 1955), 49–53; Mickel, *Footlights*, 45–46; Sturgis, *Influence*, 107–8.

135 The scenery built for Kawakami in San Francisco (and lost there) was of this type.

136 Kaneo, *Sadayakko*, 14–15; "At the Play," *Chicago Tribune*, October 22, 1899, 45; "Music and Drama," *Chicago Times-Herald*, October 23, 1899, 6; "News of the Theatres," *Chicago Tribune*, October 23, 1899, 7.

137 "Kawakami Otojirō kinshū to etari" [Kawakami Otojirō gets financial backer], *Yomiuri shimbun*, December 14, 1899, in Shirakawa, 309. Many reports in Japanese newspapers about Kawakami's tour were either written by him or based on information he supplied to the paper.

138 Kaneo, *Ōbei*, 18; Kawakami Sadayakko, "Sadayakko," 203; "Amusements. A Japanese Matinee," *Chicago Daily Inter Ocean*, October 23, 1899, 5.

139 "Plays and Play People. Entertaining Japanese," *Chicago Record*, October 23, 1899, 2. In San Francisco, as in the canon kabuki version, Banza exited after the two samurai quarreled and vowed to fight again.

140 The "fiancée's" name appeared variously as Orihime, Oshime, Onshime.

141 "News of Theatres," *Chicago Tribune*, October 23, 1899, 7; also "Music and the Drama," *Chicago Evening Post*, November 10, 1899, 5; Leroy M. Scott, "Players from the Land of Sunrise," *Chicago Journal*, November 9, 1899, 4.

142 "Amusements. A Japanese Matinee," *Chicago Daily Inter Ocean*, October 23, 1899, 5. The play appeared with such titles as *Zingoro, Jingoro, The Statue Maker, An Earnest Statue Maker*, and *The Japanese Pygmalion and Galatea*.

143 Courtesan in the kabuki versions.

144 "Plays and Play People. Entertaining Japanese," *Chicago Record*; also "Amusements. A Japanese Matinee," *Chicago Daily Inter Ocean*, October 23, 1899, 5; "News of Theatres," *Chicago Tribune*, October 23, 1899, 7.

145 "News of Theatres," *Chicago Tribune*, October 23, 1899, 7; also "Music and Drama," *Chicago Times-Herald*, October 23, 1899, 46.

146 "Music and Drama," *Chicago Times-Herald*, October 23, 1899, 46.

147 "News of Theatres," *Chicago Tribune*.

148 "Amusements. A Japanese Matinee," *Chicago Daily Inter Ocean*, October 23, 1899, 5.

149 Although I listed five statues here, I found no explicit evidence of what was shown in Chicago. The figures named were listed in a Muskegon Opera House program of November 15, 1899 (in vertical file: R977.457 Op2p, Hackley Public Library, Muskegon). This was my earliest specific documentation. The designation "Thunder God" may have been the familiar icon Raiden or the near-monster temple guardian god Fudō who was the model for the bellicose (*aragoto*) characters of kabuki (Ezaki, *Jitsuroku*, 213–14). A review of a later Kawakami *Jingorō* performance described the five statues as a Japanese soldier, a sculptor with mallet uplifted, "a black warrior," and two Japanese ladies ("Amusements," *Grand Rapids Morning Democrat*, November 14, 1899, 2). Kawakami was searching for the most impressive images.

150 Leroy M. Scott, "The Players from the Land of Sunrise," *Chicago Journal*, November 9, 1899, 4.

151 *Tableau vivant* originated in medieval religious pageants as didactic images. In the nineteenth century, many *poses plastiques* (also called "living statues") suggested the nudity of their originals but with careful suggestive concealment with tights. In contrast to the white or bronze of nineteenth century American statues, sculptures in Japan was usually painted.

152 "Amusements. A Japanese Matinee," *Chicago Daily Inter Ocean*, October 23, 1899, 5.

153 "At the Theatres," *Toledo Daily Blade*, November 22, 1899, 5.

154 Japanese, *Theatre*, 81.

155 Ihara, *Kabuki*, 7:336, 398, 511. For an account of *Jingorō* in English, see Chamberlain, *Japanese*, 84–85. Edwin Arnold in his *Seas and Lands* (London: Longmans, Green, 1891), 236–38, described a geisha dance based on a Jingorō story.

156 See Marshall, *Actresses*.

157 Kaneo, *Sadayakko*, 14; also "Amusements. A Japanese Matinee," *Chicago Daily Inter Ocean*, October 23, 1899, 5.

158 Leroy M. Scott, "Players from the Land of Sunrise," *Chicago Journal*, November 9, 1899, 4.

159 Kaneo, *Sadayakko*, 14; "Amusements. A Japanese Matinee," *Chicago Daily Inter Ocean*.

160 Dōmon, *Kawakami*, 116.

161 Kaneo, *Sadayakko*, 19 [page misnumbered as 15].

162 Ibid., 15; "Amusements. A Japanese Matinee," *Chicago Daily Inter Ocean*.

163 Kawakami Sadayakko, "Sadayakko," 203.

164 Ezaki, *Jitsuroku*, 107; Kaneo, *Sadayakko*, 15.

165 Yamaguchi, *Joyū*, 84.

166 Most dressing rooms (certainly the best ones at the Lyric) were assigned to *The Choir Invisible* company (Leroy M. Scott, "The Players from the Land of Sunrise," *Chicago Journal*, November 9, 1899, 4).

167 Kaneo, *Sadayakko*, 15.

168 Leroy M. Scott, "The Players from the Land of Sunrise."

169 "Plays and Play People. Entertaining Japanese," *Chicago Record*, October 23, 1899, 2.

170 Lyric house expenses would have ranged from $100 to $160. With the ticket scale for this matinee, a paying full house could gross about $660 (Cahn, *Theatrical 1899–1900*, 151; Kaneo, *Sadayakko*, 12). For this performance, total cash taken at the box office probably ranged from $160 to $220. Because of many free passes, attendance was larger than quick arithmetic indicates.

171 Calculated from "Amusements. McVicker's," *Chicago Daily Inter Ocean*, October 16, 1899, 5; Cahn, *Theatrical 1899–1900*, 151; Flinn, *Chicago*, 125; "McVicker's. 4th immense week," advertisement, *Chicago Tribune*, October 29, 1899, 40.

172 Kaneo, *Sadayakko*, 16.

173 Ibid.; Lyric Theatre, Chicago, program, September 24, 1899, item 9F 38RN PG L985, CHS; Leroy M. Scott, "The Players from the Land of Sunrise."

174 Kaneo, *Sadayakko*, 16.

175 Yanagi, *Shimpa no rokujūnen*, 156.

176 Kawakami Sadayakko, "Sadayakko," 204; Kaneo, *Sadayakko*, 16. Given the familiar saying "Ōsaka wa kuidore," meaning "People from Osaka can't stop eating," this tale of actors from the Osaka area who can't eat becomes ironic.

177 Kaneo, *Sadayakko*, 16–17.

178 "Shin'engeki no sossensha toshite Ōbei man'yū" [Going to Europe and America as a pioneer of the New Theatre], *Miyako shimbun*, July 25, 1900, in Shirakawa, 317–18.

Chapter 9

1 Kaneo, *Sadayakko*, 18; Kaneo, *Ōbei*, 19.

2 Kaneo, *Sadayakko*, 19 [page misnumbered as 15].

3 Kawakami included his mark-up. An average theatrical hotel with three meals a day for the whole troupe would cost about $200 a week (Hill, *Souvenir*, 150–52, 207).

4 Although Hutton found laundry an acceptable expense, the American practice was for actors to pay for laundry when they had to provide their own stage wardrobe (Whittier, *Dear*, 13–14; "Joys and Comforts, Trials and Tribulations of the Actress 'On the Road,'" *New York World*, March 25, 1900, 2E).

5 Kaneo, *Sadayakko*, 19–20 [pages misnumbered as 15–16].

6 Ibid.

7 Ibid., 20 [page misnumbered as 16].

8 Kawakami summarized these two unattributed reviews in Kaneo, *Sadayakko*, 18–20. I could not find the originals, although I searched seven Chicago newspapers. "Miyasan" was the "Miyasama" song incorporated with its Japanese lyrics into *The Mikado*.

9 "Amusements. A Japanese Matinee," *Chicago Daily Inter Ocean*, October 23, 1899, 5.

10 "Music and the Drama," *Chicago Journal*, October 23, 1899, 5.

11 D. M. H[albert], "Music and the Drama," *Chicago Evening Post*, November 10, 1899, 5.

12 Leroy M. Scott, "Players from the Land of Sunrise," *Chicago Journal*, November 9, 1899, 4.

13 Amy Leslie, "Lazy Week for Theatres. Japanese Actors at Lyric," *Chicago Daily News* October 23, 1899, 9.

14 "News of Theatres," *Chicago Tribune*, October 23, 1899, 7.

15 "Amusements. A Japanese Matinee," *Chicago Daily Inter Ocean*, October 23, 1899, 5. Comparable enthusiasm for Kawakami as an actor in "Music and the Drama," *Chicago Journal*, October 23, 1899, 5; "News of Theatres," *Chicago Tribune*, October 23, 1899, 7; "Plays and Play People. Entertaining Japanese," *Chicago Record*, October 23, 1899, 2.

16 Leroy M. Scott, "Players from the Land of Sunrise," *Chicago Journal*, November 9, 1899, 4.

17 "News of Theatres," *Chicago Tribune*; also "Plays and Play People. Entertaining Japanese," *Chicago Record*.

18 "Amusements. A Japanese Matinee," *Chicago Daily Inter Ocean*.

19 "Music and the Drama," *Chicago Journal*.

20 "Music and Drama," *Chicago Times-Herald*, October 23, 1899, 6.

21 "Amusements. A Japanese Matinee," *Chicago Daily Inter Ocean*; Leroy M. Scott, "The Players from the Land of Sunrise," *Chicago Journal*.

22 "News of Theatres," *Chicago Tribune*.

23 "Music and Drama," *Chicago Times-Herald*.

24   "Plays and Play People. Entertaining Japanese," *Chicago Record*.

25   Barba, *Dictionary*, 88.

26   Ichikawa Ennosuke III, "Ennosuke Kabuki," lecture, New York: Dag Hammarskjöld Auditorium, September 13, 1989.

27   The fixed schedule for first-class American theatres in the Midwest and East was six evening and two matinee performances a week. In contrast to this, Chicago's leading stock company at the Dearborn Theatre performed seven nights and five matinees a week, while also rehearsing the next week's play (advertisements, Chicago newspapers, October 11–November 5, 1899).

28   The Sunday matinee that the troupe first played at the Lyric was unusual because the regular show for the week, *The Choir Invisible*, was not scheduled to perform at that time.

29   Documentation of Kawakami's performances in Chicago was contradictory. My conclusions were based on advertisements cited above and in "Lyric. Bob Fitzsimmons," advertisement, *Chicago Daily News*, November 1, 1899, 2. Japanese sources conflicted with these notices. Kaneo, *Sadayakko*, 20 [page misnumbered as 16], listed no dates but stated there were "two weeks" of performances in Chicago. The day-by-day accounts in Kaneo, *Ōbei*, 19–20, listed performances only on Tuesday, October 31, and Friday, November 3. This source further recorded a Kawakami performance at the "Chicago Opera" on Saturday, October 28, but there was no American evidence for this. "Chicago Opera" could refer to either the Chicago Opera House or the Grand Opera House. Both were fully occupied on that date with much higher yielding shows. The former had an exclusive policy of vaudeville and the latter had Richard Mansfield in matinee and evening performances. Kaneo, *Ōbei*, 19, also listed a Sunday, October 29, performance by Kawakami at the Lyric, but this too was impossible as the main attraction at that time, the Bob Fitzsimmons show, played both matinee and evening. Other evidence about dates was in "Chicago Opera House … Week of 23 October," advertisement, *Chicago Tribune*, October 22, 1899, 44; "Grand Opera House," advertisement, *Chicago Tribune*, October 22, 1899, 44; "Lyric. Week starting matinee today," advertisement, *Chicago Tribune*, October 29, 1899, 40.

30   "Amusements. Japanese Matinees," *Chicago Daily Inter Ocean*, October 29, 1899, 35.

31   "Music and Drama," *Chicago Journal*, November 2, 1899, 4.

32   Ibid.

33   "Lyric. Today," advertisement, *Chicago Record*, November 2, 1899, 2. This was apparently the first time the troupe was called the Imperial Japanese Dramatic Company.

34   "Lyric. Week starting matinee today," advertisement, *Chicago Tribune*, October 29, 1988, 40; "News of Theatres. Lyric Theatre," *Chicago Tribune*, October 30, 1899, 7. "Lyric. Bob Fitzsimmons," advertisement, *Chicago Daily News*, November 1, 1899, 2.

35   "Music and the Drama," *Chicago Journal*, November 1, 1899, 4.

36   Ibid.; Lardner, *Legendary*, 100, 104; also "Lanky Bob to Box Here," *Chicago Times-Herald*, October 23, 1899, 4; also Musser, *Emergence*, 195–200.

37   "Lyric. Bob Fitzsimmons," advertisement, *Chicago Daily News*, November 1, 1899, 2. The reading aloud of blow-by-blow telegraph reports of a bout while boxers on stage imitated the punches was a frequent theatrical attraction of the period, but was being technologically replaced by the rapid processing of moving pictures of actual fights or by fake restagings before a movie camera.

38   Most states prohibited live boxing bouts but moving pictures with real or fake bouts inaugurated a new and legal way to make money.

39   W. J. Henderson, "The Business of a Theatre," *Scribner's* 25 (March 1899): 299.

40   Bernheim, Business, 49–50, 93; Cahn, *Theatrical 1899–1900*, 733–34; Hornblow, *History*, 1:319–20; Strang, *Players*, 2:216–17. The restrictive practices of the monopolistic Syndicate were accelerating the conversion of legitimate theatres to vaudeville.

41 Lardner, *Legendary*, 111; "Rounds of the Theatrical Circle," *Seattle Daily Times*, September 2, 1899, 18, Rahill, World, 272.

42 Gilbert E. Odd, *The Fighting Blacksmith: A Biography of Bob Fitzsimmons* (London: Pelham, 1976), 74, 80, 97, 151; Lardner, Legendary, 99–100, 104–7.

43 Musser, *Emergence*, 194–95, 198.

44 Glover, *Story*, 108; "Amusement Notes," *Chicago Weekly Amusement Guide*, August 20, 1899, 13; Lincoln Theatre, Chicago, programs, 1895, in Box Misc. 2 (LIN), CTPC CPL; "Choice Open Time," advertisement, *NYDM*, November 19, 1898, 11.

45 Charles Washburn, *Come into My Parlor* (New York: Knickerbocker, 1936), 23. On days when the theatre was dark, Hutton rented the Alhambra for political rallies to groups opposed to drinking and prostitution (Lloyd Wendt and Herman Kogan, *Lords of the Levee* [Indianapolis: Bobbs-Merrill, 1943], 287).

46 "Where to Go. Lyric." *Chicago Weekly Amusement Guide*, December 3, 1899, 7, 9; "Amusement Notes" and "Where to Go," *Chicago Weekly Amusement Guide*, January 7, 1900, 31 and 1; Odd, The Fighting Blacksmith, 166.

47 Cahn, *Theatrical 1899–1900*, 139, 143–55; "Amusement Notes," *Chicago Weekly Amusement Guide*, January 14, 1900, 11; Orpheon Music Hall, Chicago, program, week of October 13, 1901, in program file: Whirl-I-Gig, BRTC. The Lyric and subsequent theatre activity under other names at its 124 Washington Street address disappeared from city directories after 1902 (Reuben H. Donnelley, compiler, *The Lakeside Annual Directory of the City of Chicago*, 1902 [Chicago: Chicago Directory, 1903], et seq.)

48 Odd, *The Fighting Blacksmith*, 166.

49 Kaneo, *Ōbei*, 20; Kaneo, *Sadayakko*, 13–14. Dates were confused in these sources. Chicago newspapers seemed more reliable and offered a consensus about performances of *The Geisha and the Knight* and *Jingorō* on the three dates noted.

50 Kawakami Sadayakko, "Sadayakko," 202–3; Kaneo, *Sadayakko*, 13–14; "First Fall of Snow," *Chicago Times-Herald*, November 3, 1899, 7.

51 Kaneo, *Ōbei*, 20. Also "Kawakami Otojirō kinshū to etari" [Kawakami Otojirō gets financial backer], *Yomiuri shimbun*, December 14, 1899, in Shirakawa, 309. This listed another troupe parade on November 9, but I found no Chicago account of this. Indicative of the confusion: Sadayakko in Kawakami Sadayakko, "Sadayakko," 201, recalled a parade in Chicago snow sometime in December. This was long after the troupe departed for the East.

52 "From Other Points. Chicago," *NYC*, November 11, 1899, 764; also "Weather Indicators," *Chicago Daily Inter Ocean*, November 1–6, 1899.

53 "From Other Points. Chicago," *NYC*, November 4, 1899, 742; Biff Hall, "Telegraphic News. Chicago," *NYDM*, November 11, 1899, 12.

54 Kaneo, *Sadayakko*, 20 [page misnumbered as 16].

55 Arthur Row, "New York vs. Chicago as a Dramatic Center," *Poet Lore* 22 (March 1911): 151.

56 "News of Theatres," *Chicago Tribune*, October 30, 1899, 7; "Academy—Bob. Fitzsimmons," advertisement, *Chicago Tribune*, November 5, 1899, 40.

57 "Amusements. Alhambra," *Chicago Daily Inter Ocean*, October 29, 1899, 35. Prior to the Alhambra South Side run, *On the Wabash* did a week at the Academy on the West Side ("Academy. 25¢ Matinees," advertisement, *Chicago Tribune*, October 22, 1899, 44, "Lyric. Bob Fitzsimmons," advertisement, *Chicago Daily News*, November 1, 1899, 2).

58 "News of Theatres. On the Wabash," *Chicago Tribune*, November 6, 1899, 7; "Music and the Drama," *Chicago Evening Post*, November 6, 1899, 5.

59 "Notes on Amusements," *Chicago Daily News*, November 6, 1899, 3.

60 "Lyric—Joseph Arthur's Last Play," advertisement, *Chicago Tribune*, November 5, 1899, 40.

61   Matinees on November 6, 7, 9, and 10 (Monday, Tuesday, Thursday, and Friday). While these advertised dates were firmly established, sources conflicted over what was actually offered (Kaneo, *Ōbei*, 20; D. M. H[albert], "Music and the Drama," *Chicago Evening Post*, November 10, 1899, 5; "Music and the Drama," *Chicago Journal*, November 2, 1899, 4; "Plays and Play People. Japanese Players Remain," *Chicago Record*, November 6, 1899, 6; Leroy M. Scott, "The Players from the Land of Sunrise," *Chicago Journal*, November 9, 1899; and "News of Theatres. The Constant Wife," *Chicago Tribune*, November 10, 1899, 7).

62   In Japanese accounts, the title was *Kesa Moritō* (Kesa and Moritō) or *Kesa gozen*. Gozen was an honorific for women of high rank. After Chicago, *Kesa* titles appeared as *The Loyal Wife* or occasionally as *Tajo*, *Taijo*, *Teigo*, *Tago*, or *Teijo*. The first four of these T-words were variant transliterations of *teijo*, a Japanese word meaning faithful or chaste wife.

63   In most non-Kawakami versions of this story, the husband was called Wataru.

64   I adapted this synopsis from the Tremont Theatre, Boston, program, Thursday afternoon, December 14, 1899, in Tremont Theatre, HTC, and from a fragment in *Ost-Asien* 43 (n.d.): 394–95. What was performed in Chicago may have differed because Kawakami frequently shifted the order.

65   Tremont Theatre, Boston, program, Thursday afternoon, December 14, 1899. The unnamed Sumida locale was obviously Mukojima in Tokyo and was another example of the Japanese practice of incorporating actual locales into plays to engender familiar associations with a place. But the Sumida River that runs through Tokyo and passes Mukojima was a three- or four-week walking journey distant from the actual Mount Ōe of the first two scenes. It was the aura and poetic associations, not the actual geography, that mattered. This third scene of Kawakami's original Kesa was apparently dropped in latter performances as its lack of plot action did not work for foreign audiences (*Ost-Asien* [December 1901]: 396–97).

66   The famous cherry blossoms of Mukojima *indicated* romance while the dark forests of Mount Ōe indicated danger.

67   These assumptions are based on cast lists in subsequent programs.

68   Tremont Theatre, Boston, program, Thursday afternoon, December 14, 1899.

69   "At the Theatres," *Toledo Daily Blade*, November 24, 1899, 5.

70   "The Japanese Players at the Tremont Theatre," *Boston Evening Transcript*, December 9, 1899, 31. Apart from "gruesome" in this Boston review, the beheading of Kesa was not clearly described in American reports. Subsequent indirect evidence suggested Kawakami staged it with a papier mâché detachable head and imitation blood (chiwata) for several performances in Boston. This too-vivid (realistic?) business was soon dropped after American objections. According to Sadayakko, Kawakami restored the severed head with all its gore in France because "the more bloody, the more glad the [French] audience will be" (Yone[jirō] Noguchi, "Sada Yacco," *NYDM*, February 17, 1906, 11). A kabuki (?) production with a bloody severed head scene was described in Ozaki, "The Tragedy of Kesa Gozen," *Nineteenth Century* (London) 59 (January 1906): 131–34.

71   A kabuki-styled *Ōeyama* was unsuccessful when Kawakami tried it in 1895 at the Kabuki-za in Tokyo (Matsumoto, *Meiji engekiron*, 405, 411; Okamoto, *Meiji*, 176).

72   "Kabuki-za shichigatsu kōgyō; Kawakami engeki sujigaki" [Kabuki-za July performances; synopses of Kawakami plays], *Miyako shimbun*, 1895), 11–16.

73   The historical Mongaku supported Minamoto Yoritomo in his famous revolt against the ruling Taira hierarchy.

74   It was likely that Kawakami borrowed from this long play for his production as it included the Kesa sacrifice story.

75   The latter title is alternately written *Nachi no taki kisei no Mongaku*.

76   Matsumoto, *Meiji engekiron*, 42–46.

77   Ibid., 760, 934. A synopsis of a Kesa play and a general discussion of it appeared in Yei Theodora Ozaki, "The Tragedy of Kesa Gozen," *Nineteenth Century* (London) 59 (January 1906): 124–34.

78 English translations: Ryūnosuke Akutagawa, "Kesa and Morito," trans. Howard Hibbett, in Keene, *Modern*, 300–6; also *Rashomon and Other Stories*, trans. Takashi Kojima (New York: Liveright, 1952), 90–101. Lafcadio Hearn briefly recounted the tale in his 1894 *Glimpses of Unfamiliar Japan*, 2:577–79. Akutagawa was also the author of the two short stories adapted for Kurosawa Akira's 1950 motion picture *Rashōmon*.

79 New York: Scribner's, 1893. Adzuma is an alternate transliteration of Azuma, another name for the character usually called Kesa. Arnold fashioned his play to resonate with the subdued sexual ambiance of *Othello*. The full-length *Adzuma* was apparently never professionally produced.

80 Bordman, *American Theatre*, 625. One hundred years later, the characters Kesa and Morito appeared again in the Michael John LaChiusa musical *See What I Wanna See*.

81 Kaneo, *Ōbei*, 20. The average wage of an employed actor in the United States at the time was \$30–\$35 a week. Bit players received \$20 a week; supers, if employed regularly, \$5 a week. American skilled workers averaged \$16 to \$20 a week as did midlevel white-collar employees. Primary school teachers and male store clerks earned \$10 a week or less (Hill, *Souvenir*, 154; McArthur, *Actors*, 24; Pollock, *Footlights*, 28; Field, *Through*, 24).

82 "News of Theatres. Kawakami and Mme. Yacco," *Chicago Tribune*, November 6, 1899, 7; "Telegraphic News. Chicago," *NYDM*, October 28, 1899, 13.

83 "Music and Drama," *Chicago Journal*, October 21, 1899, 5; also "Amusements. A Japanese Matinee," *Chicago Daily Inter Ocean*, October 23, 1899, 5.

84 "At the Local Playhouses," *Grand Rapids Evening Press*, November 11, 1899, 2. None of these claims were accurate.

85 "Henry Miller's Hit. Mme. Yacco," *Chicago Evening Post*, November 2, 1899, 8; "Music and the Drama," *Chicago Journal*, November 2, 1899, 4; "News of Theatres. Kawakami and Mme. Yacco," *Chicago Tribune*, November 6, 1899, 7; "Plays and Play People. Japanese Play Again," *Chicago Record*, November 1, 1899, 3.

86 Advertisement in Lyric Theatre, Chicago, program, September 24, 1899, n.p., item 9F 38RN PG L985, CHS; also Fujine, *Rekishi*, 61; Fujine, *Haru*, 143; Kaneo, *Ōbei*, n.p.

87 "McVicker's—Extra!" and "McVicker's—Special," advertisements, *Chicago Tribune*, November 5, 1899, 40.

88 "Amusements. Actors' Fund Benefit," *Chicago Daily Inter Ocean*, November 3, 1899, 5; "News of Theatres. Actors' Fund Benefit," *Chicago Tribune*, November 9, 1899, and November 7 and 10, 1899, 7; "Plays and Play People. Big Receipts for Actors' Fund," *Chicago Record*, November 10, 1899, 6.

89 "News of Theatres, *Chicago Tribune*, October 30, 1899, 7.

90 "News of Theatres. Kawakami and Mme. Yacco," *Chicago Tribune*, November 6, 1899, 7. During his last week, Mansfield performed a different play every day, alternating *Cyrano de Bergerac*, *The First Violin*, *Beau Brummel*, and *Dr. Jekyll and Mr. Hyde* ("Amusements. Grand Opera House," *Chicago Daily Inter Ocean*," October 29, 1899, 35; "Grand Opera House. Mr. Richard Mansfield," advertisement, *Chicago Tribune*, October 29, 1899, 40). Kawakami may have also seen Mansfield in *Dr. Jekyll and Mr. Hyde* at the Grand Opera House. A confusing entry in Kaneo, *Ōbei*, 19, listed a Kawakami performance at the "Chicago Opera" on Saturday, October 28, but this most likely referred to his attendance at the Grand Opera House when Mansfield played *The First Violin*.

91 Clapp, *Players*, 231; Young, *Famous*, 2:733–34; "Hollis St. Theatre," advertisement, *Boston Herald*, January 17, 1886, 11.

92 "Music and Drama," *Chicago Journal*, October 21, 1899, 5. The play was an adaptation of a recent best-selling American novel by Jessie Fothergill and was a hit in Chicago, where its heimat ambience attracted the area's large German population. This immigrant community supported a part-time professional German-language stock company that performed every Sunday ("Amusements. The German Theatre," *Chicago Daily Inter Ocean*, October 22, 1899, and October 34 and 29, 1899, 35; "Power's Theatre," advertisement, *Chicago Tribune*, October 15, 1899, 44).

93 "At the Play," *Chicago Tribune*, October 29, 1899, 40.

94 Amy Leslie, "The Genius of Mansfield," *Chicago Daily News*, October 24, 1899, 3.

95 "Mansfield's Discipline: Actors in His Company Do Not Have an Easy Time of It," unidentified newspaper, December 19, 1899 clipping, in RLS NAFR+ v. 321, BRTC.

96 "Mansfield Company Arrives," *Chicago Daily Inter Ocean*, October 16, 1899, 5.

97 "Amusements. Grand Opera House," *Chicago Daily Inter Ocean*, October 29, 1899, 35.

98 Mansfield's portrayal was considered the first English-language *Cyrano*, even though in the United States his elegant production had to go against cheap rival versions and different translations rushed into production because of uncertainty about American copyright. The popularity of *Cyrano* immediately inspired an opera comique with music by Victor Herbert; a burlesque, *Sir Andy de Bootjack*; and a travesty, *Cyranose de Bric-à- Brac* ("'Cyrano de Bergerac.' Richard Mansfield in Rostand's Famous Play," [n.p.] *Transcript*, c. October 4, 1898, in RLS NAFR+ v. 321, p. 32, BRTC; Winter, *Life*, 1:257.)

99 Bernheim, *Business*, 49–50.

100 Wilstach, *Richard*, 325–28; McArthur, *Actors*, 25.

101 Garff B. Wilson, "Richard Mansfield: Actor of Transition," *Educational Theatre Journal* 14 (March 1962): 39; Wilstach, *Richard*, 325–28. Romantic acting that dominated American and British theatre in the last third of the nineteenth century had largely replaced the earlier "heroic" style of bombastic elocution.

102 George Henry Lewes quoted in McArthur, *Actors*, 171.

103 Norman Hapgood, "The Actor of Today," *Atlantic Monthly* 83 (January 1899): 119; also F. H. McMechan, "Acting vs. Elocution," *Theatre* (New York) No. 8 (October 1901): 18; Mullin, *Victorian*, 311–12. Mansfield had earlier attempted Richard III, Shylock, and Brutus with little success.

104 Garff B. Wilson, "Richard Mansfield: Actor of Transition," 40–41; also Alan Dale, "Who Is Our Worst Actor?," *Cosmopolitan*, April 1906, 686.

105 Garff B. Wilson, "Richard Mansfield: Actor of Transition," 38.

106 Alan Dale, "Who Is Our Worst Actor?" *Cosmopolitan*.

107 Winter, *Life*, 2:131.

108 "News of Theatres. Dr. Jekyll and Mr. Hyde," *Chicago Tribune*, November 5, 1899, 8. A representative review of Mansfield's premiere appeared in *Spirit of the Times*, May 14, 1887, n.p.

109 Garff B. Wilson, "Richard Mansfield: Actor of Transition," 38 and 41–42; also Wilstach, *Richard*, 317–18; Winter, *Life*, 1:257; "Money in Cyrano," unidentified newspaper, January 8, 1899 clipping, in RLS NAFR+ v. 321, p. 45, BRTC. A few months after this Chicago engagement, a sick Mansfield had to cancel dates despite the many comforts of his private railroad car ("Barnstorming Made Him Sick," unidentified newspaper, April 16, 1900, clipping, in RLS NAFR+ v. 321, p. 63, BRTC).

110 Winter, *Life*, 1:250; also "Amusements. Grand Opera House," *Chicago Daily Inter Ocean*, October 29, 1899, 35.

111 Arthur Ruhl, "Richard Mansfield: A Review of His Work," *Collier's* (September 14, 1907): 21.

112 Leslie, *Some*, 69, 71–71, 91, 65.

113 "At the Play," *Chicago Tribune*, October 29, 1899, 40; "Her Great Lady Macbeth," *Chicago Daily News*, November 8, 1899, 3; Biff Hall, "Telegraphic News. Chicago," *NYDM*, October 28, 1899, 13.

114 "News of Theatres," *Chicago Tribune*, November 9, 1899, 7; Coleman, *Fair*, 753, 757.

115 Coleman, *Fair*, 753; Modjeska, *Memories*, 537.

116 "News of Theatres. Kawakami and Mme. Yacco," *Chicago Tribune*, November 6, 1899, 7.

117 "News of Theatres. Macbeth," *Chicago Tribune*, November 8, 1899, 7.

118 Ibid.; "Her Great Lady Macbeth," *Chicago Daily News*.

119 "News of Theatres," *Chicago Tribune*, November 9, 1899, 7; W .F. A[pthrop], "Music and Drama. Boston Theatre: 'Much Ado about Nothing,'" *Boston Evening Transcript*, January 4, 1900, 11.

120 "News of Theatres. Mary Stuart," *Chicago Tribune*, November 7, 1899, 7. Modjeska played Mary Stuart for twenty years in a highly modified English language version by Lewis Wingfield (Coleman, *Fair*, 753; Mullin, *Victorian*, 330).

121 "News of Theatres. Macbeth," *Chicago Tribune*, November 8, 1899, 7; also "Her Great Lady Macbeth," *Chicago Daily News*, November 8, 1899, 3; "Music and the Drama," *Chicago Evening Post*, November 8, 1899, 8. A somewhat favorable review of Kellerd appeared in "Her Great Lady Macbeth," *Chicago Daily News*.

122 "Powers' Theatre. Olga Nethersole," advertisement, *Chicago Daily Inter Ocean*, October 16, 1899, n.p.

123 Joel H. Kaplan, "Pineroticism and the Problem Play: Mrs. Tanqueray, Mrs. Ebbsmith, and 'Mrs. Pat,'" in Foulkes, *British*, 40; "Miss Nethersole in 'The Profligate,'" *Chicago Times-Herald*, October 15, 1899, 2:6; Mullin, *Victorian*, 352–53; Joy Harriman Reilly, "A Forgotten 'Fallen Woman,' Olga Nethersole's Sapho," in Fisher, *When*, 106.

124 Arthur W. Pinero, *The Second Mrs. Tanqueray* (New York: Baker, 1894). With this play Pinero discarded asides, tableaux, soliloquies, and much of the craft he had perfected as a maker of nineteenth-century plays. Now he took style and subject from Ibsen but remained committed to current middle-class sensibilities and drawing room polite melodrama (Joel H. Kaplan, "Pineroticism and the Problem Play: Mrs. Tanqueray, Mrs. Ebbsmith, and 'Mrs. Pat,'" in Foulkes, *British*, 38–39).

125 Joel H. Kaplan, "Pineroticism and the Problem Play," 38, 45. Mrs. Tanqueray's sensational suicide provided satisfactory closure of the play.

126 D. M. H[albert], "Music and the Drama," *Chicago Evening Post*, October 17, 1899, 5; also "Amusements. Powers,'" *Chicago Daily Inter Ocean*, October 25, 1899, 5; Amy Leslie, "Offered at the Theatres," *Chicago Daily News*, October 17, 1899, 3.

127 Biff Hall, "Telegraphic News. Chicago," *NYDM*, November 11, 1899, 12; "News of Theatres. Sapho," *Chicago Tribune*, November 1, 1899, 4.

128 James O'Donnell Bennett, "Miss Nethersole Produces 'Sapho,'" *Chicago Journal*, November 1, 1899, 8; T[iffiny] B[lake], "Review of the Play," *Chicago Journal*, November 1, 1899, 8.

129 Clapp, *Players*, 256.

130 Howard Kyle, "On Tour with Modjeska," *Metropolitan* (January 1910): 446. Sienkiewicz is best known outside Poland for his novel, *Quo Vadis*.

131 Clapp, *Players*, 256; Hartnoll, *Concise Oxford*, s. v. "Modjeska, Helena."

132 Young, *Famous*, 1:805–6; Mullin, *Victorian*, 330. *The Doll's House* production was not successful.

133 McArthur, *Actors*, 170–71.

134 "Novelty's Stage Value," *New York Sun*, March 4, 1900, 3:7.

135 Mullin, *Victorian*, 333–34.

136 Leslie, *Some*, 1, 24.

137 Amy Leslie, "Frenchy Play by Fitch," *Chicago Daily News*, November 1, 1899; 6.

138 Amy Leslie, Some, 297–98. A metacritical male found Leslie the most talented of Chicago writers about theatre (Gordon Bowman, "Chicago Dramatic Critics," *Dramatic Magazine* [Chicago] 8 [October 1899]: 215).

139 Amy Leslie, "Frenchy Play by Fitch," *Chicago Daily News*. Other Chicago critics found the production "morally repugnant" ("Amusements," *Chicago Daily Inter Ocean*, November 5, 1899, 34; "Plays and Play People. 'Sapho' at Powers' Theatre," *Chicago Record*, November 1, 1899, 3).

140 "At the Play," *Chicago Tribune*, November 5, 1899, 41.

141 "Amusements. McVicker's," *Chicago Daily Inter Ocean*, October 16, 1899, 5.

142 "Shimpa hanseiki o kataru, 15, fūgawari na hitotachi: Fujii, Kojima, Nozaki-ra" [Talking about a half century of shimpa, 15; eccentric people: Fujii, Kojima, Nozaki, and others], *Miyako shimbun*, n.d. 1937, in "Shimpa gojūnen," n.p.; Matsumoto, *Meiji engekiron*, 428.

143   "The Man with the Lorgnette," *Boston Evening Record*, February 5, 1900, 5; "Daly's—The Great Ruby,"
        NYDM, February 18, 1899: 16; Incog [sic], "What a very queer sort of play," unidentified New York news-
        paper, c. February 1899, in clipping file: "The Great Ruby," BRTC.

144   "Daly's—The Great Ruby," *NYDM*, February 18, 1899, 16.

145   "Drama. This Week," *Athenaeum* (London) 112 (September 24, 1898): 427; T[iffiny] B[lake], "Music and
        the Drama: 'The Great Ruby,'" *Chicago Journal*, October 9, 1899, 7. The show had twelve massive sets and
        difficult set changes ("Daly's—The Great Ruby," *NYDM*, February 18, 1899, 16).

146   Alan Dale, "'The Great Ruby' at Daly's," *New York Journal*, February 10, 1899, n.p.

147   Kaneo, *Sadayakko*, 20 [page misnumbered as 16].

148   "Music and the Drama," *Chicago Journal*, November 2, 1899, 4.

149   "Amusements. Comstock's Japs," *Battle Creek Daily Journal*, November 11, 1899, 3. As this was a notice
        circulated by Comstock's publicist, it was probably not entirely accurate.

150   Kaneo, *Sadayakko*, 20 [page misnumbered as 16]. Details of this contract were unclear. Although Kawakami
        in Kaneo, *Ōbei*, 20, stated it was for forty weeks, elsewhere he reported a shorter tour (Kaneo, *Sadayakko*,
        20 [page misnumbered as 16]). A Tokyo newspaper reprinted a report from a Japanese paper in San
        Francisco that Kawakami signed a $28,990 contract for a twenty-week tour of the eastern United States to
        be followed by six months in England, France, and other European countries ("Kawakami Otojirō kinshū
        to etari" [Kawakami Otojirō gets financial backer], *Yomiuri shimbun*, December 14, 1899, in Shirakawa,
        309). A similar report appeared in "Zaibei Kawakami ichiza" [The Kawakami troupe in America], *Jiji
        shimpō*, December 24, 1899, in Shirakawa, 309–10.

151   Leavitt, *Fifty*, 273; T. Allison Brown, *History*, 3:216–20; "Death of Alexander Comstock," *NYDM*, January
        1, 1909, 7.

152   "Shin'engeki no sossensha toshite Ōbei o man'yū" [Going to Europe and America as a pioneer of the New
        Theatre], *Miyako shimbun*, July 25, 1900, in Shirakawa, 317–18.

153   "Right from Japan," *Grand Rapids Evening Press*, November 13, 1899, 3; "Amusements," *Muskegon Daily
        Chronicle*, November 16, 1899, 1; Kaneo, *Ōbei*, 21; also "Railroad Time-Tables," *Chicago Daily Inter Ocean*,
        November 10, 1899, 11.

154   Seemingly less accurate reports of the departure appeared in "Kawakami Otojirō kinshū to etari," *Yomiuri
        shimbun*; "Shin'engeki no sossensha toshite Ōbei o man'yū," *Miyako shimbun*.

155   Kaneo, *Ōbei*, 19. An argument for Chicago as the theatrical equal of New York appeared in Gordon
        Bowman, "Chicago Dramatic Critics," *Dramatic Magazine* (Chicago) 8 (October 1899): 213.

156   "Gikyōshin," Kaneo, *Sadayakko*, 12.

157   "Divine Spirit and Buddha" was my translation of "kamihotoke."

158   Kaneo, *Sadayakko*, 20 [page misnumbered as 16].

159   Chicago newspapers, September 14–November 15, 1899.

160   "War in Asia," *Grand Rapids Herald*, November 13, 1899, 1.

161   Biff Hall, "Telegraphic News. Chicago," *NYDM*, November 11 and October 12 and 28, 1899, 13.

162   D. M. H[albert], "Music and the Drama," *Chicago Evening Post*, November 10, 1899, 5.

Chapter 10

1   Kaneo, *Sadayakko*, 21; "Right from Japan," *Grand Rapids Evening Press*, November 13, 1899, 3.

2   Grand Rapids," *Grand Rapids Sunday Democrat*, November 5, 1899, 2:1; also Michigan, *Michigan*, 306;
        "The Furniture City," *Grand Rapids Morning Democrat*, November 5, 1899, 2:3.

3   Michigan, *Michigan*, 158; *R. L. Polk and Co.'s Grand Rapids City Directory 1899* (Grand Rapids, Michigan:
        Grand Rapids Directory, 1899), 33.

4   Lewis, *Trouping*, 6–7.

5   "Grand—The Great Triple Alliance," *Grand Rapids Herald*, November 5, 1899, 14; "Provincial Notices," *NYDM*, November 25, 1899, 6; "Smith's—Rose Hill Company," *Grand Rapids Herald*, November 5, 1899, 14; "The Plays This Week," *Grand Rapids Herald*, November 12, 1899, 14.

6   *The Old and New Powers Theatre Building* (Grand Rapids: Powers Theatre, 1915), 3, 9–10; Z. Z. Lydens, ed., *The Story of Grand Rapids* (Grand Rapids, Michigan: Kregel, 1967), 426. Located on the lower floors of an office building in the financial district, it closed as a movie theatre in 1975 (Lynn Mapes and Anthony Travis, *Pictorial History of Grand Rapids* [Grand Rapids: Kregel, 1976], 144).

7   "We Perfume the Opera House," advertisement, *Grand Rapids Herald*, November 10, 1899, 3. The perfume currently permeating the theatre was available retail for 75¢ an ounce.

8   "Amusements," advertisements, *Grand Rapids Herald*, November 19, 1899, 14; "Amusements," *Grand Rapids Herald*, November 14, 1899, 4; Kaneo, *Sadayakko*, 21.

9   "Amusements," *Grand Rapids Herald*, November 13, 1899, 4; "Provincial Notices," *NYDM*, November 25, 1899, 6.

10   Kaneo, *Ôbei*, 21; "Grand Rapids and Indiana Railway," advertisement, *Grand Rapids Herald*, November 11, 1899, 6.

11   Michigan, *Michigan*, 351–52; Cahn, *Theatrical 1899–1900*, 487. The Opera House was later converted into an Elks Lodge. Fire destroyed it on New Year's Day, 1913. ("Occidental Hotel Book" file, in Muskegon Picture Collection, Hackley Public Library, Muskegon). *At Piney Ridge* played at the Opera House earlier the same year.

12   "Opera House. At Piney Ridge," advertisement, *Muskegon Daily Chronicle*, November 6, 1899, 3; "Opera House. The Spy of the Tennessee," advertisement, *Muskegon Daily Chronicle*, November 22, 1899, 3.

13   Kaneo, *Ôbei*, 21.

14   *Battle Creek City Directory, 1979* (Taylor, Michigan: Polk, 1979), viii.

15   Bernice Bryant Lowe, *Tales of Battle Creek* (Battle Creek: Miller Foundation, 1976), 81.

16   Julian Street, *Abroad at Home* (New York: Century, 1914), 113–18; Elizabeth Rose Orlick, "Hamblin's of Battle Creek: The History of an Opera House 1869–1902," thesis, East Lansing: Department of Speech, Michigan State University, 1970, 2, 13.

17   Orlick, "Hamblin's of Battle Creek," 21, 34, 199. Hamblin's became a vaudeville theatre in 1905 and was remodeled into a department store in 1911 (Bernice Bryant Lowe, *Tales of Battle Creek*, 161).

18   Sôseki Natsume, *Grass on the Wayside (Michikusa)*, trans. Edwin McClellan (Chicago: University of Chicago Press, 1969), 3.

19   Whittier, *Dear*, 22; Horton, *Driftwood*, 201–3; Rudolph De Cordova, "The Stage as a Career: An Actor's Experience," *Forum* 17 (July 1894): 624–25. Hot water and soap made removing grease paint so much easier.

20   Madge Kendal, "Some Pros and Cons of Theatrical Life," in *Education and Professions. The Woman's Library* (London: Chapman and Hill, 1903), 1:230. Kendal was describing rooms in theatrical lodging houses but similar residue was in dressing rooms.

21   De Cordova, "The Stage as a Career: An Actor's Experience," 624–25; author's personal experience.

22   Winter, *Wallet*, 1:18; also Winter, *Other*, 309–10; McArthur, *Actors*, 108–9.

23   Kaneo, *Ôbei*, 21–22.

24   Cahn, *Theatrical 1899–1900*, 412; Washington Cooke, "A History of the Croswell Opera House," n.p., manuscript, June 1932, item H792.09 Co, Adrian Public Library.

25   "News and Notes," *Adrian Daily Telegram*, November 17, 1899, 3.

26   Cooke, "History of the Croswell Opera House," n.p. On November 23 and 24, local amateurs produced *The Virginia Spy* to SRO business ("Virginia Spy," *Adrian Daily Times and Expositor*, November 24, 1899,

3). This theatre continued to be active as a remodeled nonprofit community theatre for decades, personal observation, July 31–August 2, 1980; also www.croswell.org. 4/2/10).

27   Léon Beauvallet, *Rachel and the New World*, trans. Colin Clair (London: Abelard-Schuman, 1967), 37.

28   "Careless Waiter Narrowly Escapes Annihilation at the Hands of an Irate Jap," *Adrian Daily Times and Expositor*, November 21, 1899, 3.

29   Kaneo, *Ôbei*, 22; "Railroad Directory," *Tiffin Daily Advertiser*, November 20, 1899, 3.

30   George Gundlach, "Rambling Comments on Tiffin," manuscript, n.d. (c. 1960), 26, 37, Gen. Ohio 977.124 Tiffin 2g, Tiffin-Seneca Public Library; "Advertiser Dedication Edition, 22 December 1928," in Myron B. Barnes, comp., *Tiffin Theatre: A Collection of Articles Dealing with Stage and Screen in Tiffin, Ohio* (Tiffin: Barnes, 1980) 14; Myron Bruce Barnes, *Between the Eighties: Tiffin, Ohio, 1880–1980* (Tiffin: Seneca County Museum, 1982), 108–21.

31   "Amusements," *Tiffin Daily Tribune and Herald*, November 21, 1899, 5; "Entertaining Japanese," *Tiffin Daily Advertiser*, November 21, 1899, 4.

32   "Noble's Opera House," advertisements, *Tiffin Daily Tribune and Herald*, November 11, 1899, 4; *Tiffin Advertiser*, November 16, 1899, 2.

33   *Sidewalks, Streets, and Alleys: Iron Horse Days* (Tiffin: Tiffin Historic Trust, c. 1980), n.p.

34   *Toledo at the Threshold of the 20th Century* (Toledo: Toledo Bee, 1902), 40; Writers Program, *The Ohio Guide* (New York: Oxford University Press, 1940), 329–30.

35   "Valentine. Engagement Extraordinary," *Toledo Bee*, November 19, 1899, 1:2. *Kusunoki Masahige* and *Sarashi—Three Colors* had been played in San Francisco. *Nisshin Senso* (The Sino-Japanese War) was of one of Kawakami's spectacular ("but true") war plays staged several years earlier. Identification of *Japanese Fables* could not be found.

36   "The Stage," *Toledo Bee*, November 22, 1899, 4.

37   "Ohio. Toledo," *NYC*, November 11, 1899, 767.

38   "The Stage," *Toledo Bee*.

39   "Ohio. Toledo," *NYC*, December 2, 1899, 831; also "Provincial Notices," *NYDM*, December 2, 1899, 6.

40   "Madame Yacco and Her Japs," *Toledo Daily Blade*, November 23, 1899, 3.

41   Kaneo, *Ôbei*, 22.

42   Louis R. Effler, *My Memoirs of the Gay 90's* (Toledo: Buettner and Breska, 1942), 336; Valentine Theatre, Toledo, program, week of December 25, 1896, "Local History" item qR792, Toledo-Lucas Public Library; Marion S. Revett, *A Minstrel Town* (New York: Pageant, 1955), 107–9. In 1918, Loew's Inc. took over this theatre and converted it to vaudeville and movies. By 1990, the City of Toledo owned the building and it housed the Toledo public television station (Marion [S.] Revett, "On the Road," manuscript, Toledo, 1957, 166, in Local History, item qR780.9771, Toledo-Lucas Public Library; John W. Frick and Carlton Ward, eds., *Directory of Historic American Theatres* (New York: Greenwood, 1987), 214–15); personal observation.

43   "Curtain in Valentine Theatre," *Toledo Bee*, January 9, 1898, n.p.

44   "Kawakami no yōkō miyage" [Souvenirs from Kawakami's trips abroad], *Kabuki* 34 (March 1903): 32.

45   *Toledo at the Threshold of the 20th Century* (Toledo: Toledo Bee, 1902), 40; Cahn, *Theatrical 1899–1900*, 211.

46   "The Stage," *Toledo Bee*, November 19 and 24, 1899, 10; "At the Theatres," *Toledo Daily Blade*, November 24, 1899, 5.

47   Kaneo, *Ôbei*, 22; "Railroad Time Tables," *Toledo Bee*, November 27, 1899, 6; *Williams' Dayton Directory for 1899–1900* (Cincinnati: Williams, 1900), n.p.

48   "Japanese Drama," *Dayton Daily Journal*, November 28, 1899, 5; Kaneo, *Ôbei*, 22.

49   "Theatrical Patronage," *Dayton Daily News*, November 27, 1899, 4.

50   Cahn, *Theatrical 1900–01*, 554.

51   Cahn, *Theatrical 1899–1900*, 733–34. Built in 1862, the interior of this theatre was damaged several times by fire and flood (interview with Jack Keyes, manager of Victoria Theatre, Dayton, January 18, 1978; Landmark Committee of Montgomery County, *Report: A Study and Evaluation of the Significant Structures and Sites of Montgomery County, Ohio*, [Dayton: Landmark Committee, 1968], 44).

52   "Victoria Theatre," advertisement, *Dayton Daily News*, November 16, 1899, 5; "Amusements," *Dayton Evening Herald*, November 25, 1899, 6.

53   "Amusements. The Air Ship Today," *Dayton Evening Herald*, November 14, 1899, 9.

54   "Amusements," *Dayton Daily Journal*, November 28, 1899, 5; "Amusements," *Dayton Evening Herald*, November 9, 1899, 24.

55   "At the Theatres," *Toledo Daily Blade*, November 25, 1899, 10. It was not clear whether Sadayakko or shamisen specialist Kineya Kimisaburô played the *koto*.

56   "The Japanese Play," *Dayton Daily Journal*, November 29, 1899, 5.

57   Kaneo, *Ôbei*, 22; "Time Card. Union Depot," *Dayton Daily News*, November 25, 1899, 10.

58   "Opera House," advertisement, *Mansfield Daily Shield*, November 27, 1899, 8; "Amusements," *Mansfield News*, November 29, 1899, 5.

59   Kaneo, *Ôbei*, 22–23; "Railway News," *Bucyrus Evening Telegram*, November 30, 1899, 8; Daniel G. Arnold, *About Bucyrus* (Indianapolis: McM [*sic*] Corporation, 1971), 47–50.

60   Kaneo, *Ôbei*, 22–23.

61   "The Japanese," *Bucyrus Evening Telegraph*, December 1, 1899, 3.

62   Kaneo, *Ôbei*, 23; "Erie Railroad," advertisement, *Mansfield Daily Shield*, November 29, 1899, 7.

63   "Provincial Notices," *NYDM*, November 25 and December 2, 1899, 6; "Amusements," *Muskegon Daily Chronicle*, November 16, 1899, 1; "Amusement," *Adrian Daily Telegram*, November 20, 1899, 3; "Amusements," *Tiffin Daily Tribune and Herald*, November 21, 1899, 5; "Ohio. Toledo," *NYC*, December 2, 1899, 831; "The Japanese Play," *Dayton Daily Journal*, November 29, 1899, 5; "The Japanese," *Bucyrus Evening Telegraph*, December 1, 1899, 3.

64   The typical seating capacity of theatres played on the tour was twelve hundred, although theatres in the larger cities of Dayton and Toledo could hold up to two thousand. The smallest venue was the Vollrath in Bucyrus, which had less than seven hundred seats (Cahn, *Theatrical 1899–1900*; W. M. Harford, ed., *Muskegon and Its Resources* [Muskegon: Harford and Latimer, 1888], 54; Orio M. Knapp, "Succession of Old Stage Favorites That Charmed and Entertained Three Generations of Our Theatre People," in Myron B. Barnes, comp., *Tiffin Theatre* [Tiffin: Barnes, 1980], 43; Marion S. Revett, *A Minstrel Town* [New York: Pageant, 1955], 107).

65   "Victoria Theatre," advertisement, *Dayton Daily News*, November 16, 1899, 5; "Grand. At Piney Ridge," advertisement, *Grand Rapids Herald*, November 12, 1899, 14; "Noble's Opera House," advertisement, *Tiffin Advertiser*, November 16, 1899, 2.

66   For instance: "The Stage," *Toledo Bee*, November 19 and 24, 1899, 10; "The Theatres," *Grand Rapids Herald*, November 12, 1899, 14; "At the Theatres," *Toledo Daily Blade*, November 24, 1899, 5.

67   "Amusements," *Adrian Daily Times and Expositor*, November 20, 1899, 2; also "Amusements," *Grand Rapids Herald*, November 14, 1899, 4.

68   "Amusements," *Muskegon Daily Chronicle*, November 16, 1899, 1.

69   "At the Theatres," *Toledo Daily Blade*, November 22, 1899, 5.

70   "The Stage," *Toledo Bee*, November 22, 1899, 4; *Toledo Bee*, November 19, 1899, 10.

71   "A High Motive," *Adrian Daily Telegram*, November 30, 1899, 3; also "At the Local Playhouses," *Grand Rapids Evening Press*, November 11, 1899, 2; "Amusements," *Grand Rapids Morning Democrat*, November 14, 1899, 2.

72   "Amusements," *Muskegon Daily Chronicle*, November 16, 1899, 1. Concurring opinions: "Amusements," *Grand Rapids Herald*, November 14, 1899, 4; "Amusements," *Grand Rapids Morning Democrat*, November 14, 1899, 2; "Entertaining Japanese," *Tiffin Daily Advertiser*, November 21, 1899, 4.

73   "The Stage," *Toledo Bee*, November 22, 1899, 4.

74   "The Japanese Play," *Dayton Daily Journal*, November 29, 1899, 5.

75   "Amusements," *Muskegon Daily Chronicle*, November 16, 1899, 1.

76   "Provincial Notices," *NYDM*, December 2, 1899, 6.

77   "Entertaining Japanese," *Tiffin Daily Advertiser*, November 21, 1899, 4.

78   "Amusements," *Adrian Daily Times and Expositor*, November 20, 1899, 2.

79   "Amusement," *Adrian Daily Telegram*, November 20, 1899, 3.

80   Donald Thomas Shanower, "A Comparative and Descriptive Study of Three Opera Houses in Southern Michigan 1880–1900," dissertation, University of Michigan, Ann Arbor, 1959, 224.

81   "On the Road," *NYC*, November 25, 1899, 810–11. The *New York Dramatic Mirror* listed 427 dramatic productions out of a total of 572 shows ("An Unparalleled Record," *NYDM*, October 28, 1899, 14).

82   "Traveling Shows," *NYC*, September 23, 1899, 602–3; "An Unparalleled Record," *NYDM*. Notice of Kawakami's route no doubt came from Comstock, his junior partner Bailey, or their advance agent Barnes.

83   "An Unparalleled Record," *NYDM*, October 28, 1899, 14.

84   Poggi, *Theatre*, 6–10.

85   Informal conversations with old-time prairie actors, Theatre Museum of Repertoire Americana, Mt. Pleasant, Iowa, summers 1980s; Lewis, *Trouping*, 9; "Theatrical Season of 1893," unidentified newspaper c. 1894 clipping, in Alfred Edgar Mullet Scrapbook **T.11.9, RBD BPL.

86   Horton, *Driftwood*. 202–3.

87   Modjeska, *Memories*, 377.

88   William H. Crane, "The Modern Cart of Thespis," *North American Review* 154 (April 1892): 475–77; Sturgis, *Influence*, 109.

89   The burlesque show and two of the farces could be termed, in the jargon of the day, "risqué."

90   "Ohio. Toledo," *NYC*, November 11, 1899, 767; "Victoria Theatre," advertisement, *Dayton Daily News*, November 16, 1899, 5; "Amusements," *Dayton Evening Herald*, November 25, 1899, 6.

91   "Brevities," *Battle Creek Daily Journal*, November 13, 1899, 3; "Joys and Comforts, Trials and Tribulations of the Actress 'On the Road,'" *New York World*, March 25, 1900, 2E; Kirke La Shelle, "The Theatrical Advance Agent," *Cosmopolitan* (January 1900): 326–27.

92   Ibid.; "The Theatres," *Grand Rapids Herald*, November 12, 1899, 14; "Amusements," *Grand Rapids Morning Democrat*, November 14, 1899, 2; *Grand Rapids Evening Press*, *Herald*, and *Morning Democrat*. October 16–November 30, 1899.

93   "Lyric. Today," advertisement, *Chicago Record*, November 3, 1899, 2.

94   Random examples: "Powers. Imperial Japanese Dramatic Company," advertisement, *Grand Rapids Herald*, November 10, 1899, 4; "Amusements," *Muskegon Daily Chronicle*, November 16, 1899, 1; "Amusements," *Adrian Daily Times and Expositor*, November 20, 1899, 2; "Provincial Notices," *NYDM*, November 25 and December 2, 1899, 6; "Right from Japan," *Grand Rapid Evening Press*, November 13, 1899, 3; "Japanese Drama," *Dayton Daily Journal*, November 27, 1899, 5.

95   "Vaudeville," *Dramatic Magazine* 7:1 (May 1899): 28; also "Plain Tales of Stageland," *Boston Journal*, December 24, 1899, 10.

96   Estavan, *San*, 15:1:68; Odell, *Annals*, 8:217–18; Mihara Aya, "Beikoku kōgyō ni kaketa geinō rokuza no dōkō: 1687nen o chūshin ni" [What happened to six troupes of entertainers who took their chances in American show business: focusing on the year 1867], *Geinō shi kenkyū* No. 127 (1994): 1–24.

97   "Adam 4-Paw Shows. Circus. Menagerie. Museum," poster, Philadelphia: Morell Brothers, c. 1893.

98   Temple Theatre, Philadelphia, programs, weeks of February 8 and May 17, 1886, in program file: The Little Tycoon, BRTC.

99   Toll, *Blacking*, 172.

100 Odell, *Annals*, 15:437.

101 Ibid., 12:307.

102 Orpheum Theatre, San Francisco, program, April 21, 1890, in scrapbook NWEZ+ n.c. 709, BRTC.

103 Odell, *Annals*, 15:357, other references: 8:583; 10:142; 11:597; 12: 521; 14:634; 15:225, 437, 418, 437, 506, 437.

104 The Imperial appellation was a hoax on two continents. The troupe was even called Imperial in Russia where there really were imperial theatres.

105 There was a long history of major patronage of nō troupes by non-regal but ruling daimyō.

106 Show business publicity in American and Europe throughout the nineteenth century featured many reports, genuine or contrived, of performers showing before European royalty. For instance, Mark Cosdon, "Prepping for Pantomime: The Hanlon Brothers' Fame and Tragedy, 1833–1870," *Theatre History Studies* 20 (2000): 74–79; Miln, *When*, 196–97, 230–31.

107 "Amusements. Comstock's Japs," *Battle Creek Daily Journal*, November 11, 1899, 3.

108 "Madame Yacco and Her Japs," *Toledo Daily Blade*, November 22, 1899, 3.

109 "Japanese Drama," *Dayton Daily Journal*, November 27, 1899, 5.

110 "Brevities," *Battle Creek Daily Journal*, November 13, 1899, 3; also "Amusements," *Grand Rapids Morning Democrat*, November 14, 1899, 2.

111 "Japanese Drama," *Dayton Daily Journal*.

112 "The Theatres," *Grand Rapids Herald*, November 12, 1899, 14.

113 "At the Local Playhouses," *Grand Rapids Evening Press*, November 11, 1899, 2; also "Amusements," *Grand Rapids Herald*, November 10, 1899, 4.

114 "Amusements," *Muskegon Daily Chronicle*, November 16, 1899, 1; also "Amusements. Victoria Theatre," advertisement, *Dayton Evening Herald*, November 28, 1899, 7. Anna Held was Flo Ziegfield's new foreign star publicized as a world-class beauty.

115 "Japanese Henry Irving–Ellen Terry," *San Francisco Examiner Magazine*, June 25, 1899, 27.

116 "Amusements. Comstock's Japs," *Battle Creek Daily Journal*, November 13, 1899, 3; "Amusement," *Adrian Daily Telegram*, November 20, 1899, 3; "The Stage," *Toledo Bee* November 24, 1899, 10; "Japanese Drama," *Dayton Daily Journal*, November 27, 1899, 5; "Provincial Notices," *NYDM*, December 2, 1899, 6. Sadayakko's tea receptions were held onstage or in the theatre lobby.

117 Mayer, *Once Upon a City*, 156; "Atlantic City. Society by the Sea," *Philadelphia Inquirer*, July 19, 1900, 18.

118 "Amusements," *Muskegon Daily Chronicle*, November 16, 1899, 1.

119 "The Stage," *Toledo Bee*, November 22, 1899, 4. As almost everywhere, Kawakami's printed programs also had explanatory notes and synopses.

Chapter 11

1   "Erie Railroad, advertisement," *Mansfield Daily Shield*, November 29, 1899, 7; Kaneo, *Ōbei*, 23; Field, *Through*, 9.

2   Kaneo, *Ōbei*, 23; Bromley, *Atlas*, 6–10, 12.

3   Sweetser, *Greater*, n.p.; Sarah Truax, *A Woman of Parts: Memories of a Life on Stage* (New York: Longmans, Green, 1949), 51.

4   "Drama and Music," *Boston Globe*, December 10, 1899, 22.

5   Sweetser, *Greater*, 12.

6   At 570 Columbus Avenue (Kaneo, *Ōbei*, 23; Bromley, *Atlas*, 28).

7   Bainbridge Bunting, *Houses of Boston's Back Bay* (Cambridge, Massachusetts: Belknap, 1967), 43, 73 484 fn. 27; Woods, *City*, 30–31, 35; Bromley, *Atlas*, 28; Wolfe, *Lodging*, 22. People who were not Bostonians called these bulging buildings "bow fronts."

8   Woods, *City*, 50, 88; Wolfe, *Lodging*, 7, 9, 20–26, 81, 192.

9   Wolfe, *Lodging*, 29, 21. 32; Woods, *City*, 69, 185–86, 189, 197.

10   Anna Bergengren, *Her Boston Experience* (Boston: Page, 1900), 67, 68.

11   Wolfe, *Lodging*, 32; Woods, *City*, 159–64.

12   Woods, *City*, 10; Wolfe, *Lodging*, 12, 27–29, 46–47, 102–34, 139; Duis, *Saloon*, 193–96.

13   Kawakami Otojirō, "Kawakami ikkō no shibōsa" [The death of a member of the Kawakami troupe], *Miyako shimbun*, March 2, 1900, in Shirakawa, 312.

14   I found no evidence that the troupe was afflicted.

15   Hanley, *Everyday*, 100–1; Wolfe, *Lodging*, 26, 35–36; Woods, *City*, 64–67.

16   Marilyn Thornton Williams, *Washing "The Great Unwashed"* (Columbus: Ohio State University Press, 1991), 18, 72.

17   Kaneo, *Ōbei*, 23; America also had its chalk white–faced actors but they were comedians or clowns (Stephen Jenkins, *The Greatest Street in the World* [New York: Putnam's, 1911], 213).

18   Kaneo, *Sadayakko*, 24; Muramatsu Shōfu, *Kawakami*, 1:275.

19   "Morphine!" advertisement, *NYDM*, March 25, 1899, 3.

20   "Arizona," *NYDM*, September 15, 1900, 17; Tremont Theatre, Boston, program, week of December 18, 1899, in Tremont Theatre programs **T.10.27, RBD BPL.

21   These matinees were scheduled to begin at 2:30 and end at 4:45 (Kaneo, *Ōbei*, 23; "Tremont. Arizona," advertisement, *Boston Herald*, December 8, 1899, 9; Tremont Theatre, Boston, program, week of November 27, 1899, 11, in Tremont Theatre programs **T.10.27, RBD BPL).

22   Henry Irving, "The American Audience," *Fortnightly Review* 37 (February 1, 1885): 201.

23   McConachie, *Melodramatic*, 204; Dennis Kennedy, "The New Drama and the New Audience," in Booth, *Edwardian*, 136–40.

24   Cahn, *Theatrical 1899–1900*, 71.

25   "Agnes Booth," unidentified magazine, c. 1892, p. 40, in clipping file: Jewett, Henry, BRTC.

26   Tremont Theatre, Boston, programs, weeks of November 13 and December 11, 1899, in Tremont Theatre programs **T.10.27, RBD BPL; "Tremont Theatre," advertisement, *Boston Herald*, December 13, 1899, 9.

27   "Drama and Music," *Boston Globe*, December 10, 1899, 22.

28   "Japan's … [illegible]," unidentified Boston newspaper, c. December 9 or 10, 1899, fragment in my archive.

29   Tremont Theatre, Boston, program, week of November 27, 1899.

30   "A Glimpse of the Japanese Drama," *Boston Evening Transcript*, December 6, 1899, 18.

31   "The Japanese Play," *Boston Post*, December 5, 1899, 4.

32   "Japanese Players," *Boston Daily Advertiser*, December 6, 1899, 4; "The Japanese Play," *Boston Post*; "The Man with the Lorgnette," *Boston Evening Record*, December 18, 1899, 5.

33   "Music and Drama. The Japanese Stage," *Boston Evening Transcript*, December 16, 1899, 28.

34   "A Glimpse of the Japanese Drama," *Boston Evening Transcript*; "Japanese Players," *Boston Daily Advertiser*. It was likely that Ellen Terry's daughter, Edith Craig, who was traveling with Irving's company, attended this or a latter Kawakami performance (Belford, *Bram*, 285.)

35   "Music and Drama," *Boston Evening Transcript*, December 7, 1899, 9.

36   "A Glimpse of the Japanese Drama," *Boston Evening Transcript*; "Japanese Players," *Boston Daily Advertiser*.

37   "Japanese Players," *Boston Daily Advertiser*; "Calvé and 'Carmen,'" *Boston Globe*, December 5, 1899, 13.

38   "A Glimpse of the Japanese Drama," *Boston Evening Transcript*.

39   Miss Carabee, "Stage-Naughty Mlle. Fougere Is Demure in Private Life," *Boston Traveler*, December 8, 1899, 5.

40   Jay Benton, "Telegraphic News. Boston," *NYDM*, September 2, 1899, 12.

41   Bingham, *Henry*, 259.

42   "Theatres," *Boston of Today*, 99.

43   Grandgent, "Stage," 395; "Theatres," *Boston of Today*, 98; Cahn, *Theatrical 1899–1900*, 71; Cashin, *Boston*, 6 Tucci, *Boston*, 7; Norton, *Broadway*, 137.

44   "Tremont Theatre Damaged," *Boston Globe*, June 3, 1981, 26. In 1983, in commemoration of Kawakami's American performances, a brick salvaged from the Tremont stage door entrance was embedded in the foundation of Teishōji, the temple Sadayakko built as affirmation of her Buddhist faith and as a memorial to the shimpa tradition pioneered by her husband.

45   "Japanese Players," *Boston Globe*, December 10, 1899, 1:18. Later reviews of the opening included "Japanese Drama," *Boston Traveler*, December 6, 1899, 5; "The Japanese Play," *Boston Post*, December 5, 1899, 4; "Japanese Players," *Boston Daily Advertiser*; "The Japanese Plays," *Boston Dramatic Review* 6 (December 9, 1899): 1; "The Man with the Lorgnette," *Boston Evening Record*, December 18, 1899, 5.

46   "Japanese Plays in Boston," *New York Times*, December 6, 1899, 8.

47   "A Glimpse of the Japanese Drama," *Boston Evening Transcript*; also "The Japanese Play," *Boston Post*; "Japanese Players," *Boston Globe*; Jay Benton, "Telegraphic News. Boston," *NYDM*, December 9, 1899, 12.

48   "Music and Drama. The Japanese Stage," *Boston Evening Transcript*, December 16, 1899, 28.

49   "Japanese Players," *Boston Daily Advertiser*; also "Japanese Drama," *Boston Traveler*, December 6, 1899, 5.

50   "Players from Far Japan," *Boston Journal*, January 7, 1900, 4:4. The reporter's impressions were from the early Boston performances but were not published until this later interview with Kawakami. Also "The Japanese Play," *Boston Post*, December 5, 1899, 4,

51   "Japanese Drama," *Boston Traveler*; also "Japanese Players," *Boston Daily Advertiser*, December 6, 1899, 4.

52   These were vigorous but simple stunts compared to masterful kabuki techniques.

53   "Japanese Players," *Boston Daily Advertiser*. Henry Austin Clapp, the nationally known theatre scholar and principal drama critic of the *Advertiser*, probably wrote this unsigned review.

54   "Plain Tales of Stageland," *Boston Journal*, December 17, 1899, 1:4.

55   "A Glimpse of the Japanese Drama," *Boston Evening Transcript*, December 6, 1899, 18.

56   "Plain Tales of Stageland," *Boston Journal*.

57   Penciled note on a Tremont Theatre, Boston, program, December 14, 1899, in Tremont Theatre programs **T.10.27, RBD BPL.

58   "Stories of the Players, Virginia Harned's Stage Gowns," *Boston Herald*, December 18, 1899, 10.

59   "Those Japanese Players," *Boston Herald*, December 12, 1899, 9; Alexander Corbett Jr., "Japan's Foremost Actors," *Boston Globe*, December 11, 1899, 5; "Japanese Drama," *Boston Traveler*, December 6, 1899, 5; "Japanese Players," *Boston Daily Advertiser*.

60   "Japanese Players," *Boston Daily Advertiser*; "The Japanese Play," *Boston Post*.

61   Alexander Corbett Jr., "Japan's Foremost Actors," *Boston Globe*.

62   "A Glimpse of the Japanese Drama," *Boston Evening Transcript*; also "Japanese Players," *Boston Daily Advertiser*.

63   The Calcium Man, "Stage Doings and Sayings in the Limelight," *Boston Traveler*, December 16, 1899, 5.

64   Anna Farquhar, "Convictions. The Japanese Drama," *National Magazine* 11 (February 1900): 563.

65   Alexander Corbett Jr., "Japan's Foremost Actors;" echoed in Anna Farquhar, "Convictions. The Japanese Drama," 563.

66   "The Japanese Play," *Boston Post*, December 5, 1899, 4; also "The Man with the Lorgnette," *Boston Evening Record*, December 18, 1899, 5,

67   Alexander Corbett Jr., "Japan's Foremost Actors," *Boston Globe*.

68   "Japanese Players," *Boston Globe*, December 10, 1899, 1:18.

69   The Calcium Man, "Stage Doings and Sayings in the Limelight," *Boston Traveler*; also Jay Benton, "Telegraphic News. Boston," *NYDM*, January 6, 1900, 12. Anna Farquhar in "Convictions. The Japanese Drama," 563, found the gestures of the Japanese actors were "though generally speaking graceful, frequently [were] verging upon the affected and bizarre."

70   "The Japanese Plays," *Boston Dramatic Review* 6 (December 9, 1899): 1; also "The Chatterer," *Boston Herald*, December 13, 1899, 6.

71   The Calcium Man, "Stage Doings and Sayings in the Limelight," *Boston Traveler*; also "The Japanese Plays," *Boston Dramatic Review*.

72   "The Japanese Play," *Boston Post*, December 5, 1899, 4; "The Man with the Lorgnette," *Boston Evening Record*, December 18, 1899, 5.

73   "The Japanese Players," *Boston Herald*, December 17, 1899, 14.

74   "Theatrical Matters," *Boston Post*, December 8, 1899; 5.

75   Alexander Corbett Jr., "Japan's Foremost Actors," *Boston Globe*, December 11, 1899, 5.

76   "Massachusetts, Boston," *NYC*, December 23, 1899, 896.

77   "Copley Hall," advertisement, *Boston Evening Transcript*, January 8, 1900, 7. Copley Hall had no boxes.

78   The exceptions to this conclusion were inflated admissions charged for charity-related events.

79   Boston newspapers, November 1899–January 1900; Cahn, *Theatrical 1899–1900*, 63–71; *Handy*, 64–67; Woods, *City*, 178, 180–95, 183–88.

80   Theatre advertisements, *Boston Herald*, December 3, 1899, 14–15.

81   Boston newspapers, December 3, 1899–January 21, 1900. Unless their admissions were greater or less than the so-called standard scale, first-class theatres tended not to list ticket prices in advertisements. This contrasted with lesser venues that extensively advertised their low prices.

82   "The Usher," *NYDM*, November 4, 1899, 4.

83   Poggi, *Theatre*, 43–44; Weldon B. Durham, "The Revival and Decline of the Stock Company Mode of Organization 1886–1930," *Theatre History Studies* 6 (1986): 176–77.

84   Boston newspapers, November 1899–January 1900; Cahn, *Theatrical 1899–1900*, 63–71; *Handy Guide*, 64–67; Woods, *City*, 178, 180–95.

85   "Castle Sq. Theatre," advertisement, *Boston Evening Transcript*, December 7, 1899, 7; Charles Elwell French, *Six Years of Drama at the Castle Square Theatre* (Boston: French, 1903), 8–9, 240–2; Woods, *City*, 190–93.

86   *Boston Art Guide and Artists' Directory* (Boston: Wheat, 1893), 23–24; S. Foster Damon, *Amy Lowell: A Chronicle* (Boston: Houghton Mifflin, 1935), 47–48.

87   Cashin, *Boston*, 4; "Theatres," in *Boston of Today*, 96; Clapp, *Reminiscences*, 50–51; Bruce A. McConachie, "Museum Theatre and the Problem of Respectability for Mid-Century Urban Americans," in Engle, *American*, 74–77.

88   Hornblow, *History*, 2:307–8; Atherton Brownell, "Boston Theatres of To-Day," *Bostonian* 2 (September 1895): 655–73; Grandgent, "Stage," 393. Its stuffed birds and animals became an important addition to the nonprofit and more serious Boston Society of Natural History; Cashin, *Boston*, 4; "Theatres," in *Boston of Today*, 96.

89   Dennett, *Weird*, 23–25. See same, 8–22, for Barnum's predecessors.

90   Snyder, *Voice*, 7; Allen, *Horrible*, 181; Gilbert, *American*, 20, 23; Wilmeth, *Language*, 73–74; *Handy*, 67–68; Woods, *City*, 178–77, 196–97; "Theatres," in *Boston of Today*, 100.

91   Those that charged only five cent admissions were often called "nickelodeons."

92   Fred Allen, *Much Ado about Me* (Boston: Little, Brown, 1956), 81.

93   John W. Frick, *New York's Theatrical Center: The Rialto at Union Square* (Ann Arbor: UMI, 1985), 102; Nasaw, *Going*, 18–20.

94   Gilbert, *American*, 20, 22–23; Fred Allen, *Much Ado about Me*, 81–82.

95   "Grand Theatre," advertisement, *Boston Herald*, January 21, 1900, 15.

96   "Grand Dime Theatre," advertisement, *Boston Globe*, December 3, 1899, 18; "Grand Theatre," advertisement, *Boston Herald*, December 3, 1899, 15; Woods, *City*, 175; "At the Grand Museum," *Boston Herald*, January 26, 1896, 11; "Theatres," in *Boston of Today*, 93, 96, 100.

97   "Amusement Notes," *Boston Traveler*, January 4, 1900, 5.

98   Theatre advertisements, *Boston Herald*, December 3, 1899, 14–15.

99   Boston newspapers, November 1899–January 1900; Cahn, *Theatrical 1899–1900*, 63–71; *Handy Guide*, 64–67; Woods, *City*, 178, 180–95, 183–88.

100 Anthony Mitchell Sammarco, *Boston's South End* (Charleston, South Carolina: Arcadia, 1998), 29.

101 "At the Theatres. New York—The Man in the Moon," *NYDM*, April 29, 1899, 16.

102 "At Boston Playhouses. Columbia and Promenade," *Boston Journal*, December 12, 1899, 5; also Woods, *City*, 186–88.

103 "At the Play," *Boston Journal*, December 24, 1899, 2:2; "Columbia Theatre and Promenade Deluxe," advertisement, *Boston Evening Transcript*, December 7, 1899, 7.

104 The Grand Opera House should not be confused with the nearby Grand Theatre, formerly the Grand Dime Museum.

105 "Grand Opera House," advertisement, *Boston Herald*, December 3, 1899, 14; "At Boston Playhouses. Grand Opera House," *Boston Journal*, December 5, 1899, 5; "Grand Opera House," *Boston Traveler*, December 5, 1899, 5; Woods, *City*, 183–84, 187; Stephan Thernstrom, *The Other Bostonians: Poverty and Progress in the American Metropolis* (Cambridge: Harvard University Press, 1973), 132.

106 "Music Hall," advertisement, *Boston Herald*, December 3, 1899, 15. This venerable venue continues to booked for rock concerts.

107 "The Sunday Concert Law," *NYDM*, January 6, 1900, 18.

108 Ibid.; "Star Theatre," advertisement, *Lowell Sunday Telegram*, November 19, 1899, 8; "Austin and Stones," advertisement, *Boston Herald*, January 7, 1900, 13; "Fire Panic at Concert," *New York Times*, March 5, 1900, 1.

109 Boston Theatre, program, week of December 11, 1899, in Boston Theatre box, HTC.

110 "Boston Theatre," advertisement, *Boston Herald*, December 17, 1899, 15; "Opera Concerts and Repertoire," *Boston Post*, December 9, 1899, 9.

111 The Sunday concert scale for Grau was approximately one-fourth of weekday prices ($5 for orchestra) (Boston Theatre, program, week of December 11, 1899, in Boston Theatre box, HTC).

112 "Grand Theatre" and "New Palace Theatre," advertisements, *Boston Herald*, December 3, 1899, 15.

113 "The Sunday Concert Law," *NYDM*.

114 Jay Benton, "Telegraphic News. Boston," *NYDM*, December 9, 1899, 9.

115 "Theatre and Dancing," *New York Tribune*, April 15, 1900, 3:3. Northern Baptist churches already allowed members to go to the theatre.

116 Jay Benton, "Telegraphic News. Boston," *NYDM*, December 9, 1899, 9.

117 "Modern Stage Attacked," *New York Times*, February 19, 1900, 7.

118 "Gossip of the Town," *NYDM*, January 13, 1900, 17; "A Conference of Citizens on Sunday Amusements," *NYDM*, February 4, 1900, E5.

119 Slide, *Encyclopedia*, 72–73.

120 Edwin Milton Royle, "The Vaudeville Theatre, *Scribner's* 26 (September 1899): 487.

121   Snyder, *Voice*, 32–34; Allen, *Horrible*, 180–87.

122   "Is Boston to be Surfeited?" *NYDM*, December 30, 1899, 16.

123   Keith's continuous vaudeville shows replicated the uninterrupted flow of spectators through a dime museum as they came when they felt like it, walked through at their own pace, and left after they had enough. Several Keith vaudeville theatres offered only two performances a day.

124   "Keith's Theatre," advertisement, *Boston Herald*, December 3, 1899, 15; also Allen, *Horrible*, 190.

125   "Austin and Stone's Museum," advertisement, *Boston Herald*, January 22, 1896, 8; *Handy*, 68; "Theatres," in *Boston of Today*, 100; "Austin and Stone's," advertisement, *Boston Herald*, November 7, 1897, 11. Biograph moving pictures were on this 1897 bill.

126   "Austin and Stone's," advertisements, *Boston Herald*, December 3, 1899, November 15 and 28, 1899, 7.

127   "Nickelodeon Museum and Theatre," advertisement, *Boston Herald*, December 3, 1899, 15; also "Theatres," in *Boston of Today*, 100; *Handy Guide*, 64–67.

128   W. D. Howells, "At a Dime Museum," in his *Literature*, 195; Woods, *City*, 196. Such wily add-on admission policies remained standard practice at carnivals and circuses. Also "Nicklodeon," advertisement, *Boston Herald*, December 17, 1899, 15; "Massachusetts," *NYC*, May 20, 1899, 223.

129   Allen, *Horrible*, 165. Variety or vaudeville acts were called olio acts when they appeared in minstrel and burlesque shows, but they were usually known as specialties when performed with dramatic productions.

130   Theatre advertisements, *Boston Herald*, December 3, 1899, 14–15; Boston newspapers, November 1899–January 1900; Cahn, *Theatrical 1899–1900*, 63–71; *Handy*, 64–67; Woods, *City*, 178, 180–95. Although I classified the Old Howard as a burlesque and it was playing only burlesque packages when Kawakami was in town, it was still in transition from a relatively polite variety policy to newer, bawdier burlesque ("Amusements in Boston," *Review* [Boston] 6 [December 2, 9, and 16, 1899]: 1). The Howard was converted into a theatre from a church building in the 1840s and was originally called the Howard Atheneum. Sometime later "Atheneum" was dropped, and by the late nineteenth century it was already known as the Old Howard until torn down in the midtwentieth century ("Howard Atheneum," advertisement, *Boston Herald*, September 25, 1887, 11: "The Old Howard," advertisement, *Boston Herald*, November 7, 1897, 11).

131   Allen, *Horrible*, 192–93, 198; *Handy*, 64–67; Woods, *City*, 178, 180–95; Snyder, *Voice*, 27–28.

132   Woods, *City*, 196. Neither the Aquarium nor the Royal advertised in the newspapers.

133   "Austin & Stone's," *Boston Herald*, December 3, 1899, 14; also "At Boston Playhouses. Austin and Stone's," *Boston Journal*, December 5, 1899, 5.

134   "Austin & Stone's," *Boston Evening Record*, November 28, 1899, 7.

135   Advertisements, *Boston Herald*, December 3, 1899, 15.

136   "Austin & Stone's," advertisement, *Boston Herald*, December 3, 1899, 15.

137   "At the Play. Austin and Stone's," *Boston Journal*, December 3, 1899, 2:5.

138   "Austin & Stone's," *Boston Herald*, December 3, 1899, 14; also "New Plays," *Boston Evening Record*, December 2, 1899, 5.

139   "Austin and Stone's," *Boston Post*, December 5, 1899, 5.

140   Boston esthete Percival Lowell discussed foreign fascination with geisha in his *The Soul of the Far East*, 6–7, even though he himself was excited more by their artistic than their sexual attractions.

141   "This Week at the Theatres. Keith's," *Boston Journal*, November 26, 1899, 2:2; Boston Theatre, Boston, program, week of May 22, 1899, in Boston Theatre programs, 1898–1899, in scrapbook MWEZ n.c. 1951, BRTC; "Keith's Theatre," advertisement, *Boston Herald*, December 3, 1899, 15.

142   Tompkins, *History*, 469; "This Week at the Theatres. Keith's," *Boston Journal*, November 26, 1899, 2:2; "Personal. Herrmann," *NYDM*, March 3, 1900, 14. Herrmann's act included such magic standards as the "Cafe de Grand Mogol" and the "Oriental Hindoo Flower Trick" (Boston Theatre, Boston, program, week of May 22, 1899, 9, in Boston Theatre programs, 1898–1899, scrapbook MWEZ n.c. 1951, BRTC).

143 "Nickelodeon Museum and Theatre," advertisements, *Boston Herald*, January 21, 1900, 14; and *Boston Post*, January 14, 1900, 14.

144 "Next Week's Theatres. Nickelodeon," *Boston Traveler*, January 13, 1900, 10.

145 "A Clever Vocal Duo," *NYDM*, December 18, 1899, 18; "Keith's Theatre," *Boston Daily Advertiser*, December 12, 1899, 5. Eckert and Berg had a long career on the Keith circuit with their *faux*-Japanese musical playlets (*Harrisburg Telegraph*, February 28, 1899, 10; *Cincinnati Commercial*, June 3, 1912, n.p.).

146 W. Yardley, lyrics; Cotsfield Dick, music, "Japanese Love Song" (Chicago: National Music, c. 1900). There was no definitive evidence that this song was sung in the "Pee Wee" act as there were several popular songs during this period entitled "Japanese Love Song."

147 "At the Play," *Boston Journal*, December 24, 1899, 2:2.

148 "Keith's Theatre," advertisement, *Boston Journal*, November 4, 1899, 3.

149 Toll, *On*, 171–72; also Odell, *Annals*, vols. 7–15, 1857–1894. A provincial showman who was assembling a packaged variety show advertised in a trade paper: "I can use a few more Minstrel People (white) [parenthesis *sic*], Comedians, Singers, Musicians, Two More Japs. Travel in [railroad private] car" ("Allan Witfield," advertisement, *NYC*, June 17, 1899, 313; also "Wanted for Forepaugh-Sells Bros.' Circus," advertisement, *NYC*, May 27, 1899, 255).

150 "Burton Holmes on Japan," *Boston Daily Advertiser*, February 6, 1900, 6.

151 "Tea Party for Sweet Charity's Sake," *Boston Herald*, November 30, 1899, 8.

Chapter 12

1 Alexander Corbett Jr., "Japan's Foremost Actors," *Boston Globe*, December 11, 1899, 5.

2 Sweetser, *Greater*, 42; *Boston Directory 1900*, 2445.

3 Kawakami's early mentor Fukuzawa Yukichi encouraged fellow countrymen to go abroad where their success would expand Japanese political influence and economic opportunity. Once overseas, these immigrants were to remain loyal to Japan and make their businesses benefit the homeland in ways that expanded the power of the nation (Yuji, *Issei*, 10).

4 Sharf, "Matsuki Chronology," 38; Kaneo, *Sadayakko*, 29.

5 Alexander Corbett Jr., "Japan's Foremost Actors," *Boston Globe*.

6 Sharf, "Matsuki Chronology," 38; Kaneo, *Sadayakko*, 29; Muramatsu Shōfu, *Kawakami*, 1:276.

7 Kaneo, *Sadayakko*, 29.

8 "The Stage," *Washington Post*, February 4, 1900, 24.

9 Envelope addressed to Kawakami from Irving (*Kabuki* [July 1903]: frontispiece).

10 John Harris, *Historic Walks in Old Boston* (Chester, Connecticut: Globe Pequot, 1982), 81.

11 "*Māchanto obu Enisu ni tsuite Kawakami Otojirō no danwa*" [Conversation with Kawakami Otojirō about *The Merchant of Venice*], *Kabuki* (July 1903): 11–12; Kaneo, *Sadayakko*, 30.

12 Sharf, "Bunkio Matsuki," 7–11, 14–20; Bunkio Matsuki, "The Bunkio Matsuki Memoir," trans. Hina Hirayama, in Sharf, *Pleasing Novelty*, 51, 58; "Those Japanese Actors," *New York Times*, March 18, 1900, 18; Julia Meech, "Collecting Japanese Art in America," in *Japonisme Comes to America: The Japanese Impact on the Graphic Arts, 1876–1925*, eds. Julia Meech and Gabriel P. Weisberg (New York: Abrams, 1990), 53; "Those Japanese Actors," *New York Times*.

13 Sharf, "Bunkio Matsuki," 21.

14 Ibid; *Boston Directory 1900*, 1059, 1880, 2445; *Beikoku*, 1386; "Japanese Art Goods," advertisement, *Boston Evening Traveler*, December 4, 1899, 1.

15 Hosley, *Japan*, 276.

16   Hina Hirayama, "Curious Merchandise: Bunkio Matsuki's Japanese Department," in Sharf, *Pleasing Novelty*, 90–91, 94–103; Sharf, "Bunkio Matsuki," 22, 27; Frederic A. Sharf and Hina Hirayama, compilers, "A Partial List of Trade Catalogues and Advertising Literature Offered by Bunkio Matsuki," in Sharf, *Pleasing Novelty*, 104–112; Bunkio Matsuki, *Catalogue of Remarkable Antique Carvings Taken from Famous Temples and Palaces of Old Japan* (New York: American Art Association, 1902), n.p.

17   Julia Meech, "Collecting Japanese Art in America," 54; *Beikoku*, 1386; Bunkio Matsuki, *Japanese Color Prints* (New York: Walpole Galleries, 1919), n.p.

18   Sharf, "Matsuki Chronology," 39–42. In 1904 Matsuki donated a large bronze lantern to the city of Boston. He claimed with excellent provenance that it came from the Momoyama Castle of shōgun Hideyoshi. The lantern remains in the Boston Public Garden near the edge of the famous swan boat pond ("Ask the Globe," *Boston Globe*, March 21, 1976, 9.

19   Kaneo, *Sadayakko*, 30; Belford, *Bram*, 278–80.

20   "Irving and Terry," *Boston Herald*, December 3, 1899, 14.

21   Kaneo, *Sadayakko*, 30.

22   "En Route with Henry Irving," *Boston Herald*, January 1, 1894, n.p.

23   "*Māchanto obu Enisu* ni tsuite Kawakami Otojirō no danwa," 12.

24   There was no evidence about who was the interpreter at this meeting.

25   Dōmon, *Kawakami*, 119; Inoue, *Kawakami*, 69; "The Japanese Players," *Boston Evening Transcript*, January 2, 1900, 11; Kaneo, *Sadayakko*, 30; Kawakami Otojirō, "Maruyama Kambi no shibō" [The death of Maruyama Kambi], *Miyako shimbun*, January 18, 1900, in Shirakawa, 310; Matsunaga, *Kawakami*, 162; Muramatsu Shōfu, *Kawakami*, 1:274; "Music and Drama," *Boston Evening Transcript*, December 7, 1899, 9; Yamaguchi, *Joyū*, 87.

26   "Bosuton-shi no Kawakami Otojirō" [Kawakami Otojirō in Boston], *Chūō shimbun*, 1 February 1, 1900, in Shirakawa, 311; Kaneo, *Sadayakko*, 30.

27   Craig, *Henry*, 27.

28   Leopold Lewis adapted the English version of Erckmann and Chatrian's *Le Juif Polonais*.

29   Laurence Irving, *Henry*, 183–91, 205–9; Strang, *Players*, 2:272; Bingham, *Henry*, 131; Henry Irving, *Drama*, 16–20, 180–81; Bulman, *Merchant*, 39–41.

30   Henry Irving, *Drama*, 35–36.

31   Laurence Irving, *Henry*, 673; H. A. Saintsbury, "Irving as Stage Manager," in Saintsbury, *We*, 409.

32   Donaldson, *Actor-Managers*, 156; Craig, *Henry*, 172; Robertson, *Time*, 172–73.

33   Quoted in Bingham, *Henry*, 125; also Craig, *Henry*, 172.

34   Laurence Irving, *Henry*, 639; Bingham, *Henry*, 257.

35   Craig, *Henry*, 172.

36   Clapp, *Reminiscences*, 195.

37   Ibid., 199–200.

38   Ibid., 203. Italics *sic*.

39   For example, Jones, *Shadow*, 53.

40   Craig, *Henry*, 61. After listening to a 1900 recording of a slightly nasal Irving, I agreed with Craig (Creegan, *Traditions*, cut 4:1, excerpts from *Richard III*).

41   Jones, *Shadow*, 17–18.

42   Craig, *Henry*, 70, 71–74, 170.

43   Craig, *Theatre*, 232–38.

44   Craig, *Henry*, 74, 76–77, italics *sic*. Alan Hughes in his *Henry Irving, Shakespearean*, 14, perhaps borrowing from Craig, made similar observations.

45   Laurence Irving, *Henry*, 183–91; "The Irving Influence in America," *Spirit of the Times* (New York),

February 2, 1896, n.p.; Edward M. Moore, "Henry Irving's Shakespearean Productions," *Theatre Survey* 17 (November 1976): 195.

46 H. A. Saintsbury, "Irving as Stage Manager," in Saintsbury, *We*, 405; George Arthur, "Irving as Corporal Brewster," in Saintsbury, *We*, 335; James Dale, "Irving as Maximilien Robespierre," in Saintsbury, *We*, 373. "Stage manager" was the term for director in 1900.

47 George Arthur, "Irving as Corporal Brewster," in Saintsbury, *We*, 335; James Dale, "Irving as Maximilien Robespierre," in Saintsbury, *We*, 377.

48 Irving Laurence, *Henry*, 630; H. A. Saintsbury, "Irving as Stage Manager," George Arthur, "Irving as Corporal Brewster," and James Dale, "Irving as Maximilien Robespierre," in Saintsbury, *We*, 405, 335, and 377; Belford, *Bram*, 278; Brereton, *Lyceum*, 313–16. Only the recently produced *Robespierre* had new scenery and costumes.

49 H. A. Saintsbury, "Irving as Stage Manager," in Saintsbury, *We*, 407–8; Bingham, *Henry*, 296.

50 William Winter, *Vagrant Memories: Being Further Recollections of Other Days* (New York: Doran, 1915), 336; "Irving Here Once Again," *New York Sun*, October 27, 1900, 7; Bingham, *Henry*, 176.

51 Tompkins, *History*, 311, 351. Irving usually played the Boston Theatre but this time he could not be accommodated because Grau's Metropolitan Opera was already booked there. Denied this large house, Irving had to take the smaller Hollis Street Theatre and this reduced his potential daily gross in Boston by 40%.

52 Alan S. Downer, "Players and Painted Stage: Nineteenth Century Acting," *Proceedings of the Modern Language Association* 61 (June 1946): 562–65.

53 Macfall, *Sir*, 109; Clapp, *Reminiscences*, 210–13.

54 Craig, *Henry*, 69.

55 Joseph, *Tragic*, 377.

56 Shaw, "Preface," *Ellen*, xx.

57 Shaw, "Better than Shakespear" [*sic*], in his *Our*, 3:1–8.

58 Richard Foulkes, "Henry Irving and Laurence Olivier as Shylock," *Theatre Notebook* 27 (Autumn 1972): 26. Foulkes commented on the many similarities between Irving's and Olivier's Shylocks.

59 Manvell, *Ellen*, 264–65; Joseph, *Tragic*, 365.

60 Shaw, "Blaming the Bard," in his *Our*, 2:207–8; also Jones, *Shadow*, 109–10.

61 Craig, *Henry*, 32, 39.

62 Ibid., 87–89, 107; Laurence Irving, *Henry*, 203; W. D. King, "When Theatre Becomes History: Final Curtains on the Victorian Stage," *Victorian Studies* 36 (Fall 1992): 56.

63 Augustin Filon, *The English Stage*, trans. Frederic Whyte (New York: Dodd, Mead, 1897), n.p.

64 Laurence Irving, *Henry*, 183–91; Bingham, *Henry*, 130.

65 Farson, *Man*, 18–19, 53, 188, 212; Harry Ludlam, *Biography of Dracula: The Life of Story of Bram Stoker* (London: Foulsham, 1962), 98; Alan Hughes, "The Lyceum Staff: A Victorian Theatrical Organization," *Theatre Notebook* 28 (1974): 12, 16.

66 David F. Cheshire, *Portrait of Ellen Terry* (Oxford: Amber Lane, 1989), 84–85; Roth, *Stoker*, 19. Barbara Belford in her biography, *Bram Stoker*, 238, was certain that Irving's nose was the model for Dracula's.

67 Roth, *Stoker*, 19; also Farson, *Man*, 18–19.

68 Menpes, *Henry*, 2, 12.

69 Manvell, *Ellen*, 250. Company Manager Bram Stoker also recalled that his boss Irving had a continuing interest in Japan (Stoker, *Personal*, 1:331–32).

70 Kaneo, *Sadayakko*, 30.

71 "Players from Far Japan," *Boston Journal*, January 7, 1900, 4:4; Alexander Corbett Jr., "Japan's Foremost Actors," *Boston Globe*, December 11, 1899, 5; "Irving and Terry," *Boston Herald*, December 3, 1899, 14;

"Music and Drama," *Boston Evening Transcript*, December 7, 1899, 9; Kaneo, *Sadayakko*, 31; Kawakami ichiza yōkō nisshi," [Journal of the foreign tour of the Kawakami troupe], *Miyako shimbun*, July 26, 1900, in Shirakawa, 318. Kawakami's character actor Fujikawa Iwanosuke wrote this last piece.

72   "Hollis St. Theatre, Farewell Week," advertisement, *Boston Evening Transcript*, December 7, 1899, 7. Kawakami's later accounts suggested that he saw the combination bill ("*Māchanto obu Enisu* ni tsuite Kawakami Otojirō no danwa" [Conversation with Kawakami Otojirō about *The Merchant of Venice*], *Kabuki* [July 1903]: 12).

73   "Hollis St. Theatre, Farewell Week," advertisement, *Boston Evening Transcript*, December 7, 1899, 7.

74   "In the City," *Boston Post*, December 8, 1899, 5; Lelyveld, *Shylock*, 93.

75   Although he had never seen Irving perform, Sardou wrote *Robespierre* to Irving's order and delivered the script in French. Irving's son Laurence adapted it into English.

76   Stoker, *Personal*, 269; Booth, *Theatre*, 34. Irving's American touring production was smaller than the original 1899 London version when Irving employed 591 persons, not including the front of the house staff of the Lyceum Theatre.

77   "At the Theatres. Knickerbocker—Robespierre," *NYDM*, November 4, 1899, 16; Brereton, *Lyceum*, 312.

78   Clement Scott, "Irving's Triumph as Robespierre," *New York Herald*, c. 1899, n.p.; also "'Robespierre' a Vivid, Striking Spectacle of the French Commune," *Detroit News*, January 25, 1900, 2.

79   "At the Theatres," *Boston Post*, November 21, 1899, 5; also J. Ranken Towse, "The Drama" *Critic* 35 (December 31, 1899): 1140.

80   Strang, *Players*, 1:290–92; also J. Ranken Towse, "The Drama."

81   Lewis C. Strang, "At the Play," *Boston Journal*, November 26, 1899, 2:2.

82   "At Boston Playhouses. Hollis Street Theatre," *Boston Journal*, December 5, 1899, 5; also "At the Theatres," *Boston Post*; Lewis C. Strang, "At the Play," *Boston Journal*.

83   "The Man with the Lorgnette," *Boston Evening Record*, November 21, 1899, 5; also Henry Austin Clapp, "Amusements," *Boston Evening Record*, November 23, 1899, 5.

84   "At the Theatres. Knickerbocker—Robespierre," *NYDM*, November 4, 1899, 16; also Octavus Cohen, "Henry Irving and Ellen Terry," *Battle Creek Daily Journal*, November 10, 1899, 6.

85   "Good English on the Stage," *Theatre* (New York) No. 9 (November 1901): 17.

86   Shattuck, *Shakespeare*, 2:166.

87   Edward M. Moore, "Henry Irving's Shakespearean Productions," *Theatre Survey* 17 (November 1976): 204; Bulman, *Merchant*, 33–41; Shattuck, *Shakespeare*, 2:162; Lelyveld, *Shylock*, 79; Macfall, *Sir*, 122–23.

88   In "Dealing with Authors" in her *Dramatic Opinions*, 100–8, Mrs. Madge Kendal discussed "cutting" as a star's indisputable prerogative. Cutting included eliminating, rearranging, and reinterpretation.

89   Knight, *Theatrical*, 303; Styan, *Drama*, 11–12. When Booth was appearing with a major female star such as Modjeska, he gave her act five ("Unusual at the Theatre," *New York Sun*, March 22, 1900, 7). James Owen O'Connor, a minor Shakespearean star, once solved the act five issue by ending the play with Shylock's suicide (Brown, *History*, 2:324). Tampering with Shakespeare in America could be dangerous. In 1879, a store clerk shot at (and missed) Edwin Booth because he was convinced the actor was deviating from what Shakespeare wrote (Levine, *Highbrow*, 72).

90   Shattuck, *Shakespeare*, 2:162; Eaton, *Actor's*, 51.

91   Winter, *Shakespeare*, 1:196–97. To make time for act five, Irving trimmed earlier scenes (Shattuck, *Shakespeare*, 2:162).

92   "Henry Irving as Shylock," *Boston Post*, December 8, 1899, 5.

93   Tompkins, *History*, 306.

94   Shaw, "Blaming the Bard," in his *Our*, 2:208. Also Lelyveld, *Shylock*, 79

95   Shaw, "The Old Acting and the New," in his *Our*, 1:286.

96   Eaton, *Actor's*, 51.

97   Hatton, *Henry*, 227.

98   Winter, *Shakespeare*, 1:175.

99   L. F. Austin, "Sir Henry Irving," in his *Points of View* (London: Lane, 1906), 9. Red wig and big hooked nose were iconic designations of Jewish characters established before the Elizabethan era when Judases and Satans of medieval mystery plays put on red wigs and big noses. Before Irving, Edmund Kean as Shylock was one of the few to abandon conventional wig and nose (Lelyveld, *Shylock*, 27, 128, 175).

100 See Ortolani, *Japanese*, 234.

101 I have seen big noses and red wigs on non-comic foreign characters in Japan even as I have seen American and European actors playing Japanese characters with skin yellowed and eyes taped to make them slanted.

102 Clapp, *Reminiscences*, 207–13, 225.

103 Shattuck, *Shakespeare*, 2:163.

104 Lelyveld, *Shylock*, 88–90.

105 Winter, *Shakespeare*, 1:180, 191– 92; Lelyveld, *Shylock*, 88; Laurence Irving, *Henry*, 342; Fitzgerald, *Sir*, 105.

106 Winter, *Shakespeare*, 1:191–95.

107 Bulman, *Merchant, Venice*, 46; Lelyveld, *Shylock*, 89. These descriptions were of Irving's original 1879 production; also Fitzgerald, *Sir*, 107.

108 Brereton, *Lyceum*, 223.

109 L. F. Austin, "Sir Henry Irving," in his *Points of View* (London: Lane, 1906), 11.

110 Lelyveld, *Shylock*, 89, 91; Jones, *Shadow*, 52.

111 Jones, 50; Winter, *Shakespeare*, 1:194–95; Robert Hichens, "Irving as Shylock," in Saintsbury, *We*, 167; Richard Foulkes, "The Staging of the Trial Scene in Irving's *The Merchant of Venice*," *Educational Theatre Journal* 28 (October 1976): 316–17; Hughes, *Henry*, 238.

112 Scott, *Drama*, 2:460–61; also Clement Scott, *From "The Bells" to "King Arthur"–A Critical Record of First-Night Productions at the Lyceum Theatre from 1871 to 1895* (London: Macqueen, 1896), 165.

113 Auerbach, *Ellen*, 227; Richard Foulkes, "Helen Faucit and Ellen Terry as Portia," *Theatre Notebook* 31 (1977): 30–32; "Ellen Terry's Portia," *Boston Post*, December 3, 1899, 16.

114 Charles Hiatt, *Ellen Terry and Her Impersonations* (London: Bell, 1898), 143.

115 Winter, *Shakespeare*, 1:218; Lelyveld, *Shylock*, 90–91.

116 Quoted in Richard Foulkes, "Helen Faucit and Ellen Terry as Portia," *Theatre Notebook* 31 (1977): 32; Bulman, *Merchant*, 48.

117 Booth, "Ellen Terry," 100; Creegan, *Traditions*, cut 4:6: Portia's mercy plea from *The Merchant of Venice*.

118 Bingham, *Henry*, 127; Ormsbee, *Backstage*, 183; Auerbach, *Ellen*, 226–29. Terry had two unfortunate marriages to undistinguished husbands. Her personal relationship with Irving fascinated most biographers and led them to various speculations; see for instance, Auerbach, *Ellen*; Sandra Richards, *Rise*, 129; David F. Cheshire, *Portrait of Ellen Terry* (Oxford: Amber Lane, 1989), 87–88; Donaldson, *Actor-Managers*, 81; Manvell, *Ellen*, 271–74, 350 fn. 25. Early in the Irving-Terry partnership, Irving was married to a wife with whom he was increasingly estranged because he refused to give up the disreputable trade of acting.

119 Hammerton, "Miss Ellen Terry," in his *Actor's Art*, 173; Richards, *Rise*, 125–26; Laurence Irving, *Henry*, 183–91.

120 Meisel, *Realizations*, 402–3.

121 Richards, *Rise*, 128–29.

122 Ibid.; Shaw, "Why Not Sir Henry Irving," in his *Our*, 1:30.

123 Shaw, "Preface," in his *Ellen*, xxi.

124 Bingham, *Henry*, 127–29; Tompkins, *History*, 351–522.

125   Quoted in Donaldson, *Actor-Managers*, 81.

126   "The Drama. Henry Irving and Ellen Terry," *New York Tribune*, March 22, 1900, 7.

127   Winter, *Shakespeare*, 1:218, 100. I confirmed these impressions from recordings made around 1911 when Terry was in her sixties and traveling the play reading circuits (Creegan, *Traditions*, cut 4:4, Ophelia's mad scene, *Hamlet*; cut 4:5, Juliet's potion speech, *Romeo and Juliet*; cut 4:6, Portia's plea, *The Merchant of Venice*). The "husky thickness" that Henry James heard had disappeared with age.

128   Michael R. Booth, "Pictorial Acting and Ellen Terry," in Foulkes, *Shakespeare*, 83.

129   Ibid., 84–85; Booth, "Ellen Terry," Stokes, *Bernhardt*, 76–81; Donaldson, *Actor-Managers*, 81; Bulman, *Merchant*, 42.

130   Richard Foulkes, "Helen Faucit and Ellen Terry as Portia," *Theatre Notebook* 31 (1977): 27; also Michael R. Booth, "Pictorial Acting and Ellen Terry," in Foulkes, *Shakespeare*, 84; Donaldson, *Actor-Managers*, 80–81.

131   John Gielgud, "My Great-Aunt Ellen Terry," *Stage* 14 (January 1937): 92.

132   Shattuck, *Shakespeare*, 2:93.

133   Manvell, *Ellen*, 271–74; Richards, *Rise*, 128–29; Christopher St. John, *Ellen Terry* (New York: Lane, 1907), 33, 50. In July 1902, Portia was the last role she played with Irving.

134   Betty Bandel, "Ellen Terry's Foul Papers," *Theatre Survey* 11 (May 1969): 43–52; Richards, *Rise*, 124.

135   "At the Boston Playhouses," *Boston Journal*, December 5, 1899, 5; H. Chance Newton, "Miss Ellen Terry and Her Art," *Sketch* 35 (July 31, 1901): 75; "Cissie in a Dilemma," unidentified newspaper, September 1, 1899, clipping, in RLS NAFR+ v. 312, p. 20, BRTC. The term for impersonator is now impressionist.

136   Manvell, *Ellen*, 250.

137   Constance Fecher, *Bright Star: A Portrait of Ellen Terry* (New York: Farrar, Straus, and Giroux, 1970), 76; also Lancaster, *Japanese*, 25.

138   H. Chance Newton, "Miss Ellen Terry and Her Art," *Sketch* 35 (1901): 75.

139   Kōri Torahiko, *The English Works* [Tokyo, 1936]; Rimer, *Toward*, 37–39.

140   Richard Foulkes, "The Staging of the Trial Scene in Irving's *The Merchant of Venice*," *Educational Theatre Journal* 28 (October 1976): 312–15.

141   Fitzgerald, *Sir*, 107.

142   Bulman, *Merchant*, 30; Fitzgerald, *Sir*, 103; Edward M. Moore, "Henry Irving's Shakespearean Productions," *Theatre Survey* 17 (November 1976): 209. There were more than eight scene changes because of the reappearance of several sets (Hollis Street Theatre, Boston, program, week of December 4, 1899, in program file: MWEZ n.c. 7577, BRTC).

143   Odell, *Shakespeare*, 422.

144   Bulman, *Merchant*, 30.

145   Precise timing of curtains was essential to Irving.

146   Lelyveld, *Shylock*, 85–86; Hughes, *Henry*, 232. James C. Bulman in his *The Merchant of Venice*, 38, suggested that Irving did not create this blocking but borrowed it from the established stage directions for Verdi's *Rigoletto*. Irving's scene as he played it did not come from Shakespeare's text but from unseen action described in act two scene eight by the character Solanio who witnessed Shylock's loud cries when he discovered Jessica missing.

147   Nigel Gardner, "Introduction to the Music," in *Henry Irving and the Bells*, ed. David Mayer (Manchester: Manchester University Press, 1980), 109; "The Irving Influence in America," *Spirit of the Times*, February 2, 1896, n.p.; Brander Matthews, "The Rehearsal of the New Play," in his *Outlines in Local Color* (New York: Harper, 1898), 161–62.

148   Hughes, *Henry*, 17–18; "The Irving Influence in America," *Spirit of the Times*. The music for the 1899 *The Merchant of Venice* was largely adapted from Gounod (Hollis Street Theatre, Boston, program, week of December 4, 1899, in program file: MWEZ n.c. 7577, BRTC).

149 "The Man with the Lorgnette," *Boston Evening Record*, December 8, 1899, 5.

150 Kaneo, *Sadayakko*, 31.

151 Kaneo, *Ōbei*, 30.

152 Kaneo, *Sadayakko*, 31.

153 Clapp, *Reminiscences*, 210–13. Charles Kean, Macready, and Madame Vestris had much earlier integrated their actors into stage pictures that had complex pictorial compositions (Meisel, *Realizations*, 3–13, 42–51).

154 Quoted in Odell, *Shakespeare*, 420; Craig, *Henry*, 122–24.

155 Meisel, *Realizations*, 402–32.

156 Henry Irving, "The Art of Acting," in his *Drama*, 82.

157 A. B. Walkley, "Henry Irving," in Rowell, *Victorian*, 136.

158 "At the Theatres. Knickerbocker—Robespierre," *NYDM*, November 4, 1899, 16.

159 "Various Dramatic Topics," *New York Times*, March 19, 1900, 18. Gordon Craig proposed that a dominant influence on Irving's pictorial conceptions was Gustav Doré (Craig, *Henry*, 122–24).

160 Meisel, *Realizations*, 416.

161 "The Irving Influence in America," *Spirit of the Times*, February 2, 1896, n.p.

162 Shattuck, *Shakespeare*, 2:164.

163 Bulman, *Merchant*, 28, 31–39. Lelyveld in *Shylock*, 87–92 and W[illiam] W[inter], "The Drama," *New York Tribune*, March 22, 1900, 7 had similar opinions.

164 Quoted by Shattuck in his *Shakespeare*, 2:160.

165 S. Fernberger, "Philadelphia," *NYDM*, December 16, 1899, 12; Brereton, *Life*, 2:284; Jay, Benton, "Telegraphic News. Boston," *NYDM*, December 9, 1899, 12.

166 "The Man with the Lorgnette," *Boston Evening Record*, November 20, 1899, 5; Brereton, *Life*, 2:283–84; "*Mâchanto obu Enisu* ni tsuite Kawakami Otojirō no danwa," *Kabuki* (July 1903): 12.

Chapter 13

1   "Drama and Music," *Boston Globe*, December 10, 1899, 22. Herne's daughters, Julia and Crystal, continued their acting careers as adults (Malcolm M. Willey, "James A. Herne's 'Sag Harbor,'" *Long Island Forum*, January 1949, n.p.).

2   "At the Play. Park," *Boston Journal*, November 26, 1899, 2:2.

3   "Plays and Players," *Boston Herald*, November 26, 1899, 14.

4   Herne, *Shore Acres* in his *Shore*, 1–121.

5   "The Man with the Lorgnette," *Boston Evening Record*, December 18, 1899, 5; The Chevalier Toupet, "Some Recent Stage Art," *Metropolitan* 12 (December 1900): 846; Malcolm M. Willey, "James A. Herne's 'Sag Harbor,'" n.p.

6   Quoted in "James A. Herne in 'Sag Harbor,'" pamphlet, n.p., 1900, 8, in clipping file: Sag Harbor, BRTC.

7   W. F. A[pthorp], "Park Theatre: 'Sag Harbor,'" *Boston Evening Transcript*, October 25, 1899, 13.

8   Henry Austin Clapp, "The Musketeers," *Boston Daily Advertiser*, January 16, 1900, 5.

9   The Chevalier Toupet, "Some Recent Stage Art," *Metropolitan* 12 (December 1900): 845.

10 Kaneo, *Ōbei*, 29–30; *Sag Harbor* prints #7809 and #7810, in Byron Studios files: #12 and #14, MWEZ+ n.c. 15,839, BRTC.

11 Kaneo, *Sadayakko*, 36–37. This was Kawakami's general impression of all American plays. He did not specifically discuss *Sag Harbor*.

12 "Herne Holds a Rehearsal," *Boston Herald*, October 25, 1899, n.p. One pair of lovers among the three was old Captain Dan (played by Herne) and a spinster.

13   Young, *Famous*, 2:507; Hartnoll, *Concise*, 247. Decades later canine melodrama reached its apotheosis in the films of Rin-Tin-Tin.

14   Because there was no role for Corcoran in *Sag Harbor* she was working in New York City during most of the 1899–1900 winter ("News, Notes, and Gossip," *Boston Herald*, December 10, 1899, 10).

15   Perry, *James*, 181–85; McArthur, *Actors*, 155–56; Charles Nirdlinger, ed., *Gallery of Players No. 2* (New York: Illustrated American, 1894), 42; "Music and Drama. Course of Modern Plays," *Boston Evening Transcript*, January 13, 1900, 22; (Edwards, *James*, v).

16   "At the Play. Park," *Boston Journal*, November 26, 1899, 2:2.

17   Edwards, *James*, v.

18   Wilmeth, *Guide*, 430.

19   Quoted in "James A. Herne in 'Sag Harbor,'" pamphlet, n.p., 1900, in clipping file: Sag Harbor, BRTC.

20   "'Shore Acres,'" unidentified Boston newspaper, October 1899, in scrapbook MWEZ+ n.c. 13,359, BRTC.

21   Edwards, *James*, 72–73.

22   "'Sag Harbor' Behind the Scenes," *Boston Evening Transcript*, December 22, 1899, 5.

23   Leslie, *Some*, 382; James A. Herne, "Art for Truth's Sake in Drama," *Arena* (February 1897): 361.

24   Perry, *James*, 140–43, 146–49; Malcolm M. Willey, "James A. Herne's 'Sag Harbor,'" *Long Island Forum*, January 1949, n.p.

25   Bordman, *American Theatre*, 467; *Sag Harbor Pilot* (New York: Hammerstein's New Republic Theatre) 2:2 (October 8, 1900), n.p.

26   Edwards, *James*, v-vii; Bordman, *American Theatre*, 467.

27   "Massachusetts. Boston," *NYC*, December 16, 1899, 878; "At the Play. Tremont," *Boston Journal*, December 10, 1899, 2:2; "At Boston Playhouses. 'Arizona,'" *Boston Journal*, December 19, 1899, 5; "The Grumbler," *Boston Dramatic Review* 6 (December 23, 1899): 6.

28   Augustus Thomas, *Arizona* (Chicago: Dramatic Publishing, 1899); Tremont Theatre, Boston, program, week of 20 November 20, 1899, 30, in Tremont Theatre programs file: **T.10.27, RBD BPL; "Plays and Players. Tremont Theatre," *Boston Herald*, December 3, 1899, 14.

29   Clark, *History*, 659.

30   At Boston Playhouses. Arizona," *Boston Journal*, December 5, 1899, 5; George T. Richardson, "Another American Play, 'Arizona,'" *Boston Traveler*, December 5, 1899, 5; Henry Austin Clapp, "Thomas's Arizona," *Boston Daily Advertiser*, December 5, 1899, 8; "In Boston Playhouses. At the Tremont," *Boston Herald*, December 12, 1899, 9; "At the Play. Tremont," *Boston Journal*, December 10, 1899, 2:2; "Arizona, an American Drama," *Boston Evening Transcript*, December 2, 1899, 24.

31   "Stories about the Stage. Thomas and Remington," *Boston Herald*, December 4, 1899, 9; "Arizona," *NYDM*, September 15, 1900, 17.

32   Bordman, *American Theatre*, 466.

33   Poggi, *Theatre*, 257; Ronald J. Davis, *Augustus*, 14; Jerry Stagg, *The Brothers Shubert* (New York: Random House, 1968), 33. This record was achieved even though the show had difficulty securing theatres because, as an independent production that was not under its control, the Theatrical Syndicate refused to book it. Nevertheless, from their very profitable backing of *Arizona*, the struggling Shubert brothers acquired the money they needed to expand their nascent theatre empire that eventually replaced the Syndicate as the controlling force in American theatre. Since 1912, there have been at least four movie versions of *Arizona*. In 1925, the play was transformed into the Sigmund Romberg musical, *The Love Call* with a stronger cowboys and Indians motif (Bordman, *American Musical Theatre*, 430; "Arizona," unidentified newspaper, n.d., clipping, in RLS NAFR+ v. 476, p. 8, BRTC).

34   Matsumoto, *Meiji engekiron*, 427–28.

35   Drayton, "Wanted: A Native Play," *Wave* (San Francisco) 29 (September 23, 1899): 16.

36   "August Thomas' 'Arizona' Nearly Realizes the Ideal Set for 'the Great American Play,'" *Philadelphia North American*, December 19, 1901, n.p.; also "Arizona, an American Drama," *Boston Evening Transcript*, December 2, 1899, 24.

37   George T. Richardson, "Another American Play, 'Arizona,'" *Boston Traveler*, December 5, 1899.

38   "The Man with the Lorgnette," *Boston Evening Record*, December 8, 1899, 5; also Henry Austin Clapp, "Thomas's Arizona," *Boston Daily Advertiser*, December 5, 1899, 8. The dramatic situation in *Arizona* was only apparently mistaken (not actual) martial infidelity.

39   In his book, Strang, *Players*, 2:191.

40   "Arizona, an American Drama," *Boston Evening Transcript*, December 2, 1899, 24; also "Arizona," *New York World*, September 14, 1900, n.p.

41   Strang, *Players*, 2:200–3; Dion Boucicault, "The Future American Drama," *Arena* (November 1890): 641; Marian Spitzer, "Ten-20–30; the Passing of the Popular-Priced Circuit," *Saturday Evening Post* (August 22, 1925): 40.

42   Frederic Edward McKay, "Plays and Players," *New York Mail and Express Illustrated Saturday Magazine*, March 17, 1900, 6–7.

43   Edwards, *James*, 92.

44   McArthur, *Actors*, 177.

45   Carter, *Howells*, 118–22; also James A. Herne, "Art for Truth's Sake in Drama," *Arena* (February 1897): 365.

46   Clara M. and Rudolf Kirk, *William Dean Howells* (New York: Twayne, 1962), 150–53; Carter, *Howells*, 122; Hamlin Garland, *Crumbling Idols* (Chicago: Stone and Kimball, 1894), 83–96; Brockett, *Century*, 147.

47   Clark, *History*, 659; Romein, *Watershed*, 511–12; Carter, *Howells*, 122.

48   Carter, *Howells*, 116; Strang, *Players*, 2:202–3.

49   "Music and Drama. The Drama of Today," *Boston Evening Transcript*, December 16, 1899, 28; Tremont Theatre, Boston, program, week of 13 November 13, 1899, 28, in Tremont Theatre programs **T.10.27, RBD BPL.

50   "Music and Drama. Course of Modern Plays," *Boston Evening Transcript*, January 13, 1900, 22.

51   "At the Theatres. Carnegie Lyceum—The Storm," *NYDM*, March 10, 1900, 16.

52   "Notes," *Boston Daily Advertiser*, January 23, 1900, 8.

53   Arthur Crispin, "A Successful Independent Theatre Movement" (New York: Syndication Department American Press Association, January 6, 1900), in clipping file: Jewett, Henry, BRTC; Lewis C. Strang, "At the Play," *Boston Journal*, November 26, 1899, 2:2; "Drama of Today," *Boston Evening Transcript*, January 6, 1900, 22; "Personal. Blair," *NYDM*, February 18, 1899, 14.

54   Lewis C. Strang, "At the Play," *Boston Journal*, November 26, 1899, 2:2; "Music and Drama. Tomorrow's Performance," *Boston Evening Transcript*, November 20, 1899, 7.

55   "A Brief Record of the Facts by John Blair," *Chicago Record*, December 20, 1908, n.p.; also "John Blair," *Boston Transcript*, February 10, 1910, n.p.; "John Blair's Career," unidentified New York newspaper, October 6, 1908, in clipping file: Blair, John, BRTC; "Music and Drama. Tomorrow's Performance," *Boston Evening Transcript*, November 20, 1899, 7.

56   "News of the Theatres," unidentified New York newspaper, c. June 1899, in clipping file: Blair, John, BRTC. Ibsen was condemned less for his own plays and more for his alleged corrupting influence on contemporary English and American playwrights.

57   Arthur Crispin, "A Successful Independent Theatre Movement;" "Mr. John Blair's Course of Modern Plays," pamphlet, Carnegie Lyceum (New York) and New National Theatre (Washington), November 1899, both in clipping file: Blair, John, BRTC; "Notes," *Boston Daily Advertiser*, January 23, 1900, 8; "Music

and Drama. Tomorrow's Performance," *Boston Evening Transcript*; "A Brief Record of the Facts by John Blair," *Chicago Record*, December 20, 1908, n.p. The Brooklyn venue was dropped before the end of the series (Bordman, *American Theatre*, 456).

58   Tremont Theatre, Boston, program, week of December 11, 1899, 20, in Tremont Theatre programs **T.10.27, RBD BPL. *El Gran Galeoto* (The Great Galeoto) played under its original Spanish title. Echegaray, later a winner of the 1904 Nobel prize for literature, was a leader among Spanish realist writers.

59   Lewis C. Strang, "At the Play," *Boston Journal*, November 26, 1899, 2:2; "Music and Drama. The Drama of Today," *Boston Evening Transcript*, December 16, 1899, 28; also Henderson, *First*, 23.

60   "Notes," *Boston Daily Advertiser*, January 23, 1900, 8; Lewis C. Strang, "At the Play," *Boston Journal*; also W. F. A[pthrop]. "Music and Drama," *Boston Evening Transcript*, December 20, 1899, 18; "The Man with the Lorgnette," *Boston Evening Record*, December 18, 1899, 5.

61   George T. Richardson, "Ibsenism in 'The Master Builder' Is at Its Zenith," *Boston Traveler*, January 24, 1900, 4. This was the first American production of the play (Bordman, *American Theatre*, 456).

62   Henry Austin Clapp, "An Ibsen Play," *Boston Daily Advertiser*, January 24, 1900, 4.

63   "A Brief Record of the Facts by John Blair," *Chicago Record*, December 20, 1908, n.p.; George T. Richardson, "Ibsenism in 'The Master Builder' Is at Its Zenith," *Boston Traveler*, January 24, 1900, 4; "Theatricals," *New York World*, January 14, 1900, 2E; "The Theatres," *New York Commercial Advertiser*, January 16, 1900, 7. The producing organization announced it would continue with two more "Ibsenesque" items: Max Dreyer's *Drei* and the Irish Literary Theatre's *The Heather Field* by Edward Martyn ("Drama of Today," *Boston Evening Transcript*, January 6, 1900, 22).

64   "A Brief Record of the Facts by John Blair," *Chicago Record*. Blair immediately re-entered the theatrical mainstream to put on a toga for a leading role in the spectacular *Quo Vadis*. Subsequently he made a living in supporting roles but his quixotic experiments and leading roles had ended ("John Blair and the Independent Theatre," chapter in unidentified book, c. 1901, 254, in clipping file: Blair, John, BRTC; Mantle, *Best 1899–1900*, 366; "John Blair," *Chicago Daily Inter Ocean*, April 21, 1907, n.p.; Mary Caroline Crawford, *The Romance of the American Theatre* [reprint, New York: Halcyon House, 1940], 475).

65   Kawatake Shigetoshi, Gaisetsu, 394; Akiba, *Nihon*, 2:83; Ōzasa, *Nihon*. 1:93–98. Not all of Osanai's associates agreed with him on how to start theatrical reform in Japan. See later chapters.

66   "E. H. Sothern and Virginia Harned in 'The Song of the Sword,'" *Boston Post*, December 10, 1899, 14. Leo Dietrichstein wrote *The Song of the Sword*.

67   Henry Austin Clapp, "First Production," *Boston Daily Advertiser*, December 12, 1899, 5; also "Sothern and Harned at Battle, Murder, and Sudden Death," unidentified newspaper, October 26, 1899, in clipping file: RLS NAFR+ v. 435, BRTC.

68   "At Boston Theatres. Hollis Street Theatre," *Boston Journal*, December 12, 1899, 5; George T. Richardson, "Mr. Sothern and Miss Harned in 'The Song of the Sword,'" *Boston Traveler*, December 12, 1899, 5; Henry Austin Clapp, "First Production," *Boston Daily Advertiser*.

69   "The Sunken Bell," *Boston Herald*, December 17, 1899, 14; Lawrence Reamer, "The Drama," *Harper's Weekly* 44 (April 21, 1900): 370.

70   George T. Richardson, "'The Sunken Bell' Is a Curious Fairy Allegory," *Boston Traveler*, December 22, 1899, 5.

71   "The Sunken Bell," *Boston Herald*, December 17, 1899, 14.

72   W. F. A[pthorp], "Music and Drama. Hollis Street Theatre," *Boston Evening Transcript*, December 22, 1899, 5.

73   Ibid.

74   Gerhart Hauptmann, "The Sunken Bell," trans. Mary Harned, *Poet Lore* 10:2 (April 1898): 161–234; "The Man with the Lorgnette," *Boston Evening Record*, December 18, 1899, 5.

75   Henry Austin Clapp, "The Sunken Bell," *Boston Daily Advertiser*, also Lewis C. Strang, "At the Play," *Boston Journal*, December 24, 1899, 2:2.

76   "Yet last night's experience proved anew," unidentified newspaper, c. March 27, 1900, in RLS NAFR+ v. 435, p. 97, BRTC; Lawrence Reamer, "The Drama," *Harper's Weekly* 44 (April 21, 1900): 370; "This Week's New Bills, Sothern in 'The Sunken Bell'," *New York Times*, March 25, 1900, 16; Henry Austin Clapp, "The Sunken Bell," *Boston Daily Advertiser*.

77   W. F. A[pthorp], "Music and Drama. Hollis Street Theatre," *Boston Evening Transcript*; Gerhart Hauptmann and the Editor, "The Sunken Bell," *Contemporary Review* 53 (February 1898): 251.

78   Jason, "The Drama in New York" *Leslie's Weekly* 90 (April 14, 1900): 291.

79   "Kawakami Otojirō yori sa no raishin ari" [The following communication from Kawakami Otojirō], *Miyako shimbun*, February 15, 1900, in Shirakawa, 311; "Stories of the Players," *Boston Herald*, December 18, 1899, 10; "Drama and Music," *Boston Globe*, December 10, 1899, 22.

80   Matsumoto, *Meiji engekiron*, 352, 831–32, 846; Cody Poulton, "Drama and Fiction in the Meiji Era: The Case of Izumi Kyōka," *Asian Theatre Journal* 12:2 (Fall 1995): 282; Akiba, *Nihon*, 1:507, 2:268–71; Ochi, *Meiji*, 43.

81   E. A. Sothern's greatest success was in Laura Keene's production of *Our American Cousin* in which he was appearing at Ford's Theatre in Washington the night President Lincoln was assassinated.

82   "E. H. Sothern," in *American*, n.p.

83   "E. H. Sothern's Stage Fights," unidentified magazine article, c. 1897, in RLS NAFR+ v. 435, p. 69, BRTC; Young, *Famous*, 2:1030–31.

84   George T. Richardson, "'The Sunken Bell' Is a Curious Fairy Allegory," *Boston Traveler*, December 22, 1899, 5.

85   Lawrence Reamer, "The Drama," *Harper's Weekly* 44 (April 21, 1900): 370.

86   E. H. Sothern, "The Actor's Need of Culture," *New York Criterion* (May 1900): 32.

87   "E. H. Sothern in Hospital," unidentified newspaper, October 25, 1900, in RLS NAFR+ v. 435, p. 69, BRTC; Young, *Famous*, 2:1031.

88   Lawrence Reamer, "The Drama," *Harper's Weekly* 44 (April 21, 1900): 370; "The New E. H. Sothern," in *Famous Actors*, 11–31; Young, *Famous*, 2:1031; "E. H. Sothern," *American Stage*, n.p.; Clapp, *Players*, 341; *Who Was Who*, 2224–25.

89   Patty S. Derrick, "Richard Mansfield's *Henry V*: The Shaping of an American Hero," *Theatre History Studies* 19 (June 1999): 3; Bordman, *American Theatre*, 466, 468.

90   Quoted in Krows, *Play*, 160.

91   "Calve, in 'Carmen,' Opens Opera Season," *Boston Post*, December 5, 1899, 1.

92   "Scenes in the Theatre," *Boston Globe*, December 5, 1899, 13.

93   Ibid.

94   "Calve, in 'Carmen,' Opens Opera Season," *Boston Post*.

95   W. F. A[pthrop], "Calve's New 'Carmen'," *Boston Evening Transcript*, December 5, 1899, 16; "Calvé and 'Carmen'," *Boston Globe*, December 5, 1899, 13; Louis C. Elson, "The Grand Opera," *Boston Daily Advertiser*, December 5, 1899, 4.

96   Gallus, *Emma*, n.p.; Austin, *Gallery*, 44; *Baker's Biographical Dictionary of Musicians* (New York: Schrimer, 1992), s.v. "Calvé, Emma;" Julia F. Opp, "Calvé at Home," unidentified magazine, Feb. 1896, in RLS NAFR+ v. 95, BRTC; Leslie, *Some*, 470; "Musical and Theatrical Gossip. Melba and Calvé," *Sketch* 34 (June 26, 1901): 399–400; "Emma Eames," unidentified magazine, c. 1899, in RLS NAFR+ v. 173, BRTC; W. F. A[pthrop], "Music and Drama," *Boston Evening Transcript*, December 6, 1899, 18.

97   Louis C. Elson, "The Grand Opera," *Boston Daily Advertiser*, December 5, 1899, 4; also Gallus, *Emma*, n.p.; Leslie, *Some*, 473.

98   Gallus, *Emma*, n.p.; "A Glimpse of Calvé," unidentified newspaper, c. April 1900, in RLS NAFR+ v. 95, p. 33, BRTC; Leslie, *Some*, 474, 469.

99   "Calvé and 'Carmen,'" *Boston Globe*.

100   "Heard about Town," *New York Times*, January 2, 1900, 7; Gallus, *Emma*, n.p.; "Calve, in 'Carmen,' Opens Opera Season," *Boston Post*, December 5, 1899, 1; "Calvé Is a Theosophist," *New York Sun*, February 10, 1900, n.p.

101   Emma Calvé, *Sous tous les ciels j'ai chanté* (Paris: Plon, 1940), 251–52. *Netsuke* were tiny fanciful ivory carvings.

102   "Calvé and 'Carmen,'" *Boston Globe*; W. F. A[pthrop], "Calve's New 'Carmen,'" *Boston Evening Transcript*; Leslie, *Some*, 473; Gallus, *Emma*, n.p.

103   "The Grand Opera," *Boston Evening Record*, November 28, 1899, 7; also "Boston Theatre: 'Lohengrin,'" *Boston Evening Transcript*, December 9, 1899, 31. It was hype. Grau did not have all of the greats.

104   Stanley Sadie, ed., *The Grove Dictionary of Opera* (New York: Macmillan, 1992), 2:519. In achieving this distinction, the unrelenting stress of opera production was said to have ruined Grau's health (Francis Robinson, *Celebration: The Metropolitan Opera* [Garden City, New York: Doubleday, 1979], 47).

105   "Massachusetts. Boston," *NYC*, December 16, 1899, 878; "The Man with the Lorgnette," *Boston Evening Record*, December 18, 1899, 5.

106   "Scenes in the Theatre," *Boston Globe*, December 5, 1899, 13; also W. F. A[pthrop], "Calve's New 'Carmen,'" *Boston Evening Transcript*, December 5, 1899, 16; "Calvé and 'Carmen,'" *Boston Globe*.

107   "Artiste Greets Artiste," *Boston Herald*, December 13, 1899, 9; "The Japanese Plays," *Boston Post*, December 13, 1899, 16; Leslie, *Some*, 473.

108   "Artiste Greets Artiste," *Boston Herald*; also "The Man with the Lorgnette," *Boston Evening Record*, December 13, 1899, 5; "The Japanese Plays," *Boston Post*, December 13, 1899, 16; Leslie, *Some*, 473.

Chapter 14

1   Kaneo, *Ōbei*, 23–24. This source listed the date of Maruyama's death as December 12. Official Boston records indicated December 11, 1999 (City of Boston, Registry Division, death certificate for Keeranda [*sic*] Maruyama).

2   Kaneo, *Sadayakko*, 24–25.

3   "Tenno heika banzai!"

4   "Shin'engeki banzai!" Kaneo, *Sadayakko*, 25.

5   Kaneo, *Sadayakko*, 25. Kawakami also recounted Maruyama's death and related events in Kaneo, *Ōbei*, 23–24, and in Hanabusa Yūgai's play, *Yōkōchū no higeki* [Tragedy while touring abroad], 10–17. These sources differed in many details and were often contradictory.

6   Kaneo, *Ōbei*, 24; Kaneo, *Sadayakko*, 24; Ezaki, *Jitsuroku*, 109.

7   City of Boston, death certificate for Keeranda [*sic*] Maruyama. Complications from either lead poisoning or morphine overdose may produce uremic poisoning symptoms. According to a diagnosis by Dr. Fred Lee in 2003, Maruyama's symptoms also suggested infection from nonsterile needles.

8   This was the same afternoon that Calvé presented Sadayakko with her diamond-studded comb.

9   Kaneo, *Ōbei*, 24; Kaneo, *Sadayakko*, 24; Sharf, "Matsuki Chronology," 38; "Railroads," *Lowell Mail*, December 11, 1899, 11; "Wednesday's Weather," *Boston Daily Advertiser*, December 13, 1899, 1; "Opera House," advertisement, *Lowell Daily Courier*, December 12, 1899, 7.

10   Jefferson, *Autobiography*, 116; "Entertainments. Opera House," *Lowell Mail*, December 13, 1899, 2.

11   Arthur L. Eno, Jr., ed., *Cotton Was King: A History of Lowell, Massachusetts* (Lowell: Lowell Historical

Society, 1976), 255; Peter F. Blewett, "The New People: An Introduction to the Ethnic History of Lowell," in Eno, 190–217.

12   "Higher Wages," *Lowell Sun*, November 27, 1899, 1; "Much Rejoicing in Collinsville," *Lowell Sunday Telegram*, December 10, 1899, 2; "To Advance Wages," *Lowell Mail*, December 12, 1899, 2.

13   Cahn, *Theatrical 1899–1900*, 400; "Massachusetts. Lowell," *NYC*, November 25, 1899, 807. The Opera House, built in 1887, eventually became a movie theatre before it disappeared in a 1956 urban renewal frenzy (Nancye Tuttle, "Picture It: Lowell Goes to the Movies," pamphlet, [Lowell: Patrick J. Mogan Cultural Center, 1993], n.p.).

14   "Opera House," advertisement, *Lowell Daily Courier*, December 12, 1899, 7; "Amusements," *Lowell Daily Courier*, December 13, 1899, 4.

15   "Amusements," *Lowell Daily Courier*, December 13, 1899, 4; "Entertainments. Opera House," *Lowell Mail*, December 13, 1899, 2; "Entertainments. Music Hall," *Lowell Mail*, December 12, 1899, 2.

16   "Amusements," *Lowell Daily Courier*, December 13, 1899, 4.

17   "Corse Payton Dies in Brooklyn at 66," *New York Times*, February 24, 1934, 13; Ward Morehouse, "Broadway after Dark," *New York Sun*, May 2, 1933, n.p.

18   Gertrude Andrews, *The Story of Corse Payton* (Brooklyn: Andrews, 1901), 83, 105; Corse Payton's Success," *New York Dramatic Mirror*, April 14, 1900, 9; Cahn, *Theatrical 1899–1900*, xxiii.

19   "10-20-30" was theatrical jargon for inexpensive companies whose admission scales were usually 10¢, 20¢, and 30¢ (Marian Spitzer, "Ten-20-30; the Passing of the Popular-Priced Circuit," *Saturday Evening Post*, August 22, 1925, 40; "10-20-30 Cent Stock Company Pioneer Has Liabilities of $9,000," *New York Times*, March 27, 1921, n.p.; Andrews, *Story of Corse Payton*, 105). Rep companies exploited the "10-20-30" expression in many ways. Dexter and O'Neil's rep company at the Lowell Opera House three weeks earlier billed "10 Specialities. 20 Educated Horses. 30 People" ("Opera House," advertisement, *Lowell Mail*, November 11, 1899, 4).

20   Lesser Japanese touring companies had a large repertoire (often more than twenty plays), and they often performed two different bills every day for as long as a week. Actors memorized key scenes and ad-libbed the rest (Muramatsu, *Tabishibai*, 67–72).

21   "Music Hall," advertisement, *Lowell Daily Courier*, December 4, 1899, 8; "Massachusetts. Lowell," *NYC*, November 25, 1899, 807; "Entertainments. Music Hall," *Lowell Mail*, December 15, 1899, 2.

22   "Music Hall," advertisement, *Lowell Daily Courier*, December 12, 1899, 7; "Entertainments. Music Hall," *Lowell Mail*, December 12, 1899, 2; "Amusements," *Lowell Daily Courier*, December 12, 1899, 4.

23   "Savoy Theatre," advertisement, *Lowell Daily Courier*, December 12, 1899, 7; "Massachusetts. Boston," *NYC*, December 16, 1899, 878; "Gaiety Theatre," advertisement, *Lowell Daily News*, December 12, 1899, 7; "People's Theatre," *Lowell Daily News*, December 12, 1899, 7; "Massachusetts. Lowell," *NYC*, November 25, 1899, 807; "Star Theatre," advertisement, *Lowell Sunday Telegram*, December 10, 1899, 5.

24   "Amusements," *Lowell Daily Courier*, December 12, 1899, 4; Hughes, *History*, 302–3; Ralph Eugene Lund, "Trouping with Uncle Tom," *Century* (January 1928): 331; "Amusements," *Lowell Daily Courier*, December 13, 1899, 4.

25   "Amusements. Music Hall," *Lowell Daily Courier*, November 21, 1899, 8; "Gaiety Theatre," advertisement, *Lowell Daily News*, December 13, 1899, 1; "People's Theatre," *Lowell Daily New*; "Massachusetts. Lowell," *NYC*, November 25, 1899, 807; "Massachusetts. Boston," *NYC*, December 16, 1899, 878; "Star Theatre," advertisement, *Lowell Sunday Telegram*, December 10, 1899, 5; Baedeker, *United States*, 129.

26   Peter F. Blewett, "The New People," in Eno, *Cotton Was King*, 190–97; Tuttle, "Picture It: Lowell Goes to the Movies," 1993, n.p. Half of the Lowell population was French-Canadian.

27   Musser, *Before*, 142.

28   "Opera House," advertisement, *Lowell Daily Courier*, December 4, 1899, 8; "Amusements," *Lowell Daily Courier*, December 6, 1899, 4.

29   These films recorded New York and Washington parades for Admiral Dewey ("Big Week for Theatres," *Lowell Sunday Telegram*, December 3, 1899, 7; "Opera House," advertisement, *Lowell Sunday Telegram*, December 3, 1899, 7; "Entertainments. Opera House," *Lowell Mail*, December 8, 1899, 2).

30   Wittke, *Tambo*, 71, 113, 120.

31   "West's Big Minstrel Jubilee" was at the Grand Opera week of January 1–6 ("Amusement Notes," *Boston Traveler*, January 4, 1900, 5). In Boston, that show was well attended, but it was not the same troupe that played Lowell. Minstrel shows at the margins of show business may not have advertised in newspapers so they were not picked up by my research.

32   Wittke, *Tambo*, 109.

33   Hughes, *History*, 300; Rahill, *World*, 252; Oenslager, *Scenery*, 203–4; "Bypaths of the Drama," *New York Sun*, July 29, 1900, 2:5.

34   "Opera House," advertisement, *Lowell Daily Courier*, December 12, 1899, 7; "Entertainments. Music Hall," *Lowell Mail*, December 8, 1899, 2. Tom shows, minstrel troupes, and circuses all did street parades (Wittke, *Tambo*, 145–46).

35   Rahill, *World*, 250–52; Harry Birdoff, *The World's Greatest Hit: Uncle Tom's Cabin* (New York: Vanni, 1947), 307–10; Hughes, *History*, 301; Wilmeth, *Guide*, 252, 474; Oenslager, *Scenery*, 205; "At the Theatres. Third Avenue-*Uncle Tom's Cabin*," *NYDM*, April 29, 1899, 16; "New York City. Star Theatre," *NYC*, March 17, 1900, 58; "Al W. Martin's Co.," *NYDM*, August 12, 1899, 3.

36   Kaneo, *Ōbei*, 24; "Railroads," *Lowell Mail*, December 11, 1899, 11.

37   Kaneo, *Ōbei*, 24–25; Kaneo, *Sadayakko*, 25–26, 28–29; Sharf, "Matsuki Chronology," 38; Dōmon, *Kawakami*, 121; Miyaoka, *Ikoku*, 73.

38   Kaneo, *Sadayakko*, 26–27; Kaneo, *Ōbei*, 25–26.

39   Muramatsu Shōfu, *Kawakami*, 1:281.

40   Kaneo, *Ōbei*, 25.

41   Kaneo, *Sadayakko*, 27.

42   Ibid., 26.

43   For instance: Dōmon, *Kawakami*, 121; Miyaoka, *Ikoku*, 73.

44   Kaneo, *Ōbei*, 24; Kaneo, *Sadayakko*, 25. The name of this famous Boston cemetery has been incorrectly listed in every Japanese source. Kawakami called it "Monto Hōru" (Mount Hole[?] or Hall[?]) in Kaneo, *Ōbei*, and "Monto Hōmu" (Mount Home) in Kaneo, *Sadayakko*. Later writers always repeated these incorrect designations; see, for instance, Muramatsu Shōfu, *Kawakami*, 1:283.

45   "Namu Amida Butsu, namu Myōhō Rengekyō," Kaneo, *Ōbei*, 25; Kaneo, *Sadayakko*, 26.

46   Kawakami Otojirō, "Maruyama Kambi no shibō" [The death of Maruyama Kambi], *Miyako shimbun*, January 18, 1900, in Shirakawa, 310–11.

47   Irokawa, *Culture*, 31.

48   "Haiyū" [Actors], *Kabuki* (January 1900): 64.

49   McArthur, *Actors*, 65–66.

50   Jennings, *Theatrical*, 464–65.

51   Hillary Bell, "Theatres," *New York Press*, January 7, 1900, 14. My casual perusal of trade papers produced many more stories of misfortune in the 1899–1900 season than reported here.

52   "Gossip of the Theatre," *Washington Post*, January 28, 1900, 24; also "The Illness of Olga Nethersole," *NYDM*, February 3, 1900, 17. In her autobiography, Modjeska described her unrelenting fatigue from touring even though she traveled by luxurious, comfortable private railroad car (Modjeska, *Memories*, 377–78).

53   "Notes and Comment," *Boston Evening Transcript*, December 6, 1899, 18; "Mrs. Carter Still Very Weak," *New York Herald*, January 21, 1900, 13.

54   Winter, *Life and Art*, 1:257; "Money in Cyrano," unidentified newspaper, January 8, 1899, and "Barnstorming Made Him Sick," unidentified newspaper, April 16, 1900, items in RLS NAFR+ v. 321, pp. 45, 63, BRTC.

55   "E. H. Sothern's Illness," *NYDM*, February 24, 1900, 16; Fredric Edward McKay, "Theatrical Gossip," *New York Mail and Express*, March 8, 1900, 8.

56   "The Illness of Olga Nethersole," *NYD*; "Gossip of the Theatre," *Washington Post*, January 28, 1900, 24.

57   "Calve, in 'Carmen,' Opens Opera Season," *Boston Post*, December 5, 1899, 1; "Calvé Is a Theosophist," *New York Sun*, February 10, 1900, n.p.

58   Bingham, *Henry*, 294; Stoker, *Personal*, 268; H. Chance Newton, "Miss Ellen Terry and Her Art," *Sketch* 35 (July 31, 1901): 75; "New York City. Review and Comment," *NYC*, March 24, 1900, 81.

59   "Cissie Loftus," *Lowell Sun*, November 18, 1899, 8.

60   "To the Editor of the Dramatic Mirror," *NYDM*, January 13, 1900, 17; John T. Warde, "Telegraphic News. Washington," *NYDM*, December 9, 1899, 9. After an officer of the Actors' Fund learned of the woman's circumstances, the Fund paid her hospital expenses. The Fund was a mutual aid society dedicated to helping distressed members of the profession.

61   "The Usher," *NYDM*, February 3, 1900, 15.

62   "Gossip of the Theatre," *Washington Post*, January 28, 1900, 24.

63   "Saying 'I Am So Tired,' Actress Dies at Table," *New York World*, January 17, 1900, 3; "Topics from Stageland," *New York Sun*, February 14, 1900, 7.

64   *New York Dramatic Mirror* and *New York Clipper*, 1899–1900.

65   "Actor Died of Starvation," *NYC*, March 10, 1900, 31.

66   "Gossip of the Town," *NYDM*, January 13, 1900, 17; also Hillary Bell, "Theatres," *New York Press*, January 7, 1900, 14.

67   "Seeks Spirit Land," *Boston Herald*, December 15, 1899; 1, 2; also Jay Benton, "Telegraphic News. Boston," *NYDM*, December 30, 1899, 10.

68   "Murder on the Stage," *Boston Post*, December 11, 1899, 2; "Mad Act of Othello," *Washington Post*, January 21, 1900, 26. Quotations from both sources are interspersed.

69   "She Is Free," *Boston Journal*, January 11, 1900, 1.

70   Augusta Howe Chambers, lyricist, Charles Coleman, composer, "The Night That She Played Her Last Part" (New York: Charles Coleman, 1899).

71   Kaneo, *Ōbei*, 34; also Sōya, *Honno*, 72–73.

72   "The Japanese Players, *Boston Herald*, December 17, 1899, 14; also Jay Benton, "Telegraphic News. Boston," *NYDM*, December 23, 1899, 79; "The Man with the Lorgnette," *Boston Evening Record*, December 18, 1899, 5; Kaneo, *Ōbei*, 26; "Saturday's Weather," *Boston Daily Advertiser*, December 16, 1899, 1.

73   "At the Theatres," *Boston Post*, December 16, 1899, 5; "At the Theatres. Herald Square—Naughty Anthony," *NYDM*, January 13, 1900, 16; "Arizona," *NYDM*, September 15, 1900, 17.

74   Japan was not yet important or rich enough to have an ambassador posted to the United States.

75   Kaneo, *Sadayakko*, 21, 33; Muramatsu, *Kawakami*, 1:274; Dōmon, *Kawakami*, 121. Kaneo listed no date for Komura's visit. Muramatsu, a secondary source, claimed Komura came to Boston for the early December opening. Dōmon, another secondary source, placed Komura's visit concurrent with the troupe's last performances in Boston seven weeks later. An early date was more likely.

76   K. K. Kawakami, "The Japanese in New England," *New England* 35 (December 1906): 443.

77   Ezaki, *Jitsuroku*, 111–12; also Inoue, *Kawakami*, 70.

78   Dōmon, *Kawakami*, 121.

79   Ibid; Kaneo, *Sadayakko*, 21, 33.

80   Kaneo, *Ōbei*, 26; "Monday's Weather," *Boston Daily Advertiser*, December 18, 1899, 1.

81   John Harris, *Historic Walks in Old Boston* (Chester, Connecticut: Globe Pequot Press, 1982), 153–54; Edward Wagenknecht, *Edgar Allan Poe: The Man Behind the Legend* (New York: Oxford University Press, 1963), 14, 23–24.

82   A typical one-season tour for a first- or second-class company (which, if lucky, played for more than one season) was that of *The Telephone Girl*. It traveled 10,552 miles and gave a total of 266 performances, including forty-eight matinees. This included five long day-and-night jumps that were more than 330 miles, ten trips that averaged 225 miles, and twenty-four of at least 110 miles. Altogether, the tour had sixty-one one-night stands with ten, twelve, and fifteen of them in a row interrupted only by an occasional Sunday rest. Less frantic were six two-day stands, nine split-weeks of three or four-nights each, twelve one-week, and three two-week stands ("Work on a Road Tour," *New York Times*, March 11, 1900, 16).

83   "Music and Drama," *Boston Evening Transcript*, December 16, 1899, 28.

84   "Arizona. Tremont Theatre," advertisement, *Boston Herald*, December 14, 1899, 9; "The Japanese Players at the Tremont," *Boston Evening Transcript*, December 9, 1899, 31.

85   "Japanese Dramatic Company," *Boston Globe*, December 19, 1899, 2; Kaneo, *Ōbei*, 26–27.

86   The Japanese title in the records continued to be *Nunosarashi*.

87   "The Stage," *Toledo Bee*, November 24, 1899, 4.

88   "Japanese Dramatic Company," *Boston Globe*, December 19, 1899, 2; "Players from Far Japan," *Boston Journal*, January 7, 1900, 4:4. Comic dancing was one of Wada's special talents, but his name did not appear in the cast list. Wada may also have substituted for Maruyama as one of the novice maidens. It was also possible that wig master Takagi Hanjirō was the country girl, as he was replacing Maruyama in onnagata roles.

89   "Around the Playhouses. The Japanese Players," *Boston Globe*, December 19, 1899, 9; "Japanese Dramatic Company," *Boston Globe*, December 19, 1899, 2; Tremont Theatre, Boston, program, December 18, 1899, in clippings file: Tremont Theatre, HTC.

90   "Japanese Dramatic Company," *Boston Globe*, December 19, 1899, 2; "Players from Far Japan," *Boston Journal*, January 7, 1900, 4:4; also Edward S. Rogers, "The Law of Dramatic Copyright," *Michigan Law Review* 1 (1902): 112. Legal conflicts discussed in this last source sustained Fuller's contested claim that she was the originator of flowing fabric and colored light dances, although she was informed that her dances could not be copyrighted because they had no literary content.

91   Walter Sorell, *Dance in Its Time* (New York: Columbia University Press, 1986), 311–12; Gay Morris, "La Loie," *Dance* 51 (August 1977): 38.

92   "Amusements.… Madame Yacco," *Seattle Daily Times*, September 9, 1899, 12.

93   In cold weather, spectators in Japan brought their own small charcoal braziers to the theatre along with warm clothing (Kurata, *Kindaigeki*, 151).

94   "Gossip of the Theatre," *Washington Post*, January 28, 1900, 24.

95   Ibid.; Claudia D. Johnson, "Elbridge T. Gerry's Obsession," *Nineteenth Century Theatre Research* 13:1 (Summer 1985): 23; Modjeska, *Memories*, 377–78; Baker, *Rise*, 114.

96   Holograph note on Tremont Theatre, Boston, program, December 14, 1899, in Tremont Theatre programs **T.10.27, RBD BPL.

97   "Gossip of the Theatre," *Washington Post*, January 28, 1900, 24. In Japan, where theatres were not heated, pneumonia was also an occupational disease (conversation with elderly ex-shimpa actor employed as a waiter at the centrally heated Lenge [*sic*] Restaurant, Manhattan, c. 1980).

98   C. S. Montgomery, "Bad Air in Theatres," *Engineering Magazine* 3 (May 1892): 190–94. Theatres that converted to electric light were slow to install heating systems to compensate for the loss of heat from gaslights.

99   "General Theatrical Notes," *New York Evening Post*, March 3, 1900, 21.

100 Osman Edwards, *Japanese Plays and Playfellows* (New York: Lane, 1901), 91.

101 Weather reports in *Boston Daily Advertiser*, December 4–23, 1899; "Such Weather! December Weather," *Boston Evening Record*, December 20, 1899, 4.

102 Kaneo, *Sadayakko*, 28; Muramatsu, *Kawakami*, 1:284. Intern Sugimoto graduated from the Boston University School of Medicine in 1902 and became a general practitioner of allopathy. He died December 1929 (Arthur Hafner, ed., *Directory of Deceased American Physicians 1804–1929* [Chicago: American Medical Association, 1993], 2:1509).

103 Kaneo, *Sadayakko*, 28.

104 Suzuki, *Way*, 42–46.

105 Gerald Groemer, "Nō at the Crossroads: Commoner Performance During the Edo Period," *Asian Theatre Journal* 15 (Spring 1998): 117–41. Townsmen could pay to see nō and nō-influenced shows performed in public venues by marginal professional troupes.

106 Muramatsu, *Kawakami*, 1:285.

107 Kaneo, *Sadayakko*, 20 [page misnumbered as 16], 28; also Inoue, *Kawakami*, 69; Ubukata, "Kawakami," 174; Muramatsu, *Kawakami*, 1:285; Sugimoto, *Madamu*, 147.

108 "The Man with the Lorgnette," *Boston Evening Record*, December 18, 1899, 5; "At Boston Playhouses. 'Arizona,'" *Boston Journal*, December 19, 1899, 5. These "professional matinees" for theatre people were performed on a weekday other than Wednesday so that those who had their own regular midweek matinees could attend. Professional matinees offered opportunities for the profession to see what their peers were doing and they provided education for less experienced players who, spending a year or so in a touring company doing the same play, had no opportunity to see or do other shows (Grau, *Business*, 86–87).

109 "The Japanese Players," *Boston Herald*, December 21, 1899, 9; "The Man with the Lorgnette," *Boston Evening Record*, December 21, 1899, 5; "Japanese Players," *Boston Globe*, December 24, 1899, 18; "The Boston Playhouses," *Boston Evening Transcript*, December 21, 1899, 11; Kaneo, *Ōbei*, 27–28.

110 Kaneo, *Ōbei*, 27–28.

111 Fujisawa Asajirō, "Kawakami fūfu o kataru" [Talking about Mr. and Mrs. Kawakami], in Fujii, *Jiden*, 264–65. Fujisawa's account of Kawakami's talk with Sadayakko had to be second- or third-hand as he was not in America.

Chapter 15

1 "The Boston Playhouses," *Boston Evening Transcript*, December 21, 1899, 11; Tremont, Theatre, Boston, program, week of December 25, 1899, 25, in Tremont Theatre Programs **T.10.27, RBS BPL; "Japanese Players," *Boston Globe*, December 24, 1899, 18; Kaneo, *Ōbei*, 27.

2 "Around the Playhouses. The Japanese Players," *Boston Globe*, December 19, 1899, 9.

3 "The Man with the Lorgnette," *Boston Evening Record*, December 27, 1899, 5; Kaneo, *Ōbei*, 27. The "new comedy" was *Sambasō*. It was eventually performed on December 28.

4 Ibid.; "Music and Drama," *Boston Evening Transcript*, December 29, 1899, 7; also "The Japanese Players," *Boston Evening Transcript*, December 27, 1899, 13; "The Japanese Players," *Boston Herald*, December 28, 1899, 9.

5 Because of Mikami's health and behavioral problems, merchant Matsuki may have been this substitute gentleman.

6 "The Man with the Lorgnette," *Boston Evening Record*, December 29, 1899, 5.

7 "Music and Drama," *Boston Evening Transcript*, December 29, 1899, 7.

8 Ibid; also "The Japanese Players," *Boston Herald*, December 28, 1899, 9.

9 Quoted by Norman Hapgood, "The Actor of Today," *Atlantic Monthly* 83 (January 1899): 125.

10   Alexander Corbett Jr., "Japan's Foremost Actors, *Boston Globe*, December 11, 1899, 5. Similar accounts in "This Japanese Actress Likes American Life," *Boston Post*, January 15, 1900, 5.

11   "Stories of the Players," *Boston Herald*, December 18, 1899, 10.

12   Alexander Corbett Jr., "Japan's Foremost Actors, *Boston Globe*; "This Japanese Actress Likes American Life," *Boston Post*; "Mme. Yacco," *Boston Post*, December 24, 1899, 16.

13   "Madame Yacco and Her Japs," *Toledo Daily Blade*, November 22, 1899, 3.

14   "Stories of the Players," *Boston Herald*, December 18, 1899, 10. Similar response earlier in "At the Theatres," *Grand Rapids Herald*, November 12, 1899, 14.

15   "Seiyō de wa onnagata wa mina onna de aru" (Kaneo, *Ōbei*, 33).

16   With the banning of females on public stages in the seventeenth century, there was no need to distinguish between female roles and the gender of the male actors who played them.

17   "Seiyōjin no onnagata" (Kaneo, *Ōbei*, 34; "Sadayakko," *Niroku shimbun*, April 11, 1900, in Shirakawa, 314–15.

18   *Māchanto ofu Enisu ni tsuite Kawakami Otojirō no danwa* [A conversation with Kawakami Otojirō about *The Merchant of Venice*], *Kabuki* (July 1903): 11.

19   Hirayama, *Joyū*, 44; Toki, "Joyū no keifu," 225; Kuwano, *Joyū*, 248; Toita, *Kindai*, 76; Ōzasa, *Nihon*, 1:61; Kawatake Toshio, *Kindai engeki*, 130.

20   Abe, *Tōkyō*, 178–82; Miyake Saburō, *Koshibai*, 122; also "Joyū no konjaku" [Actresses then and now], *Engei gahō* (July 1908): 66–68; Ihara, *Kabuki*, 7:344, 347; Leiter, *Historical*, 277.

21   Mukai, *Nippon*, 257–78; Toita, "Kabuki, Shimpa," 259; Hirayama, *Joyū*, 44–50; Miyake Saburō, *Koshibai*, 122–25; "Joyū no konjaku," *Engei gahō*; Toita, *Kindai*, 76; Coaldrake, *Women's*, 13–14. The end of the prohibition of *mixed* male and female casts appearing on the same stage came later.

22   Kurata, *Meiji*, 4:71.

23   Toki, "Joyū," 225, 228; Kuwano, *Joyū*, 248; Iwai, *Shimpa*, 177–78; Hagii, *Shimpa*, 184; Toita, *Kindai*, 25; Okamoto, *Meiji*, 121; Abe, *Tōkyō*, 178; "Meika shinsō: Ichikawa Kumehachi" [Celebrity revelations: Kumehachi], *Engei gahō* (September 1907): 107–9.

24   Toita, *Kindai*, 25; Ihara, *Kabuki*, 7:344, 363, 392, 421, 438, 563; Okamoto, *Meiji*, 118–19, 121.

25   Yanagi Eijirō, *Shimpa gojūnen*, 18–19; Marui, *Shimpa*, 17. Four years before Sadayakko went onstage in San Francisco, Kumehachi and another female apparently appeared in a mixed gender cast in a lesser play produced by Kawakami (Mukai, *Nippon*, 258; Iwai, *Shimpa*, 177; Hirayama, *Joyū*, 44–50; Ōgawa, *Nihon*, 106).

26   Toki, "Joyū," 226–28; Iwai, *Shimpa*, 177–78; "Meika shinsō roku: Ichikawa Kumehachi." Changing stage names was common in Japanese theatre.

27   Hagii, *Shimpa*, 184.

28   "Danjo gōdō kairyō engeki."

29   Kawatake Shigetoshi, *Gaisetsu*, 374–76; Ihara, *Meiji*, 233–35; Hagii, *Shimpa*, 182–84; Toita, "Kabuki, Shimpa," 267–68; Akiba, *Tōto*, 244–46; Miyake Shūtarō, *Engeki*, 86–87; Nagai Takao, *Shimpa*, 8; "Shimpa hanseiki o kataru," 14; Toki, "Joyū no keifu," 225.

30   "Nihon haiyū bansuke; shinhaiyū no bu" [Rating chart of Japanese actors; new actors (i.e., shimpa) section]. This was a comprehensive list of leading shimpa actors in 1903 (Iwai, *Shimpa*, 10).

31   The *onna kengeki* genre disappeared four decades ago. Disappeared, that is, in the sense that professional *onna kengeki* troupes were no longer active.

32   "*Taishū engeki*" (popular theatre) is another Japanese term with several referents. Here it refers specifically to small, provincial touring companies. In other contexts, the term may be broadly applied to all kinds of "nonclassical" commercial theatre, including Broadway musicals staged in Japan.

33   Personal observation based on my attendance at *taishū engeki* since 1949. While seldom discussed in

academic histories of Japanese theatre, there is a considerable literature (largely autobiographical) about *onna kengeki* and *taishū engeki*: Minami Hiroshi, *Kabuku: taishū engeki no sekai* [*Kabuku*, letting go: the world of popular theatre]; Asaka Mitsuyo, *Onna kengeki* [Female sword drama] (Gakufū Shoin, 1962); Ōe Michiko, *Onna no hanamichi: hayagawari onna kengeki ichidaiki* [A woman's hanamichi: the life of a quick change female sword player] (Kōdansha, 1982); Takezawa Ryūchiyo, *Tabi no owari ni* [At the end of the journey] (Bun'ensha, 1988); Tsukushi Misuko, *Tabi geinin no uta* [Song of a strolling entertainer] (Fukuoka-shi: Ashi Shobō, 1981); Ugai Masaki, *Taishū engeki e no tabi: Nanjō Masaki no ichinen futatsuki* [A trip to popular theatre: one year and two months with Nanjō Masaki] (Miraisha, 1971). Representative *taishū engeki* repertories are listed in *Taishū engeki* (Tōkyō Kogekijō Kumiai, 1965).

34   Author's personal experience. Typical venues were the Ponto-chō Kaburenjō in Kyoto and the old Shimbashi Embujō in Tokyo.

35   Krows, *Play*, 55; Arthur Hornblow, *Training for the Stage* (Philadelphia: Lippincott, 1916), 109; "Plays Next Week," *Boston Daily Advertiser*, December 23, 1899, 8.

36   "Continued Attractions and Attractions to Come," *Boston Evening Transcript*, December 19, 1899, 7.

37   Clapp, *Reminiscences*, 8–10. Published in 1902.

38   "Players of Mikado-Land," *Seattle Post-Intelligencer*, September 7, 1899, 6.

39   Tomita, *Nihon*, 38–41; Kawatake Shigetoshi, *Nihon no engeki*, 181; Yamaguchi, *Joyū*, 142–46, 241–49. One must distinguish between plays performed *by* children and plays performed *for* children.

40   "The Christmas Pantomime," *NYDM*, December 31, 1898, 14. In 1899, thirty-two Christmas pantomimes were staged in the London metropolitan area but only two were in the central London theatre district. Throughout Great Britain that year, there were 120 Christmas pantomimes ("English Christmas Plays, *New York Times*, January 7, 1900, 16).

41   "Little Red Riding Hood," *Boston Herald*, December 10, 1899, 17; "Plays Next Week," *Boston Daily Advertiser*, December 23, 1899, 8; "Little Red Riding Hood," *Boston Dramatic Review* 6 (December 23, 1899): 4; Booth, *Prefaces*, 203. The most successful Christmas pantomimes in Britain continued until the end of April (Booth, *Victorian Spectacular*, 86).

42   This was where Irving and Sothern recently played.

43   "Plays Next Week," *Boston Daily Advertiser*, December 23, 1899, 8.

44   "Hollis Street Theatre," advertisement, *Boston Globe*, December 24, 1899, 15; "Little Red Riding Hood," *Boston Herald*; Hollis St. Theatre, Boston, program, December 20, 1899, in program file MWEZ n.c. 7577, BRTC.

45   "Hollis Street Theatre," advertisement, *Boston Globe*; also "Music and Drama," *Boston Evening Transcript*, December 16, 1899, 28; "Plain Tales of Stageland," *Boston Journal*, December 29, 1899, 2.

46   "Little Red Riding Hood," *Boston Globe*, December 24, 1899, 18; "Plays Next Week," *Boston Daily Advertiser*.

47   "Plays Next Week," *Boston Daily Advertiser*; "Little Red Riding Hood," *Boston Globe*. Samuel McKechnie in his *Popular Entertainments through the Ages*, 30–33, attributed the shift of late nineteenth century British pantomime from its earlier innocence toward mildly risqué material to increased domination by performers from the music halls.

48   "Plain Tales of Stageland," *Boston Journal*, December 29, 1899, 2.

49   "Hollis Street Theatre," advertisement, *Boston Globe*, December 24, 1899, 15.

50   "Little Red Riding Hood," *New York Times*, January 9, 1900, 5; "A New Extravaganza," *New York Herald*, January 9, 1900, 9.

51   "A New Extravaganza," *New York Herald*, January 9, 1900, 9.

52   "Three New Plays and a Notable Night at the Grand Opera," *New York World*, January 7, 1900, 4; "New Productions," *New York Press*, January 7, 1900, 14.

53   "New Plays on Our Stage," *New York Sun*, January 9, 1900, 7.

54   Tompkins, *History*, 455, 465, 473; "Plays and Players. The Hanlons' Pantomime," *Boston Herald*, December 17, 1899, 14; "Music and Drama," *Boston Evening Transcript*, December 19, 1899, 7; George T. Richardson, "Pantomime's Charm as Illustrated by the Hanlons," *Boston Traveler*, December 19, 1899. 15.

55   "Plays and Players," *Boston Herald*, January 19, 1896, 10.

56   Ibid.; Boston Theatre, program, week of December 25, 1899, in Boston Theatre playbills **T.10.1, RBD BPL.

57   John A. McKiven, *The Hanlon Brothers: Their Amazing Acrobatics, Pantomime, and Stage Spectacles* (Glenwood, Illinois: Meyerbooks, 1998), 64–65.

58   "Hanlons Superba," advertisement, *NYDM*, Christmas Number, December 24, 1898, 124; also "The Hanlon's Christmas Pantomime," *Boston Post*, December 17, 1899, 15; "The Park—'Superba,'" unidentified Indianapolis newspaper, September 7, 1909, n.p.; "Plays and Players; The Hanlons' Pantomime," *Boston Herald*, December 17, 1899, 14; "Boston Theatre," advertisement, *Boston Herald*, December 14, 1899, 9; "Great Northern," advertisement, *Chicago Tribune*, October 29, 1899, 40.

59   "Brand name" was not a term then in use, but the perennial *Superba* was a pioneer of this marketing technique. Another brand-name show, playing Boston at another time, was the evergreen Irish-American comedy, *McFadden's Row of Flats*, that advertised "everything new except the title" ("Academy. McFadden's Row of Flats," advertisement, *Washington Evening Star*, November 15, 1899, 24).

60   *Punch and Judy* puppet shows similarly astonished audiences by mixing the over-familiar with the unexpected.

61   George T. Richardson, "Pantomime's Charm as Illustrated by the Hanlons," *Boston Traveler*, December 19, 1899. 15.

62   This approach was more operative in the old days of wilder kabuki than in later frozen affectation.

63   "Last Week of Superba," *Boston Herald*, December 26, 1899, 6; "Music and Drama," *Boston Evening Transcript*, December 19, 1899, 7.

64   "Music and Drama," *Boston Evening Transcript*; "Plays Next Week," *Boston Evening Record*, December 16, 1899, 5.

65   Boston Theatre, program, week of December 25, 1899, in Boston Theatre playbills **T.10.1, RBD BPL. Spectacular transformation scenes were essential parts of standard pantomimes as a setting slowly, awesomely changed into a fantasyland before the eyes of the audience while characters transmuted into harlequinade figures and fairies on wires flew down from the flies.

66   "The Hanlon's Christmas Pantomime," *Boston Post*; also George T. Richardson, "Pantomime's Charm as Illustrated by the Hanlons," *Boston Traveler*, December 19, 1899, 15; Music and Drama," *Boston Evening Transcript*, December 19, 1899, 7. Patriotic finales were a common feature of British pantomimes (Booth, *Prefaces*, 209).

67   Drama historians have discussed *The Black Crook* as central to the origins of modern American musical theatre (Bordman, *American Musical*, 18–20; Gänzl, *British*, 1:47–48).

68   Marcel Marceau, "Preface," in Marian Hannah Winter, *Theatre*, 9. The *féerie* was principal fare on the "Theatre of Marvels" that flourished in France from 1790–1860 on the famed Boulevard du Temple a.k.a. Boulevard du Crime (Winter, *Theatre*, 155–161).

69   "The World Famous Hanlon Bros.," advertisement, *NYDM*, Christmas Number, December 24, 1898, 67.

70   "Hanlons Superba," advertisement, *NYDM*, Christmas Number, December 24, 1898, 124; Irving Spiegel, "Two Circus Brothers Last of Long Line," *New York Times*, April 9, 1950, 73; John A. McKiven, *The Hanlon Brothers*, 62–63.

71   "Dramatic and Musical," *New York Times*, January 2, 1900, 7.

72   "At the Theatres. Victoria—Chris and the Wonderful Lamp," *NYDM*, January 13, 1900, 16; "Plays and

Players. Boston Museum Extravaganza," *Boston Herald*, December 3, 1899, 14; Boston Museum, program, week of December 11, 1899, in RLS NAFR+ v. 282, p. 20, BRTC.

73   "Boston Museum," *Boston Daily Advertiser*, December 5, 1899, 8; also "At Boston Playhouses," *Boston Journal*, December 5, 1899, 5; "Plays and Players. The Boston Museum," *Boston Herald*, December 17, 1899, 14; The Matinee Girl, "News and Gossip of the Stage," *Boston Traveler*, December 6, 1899, 5.

74   "Dramatic and Musical," *New York Times*, January 2, 1900, 7. This was followed by a national tour (Bordman, *American Musical*, 169).

75   "The Undressing of Edna Wallace Harper," unidentified newspaper, March 1899, in RLS NAFR+ v. 282, p. 16, BRTC; Wilder D. Quint, "Sousa Opera Is a Success," *Boston Traveler*, December 5, 1899, 5; also "Plays and Players. The Boston Museum," *Boston Herald*, December 17, 1899, 14; "News and Gossip of the Stage," *Boston Traveler*, December 6, 1899, 5.

76   "Lamp of Aladdin," *New York Mail and Express*, January 2, 1900, n.p.

77   "Boston Museum," *Boston Daily Advertiser*; Boston Museum, program, week of December 11, 1899, in RLS NAFR+ v. 282, p. 20, BRTC.

78   Henry Austin Clapp, "Mme. Modjeska," *Boston Daily Advertiser*, January 4, 1900. The role in the text was "A Boy" serving Benedict.

79   "At the Play. Grand," *Boston Journal*, January 7, 1900, 2:7.

80   "The Man with the Lorgnette," *Boston Evening Record*, December 27, 1899, 6.

81   "Grand Opera Theatre," advertisement, *Boston Traveler*, January 20, 1900, 5; "'Round New York in 80 Minutes," *Boston Evening Transcript*, January 23, 1900, 12; Boston Theatre, program, week of January 22, 1900, 11, in Boston Theatre playbills **T.10.1, RBD BPL.

82   "'Prince of Bohemia' for Bankers' Benefit Fund," *Boston Post*, January 4, 1900, 5; "A Prince of Bohemia," *Boston Herald*, January 7, 1900, 17; "The 'Prince,'" *Boston Daily Advertiser*, January 11, 1900, 5; "Music and Drama. 'A Prince of Bohemia,'" *Boston Evening Transcript*, January 4, 1900, 11.

83   Patty S. Derrick, "Rosalind and the Nineteenth-Century Woman: Four Stage Interpretations," *Theatre Survey* 26 (November 1985): 160; Davies, *Mirror*, 58.

84   Reed, *Victorian*, 300, 339.

85   "Famous Actresses Whose Roles Call for Trousers," unidentified New York newspaper, c. 1899, in RLS NAFR+ v. 282, p. 15, BRTC. Male characters played by females dressed as males were often called trouser roles.

86   "Pretty Amateurs Want to Act Men's Roles," *New York World*, April 5, 1900, 14.

87   Lisa Jardine, *Still Harping on Daughters: Women and Drama in the Age of Shakespeare* (Totowa, New Jersey: Barnes and Noble, 1983), 9–13, 24; Elizabeth Reitz Mullenix, "*A Doublet and Hose in My Disposition*: Sexology and the Cross-Dressed Theatrics of the Professional Women's League," *Theatre History Studies* 15 (1995): 106; Richards, *Rise*, 93–94.

88   Patty S. Derrick, "Rosalind and the Nineteenth-Century Woman: Four Stage Interpretations."

89   Mander, *Picture*, 106. A quick review of major nineteenth century actresses and their Shakespearean male roles appeared in "Actresses in Men's Roles," *Current Opinion* 30 (May 1901): 620. Romeo was the male role most frequently played by women (Brown, *History*, 3:670).

90   Sarah Bernhardt, "Men's Roles as Played by Women," *Harper's Bazar* [sic] 33 (December 15, 1900): 2113–15; also Leslie Ferris, "Introduction: Current Crossings," in his *Crossing*, 2.

91   Elaine Aston, *Sarah Bernhardt: A French Actress on the English Stage* (Oxford: Berg, 1989), 114–29; "The Paris Stage. Bernhardt as Hamlet," *NYDM*, May 13, 1899, 17. Meanwhile in London, Mrs. Patrick Campbell created the young male lead in the first English language production of Rostand's *Les Romanesques* ("The Stage in Europe," *New York Sun*, April 8, 1900, 12). This play was adapted decades later into the minimusical *The Fantastics*.

92   Sarah Bernhardt, "Men's Roles as Played by Women."

93   H. Chance Newton, "Miss Ellen Terry and Her Art," *Sketch* 35 (July 31, 1901): 75–76.

94   Bram Stoker, *Famous Imposters* (London: Sidgwick and Jackson, 1910), 227.

95   Lifson, *Yiddish*, 152, 157.

96   Elizabeth Reitz Mullenix, "*A Doublet and Hose in My Disposition*," 106; Booth, *Theatre*, 130–31. In 1903, Sadayakko put on European breeches as the juvenile lead in her children's play, *Ukare kokyū* [Violin on a spree] (Yanagi Eijirō, *Ebanzuke*, 258).

97   "The Cadets' 'Miladi and the Musketeer,'" *Boston Herald*, January 14, 1900, 26; "Plays and Players," *Boston Herald*, January 19, 1896, 10.

98   "This Year's Cadet Theatricals," *Boston Herald*, January 7, 1900, 4:34.

99   Ibid.; W. F. A[pthrop], "Music and Drama," *Boston Evening Transcript*, February 6, 1900, 9.

100 "This Year's Cadet Theatricals," *Boston Herald*.

101 "Music and Drama," *Boston Evening Transcript*, February 3, 1900, 20; also "The Cadet Play," *Boston Daily Advertiser*, February 6, 1900, 8; W. F. A[pthrop], "Music and Drama," *Boston Evening Transcript*, February 6, 1900, 9.

102 "Cadet Theatricals," advertisement, *Boston Herald*, February 4, 1900, 2:15; The Cadet Play," *Boston Daily Advertiser*; "The Cadets' 'Miladi and the Musketeer,'" *Boston Herald*; "Music and Drama," *Boston Evening Transcript*, February 3, 1900, 20.

103 W. F. A[pthrop], "Music and Drama," *Boston Evening Transcript*, December 19, 1996, 7. Concurring opinion in Jason, "Harvard's French Play," *Leslie's Weekly* (December 23, 1899): 517.

104 W. F. A[pthrop], "Music and Drama," *Boston Evening Transcript*, February 6, 1900, 9.

105 "Boston College Men in a Shakespeare Play," *Boston Globe*, December 18, 1899, 5. Jay Benton, in "Telegraphic News. Boston," *NYDM*, December 30, 1899, 10, suggested that the ban on impersonating woman was lifted at Boston College but several local newspapers reported otherwise. Other male colleges that prohibited female impersonation by students cast faculty wives or hired actresses. The latter practice aroused moral apprehension because male students had to associate with professional actresses.

106 "Boston College Men in a Shakespeare Play," *Boston Globe*.

107 "Echoes from the Green Room," *Theatre* (London) 28 (July 1, 1896): 57. In this production, *Hamlet* was performed in Latin. Evidence was not conclusive that it was at Boston College.

108 "Boston College Men in a Shakespeare Play," *Boston Globe*.

109 Kaneo, *Ōbei*, 32–33.

110 "Japanese Are Good Actors," *San Francisco Bulletin*, June 19, 1899, 6; "Geisha and the Knight," *Tacoma Daily Ledger*, September 22, 1899, 3; "Amusements," *Seattle Daily Times*, September 14, 1899, 3. Printed programs also listed Mikami as "Miss Shigeri." This was a slight feminization or misspelling of his male familiar name, Shigeru (Muskegon Opera House, program, November 15, 1899, in R977.457 Opap, Hackley Public Library, Muskegon; Copley Hall, Boston, program, Saturday, January 6, 1900, "The Japanese Players," in program file: Zingoro, BRTC). "Miss Shigera" was used in "Around the Playhouses. The Japanese Players," *Boston Globe*, December 19, 1899, 9 and "Japanese Dramatic Company," *Boston Globe*, December 19, 1899, 2.

111 "First Japanese Actress to Appear in America," *San Francisco Bulletin*, June 18, 1899, 12; "Drama of Japan," *Seattle Daily Times*, September 16, 1899, 8; "There is a vast difference," *Seattle Post-Intelligencer*, September 17, 1899, 18.

112 "The Stage," *Toledo Bee*, November 26, 1899, 10; also Leroy M. Scott, "The Players from the Land of Sunrise," *Chicago Journal*, November 9, 1899, 4.

113 See Noguchi Yonejirō's poem, "Onnagata," in Chapter 5.

114 "The Period. The Gaiety Theatre," *Far East* (Yokohama) 2:14 (December 16, 1871): 168, 170, and other

issues reporting Yokohama amateur theatricals. Although few Japanese went to this foreigners' theatre, early theatre reformers may have been among them. Professional foreign theatre companies on tour with actresses began to play Japan only after 1890 and these were seen by Japanese (Masumoto, *Yokohama*, and Masumoto, *Yokohama*, [vol.] 2). Even the earliest performance of Western-aping shingeki in the 1900s sometimes had male actors playing females.

115   Amy Koritz, "Moving Violations: Dance in the London Music Hall, 1890–1910," *Theatre Journal* 42:4 (December 1990): 426.

116   Gilbert, *American*, 167.

117   Marybeth Hamilton, "'I'm the Queen on the Bitches;' Female Impersonation and Mae West's *Pleasure Man*," in Ferris, *Crossing*, 108.

118   Bud Coleman, "The Jewel Box Revue: America's Longest Running Touring Drag Show," *Theatre History Studies* 17 (1997): 80; "Music and Drama," *Boston Evening Transcript*, February 3, 1900, 20.

119   Sarah Bernhardt, "Men's Roles as Played by Women," *Harper's Bazar* 33 (December 15, 1900): 2,114.

120   Yoko Takakuwa, "The Performance of Gendered Identity in Shakespeare and Kabuki," in Sasayama, *Shakespeare*, 202.

121   Stanhope Sams, "Lady of the Japonicas," *Collier's* (August 19, 1911): 21. The feminine voice of onnagata Kitamura Rokurō as a thirty-year-old geisha can be heard on Kitamura, *Engeki*. Kitamura was eighty when this recording was made.

122   Hanayagi Shōtarō, *Yakusha*, 180–85, 188–89, 243–44; Kawai, *Onnagata*, 237–42.

123   The playwrights and managers of shimpa were still men.

124   Mizutani Yaeko headed the consolidated postwar shimpa troupe. She was succeeded by her daughter, who is now Mizutani Yaeko II.

125   Womanliness = onnarashisa.

126   P[ierre] [J]oseph Proudhon, *La pornocratie, ou les femmes dans les temps moderns* (Paris: Lacroix, 1875), 152.

127   Despite my apparent negativity in this chapter, this is not an argument for abolition of onnagata anywhere. I want to see kabuki with male onnagata and, although nearly impossible today, I want to see shimpa with male onnagata mixed with its female actors.

Chapter 16

1   Shattuck, *Shakespeare*, 2:95–99.

2   Causerie, "Have Actors Gone out of Fashion?" *Toledo Daily Blade*, November 25, 1899, 10.

3   "The Stage," *Washington Times*, January 21, 1900, 2:4.

4   Charles Darwin felt, "It is generally admitted that with women the powers of intuition, of rapid perception, and perhaps of imitation, are more strongly marked than in man" (Darwin, *The Descent of Man, and Selection in Relation to Sex* [1871; reprint Princeton: Princeton University Press, 1981], 2:326).

5   Dijkstra, *Idols*, 120.

6   Davis, *Actresses*, 71.

7   Stokes, *Bernhardt*, 2.

8   Dijkstra, *Idols*, 25–32. Richard Findlater, "Bernhardt and the British Player Queens: A Venture into Comparative Theatrical Mythology," in Salmon, *Bernhardt*, 92–97.

9   *Magda* was the American title of Hermann Sudermann's *Heimat*.

10   Dijkstra, *Idols*, 29, 38, 50–53.

11   Modjeska commissioned this play from Clinton Stuart ("Music and Drama. Marie Antoinette," *New York Evening Post*, March 2, 1900, 7).

12   Henry Austin Clapp, "Madame Modjeska," *Boston Daily Advertiser*, January 9, 1900, 8.

13   Coleman, *Fair*, 757–60.

14   Tompkins, *History*, 6; Coleman, *Fair*, 753.

15   W. F. A[pthrop], "Music and Drama. Boston Theatre: 'Much Ado about Nothing,'" *Boston Evening Transcript*, January 4, 1900, 11. Writing decades later, theatre historians still agreed (Shattuck, *Shakespeare*, 2:132).

16   Henry Austin Clapp, "Madame Modjeska and Mr. Kellerd in 'Macbeth,'" *Boston Daily Advertiser*, January 8, 1900, 7.

17   W. F. A[pthrop], "Music and Drama. Boston Theatre: 'Much Ado about Nothing,'" *Boston Evening Transcript*; Henry Austin Clapp, "Mme. Modjeska," *Boston Daily Advertiser* January 4, 1900, 5.

18   "Boston after Dark," *Boston Traveler*, January 17, 1900, 4.

19   Shattuck, *Shakespeare*, 2:128.

20   McArthur, *Actors*, 170–71.

21   "Massachusetts, Boston," *NYC*, January 13, 1900, 961; "Amusements. Boston Theatre," *Boston Evening Record*, January 2, 1900, 5; "Massachusetts, Boston," *NYC*, January 20, 1900, 980.

22   "Boston after Dark," *Boston Traveler*; Henry Austin Clapp, "Madame Modjeska and Mr. Kellerd in 'Macbeth,'" *Boston Daily Advertiser*.

23   Carlyle Walthers, "Mrs. Carter's Triumph," *Chicago Dramatic Magazine* (July 1899): n.p.; Richard Findlater, "Bernhardt and the British Player Queens: A Venture into Comparative Theatrical Mythology," in Salmon, *Bernhardt*. 95. The Trilby-Svengali relationship was used elsewhere to describe female protégés of domineering producers and actors (see Dave Russell, "Varieties of Life: The Making of the Edwardian Music Hall," in Booth, *Theatre*, 39). The analogy referred to Herbert Beerbohm Tree's 1895 production of a dramatization of George Du Maurier's novel, *Trilby*. Belasco and Carter had no connection with any production of *Trilby*.

24   George T. Richardson, "Mrs. Leslie Carter in 'Zaza,' a Rather Fervid Play," *Boston Traveler*, January 2, 1900, 4; Young, *Famous*, 1:163.

25   "Hollis St. Theatre," *Boston Journal*, January 2, 1900, 5; "A Vance Thompson Rhapsody."

26   L. B. G., "The postponement of 'Quo Vadis' for one night," unidentified New York newspaper, c. March 1900, in RLS NAFR+ v. 101, p. 91, BRTC.

27   "Camille Was Bad, Zaza Only a Woman," *New York World*, January 15, 1899, n.p.

28   "Five New Plays," *Boston Globe*, January 2, 1900, 8; Henry Austin Clapp, "Hollis St. Theatre," *Boston Daily Advertiser*, January 2, 1900, 5.

29   "Hollis Street Theatre," *Boston Journal*, January 2, 1900, 5.

30   "Music and Drama. Mrs. Carter's Career," *Boston Evening Transcript*, December 30, 1899, 27. Crow eaters: "Hollis St. Theatre," *Boston Traveler*, January 20, 1900, 5; Lewis C. Strang, "At the Play," *Boston Journal*, January 21, 1900, 2:2; "The Man with the Lorgnette," *Boston Evening Record*, January 11, 1900, 5; "Notes," *Boston Daily Advertiser*, January 11, 1900, 5; "Five New Plays," *Boston Globe*.

31   "Notes," *Boston Daily Advertiser*. Henry Austin Clapp, "Hollis St. Theatre," *Boston Daily Advertiser*, January 2, 1900, 5.

32   "The Man with the Lorgnette," *Boston Evening Record*.

33   Mullin, *Victorian*, 104; also Henry Austin Clapp, "Hollis St. Theatre," *Boston Daily Advertiser*; Young, *Famous*, 1:164.

34   L. B. G., "The postponement of 'Quo Vadis' for one night," unidentified New York newspaper, c. March 1900 and "A Vance Thompson Rhapsody." Also "'Zaza' and Mrs. Leslie Carter," in *Famous Actors*, 202.

35   George T. Richardson, "Mrs. Leslie Carter in 'Zaza,' a Rather Fervid Play," *Boston Traveler*, January 2, 1900, 4. Similar objections in "Leslie Carter a Success in Zaza," *New York Morning Telegraph*, December 29, 1898, n.p

36 "Five New Plays," *Boston Globe*, January 2, 1900, 8.

37 George T. Richardson, "Mrs. Leslie Carter in 'Zaza,' a Rather Fervid Play," *Boston Traveler*; also "Five New Plays," *Boston Globe*, January 2, 1900, 8.

38 "Music and Drama. Mrs. Carter's Career," *Boston Evening Transcript*, December 30, 1899, 27; Robinson, *Notable*, 114; *American Stage*, n.p. Robinson, *Notable*, 115; "'Zaza' and Mrs. Leslie Carter," in *Famous Actors*, 203–5; Young, *Famous*, 1:164.

39 William Winter quoted by Richard Moody, "American Actors and Acting before 1900: The Making of a Tradition" in Williams, *American*, 70.

40 "'Zaza' and Mrs. Leslie Carter," in *Famous Actors*, 202; Young, *Famous*, 1:163; Lewis C. Strang, "At the Play," *Boston Journal*, January 21, 1900, 2:2; *The American Stage Today*, n.p.; "Notes and Comment," *Boston Evening Transcript*, December 6, 1899, 18.

41 Grein, *Premieres*, 213.

42 Robinson, *Notable*, 114–16; *American Stage*, n.p.; *Who Was Who*, 1:399–400; "A Vance Thompson Rhapsody."

43 "Mrs. Fiske as Becky Sharp," *Boston Traveler*, January 2, 1900, 5; "The Man with the Lorgnette," *Boston Evening Record*, January 12, 1900, 5; "Continuance of Many of the Sterling Attractions Now Running at the Theatres," *Boston Post*, January 7, 1900, 16; Binns, *Mrs. Fiske*, 96–97; Tremont Theatre, Boston, program, week of January 1, 1900, in Tremont Theatre programs **T.10.27, RBD BPL; "Five New Plays," *Boston Globe*, January 2, 1900, 8; "With the Players," *Brooklyn Eagle*, August 13, 1899, n.p.

44 "Mrs. Fiske as Becky Sharp," *Boston Traveler*; *The Picture Book of Becky Sharp* (Chicago: Stone, 1899), n.p.

45 "Amusements," *Boston Evening Record*, January 12, 1900, 5; also "Five New Plays," *Boston Globe*; "Mrs. Fiske as Becky Sharp," *Boston Traveler*; Henry Austin Clapp, "Becky Sharp," *Boston Daily Advertiser*, January 2, 1900, 5. Langdon Mitchell wrote the adaptation.

46 Most enthusiastic: "Mrs. Fiske as Becky Sharp," *Boston Traveler*; Henry Austin Clapp, "Becky Sharp," *Boston Daily Advertiser*.

47 "The Man with the Lorgnette," *Boston Evening Record*, January 12, 1900, 5.

48 "Mrs. Fiske as Becky Sharp," *Boston Traveler*.

49 Ibid.; "Five New Plays," *Boston Globe*, January 2, 1900, 8.

50 "Two Schools of Acting," *Boston Herald*, January 22, 1896, n.p.

51 Leslie, *Some*, 105–6; "With the Players," *Brooklyn Eagle*, August 13, 1899, n.p.; Crawford, *Romance*, 474; Forrest Lizard, *Heroines of the Modern Stage* (New York: Sturgis and Walton, 1915), 270–71; *Who Was Who*, 842–43.

52 "The Becky Sharpe [*sic*] Case," *NYDM*, October 20, 1900, 8.

53 Binns, *Mrs. Fiske*, 79, 88–99, 111–12; Strang, *Players*, 2:217. Later, when Ellen Terry urged G. B. Shaw to let the Fiskes produce the American premiere of his *Captain Brassbound's Conversion*, the socialist playwright refused on the grounds that he would earn more money from a production controlled by the Theatrical Syndicate.

54 Robinson, *Notable*, 284–85; *Who Was Who*, 842–43; "With the Players," *Brooklyn Eagle*.

55 Frank Carlos Griffith, *Mrs. Fiske* (New York: Neale, 1912), 110; *Who Was Who*, 842–43; Wilmeth, *Guide*, 183.

56 Winter, *Wallet*, 2:594.

57 Minnie Madden Fiske, "Tricks of the Trade," unidentified newspaper, in RLS NAFR + v. 202, p. 15, BRTC.

58 Patty S. Derrick, "Julia Marlowe an Actress Caught between Traditions," *Theatre Survey* 32 (May 1991): 88; McArthur, *Actors*, 175–76. An earlier evaluation was in Leslie, *Some*, 105.

59 Pendennis, "Minnie Madden Fiske on Her Art, Her Critics, and Her Plans," unidentified newspaper, n.d., in RLS NAFR+ v. 203, p. 57, BRTC. The 1915 film *Vanity Fair* (directed by Eugene Nowland, produced

by Thomas A. Edison, Inc.) demonstrated that in an era when most film acting was excessive gesture, Fiske's subtle acting and natural grace contrasted with that of her co-players (based on my viewing of the film).

60   Crawford, *Romance*, 475.

61   Robinson, *Notable*, 285–86.

62   Brockett, *History*, 427.

63   The Rounder, "The Art of Cissie Loftus, Almost Complete Deception," *Boston Traveler*, December 9, 1899, 5.

64   Ibid., "At Boston Playhouses. Keith's Theatre," *Boston Journal*, December 5, 1899, 5; "In Boston Playhouses. Keith's Theatre," *Boston Herald*, December 12, 1899, 9; "New Plays," *Boston Evening Record*, December 2, 1899, 5; "Keith's Theatre," *Boston Daily Advertiser*, December 5, 1899, 8; "Music and Drama. Keith's Theatre: Vaudeville," *Boston Evening Transcript*, December 19, 1899, 7; Lyceum Theatre, New York, program, week of April 9, 189[9?], in Scrapbook MWEZ+ n.c. 13,443, BRTC.

65   The Rounder, "The Art of Cissie Loftus, Almost Complete Deception."

66   Greenbank, *Geisha*, 120–22; Gänzl, *British*, 1:585–90, 1:619–22; Bordman, *American Musical*, 145.

67   "Cissie Loftus Scores a Hit," *New York Telegraph*, January 3, 1899. Despite its great popularity in Britain, *The Shop Girl* failed in the United States (Gänzl, *British*, 1:518–23). I found no evidence that Loftus did the dance when she sang the song.

68   Lyceum Theatre, New York, program, week of April 9, 189[9?], in scrapbook MWEZ+ n.c. 13,443, BRTC.

69   Alice C. D. Riley, lyricist; Jessie L. Gaynor, composer, "The Jap Doll" (Chicago: Summy, 1898). I could not conclusively establish that "The Japanese Dollee" sung by Loftus and "The Jap Doll" (lyrics in this text) were the same.

70   December 11–16, 1899.

71   Slout, *Theatre*, 72; Bordman, *American Theatre*, 452.

72   Walt M'Dougall, "Rose Melville as 'Sis Hopkins,'" unidentified New York newspaper, November 27, 1899, in RLS NAFR+ v. 347, p. 9, BRTC; "Grand Opera House," *Boston Daily Advertiser*, December 12, 1899, 5.

73   "Grand Opera House," *Boston Daily Advertiser*; "Rose Melville as a Star," *Boston Traveler*, December 12, 1899, 5.

74   "Rose Melville as a Star," *Boston Traveler*, Alan Dale, "Rose Melville in a 3-Act Play," *New York Journal*, November 23, 1899, n.p.

75   "At the Theatres. Herald Square—By the Sad Sea Waves," *NYDM*, March 11, 1899, 16.

76   "Grand Dime," *Boston Evening Record*, November 28, 1899, 7; "Bowdoin Sq.," *Boston Evening Record*, January 23, 1900, 15; "Drama and Music. 'On the Wabash,'" *Boston Globe*, January 21, 1900, 18. After the touring company of *On the Wabash* (that had shared the Lyric Theatre in Chicago with Kawakami) failed on the road, the script became available to local stock companies.

77   " -day's Weather," *Boston Daily Advertiser*, December 18–31, 1899, 1; "The Weather," *Boston Journal*, December 27, 1899, January 1, 1900, 1; "Snow Carnival on the Boulevard," *Boston Post*, January 1900, 3.

78   "Japanese Players," *Boston Globe*, December 24, 1899, 18; "The Man with the Lorgnette," *Boston Evening Record*, December 29, 1899, 5.

79   "Gossip," *Boston Dramatic Review* 6 (January 1900): 13.

80   "The Japanese Players," *Boston Evening Transcript*, January 2, 1900, 11.

81   "Note and Comment," *Boston Evening Transcript*, January 1, 1900, 9; "Japanese Players at Copley Hall," *Boston Globe*, January 2, 1900, 8; "Players from Far Japan," *Boston Journal*, January 7, 1900, 4:4; John T. Warde, "Telegraphic News. Washington," *NYDM*, February 3, 1900, 12.

82   R. H. Ives Gammell, *The Boston Painters 1900–1930* (Orleans, Massachusetts: Parnassus, 1986), 21;

Boston Directory 1900, 1,764–65; Jean N. Oliver, "The Copley Society of Boston," *New England* 34 (January 1905): 608–14.

83 "No Longer a Dream," *Boston Globe*, February 25, 1894, 28; also "Harvard's French Play," *Boston Post*, December 13, 1899, 16; "Copley Hall: The Orchestral Club," *Boston Evening Transcript*, February 3, 1900, 20; S. Foster Damon, *Amy Lowell: A Chronicle* (Boston: Houghton Mifflin, 1935), 105; "Night of Merriment in Copley Hall," *Boston Globe*, December 22, 1899, 5. The hall could hold two thousand for a crowded dance, but its capacity as an auditorium was much less. The small stage was twenty-five feet across.

84 *Boston Directory 1900*, 710; Bromley, *Atlas*, 19; *The Copley Society of Boston: The First 100 Years in Review* (Boston: Copley Society, 1982), 11; Gammell, *The Boston Painters*, 21. Grundmann Studios at Clarenton and St. James Streets was torn down in a 1920s reconfiguration of Boston streets. I. M. Pei's 1976 mirror-windowed John Hancock tower now sits on the site.

85 "The Japanese Dramatic Co.," advertisement, *Boston Evening Transcript*, January 1, 1900, 5.

86 Ibid.; "Copley Hall," advertisement, *Boston Herald*, January 2, 1900, 9; "Japanese Players," *Boston Herald*, January 8, 1900, 6. Comstock remained the producer of record.

87 "The Japanese Dramatic Co.," advertisement, *Boston Evening Transcript*, January 1, 1900, 5; "Copley Hall," advertisement, *Boston Herald*, January 8, 1900, 6. The decrease in the scale suggested resistance to the $1.50 tickets.

88 "The Japanese Dramatic Co.," advertisement, *Boston Evening Transcript*, January 1, 1900, 5; "Japanese Players at Copley Hall," *Boston Globe*, January 2, 1900, 8; "The Japanese Players," *Boston Evening Transcript*, January 2, 1900, 11; Kaneo, *Ōbei*, 28; Copley Hall, Boston, program, January 4 and 6, 1900, "The Japanese Players," in clipping file: Kawakami, HTC.

89 "Music and Drama," *Boston Evening Transcript*, December 29, 1899, 7.

90 "The Japanese Players," *Boston Evening Transcript*, December 27, 1899, 13.

91 Ibid.

92 "The Japanese Players," *Boston Evening Transcript*, January 2, 1900, 11.

93 Fujita Hiroshi, *Nihon*, 92, 102–18, 215–20; Sakakibara, *Nihon*, 21–25, 59–62, 162–67; Hanayagi Chiyo, *Nihon buyō*, 90–120; Suzuki, *Way*, 66–67.

94 Field, *Through*, 17–18; David Wilmore, "The Substage Equipment at Her Majesty's, London," *Theatre Notebook* 52 (1998): 39.

95 Brazel, *Traditional*, 398–407; Kabuki-za, Tōkyō, program, month of July 1975, 17–19; Fujita Chiyo, *Nihon buyō*, 74, 215–19.

96 The nō version developed from Shintō purification dances.

97 Toyoichirō Nogami, *Zeami and His Theories on Noh*, trans. Matsumoto Ryōzō (Hinoki Shoten, 1985), 4–5; Fujita Chiyo, *Nihon buyō*, 74–75, 215–20; James R. Brandon, "Form in Kabuki Acting," in Brandon, *Studies*. 23. There is a *kyōgen* version also titled *Sambasō*.

98 Fujita Chiyo, *Nihon buyō*, 216.

99 Leiter, *Kabuki Encyclopedia*, 325–26; Dunn, *Actors'*, 20; Fujita Chiyo, *Nihon buyō*, 215.

100 James R. Brandon, "Form in Kabuki Acting," in Brandon, *Studies*, 83.

101 Copley Hall, Boston, program, January 6, 1900, "The Japanese Players," in program file: Zingoro, BRTC.

102 Kaneo, *Ōbei*, 6, 44; Makimura, *Kawakami*, 2:131; Iwai, *Shimpa*, 136.

103 "Music and Drama," *Boston Evening Transcript*, December 29, 1899, 7; "Music and Drama," *Boston Evening Transcript*, December 29, 1899, 7; "The Japanese Players," *Boston Evening Transcript*, January 2, 1900, 11.

104 "Drama of Japan," *Seattle Daily Times*, September 16, 1899, 8.

105 Leroy M. Scott, "Players from the Land of Sunrise," *Chicago Journal*, November 9, 1899, 4.

106 Copley Hall, Boston, programs for January 4 and 6, 1900, "The Japanese Players," in clipping file: Kawakami, HTC.

107   "Players from Far Japan," *Boston Journal*, January 7, 1900, 4:4; Jean N. Oliver, "The Jap. Artists' Visit to the Grundmann Studios," *Boston Evening Record*, January 8, 1900, n.p.; "Japanese Actor Dead," *Boston Morning Journal*, January 31, 1900, 2; Kaneo, *Sadayakko*, 22.

108   Copley Hall, Boston, programs for January 4 and 6, 1900. The unresolved confusion (for me) was caused by 1) the decrease in Boston newspaper coverage because critics had already reviewed most of the Kawakami productions; 2) conflicting accounts in the two Kaneo (*Ōbei* and *Sadayakko*) texts; 3) contradictory listings in surviving printed programs; and 4) frequent last-minute changes of bills.

109   Kaneo, *Ōbei*, 27–28, 34; Iwai, *Shimpa*, 171, 186. Both Fujikawa and Yamamoto joined Kawakami's troupe in 1894 and stayed with him for many years. Fujikawa later became a clerical employee of Sadayakko. Yamamoto entered films as a character actor and became a silent movie star.

110   "Those Japanese Players," *Boston Herald*, December 12, 1899, 9.

111   K. K. Kawakami, "The Japanese in New England," *New England* 35 (December 1906): 442.

112   Edward S. Morse, *Japanese Homes and Their Surroundings* (c. 1888; reprint, Rutland, Vermont: Tuttle, 1972), xxxvii.

113   Hosley, *Japan*, 111; Orvell, *Real*, 42–43.

114   Morse, *Japanese Homes*, 309–10. This "accumulated misery," as Morse called the home collections, was frequently reflected in a large mirror that doubled the apparent multitude of things.

115   Orvell, *Real*, xv–xvi.

116   Hosely, *Japan*, 38–40, 55–58, 75.

117   Some of the most expensive of these folding screens are seen in paintings of wealthy Boston interiors (Trevor J. Fairbrother, *The Bostonians: Painters of an Elegant Age, 1870–1930* [Boston: Museum of Fine Arts, 1986], 149–55; also Wichmann, *Japonisme*, 155).

118   "Japanese Players," *Boston Globe*, December 24, 1899, 18; also Tremont Theatre, Boston, program, December 14, 1899, *Zingoro* and *Tajo* [*Kesa*], in clipping file: Kawakami, HTC; Tremont Theatre, Boston, program, week of December 25, 1899, 25, in Tremont Theatre programs **T.10.27, RBD BPL; "The Japanese Players," *Boston Evening Transcript*, December 27, 1899, 13.

119   "Japanese Players," *Boston Globe*; "The Japanese Players," *Boston Evening Transcript*.

120   "Boston Theatre: 'Zingoro' and 'Soga,'" *Boston Evening Transcript*, January 19, 1900, 9; Tremont Theatre, Boston, program, Thursday afternoon, December 14, 1899, *Zingoro* and *Tajo* [*Kesa*], in clipping file: Kawakami, HTC.

121   "The Japanese Dramatic Co.," advertisement, *Boston Evening Transcript*, January 1, 1900, 5; "Notes and Comment," *Boston Evening Transcript*, January 1, 1900, 9.

122   "Copley Hall," advertisement, *Boston Herald*, January 2, 1900, 9.

123   Chisholm, *Fenollosa*, 89.

124   Patricia Jobe Pierce, *Edmund C. Tarbell and the Boston School of Painting, 1889–1980* (Hingham, Massachusetts: Pierce Galleries, 1980), 30–31, 35.

125   Jonathan Swift, *Gulliver's Travels* (1726; reprint, New York: Dodd, Mead, 1950), 220–22.

126   Josef Kreiner, "Changing Images: Japan and the Ainu as Perceived in Europe," in *Rethinking Japan; Volume 2: Social Sciences, Ideology, and Thought*, eds. Adriana Boscaro, et al. (New York: St. Martin's, 1990), 135–38.

127   European searches for earthly paradises were explored in Henri Baudet, *Paradise on Earth: Some Thoughts on European Images of Non-European Man*; Earl Miner, *The Japanese Tradition in British and American Literature*, 42–43; La Farge, *Artist's*, vii; O'Toole, *Five*, 172–73; Adams, *Letters*, 3:12. Toshio Yokoyama, in his *Japan in the Victorian Mind* (London: Macmillian, 1987), 175, found that from 1880, British concepts about Japan turned increasingly toward the idea that the country was "an elf-land."

128   Lowell, *Soul*, 9, also 7. After returning to Boston, Lowell lost his interest in Japan as paradise. He took off for Arizona where for escape he looked up at the heavens through his telescope and confirmed (for

himself) the existence of canals on Mars. Later, he accurately calculated the location of the unseen (now former) planet Pluto.

129 All material from J. L. Anderson, "*The Mikado* Hits Boston," a draft excised to shorten this book.

130 Patricia Jobe Pierce, *Edmund C. Tarbell and the Boston School of Painting, 1889–1980*, 30–31, 35.

131 "No Longer a Dream," *Boston Globe*, February 25, 1894, 28; Erica E. Hirshler, *A Studio of Her Own: Women Artists in Boston: 1870–1940* (Boston: Museum of Fine Arts, 2001), 45–46, 51, 67, 73.

132 "Grundmann Studios," *Providence Journal*, December 11, 1898, 14.

133 Ibid.

134 "Players from Far Japan," *Boston Journal*, January 7, 1900, 4:4. Oliver was affiliated with the American Arts and Crafts movement that had been inspired in part by Japanese craftwork (Karen Evans Ulehla, ed., *The Society of Arts and Crafts, Boston, Exhibition Record 1897–1927* [Boston: Boston Public Library, 1981], 164; Hosley, *Japan*, 169).

135 Jean N. Oliver, "The Jap. Artists' Visit to the Grundmann Studios," *Boston Evening Record*, January 8, 1900, 6.

136 K. K. Kawakami, "The Japanese in New England," *New England* 35 (December 1906): 40–44.

137 Jean N. Oliver, "The Jap. Artists' Visit to the Grundmann Studios," *Boston Evening Record*.

138 Ibid.

139 "Players from Far Japan," *Boston Journal*, January 7, 1900, 4:4; also Janice H. Chadbourne, Karl Gabosh, and Charles O. Vogel, *The Boston Art Club: Exhibition Record 1873–1909* (Madison, Connecticut: Sound View, 1991), 194. Green tea, the national beverage of Japan, was very popular in Boston.

140 "Players from Far Japan," *Boston Journal*. Although Kawakami did not attend the reception, he briefly mentioned it in Kawakami Otojirō, "Kawakami Otojirō yori sa no raishin ari" [The following letter from Kawakami Otojirō], *Miyako shimbun*, February 15, 1900, in Shirakawa, 311.

Chapter 17

1 Despite Kawakami's prolonged absence, the troupe premiered its often announced, often postponed, undeveloped, and under rehearsed "new play," *Soga*, on a bill with *Sambasō* on January 11 ("Notes and Comment," *Boston Evening Transcript*, January 12, 1900, 9; Kaneo, *Ōbei*, 28). Definitive evidence about all the plays performed during the second week at Copley Hall could not be found. *Soga* may have been cancelled.

2 Kaneo, *Ōbei*, 28.

3 It was possible that rather than one long confinement, Kawakami was in and out of the hospital more than once.

4 Natsume, *And Then*, 72, 73.

5 Boston Theatre, program, week of January 15, 1900, *The Musketeers*, in Boston Theatre playbills **T.10.1, RBD BPL.

6 "The Man with the Lorgnette," *Boston Evening Record*, January 18, 1900, 5; Kaneo, *Ōbei*, 28–29.

7 "Music and Drama," *Boston Evening Transcript*, January 18, 1900, 9; also "The Man with the Lorgnette," *Boston Evening Record*.

8 Takahashi, "Zadankai," 83.

9 Chamberlain, *Japanese*, 455.

10 Gilbert, *American*, 199–200.

11 "At the Theatres. Star—The Mikado," *NYDM*, May 14, 1898, 14.

12 Weldon B. Durham, "The Revival and Decline of the Stock Company Mode of Organization 1886–1930," *Theatre History Studies* 6 (1986): 173; "At the Theatres. Columbus—The Silver King," *NYDM*, April 29, 1899, 16.

13 In twenty-first century Japan, *taishū engeki* troupes dressed in their costumes greet and thank patrons leaving a theatre after a performance.

14 Craig, *Henry*, 154.

15 Field, *Through*, 6. Kawakami and his company were not the first Japanese to appear at the Boston Theatre. Coming from San Francisco thirty-three years earlier, Professor Risley's Imperial Japanese Troupe of acrobats played on the same stage for two weeks (Tompkins, *History*, 134).

16 "At Boston Playhouses. Boston Theatre," *Boston Journal*, January 16, 1900, 5; Boston Theatre, program, week of January 15, 1900, in Boston Theatre playbills **T.10.1, RBD BPL.

17 Field, *Through*, 21; "Theatres," in *Boston of Today*, 96; Leverton, *Production*, 12.

18 Cahn, *Theatrical 1899–1900*, 67, 71.

19 Ibid., 23–53, 69–77, 143–56; Leverton, *Production*, 9; Sean McCarthy, "Exit the Boxes," *Tabs* (London: Strand Electric) 25:3 (September 1967): 10.

20 Kawatake Shigetoshi, *Engeki hyakka*, 2:92. The Tokyo Kabuki-za of the Shōwa era had an effective width of seventy-eight feet.

21 Tompkins, *History*, 8.

22 Quoted in Booth, *Theatre*, 124.

23 Based on my exploration in the mid-1940s of a large American theatrical warehouse filled with stock sets from the 1910s and earlier; also "Scrapbook: "Plays to June 1905," MWEX+ n.c. 297, photos pp. 44, 68, 78, 165, BRTC.

24 Hamamura, *Kabuki*, 40. The settings for old-time small theatres that made Japanese actors seem larger than life are now impossible on the monster stages of contemporary kabuki theatres.

25 Sweetser, *Greater*, 13.

26 Field, *Through*, 6; Tompkins, *History*, 8, 13.

27 Quoted in Tucci, *Boston*, 4; also 2–3, 9–11.

28 Tompkins, *History*, 8–9, 13, 431; Grandgent, "Stage," 391. The clock showed the time in numbers that changed each minute with a mechanism like that in the non-video arrival-departure boards of modern train terminals.

29 "The Matinee Girl," *NYDM*, March 10, 1900, 2. The management of the Boston claimed they were the first theatre in America to install folding seats fixed to the floor so people might easily pass in front of each other (Tompkins, *History*, 427–28; McConachie, *Melodramatic*, 201).

30 "The custom of providing water," *Boston Dramatic Review* 6 (December 2, 1899): 1. The Columbia Theatre and the Boston Museum had already stopped serving water at intermissions, but not the Tremont. Also: Wells Hawks, "How Theatres Are Managed. No. 4. The Attachés," *Theatre* (New York) No. 41 (July 1904): 165–56; "Sewell Collins Picks a Half-Dozen Types from Theatres Audiences," *New York Evening Journal*, April 9, 1900, 10. In theatres that offered specialties between acts, there was less incentive for the audience to move around.

31 Hatton, *Henry*, 218.

32 Quoted in Jefferson, *Autobiography*, 285.

33 Atherton Brownell, "Boston Theatres of To-Day," *Bostonian* 2 (September 1895): 658; Tompkins, *History*, 4.

34 Josefita, "Drama," *Argonaut* (San Francisco) June 26, 1899: 10; Ashton Stevens, "Jap Players Present Their Native Drama," *San Francisco Call*, June 19, 1899, 3; "Thespians from Mikado's Land," *San Francisco Examiner*, June 20, 1899, 6; "The Japanese Historical Company Enacting Japanese Drama at the California Theatre," *Wave* 19 (June 24, 1899): 6.

35 "There is a vast difference," *Seattle Post-Intelligencer*, September 17, 1899, 18.

36 "'Geisha and the Knight," *Portland Morning Oregonian*, September 30, 1899, 3; "Amusements. A Japanese

Matinee," *Chicago Daily Inter Ocean*, October 23, 1899, 5; "The Stage," *Toledo Bee*, November 22, 1899, 4; Amy Leslie, "Lazy Week for Theatres. Japanese Actors at Lyric," *Chicago Daily News*, October 23, 1899, 9. In Toledo, a reviewer pointed out the sparseness: "The company carries little or no scenery and the Valentine supply has to be utilized and Orientalized as well as possible" ("The Stage," *Toledo Bee*, November 22, 1899, 4).

37   Tompkins, *History*, 2, 6; 24; Hornblow, *History*, 2:303–4.

38   "Nearly 50 Years of Acting," *Boston Herald*, August 2, 1895, n.p.; "Theatres," in *Boston of Today*, 96. When Booth played Macbeth to Janauschek's German-speaking Lady Macbeth, they discreetly pinched each other when one did not pick up the other's cue.

39   Grandgent, "Stage," 392; Tucci, *Boston*, 4–5; Tomkins, *History*, 416, 429, 434, 453–54, 462, 482.

40   Tomkins, *History*, 419, 472.

41   Ibid., 483; Tucci, *Boston*, 5; "Boston Theatres of To-Day," *Bostonian* 2 (September 1895): 655. Tompkins, who took over the Boston in 1878, was considered the wealthiest theatre manager in the United States (Grandgent, "Stage," 391).

42   Tucci, *Boston*, 6.

43   Leverton, *Production*, 20 fn. 30; *Catalog Sosman*, n.p. Early in the nineteenth century, small American theatres often had only two stock sets to serve all plays: a nondescript exterior drop with trees and a generalized interior (Moody, *America*, 207–8).

44   The principal scenery problem with *Kesa* was its last part which took place inside a Japanese house. Other than the folding screens borrowed from Matsuki, there was no hint how Kawakami staged this Japanese scene using the stock resources of American theatres. In her *Memories and Impressions*, 378, Modjeska discussed her frustration in matching American stock sets to her repertoire of European classics.

45   The dazzling scenic displays now seen in first-class kabuki theatres are a modern development.

46   For instance: Tremont Theatre, Boston, program, week of December 25, 1899, in Tremont Theatre programs **T.10.27, RBD BPL; "Japanese Players," *Boston Globe*, December 24, 1899, 18; "The Japanese Dramatic Co.," advertisement, *Boston Evening Transcript*, January 1, 1900, 5; "The Japanese Players," *Boston Evening Transcript*, January 9, 1900, 9.

47   "Music and Drama," *Boston Evening Transcript*, January 12, 1900, 11; "Notes and Comment," *Boston Evening Transcript*, January 12, 1900, 9. "Japanese Dramatic Company," *Boston Globe*, January 26, 1900, 4.

48   Boston Theatre, program, week of January 15, 1900, in Boston Theatre playbills **T.10.1, RBD BPL; "The Boston Playhouses," *Boston Evening Transcript*, January 18, 1900, 9.

49   Jean N. Oliver, "Japanese Art in Boston," *Boston Evening Transcript*, January 22, 1900, 8.

50   In the United States, the common practice for scene painters was to use a small painting or sketch as a guide when roughing in the composition full scale with charcoal on vertically hung canvas (Leverton, *Production*, 9).

51   Jean N. Oliver, "Japanese Art in Boston."

52   Ibid.

53   See Tsubouchi Hakushi, *Kokugeki*, 412, 414.

54   "Modern Mise-en-Scene," *Saturday Review* (London) (29 March 1890): 376–77.

55   Meisel, *Realizations*, 406.

56   Franklin Fyles, "The Theatre and Its People," *Ladies' Home Journal* (April 1900): 8.

57   Oscar Wilde, "Shakespeare on Scenery," in *Literary Criticism of Oscar Wilde*, ed. Stanley Weintraub (Lincoln: University of Nebraska Press, 1968), 117.

58   Sharf, "Matsuki Chronology," 38; "Breakfast Hour. Japanese Artists' Work," *Boston Daily Advertiser*, February 13, 1900, 8; Gerald D. Bolas, "American Responses to Western-Style Japanese Painting," in *Paris in Japan: The Japanese Encounter with European Painting*, eds. Shûji Takashima and J. Thomas Rimer (St.

Louis: Washington University Press, 1987), 15; *Exhibition of Japanese Paintings in Water Color and Oil: H. Yoshida, H. Nakagawa* (Boston: Museum of Fine Arts, 1900), n.p.; "The Fine Arts," *Boston Evening Transcript*, February 10, 1900, 10.

59   "The Fine Arts," *Boston Evening Transcript*, February 10, 1900, 10.

60   *Exhibition of Japanese Paintings*, n.p.

61   "Breakfast Hour. Japanese Artists' Work," *Boston Daily Advertiser*, February 13, 1900, 8; also "The Fine Arts," *Boston Evening Transcript*, February 10, 1900, 10.

62   Holographic annotations in *Exhibition of Japanese Paintings*, n.p. in Library, Boston: Museum of Fine Arts.

63   Sharf, "Matsuki Chronology," 38–39; Janice H. Chadbourne, Karl Gabosh, and Charles O. Vogel, *The Boston Art Club: Exhibition Record 1873–1909* (Madison, Connecticut: Sound View, 1991), 282, 416.

64   Tremont Theatre, Boston, programs, week of November 27 and December 11, 1899, in Tremont Theatre programs **T.10.27, RBD BPL; see also "The Japanese Players at the Tremont Theatre," *Boston Evening Transcript*, December 9, 1899, 31; "Tremont. Arizona," advertisement, *Boston Herald*, December 12, 1899, 9. *Kusunoki* had the subtitle *The Faithful Servant*.

65   "The Man with the Lorgnette," *Boston Evening Record*, December 27, 1899, 5; "Music and Drama," *Boston Evening Transcript*, December 29, 1899, 7; "The Man with the Lorgnette," *Boston Evening Record*, December 29, 1899, 5.

66   "Hollis Street Theatre," advertisement, *Boston Herald*, November 19, 1899, 15.

67   Changing previous announcements of plays to be presented often resulted from a company's late but usually accurate assessment of what local audiences favored.

68   Boston Theatre, Boston, program, January 18–19, 1900, "The Japanese Dramatic Company," in program file: Zingoro, BRTC. The wording of this Boston Theatre *Jingorō* program was exactly the same as that used for Copley Hall and for the Tremont as early as December 7, 1899. It was apparently copied but not updated (Copley Hall, Boston, program, Saturday, January 6, 1900, "The Japanese Players," in program file: Zingoro, BRTC; Tremont Theatre, Boston, program, Thursday afternoon, December 7, 1899, *Zingoro*; *The Geisha and the Knight*; in Tremont Theatre programs **T.10.27, RBD BPL).

69   Sadayakko had the female lead.

70   Boston Theatre, Boston, program, January 18–19, 1900, "The Japanese Dramatic Company." No evidence was found about how *Soga* was cast for its earlier trial performances at Copley Hall ("Note and Comment," *Boston Evening Transcript*, January 12, 1900, 9; Kaneo, *Ōbei*, 28).

71   Fujine, *Rekishi*, 46; "Boston Theatre: 'Zingoro' and 'Soga,'" *Boston Evening Transcript*, January 19, 1990, 9.

72   Boston Theatre, program, January 18–19, 1900, "The Japanese Dramatic Company."

73   Ibid.; also "Shin'engeki no sossensha" [New Theatre pioneer], *Miyako shimbun*, May 17, 1900, Shirakawa, 317. In the initial part of his *Soga*, Kawakami apparently incorporated large parts of the familiar *Soga no taimen*, including its kabuki dialog and probably duplicating kabuki business (Miller, *Yomigaeru*, p. 40 and record cut 8; Engekikai Henshûbu, *Shibai meiserifu shû* [Engeki Shuppansha, 1974], 76–77).

74   This highly altered act came from *Youchi Soga kariba no akebono* (Soga attack as dawn breaks at the hunting grounds) first produced in either 1874 or 1881. Written for Ichikawa Danjûrō IX by Kawatake Mokuami, the play was popular in the Meiji era (Matsumoto, *Meiji zenki engekiron*, 331). A full text appeared in Kawatake Mokuami, *Youchi Soga kariba no akebono*, in *Mokuami zenshū, daijū-kan* [Complete works of Mokuami, vol. 10], ed. Kawatake Shigetoshi (Shunyōdō, 1925), 231–393]. The play is summarized in Leiter, *Kabuki Encyclopedia*, 438 and Halford, *Kabuki* 374–77.

75   Boston Theatre, program, January 18–19, 1900, "The Japanese Dramatic Company"; "At the Theatres. Bijou–The Japanese Players," *NYDM*, April 7, 1900, 16; "Affairs of the Theatre," *New York Sun*, March 30, 1900, 7. When the troupe later performed the play in New York, the killing of Suketsune occurred offstage.

76 Boston Theatre, program, January 18–19, 1900, "The Japanese Dramatic Company." This description was followed by a detailed account of an actual *seppuku* that was witnessed by invited British diplomats prior to the Meiji Restoration.

77 Carolyn Shipman, "The Japanese Players," *Critic* 36 (April 1900): 330. The author gave no further details about how this was staged.

78 Their widowed mother later married a man named Soga who adopted her sons.

79 The two other major revenge episodes of Japan are the forty-seven *rōnin* of *Chūshingura* and Araki Mataemon who avenged his father-in-law's murder. The most familiar kabuki version of the latter was Chikamatsu Hanji and Chikamatsu Kasaku's kabuki play, *Igagoe dōchū sugoroku* [Diversion on the way to Igagoe].

80 English language discussions of the historical Soga revenge appear in Thornbury, *Sukeroku's*, 33–54; James T. Araki, *The Ballad-Drama of Medieval Japan* (Berkeley: University of California Press, 1964), 133–39; and *The Tale of the Soga Brothers*, trans. Thomas J. Cogan (Tokyo University Press, 1987), xvi-xxxvii. Kawatake Shigetoshi in *Engeki hyakka*, s.v. "Sogamono" listed numerous Soga plays including twentieth-century dramatizations. Cogan discussed early versions of the story.

81 Kominz, *Avatars*, 2, 8–13, 38–40, 52–54; 87–88, 250–59; Brandon, *Kabuki*, 26. For a translation of a major Soga kabuki play, see Laurence Kominz, "Ya no Ne" [The arrowheads], *Monumenta Nipponica* 38 (Winter 1983): 387–407. The best-known nō play about the Soga brothers was *Youchi Soga* [The Soga attack at night]. Kominz made a translation of this in "The Noh as Popular Theatre: Miyamasu's *Youchi Soga*," *Monumenta Nipponica*, 33:4 (1978): 441–59. A convoluted version of a Soga kabuki play appeared in Frank Alanson Lombard, *Outline History of the Japanese Drama* (1928; reprint, New York: Haskell House, 1966), 191–286.

82 Kominz, *Avatars*, 2, 27–28, 102, 110–52.

83 Halford, *Kabuki*, 463.

84 Suwa Haruo, "Goryō shinkō to aragoto gei" [Spirit belief and the art of *aragoto*], *Bungaku* 47 (August 1979): 15–16; Kominz, *Avatars*, 7, 182.

85 Kominz, *Avatars*, 153–58, 166–75; Kawatake Shigetoshi, *Gaisetsu*, 255–56. For centuries, portrayals of Soga Gorō have been associated with the Ichikawa Danjūrō line of actors.

86 Kominz, *Avatars*, 5–7, 38.

87 Gunji, *Kabuki*, 44; Kominz, *Avatars*, 9, 182–94; Thornbury, *Sukeroku's*, 11.

88 Marui, *Shimpa*, 16, 19, 22.

89 The connection made here with Kawakami's plays at the New Year may be tenuous because *Soga* in Boston was two months too soon by the old Japanese calendar and almost too early for Japan's newly adapted European calendar. Moreover, Kawakami tended to follow Osaka, not Tokyo, theatre practices where seasonal Soga observances did not loom so large.

90 "Amusements," *Boston Evening Record*, January 16, 1900, 5; Henry Austin Clapp, "The Musketeers," *Boston Daily Advertiser*, January 16, 1900, 5.

91 "Mr. James O'Neill," *Collier's Weekly* (January 1917): n.p.; Myron Matlaw, "James O. Neill's Launching of *Monte Cristo*," in Fisher, *When*, 88; "The Drama of Today," *Boston Evening Transcript*, January 13, 1900, 22; Henry Austin Clapp, "The Musketeers," *Boston Daily Advertiser*.

92 Boston Theatre, program, week of January 8, 1900, 6, in Boston Theatre programs, HTC; John Clapp, *Players*, 272; "The Melodramatic James O'Neill," chapter in unidentified book, 166, 171–72, RLS NAFR+ v. 370, BRTC.

93 Broadway Theatre, New York, program, week of March 27, 1899, in RLS NAFR+ v. 43, p. 7, BRTC.

94 A.E.B., "Mirror Interviews. James O'Neill," *NYDM*, February 2, 1895, 2; Young, *Famous*, 2:894–900; *American Stage*, n.p. O'Neill's son Eugene, in his play *Long Days Journey into Night*, explored the agonies of his actor father.

95   Henry Austin Clapp, "The Musketeers," *Boston Daily Advertiser*, January 16, 1900, 5.

96   "Miss Bates Is Angry," unidentified New York newspaper, December 19, 1899, in RLS NAFR+ v. 43, p. 21, BRTC.

97   "At the Theatres. Broadway—The Musketeers," *NYDM*, March 18, 1899, 16; "Maneuvers of the Musketeers," *NYDM*, March 25, 1899, 17; "Miss Bates and O'Neill," unidentified New York newspaper, March 14, 1899, n.p., in RLS NAFR+ v. 43, p. 20, BRTC.

98   "At the Theatres. Star—The Musketeers," *NYDM*, June 10, 1899, 14.

99   Jay Benton, "Telegraphic News. Boston," *NYDM*, April 29, 1899, 12. One production in Boston was by a local stock company, followed by two touring companies coincidentally playing day and date against each other.

100   "Romantic Drama the Feature at the Novelty," *New York Journal*, March 11, 1900, 4B; "'Musketeers' for the Palace Patrons," *New York Press*, March 20, 1900, 7.

101   "At the Theatres. Broadway—The Musketeers," *NYDM*, May 27, 1899, 16; "The Cadets' 'Miladi and the Musketeer,'" *Boston Herald*, January 14, 1900, 26.

102   "The Melodramatic James O'Neill," 166, 171–72, in RLS NAFR+ v. 370, BRTC; Tompkins, *History*, 477.

103   Harrison Grey Fiske, "James O'Neil," in McKay, *Famous*, 2:307–8.

104   "At Boston Playhouses. Boston Theatre," *Boston Journal*, January 16, 1900, 5; Bordman, *American Theatre*, 435.

105   "At Boston Playhouses. Boston Theatre."

106   "O'Neill as Swordsman," *Boston Post*, December 10, 1899, 17.

107   Ibid.

108   Clement Scott, *The Wheel of Life* (London: Greenup, 1897), 57.

109   America theatrical duels typical of the period can be seen in the 1915 Triangle Film *D'Artagnan* (a.k.a. *The Three Musketeers*, Charles Swickard, director; Thomas H. Ince, supervisor). This film had no known connection with O'Neill's stage production or his own motion picture version (Edwin S. Porter, director, *The Three Musketeers*, 1912).

110   W. F. A[pthrop], "Music and Drama. Boston Theatre," *Boston Evening Transcript*, January 16, 1900, 9.

111   [Lewis C. Strang], "At Boston Playhouses. Boston Theatre," *Boston Journal*, January 16, 1900, 5.

Chapter 18

1   Conclusive evidence for one additional performance at Copley Hall was not found and hence not included in this count.

2   Kaneo, *Sadayakko*, 31.

3   "Pari e norikomi" [Embarking for Paris], *Chūō shimbun*, December 28, 1898, in Shirakawa, 295–96; Kawatake Shigetoshi, *Sōgō*, 431.

4   *"Māchanto obu [V]enisu ni tsuite: Kawakami Otojirō no danwa"* [Conversation with Kawakami Otojirō about *The Merchant of Venice*], *Kabuki* (July 1903): 11–13.

5   Kaneo, *Sadayakko* 30–31.

6   Ibid.

7   Kawatake Shigetoshi, *Engeki hyakka*, 2:229.

8   The most frequent kabuki vehicles for *kyōen* were Soga plays and *Chūshingura*. Throughout the twentieth century, shimpa, motion pictures, and kabuki produced many other *kyōen* in competition.

9   "Wants to Reform the Mimic Stage," *Portland Evening Telegram*, September 26, 1899, 3.

10   Kaneo, *Sadayakko*, 30.

11　"Kawakami ichiza yōkō nisshi" [Journal of the foreign tour of the Kawakami troupe], *Miyako shimbun*, July 26, 1900, Shirakawa, 318.

12　Kaneo, *Sadayakko*, 30.

13　Yanagi Keitarō, *Kawakami*, part 4. Kawakami's 1894 hit *Mata igai* [Surprised again] extensively relied on *kuchidate* (Yanagi Eijirō, *Shimpa no rokujūnen*, 13; Muramatsu Shunjichi, *Tabishibai*, 69). James R. Brandon in "Performance and Text in *Kabuki*" in Scholz-Cionca, *Japanese*, 184–85), discussed the importance of ad-libbing and improvisation in kabuki. Plays continue to be produced today in which actors ad-lib without dialogue fixed by a script.

14　"*Māchanto obu [V]enisu* ni tsuite Kawakami Otojirō no danwa," 13.

15　Kaneo, *Sadayakko*, 31; Kaneo, *Ōbei*, 31; "*Māchanto obu [V]enisu* ni tsuite Kawakami Otojirō no danwa."

16　*Beikoku*, 1386.

17　Kaneo, *Ōbei*, 30; Kaneo, *Sadayakko*, 31. "Namu Amida Butsu" = "Hail Amitabha," a Buddhist incantation.

18　Marukawa, *Kawakami*. 43. What Gilbert and Sullivan incorporated into their "Miyasama, Miyasama" was the fife-and-drum march, "Tonyare-bushi," one of the first Japanese compositions transposed into a semi-Western scale (Komota, *Nihon*, 15–17, 197).

19　Artaud, *Theatre*, 86, 98, 100, 124. Kawakami, of course, did not have the exact Artaud purpose of attacking rational and middle-class sensibilities or an objective of restoring theatre "to its original direction, to reinstate it in its religious and metaphysical aspects" (Artaud, *Theatre*, 70).

20　Yamaguchi, *Joyū*, 88. If this source was accurate, Kawakami was already aware of an essential problem faced by the subsequent shingeki movement: how to stage Western plays authentically so they replicated Western life and theatre.

21　"The Japanese Players," *Boston Herald*, January 9, 1900, 9.

22　Jean N. Oliver, "Japanese Art in Boston," *Boston Evening Transcript*, January 22, 1900, 8.

23　Kaneo, *Ōbei*, 29–31; Kaneo, *Sadayakko*, 31–32.

24　Inoue, *Kawakami*, 68; Kawatake Shigetoshi, *Nihon engeki bunka shiwa*, 248; Leiter, *Kabuki Encyclopedia*, 136.

25　Kawatake Shigetoshi, *Nihon engeki bunka shiwa*, 248; Yanagi Eijirō, *Shimpa no rokujūnen*, 13–14.

26　Yanagi Keitarō, *Kawakami*, n.p.

27　Barba, *Secret*, 69.

28　Thomas Rymer, *Short View of Tragedy* (London: Baldwin, 1693), 4.

29　Douglas Arrell, "Palmy Days at the Opera: Traditional Performance Style at Covent Garden in the 1890's," in Salmon, *Bernhardt*, 19–21.

30　Quoted in James W. Flannery, *W. B. Yeats and the Idea of Theatre* (New Haven: Yale University Press, 1976), 190.

31　Toshio Kawatake, *Japan*, 88, 47–48.

32　Kaneo, *Ōbei*, 29–31; Kaneo, *Kawakami*, 31–32; "*Māchanto obu [V]enisu* ni tsuite Kawakami Otojirō no danwa," 15.

33　Dōmon, *Kawakami*, 118–22; Ezaki, *Jitsuroku*, 110; Kawatake Shigetoshi, *Nihon engeki bunka shiwa*, 248; Inoue, *Kawakami*, 68–69; Marukawa, *Kawakami*, 43; Matsunaga, *Kawakami*, 159–60; Miyaoka, *Ikoku*, 71–72; Muramatsu Shōfu, *Kawakami*, 1:288; Ozaki Hirotsugu, *Joyū*, 40; Sugimoto, *Madamu*, 144–46; Toita, *Kindai*, 29; Yamaguchi, *Joyū*, 87–89.

34　Yamaguchi, *Joyū*, 89.

35　Dōmon, *Kawakami*, 118.

36　Jay Benton, "Telegraphic News. Boston," *NYDM*, December 9, 1899, 12; S. Fernberger, "Telegraphic News. Philadelphia," *NYDM*, December 16, 1899, 12.

37	Brereton, *Life*. 2:284; Frederick Kimball, "In Other Cities. Detroit," *NYDM*, February 10, 1900, 3; "The Stage," *Detroit Free Press*, January 26, 1900, 5.

38	*Travelers' Ready Reference Guide* (New York: Knickerbocker, 1897), 127.

39	Kaneo, *Sadayakko*, 32.

40	Ibid. "Outcasts" = *eta*.

41	Close examination of all sources subsequently cited here.

42	Boston Theatre, program, January 25–26, 1900, "The Japanese Dramatic Company," in program file: Zingoro, BRTC.

43	Yezo, also transliterated Ezo, was an old name for Hokkaidō. Andō Nusuke's name should have appeared throughout with the correct transliteration of Japanese as Andō Nizaburō. This was typical of the many typographical or spelling errors in Kawakami programs.

44	Boston Theatre, program, January 25–26, 1900. Whale meat was sometimes sold by linear dimensions, not by weight. "Rio" is now transliterated *ryō*. The loan was equivalent to $1,500–$2,500.

45	Yoshitake, *Kindai*, 1–3, 13, 353–56.

46	J. Scott Miller, *Adaptations of Western Literature in Meiji Japan* (New York: Palgrave, 2001), 3–7, 13–20. One way Japanese nationalized foreign narratives was to incorporate conventional literary passages about nature for mood or metaphor.

47	Keene, *Dawn Fiction*, 55.

48	Kawatake Shigetoshi, *Nihon engeki zenshi*, 779; Akiba, *Nihon*, 1:86.

49	Patrice Pavis examined theatrical appropriation, also known to him as interculturalism, in his *Theatre at the Crossroad of Culture*, 160–64, 170–72.

50	Jon Bishop, "'They Manage Things Better in France:' French Plays and English Critics, 1850–1855," *Nineteenth Century Theatre* 22 (Summer 1994): 5–29.

51	Henry Arthur Jones, "American Copyright and the Author," from his 1891 *Saints and Sinners*, reprinted in Jackson, *Victorian*, 348.

52	Jon Bishop, "'They Manage Things Better in France.'"

53	F. C. Burand, "Authors and Managers," from *Theatre* (London) February 1879, reprinted in Jackson, *Victorian*, 319.

54	Wilmeth, *Guide*, 281, s.v. "Liptzin, Keni"; Iska Alter, "When the Audience Called 'Author! Author!:' Shakespeare on New York's Yiddish Stage," *Theatre History Studies* 10 (1900): 144.

55	"Ibergesetzt un varbessert."

56	David S. Lifson, *The Yiddish Theatre in America* (New York: Yoseloff, 1965), 148.

57	Iska Alter, "When the Audience Called 'Author! Author!,'" *Theatre* 150–56; Harold Clurman, "It Was a People's Theatre," *TV Guide*, February 18, 1987, 32; Wilmeth, *Guide*, 418, s.v. "Schwartz, Maurice."

58	Dennis Washburn, "Manly Virtue and the Quest for Self: The *Bildungsroman* of Mori Ōgai," *Journal of Japanese Studies* 21 (Winter 1995): 6.

59	Keene, *Dawn: Fiction*, 71. By 1900, Japanese novelists had largely abandoned *hon'an* for their own original works although many dramatists were still *hon'an* bound (Miller, *Adaptations*, 117).

60	Shirakawa Nobuo, "Kaisetsu" (Commentary), in Shirakawa, *shimbun*, 6. Comprehensive explanations of *sekai* concepts and technique appeared in Hattori, *Kabuki*, 69–73 and Thornbury, *Sukeroku's*, 20–28.

61	Akiba, *Nihon*, 1:85, 103–4; Kawatake Shigetoshi, *Nihon engeki zenshi*, 779; Heinz Morioka and Miyoko Sasaki, *Rakugo: The Popular Narrative Art of Japan* (Cambridge: Harvard University Press, 1990), 257.

62	Kawatake Shigetoshi, *Nihon engeki zenshi*, 833; Ihara, *Engeki*, 220–22.

63	Cody Poulton, "Drama and Fiction in the Meiji Era: The Case of Izumi Kyōka," *Asian Theatre Journal* 12:2 (Fall 1995): 280–81.

64	Later only a few of his productions relied on extensive *kuchidate*.

65 Shirakawa Nobuo, comp., "Meijiki seiyōshu gikyoku jōen nempyō, 1; Meiji gonen–Meiji yonjūnen" [Chronology of performances during the Meiji Era of plays based on Western works, part 1: 1872–1907], *Engeki kenkyū* No. 17 (1993): 49–86.

66 "Japanese Shylock," *Boston Daily Advertiser*, January 26, 1900, 2; "Japanese Dramatic Company," *Boston Globe*, January 26, 1900, 4; Boston Theatre, program, January 25–26, 1900.

67 "Japanese Dramatic Company," *Boston Globe*, January 26, 1900, 4. Her instrument was either a koto or a shamisen. As a geisha, Sadayakko was an accomplished performer of both. One surviving proof of her musical talent is "Tsuru Kame" [Kawakami], Sada Yakko [*sic*] koto's solo, recorded in Berlin, 1901, preserved in the Hornbostel Collection, Berlin Phonogramm-Archiv, with a duplicate recording in the Federal Cylinder Project, Archive of Folk Culture, Library of Congress, AFS No. 10,054: B10, cylinder no. 4,076, original no. 24.

68 Boston Theatre, program, January 25–26, 1900. A similar synopsis was later printed in *"Māchanto ofu [V]enisu* ni tsuite Kawakami Otojirō no danwa," *Kabuki* (July 1903): 15. As was a common practice of Japanese dramaturgy, the Kawakami's *Sairoku* had a very specific historical and geographic setting. Matsumaye (Matsumae in contemporary transliteration) was the name of the daimyō family then ruling over Yezo/Hokkaidō and charged with subduing the indigenous Ainu people, colonizing Hokkaidō with Japanese settlers, and resisting Russian incursions from Siberia.

69 "Japanese Shylock," *Boston Daily Advertiser*, January 26, 1900, 2; Boston Theatre, program, January 25–26, 1900.

70 Boston Theatre, program, January 25–26, 1900.

71 "Japanese Shylock," *Boston Daily Advertiser*; Kaneo, *Ōbei*, 31; Matsunaga, *Kawakami*, 160; Kaneo, *Sadayakko*, 32; Dōmon, *Kawakami*, 119; Inoue, *Kawakami*, 69.

72 Boston Theatre, program, January 25–26, 1900.

73 "Japanese Shylock," *Boston Daily Advertiser*.

74 Boston Theatre, program, January 25–26, 1900.

75 "Japanese Shylock," *Boston Daily Advertiser*.

76 Kaneo, *Sadayakko*, 31.

77 Bulman, *Merchant*, 37, 41–44.

78 Lelyveld, *Shylock*, 92. During the early 1900s, several minor American stars performed the trial scene of *The Merchant of Venice* as a dramatic act in vaudeville where it worked as a highbrow ornament among lowbrow novelties (Lelyveld, 115–16).

79 "'Merchant of Venice,'" *Boston Herald*, January 23, 1900, 9.

80 "Notes," *Boston Daily Advertiser*, January 23, 1900, 8.

81 "Japanese Shylock," *Boston Daily Advertiser*. This same review appeared in "The Man with the Lorgnette," *Boston Evening Record*, January 26, 1900, 5, and was closely paraphrased in "Life and Letters," *Poet Lore* 12:1 (January–March 1900): 152–53.

82 "Music and Drama. Boston Theatre," *Boston Evening Transcript*, January 26, 1900, 9; "Japanese Dramatic Company," *Boston Globe*, January 26, 1900, 4.

83 "The Japanese Players," *Boston Herald*, January 26, 1900, 9.

84 "The Merchant in Japanese," *NYDM*, February 3, 1900, 15; "Music and Drama. Boston Theatre," *Boston Evening Transcript*; "Japanese Dramatic Company," *Boston Globe*. Several Boston papers did not review the production.

85 "Japanese Dramatic Company," *Boston Globe*.

86 Holograph notes of unknown provenance on a Boston Theatre program, January 25–26,1900, "The Japanese Dramatic Company" in "Lawrence from Uncle Charles, Merry Christmas, 1899," scrapbook, Deac Rossell collection.

87   "Japanese Shylock," *Boston Daily Advertiser*, January 26, 1900, 2. Although this review had no byline, it was probably written by the lead critic of the paper, Henry Austin Clapp, who was a major American theatre historian. See his *Reminiscences of a Dramatic Critic*. Charles H. Shattuck in his *Shakespeare on the American Stage*, 2:11, called Clapp "the fairest, soundest, best informed theatre critic of his time."

88   "Music and Drama. Boston Theatre," *Boston Evening Transcript*, January 26, 1900, 9. In his staging, Kawakami apparently had subordinate actors remain motionless to further focus on the speaking principals.

89   Desmond MacCarthy, *Drama* (London: Putnam, 1940), 20. He was writing about a later Kawakami performance in London.

90   "Japanese Shylock," *Boston Daily Advertiser*, January 26, 1900, 2; "The Japanese Players," *Boston Herald*, January 26, 1900, 9.

91   Tompkins, *History*, 474.

92   Kaneo, *Sadayakko*, 32.

93   Andrew Gerstle, "Shakespeare and Japanese Theatre: Artists' and Scholars' Use of the 'Exotic,'" in Fujita, *Shakespeare*, 69.

94   Kawatake Toshio, *Nihon*, 373; Yanagida, *Meiji*, 4:569. Literary scholar Yanagida Izumi counted a dozen brief *Hamlet* stories (most were only a page or two long) published between 1870 and 1884 (Yanagida, *Meiji*, 4:568–71).

95   Toyoda Minoru, *Shakespeare in Japan: An Historical Survey* (Tokyo: Iwanami, 1940), 8, 61; a translation of the story appeared on pp. 9–15. Also Kawatake Toshio, *Nihon*, 367; Akiba, *Nihon*, 1:84.

96   Inoue Tsutomu, "Jinniku shichiire saiban" [The trial over pawned flesh] (Kinkodō, 1883), reprinted in Meiji Bunka, *Meiji*, 312–27. An English translation of a German translation of a condensed version of "Jinniku shichiire saiban" appeared in Emil Hausknecht, "Shakespeare in Japan," *Poet-Lore* 1 (October 1889): 467–68. Also Matsunaga, *Kawakami*, 160; Toshio Kawatake, "Shakespeare in the Japanese Theatre," *Theatre Research* 2 (1960): 83; Yoshitake, *Kindai*, 17.

97   There have been many different English translations of this title, including: *A World Where Gold Rules among the Blossoming Cherries* and *Life Is as Fragile as Cherry Blossoms in a World of Money*. The Japanese title sometimes appeared as *Nanja sakura doki zeni no yononaka*.

98   Kawatake Toshio, *Nihon*, 365, 361, 374. Journalist Udagawa Bunkan, who wrote the novel, later became one of the principal supporters of kabuki actor Sōjūrō's pioneering Theatre Reform Society in Osaka.

99   Dōmon, *Kawakami*, 122; Matsunaga, *Kawakami*, 160; Kawatake Toshio, *Nihon*, 374; Kawatake Shigetoshi, *Nihon engeki zenshi*, 833. These authors speculated but did not conclusively demonstrate that Kawakami saw *Sakura doki zeni no yononaka*.

100   Kawatake Toshio, *Nihon*, 361–67. *Ie sōdō* is one of a half dozen of the most frequently used plot devices of kabuki drama.

101   Ibid.; Yoshitake, *Kindai*, 18–19, 22–25; Yoshihara Yukari, "Japan as 'Half-Civilized:' an Early Japanese Adaptation of Shakespeare's *The Merchant of Venice* and Japan's Construction of its National Language in the Late Nineteenth Century," in Minami, *Performing*, 21–32.

102   Akiba, *Nihon*, 100.

103   Kawatake Toshio, *Nihon*, 367. "Europeanization mania" = Ōkanetsu.

104   Ibid., 373; Akiba, *Nihon*, 100–1.

105   Minami, Ryuta, complier, "Chronological Table of Shakespeare Productions in Japan 1866–1994," in Sasayama, *Shakespeare*, 258–63. This often reworked play appeared in variations under other titles such as *Jinniku shichiire saiban* [The trial of pawned human flesh] and *Jigoku no saiban* [Trial in hell] (Ihara, *Kabuki*, 7:421, 7:451; Matsumoto, *Meiji*, 413; Kawatake Toshio, *Nihon*, 361; Shirakawa Nobuo, "Kaisetsu," Shirakawa, *shimbun*, 5). In his discussions of Irving's *The Merchant of Venice* and his own *Sairoku*, Kawakami sometimes called both productions *Jinniku shichiire saiban*.

106   Toyoda Minoru, *Shakespeare in Japan*, 43, 68, 71–73, 76. Also Kaneo, *Ōbei*, 29, 30; Kaneo, *Sadayakko*, 31.

107   Masumoto, *Yokohama*, 165, 201; "Japan as a Theatrical Field." *NYDM*, December 2, 1899, 2. The Miln troupe played throughout Australia and was currently port-hopping its way back to London or India. They performed in Tokyo before a small foreign audience and a few Japanese in a Japanese theatre after they had unsuccessfully tried to present their *Merchant of Venice* before the Emperor (Miln, *When*, 193, 196, 231).

108   Masumoto, *Yokohama*, 165–66. Apart from his decisive role as a translator and scholar of Shakespeare, Tsubouchi subsequently became one of the founders of the shingeki movement.

109   Other Chinese adaptations (but not translations) were *Yi bang rou* [A pound of flesh] and *Nü lüshi* [The female lawyer].

110   Ruru Li, "The Bard in the Middle Kingdom," *Asian Theatre Journal* 12:1 (Spring 1995): 52–55, 65, 68

111   Jong-hwan Kim, "Shakespeare in a Korean Cultural Context," *Asian Theatre Journal* 12 (Spring 1995): 40–41; conversations with Yu Chi-jin, Seoul, winter 1954–55.

Chapter 19

1   Boston Theatre, program, January 25–26, 1900; also "Japanese Shylock," *Boston Daily Advertiser*, January 26, 1900, 2; Kaneo, *Ōbei*, 32. Kawakami's Japanese title of the play was *Sakurada chizome no yuki* [The blood stained snow of Sakurada]. Sakurada was the southern gate of the shōgun's castle (subsequently the Tokyo palace of the emperor). Kawakami had earlier planned to do this or a similar work in 1892 (Shirakawa, *shimbun*, 18).

2   "Imperial cabinet" should have been more accurately termed "shogunal authorities."

3   This was a reference to the Opium War and the continuing Japanese fear of similar European aggression.

4   Boston Theatre, program, January 25–26, 1900.

5   "Japanese Dramatic Company," *Boston Globe*, January 26, 1900, 4; "At the Theatres. Bijou–The Japanese Players," *NYDM*, March 31, 1900, 16–17; Boston Theatre, program, January 25–26, 1900, "The Japanese Dramatic Company," *Boston Daily Advertiser*, January 23, 1900, 8; Katherine Metcalf Roof, "Concerning the Japanese Players," *Impressionist* (June 1900), 10.

6   "Music and Drama. Boston Theatre," *Boston Evening Transcript*, January 26, 1900, 9.

7   Holograph notes, "Lawrence from Uncle Charles, Merry Christmas, 1899," in scrapbook with a Boston Theatre, program, January 25–26, 1900.

8   "Japanese Dramatic Company," *Boston Globe*.

9   "At the Theatres. Bijou—The Japanese Players," *NYDM*; "Music and Drama. Boston Theatre," *Boston Evening Transcript*.

10   "Music and Drama. Boston Theatre," *Boston Evening Transcript*.

11   "Japanese Dramatic Company," *Boston Globe*. Without positive evidence, I concluded that the attack was staged under finely shredded newspaper falling as snow and with an unidentified red liquid as the splashing blood. In kabuki productions animal blood had been used at times for realism.

12   "The Japanese Players," *Boston Herald*, January 26, 1900, 9.

13   Holographic note in "Lawrence from Uncle Charles, Merry Christmas."

14   *Tairō* was a political rank equivalent to senior councilor.

15   Oppressive measures enacted under Ii's rule are now known as the Ansei Purge.

16   The play, with its limited cast, had a vastly reduced number of attackers and guards.

17   *"Sakura"* (cherry) in the title referred not only to the Sakurada Gate location but also to *sakura* as a familiar metaphor for the brief lives of samurai falling in battle (like briefly blossoming cherry trees). Another *sakura* referent was to the cherry blossom season that usually occurred in March, but in 1860, the year of

the Sakurada Gate incident, blossoming was delayed by late winter snow. Such multilevel allusions were a favorite device of kabuki playwrights. This made play titles difficult, often impossible to translate.

18   Kawatake Shigetoshi, *Sōgō*, 253; Ihara, *Kabuki*, 7:196–349. Kawakami borrowed the title *Sakura chizome no yuki* for his *Scarlet Snow* and may have incorporated other elements of that kabuki play. An audio recording of an excerpt from Kawakami's *Sakura chizome* suggested his play was largely independent of its kabuki predecessors although Ii Kamon's harangues about loyalty and patriotism rose in intensity to a robust *kabuki-chō* (kabuki declamatory style) (Miller, *Yomigaeru*, cut 18).

19   Manabe Motoyuki, ed., *Taishū bungaku jiten* [Dictionary of popular culture] (Seiabō, 1973), 230–32, 488–90. There have been many television dramas and films about Ii Naosuke. See also a translation of a shingeki play about Ii by Kichizō Nakamura: *The Death of Ii Tairō*, trans. Mock Joya (Tokyo: Japan Times), 1927. In 1953, three major works about Ii appeared as *kyōen* (rival productions). *Hana no shōgai* [A glorious life] was a dramatization of Funabashi Seiichi's recently serialized newspaper novel about Ii. It was in competition with a different original play, *Ii tairō* [Senior councilor Ii] and a three-hour epic film, *Hana no shōgai*, also based on the Funabashi novel. (Shimbashi Embujō, Tōkyō, program for Ichikawa Enosuke Gekidan, *Hana no shōgai*, October 1953. Also Kawatake Shigetoshi, *Sōgō*, 24–25; Hōjō Hideji, *Hōjō Hideji gekisaku shi* [A history of Hōjō Hideji's plays] (Nihon Hōsō Shuppan Kyōkai, 1974), 178–84, 236–40; Shinkokugeki ed. staff, *Shinkokugeki gojūnen* [Fifty years of Shinkokugeki] (Nakabayashi Shuppan, 1967), 320; Shimaji Takamaro, ed., *Nihon eiga sakuhin zenshū* [Comprehensive directory of Japanese films] (Kinema Jumpōsha: 1973), 213–14.

20   The historical Abé Masahiro was a shogunate official when the initial treaty with Perry was signed.

21   John Weidman, book; Stephen Sondheim, music and lyrics, *Pacific Overtures* (New York: Dodd, Mead, 1976), 5, 7, 15–19, 30, 81–100, 119–20.

22   Winter Garden Theatre, New York, *Playbill* program, January 1976.

23   Weidman, *Pacific Overtures*, 6–8; personal observation, 1976.

24   "Japanese Shylock," *Boston Daily Advertiser*, January 26, 1900, 2.

25   "Boston Theatre," advertisement, *Boston Traveler*, January 23, 1900, 5.

26   "Boston Theatre," *Boston Daily Advertiser*, January 23, 1900, 8.

27   "Around New York," *Boston Traveler*, January 23, 1900, 5.

28   "Boston Theatre," *Boston Daily Advertiser*; "Boston Theatre: 'Round New York in Eighty Minutes,'" *Boston Evening Transcript*, January 23, 1900, 12; Boston Theatre, program, week of January 22, 1900, HTC; "Howard Atheneum," *Boston Post*, November 21, 1899, 5; Columbia Theatre, Brooklyn, program, week of February 26, 1900, *Round the New York in Eighty Minutes*, in scrapbook MWEZ+ n.c. 79, pp. 44–45, BRTC.

29   "Boston Theatre," *Boston Daily Advertiser*, January 23, 1900, 8. The actual neighborhood was Thompson Street in lower central Manhattan where there was a two hundred-year-old African-American community known as Coontown or Little Africa (Ellis, *Epic*, 427; Sante, *Low*, 17).

30   Columbia Theatre, Brooklyn, program, week of February 26, 1900.

31   "Boston Theatre," *Boston Daily Advertiser*.

32   "Boston Theatre," advertisement, *Boston Herald*, January 21, 1900, 15. This kind of publicized chronological precision in performance was not an innovation. An 1886 Boston production of *The Mikado* advertised a similar timetable ("Thirteenth Consecutive Week. Messrs. Keith and Batcheller's Gaiety Opera Co., *Boston Herald*, April 4, 1886, 11). Of the last 294 American professional and amateur dramatic productions I attended since I began counting, only one started at the announced start time.

33   "Boston Theatre," *Boston Daily Advertiser*; "Boston Theatre: 'Round New York in Eighty Minutes,'" *Boston Evening Transcript*, January 23, 1900, 12; Columbia Theatre, Brooklyn, program, week of February 26, 1900, *Round the New York in Eighty Minutes*, Scrapbook MWEZ+ n.c. 79, pp. 44–45, BRTC.

34   "Telegraphic News. Boston," *NYDM*, January 27, 1900, 12.

35   "Around New York," *Boston Traveler*, January 23, 1900, 5; also "Boston Theatre," *Boston Daily Advertiser*, January 23, 1900, 8; "Drama and Music. 'Round NY in 80 Minutes," *Boston Globe*, January 21, 1900, 18.

36   "The Japanese Players," *Boston Herald*, January 9, 1900, 9; "The Japanese Players," *Boston Evening Transcript*, January 2, 1900, 11; "Mme. Yacco," *Boston Post*, December 24, 1899, 16.

37   "Other Local Attractions," *Boston Evening Transcript*, January 23, 1900, 12; also "Merchant of Venice," *Boston Herald*, January 23, 1900, 9. The extravaganza that Comstock promised was not produced. His last work in show business was as manager of a Japanese tea garden in Brighton Beach on Long Island ("Death of Alexander Comstock," *NYDM*, January 1, 1909, 7).

38   Yamaguchi, *Joyū*, 87; "*Māchanto obu [V]enisu* ni tsuite Kawakami Otojirō no danwa" [Conversation about *The Merchant of Venice* with Kawakami Otojirō], *Kabuki* (July 1903): 12–14.

39   "Shin'engeki no sossensha" [New Theatre pioneer], *Miyako shimbun*, May 17, 1900, Shirakawa, 318; "Kawakami ichiza yōkō nisshi" [Journal of the foreign tour of the Kawakami troupe], *Miyako shimbun*, July 26, 1900, Shirakawa, 318; "Alexander C. Comstock Fails," *New York Times*, 21 April 1900.

40   Kaneo, *Ōbei*, 6, 32.

41   The drum was one of the instruments in the kabuki *geza* ensemble that played offstage right out of sight (and should not be confused with the other big drum in front of the theatre). When Kawakami abandoned his troupe to go to France seven years earlier, his close friend and associate Fujisawa Asajirō called it an act of *doron* (Fujii, *Jiden*, 144).

42   "Shibai no chūgi wa kuso chūgi" in Muramatsu Shunkichi, *Tabishibai*, 169.

43   Searched: *Boston Directory* (Boston: Sampson, Murdock), 1901 through 1905 editions.

44   Kaneo, *Ōbei*, 32; Ezaki, *Jitsuroku*, 109.

45   "Players from Far Japan," *Boston Journal*, January 7, 1900, 4:4.

46   Boston Theatre, program, January 18–19, 1900, "The Japanese Dramatic Company." One source reported that Mikami was not again active until January 23, a date after the *Soga* and *Jingorō* performances ("Japanese Actor Dead," *Boston Journal*, January 31, 1900, 2).

47   "The Japanese Players," *Boston Herald*, January 26, 1900, 9; Boston Theatre, program, January 25–26, 1900, "The Japanese Dramatic Company." All characters in *Scarlet Snow* were male.

48   Kaneo, *Sadayakko*, 22.

49   Alexander Corbett Jr., "Japan's Foremost Actors, *Boston Globe*, December 11, 1899, 5.

50   Duis, *Saloon*, 188–89; King, *How*, 52.

51   Evidence of Benton's friendship can be detected in his "Japanese Actor Seriously Ill," *NYDM*, February 3, 1900, 17, and other reports. Benton's stories in the *New York Dramatic Mirror* about the plight of the unknown actor Mikami were more extensive and more affectionate than that trade paper's usual short notices of sickness and death among the major figures of American theatre.

52   "Japanese Actor Seriously Ill," *NYDM*, February 3, 1900, 17; also "Players from Far Japan," *Boston Journal*, January 7, 1900, 4:4.

53   Kaneo, *Ōbei*, 32.

54   "Sunday's Weather," *Boston Daily Advertiser*, January 28, 1900, 1; "Weather," *Boston Evening Record*, January 27, 1900, 1; "Weather," *Boston Evening Transcript*, January 27, 1900, 2.

55   Kaneo, *Sadayakko*, 20 [page misnumbered as 16].

Chapter 20

1   Kaneo, *Ōbei*, 32. Kawakami's account of this part of the trip was confusing because he recorded that they left Boston at 3:30 AM Sunday. According to published railroad schedules, no trains left Boston anywhere near that time ("New York All Rail and Sound Lines," advertisement, *Boston Evening Transcript*, January

29, 1900, 4; New York, New Haven & Hartford R. R., advertisement, *Boston Evening Transcript*, January 27, 1900 11; "Weather Conditions," *Washington Post*, January 29 and 30, 1900, 1.

2   Francis E[llington] Leupp, "Washington, A City of Pictures," *Scribner's* 31 (February 1902): 142.

3   Charles B. Reynolds, *The Standard Guide: Washington* (Washington: Reynolds, 1900), 12.

4   Henry Loomis Nelson, "The Capital of Our Democracy," *Century* 64 (May 1902): 25–27.

5   "Bright Outlook for Increased Business," *New York Times*, January 1, 1900, 11.

6   *Washington Times*, February 3, 1900, 8; *New York Times*, January 1, 1900, Supplement, 2.

7   "Bright Outlook for Increased Business," *New York Times*; "The Financial Situation" *New York Times*, January 1, 1900, Supplement, 1; also Jas. T. Woodward, "The United States the Envy of the World," *New York Times*, January 1, 1900, Supplement 2; Boston and Washington newspapers December 1899–January 1900.

8   "Rival for 'Oatmeal' Trust," *New York Times*, January 1, 1900, 1; "Prune Growers in a Trust," *New York Sun*, April 1, 1900, 2:8; "Clay Sewer Pipe Trust the Latest," *New York Herald*, March 4, 1900, 1:11; "Whisky Trust Case," *New York Mail and Express*, April 9, 1900, 7; "Receivers for Flour Trust," *New York Mail and Express*, February 26, 1900, 3; "Cigarette Trust Holds Assembly," *New York Evening Journal*, February 27, 1900, 9; "One Hundred Per Cent Rise in Ice," *New York Times*, May 6, 1900, 18.

9   "The Passing Throng," *New York Tribune*, February 5, 1900, 7.

10   "Filipinos Again Active," *New York Times*, February 12, 1900, 5.

11   *New York World*, March 10, 1900, 7.

12   *New York Times*, January 29, 1900, 1. Also "A British Disaster," *Washington Times*, January 29, 1900, 1; "The Spion Kop Disaster," *Washington Times*, January 30, 1900, 1; "British Whipped Twice," *New York Evening Journal*, March 22, 1900, 1.

13   "Anxiety in China," *Boston Evening Transcript*, January 29, 1900, 1.

14   R. Van Bergen, "The Pacific to the Fore," *Harper's Weekly* 44 (February 24, 1900): 169–70.

15   "Japan Preparing to Strike at Russia," *New York World*, January 28, 1900, 6; "Japan Soon to Strike," *Washington Post*, January 8, 1900, 1; "Russo-Japanese Clash Inevitable," *New York Herald*, March 7, 1900, 5.

16   *Rand, McNally*, map n.p.

17   Cahn, *Theatrical 1899–1900*, 101; theatre advertisements, *Washington Evening Star*, January 27, 1900, 21; "At the Theatres," *Washington Post*, December 5, 1899, 3; "The Stage," *Washington Post*, January 21, 1900, 24; "Amusements," *Washington Evening Star*, January 30, 1900, 12.

18   "The Stage," *Washington Evening Star*, January 20, 1900, 20.

19   *The Master Builder* was part of the series of modern European works produced by John Blair's company with whom Kawakami had shared the Tremont Theatre in Boston.

20   "The Stage," *Washington Post*, January 21, 1900, 24. Also "At the Theatres," *Washington Post*, January 20, 1900, 8; concurring: "The Stage," *Washington Evening Star*, January 20, 1900, 20.

21   "Amusements. New National Theatre," *Washington Evening Star*, January 16, 1900, 10; "District of Columbia," *NYC*, January 27, 1900, 1001.

22   "The Stage," *Washington Post*.

23   "District of Columbia," *NYC*, February 3, 1900, 1029; "The Stage," *Washington Times*, January 28, 1900, 2:4; John T. Warde, "Telegraphic News. Washington," *NYDM*, February 3, 1900, 12.

24   "Gossip of the Theatre," *Washington Post*, January 28, 1900, 24; also "The Stage," *Washington Post*, January 21, 1900, 24; "Amusements. New National Theatre," *Washington Evening Star*, January 16, 1900, 10.

25   "Gossip of the Theatre," *Washington Post*.

26   "The Passing Show," *Washington Times*, January 21, 1900, 2:4.

27   "Events of the Stage," *Washington Post*, January 16, 1900, 3; "At the Theatres. Grand—Vaudeville," *Washington Times*, January 16, 1900, 6.

28 "New Grand," advertisement, *Washington Evening Star*, January 20, 1900, 21.

29 "The Stage," *Washington Times*, January 21, 1900, 2:4; also "District of Columbia," *NYC*, January 27, 1900, 1001.

30 "Amusements," *Washington Evening Star*, December 2, 1899, 2; also "Amusements. Lafayette Square Opera House," *Washington Evening Star*, December 5, 1899, 10.

31 "At the Theatres," *Washington Post*, January 30, 1900, 3.

32 "Amusements. Bijou Theatre," *Washington Evening Star*, January 30, 1900, 12.

33 Federal, *Washington*, 659.

34 *Rand, McNally*, 143–45; author's observations, March 27, 1999; "The Lafayette Monument," *Boston Herald*, November 9, 1890, 4.

35 Lockwood, *Columbia*, 5.

36 Federal, *Washington*, 653–59. The mansions were the twin residences of historian Henry Adams and his close friend, John Hay, the current secretary of state (Federal, *Washington*, 653–59; *Rand, McNally*, 143, 145).

37 Kelly, *Washington*, 78.

38 "Lafayette Square Opera House," advertisement, *NYDM*, June 17, 1899, 6; also author's observations, March 27, 1999.

39 Federal, *Washington*, 146.

40 "Lafayette," advertisement, *Washington Times*, January 28, 1900, 2:5; Cahn, *Theatrical 1899–1900*, 98.

41 "Kawakami no yōkō miyage" [Gifts from Kawakami's trip abroad], *Kabuki* (March 1903): 32.

42 "On Lafayette Square," *Washington Post*, October 1, 1895, n.p.; "Lafayette," advertisement, *Washington Times*, January 28, 1900, 2:5; Cahn, *Theatrical 1899–1900*, 98.

43 *Rand, McNally*, 136.

44 Federal, *Washington*, 144. The term "continuously operating" was used in the usual theatrical sense. After the first National Theatre opened in 1835, it was destroyed or severely damaged by fire and rebuilt several times on the original site. The National structure operating in the twenty-first century was built in 1922 and subsequently renovated.

45 After dark as a performance venue for a hundred years, a restored Ford's Theatre reopened in 1968. During part of that earlier interim it was a Lincoln assassination museum.

46 John T. Warde, "Telegraphic News. Washington," *NYDM*, December 9, 1899, 9.

47 A. I. Mudd, "The New Belasco Theatre in Washington," *Theatre* (New York) No. 57 (November 1905): 288. For several years previously, Belasco had been booking the theatre to try out his productions (Hornblow, *History*, 2:312).

48 Federal, *Washington*, 146; Kelly, *Washington*, 78.

49 Lockwood, *Columbia*, 5.

50 *Rand, McNally*, 143, 145. The theatre building was on land leased from the widow of famous politician and one-time presidential contender, James G. Blaine.

51 Lockwood, *Columbia*, 7; A. I. Mudd, "The New Belasco Theatre in Washington," *Theatre*.

52 "Lafayette Square Opera House," advertisement, *Washington Post*, January 27, 1900, 11; "Things Theatrical," *Washington Times*, January 27, 1900, 5.

53 "Things Theatrical," *Washington Times*.

54 "District of Columbia," *NYC*, February 3, 1900, 1029.

55 "Things Theatrical," *Washington Times*; also "Telegraphic News. Washington," *NYDM*, 3 February 1900, 15. A Japanese newspaper reported delivery of new scenery in "Kawakami Otojirō ōmote" [Big welcome for Kawakami Otojirō], *Niroku shumbun*, 17 March 1900, in Shirakawa, 312–13.

56 Kaneo, *Ōbei*, 33.

57   "At the Theatres," *Washington Post*, January 30, 1900, 3.

58   "Amusements. Lafayette Square Opera House," *Washington Evening Star*, January 30, 1900, 12.

59   The earliest Washington advertisements for Kawakami listed only *Jingorō* and *The Geisha and the Samurai* on the first bill with nothing to suggest a stand-alone *The Royalist/Kojima* play ("Lafayette," advertisement, *Washington Evening Star*, January 27, 1900, 21; "Lafayette," advertisement, *Washington Times*, January 28, 1900, 2:5; "Lafayette," advertisement, *Washington Evening Star*, January 30, 1900, 12; "At the Theatres. Lafayette," *Washington Times*, January 30, 1900, 3). These advance notices indicate that *Kojima* was suddenly separated from the longer work. Four months earlier, back in Portland, before Kawakami put together the three-part *The Geisha and the Knight*, he had offered *Kojima* as a separate piece called *Faithful Servant of the Mikado* ("Wants to Reform Mimic Stage," *Portland Evening Telegram*, September 26, 1899, 3).

60   Either title was appropriate. The difference may be attributed to confusion over the *l* and *r* sounds of the English language. Although subsequently billed in America as *The Royalist*, a Japanese newspaper report called the play *Kinnōka* which means "loyalist" ("Beijin no Nihon engekihyō" [Review of a Japanese drama by an American], *Miyako shimbun*, May 17, 1900, in Shirakawa, 315–17). Similarly, the most frequently used English language title for *Kesa* was *The Loyal Wife* but it was also called *The Royal Wife* ("Things Theatrical," *Washington Times*, February 4, 1900, 2:5).

61   In Japanese reports, this play appeared variously as *Bingo no Saburō*, *Kojima*, or *Kojima Takanori*.

62   Kawakami Otojirō, "Kondo no kyakuhon to Usaburō" [Current scripts and Usaburō], *Kabuki* (June 1909): 50. Usaburō was a second-class Osaka kabuki actor who had switched to playing shimpa in Tokyo.

63   "Amusements. Lafayette Square Opera House," *Washington Evening Star*, January 30, 1900, 12.

64   "At the Theatres," *Washington Post*, January 30, 1900, 3.

65   "Amusements. Lafayette Square Opera House," *Washington Evening Star*.

66   "At the Theatres," *Washington Post*. This description was confused. A more accurate recast would be "a Japanese solo entitled 'Kanjinchō' was rendered by Sennosuke accompanied on s[ha]misen by Kineya."

67   Yamamoto who played Gorō in Boston now had only a minor part.

68   "Things Theatrical. Lafayette," *Washington Times*, January 31, 1900, 4; "At the Theatres," *Washington Post*; Boston Theatre, Boston, program, January 18–19, 1900.

69   Kaneo, *Sadayakko*, 33–34; Kaneo, *Ōbei*, 34. Shōshō was called Koshimoto in Boston.

70   "Things Theatrical. Lafayette," *Washington Times*, January 31, 1900, 4.

71   "Amusements. Lafayette Square Opera House," *Washington Evening Star*, January 30, 1900, 12; also "The Theatre," *Washington Star*, February 3, 1900, 20.

72   "The Stage," *Washington Post*, February 4, 1900, 24. Concurring: "At the Theatres. Lafayette," *Washington Times*, January 30, 1900, 3; "The Theatre," *Washington Star*, February 3, 1900, 20.

73   Reviews throughout the tour mentioned that sparks were seen as swords struck in battle

74   "Amusements. Lafayette Square Opera House," *Washington Evening Star*, January 30, 1900, 12.

75   Harvey, *Recollections*, 30.

76   Kaneo, *Ōbei*, 36, 38; Kaneo, *Sadayakko*, 34. Kawakami was here following the rough *aragoto* style of kabuki.

77   Kaneo, *Ōbei*, 36–37; Kaneo, *Sadayakko*, 34; Littlewood, *Idea*, 36. For instances of this fascination, see Chamberlain, *Japanese*, 219–22, 228 and Mitford, *Tales*, 376–409.

78   See Hattori, *Zankoku*; Hirosue Tamori, *Mō hitotsu no Nihombi* [One more Japanese beauty] (Bijutsu Shuppansha, 1965).

79   Kaneo, *Sadayakko*, 34.

80   Kawakami Otojirō, "Kawakami ikkō no shibōsa" [The death of a member of the Kawakami troupe], *Miyako shimbun*, March 2, 1900, in Shirakawa, 312.

81   Kaneo, *Ōbei*, 37; Kaneo, *Sadayakko*, 34. In most versions of the Soga revenge, one brother was killed in the attack at the camp, the other was captured later and put to death (Kominz, *Avatars*, 248).

82 Morse, *Japan*, 1:404. The headless effect was achieved by the actor drawing his head inside his kimono (personal observation).

83 "Chats with the Players" and "The Stage," *Washington Times*, February 4, 1900, 2:4; "Things Theatrical," *Washington Times*, February 4, 1900, 2:5.

84 The most likely bills were *Jingorō*, *Kojima*, and *The Geisha and the Knight* on Wednesday evening; *Jingorō* and either *Kesa* or *The Geisha and the Knight* on Thursday; then *Kojima*, *The Geisha and the Knight*, and either *Jingorō* or *Sarashi* on Friday. *Kesa* was performed at the Saturday matinee with either *Jingorō* or *Sarashi*, or possibly both..

85 "Tonight—Souvenir Night," advertisement, *Washington Star*, February 1, 1900, 16; "Lafayette," advertisement, *Washington Post*, February 1, 1900, 11.

86 "At the Theatres, *Washington Post*, February 3, 1900, 7.

87 "Chats with the Players," *Washington Times*.

88 "Aside," *Washington Evening Star*, February 3, 1900, 21.

89 The Academy, the third-class legit house of the city, specialized in spectacular melodrama.

90 Al Martin was proprietor and star of a large *Uncle Tom's Cabin* company dominated by specialty performers.

91 Forrest was usually considered America's first great tragedian. He was an older rival of Edwin Booth who was the greatest of American tragedians. McCullough had been a protégé tragedian under Forrest and played second leads to his mentor.

92 Davis and Keogh were producers of sensational melodramas.

93 Suketsune's banquet.

94 Several scenes of Kawakami's *Soga* were staged with the kabuki technique of *ikyōgen* (seated acting) in which two characters engaged in extended conversation while seated or kneeling. The two hardly moved and had little business, often little emotion. The acting challenge was to fascinate with subtle strokes of inert virtuosity.

95 Drew was one of the Barrymore dynasty of actors and a leading man in conversation-laden polite drama and light comedy.

96 Former heavyweight boxing champion.

97 Clyde Fitch was the most commercially successful American playwright of the 1890s.

98 Although advertised as a Japanese version of *Pygmalion and Galatea*, *Jingorō* was not based on W. S. Gilbert's (pre-Arthur Sullivan) popular play, *Pygmalion and Galatea*, or any other European work.

99 All three were well-known aging drama critics who were unhappy with recent modern trends.

100 It was not Mikami but Takagi Hanjirō, the overnight onnagata, who played the part.

101 Richard Harlow(e) was the best known "male ingenue" of the 1890s. His acting was distinguished by his thoroughly feminine physical behavior, countered by his obvious male falsetto (unidentified newspaper, May 20, 1899, in clipping file: Richard Harlow(e), BRTC; "Obituary," *NYDM*, February 28, 1920, 62).

102 "The Stage," *Washington Times*, February 4, 1900, 2:4. Although unsigned, Channing Pollock, the leading critic of the city, probably wrote this piece.

103 "The Stage," *Washington Post*, February 4, 1900, 24. Anne (Annie) Russell played Shakespearean comedy and was the first in America to perform the title role in Shaw's *Major Barbara*.

104 "At the Theatres," *Washington Post*, January 30, 1900, 3.

105 "At the Theatres. Lafayette," *Washington Times*, January 30, 1900, 3.

106 "The Stage," *Washington Post*, February 4, 1900, 24.

107 "Amusements. Lafayette Square Opera House," *Washington Evening Star*, January 30, 1900, 12.

108 "Things Theatrical. Lafayette," *Washington Times*, January 31, 1900, 4.

109 Ibid.

110 "The Stage," *Washington Post.*

111 "District of Columbia," *NYC,* February 10, 1900, 1,052. Also "Things Theatrical. Lafayette," *Washington Times,* January 31, 1900, 4; "The Stage," *Washington Times,* February 4, 1900, 2:4 and "The Stage," *Washington Post.*

112 "The Stage," *Washington Times.* Conversely, the *Post* reviewer called this show "clean, wholesome entertainment" ("At the Theatres," *Washington Post,* January 30, 1900, 3).

113 "District of Columbia," *NYC,* February 10, 1900, 1,052; "The Theatre," *Washington Star,* February 3, 1900, 20.

114 "Amusements. New National Theatre," *Washington Evening Star,* January 30, 1900, 12.

115 "Weather Conditions," *Washington Post,* January 30 and 31, 1900, 1; "Coldest Day of Winter," *Washington Evening Star,* January 31, 1900, 3.

116 "Offerings of the Week," *Washington Times,* February 4, 1900, 2:5. There was no mention of these extra matinees in other papers until Monday, the day of the performance.

117 "District of Columbia," *NYC,* February 10, 1900, 1052; John T. Warde, "Telegraphic News. Washington," *NYDM,* February 10, 1900, 11; Kaneo, *Ōbei,* 35.

118 "Offerings of the Week," *Washington Times.*

119 "Amusements," *Washington Evening Star,* February 6, 1900, 10.

120 "At the Theatres," *Washington Times,* February 6, 1900, 4.

Chapter 21

1 Kawakami did not directly state this (Kaneo, *Sadayakko,* 33; "Kawakami Otojirō ōmote" [Big welcome for Kawakami Otojirō], *Niroku shimpō,* March 17, 1900, in Shirakawa, 312).

2 This was in a neighborhood of middle class homes at 1310 N Street (Charles B. Reynolds, *The Standard Guide. Washington* [Washington: Reynolds, 1900], 12; F. W. Fitzpatrick, "The Centennial of the Nation's Capital," *Cosmopolitan,* December 1900; reprinted in Oppel, *Washington,* 312–13).

3 Charles M. Pepper, *Everyday Life in Washington with Pen and Camera* (New York: Christian Herald, 1900), 231; Kaneo, *Sadayakko,* 33.

4 "In the Social World," *Washington Times,* February 7, 1900, 5; "The World of Society," *Washington Evening Star,* February 7, 1900, 5.

5 *Rand, McNally,* 139.

6 Ibid., 141–42.

7 "The Stage," *Washington Post,* February 4, 1900, 24; "In the Social World," *Washington Times.*

8 "The World of Society," *Washington Evening Star,* February 6, 1900, 5.

9 Ibid.; also "In the Social World," *Washington Times*; Kaneo, *Sadayakko,* 33. In Kaneo, *Ōbei,* 36, Kawakami reported eight hundred people attended the two performances, but this was an exaggeration.

10 Ezaki, *Jitsuroku,* 111; Fujimura Michitaka, "Komura Juntarō," in *Sekai daihyakka jiten* [World comprehensive encyclopedia] (Heibonsha, 1998), 10:506.

11 Fujimura Michitaka, "Komura Juntarō," in *Kokushi daijiten* [Dictionary of national history] (Yoshikawa Kōbunkan, 1985), 6:26; "Komura Jutarō," in *Kodansha Encyclopedia of Japan,* 4:268; Robert B. Valliant, "The Selling of Japan: Japanese Manipulation of Western Opinion, 1900–05," *Monumenta Nipponica* 29 (1974): 416–24; "Japanese Minister's Goodby," *New York Herald,* April 7, 1900, 8; Wayne Patterson, "Japanese Imperialism in Korea: A Study of Immigration and Foreign Policy," in Conroy, *Japan,* 296.

12 Ezaki, *Jitsuroku,* 111–12; Inoue, *Kawakami,* 70.

13 Dōmon, *Kawakami,* 121.

14   Kaneo, *Sadayakko*, 33; Kawakami Otojirō, "Kawakami ikkō no shibōsha" [The death of a member of the Kawakami troupe], *Miyako shimbun*, March 2, 1900, in Shirakawa, 312; "Society at the Capital," *New York Herald*, February 7, 1900, 8; "The World of Society," *Washington Evening Star*, February 7, 1900, 5.

15   "Topics of Interest in Washington," *New York Mail and Express*, February 8, 1900, 6. Summarized in Kaneo, *Ōbei*, 36 and said to be taken from the *Nippon shimbun* (called in English *New York Japanese News*). I could not find the original.

16   "In the Social World," *Washington Times*; also "Society at the Capital," *New York Herald*.

17   "The World of Society," *Washington Evening Star*; "In the Social World," *Washington Times*.

18   "Topics of Interest in Washington," *New York Mail and Express*, February 8, 1900, 6; also "The World of Society," *Washington Evening Star*.

19   "In the Social World," *Washington Times*. In 1900, there were only six diplomats of ambassador grade stationed in the United States. The lesser ranks of minister plenipotentiary and chief of legation represented other countries (*Rand, McNally*, 142; Fawcett Waldon, "Envoys in Washington," *Cosmopolitan*, May 1901, 3, 5).

20   Kaneo, *Sadayakko*, 33; Kawakami Otojirō, "Kawakami ikkō no shibōsha," 312.

21   "Topics of Interest in Washington," *New York Mail and Express*, February 8, 1900, 6; "In the Social World," *Washington Times*. In his own reports, Kawakami offered conflicting accounts: "Kawakami Otojirō ōmote" in Shirakawa, 312; Kaneo, *Sadayakko*, 33–34; Kaneo, *Ōbei*, 37.

22   Kaneo, *Sadayakko*, 35–36.

23   Obscene = *waisetsu*.

24   Charles H. Shattuck in *Shakespeare on the American Stage*, 2:17, summed up the 1890s: "Tragedy lost ground during this period, and there was a steady rise of interest in comedies—young, beautiful women, whose managers (and sometimes the actresses themselves) traded less on the appeal of Shakespeare than on the appeal of good legs."

25   Kaneo, *Sadayakko*, 36.

26   Ibid., 37.

27   Matsunaga, *Kawakami*, 164.

28   Ezaki, *Jitsuroku*, 113. An almost identical passage was in Dōmon, *Kawakami*, 123.

29   This American sexual sentimentality rivals overblown pathos-ridden Japanese stories.

30   Kaneo, *Ōbei*, 35–36.

31   Kaneo, *Sadayakko*, 33, 36–37.

32   Kaneo, *Ōbei*, 35–36. Sources of these American comments are unknown.

33   Kaneo, *Sadayakko*, 34–37; Kaneo, *Ōbei*, 36.

34   Kaneo, *Sadayakko*, 33, 35.

35   Ibid., 34–35.

36   Ezaki, *Jitsuroku*, 112–13; Inoue, *Kawakami*, 70; Matsunaga, *Kawakami*, 162–63; Miyaoka, *Ikoku*, 75; Muramatsu Shōfu, *Kawakami*, 1:293; Sugimoto, *Madamu*, 150; Yamaguchi, *Joyū*, 91.

37   Kawakami Otojirō, "Kawakami ikkō no shibōsha," *Miyako shimbun*, March 2, 1900, in Shirakawa, 311–12.

38   "Kawakami ichiza yōkō nisshi" [Journal of the foreign tour of the Kawakami troupe], *Miyako shimbun*, July 26, 1900, in Shirakawa, 318.

39   Kaneo, *Sadayakko*, 33, 36. In another account, Kawakami did hint that McKinley was not there (Kaneo, *Ōbei*, 60).

40   "The World of Society," *Washington Star*, February 8, 1900, 5; "In the Social World, *Washington Times*, February 8, 1900, 5; "In the National Capital," *New York Herald*, February 8, 1900, 10.

41   *Rand, McNally*, 140–41; also Fawcett Waldon, "Envoys in Washington," *Cosmopolitan*, May 1901, 14.

42   C. S. Olcott, *The Life of William McKinley* (Boston: Houghton, 1916), 2:303; Howard Wayne Morgan, *William McKinley and His America* (Syracuse: Syracuse University Press, 1963), 51, 488, 365–67; Margaret Leech, *In the Days of McKinley* (New York Harper, 1959), 30.

43   Brereton, *Life*, 2:284; "Next Week's Theatres," *Boston Traveler*, January 6, 1900, 5.

44   Dennis, *Adventures*, 5.

45   Tyler Dennett, *John Hay*, 31–38, 147.

46   Ibid., 36. President Buchanan, who was Lincoln's predecessor, hosted the samurai embassy from Japan.

47   Tyler Dennett, *John Hay*, 36–39.

48   Ibid., 57, 59, 64, 71–72, 98, 106, 144, 150, 289; Thayer, *Life*, 2:53–55; 2:72.

49   Lorenzo Sears, *John Hay, Author and Statesman* (New York: Dodd, Mead, 1914), 74–75, 91; Thayer, *Life*, 2:156, 2:183–85, 2:364–72, 2:398–99; Dennis, *Adventures*, 184–85, 519–20; Tyler Dennett, *John Hay*, 295–323.

50   Tyler Dennett, *John Hay*, 71–78, 82, 104–15, 133–41; Thayer, *Life*, 2:17, 2:49, 2:185; "Treaty Debate will Delay Canal Bill," *New York Herald*, February 7, 1900, 5.

51   John Hay, *Poems* (Boston: Houghton, Mifflin, 1899), 126–34.

52   "Japanese Actor Dead," *Boston Journal*, January 31, 1900, 2.

53   Brain congestion = nōjūketsu = cerebral hyperemia or blood congestion in the brain.

54   Kawakami Otojirō, "Kawakami ikkō no shibōsha," *Miyako shimbun*, March 2, 1900, in Shirakawa, 311–12.

55   "Shin'engeki no sossensha" [New Theatre pioneer], *Miyako shimbun*, May 17, 1900, in Shirakawa, 317. Sadayakko, in one of her later recollections, thought Mikami died of syphilis (Ubukata, "*Kawakami*, 174; also Matsunaga, *Kawakami*, 165).

56   "Japanese Actor Seriously Ill," *NYDM*, February 3, 1900, 17; "Japanese Actor Dead," *Boston Journal*, January 31, 1900, 2.

57   "Japanese Actor Dead," *Boston Journal*.

58   Mikami majored in English at an elite private university in Kyoto run by missionaries. He quit before graduating to become a New Theatre actor and first appeared with the Fukui Mohei and Seibidan troupes which were Kawakami rivals. He lived in Kobe with his fifty-six-year-old mother, fourteen-year-old brother, and twenty-year-old pregnant fiancé (Kaneo, *Ōbei*, 33; Kaneo, *Sadayakko*, 21–22; Muramatsu Shōfu, *Kawakami*, 1:276–78).

59   Japanese for "Splendid pine woods."

60   *Boston Journal*, February 1, 1900, 2.

61   "The Death of Sugere Mikami," *NYDM*, February 10, 1900, 13.

62   "Aside," *Washington Evening Star*, February 3, 1900, 21; "Chats with the Players," *Washington Times*, February 4, 1900, 2:4.

63   Sharf, "Matsuki Chronology," 38; Duis, *Saloon*, 122; Kaneo, *Sadayakko*, 29.

64   John Leslie Durstand, *A Light in the City: 150 Years of the City Missionary Society of Boston, 1816–1966* (Boston: Beacon, 1966), 187, 196, 202–3.

65   Benton probably wrote the earlier "Japanese Actor Seriously Ill," *NYDM*, February 3, 1900, 17.

66   Chisholm, *Fenollosa*, 118–21, 154 fn. 1, 147–48, 218. McNeil followed Fenollosa's pioneering ukiyoe studies with her own book about Hiroshige whom she preferred to her husband's favorite, Hokusai.

67   Ibid., 221–22; Brooks, "Fenollosa," 63, 66.

68   Brooks, "Fenollosa," 36; Miner, *Japanese*, 127, 135.

69   Miner, *Japanese*, 23, 238. Pound, in turn, shared Fenollosa's nō materials with W. B. Yeats.

70   Chisholm, *Fenollosa*, 5, 198.

71   Mary McNeil Fenollosa [Sidney McCall, pseud.], *Truth Dexter* (1901; reprint, Boston: Little, Brown, 1909), 4.

72 Mary McNeil Fenollosa [Sidney McCall, pseud.], *The Breath of the Gods: A Japanese Romance* (1905; reprint, Boston: Little, Brown, 1912).

73 Mary McNeil Fenollosa, *The Dragon Painter* (Boston: Little, Brown, 1906), 7.

74 "With the Publishers," *New England* 35 (November 1906): 386.

75 *The Dragon Painter* (William Worthington, director; Haworth, 1919) and *The Breath of the Gods* (Rollin Sturegon, director; Universal, 1920) *American Film Institute Catalog of Motion Pictures Produced in the United States: Feature Films, 1911–1920* (Berkeley: University of California Press, 1988), 98; Richard A. Oehling, "Hollywood and the Image of the Oriental, 1910–1950," *Film and History* 8 (September 1978): 61; "Mrs. Sessue Hayakawa Is Newest of Universal Stars," *Moving Picture World* 41 (August 2, 1919): 687.

76 Quoted from Lafcadio Hearn, *Glimpses of Unfamiliar Japan* (Boston: Houghton, Mifflin, 1894), 1:40.

77 Kaneo, *Ōbei*, 24; Kaneo, *Sadayakko*, 25; Muramatsu Shōfu, *Kawakami*, 1:283. "Mikami Shigeru" was a stage name. His legal name was Mitani Torakichi (Kaneo, *Ōbei*, 33).

78 Kaneo, *Sadayakko*, 25. The two onnagata were buried seven graves apart in a field called the C. P. Plot. C. P. stood for City Poor and was a polite Boston term for potter's field. Today, this area at Mt. Hope is a remote flat expanse of grass the size of two football fields. No individual markers remain, not even a designation that this was once the C. P. plot. Surviving C. P. records at Mt. Hope read for Maruyama: "age 21, gr[ave] 8 r[ow] 31" and for Mikami: "age 27, gr[ave] 15 r[ow] 31." I sponsored a somewhat Buddhist memorial service for them at Mt. Hope during the winter of 1988–89 (in the snow).

79 "Ōsaka no Kawakami engeki" [The Kawakami play in Osaka], *Chūō shimbun*, February 2, 1901, in Shirakawa, 348–49; "Kabuki nikki" [Theatre diary], *Kabuki* (March 1901), 67–70. Hanabusa Ryūgai, one of Kawakami's house playwrights, fashioned the play with Kawakami (Akiba, *Nihon*, 1:397). Hanabusa later became an Ibsenite who transformed several Ibsen plays into *hon'an* (Akiba, *Nihon*, 1:207, 1:481–85; Matsumoto, *Meiji engekiron*, 309–10).

80 Kaneo, *Ōbei*, 24.

81 Hanabusa, *Yōkōchū*, 1–17.

82 "Kawakami no kōgyō" [Kawakami's performances], *Miyako shimbun*, January 25, 1901, in Shirakawa, 348.

83 In American theatres, this moving stage panorama of several settings (all set inside the Chicago Lyric Theatre) would be impossible to produce so smoothly.

84 Hanabusa, *Yōkōchū*, 6.

85 Ibid., 1–10.

86 There was once a modern folk belief that eating Western food helped to make one cultured (in the Western sense).

87 "Final words" = yuigon.

88 "Great loyal samurai" = daichūshin.

89 60¢.

90 "Foreigners in their enclaves" = kyoryūchi.

91 A decade earlier, the Japanese government promulgated the official national cheer "Tennō heika banzai" that literally means "His Majesty the Emperor (tennō heika) 10,000 years." Banzai suggested infinity and was equivalent to "hurrah" (Sawada, *Tokyo*, 70; Luck, *Japan's*, 45).

92 "New Theatre" = shin'engeki.

93 The Japanese national anthem.

94 Hanabusa, *Yōkōchū*, 10–17.

95 Kawakami Otojirō, "Kawakami ikkō no shibōsha." *Miyako shimbun*, March 2, 1900, in Shirakawa, 311–12.

96 Kaneo, *Ōbei*, 33.

97 Kaneo, *Sadayakko*, 21–26.

98 Ibid., 23–25.

99   "Ōsaka no Kawakami engeki" [The Kawakami play in Osaka], *Chūō shimbun*, February 2, 1901, in Shirakawa, 348–49.[1] Yanagi, *Ebanzuke*, 121–22.

100 Yanagi, *Ebanzuke*, 121–22.

101 Hirooka Ryūkō wrote *Bushiteki kyōiku* with *hon'an* parts taken from *The Great Ruby*, *Arizona*, and a third (unidentified) play that Kawakami saw in America ("Ōsaka no Kawakami engeki" [The Kawakami play in Osaka], Shirakawa, 348–49; "Kabuki nikki" [Theatre diary], *Kabuki* (March 1901), 67–70; "Kōbe Aioi-za ni okeru Kawakami engeki no keikyō" [Viewing the Kawakami play at the Kobe Aioi-za], *Miyako shimbun*, February 8, 1901, in Shirakawa, 351; Miyake Shūtarō, *Engeki*, 91.)

102 [Ihara] Seiseien, "Kichō seru Kawakami Otojirō" [Kawakami Otojirō returns to Japan], *Kabuki* (March 1901): 59–60; Ihara Seiseien, "Shinsaku annai" [Guide to new works], *Kabuki* (March 1901), 11; also Matsunaga, Kawakami, 182–83. Looking back on the premiere production seven decades later, historian Ozaki Hirotsugu called *Yōkōchū no higeki* a "very simple, artless play" but one that projected "a fair image of a past era" (Ozaki, Joyū, 41).

103 "[T]he actor is in the ironic situation of both being and not-being himself and the character he is playing while the audience is in the ironic attitude of detached observation of life and acting" (Sharpe, *Irony*, 30).

104 Miyake Shūtarō, *Engeki*, 91. Ihara Seiseien termed *Yōkōchū no higeki* an "actuality dramatization" (jujitsu kyakushoku) ([Ihara] Seiseien, "Kichō seru Kawakami Otojirō;" Ihara Seiseien, "Shinsaku annai," 11).

105 In America, so-called "autobiographical" plays were often stories of boxers or notorious persons who played themselves—and who were seldom competent actors. When Kawakami was playing his matinees at the Lyric Theatre in Chicago, boxer Bob Fitzsimmons was the main evening attraction in a vaudeville show. Later, around the time *Yōkōchū no higeki* opened in Japan, Fitzsimmons was touring in *The Honest Blacksmith*, the story of his melodramatic rise from village blacksmith to villain-trouncing prize fighter (Bordman, *American Theatre*, 474).

106 One might call these endeavors do-it-yourself hagiography.

107 Overseas, the best-known work in this "entertainment world" genre has been Mizoguchi Kenji's 1939 motion picture version of the popular shimpa drama, *The Last Chrysanthemum* (*Zangiku monogatari*).

Chapter 22

1   Van Dyke, *New*, 181.

2   Wells, *Future*, 37, 51.

3   Kaneo, *Ōbei*, 37; DiMeglio, *Vaudeville*, 136; *Appleton's Directory*, 35; Sante, *Low*, 34; King, *Handbook*, 199, 214.

4   Keene, *Modern*, 15, 192, 205.

5   Zeisloft, *New*, 266–68.

6   Kaneo, *Ōbei*, 37; Mayer, *Once*, 3; Jeff Hirsh, *Manhattan Hotels 1880–1920* (Dover, New Hampshire: Arcadia, 1997), 2:97. Named for the sculptor of the Statue of Liberty this hotel advertised "Newly fitted with Porcelain Baths … Electric Elevators" ("Hotel Bartholdi," advertisement, Broadway Theatre, program, week of December 18, 1899, in clipping file: Foxy Quiller, BRTC).

7   *Harper's Guide to Paris and the Exposition of 1900* (New York: Harper's, 1900), 19. Fancier accommodations at five dollars a day were available at the Plaza, Savoy, and Waldorf-Astoria Hotels.

8   Fujikawa Iwanosuke, "Kawakami ichiza yōkō nisshi" [Journal of the overseas tour of the Kawakami troupe], *Miyako shimbun*, July 26, 1900, in Shirakawa, 318; B. M. Sherman, "A Pioneer in Managerial Fields," *New York Evening Telegram*, March 3, 1900, 4; Frederic Edward McKay, "Theatrical Gossip; These Actors Are So and So from Royal Stage of Tokio," *New York Journal*, February 22, 1900, 4.)

9   "At the Theatres," *New York Mail and Express*, February 20, 1900, 7; "Next Week's Plays," *New York Mail*

and Express, February 17, 1900, 18; "Huber's Museum," advertisement, *New York Times*, February 18, 1900, 9.

10   "Bypaths of the Drama," *New York Sun*, July 29, 1900, 3:5 (reprinted from a trade paper); also "Proctor's," advertisement, *New York Herald*, April 1, 1900, 4:5; "Vaudeville," *NYDM*, 7 April 1900, 18.

11   "Continuous Attractions," *New York Press*, February 11, 1900, 14; "The New York," advertisement, *New York Herald*, March 4, 4:5; "Proctor's," advertisement, *New York Herald*, April 1, 1900, 4:5.

12   Clement Scott, "'Ballet! Beauty! Brains!' Exclaims Clement Scott," *New York Herald*, January 28, 1900, 4:10.

13   "New York—Broadway to Tokio," *NYDM*, February 3, 1900, 16; also "The Elaborate and Dazzling Japanese Scene in 'Broadway to Tokio,' at the New York Theatre," *Leslie's Weekly* 90 (February 10, 1900): 118; "Broadway to Tokio," *New York Commercial Advertiser Pictorial Review*, February 3, 1900, 11.

14   "Incidents in Stageland," *New York Sun*, February 9, 1900, 7; New York Theatre, New York, program, week of January 23, 1900, in clipping file: Broadway to Tokio, BRTC.

15   "Isadora Duncan, an American Girl, Gets $250 a Performance from Society," *New York World*, March 4, 1900, E1; "Society to Hear the 'Rubaiyat,'" *Boston Evening Transcript*, January 31, 1900, 4.

16   "Japanese Dances," *New York Press*, April 1, 1900, 15.

17   Gerald R. Wolfe, *New York: A Guide to the Metropolis* (New York: New York University Press, 1975), 163–84; Zeisloft, *New*, 625; Henderson, *City*, 144–47.

18   "Wanamaker's," advertisement, *New York Times*, January 26, 1900, 4; "Things of Beauty from the Orient," advertisement, *New York Times*, January 24, 1900, 4.

19   "Dancing Costumes for Young Party Goers," *New York Press*, January 14, 1900, 17; "Fifth Avenue Auction Rooms," advertisement, *New York Tribune*, February 19, 1900, 2; "Japanese-American Type," *New York World*, January 23, 1898, 26.

20   "From Japanese Standpoint," *New York Times*, May 20, 1900, 20; Mitziko Sawada, "Japanese," in Kenneth Jackson, *Encyclopedia*, 613. Population figures were rough estimates because the U.S. Census Bureau used its broad classification of "Colored" to include African-American, Chinese, Japanese, and "civilized [American] Indian" without differentiation. For the 1900 census, the category was split into "Negro" and "Colored" (other non-Caucasian) (Riis, *Just*, 211 fn. 13).

21   "Rush of Japanese Here," *New York Press*, April 20, 1900, 6; "Many Japanese Immigrants," *New York Times*, April 20, 1900, 3; "7,000 Immigrants from Japan," *New York Times*, April 27, 1900, 8; "Japan Puts up Bars," *New York Sun*, June 13, 1900, 1; "Japanese to Be Sent Home," *New York Commercial Advertiser*, April 20, 1900, 3.

22   "Haruyama Jasutein bokushi" [Pastor Justin Haruyama], *OCS nyūsu* (New York), March 4, 1977, 3; Sawada, *Tokyo*, 21; "Japanese Editor Talks," *New York Mail and Express*, February 23, 1900, 4. Male stars of the American theatre were especially fond of Japanese valets (Edith Davids, "The Art of Theatrical Make-up," *Cosmopolitan* [August 1901]: 354; Lifson, *Yiddish*, 147; "Seventh Sister," exhibit at William Gillette Castle, Hadlyme, Connecticut, 1984).

23   "New York Society's Latest—The Japanese Servant in Fashionable Homes," *New York World*, February 25, 1900, 2.

24   "Japanese House Servants," *New York Times*, May 20, 1900, 20.

25   Ibid.; "Servants and their Woes," *Portland Morning Oregonian*, September 29, 1899, 3; "From Japanese Standpoint," *New York Times*, May 20, 1900, 20.

26   Nagai, "Akatsuki" [Dawn], in his *Amerika*, 56–59.

27   Mayer, *Once*, 53; Thomas, *Print*, 277.

28   Davis, "Broadway," 24.

29   Crane, *Last*, 173.

30   Trager, *West*, 131; "Fifth Avenue as a Thoroughfare for Business Traffic," *New York Mail and Express Illustrated Saturday Magazine*, January 6, 1900, 4; Howells, *Story*, 171.

31   Nagai, "Yowa no sakaba" [A saloon in the dead of night], in his *Amerika*, 67; Rudyard Kipling, "Across a Continent," in *Works of Rudyard Kipling*; *Letters of Travel* (London: Macmillan, 1913), 13–14.

32   Van Dyke, *New*, 48–49; "The Weather," *New York Times*, February 10–17, 1900, 2, 4; Sante, *Low*, 47.

33   "Public Demands Repaired Street," *New York Evening Telegram*, April 17, 1900, 8.

34   Sante, *Low*, 47; Allen Churchill, *The Upper Crust* (Englewood Cliffs, New Jersey: Prentice-Hall, 1970), photograph, 204; "Fifth Avenue as a Thoroughfare for Business Traffic," *New York Mail and Express Illustrated Saturday Magazine*; Baedeker, *United*, 12; Ellis, *Epic*, 462; *Appleton's Directory*, 41; J. Walton McMillar, "The Whirlpools of New York," *Metropolitan* 11 (May 1900): 590; Muirhead, *Land*, 196.

35   Mayer, *Once*, 61; Henry Collins Brown, *Golden*, 65; Ellis, *Epic*, 461; "All about Automobiles," *New York Journal Magazine*, February 4, 1900, 22.

36   Jesse Lynch Williams, *New*, 47.

37   Davis, "Broadway," 25.

38   Strang, *Players*, 2:194–95.

39   William H. Crane, "The Modern Cart of Thespis," *North American Review* 154 (April 1892): 476–77.

40   Poggi, *Theatre*, 45, 28.

41   W. J. Henderson, "The Business of a Theatre," *Scribner's* 25 (March 1899): 311–12.

42   "Brooklyn Amusements, *NYDM*, March 10, 1900, 17.

43   Quoted in Bernheim, *Business*, 49; also 47.

44   Leander Richardson, "The Month in Theatricals," *Metropolitan* 11 (January 1899): 87.

45   Many productions on the road were extending their tours because they could not get into a Manhattan theatre.

46   Bordman, *American Musical*, 159.

47   Cahn, *Theatrical 1900–01*, 19–48. The Metropolitan Opera House had 3,400 seats (Brown, *History*, 3: 454).

48   Ned A. Bowman, "American Theatre Architecture: The Concrete Mirror Held up to Yankee Nature" in Williams, *American*, 215.

49   Leander Richardson, "The Month in Theatricals;" also Jenkins, *Greatest*, 269.

50   "Price of Theatre Tickets," *New York Sun*, February 9, 1900, 5; Wells Hawks, "How Theatres Are Managed. No. 1: The Box Office Man," *Theatre* (New York) No. 38 (April 1904): 9.

51   "Ticket Speculators Object," *New York Times*, February 9, 1900, 7; Bernheim, *Business*, 192–93.

52   W. J. Henderson, "The Business of a Theatre," *Scribner's* (March 1899): 299; Grau, *Business*, 84–85; Hawks, "How Theatres Are Managed. No. 1: The Box Office Man;" Felix Isman, *Weber and Fields* (New York: Boni and Liveright, 1924), 256–57.

53   Gilbert, *American*, 245–46.

54   "Ticket Sellers Excuse," *New York Commercial Advertiser*, February 10, 1900, 7.

55   Statistics were based on weekly listings in the "Current Amusements" of the *New York Dramatic Mirror* (throughout 1899–1900), 16. This did not include all minor theatres.

56   As there were no common definitions for classes of New York theatres, my arbitrary criteria were based on 1) admission scales, 2) status of leading players and productions, 3) production budgets, and 4) critics' impressions. Principal sources were trade reviews in the *New York Dramatic Mirror* and *New York Clipper*, weekly listings in the "Current Amusements" section of the *Dramatic Mirror*, and reviews in the New York daily press. I gave little weight to theatre size, accoutrements, and reputation in theatrical histories.

57   There was only one second-class theatre for drama in Brooklyn.

58 Two first-class theatres on Broadway (the Criterion at 44th and the New York at 45th) were north of this demarcation. Another, the old Lyceum, was south of the new theatre area.

59 Four of these shows would still be running when Kawakami left New York at the end of April: the toga spectacle *Ben Hur*, William Gillette's *Sherlock Holmes*, Weber and Fields's burlesque *Whirl-i-gig*, and the down-on-the-farm melodrama *Way Down East*. Two major hits that closed in this period were Anna Held in *Papa's Wife* (at twenty weeks) and May Irwin in *Sister Mary* (at seventeen weeks).

60 Of these, seven had runs of at least eleven weeks. Other long runs continuing after the Kawakami troupe arrived in the city, but closing before they left, were Maude Adams in a repeat engagement of *The Little Minister*, David Belasco's *Naughty Anthony*, the extravaganza *Broadway to Tokio*, the officers-as-gentlemen story *Brother Officers*, and Weber and Field's *Barbara Fidgety*.

61 "Current Amusements," *NYDM*, February 3–April 28, 1900, 16.

62 *The Degenerates*, Lillie Langtry; *The Little Minister*, Maude Adams; *Papa's Wife*, Anna Held; *Naughty Anthony*, Blanche Bates; *Broadway to Tokio*, Fay Templeton; *Sister Mary*, May Irwin; *When We Were Twenty-one*, Maxine Elliott; *Sapho*, Olga Nethersole; *The Whirl-i-gig*, Lillian Russell; and *Chris and the Wonderful Lamp*, Edna Wallace Hopper in drag ("Current Amusements," *NYDM*, February 10, 1900, 16). My "top" designations came from analysis of reviews in the *NYDM*, September 2 1899–February 12, 1900.

63 Edward A. Dithmar, "At the Play and with the Players," *New York Times*, January 14, 1900, 16.

64 H[illary] B[ell], "Mrs. Langtry Gives a New Play; Old Successes Still Run On," *New York Press*, January 16, 1900, 7.

65 "At the Play," *New York World*, January 7, 1900, 2E.

66 "The Theatres," *New York Commercial Advertiser*, February 5, 1900, 7.

67 "At the Theatres. Manhattan—Papa's Wife," *NYDM*, November 18, 1899, 16.

68 Clement Scott, "'Ballet! Beauty! Brains!' Exclaims Clement Scott," *New York Herald*, January 28, 1900, 4:10; also "The Elaborate and Dazzling Japanese Scene in 'Broadway to Tokio,' at the New York Theatre," *Leslie's Weekly* 90 (February 10, 1900): 118.

69 H[illary] B[ell], "Mrs. Langtry Gives a New Play; Old Successes Still Run On," *New York Press*, January 16, 1900, 7.

70 "Dramatic and Musical," *New York Times*, January 16, 1900, 7; "The Theatres," *New York Commercial Advertiser*, January 16, 1900, 1900, 7; Frederic Edward McKay, "The Degenerates," *New York Mail and Express*, January 16, 1900, 7.

71 "This Week on Our Stage," *New York Sun*, February 11, 1900, 2:7.

72 The show starred the exotic foreign wannabe-an-American star, Anna Held who was the wife of the show's young producer, Flo Ziegfield. It ran four and a half months and put Ziegfield into the big time.

73 Manhattan Theatre, New York, program, week of January 22, 1900, "Papa's Wife," in Erlanger Collection, *ZAN-*T33 reel 12, item 269, BRTC.

74 "Dramatic and Musical. Madison Square Theatre," *New York Times*, February 6, 1900, 6; "Reviews of the New Plays," *New York Evening Telegram*, February 6, 1900, 4. One critic wrote that he was grateful the original had been cleaned up but felt the American version was still "dirty enough to disgust many" ("New Dramatic Material," *New York Sun*, February 6, 1900, 7).

75 "Reviews of the New Plays," *New York Evening Telegram*, February 6, 1900, 4; "The Theatres," *New York Commercial Advertiser*, January 16, 1900, and February 6, 1900, 7; "Four New Plays. 'Coralie & Co.,'" *New York Mail and Express*, February 6, 1900, 7. *Coralie & Co.* opened February 5 and closed March 31.

76 "Theatrical Amusements," *New York Sun*, April 22, 1900, 3:9; Hillary Bell, "The Theatres," *New York Press*, March 4, 1900, 14; "Reviews of the New Plays," *New York Evening Telegram*, February 6, 1900, 4; "Good

and Evil in Plays," *New York Sun*, February 11, 1900, 2:7; "Dramas and Audiences. Do Our People Need Protection against the Theatres?" *New York Sun*, February 18, 1900, 3:7.

77   February 24, 1900, and March 9 and 17, 1900, all p. 14.

78   Sidney Sharp, "Three New Plays and a Notable Night at the Grand Opera," *New York World*, January 7, 1900, 4; "New Plays on Our Stage," *New York Sun*, January 9, 1900, 7; "The Licentious Drama: Is the American Stage Degenerate?" *Metropolitan* 11 (June 1900): 654–55.

79   Hillary Bell, "The Theatres," *New York Press*, March 4, 1900, 14.

80   "Time to Call Halt to Dramatic Ptomaines," *New York World*, January 21, 1900, 2E; "The Usher," *NYDM*, November 4, 1899, 4; "Dramas and Audiences. Do Our People Need Protection against the Theatres?" *New York Sun*; "Immorality Has Been the Cause of This Season's Dramatic Failures," *New York World*, April 15, 2E.

81   Hillary Bell, "The Theatres," *New York Press*.

82   "Dramatic and Musical," *New York Times*, January 16, 1900, 7; Edward A. Dithmar, "At the Play and with the Players," *New York Times*, January 21, 1900: 2:16.

83   Hillary Bell, "The Theatres," *New York Press*, March 4, 1900, 14.

84   Bijou Theatre, New York, program, week of December 4, 1899, and "'Sister Mary;' May Irvin's Smile," unidentified New York newspaper, December 11, 1899, in RLS NAFR+ v. 297, pp. 15, 65. BRTC.

85   Bordman, *American Theatre*, 414.

86   Marguerite Vance, *Hear the Distant Applause!* (New York: Dutton, 1963), 141; Edward A. Dithmar, "At the Play and with the Players," *New York Times*, January 14, 1900, 16.

87   Jason, "The Dramatic Season in New York," *Leslie's Weekly* 89 (December 23, 1899): 510.

88   "Pictures New England Scenes," unidentified Chicago newspaper, August 20, 1900, in clipping file: Way Down East, BRTC; "This Week's Novelties," *New York Journal*, February 18, 1900, 38; "Way Down East Encyclopedia," brochure (New York: Plato, 1901), n.p.; "Current Amusements," *NYDM*, February 10–May 28, 1900, 16.

89   "Way Down East Encyclopedia," brochure.

90   "Themes from Stageland," *New York Sun*, June 17, 1900, 39; also "About Current Plays," *Boston Dramatic Review* (November 25, 1899), 2; William Gillette, *Sherlock Holmes* (Garden City: Double, Day, 1935).

91   "Sights at the Theatre," *New York Sun*, February 22, 1900, 7. Posh melodramas imported from Great Britain reflected the growing commercial dominance in Britain of the London West End over the East End theatres that played melodramatic fare at affordable, working class prices (Michael R. Booth, "Introduction," in ed. Booth *English Plays of the Nineteenth Century, Vol. 2, Dramas 1850–1900* [Oxford: Clarendon, 1969], 5).

92   Garden Theatre, New York, program, February 26, 1900, in scrapbook MWEZ+ n.c. 699; p. 132, BRTC; "Things in the New Plays," *New York Sun*, February 25, 1900, B7.

93   New York Theatre, New York, program, week of January 23, 1900, in clipping file: Broadway to Tokio, BRTC; "New York—Broadway to Tokio," *NYDM*, February 3, 1900, 16. Most of the scenic elements for this show were not built in solid three-dimensions but were painted in perspective on flats.

94   In Manhattan these shows respectively played twelve, twenty, and sixteen weeks (Bordman, *American Theatre*, 444–45).

95   These followed the established dramatic tradition of burlesque as parody and were not part of the emerging burlesque business of bawdy variety shows (discussed later).

96   Bordman, *American Musical*, 167.

97   "New Dramatic Material," *New York Sun*, February 6, 1900, 7.

98   "The Theatres," *New York Commercial Advertiser*, February 5, 1900, 7; "Dramatic and Musical. Madison Square Theatre," *New York Times*, February 6, 1900, 6.

99   "The Point of View," *Scribner's* 26 (July 1899): 123.

100 Ibid., 123–24.

101 Bernheim, *Business*, 30; "This Week on Our Stage," *New York Sun*, March 18, 1900, 11; "Affairs of the Theatre," *New York Sun*, March 30, 1900, 7.

102 The former ran sixteen weeks, the latter eleven (Bordman, *American Theatre*, 445, 456).

103 Bordman, *American Theatre*, 452, 454, 456, 457, 460, 461; "Current Amusements," *NYDM*, September 9, 1899–May 12, 1900, 16; "Affairs of the Theatre," *New York Sun*, March 30, 1900, 7; Leander Richardson, "The Month in Theatricals," *Metropolitan* 11 (March 1900): 322.

104 Leading players in a stock company such as the Donnelly were often expected to copy the mannerisms of the actors who originated the roles on Broadway ("Extravaganza Unready," *New York Sun*, March 13, 1900, 7).

105 "The Theatrical Syndicate," *NYDM*, January 13, 1900, 3; also "Topics from Stageland," *New York Sun*, April 19, 1900, 17; "Murray Hill," advertisement, *New York Herald*, March 18, 1900, 4:5; Leander Richardson, "Revival of the Stock Company," *Metropolitan* 11 (May 1900): 535–40; Poggi, *Theatre*, 5–7.

106 "In Theatrical Affairs," *New York Sun*, February 23, 1900, 7.

107 "Topics from Stageland," *New York Sun*, February 14, 1900, 7.

108 Weldon B. Durham, "The Revival and Decline of the Stock Company Mode of Organization 1886–1930," *Theatre History Studies* 6 (1986): 165–67.

109 Actors were usually hired and cast according to their specialized lines of business, such as leading man or woman, juvenile, old woman, genteel heavy, character heavy, ingénue, low comic, soubrette, grand dame (*Actors' Society Monthly Bulletin* [January 1900], 16–20). In earlier times, plays were often tailored to these specific character types. In their hiring of closely defined character types, American stock companies resembled kabuki employment although, of course, Japanese lines of business were different and the selection of plays more limited.

110 Jefferson, *Autobiography*, 7, 243.

111 Bloom, *Joseph*, 177.

112 Poggi, *Theatre*, 43–44; Weldon B. Durham, "The Revival and Decline of the Stock Company Mode of Organization 1886–1930," 176–77, 182–83. In the western United States, where church influence was less pervasive, Sunday performances were possible. This West Coast standard was explicit in the title of Cecil Matson's *Seven Nights—Three Matinees: Seventy Years of Dramatic Stock in Portland, Oregon 1863–1933* (Portland: Matson, 196?).

113 McArthur, *Actors*, 8; Leander Richardson, "Revival of the Stock Company," *Metropolitan* 11 (May 1900): 535–40; "In a Stock Company," *New York Times*, April 22, 1900, 18.

114 Ada Patterson and Victory Bateman, "Autobiography of an Actress," in *By the Stage Door* (New York: Grafton, 1902), 41. This fictional work was based on the authors' experiences as actresses.

115 "American. Castle Sq. Opera Co.," advertisement, *New York Times*, January 28, 1900, 9. This musical company originated at the famous Castle Square Theatre in Boston but moved on when that theatre converted to resident dramatic stock.

116 "American. Castle Sq. Opera Co.," advertisements, *New York Tribune*, February 25, 1900, 12, and *New York Herald*, March 11, 1900, 4:5; Leander Richardson, "The Month in Theatricals," *Metropolitan* 11 (March 1900): 326–27.

117 "Programme for Last Opera Performance," *New York Sun*, April 19, 1900, 7. The Metropolitan Opera winter season ran January through April.

118 "Metropolitan Opera House, Grand Opera House Season 1899–1900," advertisement, *New York Mail and Express*, February 7, 1900, 7; "Metropolitan Opera House, Grand Opera House Season 1899–1900," advertisement, *New York Herald*, March 11, 1900, 4:5.

119 Hillary Bell, "Player Folk," *New York Press*, April 20, 1900, 6; "Metropolitan Opera House," advertisement,

New York Herald, February 8, 1900, 18; "Metropolitan Opera House," advertisement, *New York Herald*, March 11, 1900.

120   John Dizikes, *Opera in America: A Cultural History* (New Haven, Connecticut: Yale University Press, 1993), 288–90.

121   Hillary Bell, "Player Folk," *New York Press*; "New York to Have a New Opera House?" *New York Herald*, April 18, 1900, 3.

Chapter 23

1   "Current Amusements," *NYDM*, September 9, 1899–May 12, 1900, 16; "News and Views of Theatricals," *New York Evening Telegram*, February 7, 1900, 4; Baedeker, *United States*, 15–16.

2   "Current Amusements," *NYDM*, September 9, 1899–May 12, 1900, 16.

3   For example, "At the Theatres. Star—The Musketeers," *NYDM*, July 8, 1899, 14.

4   Michael R. Booth, *English Melodrama* (London: Jenkins, 1965), 13. Bruce McConachie, in the opening sentence of his *Melodramatic Formations: American Theatre and Society, 1820–1870*, claimed, "Melodrama was ubiquitous in American culture between 1820 and 1870." Melodrama, in high or low forms, was still pervasive in 1900.

5   "News and Views of Theatricals," *New York Evening Telegram*; Baedeker, *United States*, 15–16.

6   Brooks McNamara, "Popular Entertainment," in Wilmeth, *History*, 399; Rahill, *World*, 271; Marian Spitzer, "Ten-Twenty-Thirty," *Saturday Evening Post*, August 25, 1914, 40, 42.

7   "At the Theatres. Metropolis—The Bowery after Dark," *NYDM*, January 20, 1900, 16; "At the Theatres. Star—The Queen of Chinatown," *NYDM*, August 26, 1899, 15; "At the Theatres. Third Avenue—The Sleeping City," *NYDM*, August 26, 1899, 15; "News and Views of Theatricals," *New York Evening Telegram*.

8   Levine, *Highbrow*, 179, 195–99.

9   See Eco, *Travels*, 153.

10   Levine, *Highbrow*, 194–99.

11   "Themes from Stageland," *New York Sun*, June 17, 1900, 39; Edward A. Dithmar, "Two Successful Plays," *Harper's Weekly* 43 (November 25, 1899): 1183; "At the Theatres. Third Avenue—The Sleeping City," *NYDM*; "Things in the New Plays," *New York Sun*, April 15, 1900, 3:7.

12   "The Gunner's Mate," *New York Mail and Express*, January 9, 1900, 7; "At the Theatres. Third Avenue—The Sleeping City," *NYDM*; "At the Theatres. Star—The Queen of Chinatown," *NYDM*, August 26, 1899.

13   The term "critic" was first applied in the theatre to those who made their opinions known by yelling out during a performance (Elizabeth Burns, *Theatricality: A Study of Convention in the Theatre and in Social Life* [London: Longman, 1972], 189).

14   Dutton Cook, "The Right to Hiss," *Theatre* (London) (October 1, 1883): 178–84. With due discretion, managers had the right to eject people if they felt demonstrations were excessive.

15   Fredric Edward McKay, "A New Melodrama," *New York Mail and Express*, January 30, 1900, 7.

16   Plays so readily called tragedies did not necessarily conform to classic definitions of tragedy.

17   Strang, *Players*, 1:24.

18   Brooks, *Melodramatic*, 205; William Archer, *About the Theatre* (London: Unwin, 1886), 320.

19   Norman Hapgood, "The Actor of Today." *Atlantic Monthly* 83 (January 1899): 123, 125.

20   Henry Tyrell, "Drama and Yellow Drama," *Theatre* (New York) No. 42 (August 1907): 193; also Fredric Edward McKay, "A New Melodrama, *New York Mail and Express*, January 30, 1900, 7.

21   Stephen Crane, "Maggie: A Girl of the Streets," in *Stephen Crane: Prose and Poetry* (New York: Library of America, 1984), 36.

22   David Grimsted, *Melodrama Unveiled: American Theatre and Culture, 1800–1850* (Chicago: University of Chicago Press, 1968), 229; also Michael R. Booth, "Introduction," in Booth, *Hiss*, 9.

23   Henry Tyrell, "Drama and Yellow Drama," 192.

24   Brooks, *Melodramatic*, ix. Brooks focused primarily on novelistic rather than theatrical concerns. Like him, I did not consider "melodrama" or "melodramatic" pejorative.

25   William Archer, *About the Theatre*, 320.

26   McConachie, *Melodramatic*, 225–26.

27   Eric Bentley, *Life of Drama* (New York: Atheneum, 1967), 216 and 198.

28   "Way Down East," unidentified New York newspaper clipping, February 8, 1898, n.p.

29   Levine, *Highbrow*, 46–49.

30   Michael Hays, "Representing Empire: Class, Culture, and the Popular Theatre in the Nineteenth Century," in Gainor, *Imperialism*, 132–47. Hays discussed melodrama in a British, not an American, context.

31   Moore, "Class and Ethnicity," 139–40; Ellis, *Epic*, 458. Three-fourths of the residents of New York in 1900 were immigrants or second-generation Americans.

32   Star Theatre, New York, program, week of February 7, 1898, in program file: The Great Train Robbery, BRTC; "Some Dramatic Subjects," *New York Sun*, February 16, 1900, 7; "At the Theatres. Star," *NYDM*, November 18, 1899, 16.

33   "Success of King of the Opium Ring," *NYDM*, May 20, 1899, 22; "At the Theatres. Third Avenue—The Queen of Chinatown," *NYDM*, March 24, 1900, 17.

34   "Topics of the Theatre," *New York Sun*, April 26, 1900, 7.

35   "'Great Train Robbery' in Brooklyn," *New York Press*, February 6, 1900, 7; "Some Dramatic Subjects," *New York Sun*, February 16, 1900, 7.

36   "At the Theatres. Star—The Bowery after Dark," *NYDM*, January 6, 1900, 17. Similar reptile realism was repeated in the climax of *A Night in Chinatown* ("Third Avenue—A Night in Chinatown," *NYDM*, January 27, 1900, 16).

37   "At the Theatres. Star—The Queen of Chinatown," *NYDM*, August 26, 1899, 15.

38   *Meiboku Sendai hagi* was adapted from a *bunraku* puppet where rats were easier to play as puppets.

39   "New Plays on Our Stage," *New York Sun*, January 9, 1900, 7.

40   "News and Gossip of the Stage," *New York Evening Telegram*, April 18, 1900, 4.

41   "Star—Across the Pacific," *NYDM*, March 24, 1900, 16.

42   Fredric Edward McKay, "A New Melodrama, *New York Mail and Express*, January 30, 1900, 7; Booth, "Introduction," in Booth, *Hiss*, 16.

43   "Current Amusements," *NYDM*, March 17, 1900, 16; Bordman, *American Theatre*, 167; "Michael Strogoff," *Illustrated London News* (June 18, 1881): n.p.

44   "At the Theatres. Star—The Bowery after Dark," *NYDM*, January 6, 1900, 17; "Third Avenue," *NYDM*, February 24, 1900, 16; "At the Theatres. Third Avenue—Just before Dawn," *NYDM*, March 17, 1900, 16; "Success of King of the Opium Ring," *NYDM*, May 20, 1899, 22; "At the Theatres. Third Avenue— "Night in Chinatown," *NYDM*, January 27, 1900, 17; Third Avenue Theatre, New York, program, week of January 22, 1900, in scrapbook MWEZ+ n.c. 713, p. 220, BRTC; "The Theatres," *New York Commercial Advertiser*, January 9, 1900, 7; "New Plays on Our Stage," *New York Sun*, January 9, 1900, 7.

45   "At the Theatres. Third Avenue—The California Detective," *NYDM*, April 7, 1900, 16; "Topics of the Theatre," *New York Sun*, April 26, 1900, 7; Bordman, *American Theatre*, 383; "Current Amusements," *NYDM*, February 23, 1900 16; "News and Views of Theatricals," *New York Evening Telegram*, February 7, 1900, 4.

46   "Star—Across the Pacific," *NYDM*, March 24, 1900, 16.

47   Rahill, *World*, 276; Davies, *Mirror*, 56.

48   "News and Gossip of the Stage," *New York Evening Telegram*, April 18, 1900, 4; "Vice Gets Hard Knocks," *New York Press*, January 16, 1900, 7; "At the Theatres. Star—The Queen of Chinatown," *NYDM*, August 26, 1899, 15.

49   "Current Amusements," *NYDM*, September 9, 1899–May 12, 1900, 16.

50   Sante, *Low*, 144–45. These plays centered on Chinese in the United States, especially in San Francisco. The beginning of the Boxer Rebellion, with its attacks on Europeans, was as yet hardly perceived in the United States ("Missionaries in Northern China," *New York Sun*, June 3, 1900, 3:9).

51   Rahill, *World*, 277; Bordman, *American Theatre*, 435, 443, 456, 471. Not all of these titles played New York in the 1899–1900 season.

52   Margret Dietrich, "The Far East—Its Reflection in and Influences on the European Theatre," trans. Bindon Russell, *Theatre Research* 4 (1962): 172–80.

53   "Success of King of the Opium Ring," *NYDM*, May 20, 1899, 22; Academy of Music, New York, program, week of May 15, 1899; in program file: The King of the Opium Ring, BRTC; "At the Theatres. Third Avenue—Night in Chinatown," *NYDM*, January 27, 1900, 17; "At the Theatres. Star—The Queen of Chinatown," *NYDM*, August 26, 1899, 15; "At the Theatres. Columbia—The King of the Opium Ring," *NYDM*, March 18, 1900, 16; "New Plays," *NYC*, March 3, 1900, 3; "Success of King of the Opium Ring," *NYDM*, May 20, 1899, 22; "At the Theatres. Third Avenue—Night in Chinatown," *NYDM*, January 27, 1900, 17; "At the Theatres. Star—The Bowery after Dark," *NYDM*, January 6, 1900, 17.

54   "At the Theatres. Columbus—The King of the Opium Ring," *NYDM*, March 18, 1899, 16.

55   "Chas. E. Blaney's The Chinese-American Sensation. King of the Opium Ring," pamphlet, Academy of Music, New York, January 9, 1900, in clipping file: The King of the Opium Ring, BRTC. A man, a woman, and three small acrobatic children were the entire royal Sam-Pee-Lee troupe.

56   "At the Theatres. Third Avenue—Night in Chinatown," *NYDM*, January 27, 1900, 17.

57   "At the Theatres. Star—The Queen of Chinatown," *NYDM*, August 26, 1899, 15; "Success of King of the Opium Ring," *NYDM*, May 20, 1899, 22; Academy of Music, New York, program, week of May 15, 1899; in program file: The King of the Opium Ring, BRTC.

58   "At the Theatres. Third Avenue—Night in Chinatown," *NYDM*.

59   Academy of Music, New York, program, week of May 15, 1899.

60   "At the Theatres. Star—The Queen of Chinatown," *NYDM*.

61   Academy of Music, New York, program, week of May 15, 1899.

62   "Current Amusements," *NYDM*, September 9, 1899–May 12, 1900, 16.

63   "This Week's Novelties," *New York Journal*, February 18, 1900, 38.

64   My calculations of the number of rube dramas in New York included only the touring productions although both the Donnelley (Manhattan) and the later Corse Payton (Brooklyn) resident stock companies played them. The distribution of engagements of touring rube dramas playing the eight third-class theatres of New York was uneven. More of them played at venues that also booked *Uncle Tom's Cabin* and minstrel shows.

65   John and Mollie Gassner, *Best Plays of the Early American Theatre from the Beginning to 1916* (New York: Crown, 1967), xxviii.

66   Francis Hodge, *Yankee Theatre: The Image of America on the Stage: 1825–1850* (Austin: University of Texas Press, 1964), 4–8, 44–45, 262; Toll, *On*, 11–12, 155–56; Bordman, *American Theatre*, 250, 272, 539; Tice L. Miller, "Plays and Playwrights: Civil War to 1896," in Wilmeth, *Guide*, 252. *The Contrast* and *The Old Homestead* were not the only foundation of American rural plays.

67   "Drama" in this context meant a mixture of melodramatic and comedic elements.

68   Quoted in Clark, *History*, 417.

69 "Third Avenue," *NYDM*, February 24, 1900, 16.

70 "At the Theatres. Third Avenue—The Missouri Girl," *NYDM*, March 10, 1900, 16.

71 Bordman, *American Theatre*, 477.

72 "At the Theatres. Third Avenue—Hi Hubbard," *NYDM*, January 20, 1900, 16.

73 "At the Theatres. Star—At Piney Ridge," *NYDM*, April 8, 1899, 17.

74 "In Old Kentucky," unidentified newspaper fragments, 1894–1902, in clipping file: In Old Kentucky, BRTC; "At the Theatres. Metropolis—In Old Kentucky," *NYDM*, March 24, 1900, 17. Stearns, *Jazz*, 75–76. Ever increasing its elaborate staging and fancier specialties, *In Old Kentucky* continued touring for two more decades.

75 "At the Theatres. Star—At Piney Ridge," *NYDM*, April 8, 1899, 17; "At the Theatres. Metropolis—At Piney Ridge," *NYDM*, March 17, 1900, 16; Hoeber, *Gallery*, n.p. *At Piney Ridge* played concurrently at competing theatres when Kawakami was in Grand Rapids and in Dayton.

76 Bordman, *American Theatre*, 356.

77 In *At Piney Ridge* genetic purity triumphed when the hero's blue blood finally shone through and the conniving "mixed blood" imposter was outed.

78 "In Old Kentucky," unidentified newspaper fragments, 1894–1902, in clipping file: In Old Kentucky, BRTC; Stearns, *Jazz*, 75–76.

79 "On the Suwanee River," advertisement, *Toledo Daily Blade*, November 18, 1899, 10; "At the Theatres. Metropolis. On the Suwanee River," *NYDM*, December 9, 1899, 17.

80 Stearns, *Jazz*, 121–22.

81 Bordman, *American Musical*, 155, 158; "Current Amusements," *NYDM*, April 7, 1900, 16; "At the Theatres. Third Avenue—A Trip to Coontown," *NYDM*, April 9, 1898, 15; "The Week at the Theatres," *New York Herald*, April 8, 1900, 5:12; "Grand Opera House, Cole and Johnson in A Trip to Chinatown [*sic*, for Coontown]," *New York Journal*, April 8, 1900, 64; "Grand Opera House, Cole and Johnson," *New York Times*, April 8, 1900, 11; Stearns, *Jazz*, 119; Riis, *Just*, 75–77. Bob Cole and Billy Johnson, already established writers of coon songs for white singers, were the stars, writers, and composers.

82 "New Show at Koster's," *New York World*, April 3, 1900, 4. It closed after two weeks ("Current Amusements," *NYDM*, April 21, 1900, 16). Bert Williams and George Walker were the headliners. Most of the elements of this show appeared earlier in two separate weeklong engagements at the Star Theatre during the current season (T. Allison Brown, *History*, 2:341).

83 Riis, *Just*, 30.

84 Don B. Wilmeth and Jonathan Curley, "Timeline: Post-Civil War to 1945," in Wilmeth, *History*, 2:50. As early as 1821, an African-American theatre in Manhattan staged plays from the common American repertoire but there were too few affluent African-Americans and interested Caucasians to form a critical mass of support (E. G. Hill, "Black Theatre," in Kenneth T. Jackson, *Encyclopedia*, 115; Henderson, *City*, 58).

85 "Carmen Sung by Negroes," *NYDM*, May 26, 1900, 16.

86 Tompkins, *History*, 374, 385, 427.

87 Troupes from Ireland were performing plays in English as early as 1858. American touring companies doing plays about Irish life were continuing commodities (Odell, *Annals*, 7:27–28; Tompkins, *History*, 348; Thomas Postlewait, "The Hieroglyphic Stage: American Theatre and Society, Post-Civil War to 1945," in Wilmeth, *History*, 2:137).

88 Ellis, *Epic*, 458; Moore, "Class and Ethnicity," 139–41; "Current Amusements," *NYDM*, January 15–May 5, 1900, 16.

89 Gilbert, *American*, 61–62; Snyder, *Voice*, 48.

90 Several had previously premiered in New York.

91 "Current Amusements," *NYDM*, January 20–May 5, 16; "Topics of the Theatres," *New York Sun*, May 2,

1900, 7; "Many Laughs in Monroe's Comedy," *New York Journal*, March 6, 1900, 4. Interludes, the primarily attraction for this kind of show, were nostalgic Irish songs and dancing.

92   "Many Laughs in Monroe's Comedy;" "At the Theatres. Metropolis—Mrs. B. O'Shaughnessey," *NYDM*, March 10, 1900, 16–17. Monroe performed this play in Boston while Kawakami was there.

93   "At the Theatres. Star—The Kerry Gow," *NYDM*, November 25, 1899, 16; "Current Amusements," *NYDM*, January 20, 1900, 16; Bordman, *American Theatre*, 96; "Columbia," advertisement, *Boston Herald*, November 14, 1897, 11. Murray had *The Shaughraun* in his active repertoire for at least fourteen years ("Opera, Drama, Concert," *Boston Globe*, March 14, 1886, 10).

94   "Themes from Stageland," *New York Sun*, September 2, 1900, 3:7; "Dramatic and Musical," *New York Times*, August 31, 1900, 6.

95   "Topics of the Theatres," *New York Sun*, May 2, 1900, 7; "14th St. Theatre," advertisement, *New York Times*, February 25, 1900, 10; Bordman, *American Musical*, 164. The principal attraction was star Chauncey Olcott and "his Irish ballads."

Chapter 24

1   "Current Amusements," *NYDM*, January 20–May 5, 1900, 16. The eight legitimate theatres of Brooklyn usually played English-language productions, although several had an occasional week with a foreign language troupe.

2   Moore, "Class and Ethnicity," 139–41; Ellis, *Epic*, 458; Sante, *Low*, 15. This population count included 160,000 from Austria-Hungary. By 1900, the main flow of immigration was from Southern and Eastern Europe.

3   "Irving Place Theater," advertisement, *New York Times*, January 21 and 28, 1900, and February 4, 1900, all p. 9; "New York City. Irving Place Theater," *NYC*, February 10, 1900, 1053; "New York City. Irving Place Theater," *NYC*, March 24, 1900, 81; "At the Theaters. Irving Place—Der Godene Kasig," *NYDM*, March 24, 1900, 16; "At the Theaters. Irving Place—Cornelius Voss," *NYDM*, April 7, 1900, 16; "Irving Place Theater," *New York Mail and Express*, February 2, 1900, 7; Irving Place Theater," advertisement, *New York Herald*, April 1, 1900, 4:5; "Theatrical Amusements," *New York Sun*, April 18, 1900, 7.

4   "Current Amusements," *NYDM*, January 15–May 5, 1900, 16; "The Theatres," *New York Commercial Advertiser*, March 6, 1900, 7. In March, the "Irving Place Company in repertoire" played a week in Brooklyn.

5   "The Week's New Bills," *New York Times*, January 7, 1900, 16; "Irving Place Theater," advertisement, *New York Times*, January 21 and 28, 1900 and February 4, 1900, all p.9.

6   "The Theatres," *New York Commercial Advertiser*, February 24, 1900, 7; "New York City. Irving Place Theater," *NYC*, February 10, 1900, 1053; "New York City. Irving Place Theater," *NYC*, March 24, 1900, 81; "At the Theatres. Irving Place—Der Godene Kasing," *NYDM*; "At the Theatres. Irving Place—Cornelius Voss," *NYDM*; "Irving Place Theater," *New York Mail and Express*, February 2, 1900, 7; "Irving Place Theater," advertisement, *New York Herald*, April 1, 1900, 4:5; "Theatrical Amusements," *New York Sun*, April 18, 1900, 7.

7   "The Week's New Bills," *New York Times*, January 7, 1900, 16; "Irving Place Theater," advertisement, *New York Times*, January 21 and 28, 1900, and February 4, 1900, all p. 9.

8   "At the Theatres. Irving Place—Fuhrmann Henschel," *NYDM*; "New York City. Irving Place Theater," *NYC*, February 10, 1900, 1053; "New York City. Irving Place Theater," *NYC*, March 24, 1900, 81; "At the Theatres. Irving Place—Der Godene Kasig," *NYDM*; "At the Theatres. Irving Place—Cornelius Voss," *NYDM*; "Irving Place Theater," *New York Mail and Express*, February 2, 1900, 7; "Irving Place Theater," advertisement, *New York Herald*, April 1, 1900, 4:5; "Theatrical Amusements," *New York Sun*, April 18, 1900, 7.

9   DeMille, *Autobiography*, 28.

10   More than 750 theaters throughout Europe employed actors who played in the German language (*Neuer Theater Almanach* 1901 [Berlin: Günther, 1901], vii–xi).

11   "The Theatres," *New York Commercial Advertiser*, April 16 and January 24, 1900, 7; John Corbin, "A Clever German Character Comedian," *Harper's Weekly* 44 (January 13, 1900): 42.

12   "Current Amusements," *NYDM*, January 15–May 5, 1900, 16; "Manager Amberg's Plans," *New York Times*, April 7, 1900, 7; "Germania Theater," advertisement, *New York Herald*, March 2, 11, and 18, 1900, 4:5.

13   "Germania Theater," advertisement, *New York Herald*, March 2, 11, and 18, 1900, 4:5.

14   Wilmeth, *Guide*, 199–200, 441–42; T. Allston Brown, *History*, 2:119, 2:224, 2:234, 2:303, 2:356.

15   "Manager Amberg's Plans," *New York Times*; Deborah Dash Moore, "Class and Ethnicity in the Creation of New York City Neighborhoods: 1900–1930," in Bender, *Budapest*, 149, 152.

16   Arthur Hornblow, "How a Play Is Produced," *Frank Leslie's Popular Monthly* 36:5 (November 1893): 622.

17   Ibid.

18   John H. James, "The Theatres of the Ghetto," *NYDM*, July 28, 1900, 3.

19   "Current Amusements," *NYDM*, January 15–May 5, 1900, 16.

20   Van Dyke, *New*, 157–58; James, "The Theatres of the Ghetto"; Sante, *Low*, 91; Ellis, *Epic*, 458–49; Baedeker, *United States*, 22.

21   James, "The Theatres of the Ghetto"; Silver, *Lost*, 48–49.

22   Ibid.; Sante, *Low*, 91–92; Backalenich, *East*, 9–11; "Yiddish Theatres," *Detroit News*, January 21, 1900, 18; Saqui Smith, "New York's Strange Theatres: Things at the Chinese and Hebrew Play-Houses That Strike the Stranger as Very Odd," *Leslie's Weekly* 89 (November 18, 1899): 399; Lifson, *Yiddish*, 166–69.

23   Silver, *Lost*, 48–49.

24   James, "The Theatres of the Ghetto"; Backalenich, *East*, 10.

25   N. Sandrow, *Vagabond Stars: A World History of the Yiddish Theatre* (New York: Harper and Row, 1977), 79; "The Theatres," *New York Commercial Advertiser*, February 3, 1900, 7.

26   "The Theatres," *New York Commercial Advertiser*, March 20, 1900, 7.

27   Mel Gordon, "The Yiddish Theatre in New York: 1900," in Gerould, *Melodrama*, 70–71; James, "The Theatres of the Ghetto"; "Yiddish Theatres," *Detroit News*.

28   James, "The Theatres of the Ghetto."

29   Ibid.; Fujii, *Jiden*, 197.

30   Baedeker, *United States*, 23; "Current Amusements," *NYDM*, January 15–May 15, 1900, 16.

31   Saqui Smith, "New York's Strange Theatres: Things at the Chinese and Hebrew Play-Houses That Strike the Stranger as Very Odd."

32   "Chinese Opera House," advertisement, *Theatre* (New York) No. 28 (June 1903): iii; "A Chinese Production," *NYDM*, February 18, 1899, 13.

33   Henry Tyrell, "The Theatre of New York's Chinatown," *Theatre* (New York) No. 29 (July 1903): 170; also T. Allison Brown, *History*, 2:589; Dimmick, *Our*, 64.

34   Moore, "Class and Ethnicity," 139–40; "Map of New York City Showing Foreign Colonies," *New York Herald*, January 28, 1900, 4:11; Charles Hemstreet, *Nooks and Corners of Old New York* (New York: Scribner's, 1899), 52.

35   Van Dyke, New, 248; Dimmick, Our, 57; Odell, *Annals*, 14:336, 14:616, 15:107–11; "The Theatres," *New York Commercial Advertiser*, March 20, 1900, 7.

36   "At the Teatro Italiano," *New York Times*, January 28, 1900, 20; "An Italian Drama Acted Here," *NYDM*, March 24, 1900, 9.

37   "At the Teatro Italiano."

38   Ibid.

39   "The Theatres," *New York Commercial Advertiser*, March 20, 1900, 7.

40   "Italian Passion Play Stopped," *New York Sun*, April 17, 1900, 7; "The Theatres," *New York Commercial Advertiser*, February 24, 1900, 7.

41   "The Theatres," *New York Commercial Advertiser*, February 24, 1900, 7; Kathy Peiss, *Cheap Amusements: Working Women and Leisure in Turn-of-the-Century New York* (Philadelphia: Temple University Press, 1986), 141; Paul McPharlin, *The Puppet Theatre in America: A History* (New York: Harper, 1949), 294–96; Sturgis, *Influence*, 58.

42   "Reflections," *NYDM*, February 24, 1900, 17.

43   "At an Italian Theatre," *New York Commercial Advertiser*, March 3, 1900, 11.

44   "Current Amusements," *NYDM*, January 20–May 5, 1900, 16; "Huber's Has Old-Time Minstrelsy," *New York Press*, January 23, 1900, 7; "At the Theatres. Star—Uncle Tom's Cabin," *NYDM*, March 17, 1900, 16; "At the Theatres. Metropolis—Uncle Tom's Cabin," *NYDM*, 3 March 1900, 16; "At the Theatres. Third Avenue—Uncle Tom's Cabin," *NYDM*, April 21, 1900, 17.

45   "At the Theatres. Star—Uncle Tom's Cabin," *NYDM*, March 17, 1900, 16; also "New York City. Star Theatre," *NYC*, March 17, 1900, 58; "At the Theatres. Third Avenue—Uncle Tom's Cabin," *NYDM*. The popularity of Tom shows with their abundance of suitable-for-all-the-family specialty acts was a precursor of, if not crucial to, the emergence of polite vaudeville in the 1890s.

46   "At the Theatres. Star—West's Minstrels," *NYDM*, December 16, 1899, 16.

47   "At the Theatres. Third Avenue—Uncle Tom's Cabin," *NYDM*, April 21, 1900, 17.

48   *NYDM*, Christmas issue, December 1899, 49.

49   "At the Theatres. Herald Square—Primrose and Dockstader," *NYDM*, January 6, 1900, 17; "Brooklyn Amusements," *NYDM*, March 10, 1900, 17; "Notes of the Week," *New York Times*, March 11, 1900, 16.

50   None of the minstrel troupes then playing in New York was Vogel and Deming's, the company that Kawakami was up against in Lowell.

51   Cecil Smith, *Musical Comedy in America* (New York: Theatre Arts, 1950), 4; Thomas Postlewait, "The Hieroglyphic Stage: American Theatre and Society, Post-Civil War to 1945," in Wilmeth, *History*, 181.

52   Finson, *Voices*, 222–39; "American Popular Songs" collection, NYPLPA Music Division.

53   "Huber's Has Old-Time Minstrelsy," *New York Press*, January 23, 1900, 7; also "At Other Theatres," *New York Mail and Express*, January 23, 1900, 7. Whites managed these "real Negro" shows. White minstrel performers were often hostile to their racial competition.

54   Tom Fletcher, *One Hundred Years of the Negro in Show Business* (New York: Burdge, 1954), 61; Stearns, *Jazz*, 44, 57; Frederic Edward McKay, "Next Week's Plays," *New York Mail and Express*, March 24, 1900, 20; Wittke, *Tambo*, n.p.

55   "Society Girls in Burnt Cork Disguise," *New York World*, February 2, 1900, 9; "Clever Society Girls Who Go in for Negro Minstrelsy [sic]," *New York Herald*, February 18, 1900, 4:10. Do-it-yourself minstrel publications such as *The Witmark Amateur Minstrel Guide and the Burnt Cork Encyclopedia* offered "Greatest detail, from 'blacking up' to the fall of the curtain.… Special section devoted exclusively to lady minstrels" ("A Wonderful Reference for Professionals!" advertisement, *NYC*, February 17, 1900, 1091).

56   "'Jung Arions' Minstrel Show," *New York Commercial Advertiser Saturday Pictorial Review*, February 17, 1900, 12.

57   Tawa, *Way*, 75; Slide, *Encyclopedia*, 72–73; Allen, *Horrible*, 319–20 fn. 64.

58   Henderson, *City*, 140; also John Frick, "A Changing Theatre: New York and Beyond," in Wilmeth, *History*, 215.

59   "Dramatic and Musical," *New York Times*, May 13, 1900, 20.

60   Cahn, *Theatrical 1900–01*, 19–48; *NYDM* and *NYC*, January 15–May 15, 1900. The second-class vaude-

ville venues were Miner's 125th Street, Harlem Music Hall, Koster and Bial's, and Schley Music Hall. Among the third-class houses was Hurtig and Seamon's Music Hall which featured black performers and catered to black audiences (Riis, *Just*, 81–82; "Hurtig and Seamon's," *New York Times*, January 21, 1900, 9; "Lion Palace Music Hall," advertisement, *New York Herald*, March 18, 1900, 4:5).

61 "At a Variety Show," *Washington Evening Star*, January 20, 1900, 14; "Fire Panic at Concert," *New York Times*, March 5, 1900, 1.

62 "More Vaudeville Theatres" and "Is Boston to be Surfeited," *NYDM*, December 30, 1899, 16; "Theatre Changes Hands," *New York Times*, March 4, 1900, 9; Frederic Edward McKay, "Theatrical Gossip, *New York Mail and Express*, March 5, 1900, 7.

63 "Proctor Makes Another Coup," *New York Herald*, March 4, 1900, 10; "'The Continuous' Invades Broadway," *New York Press*, March 4, 1900, 7; "Dramatic and Musical," *New York Times*, May 13, 1900, 20; "This Week on Stage," *New York Sun*, April 15, 1900, 3:7.

64 "Current Amusements," *NYDM*, January 15–May 5, 1900, 16; "Opening of Theatre Comique," *New York World*, November 21, 1899, 5.

65 Isman, *Weber*, 255–71; Alan Dale, "Will There Be a Resurrection of Burlesque?" *New York Journal*, March 18, 1900, 29. I considered Weber and Fields productions to be legitimate (drama) theatre for they were distinct in intention, substance, and audience from the spreading "burlesque" venues.

66 This extravaganza that had shared the Boston Theatre with Kawakami was now playing in New York ("At the Theatres. Koster and Bial's—'Round New York in 80 Minutes," *NYDM*, November 18, 1899, 18; Fredric Edward McKay, "Theatrical Gossip," *New York Mail and Express*, February 2, 1900, 7).

67 Slide, *Encyclopedia*, 72–73; Irving Zeideman, *The American Burlesque Show* (New York: Hawthorne, 1967), 6; Wilmeth, *Guide*, 215. Fleshlings were nothing new in American theatre. They were worn in *The Black Crook* 1866 extravaganza and in poses plastiques which were occasional attractions at dime museums.

68 Alan Dale, "Will There Be a Resurrection of Burlesque?" *New York Journal*.

69 The minstrel show first part was the familiar seated-across-the-stage line-up of performers doing their joking banter.

70 Slide, *Encyclopedia*, 72–3; Allen, *Horrible*, 236; Cecil Smith, *Musical Comedy in America*, 5; "Comique Show as Lively as Ever, *New York Press*, January 16, 1900, 7; Zeideman, *American Burlesque Show*, 6.

71 Allen, *Horrible*, 221, 225.

72 "Current Amusements," *NYDM*, January 15–May 5, 1900, 16.

73 Andrea Dennett, *Weird*, 6, 34, 41, 86; Slide, *Encyclopedia*, 5, 72–73, 255–56; Wilmeth, *Guide*, 138; T. Allston Brown, History, 2:522–23; "Things in Mimic Shows," *New York Sun*, April 24, 1900, 7; "'Tally-Ho!' Wins Applause," *New York Press*, April 24, 1900, 7.

74 "Notes of the Week," *New York Times*, February 26, 1900, 10; Slide, *Encyclopedia*, 255–56. Huber's opened around 1881 and closed in 1910.

75 "Notes of the Week," *New York Times*, February 11, 1900, 16; "Huber's Has Old-Time Minstrelsy," *New York Press*, January 23, 1900, 7; "Huber's Museum," advertisement, *New York Times*, February 18, 1900, and March 9 and 11, 1900, 9; "Where Variety Pleases," *New York Evening Telegram*, March 17, 1900, 5; "Huber's Museum," advertisement, *New York Herald*, April 1, 1900, 4:5; Andrea Dennett, *Weird*, 68.

76 "Huber's Museum," advertisement, *New York Times*, March 11, 1900, 9.

77 "Eden Musée," advertisement, *New York Herald*, April 1, 1900, 4:5; Slide, *Encyclopedia*, 154.

78 Andrea Dennett, *Weird*, 45–51.

79 "Sewell Collins Meets Wax Actors at the Eden Musée," *New York Evening Journal*, March 17, 1900, 10; "Where Variety Pleases," *New York Evening Telegram*, March 24, 1900, 9.

80 "Notes of the Week," *New York Times*, February 26, 1900, 10; Andrea Dennet, *Weird*, 53.

81 *Eden Musée Catalog* (New York: Eden Musée, 1896).

82   Eco, *Travels*, 44.

83   Musser, *Before*, 117.

84   "Where Variety Pleases," *New York Evening Telegram*; "News of the Theatres," *New York Mail and Express*, January 27, 1900, 18; "'Moving Day' at Theatres," *New York World*, February 4, 1900, 6E; "This Week on Our Stage," *New York Sun*, February 4, 1900, 2:6. Most moving pictures of the war in South Africa showed only behind-the-lines activities or action staged for the camera.

85   "Announcements of Dramatic and Musical Entertainments," advertisements, *New York Times*, March 11, 1900, 9; "Proctor's" and "Palace," advertisements, *New York Times*, February 11, 1900, 9; "This Week on Our Stage," *New York Sun*, March 25, 1900, 3:7; "Schley Music Hall," advertisement, *New York Times*, April 8, 1900, 8; "Topics from Stageland," *New York Sun*, February 14, 1900, 7; "The Dewey" and "Comique," advertisements, *New York Times*, April 8, 1900, 8; "Huber's Museum," advertisement, *New York Times*, February 18, 1900, 9 and *New York Herald*, April 1, 1900, 4:5; "Announcements of Dramatic and Musical Entertainments," advertisements, *New York Times*, March 11, 1900, 9.

86   "Amusements," *Washington Evening Star*, January 30, 1900, 12. Technological limitations, not content, determined the short length of early films.

87   "Theatres and Music Halls," *New York Times*, March 13, 1900, 9.

88   "This Week on Our Stage," *New York Sun*, March 18, 1900, 11; "Incidents of the Stage," *New York Sun*, March 11, 1900, 3:7; Musser, *Before*, 103, 121–25. The original 1898 production was apparently two hours long.

89   Mantle, *Best*, 362–63; "The Theatres," *New York Commercial Advertiser*, February 22, 1900, 5. These were not the first live-on-stage dramas to incorporate moving pictures.

90   "Themes from Stageland," *New York Sun*, June 24, 1900, 3:9; "Current Amusements," *NYDM*, February 10, 1900, 16; Bordman, *American Theatre*, 433. The commingling of live drama onstage with scenes on film never caught on in the United States, but in Japan this mixed form became a major entertainment form known as *rensageki* ("chained drama") that rivaled both live drama and "regular" moving pictures (J. L. Anderson, "Spoken Silents in the Japanese Cinema; or, Talking to Pictures: Essaying the Katsuben, Contexturalizing the Tests," in *Reframing the Japanese Cinema: Authorship, Genre, History*, eds. Arthur Nolletti, Jr. and David Desser [Bloomington: University of Indiana Press, 1992]: 271–73). There was no evidence that Kawakami had any direct connection with chained drama, although leading shimpa actors worked in this mixed medium.

91   Sante, *Low*, 12–14, 74, 92; Andrea Dennett, *Weird*, 41–67.

92   "Current Amusements," *NYDM*, April 29, May 27, and August 26, 1899, 16; King, *Handbook*, 199, 214.

93   For example, "'Women and Wine' Is 'Warm,'" *New York Evening Telegram*, April 12, 1900, 4; Alan Dale, "'Quo Vadis' at the Herald Square Is Bowery Melodrama in a Roman Toga," *New York Journal*, April 10, 1900, 8.

94   "Bowery" in Kenneth Jackson, *Encyclopedia*, 131–32; Nagai, "Yowa no sakaba" [A saloon in the dead of night], in his *Amerika*, 68.

95   Andrea Dennett, *Weird*, 61–65; Van Dyke, *New*, 247; Charles Lockwood, *Manhattan Moves Uptown: An Illustrated History* (Boston: Houghton Mifflin, 1976), 120; "Dancers in the Ballet," *New York Sun*, March 18, 1900, 3:11; Nasaw, *Going*, 20.

96   "The Bowery Actually Closed," *New York Commercial Advertiser*, January 6, 1900, 1; Sante, *Low*, 98–100.

97   Zeisloft, *New*, 518; Ellis, *Epic*, 426; Silver, *Lost*, 48–49; Henry Collins Brown, *In the Golden Nineties* (Hastings-on- Hudson: Valentine's, 1928), 120; Sante, *Low*, 106; Andrea Dennett, *Weird*, 61–65.

98   Richard Morton, lyricist, George LeBrun, composer, "The Jap" (Boston: White-Smith Music, 1893).

99   Asakusa, *Shashin*, 12–22, 152–54; Kata Kōji, *Asakusa monogatari* [The Asakusa story] (Jiji Tsūshinsha, 1988), 15–21, 107–13, 205–9; Seidensticker, *Low*, 20–21, 158–59. Kawakami performed in Asakusa theatres throughout his career.

100 Asakusa, *Shashin*, 186–98; Yoshida Mitsukuni, "Autorō no geinō" [Outlaw entertainment], in Dentō, *Dentō*, 14–28. The cheapest sideshow attractions known as misemono ("things to be seen") were increasingly popular in Japan's emerging *mono o miru bunka* (culture of the visual) (Hattori, Sakasama), 285–86.

101 Nam-lin Hur, *Prayer and Play in Late Tokugawa Japan: Asakusa Sensōji and Edo Society* (Cambridge: Harvard University Asia Center, 2000), 76–90, 105–8.

Chapter 25

1   "Southern Society Dines," *New York Times*, February 23, 1900, 3.

2   Henry Collins Brown, *Golden*, 182.

3   "Southern Society Dines," *New York Times*: also "'Open Door' Sure," *New York Mail and Express*, February 23, 1900, 7.

4   Ezaki, *Jitsuroku*, 115.

5   *New York Herald*, February 25, 1900, 13.

6   Called "chērī dansu" by Kawakami.

7   Kaneo, *Ōbei*, 37–40.

8   "Winter's Stinging Blow," *New York Times*, February 26, 1900, 2; "This Is the Coldest Day of Winter," *New York Evening Journal*, February 27, 1900, 9; "Cold Causes Much Sickness," *New York Times*, February 27, 1900, 7.

9   B. M. Sherman, "A Pioneer in Managerial Fields," *New York Evening Telegram*, March 3, 1900, 4; "Berkeley Lyceum," advertisements in *New York Tribune*, February 25, 1900, 12, and *New York World*, February 25, 1900, 6E; "These Actors Are So and So from Royal Stage of Tokio," *New York Journal*, February 22, 1900, 4.

10   "Three Japanese Plays," *New York Mail and Express*, March 2, 1900, 7.

11   B. M. Sherman, "A Pioneer in Managerial Fields."

12   "These Actors Are So and So from Royal Stage of Tokio."

13   "Kawakami Otojirō ikkō" [The Kawakami troupe], *Miyako shimbun*, April 10, 1900, in Shirakawa, 314.

14   Fragment of unidentified New York city directory c. 1900, n.p: "Mrs. Robert Osborne," in file MWEZ+ n.c. 8949, BRTC; Henry Collins Brown, *Golden*, 116.

15   Frederic Edward McKay, "Plays and Players," *New York Mail and Express Illustrated Saturday Magazine*, March 3, 1900, 6; also B. M. Sherman, "A Pioneer in Managerial Fields"; "Four New Plays," *New York Mail and Express*, February 6, 1900, 7. Osborne's costume contracts with producers covered only plays with contemporary settings and exempted gowns furnished by stars at their own expense.

16   "Mrs. Robert Osborne's Unique Society Theatre," unidentified New York newspaper, c. 1903, in clipping file: Theatres: U.S.: N.Y., Theatre Français, BRTC.

17   "Theatre Français," holograph notes on folder in clipping file: Theatres: U.S.: N.Y., Theatre Français, BRTC; Henry Collins Brown, *Golden*, 115; Mrs. Osborne's Playhouse, New York, program, week of February 16, 1903, in scrapbook MWEZ n.c. 12,566, p. 54, BRTC.

18   Berkeley Lyceum Theatre, New York, program, week of September 26, 1904, in Erlanger Collection, BRTC; Mrs. Osborn's Playhouse, New York, program, week of March 20, 1903, in Berkeley Theatre file, HTC.

19   "Mrs. Robert Osborne's Unique Society Theatre."

20   Frohman, *Memories*, 153–54.

21   Van Dyke, *New*, 214. Throughout the 1890s, Metropolitan Opera House programs included a detailed chart of its auditorium that identified boxes by the names of box holders (Henry Collins Brown, *Golden*,

137; John Dizikes, *Opera in America: A Cultural History* [New Haven, Connecticut: Yale University Press, 1993], 292).

22   "New York City. The Imperial Japanese Dramatic Company," *New York Clipper*, March 3, 1900, 10; "Mrs. Osborn a Manager," *New York Herald*, February 21, 1900, 13; "The Theatres," *New York Commercial Advertiser*, February 24, 1900, 7.

23   "The Theatres," *New York Commercial Advertiser*. What Kawakami had in mind for his *Romeo and Juliet* was not clear.

24   "Plays in Japanese," *New York Tribune*, March 2, 1900, 9; "Berkeley Lyceum," advertisement, *New York World*, February 25, 1900, 6E; Kaneo, *Ōbei*, 38–39.

25   Berkeley Lyceum, New York, program (1900), *Zingoro*, in program file: *Zingoro*, BRTC; "Japanese Actors Score a Success," *New York Herald*, March 2, 1900, 10; Copley Hall, Boston, program, January 6, 1900, Boston Theatre, Boston, program, January 18–19, 1900, "The Japanese Dramatic Company," in program file: Zingoro, BRTC. Some of these cast changes were made before New York. I found no full cast lists for the Washington performances.

26   "News and Gossip of the Players, *Washington Post*, January 28, 1900, 24; "Cues," *NYDM*, February 3, 1900, 17; "Stageland During Lent," *New York World*, March 4, 1900, 6E; "Burton Holmes Lectures," advertisement, *New York Times*, March 11, 1900, 9; "'Night in Japan' Is Clever," *New York Press*, March 6, 1900, 7. There was no confirming evidence that the troupe saw plays during the long February before they opened.

27   King, *Handbook*, 562; *Appleton's Directory*, 33.

28   Berkeley Lyceum Theatre, New York, program, January 6, 1896, in scrapbook MWEZ+ n.c., 135, BRTC; "Diagram. The Berkeley Lyceum," c. 1900, in box MWEZ+ n.c. 20,873, BRTC; advertisements in New York newspapers, January–June 1900.

29   "Diagram. The Berkeley Lyceum," Cahn, *Theatrical 1900–1901*, 21.

30   Berkeley Lyceum," advertisement, *New York World*, February 25, 1900, 6E.

31   Henry Collins Brown, *Golden*, 115–16; "Theatre Français," holograph notes. The new Berkeley Building was standing in 2007.

32   "Doings in the Mimic World," *New York Evening Telegram*, March 7, 1900, 4; "'Mamselle 'Awkins' in Boston," *New York Times*, February 13, 1900, 4; Edward A. Dithmar, "At the Play and with the Players," *New York Times*, March 4, 1900, 16.

33   "Storm over the State," *New York Times*, March 2, 1900, 1; "Cold Snap Causes Illness," *New York World*, March 2, 1900, 12; "Plays in Japanese, *New York Times*, March 2, 1900, 7.

34   "Japanese Players Appear," *NYDM*, March 10, 1900, 2; also "Plays in Japanese, *New York Tribune*, March 2, 1900, 9; "Stageland During Lent," *New York World*; "Attractions at Other Theatres," *New York Journal*, March 6, 1900, 4; "Extravaganza Unready," *New York Sun*, March 13, 1900, 7.

35   "Japanese Actors Score a Success," *New York Herald*; "Plays in Japanese," *New York Times*.

36   "Something New in Acting," *New York World*, March 2, 1900, 12.

37   Epes W. Sargent, "Dramatic Progress of the Japanese," *Metropolitan* 11 (May 1900): 497; also "Madame Sada Yacco, Japan's Greatest Emotional Actress," *Harper's Bazar* (March 24, 1900): 251.

38   "The Japanese Players," *New York Evening Post*, March 2, 1900, 7.

39   "Plays in Japanese, *New York Tribune*, March 2, 1900, 9.

40   "Japanese Players Appear," *NYDM*.

41   "The Theatres," *New York Commercial Advertiser*, March 2, 1900, 7.

42   "Plays in Japanese, *New York Tribune*.

43   Epes W. Sargent, "Dramatic Progress of the Japanese," 499.

44   "Japanese Players Appear," *NYDM*.

45   "Production of Dramas," *New York Sun*, March 2, 1900, 7.

46   "Japanese Players Appear," *NYDM*; also Epes W. Sargent, "Dramatic Progress of the Japanese," 498.

47   Hillary Bell, "Player Folk," *New York Press*, March 2, 1900. 6. Polygamy in Utah was a current newspaper topic of hostile concern.

48   Ibid.

49   "The Theatres," *New York Commercial Advertiser*, March 10, 1900, 5; "Japanese Players Appear," *NYDM*.

50   "Three Japanese Plays," *New York Mail and Express*, March 2, 1900, 7.

51   Epes W. Sargent, "Dramatic Progress of the Japanese," 502.

52   Ibid., 499.

53   "Plays in Japanese, *New York Tribune*, March 2, 1900, 9.

54   "Something New in Acting," *New York World*, March 2, 1900; also "Three Japanese Plays," *New York Mail and Express*; "Japanese Players Appear," *NYDM*.

55   "Japanese Players Appear," *NYDM*.

56   Epes W. Sargent, "Dramatic Progress of the Japanese," 501–2; also "A Japanese Actress," *New York Times*, March 11, 1900, 16.

57   "Japanese Actors Score a Success," *New York Herald*, March 2, 1900, 10

58   "Plays in Japanese, *New York Tribune*.

59   "Japanese Actors Score a Success," *New York Herald*. The writer was probably the paper's drama critic and editor, T. W. White. Tommaso Salvini (1829–1916) was the most internationally renowned male actor of the late nineteenth century. His forte was Shakespearean tragedy. He performed only in Italian.

60   "Something New in Acting," *New York World*.

61   "Japanese Players Appear," *NYDM*.

62   "Japanese Actors Score a Success," *New York Herald*; also "Plays in Japanese," *New York Times*; "Nyūyōku ni okeru Kawakami ichiza no hyōban" [Reviews of the Kawakami troupe in New York], *Chūō shimbun*, March 28, 1900, in Shirakawa, 313.

63   "Japanese Players Appear," *NYDM*.

64   Scrapbook: "Plays to June 1905," MWEZ+ n.c. 297, p. 101, BRTC. One of these photographs, coupled with one from *Madame Butterfly*, appeared in "The Geisha and the Knight" with "Madam [*sic*] Butterfly" in the Sunday *New York Journal*, March 18, 1900, 29. A sampling of the many publications with the Byron photographs included: **"Madame Sada Yacco, Japan's Greatest Actress,"** *Harper's Bazar* 33 (March 24, 1900): 251; Carolyn Shipman, "The Japanese Players," *Critic* 36 (April 1900): 327; Alexander Arséne, "Théatre de la Loïe Fuller. Pantomimes Japonaises," *Theatre* (Paris) No. 41 (September 1900): 16; Jules Bois, "Le théâtre, les acteurs et les actrices du Japon," *Je sais touts* 3 (March 15, 1907): 241; "L'Expo 1900," *Encyclopédia du théatre contemporain vol. 1, 1850–1914* (Paris: Publications de France, 1959), 77. Byron took at least ten shots of *The Geisha and the Knight* at the Berkeley Lyceum, according to unidentified material in scrapbook, "Plays to June 1905," MWEZ+ n.c. 297, BRTC.

65   Holmes, *Travelogues*, 2:243, 247, 265, 275.

66   Ibid. As in most of the available sources, the photographs reproduced here were cropped. The profile trees of the sets were more discernable in wider shots seen in the scrapbook "Plays to June 1905," MWEZ+ n.c. 297, pp. 99–101, BRTC. The tree with Kojima's message to the emperor appeared in other scenes without the writing attached.

67   *Exhibition of Japanese*, n.p.

68   Sets made in San Francisco had several pairs of parallel wings placed in depth along the sides to create deeper playing space.

69   "'Geisha and the Knight,'" *Portland Morning Oregonian*, September 30, 1899, 3. Indirect evidence for disappearance of the bell was that Chicago and later reviews of *The Geisha and the Knight* did not mention it and Kawakami's new ending for the *Dōjōji* act did not require it.

70   Cahn, *Theatrical 1900–1901*, 21; "Music and Drama. The Japanese Players," *New York Evening Post*, March 13, 1900, 7.

71   In Boston, Kawakami borrowed *byōbu* (floor standing screens) from art merchant Matsuki. For New York, the troupe either carried Matsuki's *byōbu* from Boston or secured the screens from local sources.

72   "The Japanese Players, Otojiro Kawakami and Mme. Sada Yacco in a scene from 'The Loyal Wife,' at the Bijou Theatre," *New York Commercial Advertiser Pictorial Review*, April 14, 1900, 11.

73   "Kawakami and Yacco," *New York Commercial Advertiser*, March 3, 1900, 6. The actor identified as "Mozaki" was most likely Nogaki Seiichi, a skilled theatrical swordfighter.

74   "The Japanese Players," *NYDM*, March 17, 1900, 15.

75   Ibid.

76   "New York City. Review and Comment," *NYC*, March 10, 1900, 33; "The Weather," *New York Times*, March 4, 1900, 2.

77   Kaneo, *Ōbei*, 39.

78   Frederic Edward McKay, "Theatrical Gossip," *New York Mail and Express*, February 28, 1900, 7; also Hillary Bell, "Player Folk," *New York Press*.

79   "Theatrical," *New York World*, March 4, 1900, 2E.

80   Puccini saw the first London production of Belasco's *Madame Butterfly*.

81   "At the Theatres," *Boston Post*, December 16, 1899, 5; "At the Theatres. Herald Square—Naughty Anthony," *NYDM*, January 13, 1900, 16.

82   Herald Square Theatre, New York, program, week of February 5, 1900, in scrapbook MWEZ+ n.c. 713, p. 246, BRTC; Frederic Edward McKay, "Three New Plays," *New York Mail and Express*, January 9, 1900, 7.

83   "Dramatic and Musical," *New York Times*, January 9, 1900, 5; also "Blanche Bates as a Hosiery Model," unidentified newspaper, December 27, 1899, in RLS NAFR+ v. 43, p. 22, BRTC; Edward A. Dithmar, "At the Play and with the Players," *New York Times*, January 14, 1900, 16; "At the Theatres. Herald Square—Naughty Anthony," *NYDM*.

84   David Belasco, "My Life Story," *Hearst's* (September 1915): 178.

85   "Blanche Bates as a Hosiery Model"; Edward A. Dithmar, "At the Play and with the Players," *New York Times*; Krehbiel, "Historical," October 15.

86   Sidney Sharp, "Three New Plays and a Notable Night at the Grand Opera," *New York World*, January 7, 1900, 4; "Music and Drama," *New York Evening Post*, January 9, 1900, 7; Edward A. Dithmar, "At the Play and with the Players," *New York Times*; "New Plays on Our Stage," *New York Sun*, January 9, 1900, 7; Frederic Edward McKay, "Three New Plays," *New York Mail and Express*, January 9, 1900, 7; Jason, "The Dramatic Season in New York," *Leslie's Weekly* 90 (January 20, 1900): 51; Lavinia Hart, "Blanche Bates Saves 'Naughty Anthony,'" *New York World*, January 7, 1900, 4; H[illary] B[ell], "Naughty Anthony a Gay Boy," *New York Press*, January 9, 1900, 7.

87   "Incidents in Stageland," *New York Sun*, January 9, 1900, 7; also Sidney Sharp, "Three New Plays and a Notable Night at the Grand Opera," *New York World*.

88   Jason, "The Dramatic Season in New York," *Leslie's Weekly*.

89   H[illary] B[ell], "Player Folk," *New York Press*, January 10, 1900, 6.

90   "A Tricky Defense of Stage Indecency," *NYDM*, March 17, 1900, 14; H[illary] B[ell], "Naughty Anthony a Gay Boy," *New York Press*.

91   "The Matinee Girl," *NYDM*, February 3, 1900, 2; "At the Play," *New York World*, January 7, 1900, 2E; Willard Holcomb, "Theatricals in New York," *Washington Post*, January 28, 1900, 24; "News and Gossip of the Players," *Washington Post*, January 28, 1900, 24; "The Theatre," *Washington Evening Star*, February 3, 1900, 20; "Cues," *NYDM*, February 3, 1900, 17.

92   "Various Dramatic Topics," *New York Times*, February 4, 1900, 16.

93   "New Act in 'Naughty Anthony' Pleases," *New York Journal*, February 2, 1900, 5; Fredric Edward McKay, "Theatrical Gossip," *New York Mail and Express*, February 1 and 2, 1900, 1900, 7; "New 'Naughty Anthony,'" *New York World*, February 2, 1900, 8; William Halcomb, "Theatricals in New York," *Washington Post*; "At Other Theatres," *New York Mail and Express*, January 23, 1900, 7; "The Theatre," *Washington Evening Star*, February 3, 1900, 20.

94   David Belasco, "My Life Story," *Hearst's* (September 1915): 178; "The Passing Show," *Washington Times*, January 21, 1900, 2:4.

95   Krehbiel, "Historical," October 15.

96   "Belasco to Write for Blanche Bates," *New York Morning Telegraph*, January 16, 1900, n.p.

97   "Cues," *NYDM*, February 10, 1900, 13; "Personal. Belasco," *NYDM*, February 17, 1900, 12.

98   Winter, *Life*, 1:477; also Krehbiel, "Historical," October 15; David Belasco, "My Life Story," 178; "Madame Butterfly," *New York Times*, March 18, 1900, 18; Frederic Edward McKay, "New Belasco Play," *New York Mail and Express*, March 6, 1900, 7.

99   J. L. Anderson, "Representing the Musmé: Before and after Belasco's *Madame Butterfly*," draft manuscript. The lyrics of the opera mention that Butterfly is fifteen years old. This was not the youngest age for a child to be licensed as a temporary bride to foreigners in Nagasaki.

100   Winter, *Life*, 1:477.

101   "Theatrical Jottings," *New York Herald*, February 7, 1900, 10.

102   "Mr. Belasco's Japanese Play," *New York Times*, February 7, 1900, 7; also "News and Views of Theatricals," *New York Evening Telegram*, February 7, 1900, 4; "This Week's Novelties," *New York Journal*, February 18, 1900, 38.

103   Hillary Bell, "Player Folk," *New York Press*, February 16, 1900, 6.

104   Hornblow, *History*, 2:312.

105   "Offerings of the Week," *Washington Times*, February 4, 1900, 2:5; "Lafayette," advertisement, *Washington Times*, February 4, 1900, 2:5; "Lafayette," advertisement, *Washington Evening Star*, February 5, 1900, 10.

106   Kaneo, *Ōbei*, 41; Kaneo, *Sadayakko*, 42. Belknap, who was interested in Japanese theatre, later guided Kawakami around the theatrical world of New York.

107   Wagenknecht, *Merely*, 227.

108   "Madame Butterfly," *New York Times*, March 18, 1900, 18; Krehbiel, "Historical," October 15; Frederic Edward McKay, "New Belasco Play," *New York Mail and Express*, March 6, 1900, 7.

109   Belasco apparently hired a "Mr. Yeto, the Japanese Artist," to secure authentic properties for his scenic realism. According to the publicity, even the coins used onstage had to be authentic Japanese currency (Hillary Bell, "Player Folk," *New York Press*, March 2, 1900, 6; "Madame Butterfly," *New York Times*).

110   H[illary] B[ell], "This 'Butterfly' a Winged Jewel," *New York Press*, March 6, 1900, 7; also "Turns of the Theatrical Wheel," *New York Evening Telegram*, March 6, 1900, 4; "At the Theatres. Herald Square—Madame Butterfly," *NYDM*, March 17, 1900, 16; "Dramatic and Musical," *New York Times*, March 6, 1900, 9.

111   Sampling: Alan Dale, "'Mme. Butterfly' Is a Gem, and Advises Everybody to See It," *New York Journal*, March 8, 1900, 8; Leander Richardson, "Mme. Butterfly a Great Success," *New York Telegram*, March 6, 1900, n.p.; "At the Theatres. Herald Square—Madame Butterfly," *NYDM*; Frederic Edward McKay, "New Belasco Play," *New York Mail and Express*.

112   "The Matinee Girl," *NYDM*, March 17, 1900, 2; also Edward A. Dithmar, "At the Play and with the Players," *New York Times*, March 11, 1900, 16.

113   Winter, *Life*, 1:484; Timberlake, *Life*, 199; "'Naughty Anthony' to Close," *New York Herald*, March 13, 1900, 13; "Dramatic and Musical," *New York Times*, April 4, 1900, 6. The disappointed Bates was left behind in the United States.

114 "Belasco on Japan's Drama," *New York World*, March 11, 1900, 2E.

115 "Novelties at the Local Theatres. A Japanese Tragedy," *New York Herald*, March 6, 1900, 9; also Winter, *Life*, 1:482; Odell, *Annals*, 8:219; Charles Osborne, *The Complete Operas of Puccini* (New York: Atheneum, 1982), 153.

116 Belasco, *Madame Butterfly* in his *Six Plays*, 24, with the italics, dashes, and ellipsis dots *sic* in the quoted passage. Edward A. Dithmar of the *Times*, impressed by the effectiveness of the dialogue in *Madame Butterfly*, accurately noted that much of it was lifted directly from Long's original short story ("At the Play and with the Players," *New York Times*, March 11, 1900, 16).

117 Clement Scott, "Mr. Scott Reviews 'Mme. Butterfly,'" *New York Herald*, March 9, 1900, 11. The "butterflies" of Nagasaki were not geisha but another kind of available woman.

118 "Novelties at the Local Theatres. A Japanese Tragedy," *New York Herald*, March 6, 1900, 9.

119 Hillary Bell, "Player Folk," *New York Press*, March 2, 1900, 6; also "Clement Scott on Japanese Plays," *New York Herald*, March 13, 1900, 13; "At the Theatres. Herald Square—Madame Butterfly" and "At the Theatres. Bijou—The Japanese Players," *NYDM*, March 17, 1900, 16.

120 "Belasco on Japan's Drama," *New York World*, March 11, 1900, 2E.

121 "Madame Butterfly," *New York Times*, March 18, 1900, 18.

122 "Otijiro [*sic*] and Sada Yakko," *Era* (June 2, 1900), 8.

123 Brockett, *Century*, 21–24; Helen Krich Chinoy, "Directing in America, 1860–1920," in Henry B. Williams, *American*, 124–51, 126.

124 Timberlake, *Life*, 220.

125 Leiter, *From*, 1.

126 In *Other Days*, 314–19, William Winter, although he was a strong supporter of Belasco, wrote a harsh polemic against the rise of stage manager/directors. He called them "a fungus of modern growth" who constrained what actors offered as their individual talent. Winter predicted theatre would die when actors, particular the great actors, lost control of how they performed.

127 Belasco, *Theatre*, 226, also 65.

128 Ibid., 234–37; Leiter, *From*, 4–7; Winter, *Life*, 2:247.

129 Leiter, *From*, x, 1–2; Marker, *David*, 17–20; Winter, *Life*, 2:247; Belasco, *Theatre*, 226, 234–37; Hewitt, *Theatre*, 270.

130 Quoted in McConachie, *Melodramatic*, 225–26.

131 Leiter, *From*, 4; Marker, *David*, 17.

132 Quoted by Marker, *David*, 16.

133 Ibid., 20; Leiter, *From*, 8–12; John B. Stuart, "The Preparation of a Modern Play," *Metropolitan* 9 (February 1899): 166.

134 Barnard Hewitt, *Theatre*, 270; Leiter, *From*, 2–4, 15; George T. Richardson, "Mrs. Leslie Carter in 'Zaza,' a Rather Fervid Play," *Boston Traveler*, January 2, 1900, 4.

135 Robinson, *Notable*, 62; Frederic Edward McKay, "Plays and Players," *New York Mail and Express Illustrated Saturday Review*, February 10, 1900, 6; Winter, *Life*, 1:469–71; Nina Carter, "Says 'Cigarette' Bates: No Society Plays for Me," unidentified New York newspaper, April 6, 1902, in RLS NAFR+ v. 43, p. 96, BRTC; Winter, *Wallet*, 2:257–61. Bates played an audacious camp follower in *Under Two Flags*, then another demure Japanese in *The Darling of the Gods*, followed by a tough, virginal saloonkeeper in *The Girl of the Golden West*. Puccini made another opera out of the latter play (the first spaghetti Western?).

136 Mullin, *Victorian*, 58; Robinson, *Notable*, 63.

137 Winter, *Life*, 1:469–70, also 471; Leiter, *From*, 3; Young, *Famous*, 1:84.

138 Leiter, *From*, 2–4, 15.

139 Recently remodeled again as the Republic Theatre on renovated 42nd Street.

140 Wilmeth, *Guide*, 65; Leiter, *From*, 4. Opened in 1907, it was still operating as the Belasco Theatre in the early 2000s.

141 Winter, *Life*, 2:239–41, 249; Wilmeth, *Guide*, 65; Leiter, *From*, 1.

142 Belasco, *Theatre*, 237–38.

143 After Butterfly's aborted suicide attempt, Long concluded his story: "The little maid came in and bound up [Butterfly's] wound. When Mrs. Pinkerton [the American] called the next day at [Butterfly's] little house on Higashi hill it was quite empty." That is the ending of Long's story (Long, "Madame Butterfly," 152). In a subsequent introduction to a reprinting of the story, Long *explicitly* stated that Butterfly "fled with Trouble and Suzuki from the little, empty, happy house on Higashi Hill" (Long, "Madame Butterfly," xii).

144 Belasco, *Madam Butterfly*, NCOF+ manuscript, act 3, pp. 23, 25–26, BRTC.

145 Ibid., act 3, p.26. Ellipsis dots in original.

146 Belasco, *Madame Butterfly* in his *Six Plays*, 32, and Puccini, *Madama*, 71; "Turns of the Theatrical Wheel," *New York Evening Telegram*, March 6, 1900, 4. Because of religious inhibitions, theatrical custom, and a penchant for happy endings, American drama tended to shun direct portrayal of suicides by protagonists.

147 J. L. Anderson, "Representing the Musmé: Before and After Belasco's *Madame Butterfly*," early draft manuscript. In *Kesa*, the heroine did not directly commit suicide by her own hand.

148 Kaneo, *Ōbei*, 36–37; Kaneo, *Sadayakko*, 34.

149 "Blanche Bates to Do Japanese Play," unidentified New York newspaper, October 8, 1902, in RLS NAFR + v. 44, p. 6, BRTC; Winter, *Life*, 2:77; Montrose J. Moses, "The Darling of the Gods," introduction, in Belasco in his *Six Plays*, 141–42. In New York, *Darling* ran for 182 performances (Bordman, *American Theatre*, 504).

150 Montrose J. Moses, "The Darling of the Gods," Belasco in his *Six Plays*, 141; J. L. Anderson, "Representing the Musmé."

151 Belasco, *Darling of the Gods* in his *Six Plays*, 157, 161–69, 222–23; Belasco, *Theatre*, 238–39.

152 This is only a sampling of similarities.

153 Winter, *Life*, 2:109.

154 Lewis C. Strang, *Famous Actresses of the Day in America* (Boston: Page, 1902), 179–80, 183. Bergere was a leading woman in the Dearborn stock company when Kawakami was in Chicago in fall 1899.

Chapter 26

1 Lloyd Morris, *Incredible New York* (New York: Random House, 1951), 259. The Bijou Theatre was on the west side of Broadway between 30th and 31st Streets.

2 This 1867 observation, quoted in Henderson, *City*, 121, was still accurate in 1900. The concentration of theatres in one area functioned like movie complexes today by offering alternate choices nearby.

3 Dreiser, *Sister*, 323.

4 Crane, *Last*, 175.

5 Lloyd Morris, *Incredible New York*, 260.

6 Crane, *Last*, 179.

7 Ibid., 28. The electric lights of Broadway at this time were not neon but bunches of incandescent bulbs.

8 Ibid., 147–51, 185–86; Burrows, *Gotham*, 1148; *Appleton's Directory*, 39; Henderson, City, 132–33; Zeisloft, *New*, 626. Because of the tempting opportunities for personal graft, the police assigned there dubbed the neighborhood "the Tenderloin" after the expensive, delicious steak cut. In March 1900, the Tenderloin precinct police station was resisting pressure from the city district attorney to close down the worst offenders ("How It Became the Tenderloin," *Broadway Magazine* 4 [December 1899]: 180; "Police Forced to Close Big Dives," *New York Times*, March 13, 1900, 2).

9   Nagai, "Yoru aruki" [Strolling through the night], in his *Amerika*, 82.

10   Burrows, Gotham, 484, 815, 1148; Rosemarie K. Bank, "Hustlers in the House: the Bowery Theatre as a Mode of Historical Information," in Engle, *American*, 51; *Michelin London Tourist Guide* (Clermont-Ferrand, France: Michelin, 1984), 139; Seigle, *Yoshiwara*, 223.

11   "Gossip," *NYDM*, March 10, 1900, 17; Frederic Edward McKay, "At the Theatres," *New York Mail and Express*, March 10, 1900, 20.

12   "Bijou—Aunt Hannah," *NYDM*, March 3, 1900, 16; also "At the Theatres," *New York Commercial Advertiser*, February 23, 1900, 7; Frederic Edward McKay, "'Aunt Hannah,'" *New York Mail and Express*, February 23, 1900, 7.

13   "In Theatrical Affairs," *New York Sun*, February 23, 1900, 7.

14   "'Aunt Hannah' to Be Revised," *New York Times*, March 9, 1900, 7; "Professional Doings," *NYDM*, March 17, 1900, 17.

15   "Current Amusements," *NYDM*, February, 17 and 24, 1900, 16; "Theatrical Amusements," *New York Sun*, November 1, 1899, 4F; "At the Theatres. Grand—Kate Kip, Buyer," *NYDM*, April 8, 1899, 17; T. Allston Brown, *History*, 3:301–2; Hillary Bell, "Player Folk," *New York Press*, March 12, 1900, 6.

16   King, *Handbook*, 556; William C. Young, *Documents of American Theatre History: Famous American Playhouses 1716–1899* (Chicago: American Library Association, 1973), 1:93; T. Allston Brown, *History*, 3:273–74; Dimmick, Our, 55; W. J. Henderson, "The Business of a Theatre," *Scribner's* 25 (March 1899): 299.

17   Cahn, *Theatrical 1900–1901*, 19–48; Henderson, *City*, 147.

18   Musser, *Before*, 89, 65; Ralph Dengler, "The First Screen Kiss and 'The Cry of Censorship,'" *Journal of Popular Film and Television* 7:3 (1979): 268–70.

19   "The Theatres," *New York Commercial Advertiser*, February 6, 1900, 7; Hillary Bell, "Music and Drama," *New York Press*, February 25, 1900, 14.

20   Leslie, *Some*, 594.

21   "Homemade Comic Plays," *New York Times*, September 17, 1895, 5.

22   Dennison, *Scandalize*, 375–77; Hitchcock, *New*, 1:493.

23   Alan Dale, "'Bunches of Good Things' in May Irwin's New Play," *New York Journal*, October 28, 1899, 4; also "At the Theatres. Bijou—Sister Mary," *NYDM*, November 4, 1899, 17; Bijou Theatre, New York, program, week of November 13, 1899, in program file: "Sister Mary," BRTC. The "In Japan" lyrics could not be found.

24   Frederic Edward McKay, "At the Theatres," *New York Mail and Express*, March 10, 1900, 20; also Hillary Bell, "Player Folk," *New York Press*.

25   "The Japanese Actors," *New York Times*, March 13, 1900, 9.

26   "Bijou," advertisement, *New York Herald*, March 11, 1900, 4:5.

27   Zeisloft, New, 356; King, *Handbook*, 556; Stephen Jenkins, *Greatest*, 251.

28   W. J. Henderson, "The Business of a Theatre," *Scribner's* 25 (March 1899): 299.

29   "Notes of the Week," *New York Times*, March 11, 1900, 16.

30   Tawa, *Way*, 184.

31   "Fougere a Proctor Feature," *New York Press*, April 10, 1900, 7; Ella Wheeler Wilcox, "Worst Plays on New York's Immoral Stage Justly Chastised," *New York Evening Journal*, October 19, 1899, n.p.

32   Hitchcock, *New*, 1:493. Some historians trace coon song origins back to African-American folk music of the early nineteenth century (Tawa, *Way*, 181–87; Isaac Goldberg, *Tin Pan Alley: A Chronicle of the American Popular Music Racket* [1930; reprint New York: Ungar, 1961], 155). "Coon" was a racial epithet apparently derived from "raccoon," which was said to be the obnoxious meat preferred by slaves. By 1880,

"coon" was a pejorative term for African-Americans (Dennison, *Scandalize My Name*, 354; "American Popular Songs 1898–1900," microfilms *ZB-768 reels 8–12A, Music Division NYPLPA).

33   Riis, *Just*, 52; Dennison, *Scandalize*, 349, 357, 375–77.

34   John Stromberg, composer; Harry B. Smith, lyricist, "Hoity-Toity," in "Hoity-Toity," MC file, Music Division NYPLPA; also Isman, *Weber*, 272. The song never caught on in the United States but was a big hit in Europe.

35   This is the usual story of the origins of the dance and its name.

36   Stearns, *Jazz*, 22–23; Tawa, *Way* 183.

37   Quoted in Stearns, *Jazz*, 123; Riis, *Just*, 78; also "Huber's Has Old-Time Minstrelsy," *New York Press*, January 23, 1900, 7; Tom Fletcher, *One Hundred Years of the Negro in Show Business* (New York: Burdge, 1954), 103.

38   Hitchcock, *New*, 1:343.

39   Edward A. Dithmar, "At the Play and with the Players," *New York Times*, January 28, 1900, 16. For instance, "Koster & Bial's," *New York Mail and Express*, January 9, 1900, 7.

40   "This Week on Our Stage," *New York Sun*, February 4, 1900, 2:6; "New York—Broadway to Tokio," *NYDM*, February 3, 1900, 16; "At the Theatres. Star—The Queen of Chinatown," *NYDM*, August 26, 1899, 15.

41   "Atlantic City," *Philadelphia Inquirer*, July 24, 1898, 22.

42   Dennison, *Scandalize*, 352; Isaac Goldberg, *Tin Pan Alley: A Chronicle of the American Popular Music Racket*, 151.

43   "New York City. The Imperial Japanese Dramatic Company," *NYC*, March 3, 1900, 10; Bijou, advertisement, *New York Herald*, March 11, 1900, 4:5; "Notes of the Week," *New York Times*, March 11, 1900, 16; "At the Theatres. Bijou—The Japanese Players," *NYDM*, March 17, 1900, 16.

44   "Announcements of Dramatic and Musical Entertainments," *New York Times*, March 11, 1900, 9.

45   Alan Dale, "'The Pride of Jennico' Treats Impossible People Doing Impossible Things," *New York Journal*, March 7, 1900, 6. Hackett's American sword action rival at this time was E. H. Sothern.

46   "Those Japanese Actors," *New York Times*, March 18, 1900, 18.

47   Cahn, *Theatrical 1900–1901*, 21.

48   "Gleanings from the Greenroom," *New York Evening Telegram*, March 13, 1900, 4.

49   "Snow, Sleet, and Hail in March," *New York Times*, March 16, 1900, 1; "Storm Strikes City in Darkest Hour," *New York Times*, March 17, 1900, 7; "City Guide. The Weather," *New York Commercial Advertiser*, March 16, 1900, 7; "Failed to Clear Streets of Snow," *New York Herald*, March 18, 1900, 1:8; "New York City. Review and Comment," *NYC*, March 24, 1900, 81.

50   "The Japanese Actors," *New York Times*; also "At Other Playhouses," *New York World*, March 13, 1900, 4; "At the Theatres; Bijou—The Japanese Players," *NYDM*; "Japan Visits Broadway," *New York Herald*, March 13, 1900, 13; "Gleanings from the Greenroom," *New York Evening Telegram*.

51   "At Other Playhouses," *New York World*; "Japan Visits Broadway," *New York Herald*.

52   "Music and Drama. The Japanese Players," *New York Evening Post*, March 13, 1900, 7; "Gleanings from the Greenroom," *New York Evening Telegram*.

53   "Kawakami ichiza yōkō nisshi" [Journal of the overseas tour of the Kawakami troupe], *Miyako shimbun*, July 26, 1900, in Shirakawa, 318–19.

54   Mihara Aya, "Professor Risley and Japanese Acrobats: Selections from the Diary of Hirohachi Takano, a Manager for the Risley Troupe, during the World Tour 1866–1869," *Nineteenth Century Theatre* 18:1–2 (1990): 63.

55   Mihara Aya, "Beikoku kōgyō ni kaketa geinō rokuza no dōkō: 1867nen o chûshin ni" [What happened to

six troupes of entertainers who took their chances in American show business; focusing on the year 1867], *Geinō shi kenkyū* No. 127 (1994): 1–24; Odell, *Annals*, throughout vols. 8–15.

56   Odell, *Annals*, 11:481. During the 1880s, Katsunoshin and his wife appeared with master magician Alexander Herrmann and with Barnum's circus. He also had his own show and later was a specialty act in an 1881 production of *The Black Crook* (Odell, 11:28, 272, 359, 379, 391; 12:48, 316, 507, 598).

57   Ibid., 15:344–45, 354, 428, 705. On various bills, the name of this act was spelled Kawakanis, Kawikanis, Kanichanis, and Khawanis.

58   Gordon Hendricks, "A Collection of Edison Films," *Image* 8 (September 1959): 159 with photograph.

59   "Notes of the Theatres," *New York Press*, March 15, 1900, 7; also "Japan Visits Broadway," *New York Herald*, March 13, 1900, 13; "Those Japanese Actors," *New York Times*, March 18, 1900, 18.

60   "Theatrically Uncommon," *New York Sun*, March 14, 1900, 7. The writer was also referring to performances of Japanese sword fighters in dime museums.

61   "The Japanese Players," *New York Mail and Express*, March 20, 1900, 7.

62   "Extravaganza Unready," *New York Sun*, March 13, 1900, 7.

63   "Music and Drama. The Japanese Players," *New York Evening Post*, March 13, 1900, 7; also "Japan Visits Broadway," *New York Herald*; "Theatrically Uncommon," *New York Sun*.

64   "Various Dramatic Topics," *New York Times*, March 4, 1900, 16; also "Japanese Actors Score a Success," *New York Herald*, March 2, 1900, 10; "The Japanese Players," *New York Evening Post*, March 2, 1900, 7; "Production of Dramas, *New York Sun*, March 2, 1900, 7; "The Theatres," *New York Commercial Advertiser*, March 10, 1900, 5; "Japanese Players Appear," *NYDM*, March 10, 1900, 2.

65   W. W., "The Dramatic Week," *New York Tribune*, March 18, 1900, 9.

66   "Novelty Stage Value," *New York Sun*, March 4, 1900, 3:7. The writer was probably the paper's main theatre critic, Franklin Fyles.

67   "Music and Drama. The Japanese Players," *New York Evening Post*.

68   "Something New in Acting," *New York World*, March 2, 1900, 12; "Japanese Realism," *New York Commercial Advertiser*, April 20, 1900, 7; also "The Theatres," *New York Commercial Advertiser*, March 10, 1900, 5.

69   "Music and Drama. The Japanese Players," *New York Evening Post*.

70   "Amusements," *Adrian Daily Times and Expositor*, November 20, 1899, 2.

71   "The Japanese Players," *New York Times*, April 1, 1900, 2:18.

72   Bijou Theatre, New York, program, week of March 12, 1900, in Brighton Theatre 1895–1910 box, HTC.

73   "The Japanese Players," *New York Mail and Express*, March 20, 1900, 7.

74   "The Japanese Players," *NYDM*, March 17, 1900, 15.[1] "Those Japanese Actors," *New York Times*, March 18, 1900, 18; also "Three Japanese Plays," *New York Mail and Express*, March 2, 1900, 7.

75   "Those Japanese Actors," *New York Times*, March 18, 1900, 18; also "Three Japanese Plays," *New York Mail and Express*, March 2, 1900, 7.

76   "Music and Drama. The Japanese Players," *New York Evening Post*; also "At the Theatres," *New York World*, March 11, 1900, 2E; "Something New in Acting," *New York World*, March 2, 1900, 12.

77   "Turns of the Theatrical Wheel," *New York Evening Telegram*, March 6, 1900, 4; "Examples in Stagecraft," *New York Sun*, March 11, 1900, 3:7.

78   *Sairoku, Kojima*, and *The Geisha and the Knight*, and specialties ran until 11:35 pm at the Bijou ("Music and Drama. The Japanese Players," *New York Evening Post*, March 13, 1900, 7). While at the Berkeley Lyceum, the company played *Jingorō, Kojima, The Geisha and the Knight* in two hours ("Calendar for the Week," *New York Herald*, March 11, 1900, 4:4). All Kawakami plays could be readily adjusted to flexible playing times.

79   Bijou Theatre, New York, program, week of March 12, 1900.

80   "Clement Scott on Japanese Plays," *New York Herald*, March 13, 1900, 13.

81   "At the Theatres. Bijou—The Japanese Players," *NYDM*, March 17, 1900, 16.

82 "Theatrically Uncommon," *New York Sun*, March 14, 1900, 7.

83 "Clement Scott on Japanese Plays," *New York Herald*.

84 "Theatrically Uncommon," *New York Sun*; Epes W. Sargent, "Dramatic Progress of the Japanese," *Metropolitan* 11 (May 1900): 501; "At the Theatres. Bijou—The Japanese Players," *NYDM*.

85 "Japan Visits Broadway," *New York Herald*, March 13, 1900, 13.

86 "Theatrically Uncommon," *New York Sun*. The dancer was Wada Makijirō doing his comic bit in *The Geisha and the Knight*.

87 "Music and Drama. The Japanese Players," *New York Evening Post*, March 13, 1900, 7.

88 "Clement Scott on Japanese Plays," *New York Herald*.

89 Ibid.

90 "Irving Here Once More," *New York Sun*, October 27, 1899, 7; Bingham, *Henry*, 176. Irving's first New York appearance that season was in October for a limited twenty-two performances (T. Allston Brown, *History*, 3: 602).

91 "The Man with the Lorgnette," *Boston Evening Record*, November 20, 1899, 5; also H. Chance Newton, "Miss Ellen Terry and Her Art," Sketch 35 (July 31, 1901): 75. Ellen Terry's had acute rheumatism that became very painful during February and March of 1900. (H. Chance Newton, "Miss Ellen Terry and Her Art," 75; Binns, *Mrs. Fiske*, 98–99).

92 "Extravaganza Unready," *New York Sun*, March 13, 1900, 7; "Sidewalk Fun at Irving's Door," *New York Herald*, March 18, 1900, 1:13.

93 "New York City. Review and Comment," *NYC*, March 24, 1900, 81.

94 "Irving Fails to Draw Without Miss Terry," *New York World*, March 13, 1900, 4; also H. H., "Speculators Lose Money on Irving," *New York Press*, March 13, 1900, 7.

95 "Revenge on Irving," *New York Evening Journal*, March 17, 1900, 7; "Extravaganza Unready," *New York Sun*.

96 Irving's engagement four months earlier had opening night $2 gallery seats that were scalped as high as four times the printed price. For the remainder of the run, $3 orchestra tickets went for $5 ("Sidewalk Fun at Irving's Door," *New York Herald*; T. Allston Brown, *History*, 3:602–3).

97 Brereton, *Life*, 2:283; "Miss Terry's Reappearance," *New York Herald*, March 20, 1900, 11; "Current Amusements," *NYDM*, March 24, 1900, 16; "Knickerbocker Theatre," advertisement, *New York Herald*, March 18, 1900; 4:5; "Unusual at the Theatre," *New York Sun*, March 22, 1900, 7.

98 Laurence Irving, *Henry*, 183–91, 205–9; David Mayer, ed., *Henry Irving and the Bells* (Manchester: Manchester University Press, 1980); Rahill, *World*, 209–10.

99 Shirakawa Nobuo, "Meijiki ni okeru Furansushu gikyoku jōen nempyō" [Chronology of Meiji era performances of plays based on French works], *Engeki kenkyū* 9 (1979): 122, 133–38.

100 "New York City. Review and Comment," *NYC*; "At the Theatres. The Merchant of Venice," *NYDM*, November 25, 1899, 16; Brereton, *Life*, 2:284.

101 "General Theatrical Notes," *New York Evening Post*, March 3, 1900, 21; also in agreement: "Dramatic and Musical," *New York Times*, February 27, 1900, 7; "The Theatres," *New York Commercial Advertiser*, March 2, 1900, 7.

102 "New York City. Fifth Avenue Theatre," *NYC*, March 3, 1900, 10; Edward A. Dithmar, "At the Play and with the Players," *New York Times*, March 11, 1900, 16.

103 "New York City. Fifth Avenue Theatre," *NYC*, March 10, 1900, 34; "Music and Drama. 'Marie Antoinette,'" *New York Evening Post*, March 2, 1900, 7; "The Theatres," *New York Commercial Advertiser*, March 2, 1900, 7; also Frederic Edward McKay, "'Marie Antoinette,'" *New York Mail and Express*, March 2, 1900, 7; "Music and Drama," *New York Evening Post*, March 6, 1900, 7; "Modjeska as Lady Macbeth," *New York Press*, March 6, 1900, 7; "New and Old Plays Score Success," *New York Evening Telegram*, February 27, 1900, 4; Edward A. Dithmar, "At the Play and with the Players," *New York Times*. Modjeska tried out a third

Shakespearean production, *Twelfth Night*, at a special matinee during her third week ("At the Theatres. Fifth Avenue—Twelfth Night," *NYDM*, March 17, 1900, 16).

104   Shattuck, *Shakespeare*. 2:127.

105   Ibid., 2:125; "New York City. Fifth Avenue Theatre," *NYC*, March 10, 1900, 34; "Theatrical Disclosures," *New York Sun*, March 6, 1900, 7; "Modjeska in 'Macbeth,'" *New York Mail and Express*, March 6, 1900, 7.

106   "Irving Here Once Again," *New York Sun*, October 27, 1899, 7.

107   Gustav Kobbé, "Some Recent Plays and Players," *Forum* 29 (May 1900): 383–84.

108   James A. Herne, "Art for Truth's Sake in Drama," *Arena* (February 1897): 365.

109   Levine, *Highbrow*, 72.

110   "Lectures on Shakespeare," *NYDM*, April 21, 1900, 14; also "New York City. Fifth Avenue Theater Theatre," *NYC*, March 3, 1900, 10.

Chapter 27

1   "At the Theatres. Bijou—The Japanese Players," *NYDM*, March 31, 1900, 16; also "'The Japanese Players," *New York Evening Post*, March 20, 1900, 7; "New Japanese Plays," *New York Herald*, March 20, 1900, 11; "The Japanese Players," *New York Mail and Express*, March 20, 1900, 7.

2   "At the Theatres. Bijou—The Japanese Players," *NYDM*.

3   "'The Japanese Players," *New York Evening Post*. No newspaper commented in detail on the scenic aspects so there was no accurate evidence how Kawakami staged this well-known assault in the snow.

4   "At the Theatres. Bijou—The Japanese Players," *NYDM*.

5   "What Ho! Ye Dainty Casino Girl," *New York Evening Telegram*, March 20, 1900, 4.

6   "'The Japanese Players," *New York Evening Post*.

7   "At the Theatres. Bijou—The Japanese Players," *NYDM*.

8   Ibid.; also "What Ho! Ye Dainty Casino Girl," *New York Evening Telegram*.

9   Frederic Edward McKay, "Theatrical Gossip," *New York Mail and Express*, March 14, 1900, 7; "Japanese Players in 'Teijo' and 'Scarlet Snow,'" *New York Herald*, March 18, 1900, 4:4; "This Week on Our Stage," *New York Sun*, March 18, 1900, 3:11.

10   "Professional Doings," *NYDM*, March 24, 1900, 13.

11   "Theatrical Jottings," *New York Herald*, March 15, 1900, 12.

12   "'Naughty Anthony' Souvenirs," *New York Times*, March 13, 1900, 9; "This Week on Our Stage," *New York Sun*, March 11. 1900, 3:7.

13   "Plays. Continuous Attractions," *New York Press*, February 14, 1900, 14; "Notes on the Theatres," *New York Press*, February 6, 1900, 7.

14   "Manager William A. Brady," unidentified New York newspaper, 1898, in clipping file: Way Down East, BRTC; "Notes of the Week," *New York Times*, April 1, 1900, 4:5.

15   "Japan Visits Broadway," *New York Herald*, March 13, 1900, 13; also "Those Japanese Actors," *New York Times*, March 18, 1900, 18; "The Japanese Players," *New York Mail and Express*; "Gleanings from the Greenroom," *New York Evening Telegram*, March 13, 1900, 4.

16   "Clement Scott on Japanese Plays," *New York Herald*, Match 13, 1900, 13.

17   "Music and Drama. The Japanese Players," *New York Evening Post*, March 13, 1900, 7.

18   "Theatrically Uncommon," *New York Sun*, March 14, 1900, 7.

19   "Professional Doings," *NYDM*, March 24, 1900, 13; also "Those Japanese Actors," *New York Times*; "New York City. Review and Comment," *NYC*, March 31, 1900, 105.

20   "At the Theatres. Bijou—The Japanese Players," *NYDM*; "Affairs of the Theatre," *New York Sun*, March 30, 1900, 7.

21 "Ethel Henry, the Tall English Actress," *Broadway Magazine* (March 1900): n.p.; "Ethel Henry. Mrs. Langtry's leading woman in 'The Degenerates' at the Garden Theatre," *New York Mail and Express Illustrated Saturday Magazine*, January 27, 1900, 7; "Beauty Says Langtry's Jealousy Led to Her Leaving 'Degenerates,'" *New York Press*, February 18, 1900, 7; "Those Japanese Actors," *New York Times*.

22 "Langtry Actress Will Sue," *New York Times*, 13 February 13, 1900, 4; "A Little Chat with Ethel Henry," *NYDM*, c. 1900; in clipping file: Henry, Ethel, BRTC; "Transatlantic Travelers," *NYDM*, May 26, 1900, 16. Henry was staying with her mother at the same Bartholdi Hotel where Kawakami and Sadayakko were. She may also have been helped by her mentor Ellen Terry who was in town.

23 Kaneo, *Sadayakko*, 42. I was unable to further identify this person.

24 Ibid., 31.

25 "New York City. Review and Comment," *NYC*, March 31, 1900, 105.

26 "At the Theatres. Bijou—The Japanese Players," *NYDM*, March 31, 1900, 16–17.

27 Auguste Comte, *System of Positive Polity*, trans. Richard Congreve (London, 1877. Reprint. New York: Franklin, n.d.), 4:100.

28 Usually called *Camille* in the United States.

29 Knepler, *Guilded*, 171, 191. While renown for their emotional displays in other roles, Rachel and Modjeska both rejected offers to play Marguerite (Knepler, *Guilded*, 134, 193).

30 "A Japanese Actress," *New York Times*, March 11, 1900, 16.

31 Dijkstra, *Idols*, 133. Foreign ideas of "romantic love" had become a subject in the reforming modern literature of Japan (Kyoko Kurita, "The Romantic Triangle in Meiji Literature," in *New Directions in the Study of Meiji Japan*, eds. Helen Hardacre and Adam L. Kern [Leiden: Brill, 1997], 229–45).

32 Amy Koritz, "Moving Violations: Dance in the London Music Hall, 1890–1901," *Theatre Journal* 42 (December 1990): 424.

33 "A Japanese Actress," *New York Times*.

34 Dijkstra, *Idols*, 246.

35 Ibid., 243–45, 248–49. Dijkstra cited clinical examples from Krafft-Ebing.

36 Ibid., 309–15. In the basic kabuki *Dōjōji*, the dancer turns into a fierce serpent.

37 The gestures and costumes were part of the standard *Dōjōji* kabuki dance.

38 Ibid., 243–45. The sheer clothing of females in the paintings that Dijkstra examined resembled that of gauze-clad contemporary American dancer Isadora Duncan.

39 Photograph of *The Geisha and the Knight* taken in New York, 1900 in "Theatre and Theatre-Going in Japan," *Theatre* (New York) No. 41 (July 1904): 167; "The Quarrel Scene of 'The Geisha and the Knight,'" *New York Journal*, March 11, 1900, 29.

40 Lowell, *Soul*, 6–7.

41 "Japanese Players in 'Teijo' and 'Scarlet Snow,'" *New York Herald*, March 18, 1900, 4:4; "This Week on Our Stage," *New York Sun*, March 18, 1900, 3:11; Frederic Edward McKay, "Theatrical Gossip," *New York Mail and Express*, March 14, 1900, 7; "Professional Doings," *NYDM*, March 24, 1900, 13. Although serving tea to audiences was already a widespread American practice with local stock companies and third-class touring troupes, it was rare on Broadway (Weldon B. Durham, "The Revival and Decline of the Stock Company Mode of Organization 1886–1930," *Theatre History Studies* 6 (1986): 173).

42 In "Invisible Presences—Performance Intertextuality," *Theatre Research International* 19:2 (Summer 1994): 11–17, Marvin Carlson discussed how the out-of-the-play life of actors was conflated with roles they performed. The identity of actors with their roles was one consequence of realism/realist aesthetics.

43 Orvell, *Real*, xv-xx. Of course, there was old fogy opposition: "The best argument against real things in the theatre is that they are real, and reality has no place in the theatre. [Might] as well demand that Camille

should be played by consumptive actresses only, or that only a crook back should play Richard. Reality on stage is disconcerting" (Field, *Through*, 30).

44 "Amusements. Keith's Theatre," *Boston Evening Record*, December 12, 1899, 5.

45 "At the Theatres. Columbus—The King of the Opium Ring," *NYDM*, March 18, 1899, 16.

46 Andrea Dennett, *Weird*, 66–80.

47 "Japanese Drama," *Dayton Daily Journal*, November 27, 1899, 5.

48 Fischer-Lichte in *Show*, 73–77, 230–31, discussed exploitation of colonial persons in colonial exhibitions (Völkerausstellung).

49 Michael Quinn, "Celebrity and the Semiotics of Acting," *New Theatre Quarterly* 22 (1990): 154–61; Marvin Carlson, "Invisible Presences—Performance Intertextuality," *Theatre Research International* 19:2 (Summer 1994): 111–17.

50 Elsom, *Erotic*, 29.

51 Yone[jirō] Noguchi, "The Geisha Girl of Japan," *Theatre* (New York) No. 47 (January 1905): 22.

52 Gregory L. Golley, "Tanizaki Jun'ichirō: The Art of Subversion and the Subversion of Art," *Journal of Japanese Studies* 21:2 (Summer 1995): 365–404.

53 Marcelle Azra Hincks, "The Art of Dancing in Japan," *Fortnightly Review* (London) 80: (July 2, 1906): 98.

54 Boyd, *Paris*, 532; also Edmond Linval, "Les spectacles de danses à l'Exposition Universelle de 1900," *Novelle revue* 141 (February 1, 1936): 213; "Miscellaneous," *Orient* (Yokohama) (February 15, 1900): 40.

55 Hillary Bell, "Player Folk," *New York Press*, February 14, 1900, 6; also Edward A. Dithmar, "At the Play and with the Players," *New York Times*, January 14, 1900, 16.

56 Shattuck, *Shakespeare*, 2:90, 2:95; McArthur, *Actors*, 43. One result was that this increase in value gave additional clout to female stars that helped several to become managers of their own companies.

57 Norman Hapgood, "The Actor of Today," *Atlantic Monthly* 83 (January 1899): 123, 125.

58 Banta, *Imagining*, 631.

59 "Maude Adams Record Beating Role of 'Babbie'," *New York Journal*, June 19, 1898, 18; *Maude Adams in The Little Minister* (New York: Russell, 1899), n.p.; Marguerite Vance, *Hear the Distant Applause!* (New York: Dutton, 1963), 141.

60 Sidney Sharp, "New Plays Out of Place," *New York World*, November 19, 1899, E3; also "At the Theatres. Manhattan—Papa's Wife," *NYDM*, November 18, 1899, 16; "Things in the New Plays," *New York Sun*, November 19, 1900, 3:9.

61 I attributed the abundant coverage of Sadayakko to strong journalist interest rather than publicist pushing. Neither theatrical novice Mrs. Osborne nor her publicity agents could have been solely so effective in securing so many published stories.

62 "Men, Women, and Events: A Japanese Actress," *Cosmopolitan* (March 1900): 511; "Madame Sada Yacco, Japan's Greatest Emotional Actress" in *Harper's Bazar* (March 24, 1900): 251–52.

63 Shattuck, *Shakespeare*, 2:90; Howells, *Story*, 4–5; H[illary] B[ell], "Nethersole's New Play Not Wicked," *New York Press*, February 6, 1900, 7.

64 "The Stage," *Washington Post*, February 4, 1900, 24.

65 "Gowns of the Stage," *NYDM*, November 12, 1898, 13 and January 14, 1899, 2; "Dramatic and Musical," *New York Times*, January 23, 1900, 7; "Three Little Lambs," *New York Times*, January 14, 1900, 16.

66 Rymer, *Short*, 2.

67 "Kabuki-za shichigatsu kyōgen no katsura to ishō" [Wigs and costumes in July plays at the Kabuki-za], *Kabuki* (August 1901): 66–70; "Kabuki-za gogatsu kyōgen ishō" [Costumes in the May plays at the Kabuki-za], *Kabuki* (June 1901): 56–62; Itō Baisetsu, "Shibai no ishō" [Theatrical costumes], *Kabuki* (March 1909): 89–90.

68 H[illary] B[ell], "Mrs. Langtry Gives a New Play," *New York Press*, January 16, 1900, 7.

69 Hillary Bell, "Player Folk," *New York Press*, February 19, 1900, 6.

70 H[illary] B[ell], "Nethersole's New Play Not Wicked," *New York Press*.

71 Clement Scott, "'Ballet! Beauty! Brains!' Exclaims Clement Scott," *New York Herald*, January 28, 1900, 4:10.

72 "Gossip of the Theatre," *Washington Post*, January 28, 1900, 24; also "News and Gossip of the Stage," *New York Evening Telegram*, April 18, 1900, 4; "At the Theatres. Star—The Queen of Chinatown," *NYDM*, August 26, 1899 15.

73 "The Theatre," *Washington Evening Star*, February 3, 1900, 20; "The Stage," *Washington Post*, February 4, 1900, 24.

74 "Rich Dressing in Plays," *New York Times*, January 28, 1900, 16; also Ethel Barrymore, *Memories, an Autobiography* (New York: Harpers, 1955), 94. The average salary of a well established male or female actor was $40 to $50 a week. Good employment for an actor was thirty weeks. See Rudolph De Cordova, "The Stage as a Career: An Actor's Experience," *Forum* 17 (July 1894): 622).

75 "Dresses at the Empire," *New York Times*, April 15, 1900, 16.

76 "Four New Plays. The Ambassador," *New York Mail and Express*, February 6, 1900, 7; McKay, "Plays and Players," *New York Mail and Express Illustrated Saturday Magazine*, March 3, 1900, 6.

77 Bijou Theatre, New York, programs, weeks of March 12 and April 2, 1900

78 "Dramatic and Musical. Madison Square Theatre," *New York Times*, February 6, 1900, 6; "The Stage," *Washington Post*, February 4, 1900, 24.

79 "Dramatic and Musical," *New York Times*, January 16, 1900, 7.

80 "Theatrical Notes," *Washington Post*, February 4, 1900, 25.

81 Sidney Sharp, "New Plays Out of Place," *New York World*; Betty Bradeen, "A Twilight Chat," *Boston Traveler*, December 23, 1899, 4; Stokes, *Bernhardt*, 5.

82 Harold Ballagh, "Madame Yacco Urges Japanese Dress for American Women," *New York World*, April 23, 1900, 9.

83 Tomoko Sato and Toshio Watanabe, *Japan and Britain: An Aesthetic Dialogue 1850–1930* (London: Lund Humphries and Barbican Art Gallery, 1991), 49.

84 Ozaki, *Joyū*, 40.

85 "At the Theatres," *Washington Post*, January 30, 1900, 3.

86 Takahashi, "Zadankai," 83.

87 "The Japanese Players," *New York Times*, April 1, 1900, 2:18; "A Japanese Actress," *New York Times*, March 11, 1900, 16. Her stage makeup was accented with the traditional stark red highlights.

88 "Players of Mikado-Land," *Seattle Post-Intelligencer*, September 7, 1899, 6.

89 Leroy M. Scott, "Players from the Land of Sunrise," *Chicago Journal*, November 9, 1899, 4.

90 Harold Ballagh, "Madame Yacco Urges Japanese Dress for American Women," *New York World*.

Chapter 28

1 Kawakami Otojirō ikkō" [The Kawakami Otojirō troupe], *Miyako shimbun*, 10 April 1900, in Shirakawa, *shimbun*, 314; "Notes of the Theatres," *New York Press*, 21 March 1900, 7; "This Week on Our Stage," *New York Sun*, 18 March 1900, 7; "Notes of the Week," *New York Times*, 19 March 1900, 18.

2 "The Elaborate and Dazzling Japanese Scene in 'Broadway to Tokio,' at the New York Theatre," *Leslie's Weekly* 90 (February 10, 1900): 118; "Broadway to Tokio," *New York Commercial Advertiser Pictorial Review*, February 2, 1900, 11. The mummy did not get to Japan until the last act.

3 "At the Play and with the Players," *New York Times*, March 25, 1900, 16; "The Benefit Performance at Daly's," *New York Times*, March 25, 1900, 9.

4   "The Benefit Performance at Daly's," *New York Times*.

5   "Charity Matinee at Daly's," *NYDM*.

6   "The Theatres," *New York Commercial Advertiser*; also "Three Japanese Plays," *New York Mail and Express*, March 2, 1900, 7.

7   "The Japanese Players," *New York Evening Post*, March 2, 1900, 7.

8   Kaneo, *Ōbei*, 40–41; Kaneo, *Sadayakko*, 42–43.

9   Hines, *Who's*, 36; *Who Was Who in America, 1897–1942* (Chicago: Marquis, 1966), 1:79.

10   "Edwin Star Belknap," brochure, New York, 1896, in program file: Her Revenge, BRTC.

11   Hines, *Who's*, 36; "The Empire School Matinee," *NYDM*, February 2, 1895, 2. Acting school students usually performed Belknap's scripts (T. Allston Brown, *History*, 3: 535, 3:536; 3:541). Contemporary symbolist playwrights were Maeterlinck, Claudel, von Hofmannsthal, and early Yeats.

12   Reviewed in "Incidents in Stageland," *New York Sun*, October 27, 1899, 7; also "A Students' Matinee," *NYDM*, February 4, 1899, 4. *A Flower of Yeddo* was about a young Japanese girl who tested the affection of her poet lover by sending two of her girl friends to tempt him. One was disguised as a dancing geisha; the other as a male samurai ("A Flower of Yeddo," *Theatre* [New York] 1:6 [August 1901]: 15; Victor Mapes, *The Flower of Yeddo* [New York: French, 1906]).

13   Kaneo, *Sadayakko*, 43; Kaneo, *Ōbei*, 40. The AADA dollar numbers cited here were Kawakami's and were not checked in AADA archives. Also "Stanhope-Wheatcroft Dramatic School," advertisement, *NYDM*, September 10, 1898, 23; Samuel Eliot Morison, *Three Centuries of Harvard* (Cambridge: Belknap, 1936), 460.

14   The average income of an American male white collar worker was $60 to $95 a month for a six-day week.

15   McArthur, *Actors*, 23.

16   Kaneo, *Ōbei*, 40–41.

17   Kaneo, *Sadayakko*, 43–44.

18   "Success on the Stage," *New York Sun*, June 10, 1900, 3:10.

19   Kaneo, *Sadayakko*, 42–50. Kawakami's observations closely paralleled those of Bronson Howard who wrote about the AADA several months later in "Our Schools for the Stage," *Century* 56 (November 1900): 34.

20   Kaneo, *Ōbei*, 40, 45.

21   Kaneo, *Sadayakko*, 45–46; Kaneo, *Ōbei*, 40.

22   "The Japanese Players," *New York Times*, April 1, 1900, 2:18.

23   Kaneo, *Sadayakko*, 46; Kaneo, *Ōbei*, 40.

24   Miyakoya, *Yomigaeru*, cut 14; and accompanying booklet, p. 14; J. Scott. Miller, "Dispossessed Melodies: Recordings of the Kawakami Theatre Troupe," *Monumenta Nipponica* 53:2 (Summer 1998): 233.

25   Bronson Howard, "Our Schools for the Stage," 34; also Kaneo, *Sadayakko*, 41.

26   McTeague, *Before*, 75, also 60. These were based on Delsarte acting techniques.

27   Kaneo, *Sadayakko*, 47; Kaneo, *Ōbei*, 41. Advanced students also had classes in foreign history and languages, music and body exercises, psychology, physiology, and aesthetics ("Success on the Stage," *New York Sun*, June 10, 1900, 3:10).

28   The shouts quoted here are my translations of Kawakami's translations into Japanese.

29   McTeague, *Before*, 49–50, 59, also 57, 87.

30   "History—American Academy of Dramatic Arts," typewritten manuscript, c. 1969, n.p., in clipping file: Sargent, Franklin, BRTC; McTeague, *Before*, xiv–xv, 45, 91; A.E.B., "Mirror Interviews," *NYDM*, March 21, 1896, 23, 45; Fred C. Blanchard, "Professional Theatre Schools in the Early Twentieth Century," 621 and Francis Hodge, "The Private Theatre Schools in the Late Nineteenth Century," 561–63, in Wallace, *History*; Bronson Howard, "Our Schools for the Stage," *Century*, 28; Hines, *Who's*, 273.

31   David Belasco, "Dramatic Schools and the Profession of Acting," *Cosmopolitan* (August 1903): 360.

32   DeMille, *Autobiography*, 46–47; also "American Academy Matinee," *NYDM*, March 24, 1900, 9 and April 14, 1900, 13.

33   McArthur, *Actors*, 102; "Success on the Stage," *New York Sun*, June 10, 1900, 3:10.

34   "Success on the Stage," *New York Sun*; A.E.B., "Mirror Interviews," *NYDM*. By 1900, the AADA had approximately 540 graduates (McTeague, *Before*, 91).

35   A.E.B., "Mirror Interviews," *NYDM*; Hines, *Who's*, 273.

36   "Mr. John Blair's Course of Modern Plays," pamphlet, Carnegie Lyceum (New York) and New National Theatre (Washington), November 1899, in clipping file: Blair, John, BRTC; A.E.B., "Mirror Interviews," *NYDM*. The New York venue for the Blair series was the Carnegie Lyceum that Sargent managed. Located in Carnegie Hall, it had modest but adequate facilities like its closest competition, the Berkeley Lyceum.

37   Kaneo, *Sadayakko*, 43, 48–49.

38   Ikkisha, "Tōkyō ni okeru mitsu no haiyū gakkō," [Three schools for actors in Tokyo], *Kabuki* (October 1909): 84–85; Ōzasa, *Nihon*, 514.

39   Kaneo, *Ōbei*, 41; "Students of Acting Graduate," *NYDM*, April 7, 1900, 22.

40   "Themes in Theatricals," *New York Sun*, March 28, 1900, 7.

41   Kaneo, *Sadayakko*, 49.

42   "Students of Acting Graduate," *NYDM*, also Eugene W. Presbrey, "Dramatic Values in Every-Day Life," *Harper's Bazar* 33 (March 3, 1900): 176.

43   "Themes in Theatricals," *New York Sun*.

44   Unidentified newspaper fragment, c. March 28, 1900, in Locke Collection Envelope 1012, BRTC.

45   "Students of Acting Graduate," *NYDM*.

46   "Themes in Theatricals," *New York Sun*.

47   Kaneo, *Sadayakko*, 50.

48   "The Japanese Players," *New York Times*, April 1, 1900, 2:18.

49   Kaneo, *Sadayakko*, 50; "Themes in Theatricals," *New York Sun*; "Success on the Stage," *New York Sun*, June 10, 1900, 3:10. The latter source listed thirty-nine graduates. Also "Students of Acting Graduate," *NYDM*, April 7, 1900, 22.

50   Kaneo, *Sadayakko*, 50.

51   Fujii, *Jiden*, 33. Isojirō subsequently returned to Japan to join one of Kawakami's troupes (Iwai, *Shimpa*, 79). I could not positively confirm his enrollment at AADA,

52   Kaneo, *Sadayakko*, 50. Typical of actress biographies, her year of birth differed in different sources.

53   Kendal, *Dramatic*, 23; Scott, *Drama*, 2:115; William C. Young, *Famous*, 2:637. Several of her Robertson brothers and sisters were actors but never surpassed the accomplishments of Madge and T. W.

54   These dramatic burlesques were in the classic theatrical tradition.

55   Kendal, *Dramatic*, 37–39; "Mrs. Madge Robertson Kendal," article in unidentified book, Locke Collection Envelope 1012, BRTC; Eleanor Hubbell, "Mr. and Mrs. Kendal," *Metropolitan* (February 1900): 123–25.

56   Quoted in Jessie Millward, *Myself and Others* (Boston: Small, Maynard, 1924), 110.

57   Edward Gordon Craig, *Index to the Story of My Days* (New York: Viking, 1957), 22.

58   Shaw, "Miss Nethersole and Mrs. Kendal," in his *Our Theatres*, 2:165–66.

59   Sidney Sharp, "The Kendals and Mansfield Join the Theatrical Stars in Town," *New York Sun*, November 21, 1899, 5; "This Week on Our Stage," *New York Sun*, November 19, 1899, 3:9; "Return of the Kendals," *New York Herald*, November 21, 1899, 13; Madge Kendal, *Dame Madge Kendal by Herself* (London: Murray, 1933), 241–42.

60   "Return of the Kendals," *New York Herald*; "This Week on Our Stage," *New York Sun*. The Kendals played five weeks at Manhattan's Knickerbocker Theatre in December 1899 to fair business (T. Allston Brown, *History*, 602–3).

61 "At the Theatres. Knickerbocker—The Elder Miss Blossom," *NYDM*, 25 November 25, 1899, 16; "Theatrical Occurrences," *New York Sun*, November 21, 1899, 7; Clement Scott, "Mr. Scott's View of the Kendals," *New York Herald*, November 21, 1899, 13; Roland Burke Hennessy, "New Plays in New York," *Broadway* (February 4, 1900): 294–97; Henry Austin Clapp, "At the Hollis St. Theatre," *Boston Daily Advertiser*, October 24, 1899, 8. "The Kendals' New Play," *NYDM*, April 7, 1900, 17; Alan Dale, "'A Son's Inheritance' Produced by the Kendals Is Sheer and Unmitigated Rubbish," *New York Journal*, March 30, 1900, 8; "The Theatres," *New York Commercial Advertiser*, March 30, 1900, 7; Frederic Edward McKay, "A Son's Inheritance," *New York Mail and Express*, March 30, 1900, 7; Jason, "The Dramatic Season in New York," *Leslie's Weekly* 89 (23 December 1899): 510.

62 Sidney Sharp, "The Kendals and Mansfield Join the Theatrical Stars in Town."

63 "Dramatic and Musical, *New York Times*, November 21, 1899, 4; also E. J. West, "Actress between Two Schools: The Case of Madge Kendal," *Speech Monographs* 11 (1944): 110.

64 Madge Kendal, "Nuts!" *NYDM*, December 28, 1889, n.p.

65 Sandra Richards, *Rise*, 116; "The Rehearsal Club," *Boston Herald*, January 14, 1900, 32; "Actors' Fund Benefit," *NYDM*, April 7, 1900, 13; Kendal, *Dame*, 283–84; unidentified clipping, in Locke Collection Envelope 1012, BRTC; Eleanor Hubbell, "Mr. and Mrs. Kendal," *Metropolitan* (February 1900): 127–28.

66 Kendal, *Dame*, 281–86. Their friendship was part of the basis for the 1979 play and 1980 film, *The Elephant Man*.

67 Kaneo, *Sadayakko*, 42; Kaneo, *Ōbei*, 42–43.

68 Kaneo, *Sadayakko*, 51–52.

69 Benjamin McArthur, "Theatrical Clubs in the Nineteenth Century: Tradition versus Assimilation in the Acting Community," *Theatre Survey* 23 (November 1982): 201–5; Daniel J. Watermeier, "Actors and Acting," in Wilmeth, *Guide*, 447; Kobbé, *Famous*, 207, 212, 219, 345. McArthur, *Actors*, 73–75, 80. The older theatrical organizations attracted a wider range of show business people such as vaudevillians.

70 Willis Steell, "The Actors' Clubs of New York," *Theatre* (New York) No. 33 (November 1903): 279; also Kaneo, *Sadayakko*, 51–54; Kaneo, *Ōbei*, 42–43; McArthur, *Actors*, 82.

71 Kaneo, *Sadayakko*, 51; Kaneo, *Ōbei*, 43.

72 Kaneo, *Ōbei*, 42; Kaneo, *Sadayakko*, 51; Kobbé, *Famous*, 215–22; Robert A. Carter, "The Hampden-Booth Theatre Library," in *Edwin Booth's Legacy: Treasures from the Hampden-Booth Theatre Collection at The Players*, ed. Raymond Wemmlinger and Brooks McNamara (New York: Hampden/Booth Theatre Library, 1989), 12; McArthur, *Actors*, 81.

73 Kaneo, *Sadayakko*, 51–52.

74 "The Twelfth Night Club," *New York Times*, January 8, 1900, 7; Benjamin McArthur, "Theatrical Clubs in the Nineteenth Century: Tradition versus Assimilation in the Acting Community"; McArthur, *Actors*, 75.

75 Kaneo, *Sadayakko*, 42; "Madame Yacco Entertained," *NYDM*, March 31, 1900, 2; Kaneo, *Ōbei*, 43–44; "Kawakami Otojirō wa Beikoku Nyūyōku" [Kawakami Otojirō in New York], *Miyako shimbun*, May 5, 1900, in Shirakawa, 315.

76 "Things at the Theatres," *New York Sun*, May 29, 1900, 7; Yamaguchi, *Joyū*, 92; Kaneo, *Ōbei*, 43; Sara A. Palmer, "A Practical Women's Club," *NYDM*, December 3, 1898, 30–32; "Drama Day at P.W.L.," *NYDM*, March 24, 1900, 13. Kawakami may have been confused about the separate identities of the Twelfth Night Club and the Professional Women's League.

77 McArthur, *Actors*, 75; Reitz, *Wearing*, 281–82, 296; T. Allston Brown, *History*, 3:610.

78 Leslie, *Some*, 80.

79 Henry Austin Clapp, *Reminiscences*, 106.

80 "Complain about Actors," *New York Commercial Advertiser*, April 4, 1900, 8.

81 "Actors Ordered Off the Old-Time Rialto," *New York World*, April 5, 1900, 3.

82   "St. James Folks Say Actors Must Move on," *New York World*, April 7, 1900, 4.

83   Keene, *World*, 233.

84   Okamoto, *Engeki*, 269.

85   Davis, *Actresses*, 71–72.

86   Chieko Ariga, "Dephallicizing Women in *Ryūkyō shinshi*: A Critique of Gender Ideology in Japanese Literature," *Journal of Asian Studies* 51:3 (August 1992): 576.

87   "A Timely Resolve," *NYDM*, May 12, 1900, 14.

88   McArthur, *Actors*, 73, 105–12.

89   "A Timely Resolve," *NYDM*.

90   "General Theatrical Notes," *New York Evening Post*, April 14, 1900, 17; "A Theatre for Children," *NYDM*, April 7, 1900, 14.

91   "At the Theatres. Carnegie Lyceum—Jack the Giant Killer," *NYDM*, 21 April 21, 1900, 16; "New York City. Carnegie Lyceum," *NYC*, April 21, 1900, 178; "Wayward Ones in Plays," *New York Sun*, April 17, 1900, 7; "The Children's Theatre," *NYDM*, May 5, 1900, 2; "Music and Drama. Mother Goose in the Theatre," *New York Evening Post*, April 17, 1900, 7; Alan Dale, "Jack the Giant Killer," *New York Journal*, April 17, 1900, 8; "Little Ones Gaze on Dreamland Folk," *New York Herald*, April 17, 1900, 10; Sidney Sharp, "The Mother Goose Play," *New York World*, April 17, 1900, 4. "Mother Goose play" was a generic term in America for extravaganzas with characters from Mother Goose tales. Not all Mother Goose production scenarios came from that nursery canon or were appropriate for younger audiences. The form was roughly equivalent to British pantomime.

92   "Topics of the Theatres," *New York Sun*, May 2, 1900, 7; "The Children's Theatre," *NYDM*. I found no evidence that Sargent or any other person constructed such a specialized professional theatre for children in New York in the following decades (Nellie McCaslin, *Theatre for Children in the United States: A History* [Norman: University of Okahoma Press, 1971], 15–17, 23–27; Alice Minnie Herts, *The Children's Educational Theatre* [New York: Harper, 1911], ix–x, 2–3).

93   *Chris and the Wonderful Lamp, Little Red Riding Hood*, and *Superba*.

94   Kawakami and Sadayakko played Britain in 1900 and again in 1901 but not during the Christmas pantomime season.

95   Kawatake Shigetoshi, *Nihon no engeki*, 181; Tomita, *Nihon*, 38–60, 173–75, 376; Iwaya Sazanami, "Kawakami kun to otogi shibai" [Mr. Kawakami and fairy tale plays], *Engei gahō* (December 1911): 143–44.

96   John B. Clapp, *Players*, 3:324–35; "Mrs. Alfred Brooks Fry, Retired Actress, Is Dead," *New York Herald Tribune*, December 11, 1936 and "Emma D. Frye," *NYDM*, August 9, 1890, both clippings in photograph file: Sheridan, Emma V., BRTC. Her father should not be confused with the more famous Civil War general, Philip Henry Sheridan.

97   Winter, *Life*, 1:349; John B. Clapp, *Players*, 3:324–35; "Dramatics Copyright," *Boston Dramatic Review* (November 25, 1899): 2; [Emma Sheridan Frye], "Every once in a while, I feel," fragment, *New York Review* 4 (April 1914): n.p.; "Theatrically Uncommon," *New York Sun*, March 14, 1900. 7; T. Allston Brown, *History*, 3:536, 3:539.

98   McTeague, *Before*, 60; Paul Kozelka, "Dramatics in the High Schools, 1900–1924," in Wallace, *History*, 599; Laura Gardner Salazar, "The Emergence of Children's Theatre, a Study in America's Changing Values and the Stage, 1900 to 1910," *Theatre History Studies* 7 (1987): 80; Nellie McCaslin, *Theatre for Children in the United States*, 15–17. Fry's book *Educational Dramatics: A Handbook on the Educational Player Method* (New York: Moffat, Yard, 1913), was an early classic in the field ("Mrs. Alfred Brooks Fry, Retired Actress, Is Dead," *New York Herald Tribune*). Most of her productions were either simplified Shakespeare or fairy tales.

99   *Ōbei*, 41–42. The play was identified as *The Traitor Mandolin* in *Who Was Who in America, 1897–1942* (Chicago: Marquis, 1966), 1:79.

100 Kaneo, *Sadayakko* 42–43, 47. Kawakami's *shosagoto* and his fighting scenes that had no dialog were sometimes described in the American press as "pantomime." Classic pantomime (silent) acting forms should not be confused with British harlequinade extravaganzas called (Christmas) pantomimes.

101 The AADA and Belknap considered pantomime "the purest expression of emotion" (McTeague, *Before*, 82–83). In performance, *The Traitor Samisen* may have had piano accompaniment.

102 "Ōsaka no Kawakami engeki" [Kawakami's play in Osaka], *Chūō shimbun*, February 2, 1901, in Shirakawa, 349.

103 These were played without speech but with musical accompaniment (Kawatake Shigetoshi, *Engeki hyakka*, 3:547–48).

104 Kaneo, *Ōbei*, 41; Kaneo, *Sadayakko*, 42.

105 Kaneo, *Sadayakko*, 42; *Ōbei*, 42. In May 1901, between Kawakami's two major trips abroad, the magazine *Kabuki* noted that Kawakami "had" a Japanese version of *The Traitor Samisen* (*Shamisen no muhon*) ("Kabuki nikki" [Theatre diary]. *Kabuki* [May 1901], 65). I found no indication that it was performed.

Chapter 29

1   "The Japanese Players," *NYDM*, March 17, 1900, 15. Most likely there were no other suitable productions available to move into the Bijou despite a surplus of shows looking for a theatre.

2   "This Week on Our Stage," *New York Sun*, March 25, 1900, 3:7; "Last Night's Plays," *New York Mail and Express*, March 27, 1900, 9; "Bijou," advertisement, *New York Times*, March 25, 1900, 9; "Notes on the Stage," *New York Tribune*, March 25, 1900, 8.

3   "At the Theatres. Bijou—The Japanese Players," *NYDM*, April 7, 1900, 16; also "This Week on Our Stage," *New York Sun*; "Sawdust Scent and Lime Light Glare," *New York Evening Telegram*, March 29, 1900, 4.

4   "Affairs of the Theatre," *New York Sun*, March 30, 1900, 7.

5   Carolyn Shipman, "The Japanese Players," *Critic* 36 (April 1900): 330. *Soga* may have had cast changes, or maybe it was only reviewers' confusion about actors' names. The younger brother Gorō (who was the central character, the more violent figure, and the most challenging role) was initially played by Yamamoto Kaichi in Boston, but he moved into a secondary part (Gosha) when Kawakami took over Gorō ("At the Theatres. Bijou—The Japanese Players," *NYDM*; Bijou Theatre, New York, program, week of April 2, 1900, *Zingoro, an Ernest Statue Maker* and *Soga*; Boston Theatre, Boston, program, January 18–19, 1900, "The Japanese Dramatic Company;" "Things Theatrical. Lafayette," *Washington Times*, January 31, 1900, 4). All of these sources had Fujikawa Iwanosuke playing Jūrō, the older brother.

6   "The Theatres," *New York Commercial Advertiser*, March 30, 1900, 7.

7   "Music and Drama. The Japanese Players," *New York Evening Post*, March 13, 1900, 7; also "At the Theatres. Bijou—The Japanese Players," *NYDM*; "Something New in Acting," *New York World*, March 2, 1900, 12.

8   Epes W. Sargent, "Dramatic Progress of the Japanese," *Metropolitan* 11 (May 1900): 503.

9   "The Theatres," *New York Commercial Advertiser*, March 27, 1900, 7.

10   Ibid., March 10, 1900, 5; Katherine Metcalf Roof, "Concerning the Japanese Players," *Impressionist* (June 1900), 6.

11   "Japanese Realism," *New York Commercial Advertiser*, April 20, 1900, 7.

12   Henry Irving, "The Art of Acting," in his *Drama*, n.p.

13   "The Theatres," *New York Commercial Advertiser*, March 10, 1900, 5. The writer was most likely Norman Hapgood who was the drama editor of the paper.

14   "Players from Far Japan, *Boston Journal*, January 7, 1900, 4:4. Although this review was unattributed, indirect evidence suggested Lewis C. Strang wrote it.

15   Littlewood, *Idea*, 64; Miner, *Japanese*, 33–35.

16   Kipling, *From*, 1:283–94.

17   Edwin Arnold, *Seas and Lands* (London: Longmans, Green, 1891), 163.

18   Luigi Illica and Giuseppe Giacosa, lyricists; Giocomo Puccini, composer, trans. Stanley Appelbaum, *Madama Butterfly* (New York: Dover, 1983), 9.

19   W. S. Gilbert, *The Mikado; or, The Town of Titipu* (reprint, New York: Macmillan, 1979), 3.

20   For summary discussions of the pictorial in Japanese theatre see Gunji, *Kabuki*, 17, 47–48; Toshio Kawatake, *Japan on Stage*, 86–87, 91–99, 117; Ronald Cavaye, *Kabuki: A Pocket Guide* (Rutland, Vermont: Tuttle, 1993), 44, 61–63; Ernst, *Kabuki*. 82–83, 112, 178–80.

21   Somewhat like the effect of a freeze frame in a motion picture.

22   The Japanese term for performing a *mie* is "*mie o kiru,*" that is "to cut a *mie.*" There are at least ten established *mie* kata.

23   This conclusion was not based on direct evidence but on the *absence* of any hint of a *mie* in published American reports.

24   Camille Mauclair, "Sada Yacco et Loïe Fuller," *Revue blanche* 23 (October 15, 1900): 281.

25   Paul Klee, *The Diaries of Paul Klee*, ed. Felix Klee (Berkeley: University of California Press, 1964), 110.

26   Faith Bach, "Breaking the *Kabuki* Actors' Barriers: 1868–1900," in Leiter, *Kabuki Reader*, 159.

27   Max Beerbohm, "Almond Blossom in Piccadilly Circus," *Saturday Review* (London) 91 (June 22, 1901): 799–800.

28   Gilbert B. Cross, *Next Week—East Lynne: Domestic Drama in Performance* (Lewisburg, Pennsylvania: Bucknell University Press, 1977), 136–37. During most of the nineteenth century, a tableau might also be struck midway during an ongoing scene to emphasize an action or to highlight a sudden plot development (Meisel, *Realizations*, 39–41).

29   Burns, *Theatricality*, 189, 196. Only later were "critics" expected to write down and propagate their opinions outside the theatre.

30   Levine, *Highbrow*, 195.

31   Bloom, *Joseph*, 37; Gilbert B. Cross, *Next Week—East Lynne*, 124–26.

32   "A Theatrical Occasion," *New York Sun*, October 31, 1899, 7; "Mrs. Fiske as Becky Sharp," *Boston Traveler*, January 2, 1900, 5; "How the Plays Went Last Night," *New York Herald*, March 27, 1900, 13; "The Carpetbagger," *New York Times*, March 6, 1900, 9; "Sewell Collins Begins a Crusade Against the 'Curtain Call,'" *New York Evening Journal*, March 19, 1900, 10. An American male actor frequently executed his curtain call with a bow and his right hand over his heart, while women curtseyed (Frederic Edward McKay, "Plays and Players," *New York Mail and Express Illustrated Saturday Magazine*, March 17, 1900, 6).

33   "Dramas and Audiences. Do Our People Need Protection against the Theatres?" *New York Sun*, February 18, 1900, 3:7; Jack W. McCullough, "The East Wind," *Winging It* 2:4 (Spring 1996): 4; "At the Theatres. Columbia—The King of the Opium Ring," *NYDM*, March 18, 1899, 16.

34   Walter Herries Pollock, "Hissing in Theatres," *Theatre* (London) No. 145 (March 1, 1895): 148–49.

35   "Sewell Collins Begins a Crusade Against the 'Curtain Call,'" *New York Evening Journal*.

36   Frederic Edward McKay, "Dramatic World," *New York Mail and Express*, April 28, 1900, 20.

37   Amy Leslie, "Frenchy Play by Fitch," *Chicago Daily News*, November 1, 1899, 6.

38   "The Theatres," *New York Commercial Advertiser*, April 17, 1900, 7.

39   "Tremont. Arizona," advertisement, *Boston Post*, December 7, 1899, 7.

40   Unidentified New York newspaper, February 1899, RLS NAFR+ v. 43; p. 7, BRTC; also "Incidents of the Stage," *New York Sun*, March 23, 1900, 7.

41   "'Robespierre' a Vivid, Striking Spectacle of the French Commune," *Detroit News*, January 25, 1900, 2; Leslie, *Some*, 64; "Sewell Collins Begins a Crusade Against the 'Curtain Call,'" *New York Evening Journal*.

42   "Dramatic and Musical," *New York Times*, April 17, 1900, 9.

43   Hillary Bell, "The Stage," *New York Press*, April 22, 1900, 2:4; also "Sewell Collins Begins a Crusade Against the 'Curtain Call,'" *New York Evening Journal*; "Dramatic and Musical," *New York Times*, January 16, 1900, 7; Clement Scott, "Clement Scott and 'The Casino Girl,'" *New York Herald*, March 20, 1900, 11.

44   "Japan's [illegible]," unidentified Boston newspaper, c. December 10, 1899.

45   "The Theatres," *New York Commercial Advertiser*, March 2, 1900, 7.

46   "What Ho! Ye Dainty Casino Girl," *New York Evening Telegram*, March 20, 1900, 4.

47   "The Japanese Players," *New York Times*, April 1, 1900, 2:18; also "Sada Yacco Plays Sapho," *New York Press*, April 17, 1900, 7.

48   Tamura Jujirō, "Watakushi ga mita Nyûyōku no shibai to yose," [Plays and vaudeville I saw in New York], *Kabuki* (May 1907), 38.

49   "Matte imashita!"

50   "Nippon-ichi!"

51   Raz, *Audience*, 185, 227–29. *Kakegoe* on a more limited and formal basis have continued to today.

52   Muramatsu Shunkichi. *Tabishibai*, 88. Tangerines (the native *mikan*) was a favorite snack in theatres. Audiences sat on cushions.

53   "'End of Babylon' Cut Out," *New York Sun*, March 19, 1900, 4.

54   Gunji, *Kabuki*, 62.

55   Kurata, *Kindaigeki*, 157.

56   Jun'ichirō Tanizaki, *Some Prefer Nettles (Tade kuu mushi)*, trans. Edward G. Seidensticker (Tokyo: Tuttle, 1955), 137, 142–43. I've personally tried it. It works.

57   "Phoebe Davies," unidentified New York newspaper, 1898, in clipping file: Way Down East, BRTC.

58   "The Japanese Players," *New York Times*, April 1, 1900, 2:18.

59   "Notes of the Week," *New York Times*, March 25, 1900, 16; "News and Views of Stageland," *New York Evening Telegram*, March 30, 1900. 4. I counted 105 performances by the troupe in regular American theatres up to April 2 and did not include the thirty shows targeted to Japanese audiences on the West Coast, in Hawaii, and at the New York Hinode Club. I also did not include performances at the Washington Legation and the recent benefit at Daly's Theatre.

60   "Bijou," advertisement, *New York Herald*, April 1, 1900, 4:5; "Souvenir Ngt. Mond. Apr. 2," advertisement, *New York Herald*, April 1, 1900, 4:5; "The Theatres," *New York Commercial Advertiser*, March 31, 1900, 7. Advertisements for this anniversary billed the troupe as the "Famous Japanese Players" under the "Management of Mrs. Robert Osborn."

61   "Theatrical Jottings," *New York Herald*, March 15, 1900, 12.

62   "Continuous Attractions," *New York Press*, April 1, 1900, 14; "Notes of the Week," *New York Times*, April 1, 1900, 2:18; "Theatrical Jottings," *New York Herald*, April 6, 1900, 10.

63   Bijou Theatre, New York, program, week of April 2, 1900.

64   Kaneo, *Sadayakko*, 42.

65   "Japanese Realism," *New York Commercial Advertiser*, April 20, 1900, 7.

66   "The Theatres," *New York Commercial Advertiser*, March 30, 1900, 7.

67   Carolyn Shipman, "The Japanese Players," *Critic* 36 (April 1900): 330. Her opinion was seconded by a *Dramatic Mirror* critic who reported that Tsusaka played Suketsune with "comic dignity" ("At the Theatres. Bijou—The Japanese Players," *NYDM*, April 7, 1900, 16). In *Soga*, Tsusaka also doubled as the old mother

of the Soga brothers, and Yamamoto Kaichi often substituted without notice for Kawakami in the leading role of Gorō. Kawakami may have had health problems so he was unable to appear.

68   Carolyn Shipman, "The Japanese Players," 328, 330, 327.

69   "Japanese Realism," *New York Commercial Advertiser.*

70   "Affairs of the Theatre," *New York Sun*, March 30, 1900, 7.

71   For a discussion of liquid blood effects in kabuki, see Kawatake Toshio, *Japan*, 213–14.

72   "Japanese Realism," *New York Commercial Advertiser.* It was not clearly established in other sources that Kawakami carried a severed head onstage in Boston, although such props were common in nineteenth-century kabuki. In Boston, *Kojima* was still played as the first part of *The Geisha and the Knight.*

73   Ibid.

74   "Theatrical Jottings," *New York Herald*, April 6, 1900, 10.

75   "At the Theatres. Bijou—The Japanese Players," *NYDM*, April 7, 1900, 16; "Notes on the Stage," *New York Tribune*, March 25, 1900, 8; "Notes of the Week," *New York Times*, April 1, 1900, 2:18; "At Other Theatres," *New York Mail and Express*, April 3, 1900, 9; "At Other Playhouses," *NYDM*, April 7, 1900, 16.

76   "'Quo Vadis' at Herald Square," *New York Times*, April 3, 1900, 9; "Theatrical Notes, *New York Sun*, March 31, 1900, 8.

77   "Notes of the Week," *New York Times*; "Themes from Stageland," *New York Sun*, June 24, 1900, 3:9.

78   The Fourteenth Street Theatre was two-thirds of a mile south of the main Broadway theatre district.

79   "New York City. Fourteenth Street Theatre," *NYC*, March 10, 1900, 34; "Current Amusements," *NYDM*, March 24, April 21 and 23, 1900, 16; "The Theatres," *New York Commercial Advertiser*, March 6, 1900, 7.

80   "'Carpet Bagger' Has One Good Character," *New York World*, March 6, 1900, 14; also "The Carpet-bagger," *New York Mail and Express*, March 6, 1900, 7; "Music and Drama," *New York Evening Post*, March 6, 1900, 7.

81   "At the Theatres. Fourteenth Street—The Carpetbagger," *NYDM*, March 10, 1900, 16.

82   "Notes," *New York Evening Post*, April 10, 1900, 7; "At the Theatres. Bijou—The Carpetbagger," *NYDM*, April 14, 1900, 17; "Tim Murphy," *Collier's Weekly*, January 1911, n.p.

83   "Rehearsing 'Quo Vadis,'" *New York World*, April 3, 1900, 4; "Bijou's Odd Double Bill," *New York Press*, April 10, 1900, 7.

84   "At the Theatres. Bijou—The Carpetbagger," *NYDM*, April 14, 1900, 17.

85   "Over the Footlights," *New York Evening Telegram*, April 10, 1900, 4.

86   Nagai, "Chainataun no ki" [Notes on Chinatown], in his *Amerika*, 78–81.

87   "At Boston Playhouses. Keith's Theatre," *Boston Journal*, December 19, 1899, 5; "Massachusetts, Boston," *NYC*, December 30, 1899, 915; "The Stage," *Washington Times*, January 21, 1900, 2:4; "Where Variety Pleases," *New York Evening Telegram*, March 24, 1900, 9; "Notes of the Week. New York Theatre," *New York Times*, April 1, 1900, 18.

88   "Music and Drama. Keith's Theatre: Vaudeville," *Boston Evening Transcript*, December 19, 1899, 7; also "Mme. Ching Ling Foo," *Washington Post*, January 21, 1900, 17; "A Wonderful Conjuror. Ching Ling Foo," *NYDM*, June 3, 1899, 16; "At Boston Playhouses. Keith's Theatre," *Boston Journal.*

89   "Vaudeville," *Dramatic Magazine* 7:1 (May 1899): 25.

90   "Music and Drama. Keith's Theatre: Vaudeville," *Boston Evening Transcript.*

91   Gilbert, *American*, 173.

92   Throughout the history of the American theatre and long before the Syndicate, many small companies and individual actors toured relying on primitive transportation.

93   William H. Crane, "The Modern Cart of Thespis," *North American Review* 154 (April 1892): 475; "Theatrical Season of 1893," unidentified newspaper c. 1894, clipping in Alfred Edgar Mullet Scrapbook **T.11.9, RBD BPL.

94   "Back to Vaudeville Again," *New York World*, April 17, 1900, 4; "Koster and Bial's Changes," *New York World*, April 24, 1899, 4; "Opening of Theatre Comique," *New York World*, November 21, 1899, 5.

95   "Crane Brothers Bankrupt," *New York Times*, April 3, 1900, 9; "Edward E. Rice a Bankrupt," *New York Times*, May 1, 1900, 8. Rice's last show was *Little Red Riding Hood*, which played Boston while Kawakami was there.

96   "Notes on New Theatres," *NYDM*, May 27, 1899–August 4, 1900.

97   "Theatres Burned," *NYDM*, May 27, 1899–August 4, 1900.

98   Larry T. Menefee, "A New Hypothesis for Dating the Decline of the 'Road,'" *Educational Theatre Journal* 30 (October 1978): 343–44; Brockett, *History*, 417; Bernheim, *Business*, 34–35.

99   Only a few theatres on any circuit were under common ownership.

100 Bernheim, *Business*, 36–47; John Frick, "A Changing Theatre: New York and Beyond," in Wilmeth, *History*, 21.

101 For reasons of business secrecy, exaggerated publicity, and continual shifts in affiliation, the number of theatres signed with the Trust at any one time was difficult to determine, see Cahn, *Theatrical Guide* for year-to-year listings.

102 Norman Hapgood, "The Theatrical 'Syndicate,'" *International Monthly* (January 1900), 93–94 reprinted in *NYDM*, January 13, 1900, 3; Bernheim, *Business*, 52; "The Split in the Theatre 'Trust,'" *New York Herald*, April 6, 1900, 10; Poggi, *Theatre*, 12–13; "Theatrical Syndicate Plans," *New York Times*, April 6, 1900, 7; Winter, *Life*, 2:157–79.

103 Poggi, *Theatre*, 10–12; Bernheim, *Business*, 37–40, 49–50, 56; Winter, *Life*, 2:155–56; Brockett, *History*, 425; "The West Wiped Out," *NYDM*, May 12, 1900, 14; Cahn, *Theatrical 1899–1900*, 733–34.

104 Churchill, *Great*, 45–48; W. J. Henderson, "The Business of a Theatre," *Scribner's* 25 (March 1899): 310–11.

105 Bernheim, *Business*, 51–53; Henderson, *City*, 189; Churchill, *Great*, 45–48; W. J. Henderson, "The Business of a Theatre"; Jerry Stagg, *The Brothers Shubert* (New York: Random House, 1968), 17. In later years, the Theatre Syndicate weakened, not so much from competition from local stock companies and expanding vaudeville but from the rise (and subsequent dominance) of yet another theatrical trust, the Shubert Brothers (Poggi, *Theatre*, 11–26; John Frick, "A Changing Theatre: New York and Beyond," in Wilmeth, *History*, 216).

106 Norman Hapgood, "The Theatrical 'Syndicate;'" also Brockett, *History*, 426; Henry Tyrell, "The Recent Dramatic Season: A Study in Theatrical Evolution," *Forum* 35 (July–September 1903): 93. For typical examples of independent theatres' scrounging for bookings, see classified advertisements, *NYDM*, March 17, 1900, 24.

107 John Frick, "A Changing Theatre: New York and Beyond," in Wilmeth and Bigsby, *History*, 213; Cahn, *Theatrical 1900–01*, 733–34. The Kawakami company was considered to be noncompetitive, too insignificant, and too different to be excluded from Syndicate theatres.

108 Bernheim, *Business*, 52; Bordman, *American Musical Theatre*, 155–56; Sturgis, *Influence*, 109.

109 Norman Hapgood, "The Theatrical Syndicate," *International Monthly* (June 1900): 93–94.

110 Ibid.

111 Ibid; Bernheim, *Business*, 93.

112 Kaneo, *Sadayakko*, 49; Cahn, *Theatrical 1900–01*, 733–34. In addition to his American holdings, Charles Frohman controlled five theatres in London (Brockett, *History*, 426; Hewitt, *Theatre*, 257).

113 Bernheim, *Business*, 48; "A Tricky Defense of Stage Indecency," *NYDM*, March 17, 1900, 14; Wilmeth, *Guide*, 478.

114 Bernheim, *Business*, 59; "The Theatrical 'Syndicate,'" *NYDM*, January 13, 1900, 3.

115 Winter, *Life*, 2:168; also Shattuck, *Shakespeare*, 2:25, 2:29.

116 Poggi, *Theatre in America*, 6–10.

117 Strang, *Players*, 2:211–12; "Current Amusements," *NYDM*, January 20–May 5, 1900, 16; "Affairs of the

Theatre," *New York Sun*, March 30, 1900, 7; Leander Richardson, "The Month in Theatricals," *Metropolitan* 11 (March 1900): 322; Shattuck, *Shakespeare*, 2:259.

118   "New Dramatic Material," *New York Sun*, February 6, 1900, 7. Daly had been an important figure in American theatre as a manager, director, dramatist, and critic. Daniel Frohman preferred high society comedies from London (Frohman, *Memories*, 154).

119   From a series of "Bunk Ballads" by Thomas J. Gray quoted in Bernheim, *Business*, 48.

Chapter 30

1   The Kawakami couple passed the Fifth Avenue Theatre on their daily walk up Broadway from their hotel to the Bijou.

2   "Current Amusements," *NYDM*, April 21 and 28, 1900, 16; "Things in Mimic Shows," *New York Sun*, April 24, 1900, 7; "Music and Drama," *New York Evening Post*, April 17, 1900, 7.

3   Lawrence Reamer, "The Drama," *Harper's Weekly* 44 (May 12, 1900): 442.

4   "Dramatic and Musical," *New York Times*, April 24, 1900, 8; Bloom, *Joseph*, 55.

5   "Topics of the Theatre," *New York Sun*, April 26, 1900, 7.

6   "The Theatres," *New York Commercial Advertiser*, April 17, 1900, 7.

7   "Sewell Collins Pays His Respects to Joseph Jefferson," *New York Evening Journal*, April 17, 1900, 10; "Alan Dale Says: The Dean of the American [missing] Audience by His Portrayal of Dipsomania," *New York Journal*, April 18, 1900, 8; "Music and Drama," *New York Evening Post*; "At the Theatres," *New York Mail and Express*, April 17, 1900, 9.

8   James B. Runnion, "Joseph Jefferson," *Lippincott's* (August 1869): 174; "Topics of the Theatre," *New York Sun*; Mullin, *Victorian*, 274. Jefferson's recorded voice on Creegan, *Traditions*, cuts 2:1–3 from *Rip Van Winkle*, 1898, 1903, revealed that unlike many of his contemporaries—including the younger ones—there were few traces of declamatory acting other than his slight theatrical trilling of "r." His acting voice was that of the new century.

9   W[illiam] W[inter], "The Drama—Music," *New York Tribune*, April 17, 1900, 6.

10   Quinn, *History*, 330; Odell, *Annals*, 7:222; Banham, *Cambridge*, s. v. "Jeffersons, The"; W[illiam] W[inter], "The Drama—Music," *New York Tribune*; Wittke, *Tambo*, n.p.; Marian Hannah Winter, *Theatre*, 66. In later years when Jefferson was ill, his son Thomas stepped in to play Rip (Leslie, *Some*, 288).

11   Ben Graf Henneke, *Laura Keene: Actress, Innovator, and Impresario; a Biography* (Tulsa: Council Oak Books, 1990), 68, 71–72, 91–92. *Our American Cousin* also made a star of Keene's eccentric comedian, E. A. Sothern, the father of E. H. Sothern.

12   "Things Theatrical," *Spirit of the Times*, June 23, 1860, 240, and June 14, 1860, 280.

13   Jefferson, *Autobiography*, 172–73.

14   Ibid., 171–73, 225–26; Quinn, *History*, 330.

15   Winter, *Other*, 71–72; Quinn, *History*, 325–30; also "At the Theatres. People's—Rip Van Winkle," *NYDM*, April 8, 1899, 17. Jefferson had unsuccessfully tried an earlier *Rip* script.

16   Jefferson, *Autobiography*, 286.

17   "Alan Dale Says: The Dean of the American Drama …," *New York Journal*.

18   Winter, *Other*, 72–73.

19   "Dramatic and Musical," *New York Times*, April 24, 1900, 8

20   Jefferson, *Autobiography*, 335–36.

21   Audience enthusiasm to catch repeated performances of the same role by the same actor has largely disappeared from the American theatre but remains fundamental to the appeal of popular music today.

22   Sigmund Freud, *Beyond the Pleasure Principle*, trans. James Strachey (New York: Liveright, 1924), 29, 30.

23   Lawrence Reamer, "The Drama," *Harper's Weekly* 44 (May 12, 1900), 441.

24   Ben Graf Henneke, *Laura Keene*, 106.

25   Attributed to Jefferson in untitled newspaper clipping: Jefferson, Joseph file, HTC.

26   William Winter, "Joseph Jefferson—A Great Actor Gone," *Theatre* (New York) No. 52 (June 1905): 139.

27   "Garrick," advertisement, *New York Herald*, March 11, 1900, 4:5.

28   Edward A. Dithmar, "Two Successful Plays," *Harper's Weekly* 43 (November 25, 1899): 1183; "At the Theatres. Garrick—Sherlock Holmes," *NYDM*, November 18, 1899, 16; "About Current Plays," *Boston Dramatic Review* (November 25, 1899): 2; "'Sherlock Holmes:' The Conan Doyle-Gillette Detective-Drama Arrives in London," *Sketch* 35 (July 24, 1901): 316.

29   "About Current Plays," *Boston Dramatic Review.*

30   "At the Theatres. Garrick—Sherlock Holmes," *NYDM.*

31   Edward A. Dithmar, "Two Successful Plays," *Harper's Weekly*; "'Sherlock Holmes:' The Conan Doyle-Gillette Detective-Drama Arrives in London," *Sketch*, n.d. Subsequent iconization of the Holmes character was largely based on Gillette's characterization and appearance in this production

32   Dithmar, "Two Successful Plays;" also McArthur, *Actors*, 174–75; "At the Theatres. Garrick—Sherlock Holmes," *NYDM*; "The Stage," *Toledo Bee*, November 19, 1899, 10. The *Bee* correspondent was reporting on the New York performance.

33   "About Current Plays," *Boston Dramatic Review.* Gillette's business for Holmes included smoking a cigar, a pipe, and cigarettes ("At the Theatres. Garrick—Sherlock Holmes," *NYDM*).

34   Ibid.; Edward A. Dithmar, "Two Successful Plays," *Harper's Weekly.*

35   Clapp, *Players*, 119; *Who Was Who*, 938; Leader Richardson, "The Month in Theatricals," *Metropolitan*, February 1900, 212; Wilmeth, *Guide*, 202.

36   Edward A. Dithmar, "Secret Service," *Harper's Weekly* 40 (October 31, 1896): 1074.

37   Lewis C. Strang, *Famous Actors of the Day in America* (Boston: Page, 1900), 178.

38   Montrose J. Moses, "William Gillette Says Farewell," *Theatre Guild* 7 (January 1930): 33–34.

39   Leslie, *Some*, 301–4.

40   William Gillette, "The Illusion of the First Time in Acting," in *Papers on Acting*, ed. Brander Matthews (New York: Hill and Wang, 1958), 124–35. Although Gillette is most closely associated with this concept, Joseph Jefferson had earlier and independently proposed his own ideas about the illusion of the first time.

41   This was a weak and subsequently unsuccessful drama written by Irving's son, Lawrence.

42   Belford, *Bram*, 251.

43   "Live Topics about Town," *New York Sun*, May 29, 1900, 7.

44   Ibid. Japan also had its own counterfeit stars and productions outside the big cities.

45   Wilmeth, *Guide*, 202; *Who Was Who*, 938; "Themes from Stageland," *New York Sun*, June 17, 1900, 3:9. Gillette died in 1937.

46   On this first time out, *Sherlock Holmes* played 256 performances in New York. The longest running show of the 1899–1900 season was Weber and Fields's *Whirl-i-gig* that did 264 (Bordman, *American Theatre*, 451; T. Allston Brown, *History*, 3:572; Bordman, *American Musical Theatre*, 168).

47   "At the Theatres. Garrick—Sherlock Holmes," *NYDM.* Lights slowly or quickly faded to black or came up according to the appropriate pace for the scene (Edward A. Dithmar, "Two Successful Plays," *Harper's Weekly* 43 (November 25, 1899): 1183).

48   Fredric Edward McKay, "Theatrical Gossip," *New York Mail and Express*, March 29, 1900, 9.

49   Ibid. *Little Nell* played Boston while Kawakami was at the Boston Theatre, but there was no record that Frohman was in the city at that time. *Little Nell and the Marchioness* was also identified by the title of its source novel, *The Old Curiosity Shop.*

50   "Kawakami and Yacco," *New York Commercial Advertiser*, March 3, 1900, 6.

51 "A Glimpse of the Japanese Drama," *Boston Evening Transcript*, December 6, 1899, 18. Kawakami had used a blackout technique to begin and end scenes in his 1894 *Igai* (Kawatake Shigetoshi, *Nihon engeki zenshi*, 1,006). Japanese theatres with electricity apparently lacked precise control of light levels that dimmers made possible.

52 "Music and Drama. The Japanese Stage," *Boston Evening Transcript*, December 16, 28; also "Amusements," *Lowell Daily Courier*, December 13, 1899, 4; "Music and Drama. The Japanese Stage," *Boston Evening Transcript*, December 16, 1899, 28. In a review of Kawakami's Washington performances, a critic noted that Kawakami's setting coming out of darkness to begin a scene and then ending by going to darkness reminded him of techniques used earlier for melodramas at a Washington theatre ("The Stage," *Washington Times*, February 4, 1900, 24).

53 "A Glimpse of the Japanese Drama," *Boston Evening Transcript*, December 6, 1899, 18. Other descriptions in "The Man with the Lorgnette," *Boston Evening Record*, December 7, 1899, 5; "Japanese Drama," *Boston Traveler*, 6 Dec. 1899, 5. Kawakami did not consistently employ this lighting technique.

54 "Darkness and the Curtain," *Grand Rapids Evening Press*, November 18, 1899, 2; "At the Theatres," also *Toledo Daily Blade*, November 25, 1899, 10.

55 Bram Stoker, "Irving and Stage Lighting," *Nineteenth Century and After* No. 411 (May 1911): 907; Mazer, *Shakespeare*, 37.

56 *Kurombō* were also called *kurogo*.

57 Of the American reviews and descriptions of the troupe's performances examined in this study, none mentioned anything resembling a *kurombō*, although Sadayakko may have had an onstage assistant—it was not clear—to assist her quick changes with the *Dōjōji* dances.

58 The *furiotoshi* was rarely used.

59 Nicoll, 201; Bailey, "Introduction," in *British Plays of the Nineteenth Century*, ed. J. O. Bailey (New York: Odyssey, 1966), 7.

60 A *hikimaku* was usually drawn from audience right to left. Theatres changed *hikimaku* frequently because these decorated curtains were received as gifts from stars' fan groups and required display when that actor was appearing.

61 Minor theatres were called *koshibai* or *shōgekijō* (both meaning small or lesser theatre) but were also known as *donchō shibai* (drop curtain theatre).

62 Miyake Saburō, *Koshibai*, 5–7; Faith Bach, "Breaking the *Kabuki* Actors' Barriers: 1868–1900," *Asian Theatre Journal* 12:2 (Fall 1995): 267, 274–76; Komiya, *Japanese*, 183–84, 314–15. In Osaka and Kyoto, there were fewer restrictions on actors' employment (James R. Brandon, "Kabuki and Shakespeare: Balancing Yin and Yang," *Drama Review* [TDR 162] 43:2 [Summer 1999]: 19).

63 "Darkness and the Curtain," *Grand Rapids Evening Press*, November 18, 1899, 2.

64 Schaffner, *Fabulous*. 27. St. John Ervine in *Theatre in My Time*, 33, reminisced and gave fuller meaning to that thud: "Even now, three decades after I last saw one [a roller drop curtain], I can hear the thud with which it rolled down on a tense scene, closing it with a bang that was as effective as an orator's thump on a table.… [It] hit the stage with dramatic deliberation. There! [I]t announced, making its tactful thump, *that's* a conclusion."

65 Gilbert, *American*, 169. An additional American indication of front curtain signification could be seen at "Sunday concerts" in the drama theatres that were skirting blue laws against Sunday theatrical performances. On Sundays, they kept their front curtains out of sight to prove they were not offering plays but only non-prohibited "performances" ("The Sunday Concert Law," *NYDM*, January 6, 1900, 18).

66 Kawajiri, *Shibai*, 45–50, 56, 60–61, 91–97; Gunji, *Kabuki*, 56; Nakamura, *Kabuki*, 174.

67 "Players from Far Japan," *Boston Journal*, January 7, 1900, 4:4.

68 "The Stage," *Washington Times*, February 4, 1900, 2:4.

69   "A Glimpse of the Japanese Drama," *Boston Evening Transcript*, December 6, 1899, 18.

70   Kawatake Shigetoshi, *Gaisetsu*, 376; "Kawakami dentō no kōka o tsukau" [Kawakami uses electric lighting effects], *Yorozu chōbō*, January 24, 1894, in Shirakawa, 145; Ōba, *Butai*, 4; Tsubouchi Hakubutsukan, *Kokugeki*, 414.

71   Quoted in John Balance, "The Use of Gas in Theatres," *Mask* 10:4 (October 1924): 164; also Fitzgerald, *Art*, 32, 188.

72   Matthews, *Development*, 339–40.

73   Bram Stoker, "Irving and Stage Lighting," *Nineteenth Century and After* No. 411 (May 1911): 907.

74   Craig, *Henry*, 113; also Bram Stoker, "Irving and Stage Lighting," 911.

75   Brockett, *Century*, 48.

76   Alan Hughes, "Limelight: Control and the Independent Lighting Designer," *Theatre Survey* 26 (November 1985): 189; Schivelbusch, *Disenchanted*, 202.

77   Johnston Forbes-Robertson, *A Player under Three Reigns* (Boston: Little, Brown, 1925), 247.

78   Brian Legge, "Stage Lighting in the Nineteenth Century," *Tabs* 25:3, p. 18; Rees, *Theatre*, 129–42; Tim Fort, "The Introduction of Electrical Incandescence in American Theatres," *Theatre Design and Technology* 29 (Spring 1993): 22.

79   Driver, *Romantic*, 62; Brockett, *Century*, 40–41; Booth, *Theatre*, 84–87; Eric Irvin, ""Notes and Queries. Auditorium Darkening," *Theatre Notebook* 34:1 (1980): 38–39; Victor Emeljanow, "Erasing the Spectator: Observations on Nineteenth Century Lighting," *Theatre History Studies* 18 (1998): 110–11; Rees, *Theatre*, 227 fn. 9.

80   Shaw, "Olivia," in his *Our*, 3:36.

81   Kawatake Shigetoshi, *Nihon engeki zenshi*, 779.

82   Kaneo, *Ōbei*, 29.

83   Ogawa, *Nihon*, 85; Ōba, *Butai*, 1.

Chapter 31

1   "Good English on the Stage," *Theatre* (New York) No. 9 (November 1901): 17.

2   Shattuck, *Shakespeare*, 2:166.

3   Japanese theatre accented the visual even though treatises and training for actors stressed the importance of voice over most of the visual aspects (see Zvika Serper, "Exploration through a Concept: Japanese Classical Acting as a model of Harmonic Contrasts," *Contemporary Theatre* 1 (1994): 2, 68–72).

4   "Hearts Are Trumps," advertisements, *New York Sun*, March 18, 1900, 4:5 and *New York Herald*, March 11, 1900, 4:4. Of the 300 persons advertised, 100 were stagehands, 100 were supers, and only fifty were actors who had speaking roles or significant business ("Having a Look at the Seamy Side of a Popular Melodrama," *New York Herald*, March 11, 1900, 6:4).

5   Columbia Theatre, Boston, program, week of December 4, 1899, in Chapman Scrapbooks **T.12.14 v. 1, BPL RBD; also "Daly's—The Great Ruby," *NYDM*, February 18, 1899, 16; "What a very queer sort of play," fragment of unidentified New York newspaper, c. February 10, 1899, in program file: The Great Ruby, BRTC.

6   "Notes of the Week," *New York Times*, March 11, 1900, 16.

7   "Daly's—The Great Ruby," *NYDM*.

8   Michael R. Booth, "Spectacle as Production Style on the Victorian Stage," *Theatre Quarterly* 8 (1979): 16.

9   "Modern Mise-en-Scene," *Saturday Review* (London) 69 (March 29, 1890): 376–77; Jefferson, *Autobiography*, 94–95: Fitzgerald, *Art*, 169; Mazer, *Shakespeare*, 34–36. "Carpenter" = stagehand.

10   "Incidents of the Stage," *New York Sun*, March 23, 1900, 7.

11   "Shimpa hanseiki o kataru, jūgo: fūgawari na hitotachi; Fujii, Kojima, Nozaki-ra" [Talking about a half

century of shimpa, 15: eccentric people: Fujii, Kojima, Nozaki, and others], *Miyako shimbun*, n.d. 1937, in "Shimpa gojūnen kaiko kiji;" Matsumoto, *Meiji engekiron shi*, 428.

12   Kaneo, *Ōbei*, 30.

13   "Music and Drama. The Japanese Stage," *Boston Evening Transcript*, December 16, 1899, 28.

14   Various techniques to speed the shifting of scenery appeared in America and Europe during the late nineteenth-century. The most common was tall gridiron fly space above the stage where scenery could be hung and quickly lowered or raised as required. For Japan, see Samuel L. Leiter, "'What Really Happens Backstage:' A Nineteenth-Century *Kabuki* Document," *Theatre Survey* 38:2 (November 1997): 108–28.

15   Field, *Through*, 17–18. For lists of equipment and descriptions of individual stages in the theatres Kawakami played, see Cahn, *Theatrical 1899–1900*.

16   Kaneo, *Ōbei*, 29–30.

17   American actors had to keep out of defined audience space.

18   I found only vague evidence about Kawakami's attendance at specific American productions.

19   "The Theatres," *New York Commercial Advertiser*, March 31, 1900, 7. Sothern's *The Sunken Bell* played Boston while Kawakami was there and had come briefly to New York in April.

20   "Contest of Dramatization," *Boston Herald*, April 15, 1900, n.p.; Mantle, *Best*, 366.

21   "The Usher," *NYDM*, April 21, 1900, 15; "Quo Vadis at Two Theatres," *NYDM*, April 7, 1900, 13; "Two Versions of Sienkiewicz's Religious Novel. Stange's 'Quo Vadis' a Success; Gilder Version Lacks Preparation," *New York World*, April 10, 1900, 14; "At the Theatres. New York—Quo Vadis," *NYDM*, April 14, 1900, 16. Stanislaus Stange adapted the New York Theatre six-act version of *Quo Vadis*; Jeannette L. Gilder adapted the Herald Square version in five acts (Mantle, *Best*, 366);

22   "Rehearsing 'Quo Vadis,'" *New York World*, April 3, 1900, 4; "Topics of the Theatre," *New York Sun*, April 4, 1900, 7. The usual rehearsal period for a show of that scale was at least two weeks.

23   "At the Theatres. Herald Square—Quo Vadis," *NYDM*, April 14, 1900, 16.

24   "Topics of the Theatre," *New York Sun*; "The Theatres," *New York Commercial Advertiser*, April 10, 1900, 7; "At the Theatres. New York—Quo Vadis," *NYDM*; "Alan Dale Says 'Quo Vadis' at the Herald [Is a] Bowery Melodrama in a Roman Toga," *New York Journal*, April 10, 1900, 8; "Events of the Stage," *Washington Post*, January 16, 1900, 3. *The Sign of the Cross* company was a British production that toured America several times and had a plot closely resembling that of the *Quo Vadis* novel.

25   Lawrence Reamer, "The Drama," *Harper's Weekly* 44 (April 28, 1900): 394.

26   Many considered the New York Theatre with its usual run of shows, its male audience, and convivial male-female activity in the foyer as an extension of the Tenderloin.

27   "Themes from Stageland," *New York Sun*, June 24, 1900, 3:9; Lawrence Reamer, "The Drama," *Harper's Weekly*; "At the Theatres. New York—Quo Vadis," *NYDM*; Edward J. Dithmar, "At the Play and with the Players," *New York Times*, April 15, 1900, 16; Alan Dale, "The New York 'Quo Vadis' Is Good for Those Who Want a Penitential Evening," *New York Journal*, April 13, 1900, 8; "Theatrical Amusements," *New York Sun*, April 22, 1900, 3:9. The Herald Square production ran for thirty-two performances (Mantle, *Best*, 366).

28   "At the Theatres. Herald Square—Quo Vadis," *NYDM*; "Miss Gilder's 'Quo Vadis,'" *New York Herald*, April 10, 1900, 10; "Alan Dale Says 'Quo Vadis' at the Herald [Is a] Bowery Melodrama in a Roman Toga," *New York Journal*; "The Theatres," *New York Commercial Advertiser*, April 10, 1900, 7

29   "Two Versions of Sienkiewicz's Religious Novel," *New York World*. April 10, 1900, 14; "At the Theatres. Herald Square—Quo Vadis," *NYDM*.

30   "Things in the New Plays," *New York Sun*, April 15, 1900, 3:7.

31   "Alan Dale Says 'Quo Vadis' at the Herald [Is a] Bowery Melodrama in a Roman Toga," *New York Journal*; also Lawrence Reamer, "The Drama," *Harper's Weekly*, 394.

32   "The Theatres," *New York Commercial Advertiser*, April 10, 1900, 7; "Miss Gilder's 'Quo Vadis,'" *New York Herald*; Edward J. Dithmar, "At the Play and with the Players," *New York Times*, April 15, 1900, 16; "The Usher," *NYDM*, April 21,1900, 15.

33   "Contest of Dramatization," *Boston Herald*, April 15, 1900, n.p.

34   "Topics of the Theatre," *New York Sun*, April 4, 1900, 7; "Various Dramatic Topics," *New York Times*, April 22, 1900, 18; "Quo Vadis," advertisement, *NYDM*, January 20, 1900, 21.

35   "The Theatre," *New York Commercial Advertiser*, April 21, 1900, 7; Frederic Edward McKay, "Theatrical Gossip," *New York Mail and Express*, February 28, 1900, 7.

36   Frederic Edward McKay, "Plays and Players," *New York Mail and Express Illustrated Saturday Magazine*, April 14, 1900, 10.

37   Marian Spitzer, "Ten-20-30; the Passing of the Popular-Priced Circuit," *Saturday Evening Post* (August 22, 1925): 40.

38   *Rōnin* = masterless samurai.

39   Yanagi, *Shimpa no rokujunen*, 154; John Masefield, *The Faithful* (New York: Macmillan, 1915). Most major kabuki productions in the largest Japanese cities had full casts with forty-seven *rōnin*. *The Faithful* was produced in 1919 in New York (*Theatre* [New York] No. 225 [1919]: 348, 350).

40   Gustav Kobbé, "Some Recent Plays and Players," *Forum* 29 (May 1900): 379–81. Aware of the trend toward dramatic adaptations with the potential for additional royalties, many American popular novelists were writing their works to make them more readily adaptable to the stage. Two easy tricks were more dialog passages and fewer locations (Lawrence Reamer, "The Drama," *Harper's Weekly* 44 [April 28, 1900]: 394).

41   For example: *Takino Shiraito* and *Konjiki yasha* (Demon of gold). Play titles were not always the titles of the original novels. The trends toward dramatization of novels in both countries were not directly related.

42   American copyright laws did little to discourage adapters from disguising copyrighted sources.

43   Frederic Edward McKay, "Plays and Players," *New York Mail and Express Illustrated Saturday Magazine*, April 14, 1900, 10; "Topics of the Theatre," *New York Sun*, April 4, 1900, 7.

44   "Current Amusements," *NYDM*, May 12, 1900, 16. *Ben Hur* ran twenty-three weeks.

45   T. Allston Brown, *History*, 3:418; Jason, "The Dramatic Season in New York," *Leslie's Weekly* 89 (December 23, 1899): 510; "At the Theatres. Broadway—Ben-Hur," *NYDM*, December 9, 1899, 16; Barnard Hewitt, *Theatre U.S A.: 1665–1957* (New York: McGraw-Hill, 1959), 276–77.

46   Jason, "The Dramatic Season in New York," *Leslie's Weekly*, 510; also Leander Richardson, "The Month in Theatricals," *Metropolitan* 11 (March 1900): 321; "At the Theatres. Broadway—Ben-Hur," *NYDM*.

47   Alan Dale, "Does the So-Called 'Religious' Play Save Souls?" *New York Journal*, April 15, 1900, n.p.

48   "At the Theatres. Broadway—Ben-Hur," *NYDM*.

49   "Italian Passion Play Stopped," *New York Sun*, April 17 1900, 7; "Reflections," *NYDM*, April 28, 1900, 2.

50   "Improvement in Chariot Race," *New York Times*, March 9, 1900, 7; Bordman, *American Theatre*, 452.

51   Leander Richardson, "The Month in Theatricals," *Metropolitan* 11 (February 1900): 211.

52   "Things in the New Plays," *New York Sun*, April 15, 1900, 3:7.

53   Garden Theatre, New York, program, February 26, 1900, in Scrapbook MWEZ+ n. c. 699; p. 132, BRTC; Leander Richardson, "The Month in Theatricals," *Metropolitan* 11 (April 1900): 428. Charles Frohman was the producer.

54   "Women Gamblers and 'Spicy' Scenes in 'Hearts Are Trumps,'" *New York World*, February 22, 1900, 14; also "Garden—Hearts Are Trumps," *NYDM*, March 3, 1900, 16; "Having a Look at the Seamy Side of a Popular Melodrama," *New York Herald*, March 11, 1900, 6:4; "Sights at the Theatre," *New York Sun*, February 22, 1907, 7.

55   "This Week's Novelties," *New York Journal*, February 18, 1900, 38; Lawrence Reamer, "The Drama,"

Harper's Weekly 44 (April 28, 1900): 322; William Raymond Hill, "'Hearts Are Trumps' Contains Two Stars and Four Mysteries," *New York World*; "Things in the New Plays," *New York Sun*, February 25, 1900, B7; "Dramatic and Musical," *New York Times*, February 22, 1900, 7; Edward A. Dithmar, "At the Play and with the Players," *New York Times*, February 26, 1900, 16.

56 "The Theatres," *New York Commercial Advertiser*, February 22, 1900, 5; also "Things in the New Plays," *New York Sun*.

57 "A New Pictorial Play," *New York Times*, February 18, 1900, 16; "Things in the New Plays," *New York Sun*; "Women Gamblers and 'Spicy' Scenes in 'Hearts Are Trumps,'" *New York World*; William Raymond Hill "'Hearts Are Trumps' Contains Two Stars and Four Mysteries," *New York World*.

58 This was not the first time that a play had scenes set in a theatre. One instance was Henry Irving's similar staging in his 1880 *The Corsican Brothers* (Clement Scott, *From "The Bells" to "King Arthur"–A Critical Record of First-Night Productions at the Lyceum Theatre from 1871 to 1895* [London: Macqueen, 1896], 187).

59 "Sights at the Theatre," *New York Sun*; "Doubling of a Stage Mob," *Washington Chronicle*, January 22, 1900, 1.

60 Typical of a long running show, *The Great Ruby* had been extensively recast (Tompkins, *History*, 474. Also "At the Theatres. Fourteenth Street—The Great Ruby," *NYDM*, March 24, 1900, 17; Fourteenth Street Theatre, New York, program, March 1900, in program file: The Great Ruby, BRTC.

61 Alan Dale, "'The Great Ruby' at Daly's," *New York Journal*, February 10, 1899, n.p.

62 "Things in the New Plays," *New York Sun*, April 15, 1900, 3:7.

63 "'Women and Wine' Is 'Warm,'" *New York Evening Telegram*, April 12, 1900, 4; Alan Dale, "'Women and Wine' Is Sizzling, Bubbling Melodrama," *New York Journal*, April 12, 1900, 8; "New Theatrical Things," *New York Sun*, April 12, 1900, 7; "Dramatic and Musical. A Sensational Melodrama at the Manhattan Theatre," *New York Times*, April 12, 1900, 8.

64 "City Guide. Weather," *New York Commercial Advertiser*, April 10, 1900, 7; "Evening Telegram's Weather Service," *New York Evening Telegram*, April 6, 1900, 4; Van Dyke, *New*, 48–52; "In Easter Parade from Dewey Arch to Park Plaza," *New York Journal*, April 16, 1900, 2.

65 Nagai, "Chōhatsu" [Long hair], in his *Amerika*, 22.

66 "Old Plays Prosperous," *New York World*, April 10, 1900, 14; "Current Amusements," *NYDM*, April 14, 1900, 16.

67 "In Easter Parade from Dewey Arch to Park Plaza," *New York Journal*.

68 "Adam Forepaugh and Sells Bros.," advertisement, *New York Times*, March 25, 1900, 9.

69 "Circus an Ocular Table d'Hote," *New York Herald*, April 5, 1900, 11.

70 "Things in Mimic Shows," *New York Sun*, April 24, 1900, 7; "Madison Square Garden," advertisement, *New York Herald*, April 15, 1900, 4:5.

71 "Buffalo Bill's Wild West," advertisement, *New York Press*, April 22, 1900, 10.

72 "In the Stage Coach," *New York Mail and Express*, April 28, 1900, 20; "Wild West on View," *New York Mail and Express*, April 24, 1900, 6.

73 "Buffalo Bill's Wild West," advertisement, *New York Press*.

74 "Wild West on View," *New York Mail and Express*.

75 "Madison Square Garden," advertisement, *New York Herald*, April 15, 1900, 4:5.

76 Ibid.; "Wild West on View," *New York Mail and Express*.

77 "Things in Mimic Shows," *New York Sun*, April 24, 1900, 7.

78 Ibid.; "Big Crowd Greets Wild West Show," *New York Press*, 24 April 24, 1900, 7.

79 Kaneo *Ōbei*, 44.

80 "Amusements. A Japanese Matinee," *Chicago Daily Inter Ocean*, October 23, 1899, 5; Muskegon Opera

House, program, November 15, 1899; Copley Hall, Boston, program, January 6, 1900, "The Japanese Players;" Boston Theatre, Boston, program, January 18–19, 1900, "The Japanese Dramatic Company," "Japanese Actors Score a Success," *New York Herald*, March 2, 1900, 10.

81   "Plays in Japanese, *New York Tribune*, March 2, 1900, 9.

82   Epes W. Sargent, "Dramatic Progress of the Japanese," *Metropolitan* 11 (May 1900): 499. In a photograph taken by Byron at the Berkeley Lyceum around March 2, Watanabe appeared as Orihime (Scrapbook "Plays to June 1905," MWEZ+ n.c. 297, pp. 99–101, BRTC).

83   Boston Theatre, Boston, program, January 25–26, 1900, "The Japanese Dramatic Company;" Bijou Theatre, New York, program, week of March 12, 1900; "Japan Visits Broadway," *New York Herald*, March 13, 1900, 13.

84   Boston Theatre, Boston, program, January 18–19, 1900; "The Japanese Dramatic Company," in program file: Zingoro, BRTC; "Things Theatrical. Lafayette," *Washington Times*, January 31, 1900, 4; Bijou Theatre, New York, program, week of April 2, 1900, *Zingoro, an Ernest Statue Maker* [and] *Soga: Two Brothers*. Cast lists printed in Kawakami's programs were curiously unreliable. Among the many inconsistencies was the continuing appearance of the names of Maruyama and Mikami in programs and publicity several weeks after both were dead. The defector Watanabe's name appeared in a program for a Kawakami performance in London (Coronet Theatre, London, program, May, 22–25, May 29–June-1, 1990, in program file: The Loyalist, BRTC).

85   "Ikyō no ani to natta mono mo futari arimasu" (Kaneo, *Sadayakko*, 17).

86   "Vaudeville," *NYDM*, April 7, 1900, 18.

87   Frederic Edward McKay, "Theatrical Gossip," *New York Mail and Express*, April 16, 1900, 9.

88   "Over the Footlights," *New York Evening Telegram*; "'The Mikado' Revived," *New York Herald*, April 17, 1900, 10; "An Amusing Ko-Ko," *New York World*, 17 April 17, 1900, 4; "'Mikado' Gayly Sung at American," *New York Journal*, April 16, 1900, 5; "Topics from Stageland," *New York Sun*, April 19, 1900, 7; "'The Mikado' at the American," *New York Times*, April 17, 1900, 9.

Chapter 32

1   "Time to Call Halt to Dramatic Ptomaines," *New York World*, January 21, 1900, 2E; "The Usher," *NYDM*, November 4, 1899, 4; "Dramas and Audiences. Do Our People Need Protection against the Theatres?" *New York Sun*, February 18, 1900, 3:7; "Immorality Has Been the Cause of This Season's Dramatic Failures," *New York World*, April 15, 1900, 2E.

2   "Gossip of the Theatre. Wicked Women of Stageland," *Washington Post*, January 28, 1900, 24.

3   "Fight in League over Jersey Lily," *New York Herald*, February 16, 1900, 12; "Crowd at Langtry Tea; and Police Stay Away," *New York Press*, February 14, 1900, 1; "Stage Immorality to Be Attacked," *New York Herald*, February 15, 1900, 6.

4   "Dramatic and Musical," *New York Times*, January 16, 1900, 7.

5   "The Theatres," *New York Commercial Advertiser*, January 16, 1900, 7; "'Mlle. Fifi' Is a Clever Farce," *New York Herald*, February 7, 1899, n.p.

6   "Four New Plays. 'Coralie & Co.,'" *New York Mail and Express*, February 6, 1900, 7; "Reviews of the New Plays," *New York Evening Telegram*, February 6, 1900, 4; "Good and Evil in Plays," *New York Sun*, February 11, 1900, 2:7; "'Coralie & Co.' Is Dull," *New York Press*, February 6, 1900, 7; "New Dramatic Material," *New York Sun*, February 6, 1900, 7.

7   "The Theatres," *New York Commercial Advertiser*, February 5, 1900, 7.

8   "Dramatic and Musical. Madison Square Theatre," *New York Times*, February 6, 1900, 6.

9   "Theatrical Amusements," *New York Sun*, April 22, 1900, 3:9; "Dramas and Audiences. Do Our People

Need Protection against the Theatres?" *New York Sun*, February 18, 1900, 3:7; "Lewdness on the Stage," *NYDM*, February 24, 1900, 9.

10 "A Tricky Defense of Stage Indecency," *NYDM*, March 17, 1900, 14.

11 Sidney Sharp, "Three New Plays and a Notable Night at the Grand Opera," *New York World*, January 7, 1900, 4; also "New Plays on Our Stage," *New York Sun*, January 9, 1900, 7.

12 "Dancers in the Ballet," *New York Sun*, March 18, 1900, 3:11; "Good and Evil in Plays," *New York Sun*; Hillary Bell, "Player Folk," *New York Press*, March 7, 1900, 5; "Amusements. Hollis St. Theatre," *Boston Journal*, January 2, 1900, 5.

13 "Mrs. Fiske as Becky Sharp," *Boston Traveler*, January 2, 1900, 5; "Dancers in the Ballet," *New York Sun*.

14 "Lewdness on the Stage," *NYDM*; also "The Usher," *NYDM*, February 24, 1900, 15; "A Tricky Defense of Stage Indecency," *NYDM*.

15 "An Awakening," *NYDM*, March 17, 1900, 14; "The Revolt against Vile Plays," *NYDM*, April 21, 1900, 14; "Dramatic and Musical," *New York Times*, March 7, 1900, 6.

16 "Four New Plays. 'Coralie & Co.," *New York Mail and Express*, February 6, 1900, 6.

17 "Manager Frohman His Own Play-Censor," *New York World*, April 12, 1900, 4.

18 "Mgr. Gibbons Gets a Scolding," *New York Press*, February 14, 1900, 7; "Club Women Much Provoked," *New York Sun*, February 14, 1900, 7.

19 Reported in "The Fountain Head of Filth," *NYDM*, April 21, 1900, 14.

20 "Dramas and Audiences. Do Our People Need Protection against the Theatres?" *New York Sun*, February 18, 1900, 3:7.

21 "Affairs of the Theatre," *New York Sun*, March 30, 1900, 7.

22 "The Stage," *Washington Post*, January 21, 1900, 24; "Events of the Stage," *Washington Post*, January 16, 1900, 3; "Amusements. New National Theatre," *Washington Evening Star*, January 16, 1900, 10; also "At the Play," *Chicago Tribune*, November 5, 1899, 41.

23 H[illary]B[ell], "Nethersole's New Play Not Wicked," *New York Press*, February 6, 1900, 7; "Events of the Stage," *Washington Post*; T[iffiny] B[lake], "Review of the Play," *Chicago Journal*, November 1, 1899, 8; *Olga Nethersole*, souvenir booklet (New York: Russell, 1900), n.p.

24 H[illary]B[ell], "Nethersole's New Play Not Wicked," *New York Press*.

25 "The Theatres," *New York Commercial Advertiser*, February 6, 1900, 7; also "News of Theatres. Sapho," *Chicago Tribune*, November 1, 1899, 4.

26 "'Sapho' Described by a Theatre-Goer," *New York World*, February 25, 1900, 3.

27 H[illary]B[ell], "Nethersole's New Play Not Wicked," *New York Press*; "Drama Not Degenerate," *New York Sun*, February 28, 1900, 7.

28 For instance, "The Drama. Olga Nethersole's Holy Work, 'Sapho,'" *New York Tribune*, February 6, 1900, 6; "New Dramatic Material," *New York Sun*, February 6, 1900, 7.

29 H[illary]B[ell], "Nethersole's New Play Not Wicked," *New York Press*.

30 "Reviews of the New Plays," *New York Evening Telegram*, February 6, 1900, 4.

31 Gustav Kobbé, "Some Recent Plays and Players," *Forum* 29 (May 1900): 378.

32 "New Dramatic Material," *New York Sun*; "Reviews of the New Plays," *New York Evening Telegram*.

33 "The Theatres," *New York Commercial Advertiser*, February 6, 1900, 7; similar predictions in "Dramatic and Musical: 'Sapho,'" *New York Times*, February 6, 1900, 6; "Player Folk," *New York Press*, April 18, 1900, 6.

34 "The Theatres," *New York Commercial Advertiser*.

35 Alan Dale, "The Attention of the Police Is Called to Nethersole's Play," *New York Journal*, February 6, 1900, 1.

36 "'Sapho' Breathes Defiance from the Stage," *New York Journal*, February 23, 1900, 4; W. R. Hearst, "The 'Sapho' Indecency," *New York Evening Journal*, January 30, 1900, n.p.; "'Sapho' Denounced by Many Ministers," *New York Evening Journal*, February 2, 1900, 3.

37   "Drama. 'Sapho,' the Salacious," *New York World*, February 11, 1900, 2E.

38   "New Dramatic Material," *New York Sun*. This piece was probably written by the paper's drama critic and editor, Franklin Fyles, who was an established playwright and a Belasco collaborator. Also T. S. Moran, "New York's Dramatic Critics," *Metropolitan* (February 1899): 105–09; W. T. Price, "Critics and Criticism," *Theatre* (New York) No. 7 (September 1901): 12–14.

39   "Good and Evil in Plays," *New York Sun*, February 11, 1900, 2:7.

40   "Music and Drama," *New York Evening Post*, February 7, 1900, 7.

41   Randy Kapelke, "Preventing Censorship: The Audience's Role in *Sapho* (1900) and *Mrs. Warren's Profession* (1905)," *Theatre History Studies* 18 (1998): 126.

42   "Unchanged and Unclear as Ever, 'Sapho' Still Thrust at the Public," *New York World*, February 22, 1900, 1; "Mgr. Gibbons Gets a Scolding," *New York Press*, February 14, 1900, 7; "W. C. T. U. after 'Sapho,'" *New York Sun*, February 21, 1900, 7.

43   "Rouse Critic and Pulpit," *New York Herald*, February 19, 1900, 6.

44   "All Denounce 'Sapho' Plague," *New York World*, February 24, 1900, 3.

45   Editorial cartoons were major weapons of this opposition.

46   "Should There Be a Censor of the Drama in New York?" *New York World*, February 18, 1900, 2E.

47   Hillary Bell, "Music and Drama," *New York Press*, February 25, 1900, 14. As early as the opening of *Sapho*, the *Commercial Advertiser* chastised the yellow press for turning the play into a scandal ("The Theatres," *New York Commercial Advertiser*, February 6, 1900, 7).

48   "'Sapho' Evokes Lusty Cheers," *New York Herald*, February 6, 1900, 9.

49   Contemporary sources, as well as later accounts, gave her birth year as 1863, 1866, 1870, or 1872.

50   Hartnoll, *Concise*, 381; *Who Was Who*, 1792; Banham, *Cambridge*, 709; Young, *Famous*, 2:864–65; Lavinia Hart, "Olga Nethersole," *Cosmopolitan* (May 1901): 14–21; Joy Harriman Reilly, "A Forgotten 'Fallen Woman:' Olga Nethersole's *Sapho*," in Fisher, *When*, 108; Emma E. Thorne, Olga Nethersole," *Metropolitan* 9 (April 1899): 399; H[illary] B[ell], "Player Folk," *New York Press*, April 6, 1900, 6; Young, *Famous*, 1:869; "The Stage," *Washington Post*, January 21, 1900, 24.

51   C. Reclus, "Olga Nethersole as Mrs. Tanqueray," *Criterion* (January 21, 1899): 50; "Olga Nethersole—Actress and Philanthropist," *Theatre* (New York) (July 1907): 104–95.

52   Archie Bell, *Olga Nethersole* (Paris: Clarke, 1907), 7; Olga Nethersole, "Sex Dramas: Today and Yesterday," *Green Book* (c. 1913): 33, in Scrapbook MWEZ+ n.c. 6484, BRTC; *Who Was Who*, 1,792–93; Banham, *Cambridge*, 709.

53   Emma E. Thorne, "Olga Nethersole," *Metropolitan*.

54   "Plea for Stage Sin," *Chicago Inter Ocean*, November 5, 1899, 37.

55   Leslie, *Some*, 298; also H. Gordon Johnson, "Olga Nethersole and Her Genius," *Looker-On* (December 1895): 235.

56   Joy Harriman Reilly, "A Forgotten 'Fallen Woman:' Olga Nethersole's *Sapho*," in Fisher, *When*, 108.

57   Leslie, *Some*, 298.

58   Ibid., 297.

59   Marwell Hall, ed., *Gallery of Players No. 4* (New York: Illustrated American, 1894), 36.

60   Max Beerbohm, "An Actress, and a Play," in his *Around Theatres* (New York: Knopf, 1930; reprint: New York: Taplinger, 1969), 264.

61   Lyman B. Glover, "Miss Nethersole in 'Sapho,'" unidentified Chicago newspaper, October 29, 1899, in RLS NAFR+ v. 361, p. 101, BRTC.

62   Marwell Hall, ed., *Gallery of Players No. 4*, 36.

63   Kaneo, *Sadayakko*, 37.

64   Shaw, "Miss Nethersole and Mrs. Kendal," in his *Our Theatres*, 2:160, 163. Nethersole's dramatic version followed Prosper Merimée's novel more closely than Bizet's opera.

65   Respectively, H. Gordon Johnson, "Olga Nethersole and Her Genius," *Looker-On* (New York) (December 1895): 235; "The Licentious Drama: Is the American Stage Degenerate?" *Metropolitan* 11 (June 1900): 649; Alan Dale, "A Vesuvian Episode," *New York Journal*, December 28, 1896, 30–31.

66   "The Theatres," *New York Commercial Advertiser*, February 6, 1900, 7; Hillary Bell, "Music and Drama," *New York Press*, February 25, 1900, 14; Hapgood, *Stage*, 356.

67   Banham, *Cambridge*, 709; "Nethersole at B. F. Keith's," *Boston Herald*, October 28, 1913 n.p.

68   Clement Scott, "Clement Scott Scores the Decadent Drama of Today," *New York Herald*, February 11, 1900, 4:8.

69   Hillary Bell, "Player Folk," *New York Press*, March 7, 1900, 5.

70   Edward Fredric McKay, "Plays and Players," *New York Mail and Express Illustrated Saturday Review*, February 10, 1900, 6.

71   Hillary Bell, "Player Folk," *New York Press*, February 16, 1900, 6.

72   For example, "Sapho-Crazed Women Throng to See the Nethersole Play," *New York World*, February 18, 1900, 2.

73   H[illary] B[ell], "Player Folk," *New York Press*, February 9, 1900, 6.

74   "Sapho-Crazed Women Throng to See the Nethersole Play," *New York World*.

75   "Unchanged and Unclear as Ever 'Sapho' Still Thrust at the Public," *New York World*, February 22, 1900, 1; "'Sapho' and the Young Girl," *New York Evening Telegram*, April 6, 1900, 4.

76   "Good and Evil in Plays," *New York Sun*, February 11, 1900, 2:7

77   "Arrest of Nethersole," *New York Sun*, February 22, 1900, 7. This arrest, although perfunctory, was more severe than any other legal action Nethersole faced on tour (Randy Kapelke, "Preventing Censorship: The Audience's Role in *Sapho* [1900] and *Mrs. Warren's Profession* [1905]," *Theatre History Studies* 18 [1998]: 121–22).

78   "Arrest of Nethersole," *New York Sun*.

79   "More on Sapho," *New York Tribune*, February 24, 1900, 9; "Arrest of Nethersole," *New York Sun*; "War against 'Sapho,'" *New York Mail and Express*, February 21, 1900, 1.

80   *New York World*, February 22, 1900, 1.

81   "Olga Nethersole to the Bar!" *New York Evening Journal*, February 21, 1900, 2.

82   "'Sapho' Taken to Court," *New York Times*, February 22, 1900, 3; "'Sapho' Breathes Defiance from the Stage," *New York Journal*, February 23, 1900, 4; "Miss Nethersole Ill; Wallack's Closed," *New York World*, February 23, 1900, 1.

83   "Drama Not Degenerate," *New York Sun*, February 28, 1900, 7; also "Sapho Stopped," *NYPM*, March 10, 1900, 17.

84   "Nethersole Sips a Tonic," *New York Sun*, March 2, 1900, 7.

85   "Sapho Stopped," *NYDM*.

86   "'Sapho' Judged in Tribunal of Public Opinion Finds Foes and Friends," *New York Herald*, February 25, 6:2.

87   "Drama Not Degenerate," *New York Sun*; "This Week on Our Stage," *New York Sun*, March 4, 1900, 3:7.

88   "Paying Back Sapho Money," *New York Sun*, March 7, 1900, 7.

89   "'Sapho' Suppressed as Immoral; Wallack's Closed by Police," *New York World*, March 6, 1900, 1.

90   "'Sapho' Off the Boards," *New York Tribune*, March 6, 1900, 1.

91   "Theatrical Disclosures," *New York Sun*, March 6, 1900, 7.

92   "Miss Nethersole Reappears," *New York Times*, March 7, 1900, 6.

93   "Notes of the Week," *New York Times*, March 11, 1900, 16; "Current Amusements," *NYDM*, March 17 and 24, 1900, 16; Mantle, *Best*, 361–62.

94   Hillary Bell, "Music and Drama," *New York Press*, February 25, 1900, 14; "Affairs of the Theatre," *New York Sun*, March 30, 1900, 7; "Clyde Fitch Sails Away," *New York Telegraph*, March 25, 1900, n.p.

95   "Jury Box Filled in 'Sapho' Case" *New York Press*, April 4, 1900, 1.

96   H[illary] B[ell], "Player Folk," *New York Press*, April 6, 1900, 6.

97   "The Acquittal of Olga Nethersole," *NYDM*, April 14, 1900, 13; "'Sapho' Case Closed, Acquittal Is Expected," *New York Herald*, April 5, 1900, 5, 1:13; "Nethersole Acquited," *New York Sun*, April 6, 1900, 1; "Jury Soon Acquits Miss Nethersole," *New York Times*, April 6, 1900, 7; "'Sapho' Again Tomorrow," *New York Times*, April 6, 1900, 7.

98   "Rush for 'Sapho' Tickets," *New York Times*, April 7, 1900, 7; "New Brood of Saphos to Bask in Limelight," *New York World*, April 7, 1900, 4.

99   "Revised Sapho Wildly Welcomed," *New York Herald*, April 8, 1900, 2:5; "'Sapho' Gets an Ovation," *New York Times*, April 8, 1900, 7; "Nethersole Acquited," *New York Sun*; "Loud Greeting for Return of 'Sapho,'" *New York World*, April 8, 1900, 10. Reports differed on the number of jurors attending.

100   "'Sapho' Gets an Ovation," *New York Times*, April 8, 1900, 7.

101   "Loud Greeting for Return of 'Sapho,'" *New York World*.

102   H[illary] B[ell], "Player Folk," *New York Press*, April 6, 1900, 6; also "The Theatres," *New York Commercial Advertiser*, April 14, 1900, 7. *Sapho* played an additional fifty-five performances until the season ended (Mantle, *Best*, 361–62). In his review of the 1899–1900 theatrical season, Gustav Kobbé thought that if the *Sapho* run had not been interrupted by the city, it would have been the most financially successful production of the season (Gustav Kobbé, "Some Recent Plays and Players," *Forum* 29 [May 1900]: 377).

103   I found no significant evidence of influential British support of Nethersole.

104   Kaneo, *Sadayakko*, 39–40; Kaneo, *Ōbei*, 38–39.

105   "Olga Nethersole to the Bar!" *New York Evening Journal*, February 21, 1900, 2.

106   "Theatrical Discussion," *New York Sun*, January 7, 1900, 9.

107   Gustav Kobbé, "Some Recent Plays and Players," 377.

108   James O'Donnell Bennett, "Miss Nethersole Produces 'Sapho,'" *Chicago Journal*, November 1, 1899, 8. As this was from an earlier performance in Chicago, the line and scene may have disappeared by New York.

109   "The Licentious Drama: Is the American Stage Degenerate?" *Metropolitan* 11 (June 1900): 654–55. Internal evidence suggested the author was male.

110   "W.C.T.U. after 'Sapho,'" *New York Sun*, February 21, 1900, 7.

111   "Dancers in the Ballet," *New York Sun*, March 18, 1900, 3:11; also Hillary Bell, "Player Folk," *New York Press*, March 7, 1900, 5.

112   The original versions of both plays were set in distant historical periods. Kawakami's geisha were an anachronism.

113   Kaneo, *Sadayakko*, 38.

114   Joy Harriman Reilly, "A Forgotten 'Fallen Woman:' Olga Nethersole's *Sapho*," in Fisher, *When*, 108; Young, *Famous*, 1:869; C. Reclus, "Olga Nethersole as Mrs. Tanqueray," *Criterion*, January 21, 1899, n.p.

115   "Is the Moral or Immoral Woman the Greater Power in the World?" *New York World*, March 11, 1900, E3.

116   "Victoria's Virtue. Cleopatra's Lure," *New York Herald*, March 1, 1900, 19; also "Man's Ideal Woman Just a Bit Wicked," *New York World*, March 1, 1900, 1.

117   "Theatrical Amusements," *New York Sun*, April 22, 1900, 3:9. Daniel Frohman and his four Syndicate theatres were the principal importers.

118   Clement Scott, "Scott's Defense of Mrs. Langtry," *New York Herald*, February 25, 1900, 6:2.

119   "Two New Mysteries of Poison; Woman's Most Insidious Weapon," *New York World Sunday Magazine*,

January 28, 1900, 8. Newspapers found that arsenic and strychnine were women's favorite poisons because they were said to be undetectable in either wine or cake.

120   Banta, *Imagining*, 620.

121   Ibid., 620–21, 623.

122   Quoted in Dijkstra, *Idols*, 334.

123   Amy Leslie, "Frenchy Play by Fitch," *Chicago Daily News*, November 1, 1899; 6.

124   Warren Susman, "'Personality' and the Making of Twentieth Century Culture" in *New Directions in American Intellectual History*, ed. John Higham and Paul K. Conkin (Baltimore: John Hopkins University Press, 1979), 212–25.

125   "The Theatres," *New York Commercial Advertiser*, January 16, 1900, 7. Concurring: Frederic Edward McKay, "The Degenerates," *New York Mail and Express*, January 16, 1900, 7; Leander Richardson, "The Month in Theatricals," *Metropolitan* 11 (March 1900): 326.

126   "The Theatres," *New York Commercial Advertiser*. Textural evidence suggested the writer was the paper's drama critic and editor, Norman Hapwood.

127   "Dancers in the Ballet," *New York Sun*, March 18, 1900, 3:11.

128   Winter, *Wallet*, 2:309, 2:114, 2:315.

Chapter 33

1   Hillary Bell, "Player Folk," *New York Press*, April 18, 1900, 6.

2   *Sapolio* replaced *Barbara Fidgety* on a two-part bill with the continuing main attraction, *Whirl-i-Gig*. The latter was a musical burlesque of Georges Feydeau's farce, *The Girl from Maxim's*, which played earlier on Broadway. *Barbara Fidgety* was a burlesque of Clyde Fitch's recent Civil War drama, *Barbara Frietchie* ("Weber and Fields," advertisement, *New York Herald*, March 4, 1900, 4:5; "News and Gossip of the Stage," *New York Evening Telegram*, March 9, 1900, 4; Isman, *Weber*, 257). *Sapolio* had been in preparation for several weeks.

3   Weber and Fields Music Hall maintained old burlesque values and dramatic form, while elsewhere the "burlesque" theatres of America were being transformed with risqué mixes of variety acts, chorus girls, and raucous travesty sketches. Weber and Fields were performers renowned as America's most popular "Dutch comedians." "Dutch" did not refer to the Netherlands but was an Americanization of "Deutsch" that became the generic designation for comic characterizations of Germans that saturated vaudeville, burlesque, and comedy in the United States.

4   Sidney Sharp, "'Sapho' Burlesque Extremely Mild," *New York World*, March 9, 1900, 3; "Sapolio at Weber and Fields," *NYDM*, March 17, 1900, 18; "May Robson's Hit in a 'Sapho' Skit," *New York Herald*, March 9, 1900, 11; Bordman, *American Musical Theatre*, 167–68.

5   Because its effectiveness as a laxative could not be politely mentioned, advertising for Sapolio relied on double entendre such as "If at first you don't succeed, try Sapolio" ("Sapolio," advertisement, *Seattle Post-Intelligencer*, September 13, 1899, 5).

6   "Sapolio at Weber and Fields," *NYDM*; Alan Dale, "The 'Sapho' Burlesque at Weber and Fields's Is an Indigestion of Moral Purpose," *New York Journal*, March 9, 1900, 8.

7   "News and Gossip of the Stage," *New York Evening Telegram*, March 9, 1900, 4; "Sapolio Clever Burlesque," *New York Times*, March 9, 1900, 7; "New York City. Weber and Fields' Music Hall," *NYC*, March 17, 1900, 58; "Examples in Stagecraft," *New York Sun*, March 11, 1900, 3:7; "May Robson's Hit in a 'Sapho' Skit," *New York Herald*, March 9, 1900, 11.

8   "Some Dramatic Subjects," *New York Sun*, February 16, 1900, 7.

9   "Current Amusements," *NYDM*, April 21, 1900, 16; "'Sapho' Again Tomorrow," *New York Times*, April 6,

1900, 7; T. Allison Brown, *History*, 3:206–22. The Comique Theatre building had opened twenty years earlier as the San Francisco Minstrel Hall and since then, through many financial difficulties, the name had changed numerous times.

10   "At the Theatres. Comique—Sappho," *NYDM*, April 21, 1900, 16–17; also "New 'Sappho' in the Field," *New York World*, April 17, 1900, 4; H[illary] B[ell], "One More on List of City's Saphos," *New York Press*, April 17, 1900, 7; "Two Versions of Sapho," *New York Times*, April 17, 1900, 9.

11   T. Allison Brown, *History*, 3:222.

12   "A Gigantic Sapho for the Germans," *New York World*, February 27, 1900, 3.

13   "'Sappho' Given at Germania. The Police Were on Hand to Stop Any German Translation of Daudet Drama," *New York Herald*, March 29, 1900, 12.

14   "At the Theatres. Third Avenue—Sapho," *NYDM*, May 19, 1900, 16.

15   John H. James, "The Theatres of the Ghetto," *NYDM*, July 28, 1900, 3; "The Endowed Theatre Project," *Theatre* (New York) 2:11 (January 1902): 9.

16   "Women Buy 'Sapho' Books from Fakirs," *New York World*, February 24, 1900, 3; "The Usher," *NYDM*, February 17, 1900, 13.

17   "Sapho Stopped," *NYDM*, March 10, 1900, 17; "The Sapho Case," *NYDM*, March 24, 1900, 17; "The Acquittal of Olga Nethersole," *NYDM*, April 14, 1900, 13.

18   "Street Sales of 'Sapho' Barred," *New York World*, April 5, 1900, 3; "To Exclude the Book 'Sapho,'" *New York Times*, March 24, 1900, 9; "'Sapho' Trial Is Set for April 3," *New York Journal*, March 24, 1900, 4.

19   "Dancers in the Ballet," *New York Sun*, March 18, 1900, 3:11.

20   Based on sources listed in this section; also "Theatrical Jottings," *New York Herald*, March 15, 1900, 12.

21   "New Brood of Saphos to Bask in Limelight," *New York World*, April 7, 1900, 4; "'Sapho' Again Tomorrow," *New York Times*, April 6, 1900, 7; "The Sapho Case," *NYDM*, March 24, 1900, 17; "Affairs of the Theatre," *New York Sun*, March 30, 1900, 7; "'Sapho' Barred out of Waterbury [Conn.]," *New York World*, February 27, 1900, 3.

22   "Would Not Play 'Sapho,'" *NYDM*, March 24, 1900, 17.

23   "'Sapho' a la Kalamazoo," *New York Herald*, March 15, 1900, 12; "Saw 'Sapho' Anyway," *New York Herald*, March 16, 1900, 11.

24   "'Sapho' Again Tomorrow," *New York Times*, April 6, 1900, 7.

25   "Affairs of the Theatre," *New York Sun*, March 30, 1900, 7; also "Baltimore Hissed 'Sapho,'" *New York World*, March 13, 1900, 4.

26   "New Brood of Saphos to Bask in Limelight," *New York World*.

27   "Traveling Dramatic Companies and Their Repertories, 1900–1901," *Winging It* (Mt. Pleasant, Iowa) 2 (Summer 1995): 7.

28   "As to 'The Regatta Girl,'" *New York Evening Telegram*, March 15, 1900, 4; "Regatta Girl Is Not Over Lightly," *New York Herald*, March 15, 1900, 12.

29   "Current Amusements," *NYDM*, February 24 and March 10, 1900, 16; "Harlem. Olympic," *NYC*, February 24, 1900, 1102; "This 'Sapho' Short Lived," *New York World*, February 22, 1900, 2. In April, the troupe was brought back for one week at Miner's ("Current Amusements," *NYDM*, April 28, 1900, 16).

30   "Theatres and Music Halls," *New York Times*, February 27, 1900, 7.

31   "Things at the Theatres," *New York Sun*, May 29, 1900, 7.

32   "S. Lubin M'f'ring Optician," advertisement, *NYC*, March 10, 1900, 41.

33   "Don't Be Bulldozed," advertisement, *NYC*, April 21, 1900, 192.

34   Moving picture running times were highly variable in 1900 because they depended on how fast or slow projectionists hand-cranked films through their projectors.

35   "Play Sapho Waltzes," advertisement, *New York World*, February 25, 1900, 6E; "'My Black Sapho' by Edwards," advertisement, *NYC*, March 17, 1900, 71.

36   "Stage and Society Meet at a Revel," *New York World*, March 22, 1900, 2. Jean was the name of the young hero in *Sapho*.

37   "Bijou" and "Comique," advertisements, *New York Times*, April 8, 1900, 11, and *New York Herald*, April 15, 1900, 4:4; "Bijou's Odd Double Bill," *New York Press*, April 10, 1900, 7.

38   Kaneo, *Ōbei*, 39.

39   "The Theatres," *New York Commercial Advertiser*, April 17, 1900, 7; "She Will Play Sapho but Must Not Kiss," *New York World*, April 14, 1900, 4; Kaneo, *Sadayakko*, 37; "Japanese Realism," *New York Commercial Advertiser*, April 20, 1900, 7.

40   Kaneo, *Sadayakko*, 37–39; Yamaguchi, *Joyū*, 92; also "Otojiro Kawakami and Sada Yacco," *Era* (June 2, 1900): 8.

41   Kaneo, *Ōbei*, 39–40; Ubukata, "Kawakami," 176; "The Theatres," *New York Commercial Advertiser*; "Bijou," advertisement, *New York Times*, April 14, 1900, 9.

42   Kaneo, *Sadayakko*, 39–40.

43   "She Will Play Sapho but Must Not Kiss," *New York World*; "Japs to Give 'Sapho' in Fashion Platonic," *New York Evening Journal*, April 16, 1900, 7; "Japanese Realism," *New York Commercial Advertiser*.

44   "Japs to Give 'Sapho' in Fashion Platonic," *New York Evening Journal*; also "She Will Play Sapho but Must Not Kiss," *New York World*. These two newspapers, which were the most curious about Kawakami's love scenes in his forthcoming version of *Sapho*, were the same yellow ones that led the crusade against Nethersole's *Sapho*.

45   "Japanese Realism," *New York Commercial Advertiser*.

46   "Japs to Give 'Sapho' in Fashion Platonic," *New York Evening Journal*.

47   Kaneo, *Sadayakko*, 40.

48   "Sada Yacco Plays Sapho," *New York Press*, April 17, 1900, 7.

49   "She Will Play Sapho but Must Not Kiss," *New York World*.

50   "The Theatres," *New York Commercial Advertiser*, April 17, 1900, 7; Kaneo, *Sadayakko*, 41. One advance notice credited the script to both Kawakami and Hayashi ("Japs to Give 'Sapho' in Fashion Platonic," *New York Evening Journal*). The Bijou program stated that Kawakami alone prepared the Japanese version after reading the Daudet novel ("Sada Yacco Plays Sapho," *New York Press*). It is doubtful that Kawakami read the novel.

51   Miyaoka, *Ikoku*, 76–77; Inoue, *Kawakami*, 73; Kaneo, *Sadayakko*, 37, 39; also Sugimoto, *Madamu*, 159–60. The Kawakami chronology for this period was confusing.

52   Kawatake Toshio, *Zoku hikaku engekigaku* [Continuation: Comparative studies of drama] (Nansōsha, 1974), 48. *Imoseyama* was usually performed in early spring.

53   Miyaoka, *Ikoku*, 75; "The Theatres," *New York Commercial Advertiser*, February 27, 1900, 7; Hillary Bell, "Player Folk," *New York Press*, March 2, 1900, 6.

54   In many Japanese accounts, the heroine's name and play title also appeared as *Safuō*.

55   Kaneo, *Sadayakko*, 40–41; "The Theatres," *New York Commercial Advertiser*, April 17, 1900, 7; "At the Theatres. Bijou—The Japanese Players," *NYDM*, April 21, 1900, 17.

56   "Current Amusements," *NYDM*, April 21, 1900, 16.

57   "Sada Yacco Plays Sapho," *New York Press*, April 17, 1900, 7; also "Wayward Ones," *New York Sun*, April 17, 1900, 7; "A Japanese 'Sapho,'" *New York Herald*, April 17, 1900, 10.

58   Kaneo, *Sadayakko*, 41.

59   Ibid., 40.

60   "The Theatres," *New York Commercial Advertiser*, April 17, 1900, 7; Hapgood, *Stage*, 354. What the actors

actually wore may have been native Japanese clothing and headgear unfamiliar to American viewers but it looked Western.

61   Hapgood, *Stage*, 354.

62   "At the Theatres. Bijou—The Japanese Players," *NYDM*, April 21, 1900, 17; "The Theatres," *New York Commercial Advertiser*.

63   "Shaku ni ureshiki; otoko no chikara" (Kaneo, *Sadayakko*, 41; also Kaneo, *Ōbei*, 40).

64   Kaneo, *Sadayakko*, 41. My summary of the act one plot was assembled from contradictory sources listed in preceding endnotes and from "Japanese Version of 'Sapho' Was the Novelty in the Local Dramatic World," *New York World*, April 17, 1900, 4. The romantic smile at the act one curtain was confirmed by viewer Katherine Metcalf Roof in her "Concerning the Japanese Players," *Impressionist* 8 (June 1900): 8.

65   "At the Theatres. Bijou—The Japanese Players," *NYDM*.

66   This act two description was compiled from "The Theatres," *New York Commercial Advertiser*; "Japanese Version of 'Sapho' Was the Novelty in the Local Dramatic World," *New York World*, April 17, 1900, 4; Hapgood, *Stage*, 354–55; "At the Theatres. Bijou—The Japanese Players," *NYDM*, April 21, 1900, 17.

67   "The Theatres," *New York Commercial Advertiser*; "A Japanese 'Sapho,'" *New York Herald*, April 17, 1900, 10.

68   Kaneo, *Sadayakko*, 40.

69   Toita Yasuji, *Shibai meisho hitomakuken* [Scenic views of famous locations in plays], (Hakusuisha, 1958).

70   Dōmon, *Kawakami*, 127–28; Yanagi Keitarō, *Kawakami*, part 6; Miyaoka, *Ikoku*, 79; Inoue, *Kawakami*, 42.

71   Because of their participation in Itō's festivities, members of his government were known as "the dancing cabinet."

72   "The Theatres," *New York Commercial Advertiser*, April 17 1900, 7; "Japanese Version of 'Sapho' Was the Novelty in the Local Dramatic World," *New York World*, April 17, 1900, 4.

73   The cherry blossoms of act one were described in "Japanese Version of 'Sapho' Was the Novelty in the Local Dramatic World," *New York World*, April 17, 1900, 4.

74   Either an American "fancy parlor" or a "rustic cottage" stock set was used for act two ("The Theatres," *New York Commercial Advertiser*). Newspaper descriptions were contradictory.

75   "Wayward Ones," *New York Sun*, April 17, 1900, 7.

76   Kaneo, *Sadayakko*, 40.

77   In Kaneo, *Sadayakko*, 40, Kawakami claimed that the act one garden party activities were backed by "cheerful *aikata*" (a kabuki musical accompaniment). A New York review insisted that this was "dreadful music of voice and instrument" ("Wayward Ones," *New York Sun*.)

78   Inoue, *Kawakami*, 73.

79   Kaneo, *Sadayakko*, 40. In this famous scene, Ōishi, the leader of the *rōnin* group, concealed his commitment to revenge by playing a drunken blindman's bluff in a Kyoto brothel. *Chūshingura*, with its strong themes of loyalty and samurai virtue, always appealed to Kawakami, but he apparently never had the means or opportunity to produce the play in its full splendor.

80   Pictorial examples are found in all kinds of books about kabuki.

81   Kaneo, *Sadayakko*, 40. The word *en* in Kawakami's original account is now read as *enishi* and appears as such in Sugimoto, *Madamu*, 158, and other recent works. *Tsunahiki* is a Japanese form of tug-of-war.

82   Kaneo, *Sadayakko*, 40.

83   Ibid., 41.

84   "The Matinee Girl," *NYDM*, April 22, 1899, 2.

85   Ezaki, *Jitsuroku*, 116.

86   Miyaoka, *Ikoku*, 77–78.

87   Stylistics and the problematics of kabuki love scenes were current topics in the Japanese theatrical world

of 1900. Examples: Chin Unō, "'Kotchi no nuregoto to atchi no rabushîn o yomite" [Reading *nuregoto* in our (plays) and 'love scenes' in foreign (plays)], *Kabuki* (October 1901): 28–29; Kanai Anzen, "Shibai no nuregoto" [Love scenes in plays], *Kabuki* (October 1901): 29–30; Kayōsei, "Shikan no nuregoto dan" [Love scenes in *Shikan*], *Kabuki* (November 1901): 39–40. "Nuregoto," the kabuki term for amorous scenes in plays, literally means "wet business."

88   "Japs to Give 'Sapho' in Fashion Platonic," *New York Evening Journal*, April 16, 1900, 7.

89   Sugimoto, *Madamu*, 155.

90   Nethersole's predatory females were already called "vampires." The vampire conception spread throughout American popular culture and culminated in the stereotypical vamp/vampire of Theda Bara movies during the mid-1910s. These were not the Transylvanian vampires of Bram Stoker's *Dracula*.

91   Clement Scott, "Irving's Triumph as Robespierre," *New York Herald*, April 16, 1899, 1:9.

92   Gershon Shaked, "The Play: Gateway to Cultural Dialog," trans. Jeffrey Green, in Scolnicov, *Play*, 8.

93   Discussed in Fischer-Lichte, *Show*, 135.

94   The papers—nine dailies and two trade—were the universe I surveyed. This did not include all New York dailies.

95   "Over the Footlights," *New York Evening Telegram*, April 17, 1900, 4; also "Sada Yacco Plays Sapho," *New York Press*, April 17, 1900, 7.

96   "Wayward Ones," *New York Sun*, April 17, 1900, 7.

97   "The Theatres," *New York Commercial Advertiser*, April 17, 1900, 7.

98   "At the Theatres. Bijou—The Japanese Players," *NYDM*, April 21, 1900, 17; "Two Versions of 'Sapho,'" *New York Times*, April 17, 1900, 9; "Over the Footlights," *New York Evening Telegram*; "Wayward Ones," *New York Sun*; "A Japanese 'Sapho,'" *New York Herald*, April 17, 1900, 10.

99   "Sewell Collins Deeply Affected by the Japs' 'Sapho,'" *New York Evening Journal*, April 21, 1900, 10.

100   "'Sapho' in Japanese," *New York Mail and Express*, April 17, 1900, 9.

101   "The Theatres," *New York Commercial Advertiser*.

102   "Japanese Version of 'Sapho' Was the Novelty in the Local Dramatic World," *New York World*, April 17, 1900, 4.

103   "At the Theatres. Bijou—The Japanese Players," *NYDM*, April 21, 1900, 17.

104   "The Theatres," *New York Commercial Advertiser*; concurring "At the Theatres. Bijou—The Japanese Players," *NYDM*. There may have been a last-minute cast change. Advance notices had "Fujikawa, the melodramatic actor" as the returned lover Furumatsu ("She Will Play Sapho but Must Not Kiss," *New York World*, April 14, 1900, 4).

105   "A Japanese 'Sapho,'" *New York Herald*, April 17, 1900, 10.

106   "Sewell Collins Deeply Affected by the Japs' 'Sapho,'" *New York Evening Journal*. The "absurd wooden doll" was a child's toy that "cried 'Mamma' when squeezed," according to "Wayward Ones," *New York Sun*, April 17, 1900, 7; Katherine Metcalf Roof, "Concerning the Japanese Players," *Impressionist* (June 1900), 9.

107   "Sada Yacco Plays Sapho," *New York Press*, April 17, 1900, 7.

108   "At the Theatres. Bijou—The Japanese Players," *NYDM*. *Madame Butterfly* had already closed.

109   "The Theatres," *New York Commercial Advertiser*, April 17, 1900, 7.

110   Ibid.

111   "Japanese Version of 'Sapho' Was the Novelty in the Local Dramatic World," *New York World*, April 17, 1900, 4.

112   Patrice Pavis, "Introduction: Towards a Theory of Interculturalism in Theatre?" in ed. Pavis, *The Intercultural Performance Reader* (New York: Routledge, 1996), 1.

113   Mori Mitsuya, "Thinking and Feeling: Characteristics of Intercultural Theatre," in Scholz-Cionca, *Japanese*, 358.

114   Hanna Scolnicov, "Introduction," in Scolnicov, *Play*, 2.

115   In "'Sapho' at 70 in the Shade," *New York Herald*, April 17, 1900, 10, the writer suggested that libidinous expectations were drawing audiences to *Sappho* at the Comique Theatre.

116   Kaneo, *Sadayakko*, 40; Kaneo, *Ōbei*, 40.

117   For instance, Yamaguchi, *Joyū*, 92; Sugimoto, *Madamu Sadayakko*, 160, 163.

118   "Sewell Collins Deeply Affected by the Japs "Sapho," *New York Evening Journal*, April 21, 1900, 10. Collins saw the show on Friday afternoon of its first and only week. Slight rain that day may have kept an interested audience away ("City Guide. The Weather," *New York Commercial Advertiser*, April 16–21, 1900, 7).

119   Kaneo, *Sadayakko*, 40. "Jap" was written phonetically "jappu."

120   Ibid., 37–39, 41; Kaneo, *Ōbei*, 39–40.

121   Kaneo, *Sadayakko*, 41. In 1903, Kawakami produced a double bill of *Merchant of Venice* (*Māchanto ofu Enisu*) and *Safuō* (*Sahoko*) in Japan. Sadayakko again had the title role in this *Safuō/Sahoko*, but the play was reworked almost beyond recognition from the New York version (Yamano Imosaku, "Yokohama no Kawakamiza" [The Kawakami troupe in Yokohama], *Kabuki* [August 1903], 25–29).

122   Kaneo, *Ōbei*, 44.

Chapter 34

1   "Current Amusements," *NYDM*, April 21 and 28, 1900, 16.

2   "Notes on Stage," *New York Tribune*, April 22, 1900, 3:8; "Current Amusements," *NYDM*, May 5, 1900, 16; "Amusements To-Night," *New York Evening Journal*, April 30, 1900, 7. The Bijou did not reopen until September 10, 1900 (Brown, *History*, 3:302).

3   "Kawakami ichiza yōkō nisshi," *Miyako shimbun*, July 26, 1900, in Shirakawa, 318.

4   Documentation was insufficient to make this a definitive number.

5   "Current Amusements," *NYDM*, April 21, 1900, 16. *My Daughter in Law* was a mother-in-law comedy adapted from the French with a cast imported from Britain.

6   As with most theatrical statistics, numbers were not exact ("Current Amusements," *NYDM*, August 26, 1899–May 26, 1900, 16).

7   The theatrical fringes were primarily Brooklyn, lower Manhattan, and Harlem ("Current Amusements," *NYDM*, August 26, 1899–May 26, 1900, 16; Bordman, *American Musical*, 153–70; Bordman, *American Theatre*, 409–63). The latter source counted ninety-nine "new productions" but excluded the many touring companies playing shows previously seen in New York and plays too obscure for standard records. Harlem in 1900 was predominantly Caucasian.

8   The Donnelley Stock Company was included in my count but I omitted the musical stock company at the American Theatre with its operettas and operas in English and, beginning April 9, the new Corse Payton rep company resident in Brooklyn ("Current Amusements," *NYDM*, August 26, 1899–May 26, 1900).

9   Gustav Kobbé, "Some Recent Plays and Players," *Forum* 29 (May 1900): 384.

10   Hapgood, *Stage*, 354–60.

11   "The Closing Season," *NYDM*, April 21, 1900, 14. The *Dramatic Mirror* numbers for the 1899–1900 season were further distorted because the length of the established theatre season had been extended and the paper had increased the number of locations across the country from which it received business reports. Also "The Theatre Year," *NYDM*, May 12, 1900, 14; Gustav Kobbé, "Some Recent Plays and Players," *Forum*.

12   "The Theatre Year," *NYDM*; also "Themes from Stageland," *New York Sun*, June 24, 1900, 3:9; Leander Richardson, "The Month in Theatricals," *Metropolitan* 11 (January 1899): 87.

13   Trolley lines were extending their tracks to new suburban amusement parks where vaudeville (and a few dramatic stock companies) were among the new major attractions.

14   "The Theatre Year," *NYDM*, May 12, 1900, 14.

15   "Themes from Stageland," *New York Sun*, June 24, 1900, 3:9.

16   Dimmick, *Our*, 79.

17   Edward J. Dithmar, "This Week's New Bills," *New York Times*, April 8, 1900, 18.

18   "Immorality Has Been the Cause of This Season's Dramatic Failures," *New York World*, April 15, 1900, 2E. In his extensive history of this season, T. Allston Brown concurred (Brown, *History*, 3:363).

19   "Immorality Has Been the Cause of This Season's Dramatic Failures," *New York World*.

20   "Current Amusements," *NYDM*, August 26, 1899–June 9, 1900, 16; Bordman, *American Theatre*, 446–63.

21   Mansfield's new repertoire was *Cyrano de Bergerac, Beau Brummell, Prince Carl, A Parisian Romance, Dr. Jekyll and Mr. Hyde, The First Violin*, and two George Bernard Shaw plays, *The Devil's Disciple* and *Arms and the Man*.

22   "Themes from Stageland" *New York Sun*, June 17, 1900, 3:9. Strictly speaking, he was mistaken. *Hamlet* and a condensed *Romeo and Juliet* were both performed twice in September 1899 by a small traveling repertoire company that played the third-class Star Theatre (Brown, *History*, 2:341).

23   "Themes from Stageland," *New York Sun*.

24   Edward A. Dithmar, "At the Play and with the Players," *New York Times*, March 11, 1900, 16; "Music and Drama," *New York Evening Post*, March 6, 1900, 7; Shattuck, *Shakespeare*, 2:125; "Modjeska as Lady Macbeth," *New York Press*, March 6, 1900, 7.

25   "Current Amusements," *NYDM*, March 17 and 24, 1900, 16; "Murray Hill," *New York Herald*, March 18, 1900, 4:5.

26   "Current Amusements," *NYDM*, March 3, 1900, 16; Bordman, *American Theatre*, 448; Brown, *History*, 2:650.

27   Eric Bentley, *Life of Drama* (New York: Atheneum, 1967), 179–80. The following season reversed the downward trend in New York with a powerful and historic Shakespearean array: E. H. Sothern's *Hamlet*, Richard Mansfield's *Henry V*, and Sarah Bernhardt's *Hamlet* in rapid succession (Brown, *History of the New York Stage*, 3:530–31).

28   Winter, *Other*, 303–4.

29   Ibid., 307.

30   Ibid., 214–15.

31   Clement Scott, "Clement Scott's Prophecy," unidentified book published c. 1899, 268–69, in loose scrapbook, BRTC.

32   That play was *The Master Builder* (Bordman, *American Theatre*, 456; 443–63). For other hostile contemporary opinion about Ibsen see "The Theatres," *New York Commercial Advertiser*, January 18, 1900, 7, and Edward A. Dithmar, "At the Play and with the Players," *New York Times*, January 21, 1900, 2:16.

33   W. J. Henderson, "The Business of a Theatre," *Scribner's* 25 (March 1899): 308; Wells Hawks, "How Theatres Are Managed. No. 1. The Box Office Man," *Theatre* (New York) No. 38 (April 1904): 90.

34   Kaneo, *Sadayakko*, 54; "The Japanese Players," *NYDM*, March 17, 1900, 15.

35   Kaneo, *Ōbei*, 44; Kaneo, *Sadayakko*, 54.

36   "Pari ni okeru Nihon kabuki oyobi engeki hyōban" [Comments on Japanese kabuki and plays in Paris], *Yomiuri shimbun*, April 8, 1900, in Shirakawa, 313–14.

37   "Kawakami ichiza yōkō nisshi," *Miyako shimbun*; Kaneo, *Ōbei*, 44; Kaneo, *Sadayakko*, 54. "Shipping and Foreign Mails," *New York Times*, April 28, 1900, 10; Kaneo, *Ōbei*, 44; "Steamship Company Atlantic Transport Line," advertisement, *NYDM*, May 5, 1900, 9; "Cunard Line," advertisement, *New York Times*, April 27, 1900, 15; Baedeker, *United States*, xix.

38   Fujii, *Jiden*, 171, Kaneo, *Sadayakko*, 54. Kawakami's words: "konnan, kutsū, zetsubō, kikatsu."

39   "Tsugi wa Kawakami" [Next for Kawakami], *Tōkyō asahi shimbun*, July 7, 1900, in Shirakawa, 317.

40   Ibid., 41. I could not find an original English-language source. The peculiar preciseness of the quotation suggested that Kawakami made it up.

41   Yanagi, *Shimpa no rokujūnen*, 167.

42   Yamaguchi, *Joyū*, 93; also Kaneo, *Sadayakko*, 54–55.

43   Kaneo, *Sadayakko*, 54.

44   Fujii, *Jiden*, 175.

45   The generic word for the comedy genre, *kigeki*, was only beginning to come into general use.

46   Fujii, *Jiden*, 171–74.

47   Yone[jirō] Noguchi, "Sada Yacco," *NYDM*, February 17, 1906, 11.

Chapter 35

1   Kaneo, *Ōbei*, 44.

2   "Player People," *Boston Post*, January 19, 1900, 7; "Our London Letter," *NYC*, June 23, 1900, 374; "The Criterion," *Stage* (June 20, 1901): 12; "Lyceum. Signora Eleonora Duse," advertisement, *Times* (London), May 14, June 10 and 7, 1900, 8; Brereton, *Lyceum*, 313–16.

3   Kaneo, *Ōbei*, 45; Kaneo, *Sadayakko*, 56–58; "Kawakami ichiza Eikoku ni tsuku" [The Kawakami troupe arrives in England], *Miyako shimbun*, June 24, 1900, in Shirakawa, 317. The Coronet Theatre, almost unchanged, was still in business as a second-run movie house in the 1990s and later became an active multiplex (author's observation).

4   Nicoll, *History*, 28–29.

5   Knepler, *Gilded*, 228–34.

6   "The Coronet," *Stage* (June 14, 1900): 15.

7   "Plays and Players," *Sunday Times* (London), May 27, 1900, 6; Kaneo, *Ōbei*, 45–46; Kaneo, *Sadayakko*, 58–59; P. C., "The Theatres," *Speaker* (June 9, 1900): 270; "Dramatic Gossip," *Athenæum* (May 26, 1900): 668.

8   "Japanese Plays at the Coronet Theatre," *Times* (London), June 13, 1900, 7; "Coronet," advertisement, *Era*, June 9, 1900, 14. *Dorothy*, first performed in 1886 and then sustained by several touring companies, had become the longest running musical production in nineteenth century Britain (Gänzl, *British*, 40, 309, 737).

9   Lady Colin Campbell, "A Woman Walks," *World* (June 13, 1900): 13–14.

10   Ibid.

11   Ibid., 14.

12   "Plays and Players," *Sunday Times* (London); Kaneo, *Sadayakko*, 58–59, 65.

13   "Japanese Plays at the Coronet Theatre," *Times*.

14   Kesa's *koto* solo may also have been performed as part of this play in America.

15   "Japanese Plays at the Coronet Theatre," *Times*.

16   "Kawakami ichiza Eikoku ni tsuku," *Miyako shimbun*; Grein, *Premières*, 252; Max Beerbohm, *Around Theatres* (New York: Knopf, 1930; reprint New York: Taplinger, 1969), 1:91; P. C., "The Theatre. Kawakami at the Coronet," *Speaker* (June 9, 1900), 270; "Japanese Plays at the Coronet Theatre," *Times*.

17   Lady Colin Campbell, "A Woman Walks," *World*.

18   For a more extensive survey of London reviews, see Berg, "Sada Yacco in London and Paris," 348–65.

19   Grein, *Premieres*, 252, 253.

20   Martin Esslin, *An Anatomy of Drama* (New York: Hill and Wang, 1977), 88–89.

21   Kaneo, *Ōbei*, 45–46.

22   "Dramatic Gossip," *Athenæum* (June 16, 1900): 764.

23 Brereton, *Life*, 2:284–86; "Musical and Theatrical Gossip: The Japanese Players," *Sketch* 35 (July 24, 1901): 36.

24 Kaneo, *Sadayakko*, 54–55; Kaneo, *Ōbei*, 45–46.

25 Kaneo, *Ōbei*, 46; Kaneo, *Sadayakko*, 61–62, 66; also Inoue, *Kawakami*, 150; Yanagi Keitarō, *Kawakami*, 11.

26 "Court Chronicle," *Queen* (July 7, 1900): 14; "The Court Journal," *Court Journal* (June 30, 1900): 932; Fournier, *Kawakami*, 31.

27 "The Foreign Stage. Paris," *NYDM*, July 7, 1900; 6.

28 Kaneo, *Sadayakko*, 71.

29 Kaneo, *Ōbei*, 47–48; "Le Monde et la Ville. Salons," *Le Figaro* (Paris), July 1, 1900, 2.

30 Richard Mandell, *Paris 1900: The Great World's Fair* (Toronto: University of Toronto, 1967), xi.

31 Romein, *Watershed*, 296–98.

32 *Exposition Paris, 1900* (London: Heineman, 1900), 422–25; Alfred Picard, *Exposition universelle international de 1900 à Paris* (Paris: Nationale, 1903), 7:228–36.

33 Paul Morand, *1900 A.D.* (Paris: Flammarion, 1931), 64, 77, 96–97, 102–3.

34 *Guide pratique du visiteur de Paris et de l'Exposition* (Paris: Hachette, 1900), 357–59; Berg, "Sada Yacco in London and Paris," 370–71.

35 Boyd, *Paris*, 531–34; "Japan's Exhibit in Paris," *Chicago Inter Ocean*, August 6, 1899, n.p.; Albert Quantin, *L'Exposition du siècle* (Paris: Monde Moderne, 1900), 199, 350; "La japonais," *Le Figaro* (Paris), September 12, 1900, 3; Romein, *Watershed*, 303–4. Japan had participated in international expositions since 1867 when its exhibits were sponsored by the pre-Meiji shogunate government. Japanese performance arts on this first occasion were represented by three dancing geisha (Miyaoka, *Ikoku*, 29–31; 100–2).

36 Burton Benedict, *The Anthropology of World Fairs* (Berkeley: University of California Press, 1982), 28, 52–53; Alfred Picard, *Exposition universelle international de 1900 à Paris*, 7:228–36; *L' Exposition illustrée* (Paris: Montegredien, 1900), n.p.; R. S., "The Exposition Theatres," *New York Times*, September 16, 1900, 18; Albert Quantin, *L'Exposition du siècle* (Paris: Monde Moderne, 1900), 359–63; René Maizeroy, "La rue de Paris," *Théâtre* (Paris) (July 1900): 19–23.

37 "Side Shows at the Paris Exhibition," *NYDM*, July 21, 1900, 3.

38 The theatre was also called Théâtre Loïe Fuller and, in Japanese, Roi Fūrū-za (Loïe Fuller Theatre).

39 "Small Talk of the Week," *Sketch*, 30 (May 23, 1900): 196; "Paris Briefs," *NYDM*, July 24, 1900, n.p.; "In the Theatrical Way," *New York Sun*, June 12, 1900, 7.

40 "Our European Letter," *NYC*, July 14, 1900, n.p.

41 Paul Morand, *1900 A.D.*, 65.

42 Margaret Haile Harris, *Loie Fuller, Magician of Light* (Richmond: Virginia Museum, 1979), 16; Bordman, *American Musical*, 115.

43 Amy Koritz, "Moving Violations: Dance in the London Music Hall, 1890–1910," *Theatre Journal* 42:4 (December 1990): 420; Walter Sorell, *Dance in Its Time* (New York: Columbia University Press, 1986), 297–302.

44 Romein, *Watershed*, 522, citing A. Moeller von den Bruck, *Das Variété* (Berlin, 1902), 2:167; Clement Scott, "'Ballet! Beauty! Brains!' Exclaims Clement Scott," *New York Herald*, January 28, 1900, 4:10.

45 Bernard Champigneulle, *Art Nouveau*, trans. Benita Eisler (Woodbury, New York: Barrow's, 1976), 207.

46 Banta, *Imagining*, 625–31.

47 Takahashi, "Zadankai," 79–80.

48 Quoted by Nesta Macdonald in "Isadora Reexamined: Lesser-Known Aspects of the Great Dancer's Life: Part 12: Paris and After, 1900–1904," *Dance* 51 (August 1977): 42.

49 Margaret Haile Harris, *Loie Fuller, Magician of Light* (Richmond: Virginia Museum, 1979), 36–93.

50   Sally R. Sommer, "The Stage Apprenticeship of Loie Fuller," *Dance Scope* 12 (Winter 1977–78): 23–34.

51   Gautier, *Les musiques*. 21. Utility player Takanami Sadajirō, who previously performed both male and female minor roles, now took the onnagata part of Orihime in *The Geisha and the Knight*. The deceased Maruyama had originated Orihime in America, but after his death, apprentice Watanabe Toichi who quit in New York sometimes assumed the role. An unidentified "Kitamura" was credited in the Orihime role at the Bijou and Coronet Theatres. Kitamura may have been Kawakami's equivalent of "George Spelvin" as well as a subtle homage to Kitamura Rokurō who was the most famous onnagata of the New Theatre back in Japan. In *Jingorō*, Takanami continued to play the wife, a role he first assumed in New York.

52   Fujii, *Jiden*, 151. The theatre capacity was five hundred.

53   Ibid., 150–53; Kaneo, *Ōbei*, 48–49; Takahashi, "Zadankai," 77. On some weekends, there were as many as four performances a day, with each show reduced to as little as thirty-five or fifty minutes by condensing the plays.

54   Grand Guignol was a new theatre troupe in Paris with a popular style that specialized in horror, blood, brutality, suspense, and occasionally farce.

55   Kaneo, *Ōbei*, 48–49; Fujii, *Jiden*, 152; "Pari no seppuku" [Seppuku/harakiri in Paris], *Niroku shimbun*, November 9, 1900, in Shirakawa, 332–33; Judith Gautier, *Les musiques bizarres de l'Exposition* (Paris: Enoch, 1900), 22. Killing off historical personage Morito in this *Kesa* episode so early in his long life was like George Washington freezing to death at Valley Forge.

56   Fujii, *Jiden*, 152.

57   Kaneo, *Ōbei*, 49–50; also Kaneo, *Sadayakko*, 74.

58   "Pari no Kawakami ichiza" [The Kawakami troupe in Paris], *Chūō shimbun*, September 2, 1900, in Shirakawa, 328; Fournier, *Kawakami*, 13; Hagii, *Shimpa*, 38.

Chapter 36

1   Henri Fouquier, "Sada Yacco," *Théâtre* (Paris) (October 1900): 2:9.

2   For instance, see, Jean-Jacques Tschudin, "The French Discovery of Traditional Japanese Theatre," in Scholz-Cionca, *Japanese*, 43–44, 57.

3   Symons, *Plays*, 89.

4   Gay Morris, "La Loie," *Dance* 51 (August 1977): 39; "The Japanese at the Criterion," *Pall Mall Gazette*, June 20, 1901, 9.

5   Adolphe Brisson, "Promenades et visites à l'Exposition: Madame Sada Yacco," *Le Temps*, August 1, 1900, 4–5.

6   Camille Mauclair, "Sada Yacco et Loïe Fuller," *Revue Blanche* (October 15, 1900): 278.

7   Émile Verharren, "Chronique de l'Exposition," *Mercure de France* No. 131 (December 1900): 782.

8   Arsène Alexandre, "Pantomimes Japonaises," *Théâtre* (Paris) (September 1900): 18.

9   André Gide, "Lettre à Angéle," *Hermitage* 11 (November 1900): 390. For an extensive survey of French critical reception, see Berg, "Sada Yacco in London and Paris," 375–94.

10   Holmes, *Travelogues*, 2:230.

11   Fournier, *Kawakami*, 13; "The Foreign Stage. Paris," *NYDM*, September 29, 1900, 7; Nesta Macdonald, "Isadora Reexamined: Lesser-Known Aspects of the Great Dancer's Life: Paris and After, 1900–1904," *Dance* 51 (August 1977): 43.

12   Robert Horville, "The Stage Techniques of Sarah Bernhardt," in Eric Salmon, ed., *Bernhardt and the Theatre of Her Time* (Westport, Connecticut: Greenwood, 1984), 58; also Gerda Taranov, *Sarah Bernhard: The Art within the Legend* (Princeton: Princeton University Press, 1972), 90, 92.

13   Taranov, *Sarah Bernhardt*, 89–90.

14   Symons, *Plays*, 88.

15   Fournier, *Kawakami*, 34.

16   Stoullig, *Annals: 1900*, 191, 202.

17   Gawain, "The Foreign Stage. London," *NYDM*, July 6, 1901, 20. The quoted material was reporter Gawain's language, not Kawakami's.

18   Sauter, *Theatrical*, 130. Gerda Taranov in *Sarah Bernhardt*, 207–8, listed thirty Bernhardt plays with death scenes.

19   Morand, *1900 A.D.*, 95.

20   André Gide, "Lettre à Angèle," *Hermitage* 11 (November 1900): 390–92.

21   Paul Klee, *The Diaries of Paul Klee*, 109–10, 86–87; also Felix Klee, *Paul Klee: His Life and Work in Documents* (New York: Braziller, 1962), 93; Nello Ponente, *Klee*, trans. James Emmons (Lausanne: Skira, 1960).

22   Vincent Cronin, *Paris on the Eve: 1900–1914* (New York: St. Martin's, 1990), 36–37, 164–65.

23   Colta Feller Ives, *The Great Wave: The Influence of Japanese Woodcuts on French Prints* (New York: Metropolitan Museum of Art, 1974), 9.

24   Anne Leslie, *Rodin: Immortal Peasant* (New York: Prentice-Hall, 1937), n.p.; Judith Claudel, *Auguste Rodin: l'oeuvre et l'homme* (Bruxelles: Librarie Nationale d'art et d'historie, 1908), 92, 123; *Exposition Paris, 1900* (London: Heineman, 1900), 422–25.

25   Takahashi, "Zadankai," 79.

26   Sawada Suketarō, *Little Hanako* (Nagoya: Chūnichi, 1984, 22–64). Hanako was Fuller's subsequent endeavor to continue her Sadayakko show business success.

27   H. Montgomery Hyde, *Oscar Wilde: A Biography* (New York: Farrar, Strauss, and Giroux, 1975), 361–63; Oscar Wilde, *Letters*, ed. Rupert Hart-Davis (London: Hart-Davis, 1962), 829–31.

28   Oscar Wilde, *Letters*, ed. Hart-Davis, 120, also 119–24.

29   Dorée Duncan et al., *Life into Art* (New York: Norton, 1993), 38; also Nesta Macdonald, "Isadora Reexamined: Lesser-Known Aspects of the Great Dancer's Life; Part 12: Paris and After, 1900–1904," *Dance* 51 (August 1977): 43; Nancy Lee Chalfa Ruyter, *Reformers and Visionaries: The Americanization of the Art of the Dance* (New York: Dance Horizons, 1979), 41, 43; Deborah Jowitt, *Time and the Dancing Image* (Berkeley: University of California Press, 1989), 90–91.

30   Isadora Duncan, *My Life* (New York: Liveright, 1927), 68–69; also Victor Seroff, *The Real Isadora* (New York: Dial, 1971), 40.

31   Peter Kurth, *Isadora: A Sensational Life* (Boston: Little, Brown, 2001), 71.

32   Fredricka Blair, *Isadora* (New York: MacGraw-Hill, 1986), 40.

33   Ruyter, *Reformers and Visionaries*, 37–39; also Deborah Jowitt, *Time and the Dancing Image*, 80.

34   Walter Terry, *Isadora Duncan: Her Life, Her Art, Her Legacy* (New York: Dodd, Mead, 1963), 150; Julie Ince Thompson dance performance, "To Dance Is to Live: Isadora Duncan," MIT Kresge Little Theatre, March 22, 1991.

35   Isadora Duncan, *Isadora Speaks* (San Francisco: City Lights, 1981), 52.

36   Deborah Jowitt, *Time and the Dancing Image*, 116–17, 345; Elizabeth Kendall, *Where She Danced* (New York: Knopf, 1979), 47.

37   Ruth St. Denis, *An Unfinished Life* (New York: Harper, 1939), 40.

38   Elizabeth Kendall, *Where She Danced*, 40–41, 48, 81. Before she arrived in Paris, Ruth St. Denis completed a London engagement in Belasco's *Zaza*, where she danced a conventional solo and spoke a few lines. In her later career in modern dance, other exotic influences, particularly Egypt and India, dominated.

39   Bordman, *American Musical*, 145.

40   "Society to Hear the 'Rubaiyat,'" *Boston Globe*, January 31, 1900, 4; also "The 'Rubaiyat' Danced and Gestured," *Boston Evening Record*, February 1, 1900, 6.

41   Isadora Duncan, *My Life*, 94–99; Fuller, *Fifteen*, 223–31; Dorée Duncan et al., *Life into Art*, 43.

42   Ibid., 47. Despite her affiliation with Belasco, St. Denis had no known direct connection with his productions of *Madame Butterfly*.

43   Ruth St. Denis, *An Unfinished Life*, 46. St. Denis, like Duncan, had extensive training in Delsarte gestural language as a young actress.

44   Gautier, *La musique bizarres*.

45   Ibid., 5–6.

46   Ibid., 5.

47   Judith Gautier, *Les parfums de la pagode* (Paris: Charpentier, 1919); "Kabuki nikki," *Kabuki* (May 1901), 65.

48   Berg, "Sada Yacco in London and Paris," 389–90; Baird Hastings, "The Denishawn Era (1914–1931)," *Dance Index* 1 (June 1984): 91; Elizabeth Kendall, *Where She Danced*, 89; "Miss Ruth St. Denis in Poetic Play-Dances," *Town and Country*, March 29, 1913, 47. St. Denis considered (perhaps mistakenly) her "O-Mika," to be more of a nō dance. In America, she often performed with inexperienced Japanese males because she valued their racial ambience more than their acting or dancing abilities.

49   Deborah Jowitt, *Time and the Dancing Image*, 128 fn, 131, 138. The performances of St. Denis's troupe in Japan encouraged the beginning of modern (Western) dance there.

50   Ibid., 123–238.

51   Joanna Richardson, *Judith Gautier: A Biography* (New York: Watts, 1987), 152–59, 176–78.

52   Miner, *Japanese*, 68; Richardson, *Judith Gautier*, 223–27, 284.

53   Richardson, *Judith Gautier*, 152, 178.

54   Judith Gautier and Saionji Kimmochi, trans., *Poëms de la libellule* (Paris: Gillot, 1885); Katō, *History*, 89.

55   Richardson, *Judith Gautier*, 152–54. It had a one-week run in New York. "Ruby" was supposedly an English translation of the courtesan's "Japanese" name. Numerous foreign authors of works set in Japan named their characters with "translations" of Japanese names; hence Madame Butterfly for Cho-Cho; Madame Chrysanthème for O-Kiku; Sir Big-Rock for Ōishi in the *Chūshingura* of Edward Greey's *The Loyal Ronins* (New York: Putnam's Sons, 1880); and Lotus Blossom in the 1950s novel, play, and film, *Teahouse of the August Moon*.

56   "Orientalism at Daly's. 'Heart of Ruby,'" unidentified New York newspaper, January 15, 1895, in clipping file: The Heart of Ruby, BRTC; "Music and Drama," *Boston Evening Transcript*, May 3, 1895, n.p.

57   Kubota Onore (a.k.a. Beisai), "Pari no Kawakami shibai" [Kawakami's plays in Paris], *Yomiuri shimbun*, August 31 and September 1, 2, and 4, 1900, in Shirakawa, 324–27.

58   Kubota's pejorative descriptions were accurate but irrelevant to the reception of Kawakami's productions in Europe.

59   Toita Yasuji, *Engeki gojūnen* [Fifty years of theatre] (Jiji Tsūshinsha, 1955), 36.

60   "Zai Parî Kawakami yori," [From Kawakami in Paris], *Yomiuri shimbun*, December 3, 1900, in Shirakawa, 333–35.

61   Hagii, *Shimpa*, 38–45, 50–51. This was probably scenery that Yoshida and Nakagawa painted in Boston.

62   Hokuō, "Kawakami Sadayakko: Berugii yori" [From Belgium: Kawakami Sadayakko], *Yomiuri shimbun*, December 29, 1900, in Shirakawa, 336–38.

63   Kaneo, *Ōbei*, 51.

64   This film apparently survived the Expo and was shown in Tokyo after 1908 with the title *Pari no Nihongeki* [Japanese play in Paris] (Tanaka Jun'ichirō, *Nihon eiga hattatsu shi* (Chūō Kōronsha, 1957), 1:177–76). This *Pari no Nihongeki* may also have been another film shot in December 1907 when Kawakami and Sadayakko were again in Paris. Years ago, I saw a listing of a "Japanese sword fighting film" in a c.1903 Pathê catalog. Unable to subsequently locate this publication or any reference to it, I assume it has been lost in computerization projects at the NYPLLC.

65 Miller, *Yomigaeru*, record cut 1.

66 Ibid., 3, 6, 7, 8, 13, 18, 22, 24, 25, and 26. Apparently no authentic recordings of Kawakami's voice have survived, but in these imitations one can try to guess what he sounded like.

67 Ibid., 11, 16, and 23.

68 Ibid., cuts 4, 6, 7, 12, 22 24, 25, and 26.

69 Ibid., cut 12. "Miya sama Miya sama" in *The Mikado*.

70 Ibid., cuts 3, 8, 13, and 18.

71 Ibid., cuts 9, 20, 21, and 27.

72 Ibid., cuts 6, 8, 14. 24, 25, and 26.

73 Ibid., cuts 2, 5, 10, 15, 17, and 28.

74 Ibid,, cuts 2, 5, 9, 10, 15, 17, 20, 21 and 28. Kineya and Fujita were the most experienced theatre professionals in the troupe.

75 Miller, *Yomigaeru*, booklet, n.p. Earlier in March 1900, when New York theatrical photographer Byron took publicity pictures at the Berkeley Lyceum, Kawakami was similarly absent in several so others appeared in his roles (Scrapbook: "Plays to June 1905," MWEZ + n.c. 297, pp. 99–101, BRTC; Berkeley Lyceum, New York, program, March 1, 1900.)

76 Berliner Gramophone made these recordings for commercial release in Europe and probably in Japan, but they were not widely distributed. Nine decades later, they were discovered in a British archive and processed for commercial CD release by Toshiba EMI in 1997. With the limits of recording technology in 1900, each piece was only a few minutes long.

77 *Kowairo* imitations were also individual acts in the small variety theatres (*yose*) (Anderson, "Spoken," 270–71).

78 Jean Schopper, "Amusements of the Paris Exposition," *Century* 60 (August 1900): 483–95; Albert Quantin, *L'Exposition du siècle* (Paris: Monde Moderne, 1900), map n.p.; "L'Exposition," *Le Figaro* (Paris), July 8 and August 15, 1900, 5; "Programme des theatres," *L'Intransigeant* (Paris), August 4, October 15, and November 2, 1900, 4; Berg, "Sada Yacco in London and Paris," 371–72.

79 *Guide pratique du visiteur de Paris et de l'Exposition* (Paris: Hachette, 1900), 361–64; Mandell, *Paris*, 69.

80 *L'art theatral* (Paris: Pariset, 1901), n.p.; *Harper's Guide to Paris and the Exposition of 1900* (New York: Harper's, 1900), 186–88.

81 "L'Exposition: Le fète de l'Elysee," *Le Figaro*, August 19, 1900, 3.

82 Takahashi, "Zadankai," 78; Kaneo, *Ōbei*, 57.

83 The Exposition opened April 14 and closed November 12, 1900.

84 Kaneo, *Ōbei*, 55. Kawakami's numbers suggested that the troupe did not always perform two plays at each performance and did not perform three performances every day.

85 Ibid., 51–55. According to the contract, if they were held over beyond the initial period, the troupe's fee rose to $1,500 a week. Unlike their Théâtre de la Loïe Fuller schedule, they were to play no more than six evening and two matinee performances a week.

86 Ibid., 57; Hokuō, "Geijutsu Kyōkai ni okeru Kawakami ichiza" [From Belgium: the Kawakami troupe at the Arts Association], *Yomiuri shimbun*, December 28, 1900, in Shirakawa, 335–36.

87 Kaneo, *Ōbei*, 58–59; Kawatake Shigetoshi, *Nihon engeki bunka shiwa*, 250.

88 Fujii, *Jiden*, 174.

89 Kaneo, *Ōbei*, 60.

90 Fournier, *Kawakami*, 38–39.

91 [Ihara] Seiseien, "Kichō seru Kawakami Otojirō" [Kawakami Otojirō returns to Japan], *Kabuki* (March 1901): 59–60. Ihara Seiseien was chief critic of the new monthly *Kabuki* and a leading advocate of theatrical *literary* reform.

92   Shirakawa, *shimbun*, 10; Miyake Shūtarō, *Engeki*, 91; Tsubouchi, *Kokugeki*, 414; Fujii, *Jiden*, 172–73; Ihara, *Meiji*, 673; Inoue, *Kawakami*, 85–86. The list is an aggregation of proposals and accomplishments over several years. Kawakami did not hope to realize all of these at any one time.

93   "Kabuki nikki" [Kabuki diary], *Kabuki* (March 1901): 68; Kaneo, *Ōbei*, 61–63; Fujii, *Jiden*, 175; "Haiyū gakkō no setsuritsu" [Establishing a school for actors], *Miyako shimbun*, March 6, 1901, in Shirakawa, 353.

94   Fujii, *Jiden*, 172–73.

95   "Kōbe Aioi-za ni okeru Kawakami engeki no keikyō"[Viewing Kawakami's plays at the Kobe Aioi-za], *Miyako shimbun*, February 8, 1901, in Shirakawa, 351; Miyake Shūtarō, *Engeki*, 91.

96   Ihara, *Kabuki*, 8:67; Matsunaga. *Kawakami*, 181.

97   Ōsaka Asahi-za no nyūjōryō [Admission prices at the Osaka Asahi-za], *Miyako shimbun*, February 7, 1901, in Shirakawa, 350; "Kōbe Aioi-za ni okeru Kawakami engeki no keikyō," *Miyako shimbun*; "Kabuki nikki," *Kabuki* (March 1901), 67–70; Akiba, *Nihon*, 1:378; Ihara, *Meiji*, 673; Ogawa, *Nihon*, 115.

Chapter 37

1   Apparently finding he needed stronger acting support, Kawakami called Yamamoto to join him for the tour of Europe ("Kawakami ichiza" [The Kawakami troupe], *Miyako shimbun*, March 24, in Shirakawa, 357; "Kawakami no ikkō" [The Kawakami troupe], *Miyako shimbun*, March 26, 1902, in Shirakawa, 361; Yamaguchi, *Joyū*, 113). In 1917 Yamamoto began to appear in films. He had been in eighty-eight films when he died in 1939.

2   Raikichi died when he was 17.

3   Matsunaga, *Kawakami*, 183.

4   "Shinhaiyū yōkō kaobura" [Lineup of New Theatre actors going abroad], *Miyako shimbun*, March 26, 1901, in Shirakawa, 354.

5   Sadayakko had five relatives in this troupe.

6   The first Tsuru was now thirteen in California and was known as Tsuru Aoki.

7   Ōta Nami, 22; Hamada Tane (a.k.a Tani/Taka), 17; and Nishio Toshi, 17.

8   Inoue, *Kawakami*, 88; "Shinhaiyū yōkō no kaobura;" Yamaguchi, *Joyū*, 109.

9   "Shinhaiyū yōkō kaobura;" Kurota, *Kindaigeki*, 150; "Kawakami no shōsoku" [News of Kawakami], *Miyako shimbun*, July 13, 1901, in Shirakawa, 355. In these and other sources, the total number of persons reported in the group going to Europe was confusing. Sometimes either Raikichi or Doi was omitted. It was not clear whether another actor, Yamato Kikuo, 33, dropped out at some early point.

10   "Kawakami ichiza," *Miyako shimbun*, November 24, 1901, 357; Takahashi, "Zadankai," 82.

11   Criterion playdates: June 18–July 13; Shaftesbury: July 15–August 7. The small Criterion remains an active theatre today. The Shaftesbury of 1901 was destroyed in the Second World War bombing of London.

12   "The Criterion," *Stage* (June 20, 1901): 12.

13   Kawakami may have used more than one English language introducer in London.

14   "The Criterion," *Stage* (July 11, 1901): 12.

15   "Theatrical Gossip," *Era* (June 22, 1901): 12.

16   Wearing, *London*, 104–5, 108–9, 112–13.

17   Takahashi, "Zadankai," 82–83; "The Japanese Players," *Sketch* (July 24, 1901): 36; Wearing, *London*, 109; "Dramatic Gossip," *Athenæum* (July 20, 1901): 104; William Archer, "The Theatre," *World*, July 24, 1901, 28. *Sairoku* was not offered in London the previous year.

18   "The Playhouses," *Illustrated London News* (July 20, 1901): 84.

19   "Shaftesbury Theatre. A Japanese Shylock," *Daily Chronicle* (London), July 16, 1901, 6.

20 "Foreign Show News," *NYC*, July 27, 1901, 462; "Théâtres," *L'Intransigeant* (Paris), September 27, 1901, 3.

21 Charles Ricketts, *Self Portrait* (London: Davies, 1939), 60–62.

22 H.A.K., "Plays and Players," *Sunday Times* (London), July 7, 1901, 6.

23 "Ōshū ni okeru Kawakami ichiza" [The Kawakami troupe in Europe], *Chūō shimbun*, December 9, 1901, in Shirakawa, 257. In the fifteenth century, the historical Yoshinori was the sixth Ashikage shogun. The historical Yoshiaki, a hundred and forty years later, became the fifteenth and last Ashikaga (a.k.a. Muromachi) shōgun. The Ashikage forces earlier defeated Kusunoki, Kojima, and their emperor Godaigo to establish the sweeping power of shogunate rule. After the fall of Ashikage dominance, widespread internal warfare broke out until the Tokugawa shogunate achieved supremacy throughout the country in the late seventeenth century.

24 Ibid.; "The Theatre," *World* (July 10, 1901): 31; H.A.K., "Plays and Players;" "Criterion Theatre, *Times* (London), July 8, 1901, 3. Self-sacrifice by substituting for superiors frequently occurred in kabuki plays.

25 Yoshitsune was the central figure in the last third of *Heike monogatari* (Tales of the Heike) and the definitive protagonist of many subsequent oral and written narratives, nō, and kabuki plays.

26 Takahashi, "Zadankai," 86, 89; *Era* (July 6, 1901): 17.

27 "The Theatre," *World*.

28 "Our Captious Critic: A Japanese Rehearsal," *Illustrated Sporting and Dramatic News* (June 29, 1901): 729. "The Japs' at the Criterion," *Sketch* 34 (June 26, 1901), 400.

29 "The Theatre," *Speaker* (July 13, 1901: 412; "The Theatre," *World*.

30 "Criterion Theatre," *Times* (London), June 19, 1901, 10.

31 Several of these reviews were by the same reviewer but for different Kawakami bills.

32 Max Beerbohm, "Almond Blossom in Piccadilly Circus," *Saturday Review* (London) (June 22, 1901): 799.

33 "Japanese Plays and Players," *Era* (June 22, 1901): 11. Archer also disliked Fuller's "colour dances" as well as the kimono drapery that obscured Sadayakko's body.

34 "The Theatre," *World*, July 24, 1901, 28.

35 "Criterion Theatre," *Times* (London), June 19, 1901, 10. The Théâtre de l'Œuvre was inactive in 1901.

36 "Criterion Theatre," *Times* (London), July 8, 1901, 3.

37 Wearing, *London,* 104, 109; Shaftesbury Theatre, London, program, July 15, 1901.

38 Matsunaga, *Kawakami*, 183.

39 Ibid., 104, 112.

40 In different reviews, Orihime was identified as either the wife or the fiancé of Nagoya.

41 Wearing, *London,* 1:104, 108, 112; Stoullig, *Annales 1901*, 414.

42 "The Japanese at the Criterion," *Pall Mall Gazette* (June 21, 1901): 9; Gawain, "The Foreign Stage. London," *NYDM*, July 6, 1901, 20.

43 "The Foreign Stage. London," *NYDM*, July 27, 1901, 8.

44 "The Japanese at the Criterion," *Pall Mall Gazette* (June 21, 1901), 9; Gawain, "The Foreign Stage. London," *NYDM*, July 6, 1901, 20.

45 "Japs at Nottinghill," Sketch 30 (May 23, 1900): 222.

46 "Theatrical Gossip," *Era* (August 10, 1901): 12.

47 Stoullig, *Annales 1901*, 406. The Athénée, newly opened when Kawakami played there, was the future home of Louis Jouvet's masterful productions during the 1930's and 1940's. The theatre was still operating a century after Kawakami played there (author's observation).

48 "Rondon no Kawakami" [Kawakami in London], *Miyako shimbun*, August 27, 1901, in Shirakawa, 357; "Courrier des théâtres," *Le Figaro* (Paris), September 14, 1901, 4; Stoullig, *Annales 1901*, 402, 414.

49 "Théâtres," *L'Intransigeant* (Paris), September 27, 1901, 3; Stoullig, *Annales 1901*, 414.

50   "Theatrical Notes," *New York Herald* (Paris) October 11, 1901, 5. The interruption in Kawakami's Paris run resulted from a prior two-week hard booking at the Athénée of Jane Hading in *Les Demi-vierges* (Stoullig, *Annales 1901*, 406, 414).

51   Stoullig, *Annales 1901*, 414; also "Courrier des théatres," *Le Figaro* (Paris), October 25, 1901, 5; "Théatres," *L'Intransigeant* (Paris) October 31, 1901, 3; "Ōshū ni okeru Kawakami ichiza" [The Kawakami troupe in Europe], *Chūō shimbun*, December 9, 1901, in Shirakawa, 357–58.

52   *Hon'an* variations of *Camille*/*La dame aux camellias* were often titled *Tsubaki hime* ("The Camellia Princess" or "Princess of the Camellias") and were popular in many subsequent shimpa repertoires ("Teikoku-za no "Tsubaki hime"" ['Princess Camellia' at the Teikoku-za], *Ōsaka mainichi*, February 15, 1911, in Shirakawa, 490–91; "Kawakamiza Doitsu ni mukau" [The Kawakami troupe in Germany], *Miyako shimbun*, December 22, 1901, in Shirakawa, 358; Matsumoto, *Meiji engekiron*, 382–83).

53   Stoullig, *Annales 1901*, 281–82, 286; "Courrier des théatres," *Le Figaro* (Paris), September 26, 1901, 5. Bernhardt was also in *La dame aux camélias* in London while Kawakami was there (Wearing, *London*, 106).

54   "Loïe Fuller dansant. Scènes de théâtre japonais: Sada Yacco et Otojiro Kawakami, Théâtre de l'Athénée, Paris, 1901," photographs, in ICO Rondel, Département des Arts du spectacle, Bibliothèque nationale de France. This set of performance photographs showed Fuller dancing in a poorly lit set of neutral drapes and also in Kawakami's *Dōjōji* set.

55   Inoue, *Kawakami*, 79; Fujine, *Haru*, 147. Sadayakko's costume in this photograph was much more elaborate than the one she wore in the "Loïe Fuller dansant" photographs. Incorporation of national flags into geisha kimono patterns was a special salute when performances in Japan were tailored for specific foreign audiences (Clara Whitney, *Clara's Diary: An American Girl in Meiji Japan* [1879; reprint; Tokyo: Kōdansha International, 1979], 260–61; "Kabuki-za Beikoku kantai kangei engei" [Welcoming performance for the American naval squadron at the Kabuki-za], *Engei gahō* [December 1908], frontispiece).

56   *Leipziger Illlustrierten Zeitung*, n.d., n.p. at w w w.dig–muenchen.de/veranst.htm [2006].

57   "Kawakamiza Doitsu ni mukau" (The Kawakami troupe in Germany), *Miyako shimbun*, December 22, 1901, in Shirakawa, 358; "Central Theater," advertisement, *Berliner Tageblatt*, November 14, 1901, 2:2; "Sada Yacco in Berlin," *Berliner Tageblatt*, November 19, 1901, 2:2; "Theater und Musik," *Berlin Neue Preussiche Zeitung*, November 20, 1901, 1.

58   "Central Theater," advertisement, *Berliner Tageblatt*, December 8, 1901, 2:2.

59   Jelavich, *Berlin*, 36–39, 44–45. Also Frank Eberhardt, "Das Bunte [*sic*] Theater in der Köpenicker Straße," *Probleme*/*Projekte*/*Prozesse* (Berlin: Berlinsche Monatsechrift, 2000), 49–51. His goal was "ennoblement of vaudeville" in a form he described as "überbrettl." This term was literally translated as "over the boards" but the "über" meant "superior to" and "bretll" referred to the boards of the stage and what appeared on those boards. It would distinguish von Wolzogen's entertainment from variety theatres that offered conventional "tingel-tangel."

60   Ibid., 53–57, 23–24.

61   Eberhardt, "Das Bunte Theater," 51–56.

62   Malcolm MacDonald. *Schoenberg* (New York: Oxford University Press, 2008), 43–44; http//www de.wikipedia.org/wiki/Überbretti 05/04/2010).

63   Pantzer, *Japanischer*, lxxi-lxxii, 74–212.

64   "Ensemble des Kaiserl. Hoftheaters" in "Central Theater," advertisement, *Berliner Tageblatt*, November 14, 1901, 2:2 and "Japanischen Hoftheaters" in "Theatre und Vergnügungen," *Wien Neue Freise Presse*, February 1, 1902, 14. Earlier in Britain they were "the Celebrated Japanese Court Company" (Coronet Theatre, London, program, May 22, 1900).

65   Pantzer, *Japanischer*, 75, 80; Passage Theater, advertisement, *Berliner Tageblatt*, November 22, 1901, 2:2.

66   Jelavich, *Berlin*, 44–35; "E. von Wolzogens Buntes Theater," advertisement, *Berliner Tageblatt*, December 10 and 17, 1901, 2:2; Lisa Appignanesi, *The Cabaret* (New London: Yale University Press, 2004), 32–33.

67   Jelavich, *Berlin*, 50–51, 57; Eberhardt, "Das Bunte Theater," 55–56.

68   Matsunaga, *Kawakami*, 140; Yamaguchi, *Joyū*, 111–12; "E. von Wolzogens Buntes Theater," advertisement, *Berliner Tageblatt*, December 17 and 20, 1901, 2:2; "Seccessions Theater," advertisement, *Berliner Tageblatt*, January 12 and 14, 1902, 4:2.

69   [Kawakami] Sada Yakko [*sic*], koto solo, "Tsuru Kame" and [Kineya a.k.a. Sugibashi Kimisaburō], shamisen solo, "Osazuma," recordings in the Hornbostel Collection, Berlin Phonogramm-Archiv, duplicates in Federal Cylinder Project, Archive of Folk Culture, Library of Congress, Washington: AFS Nos. 10,054: B10 and B11; cylinders No. 4,076 and 4,077 respectively; original Nos. 24 and 25.

70   "Kawakami ikkō no raishin" [Letter from the Kawakami troupe], in *Miyako shimbun*, January 19, 1902, in Shirakawa, 361.

71   Pantzer, *Japanischer*, lxxiii. They played at the Theater an der Wien.

72   Fuller, *Fifteen*, 223, 231.

73   Pantzer, *Japanischer*, lxxxiv-lxxxv.

74   Ibid., 87–89; Yanagi, *Kawakami*, 11; Yamaguchi, *Joyū*, 120–21; Ozaki, *Joyū*, 14; Takahashi, "Zadankai," 87–89.

75   Hagii, *Shimpa*, 57–59.

76   Kurota, *Kindaigeki*, 171; Takahashi, "Zadankai," 89–92.

77   For a survey of 1900–02 reviews, see Peter Pantzer, "Sadayakko. Eine japanische Diva auf Tournee durch Österreich," *Beiträge zur Japanologie* 17 (1981): 61–91. See also "Sekaishū yūdan" [Report on a trip around the world], *Miyako shimbun*, August 24, 27, and 28, 1901, in Shirakawa, 365–67; Abel Mercklein, "Les dernières de Sada Yacco," *Le Figaro* (Paris), November 4, 1901, 4; Gustave Larroumet, "Chronique théatrale," *Le Temps* (Paris), September 23, 1901, 1–2; Camille Mauclair, "Sada Yacco et Loïe Fuller," *Revue Blanche* (October 15, 1900: 277–83; "Sada Yacco in Berlin," *Berliner Tageblatt*, November 19, 1901, 2:2; "Theater und Musik," *Berlin Neue Preussiche Zeitung*, November 20, 1901, 1–2; Theodor Herzl, "Feuilleton: Japanische Schauspiellnust," *Vienna Neue Freie Presse*, February 8, 1902, 1–2; Shionoya, *Cyrano*, 32–51; Ericka Fischer-Lichte, "The Reception of Japanese Theatre by the European Avant-Garde (1900–1930)," in Scholz-Cionca, *Japanese*, 37, 38.

78   Ferdinand Herold, "Les theatres," *Mercùre de France* (November 1901): 549–50; Abel Mercklein, "Les dernières de Sada Yacco," *Le Figaro* (Paris), November 4, 1900, 4; Stoullig, *Annales 1901*, 408–9.

79   In Peter Pantzer's definitive compilation of European coverage of Sadayakko and Kawakami in Europe, at least sixty items (largely reviews) use the phrase "japanische Duse" in describing Sadayakko (Pantzer, *Japanischer*, 14–1046).

80   "The Playhouses," *Illustrated London News* (June 22, 1901) 2; André Hallays, "Sada Yacco et Loïe Fuller," *L'Independance Belge Édition d'outre-mer* (Brussels), September 29, 1901, 1. The Hanlons' extravaganza *Superba* played Boston when the Kawakami troupe was there.

81   "Criterion Theatre," *Times* (London), June 19, 1901, 10.

82   Fuller, *Fifteen*, 207–8.

83   Ibid., 208–16; Sawada Suketarō, *Little Hanako* (Nagoya: Chūnichi, 1984), 11–39.

84   Loïe Fuller, "A Little Japanese Girl: A Play in One Act," typescript, London, c. 1907; NCOF p.v. 241, BRTC.

85   At the Neues Deutsches Theater.

86   At the Urania Színház (Theatre). Urania, Theater an der Wien, and the Neues Deutsches Theater (now the Státní Opera Praha [Prague State Opera] were all still operating in the late 1990's after various renovations (author's observations).

87   "Kawakami sekaishū yūdan" [Report on a trip around the world], *Miyako shimbun*, August 24, 1901, in Shirakawa, 364. Partially reported in "Vermischets," *Ost-Asien* (February 1902): 493; Dōmon, *Kawakami*, 148.

88   Kurota, *Kindaigeki*, 172.

89   Hagii, *Shimpa*, 37.

90   Ibid.; also Inoue, *Kawakami*, 89; Fujii, *Jiden*, 171–74.

91   Matsunaga, *Kawakami*, 188; Kurota, *Kindaigeki*, 172.

Chapter 38

1   For instance, Peter Pantzer, "Sadayakko. Eine japanische Diva auf Tournee durch Österreich," *Japanerin in Vergangenheit und Gegenwart* 17 (1981): 61–91. Pantzer's outstanding compilation in *Japanischer Theaterhimmel über Europas Bühnen* offers definitive coverage of the critical reception of Kawakami in Europe.

2   In an interview, Kawakami claimed he saw stage productions in Britain but mentioned no titles ("Otojiro Kawakami and Sada Yacco," *Era*, June 2, 1900, 8). His responses seem to have been more professional civility than based on firsthand experience.

3   Ericka Fischer-Lichte, "The Reception of Japanese Theater by the European Avant-Garde (1900–1930)," in Scholz-Cionca, *Japanese*, 31.

4   Fischer-Lichte, *Show*, 118.

5   Konstantin Rudnitsky, *Meyerhold the Director*, trans. George Petrov (Ann Arbor: Ardis, 1981), 22, 32–34; Edward Braun, *The Theater of Meyerhold: Revolution on the Modern Stage* (New York: Drama Book Specialists, 1979), 28; Juri Jelagin (Yuriĭ Yelagin), *Temnyĭ geniĭ* [Dark Genius] (London: Overseas Publishing, 1982), 80–83.

6   Noted by Braun in Meyerhold, *Meyerhold on Theater*, trans. Edward Braun, 98.

7   Braun, *Theater of Meyerhold*, 48.

8   Nikolai Volkov, *Meĭerkol'd* (Moscow: Academia, 1929), 2:51; also V. E. Meĭerk'old, *Stat'i, pis'ma, rechi, besedi* [Articles, letters, speeches, conversations] (Moscow: Iskusstvo, 1968), 2:84.

9   Meyerhold, *Meyerhold on Theater*, 141.

10   Meĭerk'old, *Stat'i, pis'ma, rechi, besedi*, 2:84; Eugenio Barba, "Meyerhold: The Grotesque, That Is, Biomechanics," in Barba, *Secret*, 154. Meyerhold referred to what he saw in the performances of both Sadayakko and the later Hanako.

11   Quoted in Eugenio Barba, "Meyerhold: The Grotesque," 157.

12   Meyerhold paraphrased in Eugenio Barba, "Meyerhold: The Grotesque," 156; Meyerhold, *Meyerhold on Theater*, 141.

13   Meyerhold, *Meyerhold on Theater*, 112 fn.

14   This was the 1928 tour of Ichikawa Sadanji and his kabuki actors.

15   Denis Bablet, *Edward Gordon Craig*, trans. Daphne Woodward (New York: Theater Arts, 1966), 41–42, 46–47, 178.

16   Wm. Barclay Squire, "Music. Purcell at Notting Hill," *Pilot*, March 30, 1901, 400. Craig was in London when Kawakami played there in 1900 and 1901 (Craig, *Index to the Story of My Days*, 103, 231–32; Edward Craig, *Gordon Craig: The Story of His Life* [New York: Knopf, 1968], 138).

17   Sang-Kyong Lee, "Edward Gordon Craig and Japanese Theater," *Asian Theater Journal* 17 (Fall 2000): 216.

18   Craig, *Henry Irving*, 76.

19   Edward Gordon Craig, "The Actor and the Über-marionette," *Mask*, April 1908, 5.

20 Ibid., 1–3; Gordon Craig, "Kingship," *Mask* (1914): 238–40. Craig's greatest interest in Japanese theater came after he began to concentrate on what he read about nō and not what he saw earlier in Kawakami.

21 Craig, "The Actor and the Über-marionette," 10.

22 J.v.H., "Foreign Notes: Amsterdam," *Mask* 11:2 (April 1908): 21.

23 Craig, *Index to the Story of My Days*, 213; Craig, *Henry Irving*, 203; W. D. King, "When Theater Becomes History: Final Curtains on the Victorian Stage," *Victorian Studies* 36 (Fall 1992): 56; Craig, "The Actor and the Über-marionette," 3–15.

24 Craig, "The Actor and the Über-marionette," 11.

25 Harry Graf Kessler, "Vorwort," in *Die Kunst des Theaters von E. Gordon Craig* (Berlin: Nachfolger, 1905), 4.

26 Tao [Edward Gordon Craig], "Japan: Tokio: Women in the Theatre" *Mask* (October 1910): 95–96.

27 Ibid., 96.

28 An actress "is but a little thing, a little picturesque atom" (Craig, "The Actor and the Über-marionette," 6).

29 Carlson, *The French Stage in the Nineteenth Century*, 213–14.

30 In 1908, an American adaptation of Humière's *Kesa* play appeared in New York as *The Flower of Yamato* (Bordman, *American Theater*, 625).

31 Quoted in Ericka Fischer-Lichte, "The Reception of Japanese Theater by the European Avant-Garde," 37–39.

32 John A. Henderson, *The First Avant-Garde: 1887–1894: Sources of the Modern French Theatre* (London: Harrap, 1973), 44, 46–49.

33 Antoine, *Le theatre*, 1:421. Antoine saw *Kosan, Kesa,* and *The Geisha and the Knight.*

34 Ibid., 1:420–21.

35 Edouard Gautheir, "'L'Honneur Japonais' Succès d'Odéon," *Bulletin de la Société Franco-Japonaise de Paris* 30 (1913): 47–58. The forty-seven *rōnin* of the historical incident and original play were reduced to eight in this play. The ending had a major alteration when the Japanese emperor himself excused the *rōnin* from compulsory *seppuku.* In history and drama, they all committed mass *seppuku* (William Leonard Schwartz, *The Imaginative Interpretation of the Far East in Modern French Literature: 1800–1925* (Paris: Champion, 1927), 174–75. An earlier version of *Chūshingura* in French was performed "under Japanese supervision" at the Paris Opera in 1879. The Japanese title was *Nihon bidan* [A venerable story of Japan] (Akiba, *Tōto*), 105–6.

36 Georg Fuchs, *Revolution in the Theatre*, trans. Constance Connor Kuhn (Port Washington, New York: Kennikat, 1972), 60. Original text in "Die Schauspieler," *Die Schaubühne der Zukunft* (Berlin: Schuster und Loeffler, 1905), 61–76.

37 Ibid.

38 Ibid., 49; also Fischer-Lichte, *Show*, 63.

39 Herman K. Doswald, "Hofmannsthal's Turn to Drama and the Theater," *Theatre Research International*, 6:1 (Winter 1980–81): 45–46. Hofmannsthal expressed his creative impasse in "The Letter of Lord Chandos" in *Selected Prose* (New York: Pantheon, 1952), 129–41.

40 Hugo von Hofmannsthal, "Über die Pantomime," in his *Die Berührung der Sphären* (Berlin: Fischer, 1931), 163–64; also Margret Dietrich, "The Far East—Its Reflection in and Influence on the European Theater," trans. Bindon Russell, *Theatre Research* 4 (1962): 191.

41 Herman K. Doswald, "Hofmannsthal's Turn to Drama and Theater," 46.

42 J. L. Anderson, "Representing the Musmé: Before and after Belasco's *Madame Butterfly*," subchapter cut from this Kawakami manuscript.

43 Henry Edward Krehbiel, *A Second Book of Operas* (Garden City, New York: Garden City, 1926), 186; Krehbiel, *Tribune*, October 15, 1916. Illica's co-librettist for *Madama Butterfly* was Giuseppe Giacosa.

44   Claudio Sartori, *Puccini* (Milano: Nouva Accademia, 1938), 277; Spike Hughes, *Famous Puccini Operas* (New York: Dover, 1959), 114.

45   Richard Specht, *Giacomo Puccini: The Man, His Life, His Work*, trans. Catherine Alison Phillips (New York: Knopf, 1933), 176; also Mosco Carner, *Puccini: A Critical Biography* (London: Duckworth, 1953), 138.

46   Arthur Groos, "Puccini's *Madame Butterfly*: The Sadayakko Connection," lecture with summary in *Abstracts of the 1997 Annual Meeting* (Chicago, Illinois: Association for Asian Studies, March 13–16, 1997).

47   Ibid. The scene that Puccini eliminated was set in the American Consulate and was Consul Sharpless's cautioning of Butterfly about liaisons with Americans. It was part of Long's original short story but was not in the final version of Belasco's play, although the opera tended to follow Long's story more closely than the play.

48   Stanley Applebaum, "Introduction," in *Puccini's Madama Butterfly*, Luigi Illica and Giuseppe Giacosa, librettists, trans. Stanley Appelbaum (New York: Dover, 1983), ix.

49   Reported in Arthur Groos, "Puccini's *Madame Butterfly*."

50   Appelbaum, "Introduction," in Puccini, *Madama Butterfly*.

51   Claudio Sartori, *Puccini* (Milano: Nouva Accademia, 1938), 277.

52   Groos, "Puccini's *Madame Butterfly*."

53   Léon Vallas, *Claude Debussy: His Life and Works*, trans. Maire and Grace O'Brien (London: Oxford University Press, 1933), 98, 113, 157.

54   Kimura Ki, *Kaigai ni katsuyaku shita Meiji josei* [Women of Meiji who were active overseas], (Shinbundō, 1963), 150–66, 169–72; Edward Lockspeiser, *Debussy: His Life and Mind* (New York: Macmillan, 1962), 1:113–16; Julian Phillipe, *The Triumph of Art Nouveau* (New York: Larousse, 1974), 143, 168; Takahashi, *zadankai*, 67.

55   Hagii, *Shimpa*, 47. Unlike their Japanese counterparts, Western scholars have placed less emphasis on the Japanese influence on Debussy.

56   Shimazaki Tōson, *Tōson zenshū* [Collected works of Tōson] (Chikuma Shobō, 1967), 6:204–7; Rimer, *Pilgrimages*, 11.

Chapter 39

1   Yanagi, *Shimpa*, 168; Matsunaga, *Kawakami*, 196.

2   Ihara, *Meiji*, 675–77.

3   Ihara, *Kabuki*, 508–10.

4   With insufficient information, I may not have accurately categorized all shows here or in Chapter 40. Note too that "production" has been defined throughout this study as one complete bill (show). Then, as now, almost every shimpa and kabuki *production* offered two or more plays (or parts of plays).

5   Yanagi, *Shimpa no rokujūnen*, 16–54. Because of conflicting data, none of these statistics should be be considered definitive. The total number of productions counted did not include repeat bookings or companies touring to other cities.

6   Ihara, *Meiji*, 674.

7   Okamoto, *Meiji*, 247; also Kawatake Shigetoshi, *Nihon engeki zenshi*, 866.

8   Tsubouchi, *History*, 186–188.

9   Kawai, *Onnagata*, 234–42; Hagii, *Shimpa*, 86–91.

10   Kawakami Otojirō, "Haiyū ni odori wa iranu," *Jiji shimpō*, January 30–31, 1903, in Shirakawa, 375–78.

11   Kawatake Toshio, *Kindai engeki*, 158; Kurata, *Kindaigeki*, 176–77, 183–89.

12   Kawatake Shigetoshi, *Gaisetsu*, 363–4; Machida Kashō, "Japanese Music and Dance," in Komiya, *Japanese*,

329–32, 426–33; Deborah Klens-Bigman, "Nihon Buyo Happyokai," *Journal of Dramatic Theory and Criticism* 13:2 (Spring 1999): 139–41.

13   Kawatake Toshio, *Kindai engeki*, 156; Matsunaga, *Kawakami*, 188; Matsumoto, *Meiji engekiron*, 430. *Kyōgen* and nō were outside Kawakami's concerns.

14   Marui, *Shimpa*, 37, 44; Kano, *Acting*, 107–8; "Shibai dayori" [Theatre news], *Yomiuri shimbun*, September 16, 1903, in Shirakawa, 410–11. *Shin Oseru*, in a pantomime style but with a little expository dialogue, was a partial parody of *Osero* (Tarōkan, *Shin Osero* [script], c. 1906, item *ro* 5/78 in Waseda). In the comedy *Onna tenka*, a "women's party" took over the Japanese government.

15   Akiba, *Nihon*, 263. Although the two *kanji* (characters) used to write *sei* and *geki* (drama) are usually pronounced "*seigeki*," Kawakami often preferred to voice that word as "*dorama*," a Japanese pronunciation of the English word "drama" ("Kawakami to dorama" [Kawakami and drama], *Miyako shimbun*, January 15, 1903, in Shirakawa, 374).

16   In the overall shimpa taxonomy, *seigeki* was only one form limited to the early 1900s and primarily to Kawakami.

17   Compare: John Gillies's essay, "Afterword: Shakespeare Removed: Some Reflections on the Localization of Shakespeare in Japan," in Minami, *Performing*, 238.

18   Kawakami productions for American and European audiences reduced Japanese dialogue and narration by increasing pantomimic business, accelerated pace by cutting and speeding up performances, made resolution of plots clearer, and intensified stage combat.

19   Miyake Shūtarō, *Engeki*, 92.

20   For a discussion of the literary development of both *hon'an* and direct translation of foreign originals, see Kawatake Toshio, *Kindai engeki*, 134–53; Yoshitake, *Kindai*, 1–3; Miller, *Adaptations*.

21   Toyoda, *Shakespeare*, 32–35.

22   Ibid., 108–9; Kawatake Toshio, *Nihon*, 252.

23   "Dark skin," is a relative term. See my discussion in chapter 5 of American perceptions of dark-skinned samurai in the 1860 Japanese embassy to the United States and darkness-coded theatrical makeup manufactured in America.

24   "Meiji-za nigatsu kōkyō no 'Osero'" (*Othello*, the February production at the Meiji-za), *Yomiuri shimbun*, February 3, 1903, in Shirakawa, 379.

25   For a discussion of how foreign names in *hon'an* were made into similar sounding Japanese names, see Miller, *Adaptations*, 95–96, 128–29.

26   The dialogue was somewhat conversational Japanese.

27   Yone[jirō] Noguchi, "Shakespeare in Japan," *Critic* 46 (March 1905): 231.

28   Ibid., 233.

29   Yoshitake, *Kindai*, 266–68. Iya Gōzō in *Osero* was a much more overripe (i.e., melodramatic) villain than the typical evil Iago in American nineteenth-century productions (Noguchi, "Shakespeare in Japan," 236).

30   Contending arguments: "The Staging of Shakespeare," in *Fortnightly Review*; H. Beerbohm Tree, (July 1, 1900): 52–66; William Poel (August 1, 1900): 355–56; W. Hughes Hallett (September 1, 1900): 504–19. Also Mazer, *Shakespeare*, 43–44, 49–52.

31   In order "to improve sightlines" in Euro-American scenography, sidewalls of interior rooms were usually set ("cheated") at oblique angles to an upstage wall. Japanese had independently developed a box set layout that was often placed in a larger setting of exterior space. Walls of Japanese interiors usually met at architecturally accurate right angles.

32   Akiba, *Nihon*, 1:422; [Ihara] Seiseien, "Meiji-za no Kawakami" [Kawakami at the Meiji-za], *Miyako shimbun*, February 14, 1903, n.p.; Matsumoto, *Meiji engekiron*, 433–34.

33   "Kawakami seigeki-ha no 'Osero'" [The *Othello* of the Kawakami *seigeki* faction], *Yomiuri shimbun*,

February 12, 1903, in Shirakawa, 381–82. Morizumi Gekka (a.k.a. Ichikawa Kumehachi) played O-Miya (Emilia) (Matsunaga, *Kawakami*, 190–91; "Shibai dayori," *Yomiuri shimbun*, February 13, 1903, in Shirakawa, 382).

34   One newspaper critic called the overall *Osero* style *"shizen"* (natural) ("Shibai dayori," *Yomiuri shimbun*, February 13, 1903, in Shirakawa, 382).

35   A sampling of the many opinions: "Meiji-za no 'Osero'" [*Othello* at the Meiji-za], *Kokumin shimbun*, February 10, 1903, in Shirakawa, 380–81; "Kawakami seigeki-ha no 'Osero'"; "Meiji-za nigatsu kōkyō no 'Osero'" [*Othello*, the February production at the Meiji-za], *Yomiuri shimbun*, February 3, 1903, in Shirakawa, 379; Matsumoto, *Meiji engekiron*, 433–40; "Tsubouchi no 'Osero' dan" [Tsubouchi's discussion of *Othello* and *Osero*], *Kabuki* (March 1903): 1–6; Kubota Beisen, "Kawakami no Osero" [Kawakami's *Othello*], *Kabuki* (March 1903): 13–14; Ueda Ryūson, "'Osero' no hon'an to gensaku" [The *Othello* adaptation and the original work], *Kabuki* (March 1903): 11–12.

36   Kawatake Toshio, *Nihon*, 390–91.

37   Murakami Takeshi, "Shakespeare and Hamlet in Japan: A Chronological Overview," in Yoshiko Ueno, ed., *Hamlet and Japan* (New York: AMS, 1995), 253; John Gillies, "Afterword: Shakespeare Removed: Some Reflections on the Localization of Shakespeare in Japan," in Minami, *Performing*, 246; also Andrea J. Nouryeh, "Shakespeare and the Japanese Stage," in Dennis Kennedy, ed., *Foreign Shakespeare: Contemporary Performance* (Cambridge: Cambridge University Press, 1993), 255–57, 260–68.

38   Doi Shunsho made the initial semi-translated adaptation for this *Merchant* (Ihara, *Meiji*, 674; Doi Shunsho, "'Māchanto ofu Venisu,' hōtei no ba" [*The Merchant of Venice* trial scene], holograph in "Kawakami Otojirō serifu nukigaki," item *ro* 19/61, at Waseda). Doi was the interpreter and stage manager for Kawakami's 1901–2 tour of Europe. He was a protégé of Tsubouchi Shōyō.

39   In Tokyo, the abbreviated *Māchanto* had six scenes, which may have been further reduced on tour to two ("Ōsaka no Kawakami ichiza" [The Kawakami troupe in Osaka], *Jiji shimpō*, February 5, 1904, in Shirakawa, 427).

40   Yamano, "Yokohama no Kawakamiza" [The Kawakami company in Yokohama], *Kabuki* (August 1903): 25–29; "Yokohama Kiraku-za no bon kōgyō seigekiha" [The *bon* (midsummer) performance of the *seigeki* group at the Yokohama Kiraku-za], *Miyako shimbun*, July 14, 1903, in Shirakawa, 403–4; also "Shibai dayori" [Theatre news], *Miyako shimbun*, June 3, 1903, in Shirakawa, 387.

41   Kawakami and Sadayakko may have seen Irving's *Merchant* again in London in 1900.

42   *"Māchanto ofu Enisu* ni tsuite Kawakami Otojirō no danwa" [Conversation with Kawakami Otojirō about *The Merchant of Venice*], *Kabuki* (July 1903): 14. Actress Morizumi Gekka played the Nerissa role in Tokyo, but on tour onnagata Kojima Bun'ei took the part ("Shibai dayori," *Miyako shimbun*, June 3, 1903, in Shirakawa, 387; Yamano, "Yokohama no Kawakamiza"). Shifts in casting female roles between actresses and male onnagata became a frequent Kawakami practice, although Sadayakko always had the leading female parts.

43   Kimura Kinnosuke, *Meiji-za monogatari* [The Meiji-za story] (Kabuki-za Shuppambu, 1928), 253.

44   Kawatake Shigetoshi, *Sōgō Nihon*, 248–49; "Shibai dayori," *Miyako shimbun*, June 3, 1903, in Shirakawa, 387.

45   Akiba, *Nihon*, 1:423–25; Marui, *Shimpa*, 34.

46   Ihara, *Meiji*, 674.

47   Kawatake Shigetoshi, *Nihon engeki zenshi*, 875.

48   "Gekikai no sakki," *Miyako shimbun*, July 10–28, 1903, in Shirakawa, 394–403. Reports on other shimpa vs *kyūha* (kabuki) discourses are in Shirakawa, 388–94, 404–10, and Matsumoto, *Meiji engekiron*, 451–56.

49   This is my interpretive summary of arguments that were not always explicit.

50   Matsumoto, *Meiji engekiron*, 451–52; Kawatake Shigetoshi, *Nihon engeki zenshi*, 876. An important shimpa

exception to the bipolar historical division–actually a countervailing force–was Ii Yōhō's and onnagata Kawai Takeo's *Chikamatu kenkyūgeki* [Chikamatsu study plays] project. (Akiba, *Tōto*, 362, 365–66).

51   In the 1930s, the revival of a reworked *Edo-jō akewatashi* was a success when young kabuki actors of the Zenshinza troupe performed the play (Japanese, *Theatre*, 200).

52   Sadayakko again played Sahoko, the *hon'an* name for Sapho.

53   "Ōsaka no Kawakami ichiza" [The Kawakami troupe in Osaka], *Jiji shimpō*, February 5, 1904, in Shirakawa, 425–28; "Yokohama Kiraku-za no bon kōgyō seigekiha," *Miyako shimbun*, July 14, 1903, in Shirakawa, 403–4; Yamano, "Yokohama no Kawakamiza," *Kabuki* (August 1903): 26–29; "Māchanto ofu [V]enisu ni tsuite: Kawakami Otojirō no danwa," *Kabuki* (July 1903) 10–11.

54   For a comprehensive discussion of *Hamuretto*, see Kawatake Toshio, *Nihon*, 204–42. The *Hamlet* story had cloaked appearances in Japan long before Kawakami. Throughout the latter nineteenth century, there were highly different *hon'an* in short narrative formats, in partial translations, and in kabuki plays borrowing parts of *Hamlet* (Kawatake Toshio, *Nihon*, 21–187. Also Murakami Takeshi, "Shakespeare and Hamlet in Japan," 252.

55   "Shibai dayori," *Kokumin shimbun*, October 30, 1903, 415; Kawatake Toshio, *Nihon*, 234; also "Hongō-za no 'Hamuretto'" [*Hamlet* at the Hongō-za], *Kabuki* (December 1903): 38–48; Akiba, *Nihon*, 421. On tours without Kawakami, Yamamoto Kaichi took the Hamlet part and an onnagata played Ophelia (Murakami Takeshi, "Shakespeare and Hamlet in Japan," 254).

56   Matsumoto, *Meiji engekiron*, 459–62; Kawatake Toshio, *Nihon*, 223–36; Kin'ei, "Hamuretto ni tsuite" [About *Hamlet*], *Kabuki* (December 1903): 38–48.

57   "Shibai dayori," *Kokumin shimbun*, October 30, 1903, in Shirakawa, 415.

58   Kayō, "Masago-za no Hamuretto" [*Hamlet* at the Masago-za], *Kabuki* (September 1907): 20; Kawatake Shigetoshi, *Nihon no engeki*, 169. Scenic backgrounds painted in Western realist, perspective styles had been tried and rejected by kabuki as early as 1879 (Kawatake Shigetoshi, *Nihon engeki zenshi*, 781; Yamamoto Hōsui, "Hongō-za no dōgu" [Scenery at the Hongō-za], *Kabuki* [December 1903]: 30–34).

59   Kawatake Toshio, *Nihon*, 235–37, 280.

60   Noguchi, "Shakespeare in Japan," 233.

61   Ibid., 231.

62   Yamagishi Kayō and Doi Shunsho, trans. *Shaō higeki Hamuretto* [Shakespeare's tragedy *Hamlet*] (Fūsambō, 1903), 3; also Kawatake Toshio, *Nihon*, 191, 209–10.

63   Kenneth Macgowan and William Melnitz, *The Living Stage: A History of the World Theatre* (Englewood Cliffs, New Jersey: Prentice-Hall, 1955), 323. For a sampling of similar misinterpretations, see Paul Arnold, *Le théâtre japonais* (Paris: l'Arche, 1957), 261; Earl Ernst, *The Kabuki Theatre*, 250–51; Zoe Kincaid, *Kabuki: The Popular Stage of Japan* (London: Macmillan, 1925), 345–46.

64   Kayō, "Masago-za no 'Hamuretto'"; Kawatake Toshio, *Nihon*, 242; Fujisawa [Kosetsu], "Kyōto ni okeru Kawakami no 'Hamuretto' hyō" [Critique of Kawakami's *Hamlet* in Kyoto], *Kabuki* (November 1904): 45–48; "Tsubouchi hakushi no 'Osero' dan" [Dr. Tsubouchi's discussion of *Osero/Othello*], *Kabuki* (March 1903): 1–6; Ueda Yūson, "'Osero' no hon'an to gensaku" [The *Othello* adaptation and the original play], *Kabuki* 34 (March 1903): 11–12; summarized in Kawatake Toshio, *Nihon*, 242–43.

65   Yamagishi Kayō and Doi Shunsho, trans. *Shaō higeki Hamuretto* [script], 1–2.

66   [Ihara] Seiseien, "Kangeki nichiroku" [Journal of plays seen], *Kabuki* (February 1910): 82.

67   Andrea J. Nouryeh, "Shakespeare and the Japanese Stage," 267. Motion picture director Kurosawa Akira preceded contemporary stage directors with his Shakespearean *hon'an* films: *Kumonosu-jō* (American title *Throne of Blood*, based on *Macbeth*) and *Ran* (based on *King Lear*).

68   Toyoda, *Shakespeare*, 111.

69   Ibid., 189, 243–44.

70   Ibid., 254–56, 261. A review in *Kabuki* compared the female *Hamuretto* favorably to a rival all-male shimpa production (Kayō, "Masago-za no 'Hamuretto,'" *Kabuki* [September 1907], 19–21). This Tokyo female troupe usually did kabuki plays but also drew on the growing number of shimpa scripts ("Misaki-za kembutsu" [Watching at the Misaki-za], *Kabuki* (March 1911): 80; Inoue, *Kawakami*, 94; Ihara, *Meiji*, 675; "Misaki-za no joyū no shimpa" [The shimpa plays of the Misaki-za actresses], *Kabuki* [October 1912]: 71; Kawatake Toshio, *Nihon*, 241–44; Toyoda, *Shakespeare*, 255). At the Misaki-za, actresses played major male roles, but the troupe sometimes hired a few males as onnagata. This female troupe also performed an abbreviated *hon'an* of *Timon of Athens* and *Merchant of Venice* (Minami Ryuta, "Chronological Table of Shakespeare Productions in Japan 1866–1994," in Sasayama, *Shakespeare*, 262–63).

71   Kawatake Toshio, *Nihon*, 203; Yamano, "Fukuiza no 'Yami to hikari'" ['Darkness and light' of the Fukui Troupe], *Kabuki* (September 1903): 35–38; Yanagi, *Shimpa no rokujūnen*, 33, 34, 38; Minami, "Chronological Table of Shakespeare Productions," 261–62; Urayama, *Nihon*, 105.

72   Minami, "Chronological Table."

73   Kawatake Toshio, *Nihon*, 243, 273–78.

74   Minami, "Chronological Table"; Murakami Takeshi, "Shakespeare and Hamlet in Japan," 253–58.

75   Tomita, *Nihon*, 24–26.

76   Ibid., 30–33; "Jidō kyōiku" [The education of children], *Miyako shimbun*, September 15, 1903, in Shirakawa, 410; "Shibai dayori," *Miyako shimbun*, October 2, 1903, in Shirakawa, 412; "Shintomi-za," *Jiji shimpō*, October 26, 1903, in Shirakawa, 413. *Ukare* was based on a Swedish story and *Kitsune* on a German (Kurata, *Kindai*, 200–3).

77   Tomita, *Nihon*, 49–5; Akiba, *Nihon*, 421. Japan has a long history of folk entertainment for children.

78   *Kitsune no saiban* characters were all animals. Kawakami was the Fox, actress Morizumi Gekka the Lion King, and Sadayakko the Lion Queen.

79   "Shibai dayori," *Miyako shimbun*, October 2, 1904, in Shirakawa, 412; "Otogi shibai" [Fairy tale plays], *Jiji shimpō*, January 6, 1902, in Shirakawa, 420–22; *Nihon jidō engeki no ayumi* [Surveying Japanese children's theatre], (Nihon Jidō Engeki Kyōkai, 1973), 6.

80   Kubota Beisen, "Otogi shibai to mibu kyōgen to" [Fairy tale and *mibu* plays], *Kabuki* (January 1904): 20–25; Sekine, *Meiji*, 274; Waseda, *Nihon*, 233; Akiba, *Shingeki*, 1:430–31; Waseda, *Nihon*, 233; Miyake Saburō, *Koshibai no omoide* [Memories of minor theatres] (Kokuritsu Gekijō Chōsa Yōseibu Geinō Chōsashitsu, 1986), 28–29. *Mibu* were *kyōgen*-like folk plays staged by amateurs in temples.

81   These were also called *kodomo shibai* (children's plays) and were especially popular in the late Tokugawa era.

82   Akiba, *Tōto*, 291–92; Ihara, *Meiji*, 674, 678.

Chapter 40

1   Miyake Shūtarō, *Engeki*, 52; Ihara, *Kabuki*, 8:162–74; Kawai, *Onnagata*, 76–83; Okamoto, *Meiji*, 282; Ōzasa, *Nihon*, 485–86.

2   "Hongō-za no sensō geki" [The war plays at the Hongō-za], *Kabuki* (April 1904): 10–12; Miki Takeji, "Shinkyū ryōha no sensō shibai" [The war plays of shimpa and kabuki], *Kabuki* (April 1904): 12–16. War plays performed by major kabuki troupes were not very successful (Inoue, *Kawakami*, 97).

3   Sadayakko played a nurse.

4   Matsunaga, *Kawakami*, 203–4; "Meiji-za no Ōkan" [The Crown at the Meiji-za], *Kabuki* (March 1905), 47–60.

5   "Shiki no haru" [Spring of the four seasons], *Mainichi shimbun*, November 4, 1903, in Shirakawa, 417; "Shibai dayori" [Theatre news], *Miyako shimbun*, October 15, 1903, in Shirakawa, 413; "Shibai dayori,"

Yomiuri shimbun, February 13, 1903, in Shirakawa, 382; "Ōsaka no Kawakamiza" [The Kawakami Troupe in Osaka], *Jiji shimpō*, February 5, 1903, in Shirakawa, 427–28; Kawatake Shigetoshi, *Nihon engeki zenshi*, 1,010. Teahouse control of admissions to theatres was a long established practice. Using intermediaries to engage amusements continued as the way to book geisha or expensive prostitutes.

6   Akiba, *Tōto*, 242–47; Kawatake Shigetoshi, *Gaisetsu*, 378–79. The reduction of spectator revelry in first-class theatres limited such of the intimacy between actors and audience (Raz, *Audience*, 219–25).

7   Kawatake Shigetoshi, *Gaisetsu*, 378–79; Fuji, *Jiden*, 175; Ihara, *Meiji*, 675; Waseda, *Nihon*, 230, 378–79; Toita Kōji, "The Kabuki, the Shimpa," 273; Miyake Shūtarō, *Engeki*, 91; "Shibai dayori," *Miyako shimbun*, October 15, 1903, in Shirakawa, 413; Fuji, *Jiden*, 175; Ihara, *Meiji*, 675; Waseda, *Nihon*, 378–79. Theatres at this time were beginning to offer a choice between sitting in a *masu* on the floor or in a few higher-priced chairs.

8   Romein, *Watershed*, 214. Theatres overseas had already abolished most extra fees similar to Japanese cushion, footwear, escort, and other charges (Richard Leacroft, *The Development of the English Playhouse* [Ithaca: Cornell University Press, 1973]).

9   Coincidentally, Kawakami's moves to dampen partying in Japanese theatres were remarkably similar to what Tony Pastor had done in America when he converted raucous variety shows performed as saloon entertainment into American "polite vaudeville."

10 Kawatake Shigetoshi, *Nihon engeki zenshi*, 806. Candles, gas, and electricity lit evening performances. In 1900, the government restricted performances to nine hours (an increase of one hour over the previous limit) but required that performances end by midnight (Ogawa, *Nihon butai*, 112).

11 Without built-in orchestra pits in Japanese theatres, Kawakami had to take up some of the floor seating (*masu*) in front of the stage.

12 Matsunaga, *Kawakami*, 185.

13 Kawatake Shigetoshi, *Gaisetsu*, 379; Inoue, *Kawakami*, 100. These plays were written and first performed in Europe: *Pour le couronne*, 1895; *Monna Vanna*, 1902; *Patrie*, 1869.

14 Kawakami Otojirō, discussant, "'Sokoku' ni tsuite" [About Patrie/Fatherland], *Kabuki* (November 1906), 52–54.

15 "Shibai dayori," *Miyako shimbun*, February 8, 1906, in Shirakawa, 441.

16 "Monna Wanna o mite" [Looking at *Monna Vanna*], *Kabuki* (March 1906): 1–4.

17 "Shibai dayori," *Miyako shimbun*, February 4, 1905, in Shirakawa, 436–37; Kin'ei, "Meiji-za no Ōkan" [The Crown at the Meiji-za], *Kabuki* (March 1905), 47–60; Inoue, *Kawakami*, 99–100; Kawatake Shigetoshi, *Sōgō*, 72.

18 Ōzasa, *Nihon*, 109.

19 "Kawakami ichiza no 'Sokoku'" [The Kawakami troupe's *Patrie*], *Kabuki* (October 1906): 138–39. Kawakami was attracted to plays by Sardou and had met him through Fuller in Paris, but he never comprehended the precision required to develop a Sardou well-made play (Fuller, *Fifteen*, 216–21).

20 "Shibai dayori," *Miyako shimbun*, February 8, 1906, in Shirakawa, 441.

21 "Kawakami ichiza no 'Sokoku.'"

22 Inoue, *Kawakami*, 187; Matsunaga, *Kabuki*, 196.

23 Miki Takeji, "Meiji sanjūkyūnen no gekidan" [The theatre world in 1906], *Kabuki* (January 1907): 155–59; "Kawakami seigekiha" [The Kawakami *seigeki* faction], *Miyako shimbun*, September 26, 1905, in Shirakawa, *shimbun*, 440.

24 Fujii, *Jiden*, 173; Kawatake Toshio, *Nihon*, 199–200.

25 Tanaka Jun'ichirō, *Nihon eiga hattatsu shi* [History of the development of the Japanese film] (Chūō Kōronsha, 1957), 1:125.

26 Sekine, *Meiji*, 272–73.

27   A precise count was impossible because productions originating in one city may have traveled to another (often with many changes in cast), or the same play may have been separated produced in another city.

28   Ihara, *Kabuki*, 8:238–29; Kawatake Shigetoshi, *Nihon engeki zenshi*, 875.

29   As attendance at first-class kabuki was depressed at this time, kabuki managers and actors were trying to renew repertoires with *shinkabuki* (new kabuki) plays that presented historical events with new dramaturgy and interpretation. Kabuki was slowly but successfully retreating into its emergence as classic theate (Kawatake Shigetoshi, *Nihon engeki zenshi*, 1016, 861–86).

30   Yanagi, *Shimpa no gojūnen*, 26–58; Akiba, *Shingeki*, 1:455–58; Kawatake Shigetoshi, *Nihon engeki zenshi*, 988–1,016. I developed these numbers from Yanagi, who was the most liberal of sources. Akiba counted ten principal shimpa productions in 1904, nineteen in 1905, and seventeen in 1906.

31   Playing a show for only a single month had become a standard in Tokyo (Yanagi, *Shimpa no rokujūnen*, 266–71). In the late Edo (pre-Meiji) period, kabuki bills had been scheduled at two-month intervals and usually opened around the first day of the first, third, fifth, seventh ninth, and eleventh months. Few bills lasted with good houses for a full eight weeks. The eleventh month usually marked the beginning of a new season.

32   Waseda, *Nihon*, 230–31; Kawatake Shigetoshi, *Nihon engeki zenshi*, 1,016.

33   The Masago-za was located in the small business section (*shitamachi*) of Tokyo near Nihombashi. Akiba Tarō in *Nihon shingeki shi*, 1:455–58, printed a list of 1905 shimpa productions: eleven were at Masago-za and eight at Hongō-za. The next year, Masago-za had nine and Hongō-za had eight. In 1907, even though shimpa was still strong, the Masago-za apparently had none, but the Hongō-za had seven. Also Ihara, *Kabuki*, 8:238–39; Yanagi, *Shimpa no gojūnen*, 23–44.

34   Akiba, *Shingeki*, 1:455–58.

35   The most successful newspaper novelists were often members of the *Ken'yusha* coterie that sought reform of Japanese literary language and encouraged characterization based on psychological insight.

36   Kabuki playwrights had been adapting serialized newspaper novels since the mid-1870s (Ogasawara, *Kabuki*, 188–96).

37   Marui, *Shimpa*, 23–35; Akiba, *Nihon*, 1:401–11, 1:415–19; Okazaki, *Japanese*, 477–82.

38   Tsugami, *Engeki*, 219–20; Kawashima, *Nihon*, 93, also 107–8. *Higeki* was a neologism necessary for scholars to approximate foreign critical concepts of "tragedy." Excessively sentimental shimpa *higeki* were nicknamed "*onamida chōdai*" ("please give tears") plays. This phrase was equivalent to "tear jerker."

39   Kathryn Ragsdale, in "Marriage, the Newspaper Business, and the Nation-State: Ideology in the Late Meiji Serialized Katsei Shōsetsu" (*Journal of Japanese Studies*, 24:2 [Summer 1998], 229–55), discussed how this genre reinforced the new state ideology of the "family system" as "the foundation of the nation." A few shimpa and kabuki plays had strong female characters who did not submit to fate or to males.

40   Ōzasa, *Nihon*, 453–84. Shimpa plays, like the novels from which most were adapted, were often about *giri-ninjō* conflicts. These were structurally similar to those in kabuki drama and traditional story forms but often arose from different circumstances.

41   Kawatake Shigetoshi, *Nihon no engeki*, 1,014–17; Akiba, *Nihon*, 1:472–76, 484; Yanagi, *Ebanzuke*, 149–50, 164–65; Yanagi Eijirō, "Shimpa to Taki no Shiraito," Kokuritsu Gekijō, Tokyo, program, June 1972, 45–47. "Taki no Shiraito" was the *geimei* (stage name) of the water magician heroine of the play. The title *Taki no Shiraito* is also known abroad as *Taki of the White Threds*, *The Water Magician*, and *Cascading White Threads*. In the premiere production of *Taki*, Fujisawa Asajirō played the onnagata title role. For the initial production of *Konjiki yasha*, Fujisawa wrote the dramatization and played the male lead. Kawakami did not appear in *Konjiki yasha* because he was busy at the time running for election to the Diet. While both play titles are prominent among the lists of shimpa classics, they they have no definitive versions in play script form. Their familiar stories continue in variant dramatizations on stage and in film.

42   Kawatake Shigetoshi, *Sōgō*, 95, 385, 507, 402, 489, 350.

43   Kawashima, *Nihon*, 92–94; Ihara, *Kabuki*, 8:181–83; Kawatake Shigetoshi, *Nihon engeki zenshi*, 1,015–16; Waseda, *Nihon*, 230–31; Toita Kōji, "The Kabuki, the Shimpa," 276. When a kabuki troupe produced a shimpa play, it was usually as a lesser attraction on a bill dominated by regular kabuki fare (Sekine, *Meiji*, 272–73).

44   Marui, *Shimpa*, 37–45; Yanagi, *Shimpa no rokujūnen*, 30–38.

45   Akiba, *Shingeki*, 1:452–59, 476–83. Following established practice in Japan, many shimpa dramatists were "house playwrights" who, under contract, made plays only for a specific troupe or theatre.

46   Kawatake Shigetoshi, *Nihon engeki zenshi*, 1,013; Hagii, *Shimpa*, 75–76; Yanagi, *Ebanzuke*, 257.

47   Matsumoto, *Meiji engekiron*, 440–46; Kawatake Toshio, *Kindai engeki*, 160–61. Several literary authorities then and now have objected to equating Chikamatsu with the "greater" Shakespeare (discussed in Donald Keene, "Introduction," in *Major Plays of Chikamatsu* [New York: Columbia University Press, 1961], 1–3).

48   Waseda, *Nihon*, 230–31; Toita Kōji, "The Kabuki, the Shimpa," 276; Kawatake Shigetoshi, *Nihon engeki zenshi*, 1,014. Although productions at the Asahi-za dominated Osaka shimpa, that theatre faced strong competition from rival shimpa productions at the Temma-za.

49   Yanagi, *Ebanzuke*, 261.

50   "Kabuki" could still be a general term for all kinds of drama other than nō.

51   Ōzasa, *Nihon*, 453–84.

52   Often publicized as the "Danjūrō of shimpa," Takata had no direct relationship with Danjūrō IX of kabuki who was unquestionably Japan's top actor when he died in 1903.

53   Hagii, *Shimpa*, 107–8, 113–15; Kawatake Shigetoshi, *Gaisetsu*, 383; Yanagi, *Shimpa no rokujūnen*, 254.

54   The folk belief that the stomach held the ultimate source of being was long manifest in the act of *harakiri* (literally "stomach cutting," a.k.a. *seppuku*), which opened a human body to its innermost essence.

55   Yanagi, *Shimpa no rokujūnen*, 167–68.

56   Kawashima, *Nihon*, 94. This was a second- or third-hand opinion based on what Japanese had heard about Western acting.

57   Kawatake Shigetoshi, *Nihon no engeki*, 175–77.

58   Ōzasa, *Nihon*, 453–84. "Shimpa-chō" later became a pejorative term suggesting excessive sentimentality or "overdone old-fashioned" acting.

59   Akiba, *Shingeki*, 1:452–71.

60   Toita Kōji, "The Kabuki, the Shimpa," 279.

61   Kitamura, *Engeki: Onna keizu*, phonograph record. In addition to this documentation of modern shimpa voices, early shimpa onnagata (not front-rank talent) acting can be seen in the few surviving prints of Japanese silent motion pictures made before actresses began to replace them around 1920.

62   Hagii, *Shimpa*, 86–87; also Iwai, *Shimpa*, 26–27; Yanagi, *Shimpa no rokujūnen*, 243–45; Kawatake Shigetoshi, *Gaisetsu*, 383–84.

Chapter 41

1   Kawakami Otojirō, "Gekidan fushin no riyū" [Reasons for stagnation in the theatrical world], *Kabuki* (October 1909): 87. According to my survey of the monthly "Kōgyō ichiran" [Entertainment at a glance] column in *Kabuki* over a two-year period, more theatres were dark in January than in any other month (*Kabuki* [December 1906–November 1908]).

2   "Santo gekijō shichigatsu kōgyō ichiran" [A look at theatre performances in the three major cities during July], *Engei gahō* (August 1908): 146–47. The numbers recorded may be atypical because the survey covered a summer month. Surveys such as this were an infrequent feature of *Engei gahō*.

3   In April of the previous year, this report listed four top venues playing *kyūgeki* of varying quality; the other two had shimpa ("Tōkyō engei annai" [Guide to Tokyo entertainment], *Engei gahō* [April 1907]: 110–24).

4   *Gidayū* was the highly emotional chanter accompaniment for *bunraku* and related kabuki plays. *Gidayū* by itself had become popular with amateurs who attempted to emulate the professionals.

5   An alternative Japanese term for what I have called "third-class *kyūgeki*" was *chūkabuki* (middle kabuki). These troupes and their irrepressible audiences were a class-based resistance to the spreading formal, anticonviviality of first-class theatres.

6   Play titles in the data did not sufficiently indicate the type of play.

7   Miyake Saburō, *Koshibai no omoide* [Memories of minor theatres] (Kokuritsu Gekijō Chōsa Yōseibu Geinō Chōsashitsu, 1986), 30; "Taishū engeki no rekishi" [History of *taishū engeki* (popular drama)], *Engeki Gurafu* (October 2005): 104–5. *Naniwabushi* (also called *ryōkyoku*) were narrative ballads nasally intoned and bucolically accented by a single performer to samisen accompaniment. Originating in the Osaka (Naniwa) area as a solo storyteller form (without any actor or puppet adjunct), *naniwabushi* was widely popular among the lower classes around 1900 (Minami, *Kabuku*, 103–4). In *fushigeki* shows, *naniwabushi* performers were usually more important than the actors.

8   The *onna shibai* troupe at the Misaki-za gave five percent of all professional drama performances in Tokyo during the two years surveyed.

9   Actors behind or beside the screen spoke dialogue for the filmed scenes as a kind of live dubbing.

10   The *rensageki* of Japan did not fully exploit the filmic possibilities for melodramatic thrills seen in American action (film only) movies.

11   Anderson, "Spoken," 271–72; Miyake Saburō, *Koshibai*, 29–31; Shibata Katsu, *Jitsuen to eiga: rensageki no kiroku* [Live performance and film: a record of chained drama] (Shibata Katsu, 1982); Sōya, *Nippon*, 63–64; Ōzasa, *Nihon*, 550–52. In 1908, Japan had very few theatres or other venues regularly showing movies. Imports from Europe dominated this small market.

12   The Soganoya company did not play in Tokyo until 1908 ("Shintomi-za no Soganoya ichiza" [The Soganoya troupe at the Shintomi-za], *Kabuki* [June 1908]: 64–65). The independent Soganoya troupe was eventually absorbed into the Shōchiku Shinkigeki (Shōchiku New Comedy) enterprise (Waseda, *Nihon*, 277, 316).

13   Takahashi Hiroshi, *Taishū*, 134–37; Kawashima, *Nihon*, 163–67; Mukai, *Nippon*, 11–26, 29, 41, 32–37, 81–98. At the start of his theatrical career a decade and a half earlier, Kawakami had unsuccessfully attempted to reform regional *niwaka* performed by amateurs and his merchant father in Hakata.

14   Kawatake Shigetoshi, *Nihon engeki zenshi*, 1,018–25. In his discussion of comedic forms, critic Mukai Sōya suggested that *kigeki*, the Japanese word that now means "comedy" or "comic play," emerged in the 1890s as a new and necessary generic designation for discussion of the foreign comedies of Moliere and Shakespeare (Sōya, *Nippon*, 12. Also Yamaguchi Kichi, *Ōsaka no geinō* [Osaka entertainment] (Ōsaka: Mainichi Hōsō, 1973), 99–103.

15   Kawashima, *Nihon*, 160–63.

16   Counts of shows in Tokyo varied according to source: Okamoto, *Meiji*, 278; Ihara, *Kabuki nempyō*, 7:425; Miyake Saburō, *Koshibai*, 28–29; Mukai, *Nippon*, 258; Minami, *Kabuku*, 103–4.

17   "Tōkyō engei annai" [Tokyo performance guide], *Engei gahō* (April 1907): 110–24.

18   These were the equivalent of carnival and circus sideshows or the storefront shows on the Bowery and elsewhere in America.

19   "Tōkyō engei annai."

20   He was forty-two, according to the way Japanese counted age. Nephritis is also known as Bright's disease.

21   Kurata, *Kindaigeki*, 266–67; "Kawakami Otajirō no byōki mōchōen jinzōen" [Kawakami Otajirō's ill-

nesses, appendicitis, and nephritis] and "Kawakami Otojirō byōsaihatsu" [Kawakami Otojirō's illnesses break out again], *Miyako shimbun,* May 19, 1905, and April 16, 1906, in Shirakawa, 439, 443.

22 Kurata, *Kindaigeki,* 267.

23 "Shimpa Daidō Danketsu," *Engei gahō* (August 1907): 122–23; Kurata, *Kindaigeki,* 210–11; Inoue, *Kawakami,* 104; Toita, "The Kabuki, the Shimpa," 281. This organization was also called the Shinhaiyū Daidō Danketsu (Grand Coalition of New Actors).

24 Ezaki, *Jitsuroku,* 166.

25 Matsunaga, *Kawakami,* 206–9; Yamaguchi, *Joyū,* 163–64.

26 Marie Laparcerie, "Sada Yacco est à Paris," *Femina* (November 1, 1907): 490–91.

27 "Pari no Nihon engei" [Japanese performances in Paris], *Jiji shimpō,* March 5, 1908, in Shirakawa, 453–54; Yamaguchi, *Joyū,* 164–66; "Ce que nous a dit: la Sarah Bernhardt du Japon," *Lectures pour tous* (March 1908): 513; "Foreign Notes. Amsterdam," *Mask* (April 1908): 21.

28 "Kawakami Otojirō," *Miyako shimbun,* May 14, 1908, in Shirakawa, 455; Yanagi, *Ebanzuke,* 140; Matsunaga, *Kawakami,* 186, 205–10; Yamaguchi, *Joyū,* 164–66.

29 "Ōsaka Teikoku-za" [The Osaka Teikoku-za], *Miyako shimbun,* May 17, 1908, in Shirakawa, 455; "Kawakami to shinkōgyōhō" [Kawakami and measures for reform of the entertainment business], *Miyako shimbun,* May 24, 1908, in Shirakawa, 455.

30 For example, Shioya, "Haiyū gakkō no hitsuyō o ronzu" [Arguments about the necessity for acting schools], *Kabuki* (August 1902): 12–15, and *Kabuki* (September 1902): 29–32.

31 Kurata, *Kindaigeki,* 218–225; Inoue, *Kawakami,* 108; "Parī miyage" [Gifts from Paris], *Engeki gahō* (December 1908): 95–99; "Sadayakko no kanete joyū yōsei kokoroza" [Sadayakko's training for actresses], *Miyako shimbun,* January 27, 1906, in Shirakawa, 441; Okamoto, *Meiji,* 286; "Sadayakko no joyū yōseijo" [Sadayakko's training school for actresses], *Engei gahō* (September 1908): 132; "Joyū yōseijo" [Training school for actresses], *Yorozu shimbun,* August 7, 1908, in Shirakawa, 460–61; "Joyū yōseijo kaijoshiki" [Opening ceremonies at the training school for actress], *Jiji shimpō,* September 16, 1909, in Shirakawa, 466–67; Yamaguchi, *Joyū,* 163–64. For several years previously, Sadayakko had been informally tutoring young wannabe actresses.

32 Kuwano, *Joyū,* 248.

33 "Joyū yōseijo ni taisuru zasshi hyō" [Comments in magazines about training schools for actresses], *Kabuki* (October 1908): 73–74.

34 Kurata, *Kindaigeki,* 225.

35 Tanaka, *Meiji,* 53–54, 86–87; Toita, "The Kabuki, the Shimpa," 281, 291. Afterward, derived of actresses, Fujisawa's young male students played the female roles (Tanaka, *Meiji,* 87). His school failed several years later because of financial difficulties (Kawatake Shigetoshi, *Nihon no engeki,* 171).

36 Kurata, *Kindaigeki,* 267.

37 "Tōkyō ni okeru mitsu no haiyū gakkō" [Three schools for actors in Tokyo], *Kabuki* (October 1909): 84–85; Ōzasa, *Nihon,* 80–81.

38 "Meika shinsoroku 23: Kawakami Otojirō" [Celebrity facts 23: Kawakami Otojirō], *Engei gahō* (October 1908): 34; Yamaguchi, *Joyū,* 93; Kawakami Otojirō, "Gekidan fushin no riyū" [Reasons for stagnation in the theatrical world], *Kabuki* (October 1909): 87.

39 Kawakami Otojirō, "Kakushin no jikkō" [Reform in practice], *Kabuki* (August 1909): 62–63.

40 Examined in Fujii, *Jiden,* 268.

41 Yanagi, *Shimpa no rokujūnen,* 143; Ōzasa, *Nihon,* 101–2; Okamoto, *Engeki.* 168; Akiba, *Tōto,* 474–79.

42 Conversation with Yu Ch'i-jin, Seoul, 1955; Siyuan Li, "The Impact of *Shi[m]pa* on Early Chinese *Huaju,*" *Asian Theatre Journal* 23:1 (Fall 2006): 342–45.

43 "Kawakami to shinkōgyōhō" [Kawakami and measures for reform of the entertainment business], *Miyako shimbun*, May 24, 1908, in Shirakawa, 455.

44 Lesser companies with lesser actors were already touring extensively.

45 Matsunaga, *Kawakami*, 211–22; Kawakami Otojirō, "Watakushi no kōgyō kakushin" [My theatrical reforms], *Kabuki* (July 1908): 81; Kawakami Otojirō, "Kakushin no jikkō," 62–63; Ogawa, *Nihon*, 126; Okamoto, *Meiji*, 286; Sekine, *Meiji*, 312, 316–22; Kurata, *Kindaigeki*, 213–16. Stars also toured individually, much like in the United States before the combination package system became dominant.

46 Miyake Shūtarō, *Engeki*, 118–19; Kawashima, *Nihon*, 91.

47 Akiba, *Shingeki*, 1:458; Kawakami, "Watakushi no kōgyō kakushin," 81; Inoue, *Kawakami*, 106–9; Yamaguchi, *Joyū*, 173–75; "Kakushin kōgyō," *Miyako shimbun*, May 14, 1909, Shirakawa, 470. The expanded route included Kawakami's hometown of Hakata.

48 Ogawa, *Nihon*, 126; Okamoto, *Meiji*, 286–87; Shirakawa, *shimbun*, 10, 41–42. Kawakami later attempted to expand both the range of his touring network and the number of his reformed companies but was unsuccessful ("Kawakami no kakushin daisan gun" [Kawakami's third reformed drama troupe], *Kabuki* [March 1909]: 107–8; "Hongo-za," advertisement, June 3, 1909, in Shirakawa, 471; Kurata, *Kindaigeki*, 216).

49 Kurata, *Kindaigeki*, 216; Shirakawa, *shimbun*, 41–42; Okamoto, *Meiji*, 286–87. Sadanji, an inside kabuki reformer, was already a supporter of innovative *shinkabuki* plays. He had recently returned from abroad, where he studied theatre and had briefly been a special student at a London acting school. Playwright and newspaperman Matsui Shōō accompanied him as mentor and translator.

50 Ōzasa, *Nihon*, 98; "Meiji-za ichigatsu kyōgen" [January plays at the Meiji-za], *Engei gahō* (February 1908), n.p.; Inoue, *Kawakami*, 111; Okamoto, *Meiji*, 286–87. Sadanji later allied with critic-playwright Osanai Kaoru to establish the Jiyū Gekijō (Free Theatre), one of the two major early shingeki troupes. Kawakami had to replace Sadanji with a lesser kabuki actor from Osaka.

51 A featured male in Sadayakko's troupe was veteran Tsusaka Kōichirō who had been Kawakami's main supporting actor in America, where he played the comic title role in *Jingorō*, the villain in *Soga*, Banza in *The Geisha and Knight* (in New York and London), and elderly onnagata parts ("Kawakami no kakushin kōgyō" [Kawakami's reformed drama], *Engei gahō* [September 1908]: 133; "Meiji-za," *Miyako shimbun*, June 1, 1909, in Shirakawa, 470–71). Many leading shimpa actors continued to oppose the gender mix of Kawakami's Troupe Two (Kawatake Shigetoshi, *Gaisetsu*, 379). While touring as the head of this troupe, Sadayakko was also running her actresses' school.

52 Kawakami Otojirō, "Chihō jungyō to kyakuhon" [Provincial touring and its plays], *Kabuki* (January 1909): 120–22; Ōzasa, *Nihon*, 516.

53 Kawatake Shigetoshi, *Nihon engeki zenshi*, 929–31; *Shōchiku kujūnen shi* [Ninety year history of Shōchiku] (Shōchiku, 1985), 107–11.

54 Toita, "The Kabuki, the Shimpa," 312–15; Kawatake Shigetoshi, *Nihon engeki zenshi*, 929–32. Shōchiku lost theatres in the 1923 Kantō earthquake (as it later did in the air raids of the Pacific War) but rebuilt properties to maintain its dominance of the live theatre businesses.

55 Japanese motion picture companies did not own most of the theatres in their chains but bound them with exclusive distribution contracts.

56 Kawatake Shigetoshi, *Nihon engeki zenshi*, 931, 951–52; Japanese, *Theatre*, 207–8; Engeki Hakubutsukan, *Engeki jiten* [Theater dictionary] (Tōkyōdō, 1973), s.v. "Shōchiku" and "Tōhō."

57 "Meiji-za," *Miyako shimbun*, June 1, 1909, in Shirakawa, 470–71; Inoue, *Kawakami*, 111; Ōzasa, *Nihon*, 516.

58 "Meiji-za no Sadayakko" [Sadayakko at the Meiji-za], *Kabuki* (July 1909): 77–78; Kimura Kinnosuke, *Meiji-za monogatari* [The Meiji-za story] (Kabuki-za Shuppambu, 1928), 368–69.

59 Inoue, *Kawakami*, 110; Matsunaga, *Kawakami*, 217.

60 Osanai Kaoru, "Kakushingeki zakkan" [Various impressions of reformed theatre initiatives], in *Osanai Kaoru zenshū* [The complete works of Osanai Kaoru] (Kyōto: Rinji Shobō, 1975), 7:87, 91.

61 Kawakami Otojirō. "Kōgyōsha to shite no iken" [Views of a theatrical manager], *Kabuki* (September 1909): 86; Matsunaga, *Kawakami*, 223–24; Ōzasa, *Nihon*, 516.

62 Fujii, *Jiden*, 172–73.

63 An official national theatre had been proposed in 1878 but found no support (Takahashi Yuichirō, "Kabuki Goes Official: The 1878 Opening of the Shintomi-za," *TDR* No. T147 [Fall 1995]: 143).

64 Nō had only an almost cultish following as it slowly recovered during the late Meiji era.

65 Or more accurately, the palace officials who controlled the emperor had not condescended.

66 Kawatake Shigetoshi, *Nihon engeki zenshi*, 809; Akiba, *Tōto*, 189–81.

67 "Ōsaka Teikoku-za," *Miyako shimbun*, April 25, 1907, in Shirakawa, 447–48; Matsunaga, *Kawakami*, 219–24. Meanwhile, during the years of delay in completion of Kawakami's Teikoku-za, the Yūraku-za in Tokyo opened in November 1908 as the first genuinely "modern" (i.e., Western-style) theatre in Japan (Kurata, *Kindaigeki*, 267; "Engei hyakushu" [Entertainment: a hundred topics], *Ōsaka mainichi*, May 1, 1910, in Shirakawa, 481–82).

68 "Ōsaka Teikoku-za," *Miyako shimbun*, January 22, 1910, in Shirakawa, 479; Kurata, *Kindaigeki*, 249–50; Yamaguchi, *Joyū*, 183; Urayama, *Nihon*, 105.

69 "Sakuya no Teikoku-za" [Last night at the Teikoku-za], *Ōsaka mainichi*, March 1, 1910 [sic], in Shirakawa, 480–81; also "Ōsaka Teikoku-za," *Miyako shimbun*, January 22, 1910, in Shirakawa, 479; Inoue, *Kawakami*, 111–13; Matsunaga, *Kawakami*, 219–22.

70 Quoted in Matsunaga, *Kawakami*, 225.

71 Ibid., 227.

72 "Kawakami no shibai kairyū dan" [Kawakami's discussion of theatre reforms], *Yomiuri*, June 13, 1908, in Shirakawa, 456–57.

73 Both "Teikoku-za" and "Teikoku Gekijō" mean "Imperial Theatre." *Gekijō* was a modern word replacing the older *-za* that also meant theatre.

74 Saiji, "Kaijōzen no Teikoku Gekijō" [Before the Imperial Theatre opens], *Engei gahō* (March 1911): 66–74; "Teikoku Gekijō kensetsu no keikaku" [Construction plans for the Imperial Theatre], *Kabuki* (September 1906): 130–31; Kawatake Shigetoshi, *Nihon engeki zenshi*, 884, 892, 895–98; Ōzasa, *Nihon*, 517–20; Matsunaga, *Kawakami*, 225.

75 Numerous personal observations.

76 Saiji, "Kaijōzen;" Teigeki Shihensan Iinkai, *Teigeki no gojūnen* [Fifty years of the Imperial Theatre] (Tōhō, 1966), 248. In place of the hanamichi, there were two short narrow platforms that ran along the walls from the stage one third of the way into the auditorium.

77 Toita Kōji, "The Kabuki, the Shimpa," 257–58.

78 It can be argued that during the Tokugawa era, several nō troupes were official as they were supported with the patronage of the shōgun and various *daimyo*.

Chapter 42

1 Matsunaga, *Kawakami*, 223–25; Kurata, *Kindaigeki*, 244–45.

2 Ihara Seiseien, "Hongō-za no Bondoman" [*The Bondman* at the Hongō-za], *Kabuki* (January 1910): 60–62; "Sakuya no Teikoku-za" [Last night at the Teikoku-za), *Ōsaka mainichi*, March 1, 1910, in Shirakawa, 480–81.

3 Marui, *Shimpa*, 53–59; Shirakawa, *shimbun*, 41–43; Ōzasa, *Nihon*, 519–20; Yamaguchi, *Joyū*, 263–64; Kurata, *Kindaigeki*, 252–55.

4   "Ōsaka Teikoku-za," *Ōsaka mainichi*, May 1, 1910, in Shirakawa, 481–82. The Japanese title of *The Corsican Brothers* was *Parī no adauchi* [Revenge in Paris].

5   The German original was the source of Sigmund Romberg's later operetta *The Student Prince*.

6   "Teikoku-za no 'Tsubaki hime'" [*The Camilla Princess* at the Teikoku-za], *Ōsaka mainichi*, February 15, 1911, in Shirakawa, 490–91. Adapted from *La Dame aux camélias* of Dumas fils, this was a *hon'an* set in Paris with an array of Japanese characters. Soon there was a rival shimpa *kyōen* starring Takata Minoru and Ii Yōhō with *onnagata* Kawai Takeo in the Camille part. *La Dame aux camélias* became a shimpa standard in several versions that often had the title *Tsubaki hime* (Akiba, *Nihon*, 1:469).

7   Yamaguchi, *Joyū*, 265.

8   "Sekai isshū geki" [The around the world play], *Ōsaka asahi*, June 10, 1910; "Teikoku-za," *Ōsaka mainichi*, June 8, 1910; and "Teikoku-za no shonichi" [Opening day at the Teikoku-za], *Ōsaka mainichi*, June 12, 1910, all in Shirakawa, 482–83.

9   Kano, *Acting*, 99–104; "Sekai isshū geki," Shirakawa, 482–83.

10   "Ōsaka Teikoku-za," *Miyako shimbun*, October 28, 1910; "Futsuka yori kaijō" [Opening on the second], *Ōsaka mainichi*, November 2, 1910; and "Teikoku-za," *Ōsaka asahi*, November 2, 1910, in Shirakawa, 485–86; also Kurata, *Kindaigeki*, 253. *Kaizoku* was adapted from a German or French original. *Hoshi sekai tanken* was timely, as Japanophile Percival Lowell of Boston was making international news with his discovery of canals and habitation on Mars.

11   Matsunaga, *Kawakami*, 227; Shirakawa, *shimbun*, 41–42.

12   "Teikoku-za no otogi shibai" [Fairy tale plays at the Teikoku-za], *Ōsaka mainichi*, June 12, 1910, in Shirakawa, 483; Kurata, *Kindaigeki*, 200–4; Matsunaga, *Kawakami*, 226; Yamaguchi, *Joyū*, 263–65.

13   Inoue, *Kawakami*, 118; Matsunaga, *Kawakami*, 228.

14   "Kawakami Otojirō no byōki ni tsuite" [About Kawakami Otojirō's illness], *Miyako shimbun*, May 12, 1905, in Shirakawa, 439; "Kawakami Otojirō no daishujutsu" [Kawakami Otojirō's major surgery], *Ōsaka asahi*, October 24, 1911, in Shirakawa, 496; Inoue, *Kawakami*, 120.

15   There were conflicting reports about Kawakami's last words (Matsunaga, *Kawakami*, 232–33; Kurata, *Kindaigeki*, 256; Inoue, *Kawakami*, 120; Ezaki, *Jitsuroku*, 183, 185–86).

16   Kurata, *Kindaigeki*, 256–58; Inoue, *Kawakami*, 120–29, 152; "Kawakami Otojirō shisu" [Kawakami Otojirō dies], *Ōsaka asahi*, November 12, 1911, in Shirakawa, 502; Matsunaga, *Kawakami*, 235.

17   Inoue, *Kawakami*, 121–28; Kurata, *Kindaigeki*, 260; Matsunaga, *Kawakami*, 236.

18   "Kyūjō subeku" [All theatres closed], *Miyako shimbun*, November 14, 1911, Shirakawa, 510.

19   Inoue, *Kawakami*, 123–24; Matsunaga, *Kawakami*, 235–36; "Kawakami Otojirō gi" [Ceremony for Kawakami Otojirō], *Ōsaka mainichi*, November 12, 1911, in Shirakawa, 507; Marui, *Shimpa*, 59–60.

20   "Shimpageki to Kawakami" [Shimpa and Kawakami], *Miyako shimbun*, November 12, 1911, in Shirakawa, 504–5. The number of times Kawakami was jailed is uncertain.

21   Matsunaga, *Kawakami*, 238; Dōmon, *Kawakami*, 168–70; Inoue, *Kawakami*, 130. A towering twelve-foot-high stele was erected at his Shōtenji grave in 1917. Multistory apartment houses now block the view from passing trains.

22   "Kawakami Otojirō shisu;" Matsunaga, *Kawakami*, 240–41; Inoue, *Kawakami*, 130–34; Ezaki, *Jitsuroku*, 203–6. A small memorial stone had to substitute for the statue at Sengakuji. A heroic bronze statue of Kawakami was later erected at Yanaka Ten'ōji, another temple in Tokyo, but was melted for scrap during the Pacific War.

23   [Ihara] Seiseien, "Ko-Kawakami Otojirō no koto" [About the late Kawakami Otojirō], *Kabuki* (December 1911): 104.

24   Urayama, *Nihon*, 105; also "Seikōsha to shite no Kawakami-kun" [Mr. Kawakami as a successful person], *Kabuki* (December 1911): 106.

25   Yanagi, *Shimpa no rokujūnen*, 173.

26   "Zairai kabuki no sōhaku o nameta mono" quoted in Matsumoto, *Meiji engekiron*, 426.

27   Kawashima, *Nihon*, 89.

28   Toita, "The Kabuki, the Shimpa," 306.

29   "Boku wa daikon da." Quoted in Ihara, *Dan*, 18.

30   Yanagi, *Shimpa no rokujūnen*, 166; also "Kawakami wa yakusha ka [Is Kawakami an actor?], *Miyako shimbun*, September 9, 1910, in Shirakawa, 484.

31   Yanagi, *Shimpa no rokujūnen*, 163, 167–68, 177.

32   Matsunaga, *Kawakami*, 235; Yamaguchi, *Joyū*, 193–94.

33   Yamaguchi, *Joyū*, 194–97, 202–5, 209, 265–67; Tanaka, *Meiji*, 145; Marui, *Shimpa*, 53–76, 194, 197; Mizutani, *Matsuba*, 278. In Japan, *Madame Butterfly* has the title *O-Chō fujin* [Madame Butterfly]. The source of the *Jeanne d'Arc* play, most likely France, could not be identified.

34   Yamaguchi, *Joyū*, 194, 265; Kano, *Acting*, 219–30. Magician Tenkatsu incorporated magic tricks into her slightly risqué version.

35   "Sadayakko yōkō keikaku" [Sadayakko's plans for a tour abroad], *Yomiuri*, December 23, 1911, in Shirakawa, 519.

36   Domon, *Kawakami*, 171; Ezaki, *Jitsuroku*, 194.

37   Kawakami Sadayakko, "Otto ni wakarete nochi" [After separation from my husband], *Engei gahō* (November 1912): 171; Yamaguchi, *Joyū*, 195.

38   Yamaguchi, *Joyū*, 204–6; "Sadayakko no yōkō" [Sadayakko's trip abroad], *Engei gahō* (October 1916): 198; "Sadayakko to Gaimushō" [Sadayakko and the Foreign Ministry], *Engei gahō* (November 1916): 174.

39   Yamaguchi, *Joyū*, 205.

40   Ibid.; Kano, *Acting*, 52; "Sadayakko kami o kiru" [Sadayakko cuts her hair], *Kokumin shimbun*, November 14, 1911, Shirakawa, 508–10.

41   Ezaki, *Jitsuroku*, 205–6.

42   Fukuzawa Yukichi was the great modernizer (some say Americanizer) and briefly a mentor of the young Kawakami. His daughter who married Momosuke was now dead.

43   Inoue, *Kawakami*, 136–37; Yamaguchi, *Joyū*, 194–95, 207–12, 221; Matsunaga, *Kawakami*, 220.

44   Inoue, *Kawakami*, 135; Yamaguchi, *Joyū*, 205–18.

45   Yamaguchi, *Joyū*, 241–48; Tomita Hiroyuki, *Nihon jidō engeki shi* [History of children's theatre in Japan] (Tōkyō Shoseki, 1980), 58, 173–81.

46   Toita, *Kindai*, 22; "Sakura Jinja to Kawakami fūfu" [Sakura Shrine and Mr. and Mrs. Kawakami], *Engei gahō* (January 1908): 79–82.

47   Ichikawa Danjūrō I is said to have originated the *aragoto* style inherited by the succeeding Ichikawa main line of kabuki actors.

48   Yamaguchi, *Joyū*, 250–52, 257. Fukuzawa Monosuke died in 1938.

49   Nigel Gosling, Nadar (New York: Knopf, 1976), 255.

Chapter 43

1   Marui, *Shimpa*, 55–59.

2   Ibid., 57–112. One reason for the apparent statistical increase in shimpa productions was the gradual addition of Kobe, Nagoya, and Yokohama to published counts that initially included only Tokyo, Osaka, and Kyoto.

3   Kawashima, *Nihon*, 96–98; Ōzasa, *Nihon*, 545–47; Komiya, *Kabuki*, 76–102. Increases in the number of shimpa shows were in part desperate gambles to come up with a money-making hit.

4   Kawatake Shigetoshi, *Nihon engeki zenshi*, 1,017; Tsubouchi Hakubutsukan, *Kokugeki*, 337–38. New forms included *musume* or *shōjo* (girl) musical extravaganzas (of which Takurazuka was the most successful and longest lasting), contemporary Japanese comedies (begun by Soganoya), Japanese and foreign operettas, shingeki productions (original works by Japanese playwrights and translations of foreign plays), Shinkokugeki, and definition-defying inventions and mixtures of shows by obscure performing groups. Movies in this period were a small but expanding part of the entertainment business.

5   Komiya, *Kabuki*, 110.

6   Yanagi, *Ebanzuke*, 267–72; Kawashima, *Nihon*, 96–99; Marui, *Shimpa*, 39–159. Histories of shimpa tended to be patterned after the actor-centered kabuki histories.

7   Ochi Haruo, *Kyōka to gikyoku* [Izumi Kyōka and His Plays] (Sunako Shobō, 1987), 13.

8   *Shinkabuki* were recently written kabuki plays influenced by European dramaturgy but retaining essential kabuki characteristics.

9   Tanaka, *Meiji*, 145; Yamaguchi, *Joyū*, 265–67; Shirakawa Nobuo, "Meijiki ni okeru Furansushu gikyoku jōen nempyō" [Meija era chronology of performances of plays based on French dramas], *Engeki kenkyū* 9 (1979): 132–38.

10   Matsunaga, *Kawakami*, 222.

11   Fujino Yoshio, "Shingeki undō e sokushinteki yakuwari" [Assigning roles for accelerating the shingeki movement], *Nihon engeki gakkai kiyō* 10 (1968): 9–10.

12   The early shingeki preference for foreign plays rather than indigenous new works paralleled that of many theatre reform movements outside of Japan, such as Lugné-Poe's Théâtre de l'Œuvre and J. Y. Grein's Independent Theatre in London. When Kawakami was in Boston, he gave up a matinee at the Tremont Theatre for one of "John Blair's Course of Literary Drama" shows dedicated to modern European plays.

13   With multiple-item programs, a shingeki show could have the variety and approximate length of kabuki and shimpa plays. Shimpa troupes widened their range of offerings by including original Japanese and translated short plays. Apparently, the most popular one-act foreign playwrights of the 1910 decade were Chekhov and Lady Gregory (Tanaka, *Meiji*, 91–254).

14   Akiba, *Nihon*, 2:1–82, 297–98, 305, 336–37; Kawatake Shigetoshi, *Nihon engeki zenshi*, 1,076–78.

15   Kurata, *Kindaigeki*, 181.

16   Doi Shunsho played Hamlet.

17   Akiba, *Nihon*, 2:100–13; Tanaka, *Meiji*, 8–9, 52; Kawatake Shigetoshi, *Nihon engeki zenshi*, 1,045–46; Toita, "The Kabuki, the *Shimpa*," 290–93.

18   Kawatake Shigetoshi, *Nihon engeki zenshi*, 1,047–48, 1,059.

19   Ibid., 1,060–61; Akiba, *Nihon*, 2:268; Tanaka, *Meiji*, 116–24; Ōzasa, *Nihon*, 173.

20   Kawashima, *Nihon*, 111; Ōzasa, *Nihon*, 96, 102; also Akiba, *Nihon*, 2:142–52.

21   Toita, "The Kabuki, the *Shimpa*," 300–4; Rimer, *Toward*, 29–30; Kawatake Shigetoshi, *Nihon engeki zenshi*, 1,055–57; Tanaka, *Meiji*, 91–93; Akiba, *Nihon*, 2:153–57.

22   Kawatake Shigetoshi, *Nihon engeki zenshi*, 1,057; Akiba, *Nihon*, 2:178–81.

23   Tanaka, *Meiji*, 91.

24   Akiba, Nihon, 1:529–58, 2:105–12: Ōzasa, *Nihon*, 80, 83–87, 93–96; Yamaguchi, *Joyū*, 264–65; Kawatake Shigetoshi, *Nihon engeki zenshi*, 1,027–28, 1,055–56; Kawatake Toshio, *Kindai engeki*, 162–65.

25   Kurata, *Kindaigeki*, 256; "Kawakami no jūkan" [Kawakami's serious illness], *Engei gahō* (November 1911): 163; Matsunaga, *Kawakami*, 232; Inoue, *Kawakami*, 120.

26   Kawatake Shigetoshi, *Nihon engeki zenshi*, 1,058–66; Akiba, *Nihon*, 2:199–226. Tanaka, *Meiji*, 1–40, has photographs of plays produced by more than thirty-five different shingeki troupes during this early period.

27   Tanaka, *Meiji*, 89–145, 149–69, 176–93, 197–252; Kawatake Shigetoshi, *Nihon engeki zenshi*, 1,058–59.

28   Ibid., *Meiji*, 78.

29   Kawatake Shigetoshi, *Nihon engeki zenshi*, 1,056–57.

30   Tanaka, *Meiji*, 91–94.

31   [Nagai] Kafū, "Bungei Kyōkai no 'Hamuretto'" [The Bungei Kyōkai's *Hamlet*], *Kabuki* (January 1908), 87; Tanaka, *Meiji*, 81–82; Ōzasa, *Nihon*, 77; Toita, "The Kabuki, the *Shimpa*," 290–91. The Bungei Kyōkai cast neophyte actresses in subsequent plays.

32   Ōzasa, *Nihon*, 104–5.

33   Ibid., 79.

34   Hayashi Suihō, "'Osero' to 'Hamuretto' no kata" [The kata of *Othello* and *Hamlet*], *Engei gahō*, July 1910, 100–5. Reviews of film versions of European plays (mostly the usual "classics") began to be published in *Kabuki* from 1907. By 1912, there was an active film society at a first-class legitimate theatre in Tokyo (Yoshiyama, "Bungei Katsudō Shashin Kyōkai" [Literary Moving Picture Society], *Kabuki* 143 [May 1912], 60–64).

35   Mori Mitsuya "Intercultural Problems and the Modernization of Theatre in Japan" *Theatre Research International* 20:2 (Summer 1995): 153.

36   Shinkokugeki, *Shinkokugeki*, 29–30, 40–42; Mukai, *Nippon*, 237–28. Mukai noted instances of "fiercely realistic" sword fighting in nineteenth century kabuki.

37   "Taishū geijutsu no nagare" [The flowing of popular arts], Tsurumi, *Nihon*, 366–68.

38   *Shinkokugeki*, 82, 179–87, 281–82, 293–869; Nagata, *Tate*, 48–49, 50–55; Kawatake Shigetoshi, *Nihon engeki zenshi*, 1,062; Tanaka, *Meiji*, 169–76; Ōzasa Yoshio, "Shinkokugeki kaishi" [A summary history of Shinkokugeki], in *Shinkokugeki*, 189–91.

39   Tsubouchi, *History*, 144–45; Ortolani, *Japanese*, 230.

40   *Shinkokugeki*, 82, 86, 187, 281–82; Kawatake Shigetoshi, *Nihon engeki zenshi*, 1,062. Among Sawada's mottoes for his troupe were "Art on the right, the public [popularity] on the left" and "Moving a half step ahead of the public but walking with them." When Sawada died at age thirty-seven in 1929, others emerged from the troupe to carry on his vision.

41   Nagata, *Tate*, 8, 18–20, 38–87; Kawatake Shigetoshi, *Nihon engeki zenshi*, 1,062; also Anderson, *Japanese*, 35–37, 48, 57–58.

42   *Shinkokugeki*, 215. Shinkokugeki, again at the forefront, first appeared on television in 1953, the same year regular television broadcasts began in Japan.

43   Ibid., 78.

44   The hypothesis is undeveloped anywhere.

45   The stage was well equipped by international standards although its auditorium had only hard wooden benches for five hundred people.

46   Tanaka, *Meiji*, 207–40.

47   Kawatake Shigetoshi, *Nihon engeki zenshi*, 1,052–54, 1,070–73; Akiba, *Nihon*, 2:178–181; Ortolani, *Japanese*, 234–36.

48   Kawatake Shigetoshi, *Nihon engeki zenshi*, 1,084–85; Waseda, *Nihon*, 254–63.

49   The Taishō era (the reign of Emperor Taishō) was specifically 1912–26, but it became a term for the period that extended several years beyond 1926.

50   Tanaka, *Meiji*, 216–18; Kawatake Shigetoshi, *Nihon engeki zenshi*, 1,083–84; Rimer, *Toward*, 54.

51   Kawatake Shigetoshi, *Nihon engeki zenshi*, 1,083–84, 1,093–94; Akiba, *Nihon*, 2:645–46, 656–80, 704–48; 2:728.

52   Kawarasaki was in the kabuki troupe that accompanied his mentor Sadanji II for performances in the Soviet Union and Europe in 1928.

53   Kawatake Shigetoshi, *Nihon engeki zenshi*, 864, 932, 936, 946, 1,086–87; Brian Powell, "Communist Kabuki: A Contradiction in Terms?" in Leiter, *Kabuki Reader*, 174–81.

54   Kawatake Shigetoshi, *Nihon engeki zenshi*, 950–51. Many shingeki, shimpa, and kabuki actors were in films as individuals. Zenshinza actors usually appeared as an ensemble.

55   As did every active theatre company.

56   Brian Powell, "Communist Kabuki," 178–83.

57   Japanese, *Theatre*, 207–8. "Tōhō Kabuki," a brand name, used famous kabuki actors and often attempted to modernize productions with actresses, but seldom reached the standards and clarity of classical kabuki.

58   Kawatake Shigetoshi, *Nihon engeki zenshi*, 951–52.

59   Coaldrake, *Women's*, 20–22. Male *jōruri* performers in kabuki were a gender exception.

60   Kyoto had female kabuki from the 1880s. Tokyo was a little later (Mukai, *Nippon*, 257).

61   Ibid., 257–59; Japanese, *Theatre*, 208–9.

62   Toita, "The Kabuki, the *Shimpa*," 259, 308.

63   When Kawakami was in the United States, rail and streetcar connections to amusement parks were the hottest development in the American entertainment business (along with the conversion of city theatres to vaudeville). Amusement parks added vaudeville theatres and dramatic stock companies to their many attractions of rides, games, snacks, and dance halls. I found no evidence that Kobayashi directly copied the Americans, although it was likely. In Japan, there were also other kinds of mutually reinforcing transit and commercial developments such as as department stores opened at or near railway terminals.

64   In the 1940s, "Shōjo" (girls) was dropped to shorten the name to Takarazuka Kageki (Takarazuka Opera).

65   Mukai, *Nippon*, 137.

66   Kawatake Shigetoshi, *Nihon engeki zenshi*, 1,115–16; Japanese, *Theatre*, 205–7; Mukai, *Nippon*, 135–41, 238–44. "Tōhō" is an amalgam of the *Tō* of Tōkyō and *hō*, an alternate pronunciation of the character (*kanji*) for *takara*.

67   The Shōchiku "girls'" shows underwent many name changes.

68   Kawatake Shigetoshi, *Nihon engeki zenshi*, 1,116; Mukai, *Nippon*, 141–49, 156–57; Waseda, *Nihon*, 336.

69   Mukai, *Nippon*, 248–55. Female swordfighters (*onna budō*) who fought men were a popular role for onnagata in kabuki.

70   Ibid., 270–291; Kawashima, *Nihon*, 172–80; Kata, *Asakusa*, 36–42, 119–23, 132–36.

Chapter 44

1   Kawatake Shigetoshi, *Nihon engeki zenshi*, 1,017.

2   Satō Tadao and Yoshida Chieo, *Nihon eiga joyū shi* [History of Japanese film actresses] (Haga Shobō, 1975), 8–11; Hagii, *Shimpa*, 183.

3   Yanagi, *Ebanzuke*, 271–72; Kawatake Shigetoshi, *Nihon engeki zenshi*, 1,017; Hagii, *Shimpa*, 235; Marui, *Shimpa*, 193–48, 163, 168; Ōe Ryōtarō, "Shimpa no ayumi kujūnen" [Through ninety years of shimpa], in Nagai Takeo, *Shimpa*, 26–27; Kawashima, *Nihon*, 88. *Futatsuji michi* centered on the contrasting fortunes of three geisha. One reason for its extraordinary success and that of its sequels was the robust, contrasting personalities of its female characters played by shimpa onnagata.

4   Many other shimpa plays centered on waitresses, hostesses, prostitutes, and other working women who catered to male pleasure. Often the male characters were weak, stupid, oppressive, or simply peripheral.

5   Also known as *katei dorama* (family drama).

6   Marui, *Shimpa*, 134–74; Kawatake Shigetoshi, *Gaisetsu*, 388.

7   Ōe, "Shimpa no ayumi," 27; Yanagi, *Ebanzuke*, 267–72; Kawashima, *Nihon*, 96–99.

8   These films were roughly examined in the context of an imperfect American sensibility in Anderson, *Japanese*, 318–20.

9   Kawatake Toshio, *Japan*, 125.

10 The revival repertoire was primarily plays (and their revisions) from the Golden Age. If a new play proved popular, it joined the repeatable canon.

11 The film was adapted from a 1922 American play by Austin Strong.

12 Marui, *Shimpa*, 144, 163, 173.

13 Ibid., 57–68, 134–140, 147; Toita, *Kabuki*, 134; Mizutani, *Matsuba*, 280; Shirakawa Nobuo, "Meijiki ni okeru Furansushu gikyoku jōen nempyō" [Meiji era chronology of performances of plays based on French dramas], *Engeki kenkyū* 9 (1979): 125–36; Mukai, *Nippon*, 258.

14 Sometimes known as the Second Geijutsuza, this shimpa troupe was considered the resurrection of the pioneering shingeki Geijutsuza that Shimamura and Matsui led before their deaths.

15 Ōe, "Shimpa no ayumi," 29; Japanese, *Theatre*, 188–89. Honryū Shimpa fell apart in 1942.

16 Marui, *Shimpa*, 220; Kawatake Shigetoshi, *Nihon engeki zenshi*, 930.

17 Komiya, *Kabuki*, 113–20; Marui, *Shimpa*, 145–71. Two other similar surveys (Yanagi, *Shimpa no gojūnen*, 81–98, and Kawasaki Shigetoshi, *Gaisetsu*, 388) respectively listed total yearly averages for these periods as fifteen and twenty-two.

18 Other than original screenplays, popular novels were the sources of most Japanese film scripts.

19 For discussions of Mizoguchi's work relevant to shimpa, see Keiko MacDonald, *Mizoguchi* (Boston: Twayne, 1984), 18, 30, 34, 53, 57, 138, and Dudley and Paul Andrew, *Kenji Mizoguchi* (Boston: Hall, 1981).

20 These included *Ono ga tsumi* [My sin], *Nihombashi* [Japan Bridge], *Tōjin O-Kichi* [O-Kichi the foreigner], *Taki no Shiraito*, *Gubijinsō* [Poppy], and *Orizuru O-Sen* [O-Sen of the paper cranes, a.k.a., *The Downfall of O-Sen*].

21 There was an earlier *Ugetsu* shimpa play in 1933 (Marui, *Shimpa*, 147).

22 Marui, *Shimpa*, 172, 177–78, 191–98. The titles and content of films and plays listed here were not necessarily "faithful" adaptations.

23 Donald Keene, "Realism and Unreality in Japanese Drama," *Drama Survey* 3:3 (February 1984): 350. Keene did not discuss shimpa.

24 Kawashima, *Nihon*, 209–21.

25 Iwai, *Shimpa*, 26–27, 31–32; Yanagi, *Shimpa no rokujūnen*, 318–21, 334.

26 Mizuochi Kiyoshi, "Shimpa onnagata gei no denshō" [Traditions of shimpa *onnagata* art], *Engekikai* (February 1987): 96–97; Honchi Eiki, "Shimpa no iku beki michi wa" [The road shimpa should take], *Engekikai* (February 1987): 99; Ōzasa Yoshio, "Shimpa shi shaken" [A personal view of shimpa history], *Engekikai* (February 1987): 93; personal observations, 1955–57.

27 This refers to the "realistic" acting seen in domestic stories onstage and in film.

28 Ōzasa, *Nihon*, 589–90; Kawatake Shigetoshi, *Gaisetsu*, 384–87; Japanese, *Theatre*, 187.

29 Agi Ōzuke, "Shimpa meiyū no omokage" [Memorable impressions of famous shimpa actors], *Engekikai* (February 1987), 95; Ōe Ryōtarō, "Shimpa no hitobito" [The people of shimpa], in Gekidan Shimpa, *Shimpa*, 130–33. Having created the title role of the vulnerable kabuki actor Kiku on the shimpa stage, Hanayagi repeated it in Mizoguchi Kenji's 1939 film, *Zangiku monogatari*. This led to more movie appearances in male roles.

30 Iwai, *Shimpa*, 38–39; Satō Tadao and Yoshida Chieo, *Nihon eiga joyū shi*, 12–13, 174. For those counting, Mizutani may be considered Japan's third or fourth "film actress."

31 Marui, *Shimpa*, 148. In the play *Onna kengeki* [Female sword fighting plays], Mizutani played a female actor who was an androgynous male sword-fighting star.

32 Oe, "Shimpa no ayumi," 27–28; Japanese, *Theatre*, 188–89; Kawasaki Shigetoshi, *Nihon no engeki*, 216–17.

33 Kinugasa became a film director after he lost his job as a movie onnagata.

34 Shimpa *gendaigeki* and not shingeki was a greater influence on film acting.

35   William Gillette theorized on this somewhat shopworn ideal as a basis for actor realism in performance.

36   Kawashima, *Nihon*, 203–4.

37   Hagii, *Shimpa*, 220–21.

38   Hagii's proposition; my examples.

39   Marui Fujio, "Shimpa kujūninen nempu" [A ninety-two year chronology of shimpa], in Marui, *Shimpa*, 10–12; Hōjō, *Shimpa*, 231–33.

40   Ōe Ryōtarō, "Shimpa no ayumi, 28. In *Fūryū*, a young woman is caught between her feelings and obligations that are complicated by a family crisis over money in a very traditional *shitamachi* neighborhood.

41   *Engei gahō* (March 1937).

42   Inoue, *Kawakami*, 140; Marui, *Shimpa*, 160; Nagai Takao, *Shimpa*, 74.

43   Kawashima, *Nihon*, 168.

44   Historian Yi Tŭ-hyŏn called early *sinp'a* an "exact copy" of Japanese shimpa in his "Projection of Tradition in Modern Drama," in *Korean Dance, Theatre, and Cinema*, ed. Korean National Commission for UNESCO (Seoul: Si-sa-yong-o-sa [sic], 1983), 154; also conversations with playwright Yu Ch'i-jin, Seoul, 1954–55.

45   Siyuan Li, "The Impact of *Shi[m]pa* on Early Chinese *Huaju*," *Asian Theatre Journal* 23 (Fall 2006): 342–55.

46   Marui, *Shimpa*, 162–85. For a quick summary of national policy regulations and enforcement in the war period, see Anderson, *Japanese*, 128–29.

47   Kawatake Toshio, *Japan*, 223; Miyake, *Engeki*, 394–97.

48   Yanagi, *Ebanzuke*, 278; Waseda, *Nihon*, 270–71; Ortolani, *Japanese*, 227.

49   Waseda, *Nihon*, 271–72; Marui, *Shimpa*, 185; Kawatake Shigetoshi, *Nihon engeki zenshi*, 1,096–97.

50   Kabuki, motion pictures, and shingeki were more severely subjected to wartime and U. S. Occupation censorship and "guidance" than shimpa.

51   Waseda, *Nihon*, 271–72; Kawatake Shigetoshi, *Nihon engeki zenshi*, 961–64.

52   James R. Brandon, "Myth and Reality: a Story of *Kabuki* during American Censorship, 1945–1949," *Asian Theatre Journal* 23:1 (Spring 2006): 1–110.

53   Even though Shinkokugeki and Zenshinza had extensive established repertoires set in pre-Meiji feudal times, they were better able to revise their program content in accordance with postwar policies and ambiance.

54   Waseda, *Nihon*, 271, 276–80.

55   Marui, *Shimpa*, 147, 193–210.

56   Kawatake Shigetoshi, *Nihon engeki zenshi*, 876, 1,099; Ortolani, *Japanese*, 227; Marui, *Shimpa*, 208–18.

57   Kawashima, *Nihon*, 203.

58   Yanagi, *Ebanzuke*, 267–72; Kawashima, *Nihon*, 96–99; Ōe, "Shimpa no ayumi," 27.

59   Ōe, "Shimpa no ayumi," 30; Marui Fujio, "Shimpa kujūninen nempu," in his *Shimpa*, 10, also 220. The Kansai shimpa troupe in Osaka had already disbanded.

60   Marui, *Shimpa*, 185–207.

61   Marui Fujio, "Shimpa kujūninen nempu"; Ōe, "Shimpa no ayumi," 30.

62   Agi Ōzuke, "Shimpa meiyū no omokage," 95.

63   Waseda, *Nihon*, 302–3.

64   Iwai, *Shimpa*, 253; Ōzasa Yoshio, "Shimpa shi shaken," *Engekikai* (February 1987): 93; personal observation.

65   Yanagi, *Ebanzuke*, 267–72; Kawashima, *Nihon*, 96–99.

66   Marui, *Shimpa*, 153–219. *Zangiku* was adapted from a "biographical novel," a Japanese literary genre in which life history is mixed with fiction.

67   Ibid., 66, 146, 181, 204–8; Hōjō, *Hōjō*, 597–603. Matsui Sumako was portrayed in two shimpa plays, of which the most acclaimed was Hōjō Hideki's 1963 *Joyū*, in which Mizutani Yaeko's daughter, Yoshie,

played the young Matsui and Yaeko played Mori Ritsuko, who was a student of Sadayakko and the major star of early Teigeki plays. One of the minor characters in this play was a teenage actress named Mizutani Yaeko.

68   Marui, *Shimpa*, 146, 205, 216–18.

69   Ōe, "Shimpa no ayumi," 30; Ōzasa Yoshio, "Shimpa shi shaken," 95; Ortolani, *Japanese*, 227; Marui, *Shimpa*, 193–213.

70   "Shōwa yonjūnen yori genzai made" [From 1965 to the present], in Nagai Takeo, *Shimpa*, 32; Honchi Eiki, "Shimpa no iku," 99; Ōe, "Shimpa no ayumi," 98.

71   Mizuochi Kiyoshi, "Shimpa onnagata gei no denshō," 96–97; Honchi Eiki, "Shimpa no iku beki michi wa," 99; Ōzasa Yoshio, "Shimpa shi shaken," 93; Ōe, "Shimpa no ayumi," 30; "Shōwa yonjūnen yori genzai made," 31–32; Toita, *Kabuki*, 150–55.

72   Ōzasa, "Shimpa shi shiken," 93; Kawashima, *Nihon*, 204.

73   "Shōwa yonjūnen yori genzai made," 32. The troupe enrolled middle-aged male movie stars with shingeki experience to fill the gap: Mori Masayuki (*Rashōmon*), Yasui Shōji (*The Harp of Burma*), and Sugawara Kenji.

74   Several drama critics advised him to concentrate on shimpa.

75   Waseda, *Nihon*, 335.

76   Honchi Eiki, "Shimpa no iku beki michi wa," 99; personal observations.

77   Ōzasa Yoshio, "Shimpa shi shaken," *Engekikai* (February 1987): 93; Marui, *Shimpa*, 190–220; Japanese, *Theatre*, 185. Gekidan Shimpa played regularly only in Tokyo, Osaka, Kyoto, and Nagoya.

78   "Shōwa yonjūnen yori genzai made," 32.

79   Intensive rehearsals before an opening last three to five days.

80   Satō, *Nihon*, 448. Morning performances usually began at 11:30; afternoon at 4:30.

Chapter 45

1   "Taishū geijutsu no nagare" [The flowing of popular arts] in Tsurumi, *Nihon*, 396–400; Mukai, *Nippon*, 296–98.

2   "'Onna kengeki' to iu jidai" [The era of female swordplays], *Shibai tsūshin* 2003: 188–89; Mukai, *Nippon*, 248–55, 299–307. In the early 1950's there were fifteen to twenty *sutorippu shō* (strip show) theatres (often shacks) in metropolitan Tokyo and dozens more throughout Japan.

3   Waseda, *Nihon*, 264, 270, 274; Kawatake Shigetoshi, *Nihon engeki zenshi*, 1,090, 1,101–7.

4   Shingeki translations of foreign plays were frequent throughout the early postwar decades and included: Tennessee Williams, John Osborne, Beckett, Brecht, Arthur Miller, Pinter, Ionesco, Cocteau, Camus, Lorca, Stoppard, and Sartre (Waseda, *Nihon*, 282–338).

5   Ibid., 273–332; Kaori Ashizu, "What's *Hamlet* to Japan," http//www.hamjap.htm [2/17/2008]. During the 1990s, eighteen noteworthy *Hamlet* productions were staged and a full-scale pseudo-replica of the Elizabethan Globe Theatre [Gurobu-za] opened in Tokyo in 1988. The 703-seat Gurobu-za is more architectural fantasy than reproduction.

6   Ortolani, *Japanese*, 243.

7   Mukai, *Nippon*, 222–31, 321, 328.

8   Waseda, *Nihon*, 298–347. The most renowned *angura* figures were Kara Jūrō, with his Jōkyō (Situation) Theatre, and Terayama Shūji, with his Tenjō Sajiki (Top of the Gallery) troupe.

9   Ortolani, *Japanese*, 245; also works cited later in this chapter; author's observations.

10   Waseda, *Nihon*, 319, 322, 324. Suzuki Tadashi created his own distinctive synthesis of foreign and Japanese theatre that led to the founding of the international SCOT (Suzuki Company of Toga).

11   Personal observations; Waseda, *Nihon*, 324–25.

12   Ibid., 322.

13   Also known as *neo kabuki*.

14   Natsuko Inoue, "New (Neo) *Kabuki* and the Work of Hanagumi Shibai," in Leiter, *Kabuki Reader*, 186–191.

15   Kawatake Toshio, *Japan*, 284–85.

16   "Engeki sukejūru" [Play schedules], *Pia* (May 31, 2004): 209.

17   The first known postwar proposition from abroad was the Metropolitan Opera's overture to Kurosawa Akira to direct their new staging of *Madama Butterfly* after his *Rashōmon* won at the Venice 1951 Film Festival. This did not work out (personal observation).

18   Quoted in Mukai, *Nippon*, 309–10. The first postwar Teigeki musical was *Morugan O-Yuki* (O-Yuki Morgan), based on the famous true story of the geisha who married into the J. P. Morgan family.

19   Teigeki, *Teigeki*, 88, 145–48, 226–28; Waseda, *Nihon*, 280, 308–13, 318. Puccini's *Madama Butterfly* was well known in Japan. I saw a conventional production of the opera at the old Teigeki in 1950.

20   Mukai, *Nippon*, 315, 319; Waseda, *Nihon*, 292–330; Komiya, *Kabuki*, 144–87.

21   Anderson, *Japanese*, 351, 454.

22   Ibid. 451–52, 454; Anderson, "Ken, the Noodle Vendor and Other Adventures on Japanese Television," *American Film* 1 (Spring 1976); also unpublished research conducted for NHK. Numerous reruns on television contributed to the inflation of the number of Japanese drama broadcasts. Japan did not develop the subsequent American profusion of cable channels with their unceasing reruns.

23   *Shiatā gaido* [Theatre guide] (June 2009), 151; *Engekikai* [Theatre world] (June 2009), 127.

24   These grand structures were often called "so-and-so city or prefecture *Bunka Sentā*" (Cultural Center).

25   *Pia hōru, gekijō, sutajiam* [Pia halls, theatres, and stadiums], (Pia, 2009), 16–109; *Engeki nenkan 2008* [Theatre yearbook 2008] (Nihon engeki kyōkai, 2008), 480. Small performance spaces are located all over Tokyo. There are also venues much larger than those counted here, but they are not used regularly for theatrical performance.

26   *Engeki nenkan 2008*, 9–33, 93–119. I found it impossible to accurately count the total number of active producing organizations.

27   Information in this section derived from *Pia hōru, gekijō, sutajiam*, 24–109; *Pia* (May 31, 2004; October 13, 2005; May 24, 2007); *Shiatā gaido* (March through June 2007; June 2009); *Engeki nenkan 2008*, 480.

28   *Shiatā gaido* (June 2009), 83–135.

29   In my surveys, I count shows by their total number of *performances* rather than by days or weeks played.

30   *Shiatā gaido* (June 2009), 78–81.

31   My broad category here includes *taishū engeki*, single person ("one-man") performances, singing star extravaganzas (headliners sing their hits and act in short plays), variety shows of all sizes with sketches, and improv groups. There is minor interest in current American or British popular (nonmusical) plays.

32   My survey did not include music concerts.

33   *Pia hōru, gekijō, sutajiam*, 110–11.

34   Performances of traditional Japanese dance are omitted because of a lack of adequate details and because most are amateur.

35   This includes three in suburban areas (personal observation).

36   The New York numbers are from *Time Out New York* (November 8–14, 2007; February 21–27, 2008; May 8–14, 2008).

37   Mizutani Yoshie and Tsujimura Junzaburō, "Shimpa no naka Kyōka" (Shimpa inside [Izumi] Kyōka [playwright]), *Raijingu* (January 1990): 31.

38   Tokyo, Shimbashi Embujō, November 1999 (Shimbashi Embūjō, Tokyo, program, November 1999;

"Kyūshū no būtai" [Kyūshū stages]), *Engekikai* [November 1999]: n.p., and "Kyūshū gekishin" [Kyūshū drama news]: 112; personal observation).

39   Toita, *Monogatari*, 22; Takahashi, "Zadankai," 79. In 1900, when Sadayakko was the Parisian rage, a French perfume company introduced its new scent, "Yacco."

Principal Bibliography and Works Consulted

The abridged citations (author's last name and the initial word or words of the title) in the endnotes for the main text are fully listed in this bibliography. Less important or less used sources do not appear in this bibliography but are fully cited in the appropriate endnote.

In accordance with Japanese bibliographic practice, Tokyo is omitted when it is the place of publication of Japanese language material.

The following abbreviations are used throughout.

BPL	Boston Public Library
BRTC	Billy Rose Theatre Collection, NYPLPA
CHS	Chicago Historical Society
CTPC CPL	Chicago Theatre Programs Collection, Chicago Public Library
HTC	Harvard Theatre Collection
NYC	*New York Clipper*
NYDM	*New York Dramatic Mirror*
NYPLPA	New York Public Library for the Performing Arts Research Collections
RBD	Rare Book Department
RLS	Robinson Locke Scrapbook in NYPLPA
SFPLSC	San Francisco Public Library Special Collections
Waseda	Waseda Engeki Hakubutsukan Toshoshitsu, Tokyo

Abe Yūzō. *Tōkyō no koshibai* [The small theatres of Tokyo]. Engeki Shuppansha, 1970.

Adams, Henry. *The Letters of Henry Adams, Vol. 3: 1886–1892.* Ed. J. C. Levenson et al. Cambridge: Belknap/Harvard, 1982.

Akashi Tetsuya. *Kawakami Otojirō; geinō chōkan shosetsu* [Kawakami Otojirō: a novel about show business]. Sankyō Shoin, 1943.

Akiba Tōto. *Nihon shingeki shi* [A history of *shingeki* (new drama)]. 2 vols. Risōsha, 1955–56.

———. *Tōto Meiji engeki shi* [A history of theatre in Tōkyō during the Meiji era]. Nakamura Shobō, 1937.

Allen, Robert C. *Horrible Prettiness: Burlesque and American Culture.* Chapel Hill: University of North Carolina Press, 1991.

"American Popular Songs" collection [V.P.] [brackets *sic*]; microfilm *ZB-768, reels 7–12A, 1897–1901, at Music Division, NYPLPA.

American Stage Today, The. New York: Collier, 1910.

Anderson, J[oseph] L. "Spoken Silents in the Japanese Cinema; or, Talking to Pictures: Essaying the *Katsuben*, Contexturalizing the Tests." In *Reframing the Japanese Cinema: Authorship, Genre, History*, eds. Arthur Nollett, Jr. and David Desser, 259–310. Bloomington: University of Indiana Press, 1992.

Anderson, Joseph L., and Donald Richie, *The Japanese Film: Art and Industry.* Rutland, Vermont: Tuttle, 1959. Revised edition, Princeton, New Jersey: Princeton University Press, 1982.

Antoine, Andre. *Le theatre.* Paris: Editions d'France: 1932.

Appia, Adolphe. *Œuvres complete.* Lausanne: L'Âge de Homme, 1986.

Appleton's Directory of "Greater" New York. New York: Appleton, 1898.

Arnold, Edwin. *Adzuma or The Japanese Wife. In Four Acts.* New York: Scribner's, 1893.

Artaud, Antonin. *The Theatre and Its Double.* Trans. Mary Caroline Richards. New York: Grove, 1958.

Asakura Takashi. *Geinō no shigen ni mukatte* [Facing the origins of entertainment]. Myūjikku Magajin, 1986.

Asakusa no Kai, ed. *Shashin ni miru: Asakusa geinō den* [Looking at photographs: an account of Asakusa entertainment]. Asakusa no kai, 1990.

Auerbach, Nina. *Ellen Terry: Player in Her Own Time.* New York: Norton, 1987.

Austin, Henry, ed. *Gallery of Players Nos. 8 and 9.* New York: Illustrated American, 1896.

Backalenich, Irene. *East Side Story: Ten Years with the Jewish Repertory Theatre.* Langam, Maryland: University Press of America, 1988.

Baedeker, Karl, ed. *The United States with an Excursion into Mexico.* Leipzig: Baedeker, 1899.

Baker, Michael. *The Rise of the Victorian Actor.* Totowa, New Jersey: Rowman and Littlefield, 1978.

Banham, Martin, ed. *The Cambridge Guide to World Theatre.* New York: Cambridge University Press, 1992.

Banta, Martha. *Imagining American Women: Ideas and Ideals in Cultural History.* New York: Columbia University Press, 1987.

Barba, Eugenio, and Nicola Savarese. *The Secret Art of the Performer; A Dictionary of Theatre Anthropology.* Trans. Richard Fowler. London: Routledge, 1991.

Baudet, Henri. *Paradise on Earth: Some Thoughts on European Images of Non-European Man.* Trans. Richard Fowler. London: Routledge, 1991.

Beerbohm, Max. *Around Theatres*. New York: Knopf, 1930.

Beikoku Nikkeinin hyakunen shi [A hundred year history of Japanese in the United States]. Los Angeles: Shin Nichibei Shimbunsha, 1961.

Belasco, David [attributed], *Madam* [*sic*] *Butterfly*. Typewritten manuscript with holographic notations, item NCOF+, at BRTC.

Belasco, David. *Six Plays*. Boston: Little, Brown, 1928.

——— . *The Theatre through Its Stage Door*. New York: Harper, 1919.

Belford, Barbara. *Bram Stoker*. New York: Knopf, 1996.

Bender, Thomas, and Carl E. Schorske, eds. *Budapest and New York: Studies in Metropolitan Transformation, 1870–1930*. New York: Sage, 1994.

Berg, Shelley C. "Sada Yacco: The American Tour. 1899–1900." *Dance Chronicle* 16:2 (1993): 147–96.

——— . "Sada Yacco in London and Paris, 1900: Le Rêve Réalisé." *Dance Chronicle* 18:3 (1995): 343–404.

Bergman. Gösta M. *Lighting in the Theatre*. Totowa, New Jersey: Rowman and Littlefield, 1977.

Bernheim, Alfred L. *The Business of Theatre: An Economic History of the Theatre, 1750–1932*. 1932. Reprint. New York: Blom, 1964.

Bingham, Madeline. *Henry Irving: The Greatest Victorian Actor*. New York: Stein and Day, 1978.

Binns, Archie. *Mrs. Fiske and the American Theatre*. New York: Crown, 1955.

Bloom, Arthur W. *Joseph Jefferson: Dean of the American Theatre*. Savannah: Beil, 2000.

Booth, Michael [R.]. "Ellen Terry." In *Bernhardt, Terry, Duse*, by John Stokes, Michael Booth, and Susan Bassnet, 65–118. Cambridge: Cambridge University Press, 1988.

——— . *Prefaces to English Nineteenth Century Theatre*. Manchester: Manchester University Press, [c. 1980].

——— . *Theatre in the Victorian Age*. Cambridge: Cambridge University Press, 1991.

——— . *Victorian Spectacular Theatre: 1850–1910*. London: Routledge and Paul, 1981.

——— , ed. *Hiss the Villain: Six English and American Melodramas*. New York: Arnopress, 1977.

——— , ed. *Victorian Theatrical Trades*. London: Routledge and Paul, 1981.

——— , and Joel H. Kaplan, eds. *The Edwardian Theatre: Essays on Performance and the Stage*. New York: Cambridge University Press, 1996.

Bordman, Gerald. *American Musical Theatre: A Chronicle*. New York: Oxford University Press, 1986.

——— . *American Theatre: A Chronicle of Comedy and Drama, 1869–1914*. New York: Oxford University Press, 1994.

Boston Directory 1900. Boston: Sampson, Murdock, 1901.

Bowen, Roger W. *Rebellion and Democracy in Meiji Japan*. Berkeley: University of California Press, 1980.

Boyd, James Perry. *The Paris Exposition of 1900*. Philadelphia: Ziegler, 1900.

Brandon, James R. *Kabuki's Forgotten War: 1931–1945*. Honolulu: University of Hawaii. 2008.

——— , trans. *Kabuki: Five Classic Plays*. Cambridge: Harvard University Press, 1975.

——— , William P. Malm, and Donald H. Shively. *Studies in Kabuki: Its Acting, Music, and Historical Context*. Honolulu: University Press of Hawai'i, 1978.

Brazell, Karen, ed. *Traditional Japanese Theatre: An Anthology of Plays*. New York: Columbia University Press, 1998.

Brereton, Austin. *The Life of Henry Irving.* London: Longmans, Green, 1908. Reprint. New York: Blom, 1969.

————— . *The Lyceum and Henry Irving.* New York: McClure, Phillips, 1903.

Brockett, Oscar. *History of the Theatre.* Boston: Allyn and Bacon, 1974.

————— , and Robert R. Findlay. *Century of Innovation: A History of European and American Theatre and Drama since 1870.* Englewood Cliffs, New Jersey: Prentice-Hall, 1973.

Bromley, George Washington. *Atlas of the City of Boston, Central.* Philadelphia: Bromley, 1898.

Bronson, William. *The Earth Shook, the Sky Burned.* 1959. Reprint. San Francisco: Chronicle Books, 1986.

Brooks, Peter. *The Melodramatic Imagination: Balzac, Henry James, Melodrama, and the Mode of Excess.* New Haven: Yale University Press, 1976.

Brooks, Van Wyck. "Fenollosa and His Circle." In his *Fenollosa and His Circle with Other Essays in Biography.* New York: Dutton, 1963.

Brown, Henry Collins. *In the Golden Nineties.* Hastings-on-Hudson: Valentine's, 1928.

Brown, T. Allston. *A History of the New York Stage, from the First Performance in 1732 to 1901.* 3 vols. New York: Dodd, Mead, 1903.

Bulman, James C. *The Merchant of Venice.* Manchester: Manchester University Press, 1991.

Burge, James C. *Lines of Business: Casting Practice and Policy in the American Theatre 1752–1899.* New York: Peter Lang, 1986.

Burns, Elizabeth. *Theatricality: A Study of Convention in the Theatre and in Social Life.* London: Longman, 1972.

Burrows, Edwin G., and Mike Wallace. *Gotham: A History of New York City to 1898.* New York: Oxford University Press, 1999.

Cahn, Julius. *Julius Cahn's Official Theatrical Guide Containing Information of the Leading Theatres and Attractions in America, 1899–1900.* New York: Cahn, 1899.

————— . *Julius Cahn's Official Theatrical Guide Containing Information of the Leading Theatres and Attractions in America, 1900–01.* New York: Cahn, 1900.

Carlson, Marvin. *The French Stage in the Nineteenth Century.* Metuchen, New Jersey: Scarecrow, 1972,

Carter, Everett. *Howells and the Age of Realism.* Hamden, Connecticut: Archon, 1966.

Carter, Morris. *Isabella Stewart Gardner and Fenway Court.* Hamden, Connecticut: Archon, 1966.

Cashin, Charles M. *Boston Theatres and Halls with Historical Notes Past and Present.* Boston: Jones, 1907.

Catalog: Sosman and Landis Scene Painting Studio. Chicago: Sosman and Landis, 1889.

Cavaye, Ronald, Paul Griffith, and Akihiko Senda. *A Guide to the Japanese Stage: From Traditional to Cutting Edge.* Tokyo: Kodansha International, 2005.

Chamberlain, Basil Hall. *Japanese Things: Being Notes on Various Subjects Connected with Japan.* Original title: *Things Japanese.* 1905. Reprint. Rutland, Vermont: Tuttle, 1971.

Chiba Yoko. "Sada Yacco and Kawakami: Performers of Japonisme," *Modern Drama* 35 (1992): 35–53.

Chisholm, Lawrence W. *Fenollosa: The Far East and American Culture.* New Haven: Yale University Press, 1963.

Churchill, Allen. *The Great White Way.* New York: Dutton, 1962.

Clapp, Henry Austin. *Reminiscences of a Dramatic Critic.* Boston: Houghton, Mifflin, 1902.

Clapp, John B., and Edwin Francis Edgett. *Players of the Present.* New York: Dunlop Society, 1900.

Clark, Barrett H., and George Freedley, eds. *A History of Modern Drama.* New York: Appleton-Century, 1947.

Coaldrake, A. Kimi. *Women's Gidayū and the Japanese Theatre Tradition.* Book and CD recording. London: Routledge, 1997.

Cohen, Aaron M. "Otojirō Kawakami and Yacco Sada: Japanese Actors in America at the Turn of the Twentieth Century," *Nanzan Review of American Studies* 25 (2003): 31–51.

Coleman, Marion Moore. *Fair Rosalind: The American Career of Helena Modjeska.* Cheshire, Connecticut: Cherry Hill, 1969.

Conroy, Hilary, Sandra T. W. Davis, and Wayne Patterson, eds. *Japan in Transition: Thought and Action in the Meiji Era, 1868–1912.* Rutherford, New Jersey: Fairleigh Dickinson University Press, 1984.

Coquelin, Constant, et al. *The Art of Acting.* Reprint. New York: Dramatic Museum of Columbia University, 1926.

Craig, Edward Gordon. *Henry Irving.* New York: Longmans, Green, 1930.

——— . *Index to the Story of My Days.* New York: Viking, 1957.

——— . *The Theatre Advancing.* Boston: Little, Brown, 1928.

Crane, Stephen. *Last Words.* London: Digby, Long, 1902.

Crawford, Mary Caroline. *The Romance of the American Theatre.* 1913. Reprint. New York: Halcyon House, 1940.

Creegan, George R., compiler. *Traditions of Acting.* Five 1/8" tape cassettes with booklets. Steubenville, Ohio: Crest Cassettes, Creegan Company, c. 1988.

Crocker-Langley San Francisco Directory for the Year Commencing May (1898 through 1902). San Francisco: Crocker, 1898–1902.

Daniels, Roger. *Asian America: Chinese and Japanese in the United States since 1850.* Seattle: University of Washington Press, 1988.

——— . *The Politics of Prejudice: The Anti-Japanese Movement in California.* Berkeley: University of California Press, 1962.

Davies, Robertson. *The Mirror of Nature.* Toronto: University of Toronto Press, 1983.

Davis, Richard Harding. *The Great Streets of the World.* New York: Scribner's, 1892.

Davis, Ronald J. *Augustus Thomas.* Boston: Twayne, 1984.

Davis, Tracy. *Actresses as Working Women: Their Social Identity in Victorian Culture.* London: Routledge, 1991.

DeMille, Cecil B. *The Autobiography of Cecil B. DeMille.* Englewood Cliffs, New Jersey: Prentice-Hall, 1959.

Dennett, Andrea Stulman. *Weird and Wonderful: The Dime Museum in America.* New York: New York University Press, 1997.

Dennett, Tyler. *John Hay: from Poetry to Politics.* New York: Doff, Mead, 1933.

Dennis, Alfred L. *Adventures in American Diplomacy, 1896–1906.* New York: Dutton, 1928.

Dennison, Sam. *Scandalize My Name: Black Imagery in American Popular Music.* New York: Garland, 1982.

Dentō Geijutsu no Kai. *Dentō to gendai: taishū geinō* [Tradition and the present: popular entertainment]. Gakugei Shorin, 1969.

DeWitt, Frederick M. *An Illustrated and Descriptive Souvenir and Guide to San Francisco*. San Francisco: DeWitt, 1897.

Dickson, Samuel. *The Streets of San Francisco*. Stanford: Stanford University Press, 1955.

Dijkstra, Bram. *Idols of Perversity: Fantasies of Feminine Evil in Fin-de-Siècle Culture*. New York: Oxford University Press, 1986.

DiMeglio, John E. *Vaudeville U. S. A*. Bowling Green, Ohio: Bowling Green Popular Press, 1973.

Dimmick, Ruth Crosby. *Our Theatres Today and Yesterday*. New York: Fly, 1913.

Dōmon Fuyuji. *Kawakami Sadayakko: monogatari to shiseki o tazunete* [Kawakami Sadayakko: Searching for her story and historical sites]. Seimidō, 1984.

Dōmoto Masaki. *Danshoku engeki shi* [History of male homosexual theatre]. Bara Jūjisha, 1970.

Dōmoto Yatarō. *Kamigata engeki shi* [History of theatre in the Kamigata region]. Shunyōdō, 1944.

Donaldson, Frances. *The Actor-Managers*. Chicago: Regnery, 1970.

Downer, Leslie. *Madame Sadayakko: The Geisha Who Bewitched the West*. New York: Gotham, 2003.

Dreiser, Theodore. *Sister Carrie*. 1900. Reprint and addition. Philadelphia: University of Pennsylvania, 1981

Driver, Tom F. *Romantic Quest and Modern Query: A History of the Modern Theatre*. New York: Delacorte, 1970.

Duis, Perry R. *The Saloon: Public Drinking in Chicago and Boston 1880–1920*. Urbana: University of Illinois Press, 1983.

Dunn, Charles J., and Bunzō Torigoe, eds., trans. and commentators. *The Actors' Analects*. New York: Columbia Press, 1969.

Eaton, Walter Prichard. *The Actor's Heritage: Scenes from the Theatre of Yesterday*. Boston: *Atlantic Monthly*, 1924.

Eco, Umbert. *Travels in Hyperreality*. Trans. William Weaver. New York: Harcourt Brace Jovanovich, 1986.

Edwards, Herbert J., and Julia A. Herne. *James C. Herne: Rise of Realism in the American Drama*. Orono: University of Maine Press, 1964.

Ellis, Edward Robb. *The Epic of New York City*. New York: Coward-McCann, 1966.

Elsom, John. *Erotic Theatre*. London: Secker and Warburg, 1973.

Enchi Fumiko, ed., *Jimbutsu Nihon no jōsei shi, daikyūkan: gei no michi hitosuji ni* [Personalities in the history of Japanese women, vol. 9: those dedicated to the way of art]. Sūreisha, 1977.

Engeki nenkan 2008 [Theatre yearbook 2008]. Nihon Engeki Kyōkai, 2008.

Engle, Ron, and Tice L. Miller, eds. *The American Stage: Social and Economic Issues from the Colonial Period to the Present*. New York: Cambridge University Press, 1993.

Enjōji Kiyoomi. *Tōkyō no gekijō* [Theatres of Tōkyō]. Kokuritsu Geikijō Chōsa Yōseibu, 1978.

Ernst, Alice Henson. *Trouping in Oregon Country*. Portland: Oregon Historical Society, 1961.

Ernst, Earle. *The Kabuki Theatre*. New York: Grove, 1956.

Ervine, St. John. *The Theatre in My Time*. London: Rich and Cowan, 1933.

Estavan, Lawrence, ed. *San Francisco Theatre Research*. Vols. 6, 9, 16, 17. San Francisco: Works Project Administration, 1938–42.

Exhibition of Japanese Paintings in Water Color and Oil: H. Yoshida, H. Nakagawa. Boston: Museum of Fine Arts, 1900.

Ezaki Atsushi. *Jitsuroku Kawakami Sadayakko: sekai o kaketa honoo no onna* [The true story of Kawakami Sadayakko: the impassioned woman who soared around the world]. Shinjimbutsu Ōraisha, 1985.

Famous Actors of the Day in America. N.p., n.d. [fragments of book in author's collection].

Farson, Daniel. *The Man Who Wrote Dracula: A Biography of Bram Stoker*. London: Michael Joseph, 1975.

Federal Writers' Project. *Washington: City and Capital*. Washington: Government Printing Office, 1937.

Fenollosa, Mary McNeil. *Hiroshige: The Artist of Mist, Snow, and Rain*. San Francisco: Vickey, Atkins, and Torrey, 1901.

——— [Sidney McCall, pseud.]. *Out of the Nest: A Flight of Verses*. Boston: Little, Brown, 1899.

Fergusson, Francis. *The Idea of Theatre*. Princeton: Princeton University Press, 1949.

Ferris, Leslie, ed. *Crossing the Stage: Controversies on Cross-Dressing*. New York: Routledge, 1993.

[Field, Edwin A.]. *Through the Stagedoor: A Complete Hand-Book of the Theatre*. Boston: Field, 1896.

Finson, Jon W. *The Voices That Are Gone: Themes in Nineteenth-Century American Popular Song*. New York: Oxford University Press, 1994.

Fischer-Lichte, Erika. *The Show and the Gaze of Theatre*. Iowa City: University of Iowa, 1997.

Fisher, Judith L., and Stephen Watt, eds. *When They Weren't Doing Shakespeare: Essays on Nineteenth-Century British and American Theatre*. Athens: University of Georgia Press, 1989.

Fiske, Minnie Maddern. *Mrs. Fiske: Her Views on Actors, Acting, and the Problems of Production*. Recorded by Alexander Woolcott. New York: Century, 1917.

Fitzgerald, Percy. *The Art of Acting*. London: Sonnenschein, 1892.

———. *Sir Henry Irving: A Biography*. Philadelphia: Jacobs, 1906.

Flinn, John Joseph. *Chicago: The Marvelous City of the West*. Chicago: Standard Guide, 1892.

Foulkes, Richard, ed. *British Theatre in the 1890's: Essays on Drama and the Stage*. Cambridge: Cambridge University Press, 1992.

———, ed. *Shakespeare and the Victorian Stage*. New York: Cambridge University Press, 1986.

Fournier, Louis. *Kawakami and Sada Yacco*. Paris: Brentano's, 1900.

Frick, John W. *New York's Theatrical Center: The Rialto at Union Square*. Ann Arbor: UMI, 1985.

Frohman, Daniel. *Memories of a Manager: Reminiscences of the Old Lyceum and of Some Players of the Last Quarter Century*. Garden City, New York: Doubleday, Page, 1911.

Fujii Sōtetsu, ed. *Jiden Otojirō—Sadayakko* [Autobiographies of Otojirō and Sadayakko]. San'ichi Shobō, 1984.

Fujinami Yohee. *Shibai no kodōgu* [Stage properties]. Nihon Hōsō Shuppan Kyōkai, 1974.

Fujine Iwao, ed. *Haru no hatō: NHK taiga dorama sutorî* [The rough seas of spring: the story of the NHK epic drama]. Nihon Hōsō Shuppan Kyōkai, 1985.

———, ed. *Rekishi e no shōtai; 12* [Invitation to history; no. 12]. Nihon Hōsō Shuppan Kyōkai, 1981.

Fujino Yoshio. *Mizono-za hachijūnen shi* [Eighty-year history of the Mizono-za]. Nagoya: Mizono-za, 1976.

Fujisawa Asajirō. "Kawakami fūfu o kataru" [Talking about Mr. and Mrs. Kawakami]. In ed. Fujii Sōtetsu. *Jiden Otojirō—Sadayakko*, 223–70.

Fujisawa Morihiko. *Meiji ryūkōka shi* [History of popular songs of the Meiji era]. Shun'yōdō, 1929.

Fujita Heinosuke, ed. *Daikabuki kowairo senshū* [Selected dialog passages from major kabuki plays]. Tōkyō: n.p., n.d.

———, ed. *Shimpa kowairo jūhachiban* [Dialog passages from the eighteen (best) shimpa plays]. Kokkadō, 1919.

Fujita Hiroshi. *Nihon buyō* [Japanese dance]. Dentō geinō shirîzu 1 [Traditional performing arts series, book 1]. Gyōsei, 1989.

———. *Onnagata no keizu* [The lineage of onnagata]. Shintoku Shosha, 1970.

Fujita, Minoru, and Leonard Pronko, eds. *Shakespeare: East and West.* New York: St. Martin's, 1996.

Fujiwara Satoko, writer-director. *Tachimawari* [Swordfighting] in *Kabuki no miryoku* [The spellbinding power of kabuki] series. VHS cassette. Apollon, 1990.

Fuller, Loïe. Manuscript. Autobiography. In Loïe Fuller papers, item *MGZMC Res. 5 microfilm *ZBD-112, at Dance Collection, NYPLLC.

———. *Fifteen Years of a Dancer's Life.* Boston: Small, Maynard, 1913. Reprint New York: Dance Horizons, n.d.

Furst, William, composer. *The Darling of the Gods.* Manuscript. Incidental music scores. [London: His Majesty's Theatre, 1903], item ML96 .F87D3, at Brown Collection, Music Department, BPL.

———. *Madame Butterfly.* Manuscript. Incidental music scores, item JBB 82–37, at Music Department, NYPLPA.

Gagey, Edmon. *The San Francisco Stage: A History.* New York: Columbia University Press, 1950.

Gainor, J. Ellen, ed. *Imperialism and Theatre: Essays on World Theatre, Drama, and Performance.* New York: Routledge, 1995.

Gallus, Arthur. *Emma Calvé: Her Artistic Life.* New York: Russell, 1902.

Gänzl, Kurt. *The British Musical Theatre; Vol. 1, 1865–1914.* New York: Oxford University Press, 1986.

Gardner, Vivien, and Susan Rutherford, eds. *The New Woman and Her Sisters: Feminism and Theatre 1850–1914.* Ann Arbor: University of Michigan Press, 1992.

Gautier, Judith. *Les musiques bizarres de l'Exposition.* Paris: Enoch, 1900.

Geinō Shi Kenkyūkai. *Nihon no koten geinō; dairoku-kan: buyō* [Japanese classical performance arts; vol. 6: dance]. Heibonsha, 1970.

Gekidan Shimpa, Maruii Fujio, et al., eds. *Shimpa: hyakunen e no zenshin* [Shimpa: toward a hundred years of progress]. Ōtemachi Shuppansha, 1978.

Gerould, Daniel, ed. *Melodrama.* New York: New York Literary Forum, 1980.

Gilbert, Douglas. *American Vaudeville: Its Life and Times.* 1940. Reprint. New York: Dover, 1968.

Glover, Lyman Beecher. *The Story of a Theatre.* Chicago: Powers Theatre, 1899.

Gluck, Carol. *Japan's Modern Myths: Ideology in the Late Meiji Period.* Princeton: Princeton University Press, 1968.

Golden, Joseph. *The Death of Tinker Bell: The American Theatre in the 20th Century.* Syracuse: Syracuse University Press, 1967.

Goodman, David. "The Post-Shingeki Theatre Movement in Japan," in Colby H. Kullman and William C. Young, eds. *Theatre Companies of the World.* Westport, Connecticut: Greenwood, 1986, 110–25.

Gotō Hajime. *Nihon geinō shi nyūmon* [Introduction to Japanese performance arts]. 1964. Reprint. Shakai Shisōsha, 1988.

Gotō Keiji. *Nihon gekijō shi* [History of Japanese theatres]. Iwanami Shoten, 1925.

Grandgent, Charles H. "The Stage in Boston in the Last Fifty Years." In *Fifty Years of Boston*, 391–401. Boston: Subcommittee on Memorial History on the Boston Tercentenary Committee, 1932.

Grant, Ethel Austin. "Old Buildings in Seattle, Tacoma, and Spokane." Manuscript. Item qR792 G7669o, at Seattle Public Library.

Grant, Howard F. *The Story of Seattle's Early Theatres.* Seattle: University of Washington, 1934.

Grau, Robert. *The Business Man in the Amusement World.* New York: Broadway Publishing, 1910.

Greenbank, Harry, lyricist. *The Geisha, the Story of a Tea House: A Japanese Musical Play.* Sidney Jones, composer; Owen Hall, co-librettist. London: Hopwood and Crew, 1896.

Grein, J[ames] T[homas]. *Premieres of the Year.* London, 1900. Reprint. New York: Blom, 1971.

Griffis, William Elliot. *The Mikado's Empire.* New York: Harper, 1890.

Gross, John. *Shylock: A Legend and Its Legacy.* New York: Simon and Schuster, 1992.

Gunji Masakatsu. *Buyō: The Classical Dance.* Trans. Don Kenny. New York: Walker, Weatherhill, 1970.

———. *Kabuki.* Trans. John Bester and Janet Goff. Tokyo: Kōdansha International, 1985.

———. *Kabuki to Yoshiwara* [Kabuki and Yoshiwara]. Asaji Shobō, 1956.

———. *Kabuki: yōshiki to dentō* [Kabuki: form and tradition]. Gakugei Shorin, 1969.

Hagii Kōzō. *Shimpa no gei* [The art of shimpa]. Tōkyō Shoseki, 1984.

Halford, Aubrey S., and Giovanna M. Halford. *The Kabuki Handbook.* Rutland, Vermont: Tuttle, 1956.

Hamamura Yonezo et al., *Kabuki.* Kenkyūsha, 1956.

Hammerton, J. A., ed. *The Actor's Art.* London: Redway, 1897.

Hanabusa Yūgai. *Yōkōchū no higeki* [Tragedy while traveling abroad]. In *Kawakami Otojirō Ōbei man'yūki*, ed. Kaneo Tanejirō.

Hanayagi Chiyo. *Nihon buyō no kiso* [The fundamentals of Japanese traditional dance]. Tōkyō Shoseki, 1981

Hanayagi Shōtarō. *Yakusha baka* [An actor fool]. Sangatsu Shobō, 1964.

Hanayagi Shōtarō, ed. *Nihon no geidan, daigo-kan: shimpa, Shinkokugeki, kigeki* [Conversations about Japanese performing arts, vol. 5: shimpa, Shinkokugeki, and comedy]. Sangatsu Shobō, 1964.

Handy Guide to Boston and Environs. Chicago: Rand, McNally, 1900.

Hanley, Susan B. *Everyday Things in Premodern Japan.* Berkeley: University of California Press, 1997.

Hapgood, Norman. *The Stage in America: 1897–1900.* New York: Macmillan, 1901.

Hartnoll, Phyllis. ed. *The Concise Oxford Companion to the Theatre.* Oxford: Oxford University Press, 1979.

Harvey, E. T. *Recollections of a Scene Painter.* Cincinnati: E. T. Harvey, 1916.

Hasegawa Kōen. *Shin onnagata kō* [A new treatise on *onnagata*]. Yomiuri Shimbunsha, 1970.

Hasegawa Masaharu. *Nihon buyō jiten* [Dictionary of Japanese dance]. Nihon Buyōsha, 1995.

Hasegawa Shigure. "Madamu Sadayakko" [Madame Sadayakko]. In *Kindai bijin den, ue* [Stories of contemporary beautiful women, vol. 1]. Iwanami Bunko, 1920.

Hasegawa Yoshio. *Onnagata no kenkyū* [Studies of onnagata]. Ritsumeikan, 1931.

Hattori Yukio. *Sakasama no yūrei* [Upside down phantoms]. Heibonsha, 1969.

Hazama, Dorothy Ochiai, and Jane Okamoto Komeiji. *Okage same de: The Japanese in Hawaii, 1885–1985.* Honolulu: Bass Press, c. 1986.

Hatton, Joseph. *Henry Irving's Impressions of America.* Boston: Osgood, 1884.

Hattori Yukio. *Kabuki no kōzō* [The structure of kabuki]. Chūō Kōronsha, 1970.

————. *Zankoku no bi: Nihon no dentō engeki ni okeru* [The aesthetics of cruelty in traditional Japanese theatre]. Haga Shoten, 1970.

Henderson, John A. *The First Avant-Garde: 1887–1894: Sources of the Modern French Theatre.* London: Harrap, 1973.

Henderson, Mary C. *The City and the Theatre: New York Playhouses from Bowling Green to Times Square.* Clifton, New Jersey: White, 1973.

Herman, Masako. *The Japanese in America, 1843–1973.* Dobbs Ferry, New York: Oceana, 1974.

Hearn, Lafcadio. *Glimpses of Unfamiliar Japan.* Boston: Houghton, Mifflin, 1894.

Herne, James. *Shore Acres and Other Plays.* New York: French, 1928.

Hewitt, Barnard. *Theatre U. S. A.: 1665–1957.* New York: McGraw-Hill, 1959.

Hill, Thomas E. *Hill's Souvenir Guide to Chicago.* Chicago: Laird and Lee, 1892.

Hines, Dixie ed. *Who's Who in Music and Drama.* New York: Hanaford, 1914.

Hirayama Rokō [Yoshie], et al. *Jōyū Tembō* [Surveying actresses]. Sekai Shobō, 1947.

Hitchcock, H. Wiley, and Stanley Sadie. *The New Grove Dictionary of American Music.* New York: Macmillan, 1986.

Hoeber, Arthur, ed. *Gallery of Players No. 11.* New York: Illustrated American, 1898.

Hōjō Hideji. *Shimpa gunzō* [Shimpa assembage]. Ei Shuppansha, 1976.

————, ed. *Hōjō Hideji gekisaku shi* [A history of the plays of Hōjō Hideji]. Nihon Hōsō Shuppan Kyōkai, 1974.

Holmes, Burton. *Burton Holmes Travelogues Vol. 2: Round about Paris.* New York: McClure, 1908.

Hopkins, Albert. *Magic, Stage Illusions, and Scientific Diversions.* New York: Munn, 1901.

Horioka, Yasuko. *The Life of Kakuzō.* Hokuseidō, 1963.

Hornblow, Arthur. *A History of the Theatre in America from Its Beginnings to the Present Time.* 2 vols. New York: Lippincott, 1919.

Horton, Judge. *Driftwood on the Stage.* Detroit: Winn and Hammoh, 1904.

Hosley, William. *The Japan Idea: Art and Life in Victorian America.* Hartford, Connecticut: Wadsworth Atheneum, 1990.

Howells, W. D. *Literature and Life.* New York: Harper, 1902. Reprint. Port Washington, New York: Kennikat, 1968.

————. *The Story of a Play.* New York: Harper, 1898.

Hughes, Alan. *Henry Irving, Shakespearean.* Cambridge: Cambridge University Press, 1981.

Hughes, Glenn. *A History of the American Theatre, 1700–1950.* New York: French, 1951

Hungerford, Edward. *The Personality of American Cities.* New York: McBridge, Nast, 1913.

Ichioka, Yuji. "*Ameyuki-san:* Japanese Prostitutes in Nineteenth Century America," *Amerasia Journal* 4.1 (1977): 1–21.

————. "Early Issei Socialists and the Japanese Community," *Amerasia Journal* 1 (July 1971): 1–25.

————. *The Issei: The World of First-Generation Japanese Immigrants.* New York: Free Press, 1988.

Ihara Seiseien [Toshirō]. *Engeki dangi* [Lectures on theatre]. Okakura Shobō, 1934.

Ihara Toshirō. *Dan Kiku igo* [After Danjūrō and Kikugorō]. Seiabō, 1973.

————. *Kabuki nempyō* [Kabuki chronology] Vols. 7, 8. Iwanami Shoten, 1963–64

————. *Meiji engeki shi* [History of theatre in the Meiji era]. Waseda Daigaku Shuppambu, 1933.

Ii Yōhō. *Nihon no engeki no setsu* [Opinions about Japanese theatre]. Shūhōkaku, 1925.

Illustrated American Stage. New York: Russell, 1901.

Inoue Masao. *Bakesokonata tanuki* [The badger that couldn't impersonate]. Ubunsha, 1947.

Inoue Seizō, *Hakata niwaka tokuhon* [Hakata niwaka comedy reader]. Hakata: Yoshi Shobō, 1987.

———. *Kawakami Otojirō no shōgai* [The life of Kawakami Otojirō]. Fukuoka: Yoshi Shobō, 1985.

Irokawa, Daikichi. *The Culture of the Meiji Period.* Princeton: Princeton University Press, 1985.

Irving, Henry. *The Drama: Addresses.* New York: Tait, 1892.

Irvin, Laurence. *Henry Irving: Actor and His World.* New York: Macmillan, 1952.

Isman, Felix. *Weber and Fields.* New York: Boni and Liveright, 1924.

Itō Kisaku, *Butai bijutsu* [Stage art (set design)]. Asahi Shimbunsha, 1963.

Itō Mitsuo. *Taishū engeki* [Popular Drama]. Engeki Purodakushon, 1965.

Iwai Sōzō, ed. *Shimpa hyakunen: haiyū kagami* [A 100 years of shimpa: a mirror (compendium) of actors]. Funabashi, Chiba-ken, 1990.

Iwaya Shin'ichi. *Boku no engeki henro* [My theatrical pilgrimage]. Seiabō, 1976.

Jackson, Kenneth T., ed. *The Encyclopedia of New York City.* New York: New York Historical Society, 1995.

Jackson, Russell, ed. *Victorian Theatre: The Theatre in Its Time.* New York: New Amsterdam, 1989.

Jansen, Marius, ed. *The Cambridge History of Japan; Volume 5: The Nineteenth Century.* New York: Cambridge: University Press, 1989.

Japanese National Commission for UNESCO. *Theatre in Japan.* Tokyo: Ministry of Finance, 1963.

Jefferson, Joseph. *The Autobiography of Joseph Jefferson.* 1890. Reprint. Cambridge: Harvard University Press, 1964.

Jelavich, Peter. *Berlin Cabaret.* Cambridge, Massachusetts: Harvard University Press, 1993.

Jenkins, Stephen. *The Greatest Street in the World.* New York: Putnam's, 1911.

Jennings, John J. *Theatrical and Circus Life or Secrets of the Stage, Green-Room and Sawdust Arena.* St. Louis: Barnett, 1882.

Jones, Henry Arthur. *The Shadow of Henry Irving.* 1931. Reprint. New York: Blom, 1969.

Jortner, David; Keiko McDonald; and Kevin J. Wetmore, Jr., eds. *Modern Japanese Theatre and Performance.* Lanham, Maryland: Rowman and Littlefield, 2006.

Joseph, Bertram. *The Tragic Actor.* London: Routledge and Kegan Paul, 1959.

"Kaiko suru shimpa gojūnen." [Remembering fifty years of shimpa]. Clippings from 1937 unidentified newspaper in scrapbook "Shimpa gojūnen kaiko kiji" [Articles recalling fifty years of shimpa], item *ro* 2/74, at Waseda.

Kakii Michihiro. *Hariuddo no Nihonjin* [Hollywood's Japanese]. Bungeki Shunjū, 1992.

Kamakura, Keiko, et al., eds. *International Symposium on the Conservation and Restoration of Cultural Property: Kabuki: Changes and Prospects, 1996.* Tokyo: Tokyo National Research Institute of Cultural Properties, 1998.

Kaneo Tanejirō, ed. *Kawakami Otojirō Ōbei man'yūki* [Journal of Kawakami Otojirō's journey to Europe and America; English language title on cover: *Mr. Kawakami's Travels Round the World*]. Ōsaka: Kaneo Bun'endō Shoten, 1901.

———, ed. *Kawakami Otojirō Sadayakko man'yūki* [Journal of Kawakami Otojirō and Sadayakko's journey abroad]. Ōsaka: Kaneo Bun'endō Shoten, 1901.

Kano, Ayako. *Acting Like a Woman in Modern Japan: Theatre, Gender, and Nationalism*. New York: Palgrave, 2001.

Kasahara Nobuo. *Bi to aku no dentō* [Traditions of beauty and evil]. Ōfūsha, 1969.

Kata Kōji. *Asakusa monogatari* [The Asakusa story]. Jiji Tsūshinsha, 1988.

Katō Shūichi. *A History of Japanese Literature; Volume 3: The Modern Years*. Trans. Don Sanderson. Tokyo: Kōdansha International, 1983.

Kawai Takeo. *Onnagata*. Sōgabō, 1937.

Kawajiri Seitan. *Engei meika no omokage* [Images of celebrity performers]. Uchūdō, 1910.

——— . *Shibai oboechō* [Theatre notebook]. Kokuritsu Gekijō Geinō Chosashitsu, 1985.

Kawakami, Kiyoshi K. *Asia at the Door*. New York: Revell, 1914.

Kawakami Otojirō Kenshōkai [Kawakami Otojirō Memorial Society]. *Kawakami Otojirō Sadayakko-jō ni kan suru ken mokuroku* [Catalog of items connected with Kawakami Otojirō and Madame Sadayakko]. Fukuoka: Kawakami Otojirō Kenshōkai, 1963.

"Kawakami Otojirō serifu nukigaki" [Kawakami Otojirō dialog sides]. In Kokugeki Daihon Korekushon, item *ro* 19/61 1–24, at Waseda.

[Kawakami Sada Yakko], performer. "Tsuru Kame," koto solo, recorded in Berlin, 1901, in Hornbostel Collection, Berlin Phonogramm-Archiv. Duplicate tape recording in Federal Cylinder Project, AFS No. 10,054, B10; Cylinder No. 4,076, Original No. 24; 1:59, at Archive of Folk Culture, Library of Congress.

Kawakami Sadayakko. "Sadayakko issekiwa" [Sadayakko, a short tale]. *Chūō shimbun*, September–October 1903. Reprinted in Fujii Sōtetsu, ed. *Jiden Otojirō Sadayakko* [The autobiographies of Otojirō and Sadayakko], 177–222.

Kawashima Jumpei. *Nihon engeki hyakunen no ayumi* [Through a hundred years of Japanese theatre]. Hyōronsha, 1971.

Kawatake Mokuami. *Mokuami zenshū, daijū-kan* [Complete works of Mokuami, Vol. 10]. Ed. Kawatake Shigetoshi. Shunyōdō, 1925.

Kawatake Shigetoshi. *Gaisetsu Nihon engeki shi* [Outline history of Japanese theatre]. Iwanami Shoten, 1966.

——— . *Nihon engeki bunka shiwa* [Histories of Japanese theatrical culture]. Shinjusha, 1964.

——— . *Nihon engeki zenshi* [Comprehensive history of Japanese theatre]. Heibonsha, 1966.

——— . *Nihon no engeki* [Japanese theatre]. Tōkyōdō, 1942.

——— , ed. *Engeki hyakka daijiten* [Theatre encyclopedia]. 6 vols. Heibonsha, 1961.

——— , ed. *Sōgō Nihon gikyoku jiten* [Comprehensive directory of Japanese plays]. Heibonsha, 1964.

Kawatake, Toshio. *Japan on Stage: Japanese Concepts of Beauty as Shown in the Traditional Theatre*. Trans. P. G. O'Neill. Tokyo: 3A Corporation, 1990.

——— . *Kindai engeki no tenkai* [The unfolding of modern drama]. Nihon Hōsō Shuppan Kyōkai, 1982.

——— . *Nihon no Hamuretto* [Hamlet in Japan]. Nansōsha, 1972.

Keene, Donald. *Dawn to the West: Japanese Literature of the Modern Era: Fiction*. New York: Holt, 1984.

——— . *Dawn to the West: Japanese Literature of the Modern Era: Poetry, Drama, Criticism*. New York: Holt, 1984.

——— . *Modern Japanese Literature from 1868 to Present Day: An Anthology*. Tokyo: Tuttle, 1957.

——— . *The Pleasures of Japanese Literature*. New York: Columbia University Press, 1988.

——— . "The Sino-Japanese War of 1894–95 and Its Cultural Effects in Japan." In *Tradition and Modernization in Japanese Culture*, 121–75. Ed. Donald H. Shively.

——— . *World within Walls: Japanese Literature of the Pre-Modern Era, 1600–1867*. New York: Holt, Rinehart, and Wilson, 1976.

Kellermann, Bernhard. *Sassa yo yassa: Japanische Tänze*. Berlin: Cassirer, n.d.

Kelly, Charles Suddarth. *Washington, D.C. Then and Now: 69 Sites Photographed in the Past and Present*. New York: Dover, 1984.

Kendal, Mrs. [Madge]. *Dame Madge Kendal by Herself*. London: Murray, 1933.

——— . *Dramatic Opinions*. Boston: Little, Brown, 1890.

Kennedy, John Castillo. *The Great Earthquake and Fire: San Francisco, 1906*. New York: Morrow, 1963.

King, Moses, ed. *Handbook of New York City*. Boston: King, 1892.

——— . ed. *How to See Boston*. Boston: King, 1895.

Kipling, Rudyard. *American Notes*. 1891. Reprint. Norman: University of Oklahoma Press, 1981.

——— . *From Sea to Sea: Letters of Travel*. New York: Doubleday and McClure, 1899.

Kitamura Rokurō. *Geidō raisan* [In praise of the way of performance arts]. Futami Shobō, 1943.

——— , Ishii Kan, Murata Masao II, et al, performers. *Engeki: Onna keizu; Yujima keinai no ba; Izumi Kyōka gensaku, kiyomono bansō* [Drama: The Yujima scene from *A woman's lineage*; based on the original novel by Izumi Kyōka; with *kiyomoto* accompaniment]. Phonograph record. Nihon Koromubia, c. 1960; BL-5012; recorded c. 1950.

Knepler, Henry. *The Gilded Stage: The Years of the Great International Actresses*. New York: Morrow, 1968.

Knight, Joseph. *Theatrical Notes*. London, 1893. Reprint. New York: Blom, 1972.

Kobbé, Gustav. *Famous Actors and Actresses and Their Homes*. Boston: Little, Brown, 1903.

Kobitsu Matsuo. *Nihon shingeki risō shi: Meiji chūkihen, Nihon no shingeki kairyō undō to sono risō* [A history of discourse about new theatre (*shingeki*) in Japan: the Meiji middle period, Japanese *shingeki* reform movements and their polemics]. Miraisha, 1998.

Kodansha Encyclopedia of Japan. 9 vols. Kōdansha, 1983.

Kominz, Laurence. *Avatars of Vengeance: Japanese Drama and the Soga Literary Tradition*. Ann Arbor: Center for Japanese Studies, University of Michigan, 1995.

Komiya Kiichi, comp. *Kabuki, shimpa, Shinkokugeki jōen nempyō* [Chronology of kabuki, shimpa, and Shinkokugeki performances]. Komiya, 2007.

Komiya, Toyotaka, ed. *Japanese Music and Drama in the Meiji Era*. Trans. and adapted by Edward G. Seidensticker and Donald Keene. Tokyo: Ōbunsha, 1956.

Komota Nobuo, and Shimada Yoshibumi, eds. *Nihon ryūkōka [hayari uta] shi* [History of Japanese popular song]. Shakai Shisōsha, 1970.

Krehbiel, H. E. "Historical and Critical Excursions in Opera-Land," *New York Tribune*, "'Madama Butterfly' and Its Progenitors," 15 October 1916, 4:5 and "The Tragic Outcome of 'Madame Butterfly' and Its Progenitors," 27 October 1916, 4:5.

Krows, Arthur Edwin. *Play Production in America*. New York: Holt, 1916.

Kume, Kunitake, comp. *Japanese Rising: The Iwakura Embassy to the USA and Europe*. Ed. Chushichi Tsuzuki and R. Jules Young. Cambridge: Cambridge University Press, 2009.

Kurata Yoshihiro. *Kindaigeki no akebono: Kawakami Otojirō to sono shūhen shūhen* [The dawn of modern drama; Kawakami Otojirō and related matters]. Mainichi Shimbunsha, 1981.

Kurata Yoshihiro, ed. *Meiji no engei* [Performing arts in the Meiji era]. Kokuritsu Gekijō, 1983.

Kurth, Peter. *Isadora: A Sensational Life*. Boston: Little, Brown, 2001.

Kuwano Masao. *Joyū ron* [Discourse on actresses]. Sambō Shoten, 1913.

Ladd, James William. "A Survey of the Legitimate Theatre in Seattle since 1856." M.A. thesis, Washington State University, 1935.

La Farge, John. *An Artist's Letters from Japan.* 1890. Reprint. New York: Century, 1897.

Lancaster, Clay. *The Japanese Influence in America*. New York: Rawls, 1963. Reprint. New York: Abbeville, 1983.

Lardner, Rex. *The Legendary Champions*. New York: American Heritage, 1972.

Leavitt, M. B. *Fifty Years in Theatrical Management*. New York: Broadway Publishing, 1912.

Lehmann, Jean-Pierre. *The Image of Japan*. London: Allen and Unwin, 1978.

Leiter, Samuel L. *From Belasco to Brook: Representative Directors of the English-Speaking Stage*. New York: Greenwood, 1991.

————, *Historical Directory of Japanese Traditional Theatre*. Lanham, Maryland: Scarecrow, 2006.

————, *Kabuki Reader: History and Performance*. Armonk, New York: Sharpe, 2002.

————, ed. *Kabuki Encyclopedia: An English-Language Adaptation of* Kabuki jiten. Westport, Connecticut: Greenwood, 1979.

————, ed. *Rising from the Flames: The Rebirth of Theater in Occupied Japan*, 1945–1952. Lanham, Maryland, Lexington, 2009.

Lelyveld, Toby. *Shylock on the Stage*. Cleveland: Press of Western Reserve University, 1960.

Leslie, Amy [pseud., Lillie Buck]. *Some Players; Personal Sketches*. Chicago: Stone, 1899.

Leverton, Garrett H. *The Production of Later 19th Century American Drama*. New York: Columbia University, 1936.

Levine, Lawrence W. *Highbrow / Lowbrow: The Emergence of Cultural Hierarchy in America*. Cambridge: Harvard University Press, 1988.

Levy, Harriet Lane. *920 O'Farrell Street*. Garden City, New York: Doubleday, 1947.

Lewis, Lloyd, and Henry Justin Smith. *Chicago: The History of Its Reputation*. New York: Harcourt, Brace, 1929.

Lewis, Philip C. *Trouping: How the Show Came to Town*. New York: Harper and Row, 1973.

Lifson, David. *The Yiddish Theatre in America*. New York: Yoseloff, 1965.

Littlewood, Ian. *The Idea of Japan: Western Images, Western Myths*. Chicago: Dee, 1996.

Lockwood, Mary S. *Columbia Guide to Historic and Modern Washington*. Harrisburg, Pennsylvania: Harrisburg Publishing, 1897.

Long, John Luther. *Madame Butterfly*. 1897. Reprint. "Japanese Edition" New York: Grosset and Dunlap, 1903.

Loti, Pierre. *Madame Chrysanthème*. Trans. Laura Ensor. c. 1887. Reprint. Tokyo: Tuttle, 1973.

Lowell, Percival. *The Soul of the Far East*. Boston: Houghton, Mifflin, 1891.

Macfall, Haldane. *Sir Henry Irving*. Edinburgh: Foulis, 1906.

Makimura Shiyō, ed. *Kawakami Otojirō*. Ōsaka: Shiyō Senshū Kankōkai, 1963.

Malm, William P. *Japanese Music and Musical Instruments*. Tokyo: Tuttle, 1959.

Manabe Hideo. *Shinkokugeki.* Genshū Shuppansha, 2005.

Mandell, Richard. *Paris 1900: The Great World's Fair.* Toronto: University of Toronto, 1967.

Mander, Raymond, and Joe Mitchenson. *A Picture History of the British Theatre.* New York: Macmillan, 1957.

Mantle, Burns, and Garrison P. Sherwood, eds. *The Best Plays of 1899–1900.* New York: Dodd, Mead, 1947.

Manvell, Roger. *Ellen Terry.* New York: Putnam's, 1968.

Marker, Lise-Lone. *David Belasco: Naturalism in the American Theatre.* Princeton: Princeton University Press, 1975.

Markino, Yoshio. *A Japanese Artist in London.* Philadelphia: Jacobs, 1910.

Marshall, Gail. *Actresses on the Victorian Stage: Feminine Performance and the Galatea Myth.* New York: Cambridge University Press, 1998.

Martin, Harry, and Caroline Kellogg. *Tacoma.* Virginia Beach, Virginia: Donning, 1981.

Marui Fujio et al, eds. *Shimpa nempyō* [Shimpa chronology]. Ōtemachi Shuppansha, 1978.

Marukawa Kayoko. *Kawakami Sadayakko.* Shinchōsha, 1982.

Mascagni, Pietro, composer. *Iris.* Luigi Illica, librettist. Trans. Alfred Kalisch. London: Ricordi, 1907.

Masumoto Masahiko. *Yokohama Gête-za: Meiji Taishō no Seiyō gekijō* [The Yokohama Gaiety Theatre: a Western theatre in the Meiji and Taishō periods]. Yokohama: Yokohama-shi Kyōiku Iinkai, 1978.

——— . *Yokohama Gête-za: Meiji Taishō no Seiyō gekijō, daini-han* [The Yokohama Gaiety Theatre: a Western Theatre in the Meiji and Taishō periods, vol. 2]. Yokohama: Iwasaki Hakubutsukan, 1986.

Matson, Cecil. *Seven Nights—Three Matinees: Seventy Years of Dramatic Stock in Portland, Oregon 1863–1933.* Portland: Matson, c. 1965.

Matsumoto Shinko. *Meiji engekiron shi* [A history of theatrical discourse in the Meiji era]. Engeki Shuppansha, 1980.

——— . *Meiji zenki engekiron shi* [A history of theatrical discourse in the early Meiji era]. Engeki Shuppansha, 1974.

Matsunaga Goichi. *Kawakami Otojirō: kindaigeki hatenkō na yoake* [Kawakami Otojirō: the unprecedented dawn of modern drama,]. Asahi Shimbunsha, 1988.

Matthews, Brander. *The Development of Drama.* New York: Scribner's, 1903.

Mayer, Grace C. *Once Upon a City.* New York: Macmillan, 1958.

Mazer, Gary M. *Shakespeare Refashioned: Elizabethan Plays on Edwardian Stages.* Ann Arbor: UMI Research Press, 1982.

McArthur, Benjamin. *Actors and American Culture, 1880–1920.* Philadelphia: Temple University Press, 1984.

McConachie, Bruce. *Melodramatic Formations: American Theatre and Society, 1820–1870.* Iowa City: University of Iowa Press, 1992.

McKay, Frederick Edward, and Charles E. L. Wingate, eds. *Famous American Actors of Today.* New York: Crowell, 1896.

McKechnie, Samuel. *Popular Entertainments through the Ages.* London: Sampson, Low, Marston, c. 1932.

McLean, Albert F., Jr. *American Vaudeville as Ritual.* Lexington: University of Kentucky Press, 1965.

McTeague, James H. *Before Stanislavsky: American Professional Acting Schools and Acting Theory, 1875–1925*. Metuchen, New Jersey: Scarecrow, 1993.

Meiji Bunka Kenkyūkai, ed. *Meiji bunka zenshū: dainijūni-hen; hon'yaku bungei hen* [The definitive collection of Meiji culture; vol. 22, translated literature].

"Meika shinsoroku 23: Kawakami Otojirō" [Celebrity facts 23: Kawakami Otojirō], *Engei gahō* (October 1908): 21–34.

Meisel, Martin. *Realizations: Narrative, Pictorial, and Theatrical Arts in Nineteenth Century England*. Princeton: Princeton University Press, 1983.

Menpes, Mortimer. *Henry Irving*. London: Adam and Charles, 1906.

Meyerhold, Vsevolod Emilvich. *Meyerhold on Theatre*, trans. Edward Braun. New York: Hill and Wang, 1969.

Michigan Writer's Project. *Michigan: A Guide to the Wolverine State*. New York: Oxford University Press, 1941,

Mickel, Jere C. *Footlights on the Prairie*. St. Cloud, Minnesota: North Star, 1974.

Mihara Aya, "Professor Risley and Japanese Acrobats: Selections from the Diary of Hirohachi Takano, a Manager for the Risley Troupe, during the World Tour 1866–1869," *Nineteenth Century Theatre* 18:1–2 (1990): 62–74.

Miller, J. Scott. *Adaptations of Western Literature in Meiji Japan*. New York: Palgrave, 2001.

——— and Miyakoya Utaroku. *Yomigaeru Oppekepē: 1900nen Pari banpaku no Kawakami ichiza* [Resurrecting / Resuscitating Oppekepē: the Kawakami troupe at the 1900 Paris Exposition]. Booklet and CD. Toshiba EMI, 1997. TOCG-5432.

Miln, Louise Jordan. *When We Were Strolling Players in the East*. New York: Scribners, 1894.

Minami Hiroshi, Nagai Hiroo, and Ozawa Shōichi, eds. *Kabuku: taishū engeki no sekai* [*Kabuku*, letting go: the world of popular theatre]. Hakusuisha, 1982.

Minami Ryuta, Ian Carruthers, and John Gillies, eds. *Performing Shakespeare in Japan*. Cambridge: Cambridge University Press, 2000.

Miner, Earl. *The Japanese Tradition in British and American Literature*. Princeton: Princeton University Press, 1985.

Mishō Kingo. *Shinario; Oppekepē—sōshi yakusha Kawakami Otojirō* [Oppekepē—ruffian actor Kawakami Otojirō: a scenario]. Bungaku Hyrōron, 1957.

Misumi Haruo. *Nihon buyō shi no kenkyū* [A Study of the history of Japanese dance]. Tōkyōdō, 1968.

Mita Jun'ichi. *Harukanari Dōtombori* [Distant Dōtombori]. Kyūgei Shuppan, 1978.

Mita, Munesuke. *Social Psychology of Modern Japan*. London: Kegan Paul, 1992.

Mitford, A. B. *Tales of Old Japan*. 1871. Reprint. Rutland, Vermont: Tuttle, 1966.

Miyake Saburō. *Koshibai no omoide* [Memories of Minor Theatres]. Kokuritsu Gekijō Chōsa Yōseibu Geinō Chōsashitsu, 1986.

Miyake Shūtarō. *Engeki gojūnen shi* [A fifty-year history of theatre]. Masu Shobō, 1942.

Miyaoka Kenji. *Ikoku henro: tabi geinin shimatsusho* [Pilgrims to foreign countries: accounts of what happened to travelling entertainers]. Shūdōsha, 1971.

Mizutani Yaeko. *Joyū ichidai* [Life of an Actress]. Yomiuri Shimbunsha, 1966.

——— . *Matsuba botan: butai gurashi gojūnen* [A portulaca flower: fifty years of making a living on stage]. Tsuru Shobō, 1966.

Modjeska, Helena. *Memories and Impressions of Helena Modjeska, an Autobiography.* New York: Macmillan, 1910. Reprint. New York: Blom, 1969.

Moody, Richard. *America Takes the Stage: Romanticism in American Drama and Theatre, 1750–1900.* Bloomington: Indiana University Press, 1955.

——— , ed. *Dramas from the American Theatre, 1762–1909.* Cleveland: World, 1966.

Morand, Paul. *1900 A.D.* Trans. Mrs. Romilly Fedden. New York: Payson, 1931.

Morgan, Murray. *Skid Road: An Informal Portrait of Seattle.* Seattle: University of Washington Press, 1982.

Morris, Ivan. *The Nobility of Failure: Tragic Heroes in the History of Japan.* New York: Holt, Rinehart, and Winston, 1975.

Morse, Edward S. *Japan Day by Day, 1877, 1878–79, 1882–83.* 2 vols. Boston: Houghton Mifflin, 1917.

Muirhead, James Fullarton. *The Land of Contrasts.* Boston: Lamson, Wolffe, 1898.

Mukai Sōya. *Nippon minshū engeki shi* [A history of Japanese popular theatre]. Nihon Hōsō Shuppan Kyōkai, 1977.

Mullin, Donald, ed. *Victorian Actors and Actresses in Review: A Dictionary of Contemporary Views of Representative British and American Actors and Actresses.* Westport, Connecticut: Greenwood, 1983.

Muramatsu Shōfu. *Kawakami Otojirō.* 2 vols. Taiheiyō, 1952. Reprint. Ushio Bunko, 1985.

Muramatsu Shunkichi. *Tabishibai no seikatsu* [The life of strolling players]. Yūsankaku, 1972.

Muscatine, Doris. *Old San Francisco: The Biography of a City.* New York: Putnam's, 1975.

Musser, Charles. *Before the Nickelodeon: Edwin S. Porter and the Edison Manufacturing Company.* Berkeley: University of California Press, 1991.

——— . *The Emergence of Cinema: The American Screen to 1907.* History of the American Cinema, Vol. 1. New York: Scribner's, 1990.

Nagai Kafū. *Amerika monogatari* [Stories of America]. In *Gendai Nihon bungaku zenshū 34, Nagai Kafū shū 1* [Comprehensive collection of contemporary Japanese literature, vol. 34, Nagai Kafū section 1] Chikuma Shobō, 1975.

——— . *Nagai Kafū shū* [Nagai Kafū Collection]. In *Chikuma gendai bungaku taikei 16, Nagai Kafū shū* [The Chikuma comprehensive collection of contemporary literature, vol. 16, Nagai Kafū section]. Chikuma Shobō, 1975.

Nagai Takao, and Marui Fujio, eds. *Shimpa no keizu* [The geneology of shimpa]. Gekidan Shimpa, 1977.

Nagata Tetsurō. *Tate* [Theatrical sword fighting]. San'ichi Shobō, 1974.

Nakamura, Matazo. *Kabuki Backstage Onstage: An Actor's Life.* Trans. Mark Oshima. Kodansha International, 1990.

Nasaw, David. *Going Out: The Rise and Fall of Public Amusements.* New York: Basic Books, 1993.

Nathan, George Jean. *Another Book on the Theatre.* New York: Huebsch, 1915.

Natsume, Sōseki. *And Then (Sorekara).* Trans. Norma Moore Field. New York: Perigee, 1982.

Nicoll, Allardyce. *The Development of the Theatre.* New York: Harcourt, Brace, 1966.

——— . *A History of English Drama: 1660–1900; Vol. 5, Late Nineteenth Century Drama: 1850–1900.* Cambridge: Cambridge University Press, 1967.

Niiya, Brian, ed. *Japanese American History: An A-Z Reference from 1868 to Present.* New York: Facts on File, 1993.

Nishiyama Matsunosuke. *Daily Life and Diversions in Urban Japan, 1600–1868.* Trans. and ed. Gerald Groemer. Honolulu: University of Hawai'i Press, 1997.

Noël, Édouard, and Edmond Stoullig. *Les annales du théatre et de la musique: 1893.* Paris: Charpentier, 1984.

Noguchi, Yone[jirō]. *The American Diary of a Japanese Girl.* London: Mathews, 1912.

————. *The Collected English Letters of Yone Noguchi.* Ed. Ikuko Atsumi. Tokyo: Yone Noguchi Society, 1975.

————. *Japan and America.* Tokyo: Keiō University Press, 1921.

————. *The Story of Yone Noguchi by Himself.* London: Chatto and Windus, 1914.

Nolan, Paul T. *Provincial Drama in America, 1870–1916—A Casebook of Primary Material.* Metuchen, New Jersey: Scarecrow, 1967.

Norton, Elliot. *Broadway Down East: An Informal Account of the Plays, Players, and Playhouses of Boston from Puritan Times to the Present.* Boston: Public Library, 1978.

Norton, Richard. *A Chronicle of American Musical Theatre.* New York: Oxford University Press, 2002.

Ōba Saburō. *Butai shōmei—Stage Lighting* [*sic*]. Ohmsha, 1976.

Ochi Haruo. *Meiji Taishō no gekibungaku* [Dramatic literature of the Meiji and Taishō eras]. Hanawa Shobō, 1971.

Odell, George C. D. *Annals of the New York Stage; Vols. 7–15: 1857–1894.* New York: Columbia University Press, 1931–1949.

————. *Shakespeare: From Betterton to Irving.* New York: Scribner's, 1920.

O'Donnell, Terence, and Thomas Vaughan. *Portland: A Historical Sketch and Guide.* Portland: Oregon Historical Society, 1976.

Oenslager, Donald. *Scenery Then and Now.* New York: Norton, 1936.

Ogasawara Mikio. *Kabuki kara shimpa e* [From kabuki to shimpa]. Kanrin Shobō, 1996.

Ōgawa Susumu, ed. *Nihon butai shōmei shi* [History of Japanese theatrical lighting]. Nihon Shōmei Kyōkai, 1975.

Okamoto Kidō. *Engeki no Meiji* [Theatre in the Meiji era]. Daitō Shuppansha, 1942.

————. *Meiji no engeki* [Meiji era theatre]. Dōkōsha, 1949.

Okazaki, Yoshie, *Japanese Literature in the Meiji Era.* Trans. V. H. Viglielmo. Tōkyō: Ōbunsha, 1955.

Oppel, Frank, and Tony Meisel, eds. *Washington, D.C.: A Turn-of-the-Century Treasury.* Secaucus, New Jersey: Castle, 1987.

Original Sounds of the 1890's. Rerecorded from Emile Berliner Gramophone 1894–1899 recordings. Phongraph record. Los Angeles: Westwood Records, 1979. LP 501.

Ormsbee, Helen. *Backstage with Actors: From the Time of Shakespeare to the Present Day.* New York: Crowell, 1938.

Ortolani, Benito. *The Japanese Theatre: From Shamanistic Ritual to Contemporary Pluralism.* Leiden: E. J. Brill, 1991.

Orvell, Miles. *The Real Thing: Imitation and Authenticity in American Culture, 1880–1940.* Chapel Hill: University of North Carolina Press, 1989.

Ōta Saburō, "Amerika no Nagai Kafū" [Nagai Kafū in America], *Kafū zenshū geppō* [The complete works of Kafū monthly news] 9 (August 1963): 3–7.

O'Toole, Patricia. *The Five of Hearts: An Intimate Portrait of Henry Adams and His Friends, 1880–1918*. New York: Potter, 1990.

Oyama Isao. *Kindai Nihon gikyoku shi; daiichi-kan Meiji hen* [History of modern Japanese plays; vol. 1 Meiji era section].Yamagata: Kindai Nihon Gikyoku Shi Kankōkai, 1968.

Ozaki Hirotsugu. *Joyū no keizu* [The lineage of actresses]. Asahi Shimbunsha, 1964.

Ozaki Hideki. *Taishū geinō no kamigami* [Gods of the popular performance arts]. Kyūgei Shuppan, 1978.

Ōzasa Yoshio. *Kagan no hito: Hanayagi Shōtarō den* [Person with a lovely face: the life story of Hanayagi Shōtarō]. Kōdansha, 1991.

——————. *Nihon gendai engeki shi: Meiji Taishō hen* [History of Japanese contemporary theatre: Meiji and Taishō periods]. Hakusuisha, 1985.

Pantzer, Peter. *Japanischer Theaterhimmel über Europas Bühnen: Kawakami Otojiro, Sadayakko und ihre Truppe auf Tournee durch Mittel- und Osteuropia 1901–1902*. Munich: Ludicium, 2005.

Pavis, Patrice. *Theatre at the Crossroad of Culture*. Trans. Loren Kruger. London: Routledge, 1992.

——————, ed. *The Intercultural Performance Reader*. New York: Routledge, 1996.

Penzel, Frederick. *Theatre Lighting before Electricity*. Middletown, Connecticut: Wesleyan University Press, 1978.

Perry, John. *James A. Herne: The American Ibsen*. Chicago: Nelson Hall, 1978.

Pierce, Bessie Louise, ed. *As Others See Chicago*. Chicago: University of Chicago Press, 1933.

Poggi, Jack. *Theatre in America: The Impact of Economic Forces, 1870–1967*. Ithaca: Cornell University Press, 1968.

Polk's Seattle City Directory, 1899. Tacoma: Polk, 1899.

Pollock, Channing. *The Footlights Fore and Aft, 1870–1967*. Ithaca: Cornell University Press, 1968.

Postlewait, Thomas, and Bruce A. McConachie, eds. *Interpreting the Theatrical Past: Essays in the Historiography of Performance*. Iowa City: University of Iowa Press, 1989.

Powell, Brian. *Japan's Modern Theatre: a Century of Change and Continuity*. London: Japan Library, 2002.

Puccini, Giocomo, composer; Luigi Illica and Giuseppe Giacosa, lyricists. *Madama Butterfly*. Trans. Stanley Appelbaum. Reprint. Opera Libretto Series. New York: Dover, 1983.

Pyle, Kenneth B. *The New Generation in Meiji Japan: Problems of Cultural Identity, 1885–1895*. Stanford: Stanford University Press, 1969.

Quinn, Arthur Hobson. *A History of the American Drama from the Beginning to the Civil War*. New York: Appleton-Century-Crofts, 1951.

Rahill, Frank. *The World of Melodrama*. University Park: Pennsylvania State University Press, 1967.

Rand, McNally and Co.'s Pictorial Guide to Washington. Chicago: Rand, McNally, 1901.

Ransome, Stafford. *Japan in Transition*. New York: Harper, 1899.

Raz, Jacob. *Audience and Actors: A Study of Their Interaction in the Japanese Traditional Theatre*. Leiden: Brill, 1983.

Reed, John R. *Victorian Conventions*. Athens: Ohio University Press, 1975.

Rees, Terence. *Theatre Lighting in the Age of Gas*. London: Society for Theatre Research, 1978.

Reitz, Elizabeth. *Wearing the Breeches: Gender on the Antebellum Stage.* New York: St. Martin's, 2000.

Richards, Sandra. *The Rise of the English Actress.* New York: St. Martins, 1993.

Richardson, F. H. *Richardson's Chicago Guide.* Chicago: Monarch, 1905.

Riis, Thomas L. *Just before Jazz: Black Musical Theatre in New York, 1890–1915.* Washington: Smithsonian Institution, 1989.

Rimer, J. Thomas. *Pilgrimages: Aspects of Japanese Literature and Culture.* Honolulu: University of Hawaii Press, 1988.

————. *Toward a Modern Japanese Theatre: Kishida Kunio.* Princeton: Princeton University Press, 1974.

Robertson, W. Graham. *Time Was.* London: Hamilton, 1931.

Robinson, Alice M. *Notable Women in the American Theatre: A Biographical Dictionary.* New York: Greenwood, 1989.

Romein, Jan. *Watershed of Two Eras: Europe in 1900.* Trans. Arnold Romerans. Middletown, Connecticut: Wesleyan University Press, 1978.

Roth, Phyllis A. *Bram Stoker.* Boston: Twayne, 1982.

Rowell, George. *Theatre in the Age of Irving.* Oxford: Blackwell, 1981.

————. *Victorian Dramatic Criticism.* London: Methuen, 1971.

Rymer, Thomas. *A Short View of Tragedy.* London: Baldwin, 1693.

Said, Edward W. *Orientalism.* New York: Vintage, 1978.

Saintsbury, H. A., and Cecil Palmer, eds. *We Saw Him Act: A Symposium on the Art of Sir Henry Irving.* 1939. Reprint. New York: Blom, 1969.

Sakakibara Yorimasa. *Nihon minyō to odorikata* [How to perform Japanese folk songs and dances]. Kin'ensha, 1974.

Sale, Roger. *Seattle: Past and Present.* Seattle: University of Washington Press, 1976.

Salmon, Eric, ed. *Bernhardt and the Theatre of Her Time.* Westport, Connecticut: Greenwood, 1984.

Salz, Jonah. "Intercultural Pioneers: Otojirō Kawakami and Sada Yakko," *Journal of Intercultural Studies* (Kansai University of Foreign Studies) 20 (1993): 25–74.

Sansom, George. *The Western World and Japan: A Study in the Interaction of European and Asiatic Cultures.* 1949. Reprint. New York: Vintage, 1973.

Sante, Luc. *Low Life: Lures and Snares of Old New York.* New York: Farrar Straus Giroux, 1991.

Sasayama Takashi et al., eds. *Shakespeare and the Japanese Stage.* Cambridge: Cambridge University Press, 1998.

Satō Kaoru. *Nihon no geinō.* [Japanese performing arts]. Sōgeisha, 1961.

Sauter, Willmar. *The Theatrical Event: Dynamics of Performance and Perception.* Iowa City: University of Iowa Press, 2000.

Savarese, Nicola. *Teatro e spettacolo fra Orient e Occidente.* Rome: Laterza, 1992.

Sawada, Mitziko. *Tokyo Life, New York Dream: Urban Japanese Visions of America, 1890–1924.* Berkeley: University of California Press, 1996.

Scalapino, Robert. *Democracy and the Party Movement in Prewar Japan.* Berkeley: University of California Press, 1953.

Schaffner, Neil E. *The Fabulous Toby and Me.* Englewood Cliffs, New Jersey: Prentice-Hall, 1968.

Schick, L. *Chicago and Its Environs.* Englewood Cliffs, New Jersey: Prentice-Hall, 1968.

Schilling, Lester Lorenzo. "The History of the Theatre in Portland, Oregon 1846–1959." Ph. D. diss. Madison: University of Wisconsin, 1961.

Schivelbusch, Wolfgang. *Disenchanted Night: The Industrialization of Light in the Nineteenth Century.* Trans. Angela Davies. Berkeley: University of California Press, 1995.

Schlereth, Thomas J. *Victorian America: Transformations in Everyday Life, 1876–1915.* New York, Harper Collins, 1991.

Scholes, Robert, and Robert Kellogg. *The Nature of Narrative.* London: Oxford University Press, 1966.

Scholz-Cionca, Stanca, and Samuel Leiter, eds. *Japanese Theatre and the International Stage.* Leiden: Brill, 2001.

Scolnicov, Hanna, and Holland, Peter, eds. *The Play Out of Context: Transferring Plays from Culture to Culture.* Cambridge: Cambridge University Press, 1989.

Scott, A. C. *The Kabuki Theatre of Japan.* London: Allen and Unwin, 1955.

Scott, Clement. *The Drama of Yesterday and Today.* 2 vols. London: Macmillan, 1899.

Seidensticker, Edward. *Low City, High City: Tokyo from Edo to the Earthquake.* New York: Knopf, 1983.

Seigle, Cecilia Segawa. *Yoshiwara: The Glittering World of the Japanese Courtesan.* Honolulu: University of Hawaii Press, 1993.

Seilhamer, George O. *History of the American Theatre before the Revolution.* 3 vols. 1888–91. Reprint. New York: Blom, 1968.

Sekine Mokuan. *Meiji gekidan gojūnen shi* [Fifty year history of the Meiji era theatrical world]. Gembunsha, 1918.

Senda, Akihiko. *The Voyage of Contemporary Japanese Theatre.* Trans. J. Thomas Rimer. Honolulu: University of Hawai'i Press, 1997.

Sharf, Frederic A., ed. *"A Pleasing Novelty:" Bunkio Matsuki and The Japan Craze in Victorian Salem.* Salem, Massachusetts: Peabody and Essex Museum, 1993.

Sharpe, Robert Boies. *Irony in the Drama: An Essay on Impersonation, Shock, and Catharis.* Chapel Hill: University of North Carolina Press, 1959.

Shattuck, Charles H. *Shakespeare on the American Stage: From the Hallams to Edwin Booth.* Washington: Folger, 1976.

Shaw, [George] Bernard. *Our Theatres in the Nineties.* 3 vols. London: Constable, 1932.

Shaw, [George] Bernard, and Ellen Terry. *Ellen Terry and Bernard Shaw: A Correspondence.* Ed. Christopher St. John. New York: Putnam's, 1931.

Shibai meiserifu shū [Collection of famous dialog from plays]. Engeki Shuppansha, 1974.

"Shimpa gojūnen kaiko kiji" [Articles recalling fifty years of shimpa]. Scrapbook *ro* 2/74 at Waseda.

"Shimpa hanseiki o kataru" [Discussing a half century of shimpa], *Miyako shimbun*, January, 1937. In "Shimpa gojūnen kaiko kiji."

Shinkokugeki nanajūnen eikō no kiroku [The glorious record of the seventy years of Shinkokugeki]. Shinkokugeki Kiroku Horonkai, 1988.

Shionoya Kei. *Cyrano et les samuraï: Le théâtre japonais en France dans le première moitié du XXe siècle et l'effet de retour.* Paris: Publications Orientalistes de France, 1986.

Shirakawa Nobuo, ed. *Kawakami Otojirō Sadayakko: shimbun ni miru jimbutsuzō* [Kawakami Otojirō and Sadayakko: persons as seen in newspapers). Tōkyō: Yūshōdō, 1985.

Shively, Donald H., ed. *Tradition and Modernization in Japanese Culture.* Princeton: Princeton University Press, 1971.

Shōchiku kyūjūnen shi [Ninety-year history of Shōchiku]. Shōchiku. 1985.

Siefkin, David. *The City at the End of the Rainbow: San Francisco and Its Grand Hotels.* New York: Putnam, 1978.

Silver, Nathan. *Lost New York.* New York: Schocken, 1971.

Slide, Anthony. *The Encyclopedia of Vaudeville.* Westport, Connecticut: Greenwood, 1994.

Slout, W. L. *Theatre in a Tent: The Development of a Provincial Entertainment.* Bowling Green, Ohio: Bowling Green University Popular Press, 1972.

Smith, Bradford. *Americans from Japan.* Bowling Green, Ohio: Bowling Green University Popular Press, 1972.

Smith, James L. *Melodrama.* London: Methuen, 1973.

Snyder, Robert W. *The Voice of the City.* New York: Oxford University Press, 1989.

Soeda Azembō, and Soeda [Satsuki]. *Hayari uta: Meiji Taishō shi* [History of popular songs in the Meiji and Taishō eras]. Tōsui Shobō, 1982.

Sothern, E. H. *Melancholy Tale of "Me."* New York: Scribners, 1916.

Southern, Richard. *The Victorian Theatre: A Pictorial Survey.* Newton Abbot: David and Charles, 1970.

Sōya Shinji. *Honoo to niji no fūkei: joyū Kawakami Sadayakko monogatari* [Scenes of fire and rainbows: the story of actress Kawakami Sadayakko]. Ron Shobō, 1982.

Stead, William T. *If Christ Came to Chicago.* Chicago: Laird and Lee, 1894.

Stearns, Marhall Winslow, and Jean Stearns. *Jazz Dance: The Story of American Vernacular Dance.* New York: Schimer, 1968.

Stoker, Bram. *Personal Reminiscences of Henry Irving.* 2 vols. New York: Macmillan, 1906.

Stokes, John. *Resistable Theatres: Enterprise and Experiment in the Late Nineteenth Century.* London: Elek, 1972.

Stokes, John, Michael Booth, and Susan Bassnet. *Bernhardt, Terry, Duse.* Cambridge: Cambridge University Press, 1988.

Strang, Lewis C. *Players and Plays of the Last Quarter Century.* 2 vols. Boston: Page, 1903.

Stoullig, Edmond. *Les annales du théâtre et de la musique: 1900.* Paris: Ollendorff, 1901. Also *1901* [covering 1902]; *1907* [1908]; *1908* [1909].

Sturgis, Granville Forbes. *The Influence of the Drama.* New York: Shakespeare Press, 1913.

Styan, J. L. *Drama, Stage, and Audience.* Cambridge: Cambridge University Press, 1975.

Sugimoto Sonoko. *Madamu Sadayakko, chōhen shosetsu* [Madame Sadayakko, a novel]. Yomiuri Shimbunsha, 1975.

————. *Meifu kairō* [The corridors of Hades]. 2 vols. Nihon Hōsō Shuppan Kyōkai, 1984.

Suzuki, Tadashi. *The Way of Acting: The Theatre Writings of Tadashi Suzuki.* Trans. J. Thomas Rimer. New York: Theatre Communications Group, 1986.

Sweetser, M. F. *Greater Boston Illustrated.* Boston: n.p.: c. 1898.

Symons, Arthur. *Plays, Acting, and Music.* New York: Dutton, 1909.

Takahashi Hiroshi. *Taishū geinō* [Popular entertainment]. Kyōiku Shiryō Shuppankai, 1980.

Takahashi Kunitarō, Nozaki Yoshio, Kawatake Toshio, Kikuchi Akira, Akiba Tarō, and Fujiki Hiroyuki.

"Zadankai: Kawakami Otojirō ichiza no kaigai kōen o megutte" [Symposium on the performances of the Kawakami Otojirō troupe abroad]. *Nihon Engeki Gakkai Kiyō* No. 16 (1976): 74–97.

Tanaka Eizō. *Meiji Taishō shingeki shi shiryō* [*Shingeki* historical materials from the Meiji and Taishō eras]. Engeki Shuppansha, 1964.

Tanaka Hideki, ed. *Taishū geinō shiryō shūsei, daijū-kan: butaigei 3, taishū engeki 2* [Collection of popular performance historical materials, vol. 10: stage arts 3, popular theatre 2]. San'ichi Shobō, 1981.

Tawa, Nicholas E. *The Way to Tin Pan Alley: American Popular Songs, 1866–1910.* New York: Schirner, 1990.

Teigeki Shihensan Iinkai. *Teigeki no gojūnen* [Fifty years of the Imperial Theatre]. Tōhō, 1966.

Thayer, William Roscoe. *The Life and Letters of John Hay, Vol. 2.* Boston: Houghton Mifflin, 1908.

"Theatres, The." In *Boston of Today.* Comp. Richard Herndon; ed. Edwin M. Bacon, 90–100. Boston: Post, 1892.

Thomas, Augustus. *The Print of My Remembrance.* New York: Scribner's, 1922.

Thornbury, Barbara E. *Sukeroku's Double Identity: The Dramatic Structure of Edo Kabuki.* Ann Arbor: Center for Japanese Studies, University of Michigan, 1982.

Timberlake, Craig. *The Life and Work of David Belasco: The Bishop of Broadway.* Reprint. New York: Library Publishers, 1954).

Toita Yasuji. *Kabuki kono hyakunen* [The past hundred years of kabuki]. Mainichi Shimbunsha, 1978.

Toita Kōji [Yasuji] "The Kabuki, the *Shimpa*, the *Shingeki*," in *Japanese Music and Drama in the Meiji Era,* ed. Toyotaka Komiya; trans. Edward G. Seidensticker and Donald Keene, 177–325. Tokyo: Ōbunsha, 1956.

Toita Yasuji. *Kindai joyū no tanjō* [The birth of modern actresses]. Inuyama, Aichi-ken: Hakubutsukan Meiji Mura, 1986.

———. *Monogatari kindai Nihon joyū shi* [Stories: histories of modern Japanese actresses]. Chūō Kōronsha, 1980.

———, ed. *Meiji shigeki shū* [Meiji era historical plays]. *Meiji bungaku zenshū* 85 [Comprehensive collection of Meiji literature, vol. 85]. Chikuma Shobō, 1977.

Toki Michiko. "Joyū no keifu" [The lineage of actresses]. In *Jimbutsu Nihon no josei shi, daikyū-kan: gei no michi hitosuji ni* [Persons in the history of Japanese women, vol. 9: those dedicated to the way of art], ed. Enchi Fumiko, 219–48. Shūeisha, 1977.

Toki Zenmaro. *Meiji Taishō geijutsu shi.* [History of performance arts in the Meiji and Taishō periods]. Shinchōsha, 1938.

Toll, Robert C. *Blacking Up: The Minstrel Show in the Nineteenth-Century America.* New York: Oxford University Press, 1974.

———. *On with the Show.* New York: Oxford University Press, 1976.

Tomita Hiroyuki. *Nihon jidō engeki shi* [The history of children's theatre in Japan]. Tōkyō Shoseki, 1980.

Tompkins, Eugene. *History of the Boston Theatre 1854–1901.* 1908. Reprint. New York: Benjamin Blom, 1969.

Toyoda Minoru. *Shakespeare in Japan: An Historical Survey.* Tokyo: Iwanami, 1940.

Trager, James. *West of Fifth: The Rise and Fall and Rise of Manhattan's West Side.* New York: Atheneum, 1987.

Tschudin, Jean-Jacques. *Le Kabuki devant la Modernité (1870–1930)*. Lausanne: L'Age d'Homme, 1995.

Tsubota Itsuo, ed. *Nihon no rekishi, jimbutsu tambō* [Inquiries into personalities in Japanese history]. Akatsuki Kyōiku Zusho, 1975.

Tsubouchi Hakushi Kinen Engeki Hakubutsukan. *Geinō jiten* [Performing arts dictionary]. Tōkyōdō Shuppan, 1953.

——— , ed. *Kokugeki yōran* [Survey of national (Japanese) drama]. Azusa Shobō, 1932.

Tsubouchi, Shōyō. *History and Characteristics of Kabuki*. Trans. and ed. Ryōzo Matsumoto. Yokohama: Yamagata, 1960.

Tsuchida Mitsufumi. *Meiji Taishō fūzoku goten* [Dictionary of customs of the Meiji and Taishō eras]. Kadokawa Shoten, 1986.

Tsugami Tadashi, Sugai Yukio, and Kagawa Yoshinari, eds. *Engeki shi: Nihon hen* [A history of theatre: Japan section]. Kyōto: Sekimonsha, 1976.

Tsurumi Shunsuke, and Kata Kōji, eds. *Nihon no taishū geijutsu* [Japanese popular arts]. Shakai Shisōsha, 1962.

Tsurutani, Hisashi. *America Bound: The Japanese and the Opening of the American West*. Tokyo: Japan Times, 1989.

Tucci, Douglas. *The Boston Rialto*. Boston: City Conservation League, 1977.

Ubukata Tatsue. "Kawakami Sadayakko." In *Jimbutsu Nihon no josei shi, daikyū-kan: gei no michi hitosuji ni* [Personalities in the history of Japanese women, vol. 9: those dedicated to the way of art], ed. Enchi Fumiko, 156–200. Shūreisha, 1977.

Urayama Masao. *Nihon engeki shi* (History of Japanese theatre). Ōfūsha, 1976.

——— , and Matsuzaki Hitoshi, eds. *Kabuki kyakuhonshū* [Collection of kabuki scripts]. Iwanami Shoten, 1960–61.

Van Dyke, John C. *The New New York*. New York: Macmillan, 1909.

Vardac, A. Nicholas. *Stage to Screen: Theatrical Method from Garrick to Griffith*. Cambridge: Harvard University Press, 1949.

Varley, Paul. *Warriors of Japan, as Portrayed in the War Tales*. Honolulu: University of Hawai'i Press, 1994.

Vynne, Harold. *Chicago by Day and Night*. Chicago: Thomson and Zimmermann, 1892.

Wagenknecht, Edward C. *Merely Players*. Norman: University of Oklahoma, 1966.

Wallace, Karl R., ed. *History of Speech Education in America*. New York: Appleton-Century-Crofts, 1957.

Waseda Daigaku Engeki Hakubutsukan, ed. *Nihon engeki shi nempyō* [Chronology of Japanese theatre]. Yagi Shobō, 1998.

Waseda Daigaku Gikyoku Kenkyūkai. *Genten ni yoru Nihon gikyoku shi* [History of Japanese dramas according to their original versions]. Awaji Shobō, 1956.

Watanabe Tamotsu. *Musume Dōjōji* [A maiden at Dōjōji]. Shinshindō, 1986.

Wayman, Dorothy G. *Edward Sylvester Morse: A Biography*. Cambridge: Harvard University Press, 1942.

Wearing, J. P. *London Stage: 1900–1909*. Metuchan, New Jersey: Scarecrow, 1976.

Weeks, Edward. *The Lowells and Their Institute*. Boston: Little, Brown, 1966.

Wells, H. G. *The Future of America.* 1906. Reprint. New York: Arno, 1974.

Whittier, Charles L. *Dear Dad: Our Life in the Theatre around the Turn of the Century.* Freeport, Maine: Wheelwright, 1972.

Who Was Who in the Theatre, 1912–1976. 4 vols. Detroit: Gale Research, 1978.

Wichmann, Siegfried. *Japonisme: The Japanese Influence on Western Art in the 19th and 20th Centuries.* New York: Park Lane, 1981.

Williams, Henry B. *The American Theatre: A Sum of Its Parts.* New York: French, 1971.

Williams, Jesse Lynch. *New York Sketches.* New York: Scribner's, 1902.

Wilmeth, Don B. *The Language of American Popular Entertainment: A Glossary of Argot, Slang, and Terminology.* Westport, Connecticut: Greenwood, 1981.

——— , and Christopher Bigsby, eds. *The Cambridge History of American Theatre, Vol. 2: 1870–1945.* New York: Cambridge University Press, 1999.

——— , and Tice L. Miller, eds. *The Cambridge Guide to American Theatre.* New York: Cambridge University Press, 1993.

Wilson, Robert A., and Bill Hosokawa. *East to America.* New York: Cambridge University Press, 1993.

Wilstach, Paul. *Richard Mansfield: The Man and the Actor.* 1908. Reprint. Freeport, New York: Books for Libraries, 1970.

Winter, Marian Hannah. *The Theatre of Marvels.* 1908. Reprint. Freeport, New York: Books for Libraries, 1970.

Winter, William. *Life and Art of Richard Mansfield.* 2 vols. 1910. Reprint. Freeport, New York: Books for Libraries, 1970.

——— . *The Life of David Belasco.* New York: Moffat, Yard, 1918.

——— . *Other Days: Being Chronicles and Memories of the Stage.* New York: Moffat, Yard, 1908.

——— . *Shakespeare on the Stage.* 2 vols. 1910. Reprint. Freeport, New York: Books for Libraries, 1970.

——— . *The Wallet of Time.* New York: Moffat, Yard, 1913.

Wittke, Carl. *Tambo and Bones: A History of the American Minstrel Show.* 1930. Reprint. New York: Greenwood, 1968.

Wolfe, Albert Benedict. *The Lodging House Problem in Boston.* Boston: Houghton, Mifflin, 1906.

Woods, Robert A., ed. *The City Wilderness: A Settlement Study.* Boston: Houghton, Mifflin, 1898.

Writers' Program. *Washington: A Guide to the Evergreen State.* Portland: Binfords and Mort, 1941.

Yamaguchi Kichi. *Ōsaka no geinō* [Osaka performing arts]. Ōsaka: Mainichi Hōsō, 1973.

Yamaguchi Reiko. *Joyū Sadayakko* [Sadayakko, the actress]. Shinchōsha, 1982.

Yamazaki, Tomoko. *The Story of Yamada Waka: From Prostitute to Feminist Pioneer.* New York: Kodansha, 1986.

Yanagi Eijirō. *Ebanzuke: Shimpa gekidan* [Illustrated programs: talking about shimpa]. Seiabō, 1966.

——— . *Kido airaku: Shimpa kujūnen no ayumi* [Grief and pleasure in the playhouse: going through ninety years of shimpa]. Yomiuri Shimbun, 1977.

——— . *Shimpa no gojūnen kōgyō nempyō* [Fifty year chronology of shimpa performances]. Sōgabō, 1937.

——— . *Shimpa no rokujūnen* [Sixty years of shimpa]. Kawade Shobō, 1948.

Yanagi Keitarō. *Kawakami Otojirō: shimpa no so, botsugo gojūnen kinen* [Kawakami Otojirō: the founder of shimpa; commemorating the fiftieth year of his death]. Fukuoka: Kawakami Otojirō Kenshōkai, 1960.

Yanagida Izumi. *Meiji shoki no hon'yaku bungaku* [Translated literature of the early Meiji period]. Shōhakkan, 1935.

Yokohama Kaikō Shiryōkan. *Meiji no Nihon:"Yokohama no shashin" no sekai* [Meiji era Japan: the world of "Yokohama Photographs"]. Yokohama: Yūrindō, 1990.

Yoshikawa Kiyoshi. *Izumo no O-Kuni* [O-Kuni from Izumo]. Tanaka Shobō, 1954.

Yoshitake Toshinori. *Kindai bungaku no naka Seiō* [Europe in modern (Japanese) Literature]. Kyōiku Shuppan Sentâ, 1974.

———. *Meiji Taishō no hon'yaku shi* [History of translated works in the Meiji and Taishō eras]. Kenkyūsha Shuppan, 1959.

Young, James. *Making Up.* New York: Witmark, 1905.

Young, William C. *Famous Actors and Actresses of the American Stage.* 2 vols. New York: Bowker, 1977.

Zaibei Nihonjin jimmei jiten [Directory of Japanese resident in America]. With the English language title: *Japanese Who's Who in America.* San Francisco: Nichibei Shimbunsha, 1922.

Zeisloft, E. Idell. *The New Metropolis.* New York: Appleton, 1899.

Institutional Acknowledgements

Materials used in this study have primarily come from these sources:

Adrian Public Library
Awaji Bunka Shiryōkan, Sumoto
Bajor Gizi Színészmúzeun, Budapest
Baker Memorial Library, Dartmouth College
Bancroft Library, University of California, Berkeley
Bibliothèque nationale de France
Bobst Library, New York University
Boston Public Library
British Museum
Brookline Public Library
Brown University Library
Bucyrus Public Library
California Historical Society, San Francisco
Chicago Historical Society
Chicago Public Library
Dayton and Montgomery County Public Library
Duke University Library
Emerson College Library
Free Public Library of Philadelphia
Fukuoka Shimin Toshokan
Fukuoka Shiritsu Rekishi Shiryōkan
Futaba Museum, Nagoya

Grand Rapids Public Library
Hackley Public Library, Muskegon
Harvard University Theatre Collection
Harvard-Yenching Library, Harvard University
Holy Cross College Library, Worcester, Massachusetts
Japanese American National Museum, Los Angeles
Kōbe Shiritsu Hakubutsukan
Kokuritsu Kokkai Toshokan, Tokyo
Kokusai Kōryū Kikin Toshoshitsu, Tokyo
Library of Congress
Los Angeles Public Library
Mansfield Public Library
Mason Library, Keene State College
Meiji Mura Hakubutsukan, Inuyama
Mugar Library, Boston University
Multnomah County Library, Portland
Museum of the City of New York
NHK Hōsō Bunka Chōsa Kenkyūjo, Tokyo
New York Public Library
New York Public Library for the Performing Arts Research Collections
Ohio Historical Society, Columbus
Ohio State University Library
Oregon Historical Society, Portland
Österreiches Theatermuseum, Vienna
Peabody Museum of Salem
Pollard Memorial Library, Lowell
Ryerson and Burnham Libraries, Art Institute of Chicago
San Francisco Public Library
Seattle Public Library
Seminole County Public Library
Shōchiku Ōtani Toshokan, Tokyo
Smith College Library, Northhampton
Southern Illinois University at Carbondale Library
Tacoma Public Library
Teishōji, Naritasan, Kakamigahara
Theatre Museum, London
Theatre Museum of Repertoire Americana, Mt. Pleasant, Iowa
Tiffin-Seneca Public Library
Toledo-Lucas Country Public Library
Toyoda Shobō, Kanda Jimbōchō, Tokyo
University of California Los Angeles
University of California Theatre Collection, Berkeley

Wadsworth Atheneum, Hartford
Waseda Engeki Hakubutsukan Toshoshitsu, Tokyo
Willard Library, Battle Creek
William Morris Hunt Library, Museum of Fine Arts, Boston
Personal collections in Japan and the United States

Index

D

E

H

I

J

K

L

M

N

T

Z

CPSIA information can be obtained at www.ICGtesting.com
Printed in the USA
LVOW030718230412

278727LV00001B/11/P

9 781604 943689